A NATION OF AGENTS

James E. Block

A NATION OF AGENTS

*The American Path to a Modern
Self and Society*

**THE BELKNAP PRESS OF
HARVARD UNIVERSITY PRESS**

Cambridge, Massachusetts, and London, England   2002

Frontispiece: George Caleb Bingham, *The Jolly Flatboatmen*, 1877–1878, oil on canvas, 26 ¹⁄₁₆ × 36 ⅜ in., Terra Foundation for the Arts, Daniel J. Terra Collection, 1992.15; photograph courtesy of Terra Foundation for the Arts, Chicago

Library of Congress Cataloging-in-Publication Data

Block, James E.
 A nation of agents : the American path to a modern self and society / James E. Block.
  p. cm.
 Includes bibliographical references (p.) and index.
 ISBN 0-674-00883-9 (alk. paper)
  1. United States—Civilization—1783–1865. 2. National characteristics, American.
3. Agent (Philosophy)—History. 4. United States—Intellectual life—1783–1865.
5. United States—Politics and government—1783–1865. 6. Political culture—United States—
History. 7. Protestantism—Social aspects—United States—History. 8. Protestantism—
Political aspects—United States—History. 9. Liberalism—United States—History. I. Title.

E169.1 .B654 2002
306'.0973'09034—dc21   2002018486

To Ruth

CONTENTS

PREFACE

My first encounter with George Caleb Bingham's powerful painting *The Jolly Flatboatmen* (1877–1878) at the Terra Museum in Chicago was during the long years of labor on this book. "This," I exclaimed to myself, "is the book I am trying to write." Already drawn to its subject owing to my love of American river and riverboat prints, I was no doubt led toward the particular responses I had that day by my research. For in the past I would have leapt with a prolonged sense of release at the boat's journey toward the frontier, the openness of the river itself, and the compounding aura of liberation Bingham achieves with reverberating strains of musical intoxication. All of my impious attitudes toward restraint would have been triggered by the surging sense of being "on the road."

And initially they were. But . . . the book. Working to untangle the mysterious web of liberation and constraint in America that has so infused its culture, delving into its complex synthesis of openness and limitation, I was quickly brought back from my reverie to the subtle, nearly invisible tie-lines of order in the painting, an order so intrinsic to the experience of release as to fade within it. The midwestern frontier, we know as did Bingham in 1877, was nearly settled; the river was no undemarcated field but a very clearly defined path of settlement and commerce; the music evoked not simply antinomian release but also the powerful quest for popular order, enabling the boatmen to play and dance to their own melodies, but in time, together, with more or less fixed notes and steps.

What was the relation between these two experiences? and where was the "true" story? This image, almost a sonogram of the project now realized, did not answer the questions I had put to the culture about its own inmost intentions. But in revealing these polarities interwoven, surely and tangibly in that moment, it encouraged me on the journey I was taking, that similar combination of adventure and fidelity that defines scholarly discovery itself.

As momentarily attractive as the story of the self-dependent author is, writers on journeys of this duration well understand the communities that are mobilized to complete such a project and the many debts that are accumulated at every stage. In the case of this project, I want to begin by thanking those who enabled the initial version to become a reality and have stayed with it since: Martin Marty, my guide to the world of American religions and an inspiring mentor who unflinchingly engaged the full scope of the project as it unfolded; Stephen Toulmin, my colleague and friend, who showed me the way of the independent intellectual; Herman Sinaiko, my advisor and confidant par excellence; Tony Yu, a committed supporter throughout; and Robert Pippin, who made the project possible.

The years of labor would not have been possible without the sustained support and engagement of my DePaul University colleagues and their commitment above all to a better world. I was most demanding of Charles Strain and Roberta Garner, but asked much of Harry Wray, Rose Spalding, Bob Rotenberg, Fassil Demissie, Sandi Jackson, Nena Torres, Frida Furman, Roy Furman, Mike Budde, Michael Alvarez, David Pellauer, Caryn Chaden, Beth Kelly, and others too numerous to mention, including many inspiring and challenging students over the years. Other scholars upon whose friendship and insight I have depended include Josef Barton, Richard Carwardine, David Ericson, David Greenstone, Henry May, Dana Chabot, and Arthur Wilson. To Ed Rothstein I want to acknowledge multiple debts of gratitude.

A great deal is owed to two extraordinary readers, Harry Stout and Eldon Eisenach, whose reports offered both powerful and sustained analytic guidance as well as extensive suggestions for a more complete narrative that were central to my redrafts. Great professional and personal guides to the world of publishing have been Lisa Adams and David Miller, and I was further assisted by David Follmer, Anita Samen, and Karen Wilson.

My great fortune at Harvard University Press was to have the steady and incisive support of Michael Aronson as my editor and Joyce Seltzer as an early engaged reader and advocate.

My thanks are also due for the dedicated editorial support provided by Mary Caraway, Amanda Heller, and Martin White.

The resources of several libraries were indispensable. Margaret Power and Denise Rogers and their tireless staffs at the DePaul University Library; Ken

Sawyer and the staff at the jewel of a research library, the Jesuit-Krauss-McCormick Library in Hyde Park; and the staff and collections at the Regenstein Library of the University of Chicago deserve a great debt of gratitude.

Among my inspirations was a community of friends who came to expect and perhaps even enjoy my recurring flights of abstraction. This includes Adrienne Asch, Ben Braude and Lois Dubin, my late intellectual comrade Irwin Miller, Bill Strehlow, Larry Garner, Philip Rubovitz-Seitz, Tom Hey, Murray Gruber, Daniel Halperin and Moira Killoran, Lloyd Buzzell, Judy Buzzell, Cheryl Bryson, Stan Izen, Don Lamb and Linda Gilkerson, Dick Berger, David Ciepley, Charles and Myrna Greene, Ralph and Nancy Segall, Bill Lynch, and Marshall Kaufman. Joe Kinsella deserves particular thanks for his photographic artistry. Many other family members and personal friends as well sustained my wife, Ruth, and me during this period, and are very much part of our village.

My most personal gratitude and thanks go to my parents, Herb and Mildred Block, my in-laws Jim and Dorothy Fuerst, who had everything to do with how this (and I) turned out, Tam Greene, Mike and Lillian Braude, Bill and Pearl Braude, and our brothers Glenn Block and Dan Schauben-Fuerst. Ruth and I have been particularly fortunate to have within our family circle the younger families of Dan Greenstone and Heidi Lynch, Michael Greenstone and Katherine Ozment, and Michael Ash and Krista Harper.

To our son, Matt, I owe the miracle of his presence, a judgment and wisdom beyond his years, his love and good-spiritedness about the project, and the excitement of his increasing engagement in these concerns of culture and meaning. Finally, I want to convey a gratefulness beyond words to Ruth Fuerst, my partner in all things, a dauntless assumer and sharer of risks, whose sense of what makes life matter and what is necessary to achieve it has long lit the darkness, and whose clarity, affirmation, and strength enabled this project to reach fruition. It is to her that this book is dedicated.

Character teaches above our wills. . . . [It] is this moral order seen through the medium of an individual nature.

—*Ralph Waldo Emerson*

We must begin . . . [by] watch[ing] the infant in his mother's arms; we must see the first images which the external world casts upon the dark mirror of his mind, the first occurrences which he witnesses; we must hear the first words which awaken the sleeping powers of thought, and stand by his earliest efforts,—if we would understand the prejudices, the habits, and the passions which will rule his life. The entire man is, so to speak, to be seen in the cradle of the child. The growth of nations presents something analogous to this; they all bear some marks of their origin. The circumstances which accompanied their birth and contributed to their development affect the whole term of their being.

—*Alexis de Tocqueville*

The American Narrative in Crisis

> [The] American, still thinking of freedom in the old-fashioned way
> as independence from coercive authority, may very well overesti-
> mate the extent to which he is free. . . . [T]he traditional American
> rejection of authority left a void that had to be filled somehow. The
> result, it might be argued, was not to abolish coercion but merely to
> make it more subtle and impersonal. . . . Thus social control in a vol-
> untaristic society is less a matter of regulating behavior than of shap-
> ing attitudes and character, and that is a far more complex enter-
> prise.
>
> —David M. Potter

> You overcome history with history. So with narrative and myth and
> symbol: you overcome story with story. . . . You come out from un-
> der the dominance of a symbol not by rejecting the symbol but by
> seeing that another interpretation of it gets heard.
>
> —Martin Marty

A relative absence of serious political and cultural discourse
amidst a made-for-T.V. public culture belies the churning soul of contemporary American life. As a nation we have lost our way, lulled by the drifting
stream, unmindful in Tocqueville's cautionary words of "the current" which
"hurries us away and drags us . . . towards the abyss."[1] Most striking evidence of this is the virtual disappearance from public discourse for the first
time of the central narrative of American history, the discourse on freedom.
Whatever else has been in doubt historically, the national culture has understood itself as a collective experiment in human liberty and as such a model
and symbol for the aspirations of the world.

The Challenge to American Verities

The collapse of this narrative dates from the abrupt end of the "end of ideology" in the 1960s. Beginning at that time, what Sydney Ahlstrom later called "the Traumatic Era," the view grew that a "well-behaved America had passed away, and with it the certitudes that had always shaped the nation's well-being and sense of destiny." The public response to "the sudden discovery that dry rot had weakened the supporting members of a very comfortable structure of values" was "moral shock" and "a sense of 'all coherence gone.'"[2]

What had happened? Postindustrial productivity and receding normative boundaries had unleashed unprecedented opportunities for release within an American culture asserting the centrality of individual voluntarism. These shifts transformed the conditions under which that culture had been formed and always functioned. The inevitable constraints imposed by natural economic limits and largely consensual religious and community norms could no longer sustain the consensus about freedom. These past constraints had specifically muted the two polarizing tendencies in the culture: proponents of strong limits on personal conduct could defend freedom, privately reassured by the inevitable limits to its practice; advocates of greater voluntarism were led to restrain their critique of the existing order given the limits of what could realistically be expected.

The postwar shifts in the American economy and culture changed everything. No longer were constraints inevitable. Those who believed in moral and behavioral regularity would have to defend and promote rather than merely presume it. Defenders of increased postindustrial autonomy need no longer be bound by existing institutional arrangements. The result was the beginning of a culture war, what James Davison Hunter has called "allegiances to different formulations and sources of moral authority,"[3] what Kevin Phillips identified as "a major new antagonism" between "'double-knit' populist conservative fundamentalists" and "'wine-and-cheese' neoliberals" constituted from "the most affluent, best-educated, and most technologically advanced" or "post-industrial areas of our country."[4] This division led, in Todd Gitlin's terms, to the critical fraying of "whatever consensus existed about the direction and meaning of American history" and a "coherent American identity," and in turn to "the twilight of common dreams."[5]

Given the present concern with the formation of American national identity, the contemporary policy implications of this emerging cultural division must remain for a subsequent occasion. What is crucial for present purposes is the impact of this postindustrial realignment on conceptualizing American history. For the startling increase in individualism and lifestyle diversity in our time, whether regarded as autonomy or license, has provoked an intense debate regarding the traditional premises of American life, and in particular the structure of constraints which attended the practices of this presumably free society. Embracing the extreme tendencies were two "parties," each seeking the ideological high ground by casting itself as the "party of liberty." Each in turn produced a polemical view of the historical record as a defense of its current agenda. The result has been a loss of intellectual clarity regarding both the present and what the nation from its inception was and understood itself to be.

The first party (of liberty), ironically the "party of constraint," to press its claim for present limits on autonomy argues that freedom in America has always involved significant restraints—moral, religious, familial, economic—on personal choice. For this party, a history of such limits poses no problems. What is problematic for others, however, is that such limits stimulate no rethinking of the national claim to exemplary freedom. In the words of William Bennett, "liberty . . . requires a strong measure of virtue," which in turn requires "traditions, institutions, habits and authority" that disseminate the "principles developed over time by custom, the lessons of experience, and consensus."[6] America is thereby conceived as axiomatically free, and a history of constraints as well as current efforts to control individual behavior are treated as coextensive with the project of liberty. In this view, freedom can become indistinguishable from obedience.

For the second party, the "party of autonomy," its advocacy of greater liberation leads it to identify the traditional constraints of American life, including those directed toward groups excluded from the dominant culture, as compelling evidence of national hypocrisy. The nation from this perspective, while proclaiming its belief in freedom for society and for the individual, never meant to make good on its promises. The pervasive subordination of social groups on the basis of race, ethnicity, gender, and class are treated as conclusive evidence of a project in bad faith. Robert Blauner, for example, has written: "The labor forces that built up the Western hemisphere were structured on the principle of race and color. The European conquest of Native Americans and the introduction of plantation slavery were crucial beginning points for the emergence of a worldwide colonial order."[7] For this party, the illegitimacy of the rhetoric of freedom vitiates a coherent national identity.

Both parties are right to identify how extensively freedom has been historically bounded, even subordinated to other priorities. What implications follow from this insight? Is it reasonable to suggest that this nation, long regarding itself as fulfilling a mission through its history, has proceeded by hypocritically flaunting the "truth" as it understood that truth? Is it more reasonable to conclude that a consistent pattern of institutional containment and strict normative limits reveals a primary commitment to liberty? In this debate, either the nation's motives or its rationality are rendered suspect. Ironically both parties, by taking the discourse of liberty at face value, have contributed to the public distrust of national ideals and to a retreat from reconstituting them.

Is it possible to recover the national narrative from the cul-de-sac of contemporary discourse? In a way which acknowledges both historical cohesion and postindustrial dislocations? Which reconciles the discourse on liberty and the historic realities of social constraint in terms of deeper operative priorities? These questions have framed the direction of the present work.

The Crisis in American Historiography

The fragmenting of the national narrative of liberty extends beyond current political discourse to the work of American historians. The nation's self-conceived role as heir and promoter of the Enlightenment narrative tradition has been undercut by such influential postmodern theorists as Michel Foucault and Jean-François Lyotard, who have identified European master narratives as mythologizing mystifications imposed on an otherwise intractable reality. The Western "historical consciousness," Hayden White suggests in his classic work *Metahistory,* is "little more than a theoretical basis for the ideological position" promoting "a specifically Western prejudice by which the presumed superiority of modern, industrial society can be retroactively substantiated."[8] When juxtaposed to the record of European colonialism and twentieth-century genocide, the Enlightenment vision of historical progress has been deeply eroded. Its values of liberty, equality, the rule of law, and human rights have come to be regarded as empty universals, merely "cultural statements and systems . . . constructed in this contradictory and ambivalent space of enunciation."[9]

More important to historians of the United States has been the bitter evidence of its historical record. As Eric Foner put the case in his 1994 presidential address to the Organization of American Historians, "From the very beginning of our history, freedom has been a central value for countless Americans and a cruel mockery for others." This tension has produced an enduring "American paradox" regarding what "the meaning of freedom" could be "in a land pervaded by inequality."[10] Ronald Takaki, addressing one of myriad crises of interpretation, asks what the impact on the vaunted Turner thesis of frontier liberty might be if the discussion were opened to Indians, with their "different view of this entire process."[11] The loss to contemporary scholarship of an interpretive paradigm for the national story has produced what the historian Daniel T. Rodgers has called its "conceptual confusion," the "muddle" of a "whimsically incoherent wardrobe to mix and match at will."[12]

The causes of this crisis are instructive. In recent decades, many socially progressive historians, excited by postindustrial opportunities for a more inclusive and liberated society, at first treated such advances as amplifications consistent with the national narrative of social progress. Frustrated, however, by the slow pace of change and by structural barriers to reform, these historians turned to the past to locate a dynamic more supportive of their transformative agendas. Refusing to treat the limits imposed by the nation's constitutive values as fixed, they have reimagined the nation's past at one remove from its liberal tradition, and at a double remove—their modernist antipathy added to liberalism's own secular dissociation—from its Protestant heritage. The resulting muddle is not unexpected. With liberalism and Protestantism excised from the historical record, there is little to see, and what is visible cannot be coherently rendered.

The background to this dissociative process begins with the triumph of the liberal consensus after World War II, followed, as Rodgers explains, by reactions to it beginning in the 1960s. The reigning view of the 1950s was Hartzian liberalism. For the Harvard political theorist Louis Hartz, the United States was from its origins shaped by a consensual Lockean paradigm that provided no space for alternative traditions and modes of thought. "Liberalism," whose "natural development" was for Hartz the "single factor" in American history, "shaped every aspect of . . . social thought," just as it reflected the undisputed middle-class proprietary individualism of society itself.[13] To be sure, Hartz was critical of the "danger of unanimity" to liberty from a "self-evident . . . faith" in popular "norms" amounting to "absolutism."[14] He even suggested that the postwar settlement represented "the bizarre fulfillment of liberalism," requiring "a transcending of irrational Lockeanism" with "a new level of consciousness."[15]

Yet Hartz's analysis accentuated the fearsome aspects of liberal triumphalism by reinforcing the conviction that all alternatives, including the traces of a religious heritage, had been expunged or overcome. Previous liberals had typically dealt with America's religious origins by quite deftly transforming the Puritans into early proponents of "the political ideals of the founding fathers," that is, into religious liberals who believed in "toleration" and possessed "a love of universal liberty."[16] An alternative approach dating from the eighteenth century involved "the old national pastime" of "debunking the Puritans,"[17] treating them as early authoritarian opponents against whom the traditions of liberty and democratic self-governance had triumphed.[18] In this view, the Revolution became "the true beginning of our national history."[19]

The Hartzian analysis was yet more extreme, treating the liberal consensus as powerful enough to have conjured away Puritan understandings of self and society as if by "magic" from the national record. Achieving a "curiously timeless place" and "fixity" as an innate or unconscious consensus from "the outset of colonial life,"[20] liberalism as the "American way of life" quickly became "master" of the "whole region." Emerging first "as a universal, sinking beneath the surface of thought to the level of an assumption," then "almost instantly" it was "reborn, transformed into a new nationalism." The result was for Hartz a "colossal blending and confusion" in which all opposition disappeared: "The men of the *Mayflower* sink into the ranks of the men of the Revolution."[21]

Contemporary scholarship in turn sought, though with less success, to repeat the liberal process of dissociation, this time not only from the Protestant origins of the nation but also from its liberal successor. For the generation coming of age in the 1960s, the Hartzian claim of consensus was profoundly flawed because, first, it naively ignored the realities of contestation within American history, and second, it was taken normatively—and ideologically—by postwar centrist liberalism to preclude the possibility of contemporary social conflict as well.[22] This refusal to entertain fissures in the consensus was regarded as a by-product of the anxious liberal ascendancy at home, a wish to be rid of normative and popular challenges both domestically and internationally.

The sudden return to prominence of quasi-ideological divisions with the controversies of the 1960s, that is, divisions which demanded but could not locate a theoretical framework, set critical Americanists to work challenging Hartz on both fronts. The perceived task was to link the contemporary and historical analyses, to find in effect a history with an explanatory framework that would also discern the inevitable rise of prospective social movements. The result was a surge of interpretive thrusts, both innovative and recycled, recasting the American past in terms of social conflict along lines of race, class, ethnicity, gender, the role of community or the public, generational differences, and so forth. The challenge scholars faced was to express the contested triumph of liberalism in a way that opened the future (and the past). The danger was to presume that precisely the same key opened both.

The reinterpretation of American history in terms of a republican tradition was the first of two major revisionist efforts to frame fundamental historical divisions as the precursor of a new organization of society. Growing out of the critique of liberal privatism and materialism, such advocates of a republican reading as Bernard Bailyn, Gordon Wood, and J. G. A. Pocock began in the late 1960s to recast the agenda of the American Revolution. No longer the product of an unconflicted search for a liberal polity, it was read at least in part as a quest for a participatory community composed of virtuous civic actors living for the common good rather than private interests. From this starting point, alternative republican values and commitments were identified in every corner of American social movements, in artisan and worker and regional movements, populist and women's rights struggles.

The American record, however, seemed resistant if not impervious to such fundamental reconstitution. In time, the republican thesis collapsed as proponents retreated from their historical claims, the victims of wishful thinking unsupported by historical evidence. Republicanism, Rodgers points out, had been constituted as a "shorthand for everything liberalism was not: commitment to an active civic life (contra liberalism's obsession with immunities and rights), to explicit value commitments and deliberative justice (as opposed to liberalism's procedural neutrality), to public, common purposes (contra liberalism's inability to imagine politics as anything other than interest group pluralism)."[23] The irony was that the thesis had in fact originated as a historical fiction in Hannah Arendt's *On Revolution*, whose inspiration was the Greek polis.[24] Widely read among 1960s radicals, the book put forth a vision of a birth of public life that the American Revolution might have achieved had it realized its "true" agenda, although few of its leaders possessed even a fleeting glimmer of this possibility. Arendt's dream of "public spaces" of citizen involvement had provided a nonhierarchical, broadly accessible institutional model suggestive for contemporary democratic and communitarian theorists such as Sheldon Wolin, Robert Bellah, Michael Sandel, and others.[25]

Shorn of a connection between their prescriptive agendas and the realities of the past, left in what Sandel calls the "moral void,"[26] these writers retreated from historical reconstruction. The result, ironically, was that of "reifying and reconfirming" the liberalism the republican argument had been "designed to escape."[27] With alternatives dissipating, scholars such as John Patrick Diggins, Eric Foner, Theda Skocpol, and Isaac Kramnick[28] cannot avoid reasserting the historical hegemony of the very liberal consensus they deplore, the "liberal legacy" Diggins accuses of "leav[ing] America without a sense of moral community" or "moral purpose."[29] The historians Joyce Appleby, Lynn Hunt, and Margaret Jacob, though having formerly "participated in the dethroning of once sacred intellectual icons," now conclude "that the ideas embodied in the Declaration of Independence . . . reflect the highest aspirations of an ascendant West as it moved to conquer both the world of nature and those people classified as 'backward.' . . . Then and today, America stands for a set of abstractions pointing to the superiority of individual freedom, restrained government, open opportunity, mutual tolerance, and diplomatic support for free nations."[30] Even Foner in his 1998 book *The Story of American Freedom*, while finding freedom an elusive and highly contested concept which "camouflages a host of divergent connotations and applications," nevertheless accepts our "very preoccupation" with it as "a point of unity in understanding the American past."[31] In Rodgers's image, "the Hartzian paradigm was something like a tar baby; the harder one struggled against it, the tighter its vocabulary seemed to stick."[32]

Contemporary multiculturalism suffers from related problems. Intent upon resisting liberal hegemony by opening contemporary society to the multiplicity of group solidarities and values which constitute it, proponents of multiculturalism have similarly sought to broaden the range of influences and cultures shaping the American past. As a theory emerging from modern movements for the rights of diverse groups, multiculturalism can account for the history of social conflicts as well as current struggles. It further suggests an American future both more complex and inclusive than its past. At the same time, in its haste to remake the American narrative, it is prone to ignore the actual legacy—and achievements—of the dominant culture. By, in Todd Gitlin's words, "inflat[ing] the claims . . . for multiculturalism" as a historical force,[33] its theorists confuse their influential attack on mainstream historiography with an accurate account of the locus of power in the past and present. The historian David Hollinger, notably sympathetic to the project, says, "One can write narratives calculated to include without turning the past into a retrospective mirror of the ethno-racial present."[34] Gary B. Nash notes, "If multiculturalism is to get beyond a promiscuous pluralism that gives every thing equal weight and adopts complete moral relativism, it must reach some agreement on what is at the core of American culture."[35] This project of social reconstruction, too, may in the end confuse the historical record with the programmatic need to ground contemporary social movements.

The larger conundrums therefore remain: no image of consensus could obscure the presence of either significant social turmoil over the role and application of freedom in American history or evident divisions and polarizations in our time. That is, the critics of Hartz were right on both counts—both his blindness to a conflictual past and his reification of present-day liberalism. They were also right that contemporary divisions could not have been spontaneously generated without some link with the past. But these insights, even if attached to a reform agenda, did not amount to a convincing narrative of national development. The historical record could not simply be reframed de novo. Unconvincing efforts at such reframing had the undesirable result of reinforcing the ascendancy of those liberal values now being so widely challenged.

The Liberal Flight from History

Socially progressive historians were, with Hartz, repeating a pattern of flight from historical realities within liberal theory. From its earliest English statement by Hobbes to the revolutionary myth deriving from Jefferson, Anglo-American liberalism, with its claim to a social contract arising from a prior state of nature, has presented itself in the memorable words of Eliza Doolittle as "the beginning and the end." By substituting this apocryphal beginning for the real story of its emergence, liberalism was able to imagine that it had reconstituted reality anew. As Sheldon Wolin has written: "An identity that is established by revolution is typically one that renounces the past and seeks liberation from it. A revolution . . . wants to begin history, not to continue it. And so the Declaration of Independence appealed to 'self-evident truths' rather than to historical principles."[36] Thus, it provided itself free rein to eliminate from memory the traditional realities it had overcome and to deflect attention from the extent to which it had made peace with and even appropriated them. And so that pattern has continued. Michael Lienesch notes that "until recently, historians and political theorists have tended to overlook the role of time in American politics . . . tend[ing] to see America as a uniquely modern nation."[37]

Liberal ahistoricism, shifting from a bold revolutionary futurism to the later forestalling of doubts about liberal claims of liberty and progress evident after the 1960s as conservative liberals proclaimed "the end of history" against the forces of identity politics, multiculturalism, and institutional restructuring,[38] was a consistent feature of the postwar period. In the 1950s, faced with claims of historical supersession by socialism and communism, liberalism declared the end of fundamental historical conflict—the celebrated "end of ideology"—with itself as victor. The internal buckling emerged with the effort of postwar liberal scholarship to conceptualize liberal individualism in the context of global modernization and the Western transition to postindustrial society. The most confident images of American individualism arose when it was contrasted with more traditional or authoritarian societies or with the radical American right. In such relief, an idealized profile of the modern liberal character was established along such measures as independence, self-direction, egalitarianism, and institutional participation.[39] Daniel Lerner, tracing character shifts in the modernizing Middle East, described modern Western society as a set of "social institutions founded on voluntary participation by mobile individuals . . . each having made a personal choice to seek . . . his own version of a better life."[40] David Riesman emphasized the greater incidence of "autonomy" in classic American liberal society,[41] while Alex Inkeles, like many others, trumpeted the liberal individual to vindicate cold war polarities and America's global mission: "At the core of the democratic personality lies a stress on personal autonomy and a certain distance from, if not distrust of, powerful authority . . . an absence of the need to dominate or submit such as is found in the authoritarian personality." It was easily identified as the "opposite" of "the authoritarian personality," possessing values of equality, friendship, sharing, capacity to compromise, flexibility, respect for human rights, self-control, openness, responsibility, and acceptance of difference.[42]

Parallel attempts to contrast the liberalism of the industrial period with its emerging postindustrial version proved both a more difficult and less self-validating undertaking. The evolution of the United States into a technological, organizational society was clearly altering traditional forms of American individualism in economic and social life. Yet the effort to validate the resulting characterological shifts had an unintended consequence of exposing long-standing cultural idealizations, forcing a more realistic, less ideological reassessment of its earlier structure of personal identity. Numerous theoretical models were advanced, but the result was dissensus and confusion as well as growing skepticism about the classic account of American values. The early studies explored the impact of the shift toward a more bureaucratic, organizational, suburban, consumerist, and peer-oriented society. Such writers as Erich Fromm, David Riesman, William Whyte, and Karen Horney identified trends away from nineteenth-century American individualism toward a more conformist internalization of institutional and group pressures and demands.[43] This reiteration of fears about declining individuality in modern America earlier expressed by Frederick Jackson Turner, Sinclair Lewis, Sherwood Anderson, and Lewis Mumford would have been serious enough. But a closer examination suggested that, if Tocqueville's observations were to be taken seriously, as well as those of Van Wyck Brooks, Herbert Croly, Carl Becker, and Josiah Royce, among others, conformity had been a feature of the American character from the outset.

Some writers, acknowledging this critique, suggested that postindustrial society finally provided the conditions for individual liberation. Herbert Marcuse, N. O. Brown, Theodore Roszak, Henry Malcolm, Kenneth Keniston, among others, claimed that the shift from work and self-denial to leisure and self-expression would increase autonomy by permitting a greater degree of individuality in the choice of lifestyles and priorities.[44] Other theorists, such as Christopher Lasch, Richard Sennett, Philip Rieff, and Daniel Bell, retorted that these developments augured a breakdown of the characterological fabric of liberal society.[45] The result as they saw it was not increased freedom but a retreat to primitive emotional life in which apparent autonomy and individuality concealed deep levels of psychological dependence, disorientation, and conformity. David M. Potter and Seymour Martin Lipset advanced the view that these shifts, though in seeming opposition, were simultaneously accelerating, that, in Lipset's words, both "individualism *and* conformism, innovation *and* dominance by low-level mass taste, are outgrowths of identical forces."[46] Clyde Kluckhohn, by contrast, suggested that autonomy and conformity, while both expanding, were doing so not as divergent options but as complementary strengths within a new, adaptive postindustrial character.[47] Lasch, Rieff, and Riesman responded that the two were combined in a new, degraded, conformist individualism.

The situation was becoming, in Potter's image, that of "a blind man in a dark room looking for a black cat." For if individuality and conformity, Jeffersonian self-reliance and Tocquevillian tractability were so thoroughly interrelated, then the American character "might conform to the Jeffersonian image; it might conform to the Tocquevillian image; it might conform in part to both; or it might conform to neither."[48] And the moral valences were if anything harder to read. This elusiveness of the evidence and its potentially corrosive implications for the liberal ethos resulted by the 1980s in a collapse of the inquiry on modern individualism. The combined inference emerging from the various perspectives, particularly as the collapse of the counterculture undermined more optimistic accounts, was that significant pressures toward conformity and group accommodation had shaped self-formation throughout the course of American history. Some scholars tried to save liberalism's self-idealization by treating this larger pattern of social uniformity and regularity as insignificant relative to more traditional societies or as a failure of the citizenry to realize liberalism's intrinsic opportunities.[49] These efforts were insufficient to sustain faith in the United States as the ideally free society. Yet more telling was a growing sense among theorists that such irrational pressures toward social cohesion were an invaluable and perhaps irreplaceable feature of liberal society—conceivably the last line of defense if properly constituted against the extreme individualism emerging in postindustrial culture.[50]

The results of this inquiry were devastating. The success of the nation's mission as a free society was being challenged by its own cultural defenders at the moment of its global ascendance. Moreover, the very goal of this mission, the free society itself, was being more deeply questioned than at any previous point in U.S. history. What if this society dedicated to freedom now believed that too much freedom was deleterious individually and uncontainable societally? What remained of its central convictions to ground such a society? What was the future of the unraveling American identity (to say nothing of the American mission) if the only realistic choices were now too much license or too much conformity, or if the liberal character were not strong enough to maintain its historic role as the anchor for a restrained self-reliance? In the face of such dangerous questions regarding national identity and the future of liberal society, historical inquiry became a casualty of the narratological confusion.

Contemporary theorists seeking to establish a new direction for liberalism have not, despite their best intentions, been able to transcend this loss of history. Many, recognizing a need to reshape its contemporary priorities, understand that liberalism will not and ought not to be frozen in its present condition. But whereas at midcentury the lack of historical consciousness was most evident in Hartz's exaggerated fear of a monolithic, timeless, and inflexible liberal consensus, today a contrary situation exists: reflecting a culture of seemingly endless options, we are now told by liberal reformers that liberalism itself can be whatever we wish. If we seek wider distribution or broader participation, more virtuous citizens or a stronger sense of community, a deeper belief in democracy or a stronger commitment to personal rights, there is no reason why liberalism cannot embody those values.[51] Change is made to seem no farther away than the respondent's assent to the proposals being offered at the moment. While a situation with apparent options appears more hopeful than one without them, the reality, alas, is not so different from that of Hartz. Each proposal offers only a weak sense of what liberalism and the history of liberal society is. Each assumes the irrelevance of the real origins of the liberal world and the opportunities and constraints likewise constituted by the specific course of its development. Behind the idea that we can make history any way we want because of the American can-do, all-is-possible, limits-are-there-to-be-transcended spirit lies a palpable sense that matters may be out of our control. Waving preferences (or blueprints for dams) at the passing stream may forestall Hartzian despair, but it does not begin to redirect liberal priorities.

Liberal theory in all of its variants had clearly failed to acknowledge the central role of structural boundaries and constraints in its formation of modern society and individual character. By accepting its claim of substantially diminished or negligible—rather than nontraditional—systemic demands, scholars within the tradition had isolated the values of liberalism from its larger historical and institutional project, including the history of those forces required to carry out modern nation building and of the oppositions this generated. Somehow the nation's past had to be reopened in a way that acknowledged the ambiguous legacy of freedom, insisted on a deeper understanding of the nation's historic priorities, and yet remained responsive to both historic and—perhaps quite different—contemporary challenges. Where was the key that unlocked Hartz?

Toward an American Past

A time of crisis is a time neither to gather the wagons around a tradition nor to assert the end of identity and narrative. The recovery of traction compels us, in the words of Martin Marty, to "overcome history" and "story" (but also the specter of historylessness and storylessness) "with history" and "story."[52] This search for unities is clearly on the minds of many. Foner notes "the desirability of moving beyond a portrait of the United States as a collection of fractious racial, ethnic, and sexual groups, to an appreciation of common themes that give coherence to the nation's past,"[53] while Gary Nash proposes acknowledging distinct backgrounds and "distinctive historical experiences" as well as a history of "struggle" within "a common commitment to core political and moral values."[54] Ronald Takaki asks from a multicultural perspective whether a reconstructed "common past" might enable "Americans of diverse races and ethnicities . . . to connect themselves to a larger narrative."[55] Patricia Limerick admitted in her 1996 presidential address before the American Studies Association, "In the excitement of discovering how much there was to learn about the experiences of people formerly excluded from the historical record, we have backed away from any vision of common ground" and asked whether it is "time to build some of that foundation back in."[56]

The key that begins to unlock the current impasse is the insight, to be emphasized in the modern era of revolutions, that if civilizations are not static formations but rather shift over time, those shifts do not arise ex nihilo from the visions of theorists and social movements. The intense burden associated with the American claim of "prophetic" transformation, as the Canadian historian Sacvan Bercovitch noted, with its emotional pulls alternately toward "lament and celebration," divine abandonment and triumphalism, can be lightened only by reconnecting the national project with the realities of our history and achievement.[57] This process of reconnection must by no means reject the novel features of modernity and of the specifically American variant. But it is necessary first to pierce the veil of forgetfulness, to recover the past that Protestantism and liberalism each in its own way conveniently obscured in order to propel the modern project beyond its constraining traditional European origins. The strategy of dissenting Protestantism was to draw a sharp spiritual division between a condemned and no longer meaningful history of Catholic and Anglican tyranny and the shining future of religious fellowship, and to turn believers firmly toward the project of realizing that fellowship. English liberal theorists, seeking to consolidate a modern political regime, effectively erased the collective and personal past by removing traditional social reality to a prehistoric limbo and the traditional demands on the individual to a period prior to the accessibility of personal memory.

The fantasy of beginning anew provided necessary distance from earlier encumbrances, but it also left the first liberal nation with a faulty perception of its strengths and weaknesses. The absence of a past prevented identification of the powerful resources by which it had uniquely achieved separation and independent nationhood. At the same time Americans, for fear of being reminded of "their status as dependent colonials,"[58] were never able to locate either the historical limits deriving in Robert Nisbet's terms "from the vast conservatism and stability" of "deeply rooted" primary institutions[59] or the new institutional constraints which they subsequently forged. By reopening the myth of American origins and its claim of transcending history, we can reexamine the actual grounds of our nation's self and society and the process attending the birth of this distinctively modern and individualist nation. A more balanced reading of the historical record neither idealizes nor dismisses out of hand the claims of exceptionalism. By disconnecting "the study of national history" from either "a respect for national myths" or from making the nation "a villain in other people's stories,"[60] we can assess with the party of constraint what has been achieved and with the party of autonomy what has not. It is reassuring that such a move toward realism, particularly in rethinking founding revolutions and wars of liberation, is now under way among the New Historians in Israel, France, Mexico, of course Russia, and elsewhere.[61]

The Twin Faces of American Culture

Despite the increasing recognition of an interconnection between liberation and constraint in the American project, contemporary political theorists continue to assert the conventional antinomies. The theoretical debate sparked by Michael Sandel's republican reading of American history, *Democracy's Discontent*,[62] once again pitted liberal individualists with their "'voluntarist' conception" of "individuals" who should "judge for themselves the worth of different conceptions of the good life" against proponents of the constraining values of "civic solidarity and the pursuit of a common good."[63] Yet what is most striking about the American project of nationhood—and what, finally, must be insisted upon—is its two sides: its originative journey toward a modern voluntarist society *and* the structures and boundaries that secured and stabilized that achievement.

As Tocqueville and many since have noted, in dispensing with traditional hierarchies and external controls in favor of unprecedented realms of personal initiative and participation, the United States cast modernity as the continuing project of reconciling individual prerogatives and normative order. Potter has written that "every society, to survive, must somehow coordinate the work of its members. Where authority and coercion have been displaced there must be control without command." Given these institutional limitations, "social control in a voluntarist society is less a matter of regulating behavior than of shaping attitudes and character, and that is a far more complex enterprise." This inquiry will be guided by the search for such new forms of "power without coercion," the "indirection" by which social demands "developed integrally along with freedom" structuring "the cultural and institutional aspects" of a new kind of "nation-building."[64] The enduring connection in Daniel Walker Howe's terms of "voluntarism with discipline," of "liberation and control," means, according to Daniel Rodgers, that the "rubric of Freedom" must be understood as "a synonym for everything Americans already had—for the way of life (however many compromises of freedom it might contain)," including "the institutions of the status quo."[65]

The noted historian Carl Becker described the late-nineteenth-century "individualism" of the "middle border" where he grew up as "an individualism of conformity, not of revolt. . . . While the conditions of frontier life release the individual from many of the formal restraints of ordered society, they exact a most rigid adherence to lines of conduct inevitably fixed by the stern necessities of life in a primitive community."[66] For the historian Michael Zuckerman, Americans have always had "two revolutions in train, in opposite directions, at the same time. They have grown more individuated *and* more regimented, more tolerant *and* more repressive. They have come increasingly to move, as Philip Rieff had said, in a milieu 'of orgy and routine which constitutes modernization.'"[67] In *The Democratic Wish,* James Morone links the historical pursuit of democratic reform to a deeper dynamic which inevitably produces "new bureaucracies, new public power, new political privileges, and newly legitimated groups."[68] If the dynamism and initiative released in American life result in the building of ever more elaborated institutions, then the American project is a different one than we imagined. But paradox and opposition will not explain that only apparently paradoxical "collective self" whose generation of "new individual and collective identities" laid the solid basis for a new form of polity.[69] The problem is to discern the nature and history of that self, which requires "a fundamental reworking of the whole history of freedom in America."[70]

Locating the American Path to a Modern Self

There is a growing sense today that the distinctive features of a historic American identity can be salvaged by moving away from the idealized categories of Enlightenment universalism. Foner concludes that the search for "common themes" must account for "the demise of older generalizations that claimed to distill the essence of the American saga."[71] Gordon Wood, confessing the "hopeless disarray" of traditional history, with "no coherence" or "central organizing principles" or "themes or stories" or "narratives," takes hope from the widespread "call (or is it a cry?)" to reconstitute "narrative history," with new ways of understanding the "dynamic movement" of "whole societies."[72] Geoff Eley and Ronald Suny accept that "being national is the condition of our times," though inherently sustainable henceforth only by refusing "an inclusive, illusory stability" or exclusivity.[73]

The challenge in identifying the collective dimension of the American experience, even as revised formulations of individualism such as "interest" and "rational choice" attest to its vitality, is facing the reality of authority. Normative boundaries and social constraints, cohesive communities and discrete nations, regardless of America's "obsessive . . . opposition to authority" and "distrust of power,"[74] require a supervening source of legitimation. John Higham conditions "the reconstruction of a genuinely national history" on our capacity "to rethink the vehicles of tradition and the agencies of authority in a chaotic world."[75] The reconstruction of the discourse on modern individualism and the constitution of liberal society must begin by acknowledging the primordial role of authority in constituting *all* cultures, in shaping a society's citizenry and framing its institutions. Tocqueville, it is well known, after initial incredulity at the seemingly unlimited freedom and independence of action Americans enjoyed, grew ever more aware of the pervasive order and ubiquitous routinization which characterized life in the new society. In time he concluded that a "principle of authority must . . . always occur, under all circumstances, in some part or other of the moral and intellectual world," although he could not identify the specific form of the American variant: "The old words *despotism* and *tyranny* are inappropriate:

the thing itself is new, and since I cannot name, I must attempt to define it."[76] For Tocqueville, the authority emerging in "nations of our age," in popular, post-traditional societies, was of "a different character" than ever before.[77] This was in large part what terrified him, for in its powerful and yet moderate form it operated "by the natural inclination of mind and heart" such that "the hidden force that restrains and unites . . . is not discernible" to those who submit to it.[78] Thus, he observed of Americans, "they become ever more alike, even without having imitated each other."[79]

This surreptitious process of integration before unacknowledged authority juxtaposed with the insistence on freedom confuses us to our own day. And so the words for what cannot be admitted remain elusive. Americans, Daniel Rodgers notes, still have "an embarrassingly hard time finding words to explain even to ourselves our enduring sense" of "common bonds and responsibilities," and need to evolve a language of "common happiness" and "public good."[80] For Howe, "the limitations of our concept of social control" produce a difficulty in understanding the dual nature of American cultural movements.[81]

To find a language for the formation of American society, we must return to the history we have forgotten, to the constitutive traditions of the modern West. These traditions offer valuable compensation for the later liberal tendency to understate the role of authority in society and character formation. The philosopher Charles Taylor in *Sources of the Self* inquires whether a sense of modern individuality rooted in both "freedom" or "autonomy" and "some orientation to the good" was plausible.[82] Though liberalism posits a "free, disengaged subject," for Taylor such "illusions" ignore how "the sense of who we are" arises from a "generally socially induced . . . sense of where we stand to the good." He continues: "We may sharply shift the balance in our definition of identity, dethrone the given historic community. . . . But this doesn't sever our dependence on webs of interlocution. It only changes the webs, and the nature of our dependence."[83] Yet Taylor's analysis suffers from an instructive irresolution. While tracing the emerging web of modern culture with its new sense of inwardness, voluntarism, rights, rationality, and inclusion through the major figures of early modern Western philosophy, he admits that modern "culture didn't spread outward from the formulations of epoch-making philosophers." Rather, such philosophers express "the great unsaid that underlies widespread attitudes" already present in the civilization.[84] Despite his caution in locating such popular sources, Taylor identifies the origin of the Western sense of an embedded good in the "theis-

tic context." This "unsaid," in other words, has been said: "Secular humanism . . . has its roots in Judeo-Christian faith. . . . The original form of this
affirmation [of life] was theological, and it involved a positive version of ordinary life as hallowed by God."[85] The modern doctrines of science, nature,
reason, selfhood all arise in the struggle to separate from—while retaining
the residuum from—their divine "Author."[86]

Taylor thus challenges the claim of secularization as a distinct moral project. Not just his own philosophical chronicle, but implicitly the civic republican thesis, Howe's defense of an "autonomous self" originating "in the Enlightenment,"[87] and Rodgers's pursuit of secular "contested truths" over the
"obligations" and "piety-saturated" traditionalism of the nineteenth-century revivalist "Protestant counterrevolution,"[88] all demonstrate how the
"continuing dependence" on an authorized world remains unarticulable
within a culture that "prizes autonomy."[89] These are, it is clear, flights from
the obvious: alongside the conceits of secularism, and never secretly, Anglo-
American culture consistently enunciated its founding and moving convictions in the language of Protestant religiosity. At every level from elites to
popular movements, its history is the story of religious struggles. The Western religious tradition, with its vital center in the individual's relation to authority as the precondition for personal identity and worldly role, takes as its
orientation the missing major premise in liberal modernism.

Despite the effort of American liberalism to jettison its origins, it is now
possible to surmount the revolutionary erasure and grasp the national legacy in the English Reformation and colonial religious experience. From this
perspective, the historical and conceptual formation of the American self
and society must be understood as the product and in turn one component
of that great movement whose goal was the transformative reconstitution
of authority relations in the West. The modern project of replacing traditional authority relations with a more individualist society must be discerned from "new ground," with an analysis "concentrating not on secular
thought alone, or on 'religious thought' as an alternative to it, but on the incessant interactions between these two poles."[90]

The birth of a modern relation to authority is thus both a religious *and* secular account. It evolved both in the religious relation of the essential self to
an ultimate author and in the worldly reshaping of institutional authorities
and structures. Secularization is only the later phase of the process in which
the rational apprehension of self-evident truths—that is, truths now embedded—replaces the early intuition of these truths through faith. At the same

time, grounding these truths in faith or in an ethic derived from "the good" unduly privileges religion.[91] Secularism for its part seeks the reasons for and implications of particular faith projects. It is only in arising and operating together that faith and its reasons complementarily promoted and jointly sustained the modernist transformation.

This historical understanding of the American path to modernity also provides insight into the present cultural stalemate by placing Hartz's reification of postwar liberalism in its context. Hartz had read a one-dimensional narrative into the past and the future from the consensus of the late 1940s and 1950s. Contemporary historians who deny the Hartzian thesis of a liberal consensus by the 1950s obscure the fundamental shift that it convincingly asserts: the historic triumph of the Protestant-liberal paradigm, the fact that, to paraphrase Jefferson, "we are all Protestants—we are all liberals." And yet, critically, this triumph precluded neither fundamental historical divisions nor deep divisions emerging thereafter—only the flawed assumption that we must expect them to be identical before and after that consolidation.

Historic liberalism in fact never had it as easy as Hartz feared, and its complex path to ascendancy was quite distinct from its later triumph. The American myth of liberty and the eighteenth-century idyll of progress featured in postmodernist attacks were both later idealizations of the dynamic of struggle in the Protestant-liberal world for coherence and coalescence. Similarly, as I suggested at the outset, the converging of industrial age political controversies in the 1950s was only the beginning of postindustrial divisions which now shape public discourse. To acknowledge the postwar consensus, then, represented not an acquiescence to liberal hegemony but rather the opening of new discourses and contestations as promising and troubling as any before. Restoring the focus on the nation's two formative traditions and their achievements provides—as idylls do not—not only an awareness of new contradictions but also new forms of hope.

Recovering the Language of Agency

In this book I accept Tocqueville's challenge of naming the modernist form of authority in the United States and the new character of its citizenry. The recovery of that language lies within the original national discourse of Anglo-American Protestantism: not to be located, as with most previous inquiries, in the collective values appropriated from Puritan religious experience as the basis of a national civil religion, but rather in that discourse's new understanding of the individual and its role in modern institutions. Establishing the two faces of modernist individualism enables us to recover the foundational importance of Anglo-American Protestantism. As the historian Cushing Strout suggests, surmounting Hartzian hegemony must begin from Tocqueville's insight regarding "the secular consequences of religious ideologies" in American history. The Protestant synthesis of personal "obedience" with "independence," of "restraints on constituted authority" and "obedient conformity in thought and action" with "noncoercive voluntary decisions," formed the psychosocial basis for the American way of life in "voluntary associations for chosen impersonal ends."[92]

Michael Zuckerman's work has revealed how "the American character" from its colonial origins contained the extremes of "individualism" and "community," "determined assertions of personal liberty" and "self-interest" along with "equally determined assertions of social control." He writes that "the early colonists were at once more free and more controlled, more concerned about themselves and more attentive to the opinions of their neighbors, than their European forebears had been." Colonial English Protestantism operated institutionally through covenanted communities to impose new identities that would at once "individuate and . . . aggregate."[93] Adam Seligman, tracing modern American identity to its European Reformation roots, explains how "modern individualism" and "institutionalization" in "the collective" were reconciled to become "the intensely communal nature of individual identities" in Protestant society. Through normatively mandated religious practice and ritual, individuals were socialized to internalize "within the private soul" the moral requirements for being an "individual endowed with conscience and moral agency" inside the society.[94] As the maintenance of social boundaries shifted from "the community" to "the individual's own conscience," the interpenetration of "the sacred and the secular" led to "morally responsible individuals participating with a high degree of commitment in the making of a new cultural and political order" beyond the walls of the religious community.[95]

Max Weber and Michael Walzer, while focused on the shaping impact of early modern institutions in their classic works *The Protestant Ethic and the Spirit of Capitalism* and *The Revolution of the Saints,* locate the duality of the modern character in the new theological formulations of "God's commandment to the individual." Weber writes: "We are interested rather in . . . the influence of those psychological sanctions which, originating in religious belief and the practice of religion . . . derived from the peculiarities of the religious ideas behind them . . . gave direction to practical conduct and held the individual to it."[96] The result of early modern Protestant conviction was an individualism combining "one's own ability and initiative" with "the perseverance of the individual in the place and within the limits God had assigned to him [as] . . . a religious duty."[97] Emphasizing the political dimensions of the "saint's personality," Michael Walzer explores how Protestant activists utilized a new "relation between God and man" to combine "individualism," "voluntarism," and "self-control" with "a new and impersonal discipline" demanding "civic virtue" and "duty."[98] Driven by this radically new sense of duty, they politically transformed the "established patterns of obedience and deference" of the "world of tradition" into the new voluntarist but constraining institutions of "religious discipline, household government" and "holy commonwealth" of early modern and then modern society.[99]

Seeking the principles by which the individual and society were reshaped by these theological and institutional transformations, this book treats the formation of American civilization as the product of a shift in the Western conception of human nature in the sixteenth and seventeenth centuries that achieved its fullest expression in England. In this period, English society was confronted with growing initiative on the part of historically quiescent sectors of society in religious, political, economic, and social activity. In the English Reformation, Puritan dissenters followed by religious sectarians and political insurgents generated widespread demands for greater responsibility, power, and initiative in institutional processes. Dissenting England in effect was insisting on an enhanced role in the cosmic plan and in worldly activity, a role which reconstituted rather than eliminated the legitimate supervening authority theologically and institutionally. This new role became the underlying basis of Anglo-American liberalism and American society on which the ideology of liberty was later superimposed by liberalism.

It is the concept of *agent* which I utilize to differentiate this modern form of individualism. The thesis of this book is that, while not recognized until much later, this fundamental shift of the human role in relation to authority was effectuated as a new human character type: individuals shifted from being servants of God and society carrying out rigidly defined duties on behalf of distantly formulated but fully designated ends. They became agents, that is, individuals participating actively in shaping the worldly means to be employed for realizing divine and collective purposes. The conception of agency requires a fundamental rethinking of the mainstream account of the national history as "the sacred cause of liberty" and the Declaration of Independence as its "American scripture." It further requires a reconsideration of the naive liberal claim to have constituted a society in which individuals elect their own ends rather than available preferences within a structure of organized preferences.[100] The *Oxford English Dictionary* defines *agent* as "one who does the *actual work* of anything, as distinguished from the instigator or employer, hence one who acts for another, a deputy, steward, factor, substitute, representative, or emissary." Agency exists only with reference to a principal, a designator, an author/ity.

The agent, to be sure, was constituted with a novel sense of its powers: to be turned into agents meant that individuals were to be released from traditional hierarchies and made initiatory and self-reliant worldly actors. Yet this greater latitude for the individual was never meant to include freedom regarding the formation of ends. Agents, dependent as emissaries must be on their warrant of authority and on the author who warrants them, were not at liberty to define their own ends. That was the dangerous power of self-authorization that English Protestantism and liberalism, Milton and Hobbes, had defined as the one greatest danger of an individualist age. A "free agent" was an oxymoron, *ultra vires,* and this conflation, part of the idyll of the freedom narrative, preserves in language its contradictory claim and its built-in but unacknowledged limits. While an agent operating with delegated authority could be difficult to distinguish from an individual acting freely, particularly when the frame of reference was traditional coercive society and modern ideology promoted the new status as autonomous, the agent was specifically constituted as the deferential and willing repository of collective values. It was only by an acceptance of the role and those ends that the agent was released into modern activity and to ever wider exercises of initiative, discretion, and judgment in the means by which those ends were to be fulfilled.

Those ends were in turn to be provided in a host of new ways, for the agent was resistant to being treated by the standards of traditional servitude. The very task of modernity, of Protestantism and liberalism, was to constitute entirely novel—largely majoritarian and participatory—forms of collective authority and legitimate process by which inclusive ends were to be formulated, societally institutionalized, and individually integrated. These were to take the form, as we shall see, of the open economic market, participatory political processes, voluntarist religious institutions, and community social norms. The result, which shattered traditional hierarchical civilization, was the Protestant-liberal civilization of modernity with its distinctive agency forms of authority, selfhood, and institutional organization.

The term *agency*, while associated with liberal moral theory, emerges in early English dissent as one of several parallel terms and achieves ever greater prominence in Anglo-American Protestant discourse after the late seventeenth century. Urian Oakes, president of Harvard College, writes in *The Soveraign Efficacy of Divine Providence* (1677) of humans as "created agents" who, being "second causes" of "Providence," employ "the active power and virtue of causes" as "means" for "the operations and effects He hath made for them."[101] The Boston minister Samuel Willard speaks at the end of the century of "voluntary obligation" as the work of "Rational and free Agents."[102] In the middle of the eighteenth century, the Reverend Samuel Johnson defends God's creation of "rational and moral agents" with the capacity to use "means and assistances" for "a free and voluntary conformity to these laws [of God] from a sense of duty to him."[103] William Livingston locates the human being's power of "free agency" in "a Freedom of Action, determinable by the Dictates of his own Reason, the self-resolving Exertions of his own Volition, and a Reverence to the Laws prescribed to him by his omnipotent Creator." Together these make individuals "subjects of moral government" through "a natural and moral Dependence on [their] Maker alone."[104]

The noted late-colonial-era minister Charles Chauncy praised the status of "rational, free Agents" who "can't be religious but with the free Consent of their Wills."[105] For the South Carolinian Alexander Garden, humans acted as "moral agents" in the "gradual co-operative Work of God's Holy Spirit."[106] In the period of the Revolution, the physician John Perkins writes in *Theory of Agency* (1771) of the individual as "a free agent" who is thus able "by the use of moral powers" to "approve himself to his maker in a suitable and determin'd degree."[107] The purpose of "rational moral agents" for Daniel Shute is by "the rule of their duty, according to their measure," to "promote the happiness of [God's] creation."[108] The minister Levi Hart holds that as "a moral agent," the individual has "liberty" of action and is therefore an "accountable being."[109] Yale president and Federalist leader Timothy Dwight speaks of humans as "moral agents," thus capable of fulfilling "the end, for which man was made, and for which he was redeemed . . . that he might do good, and actively glorify his creator."[110]

The conception of humans as God's agents emerged, I will suggest, early in English Puritanism, as believers came, by the turn of the seventeenth century, to a firm sense of being "a new creature" with an entirely new nature. Expressing it first in the terms of an enhanced religious status, Puritans spoke of achieving "sanctification," "regeneration," "sainthood," and "sonship" of God. At the same time, this new status involved the responsibility to act on behalf of God's ends in the world, to be in Puritan terms God's "instruments" or "stewards."

The concept of agent was in use at the time, but conveyed the capacity for independent judgment and action that Puritans, self-questioning regarding both their relation to God and their appointed role in the world, were hesitant to claim as their own. In law and diplomacy, the concept conveyed the sense of a specifically deputized appointment.[111] Agency used as a scientific term involved "the sufficiency" to "produce an effect" through "an active power" adequately independent of the direct will of God to "deserve the name." It presumed God's willingness to trust "the order" and "course He hath set in the world," that is, the powers of his "instruments" to act at a distance and with self-reliance.[112] As the outlines of the new cosmic order clarified for American Protestants, the enhanced capacity of individuals to ascertain that order through reason and faith and to act accordingly produced a stronger conviction regarding human ability. They began to regard themselves as discrete secondary causes both in their own salvation and in God's plan for the world.[113] As with eighteenth-century English moral philosophy after England's religious settlement,[114] Americans, though more religious, came to see themselves as agents as they recognized their important role in God's settlement of the New World.

The Dynamic of Reversal

Agency unlocks the paradox of Tocqueville's duality, but the question remains: How did a nation submerged in the Jeffersonian discourse, turned toward an open field of potential action, ever produce institutional boundaries and limits? Put another way, what relation did the culture of freedom have to the reality of agency? Tocqueville's difficulty in naming agency was partly because it operated beneath the level of awareness. Acting consciously to extend and exploit freedom, Americans from the outset produced structures. This counterintuitive process at the heart of national formation I have called the process of *reversal*. In order to reappropriate authority in their role as agents in a society celebrating individual freedom, they turned largely without knowing from the open field back toward the community and a place within it. Moreover, though the direction changed, the conscious intention did not. Thus the project of preserving freedom became deeply interwoven with and difficult to separate from that of building new institutions for the nation (as distinct from the state).

Liberalism, as we shall see, has always predicated freedom on this dynamic of reversal. For Hobbes and Locke, providing order in an individualist society was a challenge which required—following the Protestant reformers—that individuals shift from pursuing their own ends to acting as instruments of community ends. They also realized that individuals newly released from traditional constraints would not willingly resubordinate themselves to authority. Reversal, once recognized, was optimal because it premised integration not on a political or religious arbiter, but on voluntary consent as individuals discovered the need for limits on their own.

Liberalism in its genius offered no express ends beyond a social space secured for voluntary conduct. Its concept of negative freedom was a denial within that space of external imposition. But space for what? Liberalism assumed in its reconstitution of social order that individuals released from long-standing controls would inevitably act out the deeper—and quite likely inaccessible—imperatives of their internal lives. The inner horizons constituting modern citizens would propel them when acting in unencumbered space to create through reversal the institutions of modern agency. Shaping themselves as free agents through their own authority, establishing constraints through a process breathtakingly modern and participatory, they would be foreclosed from disputing the result. Conceived in early liberal theory, reversal emerges in the vast unregulated space of early America as the internal and social dynamic by which free citizens constituted an agency nation.

The World of the Agent

In this work, I trace the transformation to agency. In Europe, it achieved the critical mass to generate a national popular movement only in England, though after taking power in the revolutionary Commonwealth, this movement failed to establish the institutional framework necessary to create an agency society. The English insurgency, however, gave rise to a radical set of ideas and beliefs including a new view of human character and the vision of a new organization of society to complement it. The realization of that vision would occur elsewhere—in the post-traditional United States. Colonial and young republican America shared with England the collapse of traditional authority and social hierarchies, but it had not evolved those commercial and political powers that would co-opt the English path to modernity. Virtually all American colonists, indigenous elites, and common people, the John Winthrops and the Anne Hutchinsons, were dissenters, heirs to the agency transformation in England in the understanding of human nature and the human role, of institutions, forms of authority, and prerogative. They had emigrated not to live freely, but to gather together in communities dedicated to the orderly, disciplined fulfillment of transcendent and collective ends and to carry out those ends individually. And in the colonies, whether in seaboard cities or in unregulated spaces distant from imperial oversight and even effective local authority, with abundant land, a decentralized economy, and anemic class boundaries, Americans by the period of the Revolution had in the main embraced the agency character and evolved, without fully realizing it, an incipient agency civilization.

Moving beyond the self-conception of liberalism as the product of a modernist secularizing impulse, I treat both the English and American phases of the agency world as the joint creation of Protestant activists and the theorists and practitioners of liberalism. Despite their historic roles as antagonists and alternatives,[115] despite present efforts to renew the rivalry,[116] the Protestant-liberal settlement was made possible by their deep common values. Historically, Protestantism and liberalism shared a rejection of traditional social character and social organization. They both understood that individualism was inevitable and would necessarily lead to a society of expanded options. Radical Protestantism in England emerged as the religious framework for reshaping church and society to accommodate religious equality as well as greater individual activity and responsibility in matters of personal faith. It elaborated a model of universal siblingship under a common author, God. Individuals were now empowered to be agents of God, qualified to represent and actualize the divine will in their worldly activity. Agency forms the core of the Protestant worldview and is central to the ultimate Protestant-liberal synthesis. The problem for radical Protestantism as a religion of individual conscience was that there was no legitimacy accorded to worldly hierarchies which could contain the religious, political, and economic individualism being unleashed. While Protestant sects often demanded and exercised substantial influence in the lives of members, they could neither stem the proliferation of new denominations nor control the lives of nonbelievers. The result in England and in the United States was the rise of divergent and incompatible sects, together with a vast unaffiliated population beyond institutional control.

Liberalism arose after Protestantism in an effort to reverse this disorder and to reestablish social and institutional cohesion. The ingenious liberal solution was first proposed by Hobbes and refined by subsequent theorists: the formation of an individual who, in terror of the chaotic consequences of autonomy and self-authorization, willingly repudiates its own independence and combines consensually with others to adopt common overarching ends. This individual, in order to show its acceptance of those common ends, was "voluntarily" but unequivocally to acknowledge—and authorize—itself as an agent of those ends and to further support the demand for the application of this role to all members of the body politic. In this way the political enforcement of agency by the liberal polity became the basis for universal institutions that would surmount Protestant divisiveness.

As I will show, radical Protestantism and voluntarist liberalism, stymied in England, were able to operate independently and virtually without constraints in the young American republic. Each on its own, Protestantism in the First and Second Great Awakenings, liberalism in its efforts to create an antebellum Lockean-Jeffersonian proprietary republic, led to an untenable and unsustainable form of society. Together, compensating for their respective deficiencies, they were able to achieve one of the most successful and influential alternatives to traditional societies. In the American setting, Protestantism, confronted by its own fragmenting dynamic, was in time forced to acknowledge the impossibility of a doctrinal commonwealth and to accept the necessity of a liberal society and state which could provide behavioral uniformity and a more inclusive framework for the diverse members of American society. American liberalism, similarly, had to wrestle in the Jacksonian period with its own failing quest to construct a society without organizational integration. It was to rediscover in Protestant agency a model of a socially integrated and institutionally engaged self that would enable it to move from the temporary proprietary republic into modern organizational society.

I trace here for the first time the liberalization of American Protestantism in conjunction with the liberal reconciliation with its own Protestant origins. As the deficiencies of their individual movements manifested themselves by the post–Civil War period, American Protestantism and liberalism gradually united to complete an agency society. Its components were a liberal civil religion and a Protestant-based market economy and organizational society. This was, despite the rhetoric of Jefferson's Declaration, the war for independence, popular government, and the ubiquitous rhetoric of a free society of free individuals, not a society of self-authorizers but a *nation of agents*. Its vision was of individuals freed from lifelong submissiveness within authoritarian hierarchies in every domain of societal life in order to be resubordinated to the emerging institutions of liberal society, and placed *qua* individuals as equal agents capable of undertaking the realization of collective ends. The process of theoretical consolidation and societal integration was the work of the full nineteenth century, and its great propounder was the preeminent liberal theorist, who was himself from an activist evangelical background, John Dewey.

This agency model achieved such embeddedness as to make this society one discrete model of the post-traditional way of life. At every turn, its institutions and its way of life were remade into realms of agency authority which not only permitted but even demanded bounded forms of individualism, self-reliance, and initiative. At the same time, the success of this new model does not suggest an unconflicted path to dominance. To the contrary, I show how the settlement achieved coherence and centrality in the face of opposition on the right and left as well as from its own internal conflicts. Agency liberalism struggled against and overcame the traditional models of servitude and Puritan proto-agency (though the latter long lingered) embedded in early religious movements and local hierarchies, in colonial dependency, southern slave society, and early industrial organization. It was also forced to contain the still emerging individualist culture of sectarian and Emersonian self-authorization. The new coalition, finally, struggled with its own two extremes contesting its settlement: the claim of idyllic liberalism that agency was natural and required no institutional coercion, on the one hand, and the Protestant sectarian vision of an exclusive religious community, on the other.

The Path Ahead

The fact that the historical evolution and consolidation of the agency character occurred in two distinct historical stages explains the twin focus of this book. In the first stage, in England, the conception of agency emerged slowly among insurgent Puritan ministers struggling to harness new spiritual aspirations to traditional Christian life, gradually recognizing their distinctive claims, and building in time a mass movement that would generate

prolific religious and political diversity and ultimately bring down traditional society. This new character would also be the starting point for the reconstitution of society on a modern foundation by the two great theorists of
liberalism, Thomas Hobbes and John Locke.

Part I focuses on the conceptual phase of the rise of agency civilization,
the development of this new character, the emergence of beliefs about its
role in worldly and transcendent processes, and the construction of new
models of institutional practice and containment in the work of the English
religious and political insurgents and liberal theorists. At the same time,
since England would not fully implement agency society, the complex issues
of the struggles for institutionalization and their fate lie beyond our scope.
Chapters 2 and 3 offer a new reading of the emergence of the agency paradigm from traditional English culture and ideas. They trace its incubation in
the treatises, tracts, diaries, sermons, and guidebooks of dissenting Puritan
ministers beginning in the 1570s, followed by its later development in the
religious and political insurgents who brought about the Commonwealth.
Chapter 4 develops the seminal contribution of Thomas Hobbes as a response to the political chaos generated by the forces of modernity. I treat
him from a new perspective as the great theorist of agency civilization who
appropriated the agency character and the Protestant narrative of progress
from the insurgents to frame the psychosocial foundation for a new human
order. One novel aspect of this study is to treat the liberal tradition, including the Lockean-Jeffersonian variant, as dependent on the dynamic of voluntary conformity to the agency role which Hobbes regarded as the sole pal-
atable antidote to self-regarding individualism.

Chapter 5 explores the reframing of this synthesis by John Locke, a critical
stage in its later reception in the United States. While Locke's political and
characterological theories rest almost entirely on these earlier contributions,
his specific role in the subsequent influence of the agency paradigm was
to incorporate it within a voluntarist framework. His underlying concern
within his diverse discourses on politics, religion, and metaphysics was the
institutionalization and integration of the agency character as the precondition for social regularity. These diverse discourses are guides to adult behavior rooted in the most important of Locke's discourses, his treatise on education. In this discourse, the imposition of agency character formation in the
child becomes the precondition of relaxed restraints on liberal adults. The
conditions of early American society found its people receptive to this reformulation, for it largely obscured the elements of authority and compliance

within agency society and character. Locke's writing, then, is the source of the "idyll of the free agent," which would become a key component of American liberal ideals.

The remainder of the book traces the American elaboration of the agency character from its late colonial emergence into prominence through its full implementation in agency institutions by the end of the nineteenth century. Part II offers a revised reading of the dynamic of colonial American society through the period of the Revolution. In Chapter 6, I treat the central dynamic of the First Great Awakening, not its early restricted phase symbolized by Jonathan Edwards but the subsequent explosion of popular religiosity and institutional experimentation beginning in 1740. This was the period in which the dissenting culture of agency simmering in colonial society broke the bonds of traditional imperial society and the indigenous Puritan proto-agency hierarchies to become a primary force in American society. Chapter 7 offers a fundamental reinterpretation of the American Revolution as a "revolution for agency," and takes issue with previous understandings including the Hartzian thesis, the Progressive model, the civil religion paradigm, civic republicanism, and particularly the traditional notion of a struggle for liberty.

In developing this argument, I suggest how the "revolution for freedom" emerged as a distortion of the historical events. The Revolution must be seen as the product of two distinct colonial movements: the War for Independence organized by Whig commercial, religious, and liberal plantation elites, the group we associate with Jefferson, in the name of national control; and a second internal revolution by urban, rural, and particularly western commoners mobilized after the Awakening throughout the colonies for greater suffrage, disestablishment, religious noninfringement, local community autonomy, and fairer representation and taxation. Despite the heated internal debate pitting a hierarchical republic of agency virtue against a sectarian community of equal agency believers, they came together on the basis of their common dissenting roots in the English tradition of agency insurgency. The Declaration of Independence, though the later source of the national idyll of liberty, must be understood in its role at the time as central to the elite strategy of popular mobilization. In it, Jefferson effected a pragmatic alliance between the two insurgencies on the basis of mutual noninterference, offering common citizens a temporary respite from elite control. Despite overt popular discontent with elite rule since the 1740s and antipathy to the elite war, the Declaration succeeded because its universalizing language boldly signaled the elites' willingness to suspend their internal agenda for the duration of the war. This language was in their view merely symbolic and retractable, and they quickly sought to back out. But the people heard Jefferson's words, and in absorbing their broadest implication a new national myth of liberty was formed.

Part III lays forth the crisis of the young republic set loose from the imperial structure without a clear sense of its destiny or the meaning of its revolutionary claims. The result (Chapter 8) was the crisis of antebellum revolutionary liberalism as the Lockean idyll of proprietary individualism shattered in the face of unrealistic expectations and the developing economic and social institutions of the new republic. This produced in turn a prolonged period of psychological dislocation created by the absence of institutional and cultural guidelines for the new society and a desperate, though inarticulate (as it contradicted the stated aspirations), search for a cohesion deeper than freedom from institutional restraints. Through an examination of postrevolutionary literature and the evolution of Tocqueville's thinking (in Chapter 9), a clear pattern emerges of individuals venturing beyond traditional constraints in search of liberation, often in the wilderness, only to face the terror of indeterminacy. This precipitates a dramatic return to reconstitute collective life. This is the collective pattern I have called the reversal from autonomy into agency, and this narrative pattern in American literature can be newly described as the narrative of reversal.

Part IV explores the response of American society to the collapse of its revolutionary ideals. I suggest that its lack of an institutional nexus for its culture of voluntarism led it to embrace Protestant agency, the very conception from which this culture was derived, for a modern theory of the individual role within society. The most important of those searches for cohesion was the reemergence of Protestant revivalism across the land throughout the antebellum period (Chapter 10). In this extended movement of popular religiosity, older denominations, theological principles, and patterns of worship are transformed into laboratories for creating a new agency Protestantism. This becomes the crucible for the constitution of a new citizenry with agency characters and a psychosocial and programmatic receptivity for engaging in institutional life. Chapter 11 explains how the success of revivalism in disseminating the new agency self failed to extend to stable godly institutions, leading instead to cultural and religious fragmentation. The failure of renovated Protestantism to establish social order on its terms led—beginning before the Civil War and expanding thereafter—to its embrace of a liberal civil religion and its role as an ancillary to the liberal polis.

The remaining chapters trace the elaboration of an organizational liberalism substituting a Protestant model of individual integration for its failed theory of decentralized and limited institutions. Chapter 12 focuses on the rejection of proprietary individualism and the embrace of market agency with explicitly Protestant roots by the liberal economic theorists of the last third of the nineteenth century. The concluding chapter begins with the efforts by social reformers and social theorists of that period to place emerging organizational society within the liberal conceptual and normative framework. While suggestive in the reshaping of liberal ethical and structural premises, their work was unable to preserve liberal voluntarism within the overarching modern institutions and structures of integration. It was John Dewey who, in his early work, resolved the theoretical crisis of the liberal narrative by salvaging and reinscribing its values within a fully evolved organizational society through his unique characterological and institutional synthesis of Protestant agency and liberal voluntarism. In this architectonic conception which formed the Protestant-liberal settlement, the internal conflicts and mutual antipathy on the part of each was overcome to constitute a consensual model of Protestant agency character in inclusive liberal institutions. This synthesis, "the Protestant agent in liberal society," provided the operational consensus that underlay American national integration in the twentieth century. It forms in turn the world we have inherited and, as I discuss in the Conclusion, the vision which forms the starting point both for those who would restore traditional liberalism and those who would rethink its viability for the emerging global and postindustrial world.

In this new reading of the American narrative, we encounter an immense achievement, not the failed dream alleged by its detractors but something new under the sun, worthy of the great historical encomiums which were already by 1824 "a field so oft trodden."[117] At the same time, this new nation is not the paradise begun anew of its idealizers, for it bears all the limits of its achievement.[118] Agency society, cast as a "free" society relative to previous models and reinforced by its "war for national liberation," entailed from the outset an original but effective model of authority. It contains the largely unspoken forms of resubordination that Tocqueville glimpsed behind its spectacle of ubiquitous energy and seemingly unlimited independence.

His great fear was that in calling this election (and he believed that we were, despite ourselves, choosing it) of agency status by the name of freedom, Americans would forgo understanding the subtle patterns of coercion and accommodation required in an agency world and thus fail to question the institutions to which we were now beholden.

The American experiment succeeded by turning individuals into agents with internalized limits and institutional constraints using voluntarist incentives. This successful substitution accorded with the national emphasis on freedom. It anchored the American sense of mission and in turn legitimized the institutions that carried it forward. Today, however, the words of national triumph—"free agency"—must be understood as the problematic of modern political systems. Promising freedom but delivering agency is no longer tenable, for it only reinforces the popular disconnection from liberal institutions.

The renewal of democratic commitment in our time must begin with an honest appraisal of the foundations of liberalism. The confused defense of freedom today and the equally confused efforts at reform derive from an inability to grasp the complex achievement of agency civilization. This in turn makes it impossible to distinguish what might be retained and what must be reformulated. The agency narrative provides a new framework for understanding not only the past but also the contemporary political terrain. Movements such as republicanism and multiculturalism, whether their adherents recognize it or not, challenge agency premises in significant ways. Accepting the consolidation of American agency society, they now propose greater individual and collective access to the determination of ends by opening communal authority to participatory negotiation or to multiple subcultural priorities. In rejecting these claims, neoconservativism and neoliberalism are best understood as efforts to reinvigorate the agency paradigm.

Greater clarity about the foundations of American society will lead not to ideological closure or historical inevitability but to an increased ability to shape the discourses of a future faith. By seeing both ages more clearly, we may be able to grasp the reasons for the Protestant-liberal triumph as well as the fault lines of the agency settlement and the paths not taken. That is, the dislocations of our own time—with changing attitudes toward authority, a breakdown of institutional structures, and the search for new psychological and social forms—suggest a parallel with the collapse of traditional society and the birth of modernity. The agency paradigm then becomes the starting point for the struggles of our day and the possible seedbed of contemporary dreams. If we are unable to dispute Hartz, we may in this way be able to contextualize him.

The claim of American liberalism ever since the Revolution to have realized a nearly optimal degree of individual autonomy with political, market, social, and religious freedom contains discrepancies so evident that in our time they undercut its legitimacy. The result is a society in stalemate—an established agency culture with eroding validity challenged by a culture of self-authorization in the wings, a standoff between "the one and the many."[119] Perhaps the structural and characterological constraints forged by this first agency nation are still necessary. Perhaps in their existing form they are not. Only when we understand who we have been and the nation we have made shall we come to know that answer.

I

*The English Origins of the
American Self and Society*

2

The Early Puritan Insurgents and the Origins of Agency

In its place grew that old feeling . . . that there's something bigger involved than is apparent on the surface. You follow these little discrepancies long enough and they sometimes open up into huge revelations.

—Robert Pirsig

Yet, after our regeneration, by truth . . . we begin to be *Co-workers* with the grace of God.

—William Perkins

The culture of modern individualism emerged most prominently and pervasively in England in the century leading to the English Revolution. It began with the rise of a Puritan opposition in the 1560s, a popular movement which evolved far beyond its elite and intellectual origins to capture Parliament along with broad sections of the church and society. Its constituents were the product of profound changes in the English economy. During that century, the privatization of agricultural holdings and the emergence of a national market had stimulated widespread commercialization with incentives for specialized production, technological improvements, and a consolidation of holdings. The increasing role of individual initiative, business acumen, and responsibility for success in this new market economy generated a rising group of enterprising rural gentry, yeomen, and artisans. Together with London's merchant and industrial interests and its established artisan and craftsman class, a broad sector of English society was becoming prosperous, powerful, and independent of traditional restraints in a newly commercial society.

The dependence of fortune on an individual's own actions increased the reliance on personal judgment and initiative. Commercially the emerging groups were executing their own business contracts and financial arrange-

39

ments; religiously and culturally they pursued self-education, now available with the dissemination of printed materials. The expanding power and influence of new market participants and increased independence and self-reliance among yeomen and artisans were incompatible with traditional social hierarchy and the hopelessly outmoded governing nostrums of obedience and passivity. The result was a growing sense of popular dislocation and a need for adjustments to institutional structures and roles. In this early phase, these forces sought above all validation for their assumption of individual responsibility and support for the unprecedented pressures and anxieties which this generated. In time, they would demand political and economic power corresponding to their central role in the modernizing process.[1]

The Puritan Movement

English Puritanism grew through its capacity to explain and incorporate these dramatic, uncharted economic and psychosocial shifts, and to support and cushion adaptation to them. It recognized the new ambitions and confusions about place, affirming the assumption of heightened responsibility and crafting new adaptive strategies and roles. These shifts in the economy and society became perceived as part of God's plan to remake the world by utilizing individuals who willed God's purposes and would bring them forth. In their call to refashion the self for this task of reshaping the world, the Puritan ministers enabled their constituents to dispense gradually with traditional acquiescence to hierarchy, subordination, and quietism. Increasing popular acceptance followed from their effectiveness in framing aspirations for a new role.

The focus on doctrinal shifts articulated by ministers and theologians should not minimize the importance of Puritanism as a mass movement propelled into its transformative agenda, moreover, by a radicalizing laity.[2] Begun within the Marian and early Elizabethan church, this movement was carried across the land by proselytizing ministers. Given wide latitude to preach openly, and often without ecclesiastical support until Archbishop Laud's tardy reassertion of ecclesiastical control in 1628, they were at the same time denied a role in church policy. The growing energies of religious dissent were thus forced toward decentralized spaces at the margins of control, where popular influence and the support of local elites but not institutional authority could be pursued. Addressing popular concerns, the Puritan insurgency gained support among the rising cohorts in London and the countryside, until Cambridge, parishes in London, and regions throughout England had become insurgent strongholds.

Within these many unregulated spaces, in effect marketplaces of independent religious activity and innovation driven by consumer preferences, the movement evolved without rigid doctrine or centralized leadership.[3] Recruitment depended on connecting with the public and persuading them to join the fellowship. This produced in time an influential laity within the movement, and an articulate class of popular organizers highly responsive to the evolving power and self-confidence of their constituency.[4] The broad reception of a new status by mobilized segments of the population fed rising expectations of mass personal transformations and messianic hopes for the social transformation of England. Such expectations flourished first in the spheres of religious belief and ecclesiastical participation, then in economic and political roles, until the operation of a distinctive principle of empowered individualism was apparent.

This approach stresses the Puritan role in the dynamic of emerging individualism. A personal godliness in opposition to Anglican ritual conformity was the anchor for individuals pursuing new choices and responsibilities and provided the impulse for continuing theological and conceptual innovations.[5] The retreat from ecclesiastical reform in the 1590s under late Elizabethan repression accelerated this individualistic focus. Turning inward to focus on the individual soul apart from institutional supervision, the religious dissenters now pursued the growth in grace culminating in a conviction of personal sanctification, that is, of living with a sense of present godliness. This concern with spiritual development, including strategies for internal change and the ultimate role of the godly individual, increasingly shaped religious discourse. Individuals, as the ministers explained and the great epics of Milton and Bunyan later crystallized, had cast off from the collapsing city of tradition to venture on a personal journey toward redemption. William Haller writes: "Lacking the power, [the ministers] had to dwell upon the responsibility of the individual for enforcing [Puritan ideals] upon himself. They told him that his soul was a traveler through a strange country and a soldier in battle. . . . [H]is life was the story of his adventures on the road to the heavenly city, of his feats in the battle of the spirit."[6] John Preston, a Puritan leader in the early seventeenth century, wrote: "Our duty . . . is, to maintain such a constant communion with him, that we may be able to fetch help, and comfort, and direction from him, so that we need not turn aside to the creatures, and be dependent upon them. And indeed one that is acquainted with him, may be satisfied with that alone. . . . There are two companions which a man needs never to be destitute of, GOD and himself. . . . [A] man walks with himself by reflection on his own actions, and heart, and ways."[7] Yet this new individualism could be regarded as liberation only by comparison to traditional religion. For the release from traditional institutions and constraints served the overriding goal of resubordination within a new godly settlement.[8]

In this first stage, the conception of individual agency arose slowly. Like other potential revolutionaries before the rise of modern revolutionary self-consciousness, Elizabethan religious reformers struggled at the outset to harness new spiritual aspirations to traditional Christian life. Conceiving their mission as one of revitalizing English Christianity, they framed their religious expectations to accord with existing doctrines and feasible institutional adjustments. By William Perkins at the end of the sixteenth century, however, the sense emerged of a core incompatibility between the new relation to God that they were constituting and the traditional ecclesiastical model of the human role. With remarkable acuity, this generation of religious insurgents recognized within themselves an ongoing developmental transformation of human character. They described their experience of a radiant new soul, the inner surging of new powers, and the availability of new options. They withdrew their commitment to human history as the story of an initial, inevitable fall followed by patient hope for an otherworldly future grace. They reimagined it as a process of human growth and self-consolidation in earthly time. As this awareness sharpened, they explicitly constituted a new understanding of God's authority and their earthly role, the human relation to God, and the movement of human history toward an agency instantiation. Increasing self-confidence shifted the focus from reform to transformation, from containing sin to embracing sanctification, from predestination to freely affirmed participation, from subordination to agency.[9]

Until the 1640s, these religious dissenters pursued demands for personal and ecclesiastical transformation among the English citizenry. The popular penetration of the movement accounts for the dramatic collapse of traditional society and sudden onset of the Revolution despite a decade of substantial repression. The prompt mobilization of a national constituency and the explosion of sectarian visions deriving from Puritan ideals testify to the preparatory work of these ministers. As a result, the monarchy once under direct attack was, like Tocqueville's French nobility, "stricken down in a single night."[10] As the insurgency expanded, the religious discourse in which agency principles of individual identity and social practice were first fashioned combined with more secular expressions of individualism to unleash its societally transformative potential, the end not only of a monarchy but also of a worldview.

The religious development of the agency paradigm in England thus occurs in three stages: the emergence among Puritan ministers of a new human role for Protestant believers; the spread and radicalization of agency beliefs among popular constituencies willing to embrace this role through conversion and commitment; and the emerging revolutionary expectations of a mass movement demanding the transformation of English society. With the failure of the insurgents to establish a new political consensus in the Civil War, the Commonwealth devolved into a holding action, undermining the religious will to govern. As it became clear that traditional arrangements were beyond recovery, a new basis for social order was needed. Arising to formulate models of citizenship and institutional structure by which a society composed of agents might be governed, liberal theory signaled the irreversible intrusion of modernity.

Reframing the Puritan Insurgency

As an epochal event, the shifts attending the English Revolution have not received their due. Voltaire, celebrating England's head start as a free, open, and modern commercial nation in his *Philosophical Letters,* mentions in passing its few distant and isolated occasions of civil turmoil.[11] In his classic study of the French Revolution, Tocqueville contrasts his nation's violent path to modernization with the apparently orderly route of its island neighbor. England, he suggests, provided itself "a new lease of life and new energy" by introducing "quite modern . . . innovations, gradually and adroitly . . . into the old order . . . without impairing its stability or demolishing ancient forms."[12] For Marx, the English transition to modernity occurred too early to serve as a model for the later revolutions of the industrial bourgeoisie.[13] If for Continental writers England's modernism existed independent of its revolution, writers from the American perspective neglected the Revolution, conversely, for failing to modernize England. It is scarcely mentioned in *On Revolution,* Hannah Arendt's study of the modern revolutionary tradition, reflecting in part its apparent lack of contemporary relevance and in part her difficulty discerning its transformative implications.[14] Gordon Wood's important work on revolutionary America treats eighteenth-century England as the paradigmatic traditional "monarchical, hierarchy-ridden" society in "its basic social relationships and in its cultural consciousness" from which a "radical" and "revolutionary" America would distinguish itself.[15] Wood's analysis reflects an American view dating from Crèvecoeur, Franklin, Jefferson, and Emerson.

Christopher Hill preeminently among others has helped to recover the English Revolution as a history-making event on two counts: first, as a successful and unprecedented shift of political and economic power to the rising commercial class, making England the first modern, liberal society; and second, as the seedbed for post-liberal ideals of political liberty, economic equality, social justice, and instinctual release, a possible "kingdom of heaven . . . on earth now."[16] This dream of producing fundamental "changes in people's modes of thought and conduct," while, according to Hill, unsuccessful at the time, would resurface centuries later as the basis of modern social and cultural radicalism.[17] Hill's account, while restoring the Revolution to importance as a model of bourgeois modernization and as a harbinger of radical modernism, seriously understates its transformative impact. It indeed transformed thought and conduct with a new human role and society, though to recover its radical legacy we must look not to England but to the United States. Origination of the post-traditional consciousness may have been ceded to more self-conscious modernizers such as Locke, Adam Smith, and the American revolutionaries, but it derived from the reformers and radicals of the English Revolution, who conceived that new heaven on earth for their own time and pushed its logic spiritually and socially beyond the point of no return. Americans inhabit the world these insurgents made.

To grasp this transformation in human role, theological disputes and innovations must be reopened which are now regarded as relevant only to church matters or, worse, the concerns of a bygone world. For the religious discourse of the insurgents directly reflected their own effort to internally fashion and elaborate new worldly capacities. It progressively imagines the developmental advance to agency through a closer and more empowering relation to the divine Author, culminating in the new human responsibility for fulfilling its mandates on earth. To formulate this shift, the Puritans utilized the traditional theological ideas at their disposal, including predestination, original sin, justification by faith, Christian liberty, the role of Jesus, and the story of Adam, continuously revising them in the direction of individual agency.[18]

Added to the problem of a distant rhetoric are confusions which inevitably attend the effort to grasp an underlying historical process such as the characterological shift driving the insurgent agenda. To begin with, the historical actors themselves did not typically realize the full dimensions of their yearnings at the outset. Their early views were often tentative as they sought to match available discourses with their aspirations. Issues and positions shifted dramatically as the larger dimensions of the project gradually emerged. The first English Puritans understood themselves to be reforming the national church and, following Luther, *returning* to the forms of ritual and church organization mandated by Scripture.[19] Only as new internal capacities were integrated and exercised did the reality of an innovative project oriented toward the future reveal itself to the actors. The Puritan focus thus moved from the initial dispute over vestments and ceremonies to the presbyterian reform of the church, then beginning in the 1590s, to personal salvation, the pursuit of sanctification, and the covenant. In Laud's time, the attack on church hierarchy was renewed with a growing commitment to independence and separatism. Finally, by the Revolution, Puritans and their sectarian descendants framed their demands in terms of individual freedom, universal grace, and the restructuring of the Commonwealth.[20] The emergence of these later revolutionary demands from narrow doctrinal controversies can be discerned only by attending to shifts in tone, nuance, and emphasis, and to the growth in boldness, confidence, and certitude.

The complexity confounding the origins of such a historical shift similarly haunts its subsequent stages. The Puritan mainstream never fully comprehended the transformative implications of its convictions. To be sure, the radicalization of its own positions on individual knowledge, conscience, and judgment; worldly activism, open institutional dissent, popular reformism, and theological disputatiousness; godly zeal, millennialism, and Christian liberty were the very timber by which the old order was set afire and the new structure framed in.[21] Yet, as the traditional order collapsed and more extreme views surfaced, the magnitude of the dynamic that had been unleashed generated growing anxiety within the Puritan mainstream. As insurgent sects arrived at radical forms of agency and even approached human self-authorization, the moderate dissenters retrenched, moving back from reform to support a return of civil and royal order. This later retreat has obscured the Puritan contribution to the modernizing agenda and the movement's significant areas of agreement with the sectarians.

Another difficulty with grasping a complex shift in human role arises from the presence of regressive aspects within a broader role enhancement. J. Sears McGee points to the Puritan sense of "human corruption" and "human impotence," irresolution and doubt of God's will, far deeper than the Anglicans', with their more generous view of human rationality and belief that "God requires nothing of us but what is in our power to do" for entry into "his own holy city."[22] Using specific attitudes as benchmarks neglects the contrary agendas from which such attitudes arise. The Puritans' anxiety, strenuousity, and demand for unrelenting obedience derived from their effort to make a new relation with God. These reflected the pressure to demonstrate their worthiness to take and their capacity to sustain such a risky step. Their often agonized sense of sinfulness arose from fears of being inundated with corrupt patterns of deference and godless formalism. These discredited patterns, whose arduous uprooting alone made possible their higher experience of grace, were of course the very substance of Anglican religiosity. More difficult developmental tasks increased spiritual demands as well as fears about the risks and costs of failure. Anglican complacency derived not from religious optimism but from the church's support for established religious and institutional relations and the denial of any systemic discontent. An appropriate comparison, then, situates motivational imperatives and frames of mind within the larger agendas.

A final interpretive difficulty lies in the disparate and internally inconsistent formulations of authority possible within a single conceptual model. Puritans widely disagreed on matters of predestination, church structure, and the human relation with God, constituting for Janice Knight "significant differences and alternative voices within Puritan culture" rather than "a monologic . . . culture."[23] To a degree, these theological disputes are a projective screen for different leadership styles and motivational strategies. Puritan constituents were of divergent temperaments and backgrounds, variously motivated by hopes and fears, promises and threats, love and expectation, insecurity and certitude. Where theology was being framed in situ to catalyze popular constituencies, it accumulated a range of wishes concerning God and God's plan. Beyond a certain point, of course, these distinctions constituted incommensurable images of the human relation to authority. Thus growing divisions between orthodox Calvinists, liberalizing Puritan independents, and radical sectarians in time separated the major parties—proto-agency, agency, and proto-principality, respectively—contesting the shape of Anglo-American modernism.

At the same time, the conceptual complexity created by continuous theological shifts reflects the growing search within Puritan thought for doctrinal support for alternatives to orthodox Calvinism with its constricted reading of the agency advance. Limits imposed on human initiative by predestination, divine inscrutability, and human weakness were continually challenged by such mitigating doctrines as covenantalism, preparationism, voluntarism, assurance of grace, universalism, and even earthly regeneration and the kingdom in history. Some of the many apparent contradictions within Puritan theology have been well noted: a sense of overwhelming sinfulness together with the likelihood of salvation by the elect;[24] predestination juxtaposed with increasing congregational activism and voluntarism.[25] When seen in the context of an evolving ministerial and lay confidence in their religious and worldly powers,[26] recurrent doctrinal shifts and proliferating contradictions reflect the persistent effort to weave revisions of role into original doctrine. Thus, as sin is increasingly mastered, the earlier obsession with it is made to coexist with a new confidence in sanctification.[27] Similarly, as the capacity to act self-reliantly in the world in accord with God's fixed (predestined) ends evolves, a theology of greater choice and initiative is appended.

The failure to discern the emergence of agency as a distinct model of authority has led some scholars to deny the existence of major theological differences between reformers and the established church.[28] Because innovations often remain below the surface until they demand attention, such a case—though errant—could be made in 1570, or even in 1600, as in the colonies in 1770 and in France in 1780. Once it is understood that historical transformations involve gradual stages of self-definition and self-awareness, attention must be given to the way in which great divisions often flow from the logic of seemingly narrow initial differences. In the case before us, the relocation of the earthly locus of divine mediating authority, God's point of human connection, from institutional elites to the individual conscience was, if followed through systematically—as it would be—nothing less than a revolution in worldviews.

The focus on internal and role shifts in this period rather than on ideology enables us to locate the revolution, despite the tangled ideology of its participants, at the beginning of modernity.[29] Subsequent efforts in England and the United States to establish ideological distance from the religious insurgency in both countries constitute later phases in the institutionalization of this new paradigm. While reflecting the wish for a framework less burdened by traditional contentions, secular and even liberationist discourses presuppose agency.

The Anglican Model of Self and Society

A baseline for measuring the gradual emergence of the agency paradigm is the national Anglican Church, established by Henry VIII. Anglican doctrine in the age before the Revolution, with its traditional understanding of institutional authority, institutional prerogatives, and social role, formed a clear and fixed opposition for the clarification of a reformist agenda. Its continuity was maintained from its leader John Whitgift, archbishop of Canterbury during the disputes of the late 1560s and 1570s, and his followers through the great synthesis of Richard Hooker's *Laws of Ecclesiastical Polity* (1593–1597) to the views of James I upon accession and the policies of Archbishop Laud during the period preceding the Revolution. The increasingly intransigent expression of Anglican ideology, influenced by the reformers' popular success and recognition of their doctrinal innovations, sharpened those divisions.

The debate with early Presbyterian reformers over the nature and scope of church government and the relative authority of sacred and secular institutions quickly consolidated the Anglican defense of societal and episcopal hierarchy and the authority of their leaders, the Christian prince and the bishop. Although for the reformers the initial commitment to a presbyterian model of church government independent from civil authority on religious matters scarcely captured the full dimensions of their godly pursuit, Whitgift early recognized the individualistic implications of institutional decentralization. He thus accused the Puritan leader Thomas Cartwright of embracing "such a perfection in men as though they needed no laws or magistrates to govern them but that every man might be as it were a law unto himself."[30] The Anglican defense of the Henrician settlement secured civil order as a Christian commonwealth through the undivided authority of the Christian magistrate to govern both the polity and national church. The appointed ecclesiastical hierarchy, in turn, administered the church and set forth doctrine for the national membership.

The necessity of central authority and institutional hierarchy derived from human incapacity. The prevalence of human fallenness even among believers and the ubiquity of corruption as well as the inconstancy of spiritual growth made centralized control and constant discipline indispensable. The responsibility of community members was in turn to submit: "Who knoweth not that the people for the most part be ignorant and unlearned and inapt to govern? . . . In a word God both appointed the multitude, how godly and learned soever they be to obey and not to rule."[31] Individual concern with personal salvation was legitimate. Given the godly administration of English state and church, however, the path of piety lay within its directives. These authorized the proper beliefs and appropriate participation in the sacraments and other ceremonies, what Laud called "the external decent worship of God."[32] Corrupted individuals, unable to discern or order their relationship with God, were to avoid theological disputes and leave for the church to determine how to "lead . . . a godly, righteous and sober life."[33]

The Anglican defense of central authority required equal deference in society. Virtuous conduct toward others entailed obedience to the moral rules of the community and fulfillment of one's station in the societal hierarchy: "God's kingdom is . . . ordered and peaceable; in it everything is 'in its order. There is something first and something next to be observed, and every thing to be ranked in its proper place.' In the kingdom of nature things are ordered and ranked; heavy bodies do not ascend, nor do light ones descend; 'and so it is in both church and commonwealth. . . . We cannot be quiet and rest but in our own place and function.'"[34] Thus, "loyalty and obedience toward our sovereign" together with "justice and charity toward all [one's] neighbors" produced a community ordered from above.[35] By "resigning our wills up to the command of others,"[36] parishioners imitated the "meekness and humility and patience" of Christ.[37] As Protestants, Anglicans acknowledged individual conscience, but the church's message was "the duty of obedience"[38] and the subordination of private judgment to "authorized guides" speaking for the "entire society or body politic."[39] Because the fate of the individual soul was not affected by worldly conditions, personal godliness involved no public responsibilities. The spiritual failings of other citizens and abuses of political or ecclesiastical leaders were to be borne patiently and left to God's inscrutable wisdom.

This conception of the individual grounded in "subjection to the known laws"[40] of political and religious superiors and performance of a limited and prescribed social function I shall call the traditional model of *servitude*. Religious ideology shaped servitude by establishing the divine governor with its "true and infallible principles" of absolute "Justice."[41] This prepared individuals for subsequent authority relations: "It doth thus appear that the safety of all estates dependeth upon religion; that religion unfeignedly loved perfecteth men's abilities unto all kinds of virtuous services in the commonwealth."[42] Religious subordination operated "to qualify all sorts of men, and to make them in public affairs the more serviceable . . . inferiors for conscience' sake the willinger to obey." Anglican apologists, while justifying religious institutions as the product of "right reason" and the "laws" by which "God will have the world guided,"[43] recognized "that all duties are by so much the better performed, by how much the men are more religious."[44]

Although it was the early Puritans rather than Anglicans who most often identified believers as servants, this was, as we shall see, a matter of available language as well as modesty about the boldness of their claims of individual conscience, social responsibility, and self-initiating activism.[45] The Anglicans, much like the papists, by contrast rejected outright the emerging powers and qualities of Puritan agency. For Anglican Bishop Stephen Gardiner, criticizing "human laws implies injury offered to the majesty of God."[46] Altering those "positive laws" which "proceed from those superiors under whom they live" would also "overturn the world and make every man his own commander"; it "shaketh universally the fabric of government, tendeth to anarchy and mere confusion, dissolveth families, dissipateth colleges, corporations, armies, overthroweth kingdoms, churches, and whatsoever is now through the providence of God by authority and power upheld."[47] The proper standard for citizenship was a "willing and cheerful performance" of all duties and "keep[ing] quiet, without raising quarrels, or disturbing the peace of the church."[48]

The Early Puritan Insurgents

The earliest Puritans supported the separation of the English church from Catholicism but not Elizabeth's employment of religion as a bulwark of her sovereignty through a national church. Anglican inclusivity placed a premium on ritualism and outward conformity at the expense of theological clarity and personal piety. Reformers during the late 1560s and 1570s focused on changes in Anglican governance, sacraments, ceremonies, and prayerbooks and advocated the decentralization of church structure into local presbyteries. Brooking no criticism, the queen countered initiatives in Parliament and church councils by eliminating overt nonconformity and purging dissident ministers. Neutralized as a national force, insurgents were compelled to de-emphasize church policy. From bases of power in the universities and local parishes, they turned ever more to the personal demands of a Christian life.

Late Elizabethan spiritual tracts and diaries reveal the early stages in the transformative process. The writings of Puritan ministers such as Richard Rogers, Richard Greenham, and Arthur Dent present individuals moving beyond the established church to uncover the meaning of personal piety for themselves and their followers. Heretofore tightly controlled worldly energies were being set loose in a society of declining restraints, leaving individuals struggling to find order and coherence amidst the many temptations. In a 1587 diary entry Rogers writes, "I see the course of this world caryeth men, espec[ially] of our calleing, after it, and for profit and promotion to foresee or refuze no slavery nor shamefull dealinge, and to please men, howsoever god be displeased."[49] Arthur Dent, in the widely disseminated popular tract *The Plain Man's Path-way to Heaven,* paints "the world" in rhetoric of "Orient colours" as "a sea of glass, a pageant of fond delights, a Theatre of Vanity, a Labyrinth of errour, a Gulf of grief, a Stye of filthiness, a Vale of misery, a Spectacle of woe, a river of tears, a Stage of deceit, a Cage full of Owls, a den of Scorpions . . . a whirl-winde of passions, a feigned Comedy, a delectable phrensie, where is false delight, assured grief, certain sorrow, uncertain pleasure, lasting wo, fickle worth, long heaviness, short joy."[50] The inflated language captures an ambiguous attachment to worldliness leavened with fears of its seductiveness in the absence of spiritual direction.

These early reformers helped to contain the burgeoning of worldly energies through the revitalization of religious piety. They yearned for personal validation and guidance from a deeper, more intimate relation with God, and turned from the world not toward monasticism but to recover the strength of their spiritual priorities. In "torment" over his "looseness" and "unwillinge[ness] to be awakened," distracted by the emptiness and "utter daunger" of a world filled with "uncertaintie" and the "brittlenes of thinges below," Rogers adopts "a sensible contempt of this worlde" for "joyfull expectation of departure from hence."[51] He finds "great comfort" and spiritual clarity for the "many things amisse in our lives" which "we can see no cause of" by turning toward God, "careinge for the matters of god" and "our christian estate," asking "godes mercy in our calleing to the felow[ship] of the gospel."[52] Like the earlier Marian exiles, these men were Calvinists. But Calvinism's moralistic preoccupation with obedience and duty, and both its expectation and stigmatization of failure, was debilitating. The immense responsibility of reorganizing and managing one's own personal spirituality, of resisting all temptations to sin including passive (Anglican) ritualistic conformity, had to be sustained in the face of inevitable lapses. How could this fragile new relationship to God, with its as yet unclear new strengths and weaknesses, be securely established? In their diaries and books of spiritual advice, these ministers struggled for an answer.

Restoring meaning in a radically changing world required God's direction. Help is called upon initially to control worldly temptations to "injoy our peace, liberty, and other commod[ities] upon such conditions as the times doe oft offer unto us," by "keepe[ing] us . . . from the corruptions of the time and of the world" which have "great force and strenghth." Individuals must accept responsibility for their good and bad conduct: resisting "wandering and fonde desires . . . profites and pleasures" as "unlawful"; determining to "doe duty aright," to "be always doeing or seekeing occasion to do some good" with "aptness and willingnes."[53] To bolster self-control, Puritan ministers in broadly disseminated guidance books such as *A Garden of Spiritual Flowers* by Rogers, William Perkins, Richard Greenham, and George Webbe, Rogers's own *Seaven Treatises, Containing Such Directions . . . in the which, True Christians may learne how to leade a godly and comfortable life every day,* and Dent's *Path-way* detailed the temptations and the responsibilities framing Puritan life. In his *Seaven Treatises,* which Rogers asserts is the first of its kind, he elaborates these two polarities over several hundred pages: first, "setting before [God's children's] eyes as in a glasse, the infinite, secret, and deceitful corruptions of the heart"; then offering "doctrines particularlie drawne and gathered for mens lives to governe and order them, which tieth them to dailie use of the same throughout their whole course."[54] Dent details at great length the "nine very clear and manifest signs of a man's condemnation" or traditional sins and the eight "manifest signs of damnation" or Puritan faithlessness as well as the "eight infallible tokens of a regenerate mind."[55]

While framed as the moral duty to follow "good precepts" and "holy directions,"[56] the principles of godly obedience are being subsumed within the wish for God's presence in an abiding relation. They ask "that good would awaken us and bring us neerer to him." The *purpose* of obedience is to establish a personal connection, "to mak my whole life a meditation of a better life, and godliness in every part even mine occupacion and trade, that I may . . . walk with the lord for the time of our abideinge here below . . . [and] come neerer to the practize of godliness and after to have our conversation in heaven."[57] God's continuing presence no longer follows merely from fulfilling one's obligations: "All outward honesty and righteousness, without the true knowledge and inward feeling of God, availeth not to eternal life." Out of "faith, love, zeal, conscience of obedience" arises the deeper "power thereof in the heart, which is only from the sanctifying spirit." By the indwelling of this spirit, believers are elevated from performers of acts "which of themselves are good," from being "counted good honest men, good true dealers, good neighbors, and good townsmen" who nevertheless are in "great danger of losing their souls for ever,"[58] to individuals sanctified and able to withstand lapses: "There are two workings of God's spirit in us, the one inferiour, which brings but some fruit of the spirit, without any special fruits of grace; the other superior and more certain, when the spirit works an infallible sanctification . . . [which] may be dimmed . . . but . . . not finally quenched. . . . [He] regenerates us so, that we may fall, so as afterward he may raise us again, and will."[59] The Puritan catalogue of sins reflects this shift by including with traditional sins signs of an internal want of faith.[60]

The experience of sanctification provides the key to understanding Puritan spirituality. As these believers struggled to deepen and sustain the new sense of a godly presence, and radically achieved the clarity that enabled them to identify and define it, present sanctification gradually eclipsed the prospect of future salvation. This in turn produced a heightened religious confidence along with the sense of being cultural innovators and transformers. The early experience, however, was only a temporary heightening of spiritual well-being. Rogers reflects:

> God hath continued his kindness to me . . . peaceable thinkinge of the liberty and happiness in christianity so occupied that I have not meanly thought of earthly peace or provision. . . . I have not had so continual a fitnes and cheerfulnes of minde to such duties as lay uppon me in any man[ner] as here of late. . . . Among other medit[ations] . . . I [was] beholding how graciously the lord hath hedged me in on every side, what sweet knowledg of his will . . . he hath given me, and other bless[ings], good will and a good name with the godlier sort.

Rogers is periodically overcome by the escalating experience of godly sanctification. He writes at one point: "In my retourne home my minde by the way was taken upp in veary heavenly sorte, reioiceing not a litle that the lord hath so inlarged mine hart as that mine olde and accustomed dreames and fantasies of thinges belowe were vanished and drowned. The med-it[ations] of mine hart were such as caryed me to the lord."[61]

These intimations of a new sense of self and world are difficult to fathom: "This one thing much occupied me, that . . . we might grow and . . . might see in what partic[ulars] we were chaunged as well concerneing knowl-edge as pract[ice]." More troubling, these experiences of enhancement are fleeting, producing a continual "decay of grac," the "declineinges . . . in our lives, remitting of zeale, and a growinge in a short time to a comon course." With such mood swings, "gracious deliver[ances]" are often followed by "mine unwoorthiness and wants" as "I by the litle and litle fell from the strenghthe I had gotten."[62] This dependence on surging moods of spiritual-ity, on a "vehemency of zeale and my heavenly affection," lead in manic fashion to the "slake" of "feelinge of joy," to "lighthart[edness]," to "unset-ledness" and "wax[ing] colde," to a sense that one will "loose" the sense of sanctification "again, yea and worse," as "former fervency" is inevitably "abated." Such declensions increase vulnerability and shake one's sense of self-worth and self-assurance: "Again I felt the rebellion ariseinge, so that I see not how one may safely grow secure and bolde but one daunger or other may holde him from it."[63]

To sustain spiritual well-being and counter such feelings of loss, early Puritans, though lacking clarity about the process, are impelled to "grow" continually in "godliness."[64] Greenham yearns for "an infallible sanctifica-tion."[65] Dent wishes for "the new creature or work" of "sanctification"— though "always still fashioning," always "imperfect"—to be "fully fashioned in this life."[66] Rogers is obsessed with becoming "more constant" in "my course in godliness." He seeks amidst the setbacks an "increase" in God's "gifts in me," new sustaining powers and impulses: "There are evident to-kens of the sanctifying spirit, to love good, because it is good; and to hate sin, because it is sin: the more we grow in gifts, the more . . . to feel the graces of God in us, as that yet our sense and feeling is not lessened, and to fear and quake at the first degree and motions of sin; not less they full quench, but less they cool the heart of the spirit in us." They experience the result as a new internal development: "We must be like . . . them that are growing from childhood. . . . [T]hey that grow out of child-hood, do things be-seeming manhood, rather than childishness: so though babyish things both in life and doctrine become us being babes, yet having past our child-hood, the Lord looks for more manly ripeness; both in knowledge and in holiness of life."[67] A remarkable new evolutionary perspective is emerging: the religious mission may be posed theologically as the return to earlier convictions, but spiritual growth increasingly guides the meaning and direction of daily aspirations.

The determination to consolidate the experience of sanctification on some stable internal base stretched theological assumptions. Puritan religious life was framed as participation within a fellowship of believers. Yet insurgent conventicles were too unstable, and the new sensibility could find no home in existing institutions. Greenham writes: "In all which troubles notwithstanding no world of reward, no terror of tyranny, could cause [one] willingly to do the least thing displeasing to God. . . . If all the Monarchs in the world withstood us, our own consciences comforting us, we ruled above all."[68] At the same time, patient reliance on God only bolstered prevailing institutions and practices. For dissenting Puritans seeking to build a movement there was, regardless of theological mandates of predestination and salvation by faith, finally the individual and his or her willingness to embrace new commitments.

Individuals, Dent holds, needed to "awake" and begin taking "a greater care of our salvation" by "seeking after God": salvation "is not found, but of them that seek it diligently, and beg it earnestly. . . . Herein delayes are dangerous: for the longer we defer it, the worse is our case." The dissenters' religious fate, from the strenuous regimens recorded in their diaries to the detailed exortations in their guidance books, depended on their own efforts: "The end of Christ's coming shall be able to judge every man according to his works; that is, as his works shall declare him, and testifie of him; and of his faith." Then shall God "call all men to an account, and have a reckoning of every man's particular actions and to reward them according to their deeds." The individual can take assurance that "so long as I keep his commandments, and . . . as a Christian man ought to do, he will not damn my soul." This freedom, not yet the voluntarist foundation of agency evolved by Milton, John Goodwin, and others, already called individuals to enhanced responsibilities. Thus, the awesome responsibility for personal sanctification and salvation lay in one's own hands. In this emerging dispensation, each alone must pursue "some better sight of your self" in "that glass, wherein we do behold the face of our souls before God."[69]

The courage to present oneself to God for an absolute and just—not merciful—judgment explains the rigorous preparation Puritans demanded of themselves. An obsession with the minutiae of sin was a measure not of defeatism but contrarily of a readiness to be accountable in God's terms. Attending to the detailed indicators of preparation and sanctification provided a continuing measure of that readiness. Through vigilance, every accessible vice could be rigorously identified and uprooted: "I desire, to know mine owne hart better . . . and to be acquainted with the diverse corners of it and what sin I am most in daunger of and what dilig[ence] and meanes I use against any sin and how I goe under any afflic[tion]," wrote Rogers. In "great watchfullnes" he "looked to finde out any, either olde or new corruptions" in himself. Continuing self-scrutiny was the pathway toward sanctification, wherein we learn "we had not to trust to the goodness which is in us, for it soon flitteth, but to noorishe good begin[nings] in our selves with care, etc."[70]

In time, the previously unthinkable possibility emerged of sustaining this heightened condition. Without fathoming its full scope or comprehending its transformative implications, these seekers foresaw living at a higher stage of blessedness and sanctity on earth. Rogers writes the *Seaven Treatises* in order to "direct the true Christian" to a "very sweet and effectual taste of eternall happines, even here." He instructs that "the heart which is the fountaine from which the practice of godliness must grow and come, ought to be purged and clensed: and consequently, the bodie it selfe, ought to be first made a fit instrument for the same, (to the accomplishment of that which is good, and to the well ordering of the life) in which two, consisteth the sanctification of the whole Man." In this way, "the heart of man" becomes "good, and holy and pure."[71]

The growth into sanctification is characterized at this point in two ways: the development of new powers and capacities within the individual, and the attainment of a new state of being. These individual powers include a greater mastery over the "weedes" of earthly corruptions and desires needing "tillage,"[72] a heart and mind increasingly "kept pure and cleane," a greater clarity regarding God's purposes,[73] a growing stability and confidence in election and in God's commitment to "keep fast the certaintie of Gods favor daily, and constantly,"[74] amounting to a greater sense of one's inner capacities and godly role. The broader qualitative experience of a higher stage, growing out of the experience of new powers, is characterized ambiguously as both return and innovation. It is, on the one hand, "a renewing and repairing of the corrupted estate of our soul" which was "attainted" by "Adam's transgressions."[75] This view imagines for individuals a return to Adam's prelapsarian obedience, "to practice all duties commanded" now "strengthened to doe that good in their life, which they can love with their heart" and "approve . . . in their judgment" with the greater "diligence and constancie."[76] Yet, on the other hand, this inner shift is also spoken of as the "new birth" of a "new man, or new work of grace." The "new Crea-ture" transcends obedience as a godly instrument who through the "work of Gods grace within" is made "holy and unblameable" to "walk as Christ has walked" and "serve God in righteousnes and true holiness all the days of his life."[77] The wish to recover an original innocence is being contested by a pro-gressive vision of characterological development with its culmination in the integration of inner sanctification.

Growing sanctification provoked new thoughts about worldly activity. Life was still a temporary exile in preparation for salvation, but with the in-creasing sense of spiritual power it was also emerging as an arena of godly activity. After the "veary sweet bles[sing]" from "prayer and med[itation]," Rogers experienced the "knowledge and grace to be the fitter to other du-ties," feeling "unrebukeable in the middest of a wicked and froward genera-tion" to "woorck" on the spiritual tasks of earthly ministry.[78] This under-standing of the individual newly shaped to act in the world in a godly fashion is an interim stage in the development of agency that I will call *proto-agency*. Well beyond servitude, the individual experiences an inward holi-ness. Enabled but not yet empowered by the spirit, the believer's sanctity de-pends on God's immediate power and presence. A capability to act person-ally with ever more righteousness is now possible, though not yet as a full instrument to enact God's plan in the world. Under direct guidance, a con-viction regarding one's godliness is sustainable: "We must fetch the warrant of our Salvation from within our selves; even from the work of GOD within us. . . . A man's Conscience is of great force this way, and will not lye or de-ceive."[79] Sanctified individuals in turn gained radical worldly capacities, in-cluding the power to judge "the Spirits, and doctrines of the Preachers," to "discern betwixt truth and falsehood in matters of Religion . . . whether they be of God or no," to determine those preachers "which walk unblameably," and to "follow the example of those" and "flee the example of such as are offensive."[80] Above all, individuals could now "perceive, in what case you stand before God."[81]

While new spiritual powers were mandating expanded initiative and per-sonal discretion, the coherent sense of a more advanced role remained elu-sive. Traditional doctrinal restraints continued to stifle a potential release from institutional control. Individuals remained "lumps of sin, and masses of misery," with a "voluntary inclination of [their] will unto evil."[82] They alone were the cause of their own damnation, "for God is not the cause of mens condemnation, but themselves," while God received the credit for any righteousness and repentance. Yet though they presumably could not save themselves, these miserable sinners could swiftly be, with God's power, transformed and capable of the highest good, as "the causes of Election" are "only in God himself."[83] Thus they were obligated to "strive, according to that power and faculty we have," to walk in the "path of salvation" so that God might choose them.[84] Believers could never doctrinally "comprehend the reason of *God's* proceeding" or "search out the bottom of God's secrets,"[85] yet were experientially encouraged to feel "cock sure, and cease to doubt any more"[86] about his intentions. By this logical prescription, the elect remained the few, "not one out of a hundred." Nevertheless, the ministers wrote to convince the growing public that "Heaven [may] preserve us all."[87] This unresolved and incompatible combination of elements from servitude and agency, strong evidence of a culture in transition, would not evolve into a coherent theology or workable identity.

William Perkins and the Theology of Spiritual Growth

The crystalization of English Puritan spirituality occurred at the end of the century under the leadership of the influential Cambridge preacher William Perkins. Called the "new Moses" by his contemporaries,[88] he nurtured a generation of popular preachers during the reign of James I, beginning in 1603, including Richard Sibbes, William Ames, John Preston, John Cotton, William Gouge, Thomas Goodwin, Thomas Hooker, and Thomas Shepard. Building on Perkins's theological advances, these preachers and their colleagues and students spread the call to a godly life, elaborated its dynamic new powers, pinpointed the signs of its progress, developed the process for attaining it, and above all named it. Proclaiming national godliness as imminent, they brought urgency to the pursuit of a transformed character and worldly role.

Perkins's dramatic emphasis on spiritual growth provided legitimacy for and impetus to the inward turning of Puritan aspirations. Believers were exhorted to effect their own spiritual destinies, and promised in return for an active and resolute faith personal development with sanctification and its new powers of agency the culmination. The spiritual goal that "every person must have a faith of his own"[89] was now clearly the result of a distinctly individual process: "Whom must we search? The prophet answereth, Your-selves—not other men, but yourselves. . . . Every man for himself, for as every soul must be saved by itself, so must it believe, repent and search it-self."[90] The rewards were also personal: "The more we shall be made partak-ers of the graces of God and the heavenly glory; so much also more and more shall the glory of God be made manifest in us."[91] Though living amidst worldly institutions, the seeker lived apart: "We are pilgrims in this world, our life is a journey: God also hath appointed our conscience to be our com-panion and guide, to show us what course we may take and what we may not."[92] Pressures for institutional and spiritual accommodation had to be and could be withstood. One's "office regenerate is . . . to clear and defend a man against all his enemies both bodily and ghostly. . . . [I]t is neither wit nor learning, nor favour, nor honor that can" protect the individual, but "only the poor conscience directed and sanctified by the spirit of God which boldly and constantly answereth, *I know that I believe.*"[93]

To fortify personal responsibility, Perkins infused his Calvinism with prag-matic individual voluntarism. The task was complicated doctrinally. As a product of God's unconstrained choice, individual grace through "justifica-tion and sanctification" had to precede individual "repentance." This, how-ever, left individuals passive while awaiting God's favorable judgment. Dis-tinguishing religious experience from theology, Perkins simply inverts the order placing existential initiative first: "And though this repentance be one of the last in order, yet it showes it selfe first: as when a candle is brought into a roome, we first see the light before we see the candle, and yet the can-dle must neede be, before the light can be."[94] Repentance could now be "first preached,"[95] though theologically human efforts were "onely *works of preparation,*" a "preparation to . . . the applying of the remedy, the reforma-tion of conscience." God's predetermination now came to those who "above all things . . . labour to obtain it: for it is not given by nature to any man."[96]

Thus, individuals were free to sin—"sinnes proceeding from the will, are properly tearmed *voluntarie;* such as the doer mooved by his own will com-mits"[97]—or to repent: "I call Repentance a work, because it seems . . . an ac-tion of a repentant sinner. Which appears by the sermons of the Prophets and Apostles. . . . *Repent, turn to God, amend your lives, etc.*" God responds to human initiative: "In that the new birth and regeneration of a sinner is not without the motion of his own will, we are taught, that we must desire our own salvation, use the good means, and strive against our own corruptions, and endeavor earnestly by asking, seeking, knocking. . . . [T]here is no virtue or gift of God in us, without our wills: and in every good act: God's grace and mans will concur."[98] Individuals have the full capacity to search themselves, find out their sins, "confess them to God freely and ingeniously," and willingly "give free and frank obedience to God's will."[99]

With Perkins, the path toward grace becomes a developmental advance. "Original sinne," an initial state of "naturall corruption," represents only "an absence of goodnesse and uprightnes" for individuals who have not yet developed their "created qualitie of holines." One's dissatisfaction "in his first estate" must be stressed, for one "is natural and corrupt (as we are bred and born)" with "a veil before his face so that he seeth nothing."[100] Those who "live and grow" and "bring forth good fruit" in turn "by little and little are wholy renewed from evil to good."[101] Responsibility to develop must be mobilized, as those with "no more than these small beginnings must be careful to increase them, because he which goes not forward goes backward."[102] Beginning as "babes in Christ," individuals can, like "a grain of mustard seed," one of Perkins's popular religious symbols, "grow up and increase . . . to a great tree and bear fruit admirably."[103]

Personal change required intensive efforts to judge one's religious condition, by first obtaining "knowledge of the law" and of "the judicial sentence of the law," then pursuing a "*just* and *serious examination* of the conscience by the law*," and finally undergoing "a *sorrow*" for "the punishment of sin" discovered by this analysis. The injunction to search oneself "diligently, and by a serious examination" was designed expressly to discover the roots of sin and passive servitude within and to uproot them: "This duty of searching is both the beginning of all true grace and the means to stay God's judgments and therefore is so pithily and so forcibly urged by the Holy Ghost. . . . Seeing therefore that it is so necessary a duty, let every one of us endeavor . . . to rip and ransack our hearts and to search our ways to the bottom of it."[104] In reaching down to "see into himself" and "know himself," it became possible for the individual to "forsake himself and his own ways and turn to the Lord."[105]

By carefully defining the process of spiritual growth, Perkins provided markers for a self-regulated process that moved Puritans beyond a self constituted by traditional society to one grounded in emergent Protestant values. He prescribed those "special duties" necessary for a "diligent and serious examination of the conscience," specifically setting forth each type of sin to "search" and the process for evaluating and overcoming them.[106] To this end, the individual was to keep a "strict and good account" to God "for all his actions," all "graces, blessings and gifts" from God, and all "sins

[and] abuses of our gifts, all our ignorances, negligences and frailties whatsoever" just as "tradesmen . . . keep in their shops books of receipts and expenses."[107] By humbling ourselves and craving "renovation" with "all our heart," with "the whole man" as a "free and voluntary" act "without all constraint and compulsion," we are freed from the guilt of sin, original and actual.[108] The culmination, clearer and more definitive than ever before, was to be "born anew" on a new "stay or foundation," the "foundation of God, that is, the decree of Gods election," which "is like the foundation of an house, which standeth fast, though all the buildings be shaken," to then "build ourselves upon *it*."[109] This new foundation formed the characterological base for the new and modern self.

The "New Creature": The Agent

Perkins realized that this achievement of spiritual regeneration was a developmental transformation, a reshaping of the self through its "change of the minde and whole man in affection, life and conversation."[110] He spoke of it as an evolution to a higher level, as "Saints" or individuals coming "to perfection" in "conformity with Angels,"[111] as a "child" of the "father" or "*the* sonnes of God"[112] who from *"newborn babies feeding on the milk of the word"* became "new" or *"perfect men in Christ,"*[113] even to be "a brother to Christ."[114] Perkins at times framed it as a transfer or extension of the products of God's spirit to the inner self, as "the seale of Gods election imprinted in their hearts," or "the words" of "the Spirit of God" being "engraffe[d] . . . in their hearts," or "the apprehending" in "their hearts" of "the things which the spirit of God makes known to the faithful."[115] This alone certified an inner spiritual transformation, an inner righteousness by which one "cannot but understand the Scripture . . . for I feel in my heart, and have a sensible experience of that inwardly, which the Spirit of God has delivered in the Scriptures."[116] At other times, Perkins speaks more dramatically of being taken over "and truly *joined* unto Christ" in "heavenly fellowship and communion with him" such that one feels "his holy spirit moving and stirring" within, which "by his heavenly power makes him do the good which he does."[117] In the most extreme formulation, believers internalize Christ within the self: "They do in their hearts distinctly apply and appropriate Christ and his benefits to themselves" such that Christ may dwell in their hearts "by faith,"[118] integrating "the Image of God" to become crookedness made "straightnes" as "his image is renewed or restored to us."[119]

This new individual was wholly remade with "the setting or imprinting of the new qualities and inclinations in the mind, will, affections of the heart."[120] As "new creatures," spiritually developed believers now possessed sanctified capacities: a new "heart stable and unblameable" powered by "all spirituall motions";[121] a regenerate reason or mind with "knowledge of those patterns . . . in the Lord himself" as "partakers of his light and his knowledge";[122] a renovated will that can "choose . . . good" and "refuse . . . evil";[123] "sanctified affections . . . inclined to . . . good";[124] and a "conscience sanctified and renewed by the Holy Ghost" operating as God's "witnesse" on earth.[125] Regenerated individuals are moved by an inwardness sanctified by the "abolishment of . . . corruption," by an inner "apt[ness] to live well" out of a "purity and holiness."[126]

So transformed, in "harmony" rather than *"disharmonie"* with God, in "conformitie or correspondence to the will of God" in all "the substance of his body and soul" and all "Faculties and Powers," the individual was empowered to act inwardly out of God's will, spontaneously realizing it "in new and spiritual actions, as namely in thinking, willing, and desiring that which is good." Perkins sometimes defines the new role by expanding the older language of duty, as the "new obedience," as an enhanced inner willingness to obey by "the affection and desire" rather than mere obligation through "act and performance."[127] Yet it is not a return to mere obligation, for it transcends conformance with the letter of divine injunctions. An individual might "fail greatly in the action of obedience" and still if possessing "the spirit . . . in Christ" then "God will accept his affection to obey, as obedience acceptable unto him." Adhering "no longer to the world, but to that city which is above," the believer now freely actualizes the ends of God, remarkably transcending both "the *bondage* and *tyranny* of sin and Satan" and "the rigour of the law, which exacteth perfect obedience and condemneth all imperfection."[128]

Virtue through obedience has given way to a righteousness which precedes action. With godliness now distinct from the rigid execution of demands in every case, individuals are released from the submission characterizing the world of servitude. Regeneration

sets the soul at liberty, and makes her free to follow the will of God . . . to do of his own accord that which before he could not do, neither could suffer that any man could exort him to do, and has now lust in wholesome things, and his members are free and at liberty, and have power to do all things of his own accord which belong to a sound and whole man to do. . . . [O]f his own nature without any compulsion of the law, he brings forth good works. . . . [H]e works naturally the will of God.

"Christian liberty" has become the "service of God" in "perfect freedom."[129] The spontaneous will is now godly: "All our obedience must be voluntary, and come from such freeness of will, as if there were no bond in the law of God to force and compel us thereto. The people of God that are turned and guided by the free spirit of God, must be a voluntary people, and with alacrity and cheerfulness do the duties . . . even as if there were neither heaven nor hell, judge nor judgment after this life."[130]

This capacity for sustained, internally mobilized godly action in turn reconstituted the human role as instrument—or agent—of God on earth:

> Now these actions are works of God in and by a man's will: and mans will is not only a subject of them, but also an instrument. A Subject, in that God is the first and principal worker of these works in the will. An Instrument, because it pleases God to use the will, and to move it by his grace for the acting and effecting of the things which he appoints. And thus the will is not merely passive, but *passive* and *active* both: first passive, and then active. . . . It is necessary indeed that God first regenerate us and make us his children and new creatures. And in this thing we do not Co-work with God, but stand as patients, that God may work upon us and reform us. . . . Yet, after our regeneration, by truth . . . we begin to be *Co-workers* with the grace of God.

This transformed self is an active and responsible self, participating as the "instrument" in joint works on earth with God the "principal cause" or "principal agent."[131] Journeying across the "huge sea" which is the "world" toward that final end or destination determined by God, "the intended port of happiness which is the salvation of our souls," the believer now determines the means—the direction, route, and equipment—for its realization on earth: "Our ship is the conscience of every man. . . . Therefore it stands us in hand to be always at the helm, and to carry our ship with as even a course as possibly we can."[132]

Institutional Implications

By setting individuals free as God's agents, Perkins sharpened the radically individualist dimensions of Puritan faith. Unable to assume communal support, the "one rule" for "all matters" is to "ask your own conscience what you may or ought to do": "Would you men did so with you? Then do you it. Would you not be so dealt with? Then do it not. . . . So in all things ask your conscience . . . and she will teach you." Conscience supersedes rules of the body politic: "human laws made after the grant of this liberty" cannot "bind conscience of themselves . . . for that which is granted by a higher authority, namely God himself, cannot be revoked or repealed by the inferior authority of any man. . . . [I]t is against reason that human laws being subject to defects, faults, errors, and manifold imperfections, should truly bind conscience, as Gods laws do, which are the rule of righteousness."[133] Believers must evaluate human laws by divine standards and decide to obey or "not to obey" accordingly.[134] Similarly with religious institutions, individuals must judge their ministers and the "Creeds and Confessions of particular Churches" as to whether they are "ordained in [God's] own word and commanded to us as his own worship."[135] While "necessary obedience is to be performed both to civil and Ecclesiastical jurisdiction . . . that they have a constraining power to bind conscience . . . as gods laws do, it is not yet proved, neither can be."[136] "We must not," he tells us, "fall away from God for any creature . . . though we lose temporal blessings."[137]

Institutional prerogatives are further undercut. Although "mans conscience is knowne to none, besides himselfe, but to God," the individual may be compelled by it to resist institutional authority: "It may . . . be true in the laws of men, that they may in some cases be omitted without sin against God." Legal duties might be "done or not done without sin" in those cases where "peace, the common good, and comly order may be maintained and all offense avoided by any other means." In other cases, civil law should be contravened: in wartime, opening the city gates for retreating soldiers over the magistrate's contrary order would "further" and not "hinder the end of the law." Perkins finally defends the sanctity of conscience absolutely: *"What is done against conscience though it err and be deceived, it is a sin in the doer."*[138] Were Anabaptists, whose doctrines he personally rejected, to violate their godly precepts, such as the refusal to swear oaths, that would be a sin in his judgment.[139] The principle of direct internal authorization that would in time recast the world and remake institutions has been firmly established.

While the goal of spiritual development is to dwell in a transformed world, Perkins's agent was not yet a conscious or willful social activist. The revolutionary implications of this new dispensation remained just the surface, implied in the fact that "every person is a double person and under two regiments." One is "the regiment of the world" or "the temporal kingdom" in which the believer accepts social hierarchies, economic disparities, and political authority: "In the temporal regiment is husband, wife, father, mother, son, daughter, mistress, maid, subject, lord. . . . [T]here thou must do according to thine office. If thou be a father, thou must . . . bring all under obedience, whether by fair means or foul."[140] At the same time, one is also in "the regiment of the gospel" or "the kingdom of heaven." Here "there is neither father nor mother, neither master, mistress, maid nor servant, nor husband nor wife, nor lord nor subject nor inferior, but Christ is all and each to other is Christ himself. There is none better than other, but all alike good, all brethren."[141] Instructed of the need to balance the demands of both king-doms,[142] the believer is nevertheless urged toward the higher realm: "His will must be done on earth as it is in heaven . . . [as] it is done by Angels . . . willingely, speedily, and faithfully."[143]

The burden on the godly is intensified by Perkins's insistence on England's special mission:

> Thus for soul and body they were every way a nation blessed of God, a peo-ple beloved of God above all others. . . . He hath called us out of the dark-ness, first of heathenism and then of popery. His covenant of grace and sal-vation he hath confirmed with us . . . his holy word never better preached and the mysteries thereof never more plainly opened since the time of the apostles. . . . Beyond all this, we have a land also that floweth with milk and honey. It is plentiful in all good things. We have liberty and peace . . . and the companions of peace, prosperity, plenty, health, wealth, corn, wool, sil-ver, abundance of all good things that may please the heart of men.

These blessings entail increased responsibility: "Thus hath God deserved the love of England."[144] God is demanding its embrace of redemption, its being "healed to the bottom"—and promptly: "The time [is] limited. . . . God . . . will not let the chaff lie forever amongst the wheat. He hath therefore ap-pointed his fanning time, when to blow the chaff to hell and to gather his wheat into heavenly garners." This "so fearful a fanning" is, Perkins warns, "so near, as appeareth by the blast already passed over us (which are noth-ing but forerunners of a greater tempest)."[145] Perkins's urgency was driven by his vast aspirations, and his fear of losing an extraordinary opportunity: "I may cry out . . . O England, a nation not worthy to be beloved. . . . Our long peace, plenty and ease have bred great sins, so great that they reach to heaven . . . specially of Atheism, neglect of gods worship, contempt of the word, profanation of the Sabbath, abuse of the Sacraments, etc."[146] Failure, though unthinkable, presses: "A plague and a judgment, and that most fearful hangs over England . . . already pronounced . . . and shall certainly be executed, without a visible reformation." In this imminent sorting with its hints of "heaven now," the resolution to be "fanned and cleansed by his word" will spare believers and enable them to "remain pure and clean wheat, fit for the house and church of God and for his kingdom in heaven" in an England of "glorious prosperity."[147]

For agents in a larger collective destiny, the role of the "new creature" had evolved beyond any conventional prelapsarian obedience. Yet Perkins was hesitant to affirm an expanded public role, because the mass consolidation of the new self, clearly the basis of the larger redemptive agenda, remained uncertain. As vanguards in a transformative process, many exemplars of this new type would feel unresolved about the vast internal transition being demanded: "In Gods Church commonly they who are touched by the spirit, and begin to come on in Religion, are much troubled with fear that they are not Gods children; and none so much as they." They need certitude, and "are not quiet till they find some resolution."[148] The overriding concern at this point was to help them attain the necessary clarity and certainty to sustain their own individual advance. Perkins stressed internal consolidation: "The apprehending of Christ is . . . spiritually by *assurance*, which is, when the elect are persuaded in their hearts by the Holy Ghost, of the forgiveness of their sins . . . their justification, adoption, sanctification, eternall life. . . . [T]hey know the time will come when they have full redemption from all evils."[149] Promised the "certainty of salvation" as a "property of regenerate conscience," every seeker "is bound . . . to believe in his own salvation and adoption by Christ."[150]

Yet the movement needed constituents, ready or not, and Perkins evolved Puritan theology to promote confidence. Thus, he proclaimed that "a man is even at that instant already entered into the kingdom of heaven when the Lord . . . hath cast but some small portion of faith as repentance into the ground of the heart." Given the limited effect of such exhortations, Perkins further enumerated the "manifold tokens" of "election"[151] in the experience of faith as well as facility and perseverance in works which constituted reassuring "signes, whereby a sonne of God may be discerned from a child of the devill."[152] In pursuing this strenuous regimen, he encouraged reliance on "the strengthening power of Christ," which would ensure that "a Christian can not quite fall away from grace."[153]

Greatly influencing the subsequent movement, Perkins further placed at the center of his theology the doctrine of covenant. The covenant of grace was a key development in the emergence of voluntarism, integrating choice with necessity through the creation of a binding relationship with God "freely by oath."[154] In fact, a "lawfull vowe" required "libertie." Only the product of a *"voluntarie"* and *"free"* will, "libertie of conscience," or uncoerced "reason" rendered a "Judgment" possessing sound "delibera-tion."[155] Moreover, the covenant facilitated the individual's new freedom as a "stay and Proppe" to "help his own weaknes & to keep himself from fall-ing." Once the individual has "sworne" to God *"that I will keepe thy righteous judgements,"* God will also perform with covenantal certainty—opening on a "universall" basis "the promises of the Gospel."[156] This use of the covenant reflects a continuing movement away from the theology of predestination toward a more limited instrumental use of divine determinism. For Perkins, as for Dent, the role of predestination, already applied beyond its initial meaning as confirmation of the believer's own judgment, such that "whoso-ever feels himself freed through the graces of God, may be assured of his predestination," was extended even further. Now linked to the covenant, it ratified a contractually negotiated assurance by promising "election . . . cer-tain and immutable" regardless of "any of our evil defects."[157] By circum-venting predestination by which the individual is "bound by God" with the provision that one "may also bind himselfe,"[158] Perkins took a major step to-ward voluntary commitment in the shift from proto-agency to agency.[159]

In establishing agency, Perkins shaped the Protestant image of the self in the world—its now active participation through the "works and duties and la-bours of our callings to the good of the church and commonwealth and the place whereof we are members." Where institutions embody godly ends, the Puritan had a responsibility to examine the available roles in terms of his or her personal "affections" and "gifts" and choose that which "he liketh best and is every way the fittest to."[160] Although not everyone was to be elected, Perkins's God is inclusive, reflecting the goal of the ministry to reach all who would listen: *"Christ died for all men. . . .* [who] would have received Christ."[161] He accepts without distinction "rich and poor, noble or com-moner, minister or kitchen boy," for he is "like a father" and "if a child be sick . . . will not cast him forth of his doors, but pity him, and provide such things as may restore him to health." Thus "every man, of what condition soever he be," should be encouraged in "the diligent performance of his duties" in order that believers might together constitute a harmonious and mobilized community in which all serve God in their place and through their specific function.[162]

The problem for Perkins and the early Puritans was that no such community existed. Living in an unreformed world, Puritan agents had to choose God and forgo fallen institutions. Taking faith in the ultimate vindication of the new powers, they might believe "of things to come, by foretelling, and (as it were) saying inwardly in the heart; that the thing may well be done," that they are to be "the heirs of the kingdom of heaven." Puritans could moreover hope fervently and work diligently for the "glory of God . . . made manifest in us." But that vision of believers at home among other agents in a world of their joint making lay far ahead. Until then, each must attend to the discipline of internal development as an individual first, then as an "example" to teach and instill "reverence" in others.[163] Nurtured by the regimen of a godly life, the "grain of mustard seed" would become "a great tree and bear fruit" within. Coordinated effort would fulfill in time the godly plan, a cosmic order described as "the watch of the great world, allotting to every man his motion and calling and in that calling his particular office and function."[164] It was that vision of an agency world and its contrast with Stuart society which propelled the Protestant revolutionaries in the following generations.

3

The Protestant Revolutionaries
and the Emerging Society of Agents

> For when God shakes a Kingdome with strong and healthfull com-
> motions to a general reforming . . . God then raises to his own work
> men of rare abilities, and more than common industry not only to
> look back and revise what hath bin taught heretofore, but to gain
> furder and goe on, some new enlighten'd steps in the discovery of
> truth. For such is the order of Gods enlightening his Church, to dis-
> pense and deal out by degrees his beam.
>
> —John Milton

William Perkins's rhetoric of urgent transformation re-
sounded through the Puritan discourse of the new century, spreading from
the Cambridge ministers throughout the land. Faced with James I's resistance to institutional reform and his insistence on outward clerical conformity, the ministers tried to reconcile their commitment to a national church
and their spiritual mission by crafting a theology of inwardness. Deflecting
demands for church reform into a language of spiritual individualism and
millennial impatience, they boldly expanded Perkins's vision of a new developmental identity into a promise of personal sanctification. Until the accession of Archbishop Laud under Charles I, the ministers succeeded by
crafting an oppositional language which, resisting direct politicization, extended the movement's commitment to individualism, choice, independent
judgment, and harsh societal criticism.

With the Laudian repression in 1628, in a final effort to repel the forces of
change, Presbyterian moderates were forced into quietism or exile. A more
radical Independent and sectarian opposition in turn emerged—that is, both
those committed to congregational autonomy from all ecclesiastical hierarchy and those rejecting as well the larger Calvinist theological framework—
challenging an ineffective Puritan reformism with full spiritual individualism and demands for ecclesiastical and political restructuring. Yet it was the

Puritan mainstream, exhorting followers to pursue self-transformation and God's plan for the world, who initiated this ensuing torrent of popular activism which precipitated England's transition to modernity.

Spiritual Individualism and the New Self

The capacity to shape a new and empowering personal relation to God was dramatically expanding. Believers were casting off from these "ill times" of spiritual reaction marked by "the captivity of the church," a time "when God seems to cry out unto us, 'Who is on my side, who?'" In preparation for the coming "day of severing," Puritan ministers maintained, one must undertake "separation from whatsoever is contrary" and "bid defiance to all opposite power," to "the god of the world," while "setting the soul above the world, having a spirit larger and higher than the world," and "cleaving to him, and him only."[1] Henceforth on a "journey"—"walking from place to place"—the Christian, wrote John Preston, must heed God's direct words and "walk with God exactly in all things": "Fear not Abraham, thou art in a strange Country, where thou hast no body to provide for thee, yet I will be All-Sufficient."[2] To "stand at staves end with" the world's "corruptions," the believer could not, in Robert Bolton's terms, serve any longer "two principal ends" as a "double minded man," but was to be "a single hearted man that chooses God alone," and has "all [his] business now . . . with God in heaven, and not with men."[3]

Given "the uncertainty of all events here" and of "what other men think or speak," wrote Richard Sibbes, individuals must "labour to frame that contentment in and from our own selves" and not from others: "It is neither education, nor the authority of others" nor "men of great parts" that "will settle the heart, until we find an inward power and authority in the truth itself shining in our hearts." In the "book of our heart and conscience," with "no other witness but God and [one]self," individuals should seek the "unity in ourselves" which precedes "union with others": "By these means we shall never want a divine to comfort us, a physician to cure us, a counsellor to direct us, a musician to cheer us, a controller to check us, because, by help of the word and Spirit, we can be all these to ourselves."[4]

Individuals must accept personal responsibility for the project of self-transformation: "How dost thou rule in thine house, in thyself?" It is "we" who "weave the web of our own sorrow" and "deal with our souls," "take pains with ourselves," and "promoteth" our souls "to all holy duties."[5] Just as we "willingly" and "voluntarily . . . pull [sin] upon ourselves," so we can "endeavor to obtain . . . what we love." We are to "labour to know God's meaning in every thing," now capable through "a revealing of the will of God" of "a knowledge of the promises of God, as well as of his providence."[6] Given "liberty," we can "choose," utilizing a new self-reliance.[7] The seeker "may take up matters in himself" and "reason" not "contrary [to] his own principles," for "God hath set up a court in man's heart, wherein the conscience hath the office both of informer, accuser, witness, and judge."[8] Thomas Goodwin described his transformation: "I observed of this Work of God on my Soul, that there was nothing of Constraint or Force in it, but I was carried on with the most ready and willing Mind, and what I did was what I chose to do. With the greatest Freedom I parted with my Sins . . . and resolv'd never to return to them more."[9]

The language of development to a new role infuses the process: one is now a "fire worker" who is "able to set forth itself into any holy action" rather than without "any spiritual power to do any thing" but "only endure."[10] "The old man" bound by "common grace" or an "outward conformity to religion" gains a new "sense of the power of godliness"; the "weak, and narrow, and slavish" person achieves "a large command . . . over all things under him." Goodwin sought "this great Alteration" which "extends its Influence upon all things," while Sibbes demanded that "our nature itself" be "changed" to "'an instrument in tune, fit to be moved to any duty; as a clean neat glass' representing 'God's image and holiness.'"[11] Hooker writes of being newly "formed and fashioned": "As the gardener cuts off a graft to plant it in a new stock . . . so the Lord cuts a sinner off from all abomination . . . melts the heart of a poor sinner, but consumes him not, but as the goldsmith melts his gold . . . to make it a better vessel: so the Lord melts a poor sinner to make him a vessel of glory."[12] For Preston, the "new Creature" possesses "all things new within and without . . . everything is new," in "a new world" in which "his eyes see things, his ears hear things that never entered into any mans heart."[13] Goodwin explained his conversion: "I felt my Soul, and all the Powers of it, as in an instant to be clean altered and changed . . . my Spirit clothed with a new Nature."[14]

Immense expectations were advanced regarding this internal development: now "made partakers of the godly nature"[15] with a "new nature" that was "bred from heaven," one was "put into a holy frame" to become a "whole man"[16] possessed of a "divine spark" and shaped in God's "own image." As "carr[iers]" of "a divinity in them" and "capable of divine nature,"[17] one could "walk before [God], and be perfect." Having achieved "a higher condition, and made one with Christ," with God given "his own place in the soul," one became "a sanctuary and temple for God to dwell in." In Preston's terms, "the sanctifying Spirit . . . possesses and informs his soul, it joins with his soul, it is dwelling in him."[18]

Only a catalogue of expanded attributes conveys the immensity of this project of reconstitution: a new "reason" or "Judgment" to discern God's will and "the steps of *Gods* way"; a new "understanding" as "a glass of the word to see" with the "light" and truly comprehend it;[19] a "new Conscience"[20] to authorize that way; a new power—"a new and further light into the bottom of [one's] Heart"—to examine one's sin and to perceive one's self clearly; a new "soul" with the "excellency" to "reflect upon itself, and judge whatsoever comes from it"; a "new spirit" and a "new heart" now "perfectly holy"[21] upon which "the law of God" is "so written" that one is "perfect with God though [one] relapse into sin";[22] a transformed "disposition" which as "a new Indwelling"[23] was now "pure and clean . . . full of purity and brightness . . . Soul spots and greater defilements rubbed out . . . the graces of God . . . splendid and bright and clear without that mixture and dross";[24] a new internal bent "naturally inclining [one] to good" so one is "carried willingly to the ways of God."[25]

Where God "sends his Spirit to write his Laws in the heart," the result is "an inward aptness" or "disposition" which is "so ingrafted as any natural disposition . . . so rooted in the heart" that it becomes "natural . . . so as it shall never again be obliterated," enabling any so "inclined to keep the Law in all points."[26] These "new moulded" individuals have a new moral or "righteous" nature which intends "not only to do good, but to do good in ourselves"; newly spiritualized "affections" which "move us" to "walk with, and before God";[27] an inner wisdom, a "treasury and storehouse of divine truths," to discern "what is to be chosen, and what is to be refused"; a new will now "melted and soften'd . . . a Stone made Flesh, disposed" to carry out truth with "uniformity and constancy in our resolutions."[28]

The "power of godliness," all "grace and holiness . . . all power and wisdom" that "infuse" the individual generate a vastly enhanced sense of size and "divine strength."[29] With John Cotton's "power" to "march in his strength," Thomas Hooker's "new power" to "set forth itself into holy action" and "to do . . . [w]hat ever a Christian should do,"[30] humans will "rule other things beneath them" while "under the power of nothing beneath" themselves.[31] Where God's "strength is our strength, and his Armies are our

Armies," we are like "samsons," invulnerable to any "creature in heaven or earth" trying to "do [us] hurt." The promises mushroomed: "With God all things are possible . . . be it poverty in your estates, or debts" or "a blemish in your name . . . or weakness in your body" or "a lust that ye cannot overcome" or "a deadness of spirit."[32] So fortified, with "God ours" and "all other things . . . ours," we begin a "new Life" free from "the world" and all things which could once "much dismay us." As one of the "righteous," each believer will shine as "the sun in the firmament" who "borroweth not its lustre from without."[33]

The Self as Agent

A new authentic self has emerged to "appear in its own likeness," distinguishable from past inauthenticity: "A godly man counts the inner man, the sanctified part, to be himself . . . ourselves perfectly." Now "so entire" in "truth," the individual is no longer "afraid" to let "God himself look into his heart . . . that can search every cranny of it . . . yet he shall find him true."[34] Able to "approve himself to" God, one is confidently the self God himself is "glorified in making . . . happy." Having achieved mastery of the new powers to "rule over our own spirits well" made integration as a "soul" in "harmony" now attainable, with a life "of one colour, like itself," filled with "peace and joy."[35]

Yet such a roseate view of human powers and capacities also opened dangerous excesses, particularly where the individual was free of ministerial control as "a governor over himself" with "a different cup measured to every one."[36] Certain boundaries and necessary limits appropriate to this accession had to be delineated by the absolute Author superintending it: "True self . . . is under the law and government of the Spirit, and . . . works according to that principle." Empowerment and subordination were complements of the "rule" of "Christ . . . in himself."[37] John Benbrigge wrote: "Christ must be obeyed, Christ must be pleased, Christ must be honored."[38] Preston spoke of Christ as his "chiefest commander" who must be obeyed "rather than any other," not to the exclusion of worldly authority but always in any conflict of authorities.[39] This subordination was clearly a "new obedience," a commitment from faith rather than obligation such that no mere "disobedience . . . shall cause the Lord to depart from thee . . . [a]s long as you keep within bounds, and keep within the Fold, as long as you go along the paths of righteousness."[40]

What defines this new self is its dual nature—active, self-reliant, and initiatory yet wholly under orders. This reflected the two spheres of Protestant reality: heaven with its transcendant operation of ends beyond human intervention, and "this world" in which God now allowed human power to constitute "a map and shadow of the spiritual estate of the souls of men." The distinction was thus made between God's fixed ends and the means to achieve them, which in the earthly realm were within human reach. For Sibbes, God "governs" us "in [our] ends," while "man hath a freedom in working" for them.[41] In Preston's metaphor, "all men, though they have but one Journeys end, yet there are different places, from which every one of them travel." Each must therefore "think" individually "upon every action what his end is . . . busy in his study . . . his trade . . . his particular calling."[42] The result was enormous individual discretion: God "furnishes creatures with a virtue and power to work, and likewise with a manner of working suitable to their own nature; as it is proper for a man, when he works, to work with freedom."[43] By the "power of that Spirit" the individual soul will "run right," despite no "hope of reward, nor fear of revenge."[44]

This offer of divine means created, moreover, a responsibility to act. A "chief property of wisdom" is "not only to know, but to put in execution," and people are to "be judged" not on "knowledge" or "habits" but "according to the act." Once "we know what to do" and "what is best to be done," it is "dangerous" and evidence of "a false heart" to undertake "further deliberation."[45] Actions undertaken by a regenerated nature, whether to solidify one's relationship with God or to spontaneously pursue divine ends without external institutional legitimation, achieved heightened spiritual significance. Godliness is "so ingrafted . . . so rooted in the heart, it is so rivetted in . . . it shall be natural to you" and "thou bring forth good fruits . . . they flow from thee . . . they grow in thine heart as naturally as fruit grows on trees." With the new godly powers at its core, this new nature, unable to act otherwise, would be liberated to fulfill and express that nature. It became capable of undertaking great risks: "trust is bold because it is grounded upon" God and "gives boldness to the soul" and a "warrant from him for whatsoever it trusts him for." Not surprisingly, this "courage" against "the world," making the faithful "so many conquerors over that which others are slaves to," would enable the following generation of Puritans to boldly recast the world in conformity with and as a fulfillment of their new natures.[46]

This generation understood the result of this transformation as a new self. It was variously called "Saint,"[47] God's "favorites," "stewards," "so many kings and queens," the spouse of "thine Husband,"[48] a "son in the family," a

"Prince" with "royal spirits,"[49] "daughters" with "raiments" of "gold," the "wisest merchant," a "greater man,"[50] the "Image of Christ,"[51] "co-workers," the "likeness of Christ," a soul "engrafted into Christ," "fire worker."[52] Several images are used concurrently, often interweaving conflicting qualities of maturity with those of innocence or immaturity.[53] In a confusing effort to define the strengths and limits of the new role, Sibbes refers to it as both "an agent" in the "labours to help the light" and yet "a patient" in "enduring" determinations beyond one's control. Sanctification suggested Christ's earthly being, but Christ represented a dangerous model, presuming an eventual inheritance of godhood itself. No single concept grasped the simultaneous validation of new powers with the even stronger bond to authority, "a higher condition" in which one is "wiser than himself, holier than himself, stronger than himself," "more than a man" yet finally just a man, in which we are "lords over our own speeches and actions, yet under a higher lord."[54] Even Hobbes, with his unique grasp of the twin dimensions of empowerment and constraint within this new role, employed tentative formulations. Only later would these merge as the agency role, and it would be far longer yet before modern citizens would fully internalize its complex specifications.

A New Developmental Model

The continued preoccupation with achieving sanctification, in which the individual was a "double self" whose "holy man" triumphs or "win[s] ground" over "the old man," began from Perkins's model, which already presupposed a process of characterological development. With ever-increased attentiveness to daily modulations of spiritual life evident in Puritan diary keeping, this next generation provided a further experiential basis for internal growth, substituting for theological terms the movement from one form of internal organization to another.[55] Primordial impulses no longer reflected the unalterable theological curse of original sin but revealed instead instincts of nature which are "wild and untamed, and impatient of the yoke." An unformed nature certainly required "the yoke of obedience" which "makes the life regular and quiet." But the presumption that this nature was static was unacceptable, for it made abject subordination the only solution: "blind enfolded [blindfolded?] obedience." This had been the argument of the regressive theologies of Catholic and Anglican "adversaries," which "will never stand with sound peace of conscience."[56]

The deepest conviction of dissenting Protestantism was that human nature was transformable. The core of its theology was the growth of individuals from "vocation" to "justification" and then "sanctification," as they were "first called, and then justified, and then glorified."[57] The theology of the two covenants was employed to represent the two major stages of spiritual development. The covenant of works was "a Ministration of the Letter," a "naked Commandment," requiring "no aptness, no disposition" from the believer "to keep it." The controlling motivation for obedience was "only a servile fear, and an enmity" which cast God "as a hard Master, as an enemy" with "a hard and cruel law, as a heavy yoke, as an unsupportable bondage." This religion created "a Bondslave" with unaltered instincts who only "wishes there were no such law, he runs from it . . . from his Master, as far as it is in his power." The covenant of grace, by contrast, was "a ministration of the Spirit, and not of the letter[;] . . . of love, not of enmity; of freedom, not of bondage." God now was no "hard and cruel Master" but an authority "exceeding full of mercy and compassion." Reflecting a transformed nature, the new covenant offered "promises" which were "better promises" with "a larger effusion of the Spirit . . . now poured on us in greater measure, then it was distilled by drops, now the Lord hath dispensed it in a greater abundance to the sons of men."[58]

Images of development abounded. Preston asked, "Doth any man sow before he hath plowed? Doth any man make a new impression before there hath been an obliteration of the old?" To "grow in grace" was likened to "the rounds in a Ladder, that go from bottom to the top," a "perfect plant" which "when it grows up, it will be a perfect tree," a "dawning light" that "will at length clear up to a perfect day," a "Journey" in which every act, big or little, is "a step."[59] Sibbes spoke of "several ages in Christ" whereby we "see more every day into the state of our own souls," thus "growing in holiness" and self-mastery. As individuals "grow up in him," "ascend to him," "raise themselves upwards to know their election," they approach perfect agency on earth through "the paradise of a good conscience," which is the ideal condition "until we come to heaven."[60]

Personal transformation involved a radical self-uprooting of old ways. On this internal journey to "rule ourselves," the "wise traveller[s]" can expect "no satisfaction" from others, wrote Sibbes. They must rely on "supplys from our own store," for "we are most privy to our own intentions and aims, whence comfort must be fetched."[61] Ministers provided great detail on how to "make a narrow search into our souls," to the "core," to pursue the "least stirrings" and "first beginnings of any unruly passions and affections."[62] Central to the conviction that transformation was possible was the remarkable belief that the sources of unreformed nature could be fully exposed. Writes Thomas Goodwin: "The Light which Christ now vouchsafed me, and this new sort of Illumination, gave discovery of my heart in all my Sinnings, carried me down to see the Inwards of my Belly pains and searched the lower Rooms of my Heart, as it were with Candles . . . the Root and Ground of all my other Sinnings. . . . And by and through the Discovery of those Lusts, a new horrid Vein and Course of Sin was revealed also to me, that I saw lay at the bottom of my Heart." Through assiduous labors he actually reaches "the Original Corruption of my Nature, and inward evil Constitution and depravation of all my Faculties . . . as if I had in the Heat of Summer lookt down into the Filth of a Dungeon, where by a clear Light and piercing Eye I discern'd Millions of crawling things, in the midst of that Sink and Liquid Corruption."[63]

Despite the pervasiveness of sin, Puritans paradoxically gained increasing optimism as they pursued the confrontation. The willingness to engage in total combat alone made complete triumph possible: "As in war, haply they cannot take the enemy, but will drive him out of the country, and burn down all his forts, and fill up all his trenches, that he may find no provision."[64] Through radical probing, the "knot of corruption" is "loosened" and "the soldering between sin and the soul" is "removed," allowing "a passage" for removing "corruptions," so that our heart may be "severed from our sins."[65] Only radical surgery offered reconstitution of a new "centre and resting place,"[66] a shift "off from [one's] own bottom" or ground to "be so bottomed"[67] with "the foundation" of "God himself . . . to build on." The new source from which the life of the sanctified self flowed was a "radical and fundamental grace . . . as it were, the mother root and great vein whence the exercise of all graces have their beginning and strength."[68] In Goodwin's own "great" inward "Alteration," "the works of the Devil" were "dissolved in [his] Heart" and his "spirit clothed in a new Nature."[69]

The Evolving Relationship with God

The new foundation was an intimate relationship with God. The personal embrace of God's ends and mandate would mobilize the Protestant to voluntary godly activity. As the relation deepened, the theological guarantees of predestined ends and covenantal promises for security and certainty receded dramatically in importance. Predestination increasingly operated to bolster confidence, Sibbes explained: "It cannot but bring strong security to the soul, to know that in all variety of changes and intercourse of good and bad events, God, and our God, hath such a disposing hand. Whatsoever befalls us, all serves . . . his purpose to save us."[70] Preston found strength for one's voluntary preparation in "a strong stream that cannot be resisted."[71] Thomas Goodwin noted the power of predestination among Cambridge students: the voluntarist Arminians "often . . . fall away totally" and then erratically "return again to repentance"; the Puritans by contrast exhibit a "constant Perseverance . . . to their strict Religious Practices and Principles, without falling away and declining as I knew of."[72] In this shift toward developmental achievement, even crises of faith were no longer signs of predestined damnation but rather spurs to religious recommitment.

Of much greater importance in promoting the voluntary pursuit of the new role was covenant theology. The possibility of ensuring "God's gracious promises" by a personal vow embodied the heightened Puritan sense of worthiness and capacity to craft one's own fate.[73] Preston began *The New Covenant* with a human rendering of "His promise" in "His" voice: "I will make my covenant between me and thee, and I will multiply thee exceedingly. . . . I will . . . preserve thee from all evil. . . . I will be thy exceeding great reward."[74] A bilateral covenant clarified the performance required: to "choose" God meant in effect the "taking of the Covenant" with its responsibilities, while in turn locking God into a now scrutable performance of his promises and commitment to his human contractees.[75] Preston even assisted God in the articulation of his obligation: "I am willing to enter into covenant with thee, that is, I will bind my self, I will engage my self, I will enter into bond, as it were, I will not be at liberty any more." Sibbes confirmed God's willingness "to perform all things for our own good."[76] This "everlasting" commitment conveyed the double edge of immense empowerment yet trepidation at the magnitude of the relational advance: "It is an exceeding great mercy, when we think thus with our selves, he is in heaven, and we are on earth; he is the glorious GOD, we dust and ashes; he is the Creator, and we but creatures; and yet he is willing to enter into Covenant, which implies a kind of equality between us . . . that he should be willing to indent with us . . . make himself a debtor to us."[77] The covenant presuming God's performance—"the bargain is stricken up, Christ is yours"—made it obligatory: "Lord I want faith, give me it." God could even be "sued on his own bond."[78] At the same time, it reflected intense insecurity and the need for support in fulfilling the increased responsibilities: "In case of extremity, opposition, strange accidents, desertion, and damps of spirit, &c., here we may take sanctuary, that we are in covenant with him who sits at the stern and rules all." This insecurity, reflected in the conditional nature of the covenant, was simultaneously eased by providing clear "conditions and articles of agreement between the parties," strict measures of performance, and clear options for abrogation.[79]

Use of the covenant, then, while offering concrete, tangible validation of the new role of agent, reflected anxieties about the strength of the relationship which rendered it only a provisional mechanism in the ultimate quest for sanctified status with God.[80] Slowly a sense was emerging that a loving God might embrace individuals in an intimate, even familial relationship, and dispense with the rigidity and conditionality of an arm's-length transaction. God was available as never before: "Other Kings must needs govern by Deputies and Viceroys, and inferior Magistrates . . . because they cannot be everywhere. . . . But with the Lord . . . he guides immediately, and being every where present, he needs no deputies."[81] This opened the way to "an holy familiarity with God," a relationship based on love more than duty: "Our love of God must be most evident. . . . Love is the ground of all the duties that are acceptably performed to God."[82] Rooted in "the affections" and in "trust," a love relationship opened an intimacy with God for the soul "fitteth . . . to join with so gracious an object," "a communion" whereby one was "made one with Christ,"[83] a "heart united unto God" in "fellowship with him."[84]

Given this connection, God could now work directly through the affects by "convey[ing] himself and his goodness to the soul." Intimate access in turn provided God as an accessible model of selfhood: "Love is an affection of imitation; we affect a likeness to him we love."[85] In this subtle way, the affective commitment arising from identification with a loved authority was emerging to become the voluntary basis of modern identity and performance: "Where love abounds, there will be much willingness, cheerfulness, forwardness, and readiness to do what can be done to the well-pleasing of him that is loved."[86] With God's grace and his ends willingly embraced, individuals could henceforth be trusted to obey divine ends spontaneously with full choice regarding the means to achieve them.

This voluntarist ground for the relation to authority and thus for human obligation opened levels of commitment and perseverance previously unimaginable. Utilizing a freedom unavoidable in their uncontrollable religious market, the Puritans came to realize its role in a deeper and more engaged faith. Choice increased the burden and pressure of individual responsibility, which in turn mobilized all the skills and the inner self of the seeker. Distinguished from servitude, "Christian liberty" and liberty of conscience harnessed the transforming power of agency by offering the opportunity to form one's own obedience to collective ends and the power to shape its responsibilities. The proto-agent position on voluntarism, limited because of fears about its release, would, like its theological complements predestination and even the more legalistic forms of covenant, offer little competition for the dynamism that the fully voluntary agent would soon unleash. As clear and nonnegotiable systemic ends and appropriate means became accessible to believers in the subsequent decades, unhindered personal discretion became both feasible and necessary to validate the power of personal commitment. Through this logic, the powers of initiative, self-reliance, and personal judgment became part of Western selfhood.

Emboldened by the new affective bond, the ministers proclaimed the possibility of full transformation, an "assurance of preservation . . . sealed up."[87] Robert Bolton exhorted, "As certainly as he that hath a corporeal eye, knoweth that he sees: so certainly, he that is illumined with the light of faith, knows that he believes." For Sibbes, "if we believe in Christ we are as sure to come to heaven as Christ is there," and become able even now to "stand fast" and "withstand whatever opposeth us."[88] The terror of theological innovation was receding, leaving only the more limited fears of personal failure, of not traversing the "maze" of one's "heart" or being able to "stick fast to God." Even so, conviction was made easy, for "the son abides for ever."[89] Uncertainty was increasingly manageable: "Grief . . . must be bounded. . . . [T]he strong man" realizes that "despair . . . is the beginning of comfort; and trouble the beginning of peace. A storm is the way to a calm, and hell the way to heaven." Despite remnants of irresolution, a new inner orientation was to prevail: "When the soul leaves God once, and looks downward, what is there to stay it from disquiet. Remove the needle from the pole-star, and it is always stirring and trembling, never quiet till it be right again."[90] The remaining barrier was remarkably no longer sin, as "grace gathers strength" and "sin loses strength by every new fall," but—revealing a vast new confidence—*false modesty:* "Our Saviour justly taxes these men of hypocrisy . . . [w]hen a man pretends want of light in his understanding and judgment."[91]

Yet doubt, though diminished in scope and fearfulness, lingered.[92] Puritans never fully trusted the affective bond to ensure personal responsibility.

"Doubting and misgiving" believers were not close enough or committed enough to see God "face to face," but only in "some ways answerable to that blessed estate which . . . yet it enjoys not," only "at length" to "appear." Complete transformation still lay in the future, when "we shall be lift up" and "shall find a bottom and a deliverance in due time."[93] Laboring every moment to achieve agency, Puritans continued, unlike those who followed, to require mediating theological limits on voluntarism to cope with spiritual uncertainty.[94]

Toward a Worldly Role

Despite its caution, the Puritan movement sensed with messianic fervor a world in transition: "God defers, but his deferring is no empty space, wherein no good is done, but there is in that space a fitting for promises. Whilst the seed lieth hidded in the earth, time is not lost, for winter fits for spring, yea, the harder the winter, the more hopeful the spring." Transformation beckoned: "In these glorious times wherein so great a light shineth, whereby so great things are discovered . . . [o]ur hearts should be more and more enlarged, as things are more and more revealed to us." Hooker waxed rhapsodic during his early phase in 1626 about "our marvelous deliverance" as "God delivers England."[95] For Cotton, the "deliverance out of affliction" to be "washed . . . in the blood of the Lamb" was "not a description of the Saints glorified in heaven" but referred to those "upon Earth" in this "time of our visitation," the "time of . . . happiness."[96] Great hopefulness also threatened unsurpassed frustration and disappointment: a time of "misery" and "evil," of "danger on all sides," of "Jacob's trouble and Zion's sorrow," a time of the "old Worlds degeneration and destruction" in a "general Deluge," of "God" surely "going from England."[97]

With such extreme options—an "illustrious Star, shining full fair with a singularity of heavenly light . . . in the darkest midnight of Satans universal reign"—human action could now make the difference: "Consider . . . all those great plagues, that the Lord brought upon the Egyptians," urged Preston, as the prelude to the momentous decision "that saw his power in bringing [the Israelites] through the red sea."[98] Like Noah, believers were to act decisively as a saving remnant, utilizing powers of agency to "side with him . . . and his cause in ill times." While "waiting upon God" was "doing good,"[99] and belief itself motivated "a suitable conformity . . . with the holiness of that condition," this was hardly the time to attend patiently:

> Now it is high time to awake. . . . How shall I know it? . . . when God calls
> you to accept the offer of grace. . . . [W]hy the night is far spent and the day
> is at hand; a man knows his time to rise, he will for shame get up, when the
> day breaks and the Sun arises, and shines in at his window. . . . [W]hen the
> light of the Gospel shines clearly . . . we cannot but see and hear and be con-
> verted, unless we will be willfully blind: when the day dawns and the day
> star arises in our hearts, is it not now time to rise.[100]

In Preston's terms, "oftentimes God opens a door to us," but unless "it be
taken," it may "be shut up again." Those who are "idle, slack, indigent" may
be "negligent" for "missing the time," for it "is short," and we must be "doing what we do with all our might, and with all our diligence" to "take the
times, and not over-slip and over-pass them." The "godly man," he added,
"shall know the time, and the Judgment."[101]

Puritans believed that a revelation of transcendent order was emerging in
which every physical body and every being would grasp the cosmic plan and
the necessary steps for its completion, and in turn take on "the comely order
wherein every creature is placed" and given "its own and proper working."
All would know "what the times to come shall be."[102] "I will pour out my
Spirit upon all flesh, and your young men shall see visions, and your old
men shall dream dreams." Learning these "mysteries that were had from
the beginning of the world" will "guide you and direct you" toward a particular role and responsibility in the overall structure, the "nearest" and
"plainest way" which God "hath made plain . . . that men might know . . .
what you ought to do, what way you ought to choose."[103] This role involved "holy duties," those "duties of our callings" whose diligent performance is "fitted for our parts."[104] Though the way was one of "breadth" and
"latitude," the individual must "not . . . go beyond" but stay "within the
bounds" and "runneth in the due channel,"[105] which were the fit arenas for
the "new Nature." Here believers "live, and are, as it were, in heaven" and
"enjoy heaven in the world under heaven,"[106] both internally and in "present life."[107]

As the new conviction spread, the rhetoric of worldly transformation intensified, creating untenable problems for the movement. Despite this expectation of profound change, the goal was a vertically ordered society of
"holy duties" and responsible callings managed by a regime of godly authority. The human role required fixed institutional participation and commu-

nity membership: "Whatsoever the creature hath, it hath it but by participation. . . . [T]here is something else that is the whole, of which it is but the part." A "useful calling" required the keeping of "a strict account," the responsibility to "know our work, and then to do it" with "diligence," to "'serve one another in love' . . . as members of the state as well as the church" by "every one," no matter how "mean."[108] In an inclusive society of just institutions, "every man shall be rewarded according to his faithfulness, and sincerity," that is, according to the effectiveness of one's agency contribution.[109] Proto-agent controls contained popular activism within religious bounds. The weapon of the godly remained faith, that power which "works without us, conquering whatsoever is in the world" in opposition. For believers, "our work is only to do our work and be quiet, as children when they please their parents take no further thought," to "look to our place wherein God hath set us," to carry out one's obligations in faith and involvement "with God in heaven, and not with men."[110]

Despite these limits, the ever closer approach of a new world made socially transforming action ever more appealing. Existing institutions, ecclesiastical and political, were bankrupt:

> All, either personal duties, or employment of State, are by so much the better performed, by how much the men are more religious, from whose abilities the same proceed: That when Heaven is made too much to stoop to Earth; Piety to Policy; Publick Good, to private ends; there authority is embittered, inferiours plagued, and too often Law and Justice turned to Wormwood and rapine. . . . [W]hat a deal of hurt is done; what a world of mischief is many times wrought, insensibly and unobservedly; when a wicked wit, and wide conscience wield the sword of authority. For it is easy . . . putting foul business into fair language . . . to compass his own ends; either for promotion of iniquity; or oppression of innocency.[111]

Moreover, because faith will also "set God against all," the believer must be independent, "follow . . . his own conscience." They must exercise "courage and boldness in setting ourselves against whatsoever may oppose us in the way." Promised that "when we have learned to rule over our spirits well, then we may be fit to rule over others," the regenerate possessed transformative powers: "If Christians knew the power they have in the world, what were able to stand against them?"[112] They must "bid defiance to all opposite power" and "withstand whatsoever opposes us."[113] They were pressed to show "an ecstacy of zeal" for God's cause and act to reinstate "religion and justice" where it had been lost.[114]

Puritans were thus cautiously called into the world, to actions that

> tend to the good of others, the good of the Church, the good of the Commonwealth[,] the good of particular men; There is a time when (it may be) a mans voice, or suffrage would have turned the scale of a business, that concerned much the Common-wealth, or the society where he lives: but when that opportunity is past, it can be recalled no more. . . . There is an opportunity of preventing a mischief to a Common-wealth, or to a kingdom, [and] when we neglect that opportunity, it causes the misery of many to be great upon him.

Such actions may incur "the wrath of man," but silence will incur "the wrath of God." Those who do not take "such actions" have "lost their opportunity," and will suffer "eternal misery" at "the day of judgement." They will have "lost the Kingdom."[115]

Despite the rhetoric, however, Puritans remained bound by their sense of restraint. Even in this time of "beginnings," they hewed to the path of individual preparation and abundant "Good Works,"[116] hoping to produce gardeners for "the further spreading and multiplying" of God's seed. They continued patiently to look to "what the times to come shall be," the "light" that "will at length" be "dawning."[117] A transformed civilization in the future would be the reward which, if they continued to evolve spiritually and act in faith, was promised to be theirs. Others would see the task much closer at hand.

The Intensifying Opposition

It was Independents and sectarians in the Laudian underground and the early Revolution who pushed English society toward an irreversible transformation of the human role. At the same time, their increasing radicalism was, it is clear, the elaboration of Puritan innovations. They placed ever greater reliance on individual sainthood, on the sanctity of the saint's personal conscience, judgment, and independent capacity to act regarding godly ends. This in turn undermined the very forms of hierarchical authority that had always contained or restricted these incendiary powers. This growing movement has typically been regarded as marginal—if a suggestive or even prophetic sidelight—to the main thrust of the period, as merely "a larger and larger number of imaginative, idealistic, self-centered, histrionic, articulate, Quixotic dreamers and talkers."[118] Certainly, even given the vast range of emerging ideas, these rebels, insurgents, and self-appointed prophets were at the far edge of English thinking. Once the period is reframed in terms of a developmental shift, however, these groups must be given credit, though they were often driven by their "new truth" to overshoot the mark, for grasping the new paradigm and insisting on its completion. Their double move beyond the traditional assumptions of the age explains their isolation: with the Puritans they embraced the new model of agency; they in turn alone shed their remaining proto-agent constraints. Declaring this new uncompromised self the property of all in a broadly mobilized prerevolutionary society, these religious radicals in effect jettisoned all prior structures of meaning, becoming the midwives of a historical transformation.

Their complete and self-conscious defense of agency principles of self and society left Puritan equivocations transparently compromised: "Orthodox Calvinism leveled all men under the law, made all equal in their title to grace, and then denied to most all prospect of realizing their hopes. It made the individual experience of God in the soul all-important, enormously stimulating individual spiritual experience," and yet substantially limited the "freedom" of the "individual will." The revolutionary alternatives after 1630, one of the great periods of Western spiritual ferment, while drawing on Puritanism's "own premises and its own dogmas . . . swept on . . . to conclusions and practical consequences" that would shatter the dream of theocratic elitism before the forces of universalism.[119] As Laud forced Puritans into hiding or exile, hindering their interchange and mutual scrutiny, persecuted believers were driven to more antihierarchical ideas of church and state. The subsequent triumph of Parliament and collapse of the monarchy accelerated popular convictions regarding personal and national transformation.

By the early 1640s, the English laity were "joining together as they chose or as circumstances might require for their souls' satisfaction without the benefit of clergy in church, chapel, or conventicle, at home or in exile, in England, in foreign lands, in the American wilderness."[120] Individuals became self-appointed instruments of the divine will, possessed of full agency powers, to act as they or their group understood their warrant or appointment. To the extent that institutions interfered with such grants of authority, they were illegitimate. Milton wrote at the execution of Charles I that as "great a good and happiness as a just King is, so great a mischeife is a Tyrant

. . . the common enemie. Against whom what the people lawfully may doe, as against a common pest, and destroyer of mankinde, I suppose no man of cleare judgement need goe furder to be guided than by the very principles of nature in him . . . [and] their own reason."[121] Hanserd Knollys would write in 1641: "Babylon is fallen, it is fallen. . . . Babylon's destruction is Jerusalem's salvation."[122] In time, even the presbyterian Puritans would—as they retreated from revolution to the restoration of institutional controls—be called by these radicals they had mobilized "that most barbarous, inhumane, and bloody faction amongst us" which has "attempted the absolute enslaving (. . . the utter undoing) of the nation."[123]

The Full Bond of Agency

The formidable breakthrough to a thoroughgoing agency came with the dramatically enhanced confidence in the connection with God. Many sectarians and some Independents felt increasingly able to establish an intimate and mutually loving relationship with "the Divine character," a "very gracious, loving, and bountiful" being who offered "a gracious tie" of "parental kindness." William Walwyn, in the aptly named tract "The Power of Love," held that "God is love," with a place for all in "Gods family."[124] Divine love now permeated the world: "As the sun diffuses his light and heat through every part of the solar system, so God pours forth his universal goodness in number-less streams upon all his creatures, from that infinite source of love that is within him." Individuals who absorbed that love as an ever-faithful presence would be stirred into a similarly caring commitment in return: "The Spirit of God is full of the love of God, and full of zeal for God, and set upon magnifying of him in the world. . . . Now, he that is born of the Spirit must needs act and be inclined after the same manner; he will be zealous for God, bestirring himself . . . as the Spirit of God doth."[125] Love becomes one's light and strength, willingly given to a God who "so freely hath loved you."[126]

Such deep affective mutuality opened the self without internal resistance to divinity and its powers, for one whose "heart" was "moving in thoughts of thankfulnesse" would "instantly be inflamed with love, which in an instant refines the whole man." Emulation of God's character and behavior, "an absolute conformity with God, in his ways and actions," further grew into an imitation of God, later to be called identification, a "likeness unto God." From the wish to "be holy, for I am holy," in turn was constituted an ultimate "God-like" self: "How sovereign an influence must this consideration, that God is holy, needs be upon the hearts and souls of men capable of it, to persuade unto holiness! What! a mortal man . . . to be like unto God! to have communion with him in so darling an attribute as his holiness! What! . . . to ascend this high!"[127] In identifying, believers "enlarge their hearts" and become filled with a "blessedness" that is "wholly, purely, and entirely God, all God." Filled with a "higher degree of power," with "an excess of good," transformation naturally succeeds unless beset by unnatural or perverted motives. Individuals would thus be "sooner persuaded" to "abundantly preferre" the "cordes of love" over "their vanities, pressures of the law, and affrighting terrors of wrath and hell,"[128] and when they "walke in love" would find it worthy of more "trust" than "the authority of any man, or any mans relation." This "so full and absolute, so free and unexpecting love" provides "perfect reconciliation with God" regardless of one's "fears," "sinnes," and "doubtings."[129]

With this release from doubt, the certainty of earthly sanctification or godliness swelled along with a declining fear of sin. For John Goodwin, all individuals had "a sufficiency of means . . . to redeem themselves," and each had God's "strongest ground of assurance" that "upon a regular deportment of himself towards him, he shall receive protection and every good thing from him." The radical leader John Lilburne spoke as one of God's "chosen ones" whose spiritual sufferings were "a Crowne of gold . . . set upon my head, for I have in some part beene made conformable to my Lord and Master, and have in some measure drunke of the same Cupp which he himselfe drank of."[130] Walwyn pressed individuals not "to dooubt your selves" but to "reade, and know, and understand your blessed condition," exclaiming, "Good God! that free love should be suspected: that because is easie to be had." The enhanced capacity to fulfill divine obligations was attributed to our "rational nature," which "inclines [one] to an absolute conformity with God, in his ways and actions," to the "perfection of his nature which inclines him to do all things . . . like unto God."[131]

Thomas Collier, in a 1647 sermon to the radicalized popular insurgent army, expressed the growing experience of imminent transformation: "[The] old creation . . . shall be so overpowered by the glorious appearances of light, that [it] shall no more hurt or destroy the Saints' peace in their holy mountain, their enjoyment of God in the spirit." Saints should now "be in a gret measure freed from those corruptions, those distractions, which formerly were prevalent in them." Cromwell in the Putney Debates (1647)—

along with the Whitehall Debates (1648–49) one of two far-reaching discussions within the radical army leadership—thanked God that "I stand upon the bottom of my own innocence."[132] This sense of increasing infallibility, a "glorious estate of perfection,"[133] was quickly taken up by such sects as the Grindletonians, Familists, and Ranters and made the doctrine of a perfectible nature, freed of sin entirely. Ranter Lawrence Clarkson proclaimed that "sin hath its conception only in the imagination. . . . No matter what Scripture, saints or churches say, if that within thee do not condemn thee, thou shalt not be condemned." Thus, he continued, "to the pure all things, yea all things, are pure." Robert Towne claimed that if individuals "believe sin, death and the curse to be abolished, they are abolished."[134]

With the certitude of inner transformation, believers were correspondingly empowered to utilize all available worldly means to fulfill God's plan. William Haller writes: "All believed or professed to believe that their lives had been transformed from within by divine grace, that grace was also in the process of transforming the life of mankind in general."[135] Insurgents from Independent leaders to army radicals dedicated themselves without reservation to acting on behalf of God, who, Henry Ireton declared, "will so lead those that are his" in "whatever I find the work of God tending to." Whether to "destroy, not only Kings and Lords, but all distinctions of degrees—nay if it go further, to destroy all property," or whether to be "a rod of iron to dash the common enemies in pieces," they were now determined "to follow him whethersoever he goeth."[136] They had been called to "deliver the kingdom from that burden that lies upon us,"[137] to "bring about" the "destruction of Antichrist and the deliverance of his Church and people,"[138] to answer being "called of God unto . . . the accomplishment of . . . this great work and design of God in and by you."[139] George Joyce of the army declared that "his people" would "by belief . . . move mountains," achieving "such things as were never yet done by men on earth."[140] John Goodwin regarded believers as now "vigorous, active, and free in their work" and able to "do what they do with all their might," to "mount up on high, and be carried, as it were, on eagle's wings, enable to do . . . [g]reat and excellent things . . . that shall have more of heaven . . . glory . . . beauty . . . matter for admiration, than can be found . . . in the world."[141]

Spiritual regeneration of the individual, together with the encouragement to employ it in world-transforming activity, crystallized a new human role. Believers now dwelled on earth and in the social world with a new warrant defining the purpose of their lives: "Godliness is a disposition which inclines the person . . . to act for God, and to make the advancement of his glory the supreme end of their ways and actions. . . . [G]odliness respects the end of the action, and carries the agent in his intentions herein upon God." The role of agent, though rarely so named, was defined in detail as the capacity and will to undertake "actions" for "the glory of God." These acts must advance this end, be fit for the "time and place," in "proportion" and "kind," derive from detailed information and consultation "in all particulars," and, most important, stem from a consecrated "heart and soul." So doing, individuals in their earthly "endeavors and engagements" would be "able to dwell amongst lions . . . without fear or danger."[142]

Institutional demands to limit personal convictions or actions, to "relinquish their tenets," were no more feasible than getting individuals to "forsake their meat." On this "new earth," institutional legitimacy would be recast in terms of these new human powers.[143] John Goodwin offered a modern version of the classic Platonic metaphor of statecraft as a parable of universal agency:

> When the pilot or master of a ship at sea be . . . disabled, as through a phrenetical passion or sickness of any kind, so that he is incapable of acting the exigencies of his place for the preservation of the ship, being now in present danger . . . any one or more of the inferior mariners, having skill, may, in order to the saving of the ship and of the lives of all that are in it, very lawfully assume, and act according to, the interest of a pilot or master, and give orders and directions to those with them in the ship accordingly, who stand bound . . . to obey them.[144]

Believers were exhorted not to succumb to the "old threadbare trick of the profane Court" to tar political activists with the "malign reproach" of being "sectaries, seditious persons, troublers both of church and state." John Wildman urged, "Beware that ye be not frighted by the word anarchy, unto a love of monarchy, which is but the gilded name for tyranny."[145] Beyond this point of no return, the recovery of legitimate authority would require, as Hobbes came to realize, a new foundation in agency.

Though variously named, a heightened role was now the pattern. All who had been at "a lower growth in Christianity," incapable of "discerning good and evil," now had "an effectual door open" to "change and alter the property of a man." This was a "turning, as it were, course and frame of nature upside down within . . . men's hearts and disposition" which would allow "waters to break out in these deserts," the "myrtle tree to grow" in wilderness once "full of thorns and briers," and each individual to "pass unto the glorious liberty of holiness" and "conformity with itself."[146] John Goodwin identified these new self-conforming individuals as "high priests" with a "great and sacred investiture" through "God's appointment," humans "no more like unto other men" but "more excellent," now with God's "character" upon them. This made them "meet to be chosen as instruments to serve him, and . . . fitly qualified for any work or employment that shall be put into their hands."[147] Walwyn called the new individual "God-like." An anonymous pamphlet, *The Ancient Bounds,* spoke of a "microchristus, the epitome of Christ mystical," while Richard Overton referred to those "delivered of God" to be a "king, priest, prophet in his own natural circuit and compass."[148]

Roger Williams called them "stewards under God," Milton during the war "a chosen generation, a royal Priesthood."[149] For William Goffe, the insurgents were "instruments that God hath in his hands," "a company of Saints to follow" Jesus who "are chosen and called and faithful," undertaking work of "weightiness." The army radicals regarded themselves as "called forth by the Lord" to be "instruments in God's hands." Thomas Collier deemed the Saint a "new creature" who is "all righteousness" and therefore fit to undertake "the powers of the earth . . . the rule and government of the earth" in God's name.[150] John Saltmarsh regarded "the people" as now "raised up" from those who "lose their old capacity" for "compliancy and obedience and submission," to become "brethren" engaged in "consultation, [and] debating, counselling, prophesying, voting."[151] Among these various elaborations, the agent had come of age.

The Liberty of Empowered Agents

As correspondence with God's will was as available as "Manna" for "every child or babe in Christ" and divinely supported at every step, the regenerate were now to be wholly motivated by the power of positive involvement. Given the sanctified will's commitment to and engagement in divine ends, obligations would henceforth be willingly rendered. Rebellion or betrayal was unthinkable, for, declared Walwyn, "you will resolve rather to lose your life than to show your selves so basely ungrateful" to the empowering divinity. Moreover, the rising levels of popular mobilization in the insurgent cause confirmed that voluntarism, far from hindering decision, in fact promoted the sense of conviction.[152]

Early believers in congregational independence like William Bradshaw and William Ames as extreme voices in the wilderness had defended universal religious discretion, for the "judgment to discern well for a man's self, in his own Conscience, belongs to every man."[153] Early separatists including John Robinson and John Smyth had further recognized that ritual obedience without choice would not generate the necessary conviction: "As it were a ridiculous thing for a child, when he would ask of his father bread, fish, or any other thing he wanted, to read it to him out of a paper, so it is for the children of God . . . to read unto God their requests, for their own, out of a service book." Only willing and knowledgeable participation involving a "voluntary . . . communion of saints" and unfettered "personal profession" typical among dissenters would produce the requisite faith: "There is no truth of doctrine, nor evidence of Christ taught or practiced in the Church of England which we enjoy not, with far more liberty, better right, and greater purity."[154]

Henry Robinson in his popular 1643 tract "Liberty of Conscience, or The Sole means to obtain Peace and Truth" called upon individuals to "assume againe the dominion of our consciences" against "the imperiousnesse of Episcopacie, Presbyterie," and any others as "that which a mans owne judgement and understanding leads him to." Because every individual is "desirous" to "do what I will with mine own," he said, and will accept the results only "with what he does himselfe" regardless of success or failure, in religious matters eternal justice requires that "I must give account, repent and beleeve for my selfe, and can not doe either by proxie." Then "since no man knoweth the things of a man, save the spirit . . . within him, since my salvation ought to be more deare to my self than to any else; since if I miscarry through mine own choice and will, I shall easier acknowledge my destruction to be from my selfe, and declare Gods judgements to be just."[155] Overton added that anyone who would repress the liberty of conscience undermined true religion: "PERSECUTION for Conscience, maketh the Gospel of none effect, instead of Sincerity he setteth up Hypocrisy, instead of the Feare of God he setteth up the Terrour of men: instead of . . . the Word . . . the Sword . . . tumbling of them headlong without remorse to the Divell."[156] Roger Williams contended in his influential tract "The Bloody Tenet of Persecution" (1644) that spiritual coercion, while of the believer represents a "ravishing of conscience," in "unregenerate and unrepentant persons hardens up their souls" and creates "a dreadful . . . dream" of "the secure expectation of a false salvation." The prerequisite for "truth," it was now

understood even in the Independent tract *The Ancient Bounds* and in Cromwell's view, was the "liberty" of "judging and accepting what [one]
holds."[157] Moreover, the responsibility of each individual to "justify himself"
by his acts unleashed the immense power of personal commitment.[158]

No longer needing "outward administrations" or institutional rituals, neither did such individuals need the supportive constraints of predestination or God's inflexible legal conditions to freely believe and follow divine
ends.[159] An inflexible prior dispensation no longer reflected God's "merciful
and gracious" involvement: "The relation of a parent promiseth to a child a
constant desire and endeavor to promote its comfort and well-being. By virtue of this promise, parents are obliged to provide and 'lay up for their children.'" God would not permit a doctrine whose result was to "cast out of
[his] favour, and devote to everlasting misery, thousands and tens of thousands of [his] most excellent creatures" for redeemable offenses. God would
not "threaten" individuals "with the most horrid punishment" for "non-
performance" of obligations he believed they "neither are nor can be in any
capacity to perform," rendering ungodly the doctrine's insistence that God
"only is able to perform!" Given God's true gentleness, it would take a "very
great breach on the creature's part, in point of degeneracy and unworthi-
ness, before God looks upon himself as discharged from . . . all the parental
kindness to which he stood obliged by the relation of Creator."[160]

Predestination was not merely immoral but counterproductive. It provided false assurance to the sinful and enervating comfort to the spiritually
slothful. Preexisting judgment amounted to "a dispensation to sin without
danger . . . because it administereth a certain hope to it, that though it gratify
any vicious inclination or desire which may arise, yet it shall escape the future vengeance of Almighty God." This "liberty of sinning" was "more likely
to entice" saints into sin, being a "powerful temptation . . . to 'wax wanton
against Christ,'" for "when a man who stands is in danger of falling, is it
not the most likely way to procure his fall to persuade him that there is no
possibility of it?" The fallen in turn faced the absolute judgment of eternal
damnation, which was to "draw them aside from the way of faith" rather
than rekindling "a very fair and hopeful way" of recovering "true faith."[161]
Thomas Helwys concurred that predestination "makes some despair" and
"makes others deeply careless."[162]

John Goodwin moved from absolute predestinarianism to embrace Arminianism, with its free "power of believing" for those "earnestly, invited,
called, importuned, by God."[163] Given the full access of our "reasons, judg-

ments, and consciences" to "understanding and light," individuals must have "liberty to work [themselves] to any degree of inclination." Without the capacity for "voluntary negligence" and "voluntarily destroying their lives," God's call would be "pathetical" and an "insult" leading to "extremity of misery" and disbelief:

> For, to what purpose should a reward be promised to me, to persuade or induce me to engage in such or such a course, or to perform such or such a service, if I be necessitated to the same in some other way? Or what room is there left for moral inducement, where physical necessity hath done the execution. Now, that all the rewards promised in the Scriptures to those who persevere to the end, are promised . . . to work on the wills of men, to induce them to persevere, is a truth so replete with evidence, that it needs no proof.

No "doctrine" is "more powerful" in its capacity to "animate and encourage" or "promote godliness in the hearts and lives of men" than the promise of "a crown of glory and blessedness" to the godly and the threat of "the vengeance of hell-fire" to those who persist in "sin and folly."[164]

Milton in his antimonarchical tracts cautions Presbyterians "not to compel unforcible things in Religion especially, which if not voluntary, becomes a sin." The power of "reason" for him must include the "freedom to choose."[165] For John Goodwin, those assuming the new convictions had sufficient personal assurance regarding their spiritual destiny to relinquish theological certitude:

> Conditional assurance . . . will not fall much short of [absolute assurance]. Were I a person who desired to live long in the world, and God should please to grant me a lease of my life for a thousand years, only on condition that I should not wilfully destroy myself before that time; should I not be as well satisfied with such a conditional lease as . . . absolute. . . . In like manner, if it be simply the salvation of my soul which I desire, such a conditional promise as this, that I shall certainly be saved, if I abstain from folly, follow the Lord in the way of duty . . . is all the security I stand in need of.

Such conditionality in fact grounds ultimate reward, for one incapable of "falling away" is "incapable of reward from God" for "persevering to the end."[166]

Even covenant theory, important as a transitional expression of Puritan voluntarism, proved unduly formal and performance oriented. For some, including John Goodwin, the new covenant of grace remained applicable, though the onus, given the presumption of an adequate human performance, was now on God, who "promiseth to do all good things" with "infinite goodness and power," having "bound himself" to give "actual possession and enjoyment" of "justification" to us "with bands which he cannot break."[167] Many, notes Christopher Hill, including Walwyn, Saltmarsh, Collier, and other radical "preachers of free grace," sought "to liberate men and women from the formalism, the legal calculations of covenant theologians."[168] Rejecting "Old Testament" modes of "dispensation," Saints were now to be "gather[ed] up more closely, spiritually, and cordially" by "a law upon their inward parts, sweetly compelling in the consciences with power and yet not with force," through "a fulness of spirit."[169]

In place of "external compactings," the "glory of this new creature" enabled it to be "delivered from legal and fleshly actings," to be "new in respect of form, compacted together by the Spirit, not literal forms and ordinances." Grace issued not from legal principles, being "a law without them," but from "a principle of light, life, liberty, and power within" each person.[170] The "very difficult" path to salvation requiring conditionality in "our labour, industry, study, and watching" or "our beleeving, or doing, or repenting, or selfe-deniall, or Sabbath-keeping, or something or other" was to be replaced by "our blessed condition" obtainable "depending on no condition, no performance at all."[171] "The worke of Christ," wrote Walwyn, "depends not on your beleeving. . . . It is so naturall to think that [one] is still bound to do something for obtaining the love and favour of God, that you will finde it the hardest thing in the world to free your selves from it, though it be the grossest Antichristian errour that ever was. . . . [T]hough you should not beleeve, yet hee is faithfull and cannot deny himselfe to be your redeemer, your peace-maker, your Saviour."[172] A group of army leaders including John Lilburne determined no longer "to idolize the Covenant (as we fear many do)," for it was "so mixed with worldly interest" that "every party" uses it "though as far different as light and darkness." They vowed to "preserve its true and lawful ends" as "though there had been no such Covenant at all entered into."[173]

The ever-growing willingness to pursue God's ends had finally issued in the revolutionary claim that freedom—the freedom entitled to agents—was the precondition to agency's effective exercise. The collapse of civil and religious restraints with the onset of the Revolution encouraged demands for Christian liberty among believers throughout society, just as the political and economic insurgents pressed claims of natural liberty and the civil liberty of Englishmen: "The collapse of monarchical and ecclesiastical authority and the triumph of the army set all godly souls at last completely free to heed whatever call or revelation they believed had come to them, to commune with one group or another as the spirit moved them or with none at all, a law unto themselves in what seemed to many a lawless world."[174] The fractious question Cromwell put at the army debates at Putney, "to consider how far we are obliged, and how far we are free,"[175] moved like a whirlwind across the land. These discourses gradually coalesced multiple claims of entitlement in the novel demand that "true freedom . . . is the end of . . . all government," codified with the Leveller assertion that "the end of all government is the safety and freedome of the governed."[176] As in godly covenants, freedom was now the source of political obligation: "Covenants freely made, freely entered into, must be kept. . . . Take that away, I do not know what ground there is."[177] Even though the link between freedom and agency was largely implicit, this new assertion of a fundamental right to voluntary self-binding, a right inconsistent with both authoritative demands for servitude and proto-agency hierarchies of the elect, signified the crossing of a cultural divide.

Agency as a Developmental Process

With agency as a new life stage, the believer's time on earth had become a journey constituted not from a theological pattern but as a real, immanent historical achievement: a story no longer of fall from innocence into sin followed by lifelong patience in the hope of future rewards, but of movement from immature and irresponsible infancy or childhood to maturity, self-mastery, and knowledgeable responsibility sustained by an authority recognized and followed from within.

Reinterpreting both humankind's present condition and its history, John Goodwin read the death of Jesus as nullifying the "guilt and condemnation" of original sin from "Adam's transgression," so that "no man shall be condemned, but for his own personal sins." Grace was no longer equated with return to the prelapsarian state, for Adam lived within a prior dispensation of the human role: "If Adam in his innocency had a power of believing, then might he actually have believed, if he pleased. But it was not possible that Adam, during his innocency, should actually believe; because all this while there was no word of revelation from God concerning Jesus Christ, without which there was no possibility of actually believing. . . . [H]e carried nothing saving with him out of his state of innocency into this lapsed condition." Authority in the first stage of human development, whether during the "state of innocency" or after the fall, "remained under a covenant of works" with the same requirement of "absolute obedience to the whole law in all things." While original innocence was not, to be sure, like the subsequent period of "sin, misery, and condemnation," Eden was no longer the model.[178] The present "dispensation," as Thomas Collier put it, was a "new creation," a "new heaven" and "new earth," a "higher manifestation of light and glory" than in "young or middle age."[179]

Once the traditional claim of original perfection was relinquished, the theological and historical narratives of human growth could be merged.[180] The covenant of works had been necessitated by the immature condition of the people, theologically in Eden and then historically in the age of absolutism. As one participant at Putney put it: "The like thraldom . . . of the nation . . . in times past . . . hath been [due to] the stage of ignorance, and darkness, and pretence of religion, that hath been amongst us, so that, not having [had] the faith itself which we pretended to, we have [had] rather the form of godliness than the power of it." Only now, given recent advances, was it the time for a "coming forth of captives," as it is written: "I will take off every yoke and remove every burden from off the people, because of the anointing."[181] Theologically it was now possible to move from "wilderness and deserts" of sin to the "streams" of "heavenly dispositions" and "perfect righteousness," from "the law" to "grace," "the Letter" to "the Spirit."[182] Historically, the people could now "break an unrighteous engagement," one that "enslaves the people of England—that they should be bound by laws in which they have no voice at all," and become in Cromwell's terms "enlighten[ed] . . . to see our liberties."[183] Lilburne wrote that the "cruel, pitifull, lamentable and intollerable Bondage" was "no longer to be indured, suffered, nor undergone." Finally, now, "Godlinesse and true Religion being increased by faithfull Preaching and godly Discipline, in the hearts of men, will make the Common-wealth free from the necessity of so many Lawyers" and from being "oppressed with our Lawes."[184] Collier preached deliverance from "tyrannical and oppressing laws" and from "the old church," which "cannot be borne in souls who live in light."[185]

The journey from the bondage of enforced obligation to the freedom of "voluntary service" became the great narrative of Protestant development.[186] It directed the novel and unsettling experience of an age growing to new powers and responsibilities by fusing historical progress with the transcendent theology of regeneration. Believers became "actors in a universal drama" framed as "the course of the godly soul" from servitude to agency.[187] This pattern, which became the paradigm for the defining Protestant narratives from *Pilgrim's Progress* to *Robinson Crusoe* to Benjamin Franklin's *Autobiography,* was principally the work of one figure, John Milton. In his hands the developmental triumph became a cosmic epic, reordering the human role, the world, and human history.

The Agency Cosmology of John Milton

Milton in his early revolutionary tracts recognized a civilizational shift beyond the "iron yoke of outward conformity" which "hath left a slavish print upon our necks." Individuals previously could only be "slaves" who "like unruly horses that are impatient of the bit . . . will endeavor to throw off the yoke, not from the love of genuine liberty . . . but from the impulses of pride and little passions." Though "they may change their master," such persons "will never be able to get rid of their servitude."[188] God, however, now "enlightening of his Church" by "dispens[ing] and deal[ing] out by degrees his beam," was enabling humankind "not only to look back and revise what hath bin taught heretofore, but to gain furder and goe on, some new enlighten'd steps in the discovery of truth."[189]

Milton's focus in the revolutionary period, despite increasing doubts about human capacity, was on overcoming the servility of the past with a responsible, self-defined, and self-imposed commitment to God. Using "reason," individuals would relinquish their "double tyranny, of custom from without, and blind affections within" previously glorified with "the falsifi'd names of Loyalty and Obedience, to colour over their base compliances." They would embrace "Christian liberty," "the free Gospel" of "grace, manhood, freedom, and faith," over "the servile law" of "rigour, childhood, bondage, and works," becoming "sons" rather than "servants unadopted."[190] Because "absolute lordship and Christianity are inconsistent,"[191] society would in turn need transformation to the just "administration of government" by "brethren" rather than "lords." The goal of eliminating hierarchical coercion was not "license," that is, unconstrained liberty, but a "willingness" to be "freeborne of the Spirit," for "to be free is the same as to be pious, to be wise, to be temperate and just."[192] Individual "obedience to right reason and the rule of yourselves" would facilitate "civil liberty" for Christians striving to fulfill the Gospels as they saw fit.[193]

The author of *Paradise Lost* offered a radically different account. Reflecting on the Revolution after its failure to produce stable institutions or identities, Milton now understands its collapse in a new way. The insurgency was doomed not by the tenacity of the traditional world or the failure to effect revolutionary transformation of the human role but by its very success conjoined with the almost instantaneous disappearance of traditional restraints. *Paradise Lost* portrays this transformed cosmos in which a ubiquitous modern individualism driving the motivations and conduct of fallen angels and the new human race has already rent the harmony of heaven and is about to shatter Eden. The great challenge in this new world, grasped equally only by Hobbes with his original condition of uncontained individualism, was no longer the internal impact of slavish obedience or the external powers of tyrannical oppression preventing the ascension to agency (Hobbes, for one, wished for more of such obedience). It was contrarily taming those unprecedented internal forces that agency by its success had unleashed: individuals justified by a personal mandate of authorization transcending human institutions could not easily be limited by worldly constraints; moreover, the personal and self-validating nature of that warrant would beguile many agents into believing themselves the author of its mandate as well. In the populist council of fallen angels, the narcissistic self-justifying by envious Satan, naively self-absorbed Eve, and blindly rationalistic Adam, Milton exemplifies the new dangers. The primal sin of servants, a wish for the apple of knowledge which invests the agency power to independently perform one's given role, had become the primal sin of the emergent agency character, the wish to define "the edible" which invests the source of one's warrant in self-authority.

Milton's epic illuminates for modernity the overarching principles of agency which are now inscribed in the cosmic structure. At the same time a defense of this new cosmology against both its traditional rival of servitude and its newly emergent opponent, self-authorization, it presents its argument by juxtaposing two perspectives on the universe as possible frames for the creation story. The first perspective, from the viewpoint of Adam and Eve, traces their experiential development to agency. It begins with their original innocence, a dream of perpetual childhood amidst God's plenty before the fall into history. Imagining heavenly unity and a cosmos at peace, they naively foresee a life in which they can "perform / Aught whereof [God] hath need" in a world without need, simply "ceaselessly prais[ing] his works" and otherwise pursuing "choice / Unlimited of manifold delights."[194] Obedient children, they will be taken care of in their appetites while forgoing all larger responsibilities. In this narrative tracing Adam and Eve's evolving state of mind, they must face the wrenching and seemingly avoidable loss of Paradise, adjusting through painful adaptation to responsibilities beyond mere childhood obedience.

The other and controlling perspective in which the reader is situated presents a differently conceived epic narrative. Here, the experience of innocence and fall from unity is precluded by a world already inescapably sundered, for in the beginning was division. Cosmic harmony is moved back to a period before human creation and is inessential to the human narrative. Both God's creation and empowerment of Jesus and the surfacing of the heavenly rift which it provoked (but did not cause, given underlying jealousies in heaven) are irreversible. While Adam and Eve, as the "everypeople" of their age, must doubtless adjust to the shock of recent exile from "so late their happy seat,"[195] Milton's readers by contrast are to presume the loss of Eden from the opening lines of the epic.

Yet this loss, which stirs childish longings even in Milton's readers, is to be more than compensated for by the greater recognition—their irreversible attainment of human agency. From the outset, Adam and Eve are structurally defined as—their very creation mandates them to be—primordial agents in God's larger plan to repair the divisions in the cosmos. By the structure of divine purpose their role has been set through "his works / In thee and in thy Seed" to achieve the ultimate healing by which "the Earth / Shall all be Paradise, far happier place / Than this of Eden."[196] Endowed though they do not yet realize it with the modern capacities for choice and the power to act individually, they will determine not just their own destinies but the future of all being. Readers are alerted from the outset to witness what Adam and Eve must learn from experience: a dutiful commitment to the letter of God's law will fail. The conscious determination to obey the rules because they are rules, sustained only by Eve's naively ingenuous but deluded wish to please or Adam's rigidly rationalistic and equally deluded rectitude buttressed by God's formal instruction,[197] will be quickly and effortlessly overcome. It is no match for their deeper raging impulses to be "self-begot, self-rais'd / By our own quick'ning power," the "savory smell" of "prospect wide" and "high exaltation" by which "Gods of men" are made.[198] Childish obedience ignorant of personal pitfalls and human responsibilities must give way to a changed heart rooted in personal and religious understanding. Returning to a position of servitude and thus inconsequence in the cosmic drama is never an option, foreclosed in the narrative entirely by the larger reasons for human existence and the inevitability of Eden's collapse. Thus, in place of a "servile fear" of "the Law" imposed through "servitude" to the "Tyranny" of "violent Lords," they are offered the "Truth" of "Faith" in the "free / Acceptance of large Grace" and adaptation to the detailed requirements of their new role.[199]

From the reader's more knowledgeable perspective, innocence has lost much of its attraction. Adam and Eve live in a fantastical and false Paradise with regard to the state of both the cosmos and their own souls. They have no conception of the cosmic divisions that frame their existence, the decisive role they were created to play, the struggle against sin and death they must undertake, or the strengths they will need to succeed. On the internal level, unable to read themselves or each other, they lack any clue that the driving forces of personal overreaching are already active.[200] In this new world of unleashed individual impulses, a world in which "War hath determin'd us," the narcissistic drives for "Power . . . favor and preeminence" already propel Satan toward destructive behavior well before his open rage surfaces at subordination to Jesus, just as they control Adam and Eve from the moment of their creation: in Eve's first narcissistic longings and her dislike of being subordinated, but also if more veiled in Adam's cloning of a love object, his presumptuous curiosity, his profane projective idealization of Eve, and his hunger for dominance over her.[201]

Deconstructing the theology of innocence, Milton redefined the reality of the original condition in experiential terms as a psychological gap between the fantasy of harmony and the driving presence of narcissistic self-aggrandizement. Given that the primal sin is the continuing wish to appropriate the apple's (or apple-definer's) powers and not the discrete violation of the rule against ingestion, this condition is furthermore an *already fallen* internal state mirroring cosmic fragmentation. Adam and Eve are in their essential natures unwilling to live by Eden's terms, like Satan in heaven, but cannot bring themselves to leave it and grow up. Instead they naively clutch the preposterous delusion that mastery in Eden and instant gratification can be effortlessly continued without giving rise to either dangerous fantasies of self-authority or to a corresponding need for internal mastery. Thus, readers helplessly watch Eve wander off and Adam imagine himself turned always heavenward in piety, both flaunting their invulnerability under the condition of greatest vulnerability to and without any defenses against being taken over by their grandiose wishes.

The problem for Milton is to link the two narratives, to provide the experiential logic by which Adam and Eve grow to understand and embrace the reader's perspective. In a world of empowered individualists, the commitment to obey authority and to accept the constraints and responsibilities of one's agency role will be effective only if it freely arises from the will of the individual. How in a world where all things now seem possible is one to learn that a narrow range of outcomes governs our lives? They must learn through the journey of experience that Eden's infinite possibilities, like the English revolutionaries' dreams of instant paradise, mask the uncompromising moral structure governing human life. The only corrective to unconstrained impulse and fantasies of easy self-control, befitting the new powers and responsibilities of the agent but unthinkable before, is knowledge: full knowledge from God of their status (not God's) in the scheme of divine ends, and the transforming personal confrontation with the primal sin of agency through the psychological, earthly hell of collapsing delusions of grandeur and the history of human sin and pain that it initiates. From painful experience, they gain the mature insight that self-authorization is as effectively foreclosed as servitude, that only the options appropriate to agency pertain: either the believer's opportunity to "Restore us, and regain the blissful Seat," not as an unrecoverable and unenvied garden of bounded obedience but as a "commodiously" appointed "World" to be achieved "all before them," or for all others "parcht with scalding thirst and hunger fierce" the "Fruit" of "bitter Ashes."[202] As with children of divorce, one was not innocent but ignorant at first, for one did not fall into division so much as wake up to its reality, thereby gaining the recognition and strength to move beyond it.

By setting up these polarities and favorably situating readers to recognize and examine the internal causes for the failure of agency in England, Milton challenged them to internalize the proper ends and develop the corresponding constraints that would enable them to construct a new—agency—garden on earth. With greater enlightenment than in the childhood of the species, they will relive the original fall, though realizing in advance the inevitable divisions and the need to participate through human history in their overcoming. The rifts exist because of Satan's original demand for self-authorization, and the creation of humanity and its agency role precisely to vanquish these impulses ensures that humans informed of this prehistory will not seek a return to the original vulnerability and impotence.

Rather, they will *choose* the new mature healing role (not possible in Eden's monochromatic world) in God's future: "what . . . fruits on Earth . . .

/ From thy implanted Grace . . . [are] / Fruits of more pleasing savor from thy seed / Sown with contrition in his heart, than those / Which his own hand manuring all the Trees / Of Paradise could have produc't, ere fall'n / From innocence."[203] The reader's journey, rather than clutching onto or even grieving over Eden with its devastating flaws, willingly employs agency powers to propel the world—reflecting Jesus' dictum to bring "not peace, but a sword"—from division to a new higher unity.[204] The futility of unprepared agents attending (as servants would have) God's controlling ministrations is replaced by agents prepared to win God's plan, a Protestant paradise on earth reflecting the "Paradise within thee, happier far" of freely rendered obedience.[205]

Milton's epic restores a map of the future, fulfilling the early vision and logic of English Protestant agency. Adam and Eve venture in God's sight into the world as never before possible, empowered "to choose / Thir place of rest," of work and community building, as modern individuals. Such individualism could not thenceforth, as in the traditional world, be externally repressed in order to subdue egoism.[206] Rather, it had to be given a pivotal role through which its powers were affirmed and harnessed to new responsibilities so as to build a new form of human order. By linking that empowering role to a repudiation of wishes for personal authorization, Milton like Hobbes mobilized the new self against its own dangers, now understood as the sole resource for order in a post-obedient world.

The Politicization of Protestant Agency

The new sense that religious energies could be actively employed to realize divine ends, as well as the political dangers (later reflected in *Paradise Lost*) lurking within their tendency toward self-authorization, achieved its fullest expression in the Civil War. Decades of heightened spiritual and political expectations sharpening the determination to battle against sin emboldened radicals to revolutionary engagement. As those political and religious institutions increasingly identified with the forces of Antichrist collapsed, the unchecked drive emerged for systematic reformation of society. John Goodwin in 1642 called all insurgents to "Battell," to defend "to the utmost of your ability," both "freely" and "willingly," the "true Protestant Religion" and its future triumph for "sons and daughters" and "posterities . . . yet unborne" in "the Gospel." Against the forces of royal and religious reaction, which as "in Sodome . . . the Lord would destroy the place and City where they were," they must "advance" this cause of "the Saints" now rising "throughout the whole world" for its salvation. All in "houses of vision" must accept this "great and solemne invitation from God himself unto you, to do greater things for the world . . . than any particular Christian State ever did, or is likely to do while the world stands." It was a ringing affirmation of agents who now "have the patterne in the mount before you: See that according to your line and measure, you make all things like to it." They were now fully capable "to execute the judgement that is written."[207]

William Walwyn in 1643 implored the religious insurgents "when tyrants and oppressors . . . pervert the truth of God into a lie" to "be bold as Lions": "You will finde it nothing to hazzard your lives for God, in defense of his truth from errour; in defense of your brother or neighbour from oppression or tyranny . . . in the punishment of all kinde of exorbitances . . . any kind of injustice in whomsoever, and to be no respecter of persons; nor will any ones greatnesse over-sway or daunt your resolutions." Godly action was now part of the divine warrant: "You will know these things are by God referred unto you, and you will not resigne them up to him, but willingly sacrifice" all in pursuit of this mission.[208] The "duty to God and his conscience" for Thomas Rainborough at Putney required the "work" of revolutionary "service to God and the kingdom": "At the last day it can never be answered to God, that you did not do it." Cromwell called upon the army to do "our part" in remaking the kingdom, to "carry on our business, to do God's business, that which is the will of God." The Commonwealth Army in Scotland defended its campaigns in England, Ireland, and now Scotland "against all the opposers of this work of Jesus Christ" to complete "the destruction of Antichrist."[209]

As the call to "do something for the kingdom" spread through the land, the ecclesiastical and more broadly political dimensions of the new role emerged with a swiftness unthinkable within an orderly society.[210] The appropriation of the personal warrant of agency by the populace starkly revealed its incompatibility with both hierarchy and external control in spiritual matters. First, given the equivalent status of each individual's relation with God, no other individual or collectivity was in a position to assert control over it. Now that "the Spirit is . . . vouchsafed unto every man coming into the world, inasmuch as every man is enlightened," access to its full powers "includes every individual of mankind without any exception."[211] Many sectarians had long affirmed universal grace in repudiation of ministerial elites, and the laity entering the lists during the Revolution began more assertively to "stir with the belief that they were the saints."[212] Where "the meanest capacity is fully capable of a right understanding,"[213] at the extreme, individuals were increasingly regarded as spiritually equal, "God" being "in every one," such that "the same all which is in me, is in thee."[214] The warrant that "God will pour his Spirit" on both "young men" and "old men," enabling them to "see visions," amounted to universal prophecy for individuals in direct contact with the Word. Ecclesiastically, the equality of believers meant that all religious associations were equal, though they be "but of two or three" members or, finally, the individual "left utterly alone with his private God."[215]

Closely related was the collapse of ecclesiastical controls on religious activity, for unlike the performance of covenant or uniform ritual obligations which could be monitored, the internal convictions of one's distinctive heart and spirit could not. Furthermore, the sanctity of that primordial relation made worldly constraints on its expression inherently profane. John Goodwin wrote, "When men are filled with the Spirit, they . . . shall be enabled to act in a peculiar sphere by themselves, leaving the world, yea." Once "there is no place left within him for the flesh to suggest any thing to the contrary, either to take him off from, or to retard him in, the prosecution" of "honourable purposes," the individual's "being 'filled with the Spirit' will free you from all incumbrances in the ways of holiness."[216] For such individuals, there is "a strong presumption, that an act performed by such a person, is lawfull"[217] to God regardless of its institutional implications. In the remarkable Putney and Whitehall debates on the nature of magistracy and church-state relations, Cromwell and others demanded "to speak our hearts freely here" in order to discern "the counsels of God" without constraint or censure.[218]

As these arguments gained ever more adherents during the 1640s, they evolved beyond their religious formulations into fundamental new claims that equality and liberty required the restructuring of political hierarchy and control. The reasons for this are complex: the increasing influence of the newly powerful political and economic insurgents who in pursuit of greater power and independence appropriated and extended the religious arguments along with other natural law and civil law doctrines; the growing worldliness of religious activists, partly the outcome of religious promises of earthly fulfillment as they experienced the powerful pull of success and power, expanded opportunities, and reduced constraints; the inevitable expansion of political language to include competing sects. Given the priority accorded religious convictions, the demand for equal power to shape one's spiritual fate mandated greater equivalence in every institution. If "every one hath a spirit within him" such that "no man can judge so of any man," then all individuals have "a right to the kingdom" and need give their "birthright to none."[219] Kings were as "all creatures" one of "his instruments."[220]

Political legitimacy was in turn recast. Since, in Lilburne's terms, "every particular and individual man and woman . . . are . . . all equal and alike in power, dignity, authority, and majesty, none of them having by nature any authority, dominion, or magisterial power one over or above another," then all institutional authority is "by mutual agreement or consent, given . . . for the good benefit and comfort of each other."[221] Any other exercise, "spiritual or temporal," is "unjust, devilish, and tyrannical" and "enslaves the people."[222] To ground the claim of universal participation, these radicals were led toward a social contract theory of origins that people are "by nature all equal" and that states must therefore have their "foundation" in the "Law of Nature" whereby men "put" themselves "under" government each "by his own consent."[223]

Similarly, the insistence on unconstrained religious expression would necessitate a reduction of institutional constraint throughout society. Under conditions of oppression and resistance, the religious language of responsible liberty under conscience, "compulsion" which is "yet with consent,"[224] gave way to a full-blown discourse of anti-institutional freedom. As "those with no lawfull authority or power" proceeded with "hatred, and malice, and revenge" to "fall upon us, and our lives and liberties, both spiritual and civill, upon our estates, our Gospell and Religion," they had to "very lawfully be resisted."[225] Because in matters of conscience "no man or magistrate on the earth hath power to meddle," then "men" must be "freed from dependence upon others."[226] The "blessings of liberty" in their "benefit and sweetnesse" must be as "high prised with us as matter of estate is . . . a dram of that liberty . . . as pretious to us, as a drop of could water . . . to the rich man in hell . . . so grieviously tormented in those flames."[227] The "principles of right and freedom," framed variously as the "liberties of the people" and "the people's right," as freedom from unjust "engagements," a continual "enlightening" to better "see our liberties," and the right to go no "further than your own satisfactions lead you," dominated the discourse of the Revolution.[228]

The right to freedom, now "original and fundamental,"[229] entailed a restraint on institutions, "taking off tithes and other Antichristian yokes," the people's right to "free themselves from tyranny" and be "freed from dependence upon others," from interference or "power over" them.[230] Robert Everard asked at Putney, "Is there any liberty that we find ourselves deprived of" or any "hindrances" that cannot be removed?[231] It was essential to independence in matters of press, conscience, and arbitrary government intrusion upon lives or property.[232] To buttress these claims against interference, many religious radicals as well as lawyers and members of Parliament turned from the constraining theory of Christian liberty to the institutionally limiting liberties of the "Laws of Nature and Nations" as freedoms they possessed either naturally or as Englishmen, derived from a time prior to existing political society and forming original conditions or constraints on its operation.[233]

The Political Crisis of Agency

This association of freedom with the illegitimacy of institutional constraints was creating a political vacuum. Witnessing the conditions arise for the uncontrolled assertion of self-authorization, religious insurgents expressed great concern lest they release "the false prophet within us," about "mentioning our own thoughts and conceptions with that which is of God . . . whether it be of God or no."[234] John Goodwin warned of being "fervent in spirit" regarding what individuals "call, or judge to be, the service of God, although it be a service of their own fancy, or genius, or of some worse deity."[235] Many radical sectarians would "claim to be Christ or God"; Hobbes would note the incidence of those who "tell you, he were God the Father."[236] Milton and the Protestants had struggled to contain individualism within agency limits. Hobbes understood that, from the perspective of politics, unconstrained Protestant agency was no less dangerous than self-authorization. Where "every one hath the right and power alike to speak the Word,"[237] a "pretence of godliness" was no constraint.[238] As one participant at Putney expressed it: "God hath put us on such a course which I cannot but reverence, and God does not now speak by one particular man, but in every one of our hearts. . . . [I]f it were a dangerous thing to refuse a message that came from one man to many, it is a more dangerous thing to refuse what comes from God, being spoke by many to us." Cromwell himself believed that "truly we have heard many speaking to us; and I cannot but think that in many of those things God hath spoke to us."[239] For Hobbes, the danger of "inspiration," an opinion of "being in the special grace of God almighty," was with all other extreme forms of "madness" the "seditious roaring of a troubled nation."[240]

As values now inscribed in nature or national formation for each to access individually or worse, to be defined at will by individual authors, freedom and equality were attaining a transcendent priority in political life as they had in radical religious discourse. As was to happen so many times in the course of Anglo-American development, Protestantism could not contain the forces it had unleashed. The Protestant community fragmented into rival visions and internecine conflicts over power until, in Roger Williams's terms, it did "break into schisms and factions . . . yea, wholly break up and dissolve into pieces and nothing."[241] In the proliferating chaos of agents and narratives, legitimacies and validations, none of course could establish credibility. This led Williams and his ilk to give up on the world as a "wilderness, or sea of wild beasts innumerable, fornicators, covetous, idolators, &c."[242] Rainborough expressed the agony of the believer's disorientation: "I hope when I leap I shall take so much of God with me, and so much of just and right with me, as I shall jump sure."[243] Cromwell implored God for "engaged spirits."[244] Joshua Sprigge hoped that Christ would take responsibility to "provide for the maintaining of his own truth in the world."[245] They had no wish that the old system, collapsed like "a pilot" who "has run his ship upon a rock, a general [who] mount his cannon against his army,"[246] might ever be restored.[247] Yet, without political direction, Cromwell's government by the 1650s devolved to the maintenance of order by the army. For, as John Wildman admitted at Putney, the multiplying visions of political transformation had left "the principles and maxims of just government . . . as loose as can be," creating what Sprigge called "this labyrinth wherein we are."[248]

Mainstream Puritans such as Thomas Hooker, Thomas Shepard, Thomas Goodwin, Philip Nye, and William Prynne panicked at the disorder caused by a "liberty" which "men . . . know not how to use." Individuals had been left completely "at liberty (as the Principle of the times is) to choose (as men in a Market) what that Light will lead them to" with ministry now "levelled, and diffused into that bulk and commoners."[249] Shepard wrote from America: "What is the cause in our native country, notwithstanding all prayers and tears no deliverance? Truly men do not know it, but the Lord sees it, they know not how to use their liberty."[250] Stephen Marshall wrote, "Our times are times of . . . such Divisions, as (I thinke) were hardly ever known in the Christian World . . . worst of all, divisions among Gods people."[251] Shepard believed a return of authority was paramount: "Like untamed horses that will cast their rider, unless they be held under and backed, and then they are gentle, so it is here; and truly it is long before a man can learn the sweet of Christ's government: hence Israel must be long in Egyptian bondage, and many long miseries."[252] He called for the return of "a ruler of a ship" to "guide it right." This faction now demanded order through imposition of presbyterian controls and institutions, and when this failed, began to seek the return of the monarchy, for it is finally "the king who hath power."[253]

But the assault on traditional hierarchy which united the political and economic insurgents with the spreading religious movement rendered return impossible. The pragmatic leadership of the Revolution, to be sure, anxious to seize power from the court and church, had no intention of turning over authority to a Puritan ministry intent on establishing universal discipline and a theocratic state. Many religious radicals would, with Roger Williams, recognize the political stalemate and plead to be saved from disorder by a new and inclusive "civil way of union" that recognized "nonconformists." They acknowledged the necessity of ending an "enforced uniformity" of religion as the cause of "civil war," "tumults and garboils," and moreover as an impractical means of getting individuals to "forsake their meat." In fact, where religious unanimity was unobtainable, "the practice of forcing straitens men in their liberty."[254] The solution was toleration, the separation of religious belief from political controls. But no state existed or could be created by the religious factions themselves, with their pressing spiritual agendas, which could provide a stable basis for the new spiritual and political priorities and the transformed human role that had produced them.[255]

The insurgents, including notably Cromwell, had fought for a new unification, hoping from a "uniting spirit" to "seek God together" with "one heart" and "one mind"[256] and produce a "kingdom" without "divisions" for the "public good." But "the immunity and impunity of differing opinions in religion" and politics was inevitable,[257] what Cromwell feared as the "utter confusion" of intransigent beliefs producing endless "dispute" among equally "plausible" ideals leading to "an absolute desolation."[258] The result was what Christopher Hill calls "teeming freedom," a "continuous revelation" of sustained "novelty" and "originality" in which "ordinary people were freer from the authority of church and social superiors than they had ever been before, or were for a long time to be again."[259] The rejection of old rationales and narratives by saints armed and the embrace of new ones with no authority left to "deter" or "oppose" generated an innovative age with few parallels in Western history. For those at the time, however, England was a "kingdom . . . shaken" to its roots with "all authority . . . broken to pieces," in a "wilderness condition" and in danger of being destroyed.[260]

Despite their self-image of failure, we can from a distance question that assessment. The insurgents had promised, exhorted, worked ceaselessly for a "new earth," and after a great deal longer than six days and six nights, it came to pass. Even Hobbes, their implacable enemy, acknowledged modern individualism with its liberty and equality as the new original condition. What they had not answered was, How would a society of agents be governed? What was the alternative to total release? How were institutions to be reconstituted that would permit rather than repress the agency role? Moreover, how were the requisite uniformity and constancy to be assured in a culture of active, diversely warranted agents? Could the latitude and choice at the core of agency be rendered consistent with civil order? How much egalitarianism was sufficient to replace the now invalidated ascriptive hierarchies? In what manner could dangerous religious commitments be contained? Above all, how was agency itself to be conceived, in relation to what author who would be able to establish and maintain unity? Put another way, in whose sight were humans to acknowledge being legitimated where only Jesus truly saw into the human heart but yet could not, politically speaking, be counted on?

As the religious insurgents abdicated responsibility for political order, religion passed from its position at the operational center of societal life. The pattern emerged by which the maintenance of peace, no easy matter, would then be left to the secular institutions.[261] Thus, the stage was set for the emergence of liberalism, the political response to the Protestant cry for assistance. Sharing its basic assumptions, liberalism would be quite stern regarding Protestant excesses. This would create the impression of a fierce contest for the control of modern society. This impression would miss how liberalism, with its inclusive and nonsectarian priorities, saved with a defensible politics of agency the new worldview.

Christopher Hill identifies the "collapse of Calvinism" as "one of the fascinating problems" of the modern age. In one sense, its work was done with the establishment of the principles of agency. In another sense, of course, its work had just begun: to embrace Milton's challenge to make a garden in the world out of labor and faith, a garden of self-reliance and active utility, without hierarchy or external coercion, a garden no longer of Edenic servitude but of agency. English society only partly responded, muting the religious call for agency within the hierarchies, now modified, of English class society. The purer the belief in agency, the greater would be the English sense of defeat.[262]

And yet, there was not entirely cause for despair. Puritanism did not disappear so much as "start the same process over again" in the colonies with "new churches, new orthodoxies, new schisms, new exoduses to newer and newer promised lands."[263] In the United States, the people of the dream and the dream itself would reconnect, forging a dynamic by which Puritanism passed over into the Protestantism of full agency and liberalism that came to shape American life. And this new people in turn would repudiate the Puritans, in time vilifying them as prison keepers of the possibilities attainable in the new world of agency. But, then, they would not understand their own origin in the Protestant revolt, and their immense debt to the heroic and innovative age of Puritan insurgency.

4

Thomas Hobbes and the Founding of the Liberal Politics of Agency

I authorize and give up my right of governing myself . . . on this condition, that thou give up thy right to him, and authorize all his actions in like manner.

—Thomas Hobbes

Understanding Anglo-American liberalism and its historical role has been impeded by its rhetorical consecration as the theory of the "free society." Harold Laski in his classic study *The Rise of European Liberalism* located its origins in the shift from "the idea of social initiative and social control" to that "of individual initiative and individual control" by which liberalism "sought to vindicate the right of the individual to shape his own destiny, regardless of any authority which might seek to limit his possibilities." In a more critical vein, John P. Diggins similarly defines "liberalism" in *The Lost Soul of American Politics* "in a word" as "negative freedom, freedom from political power and public authority, freedom for man to pursue his own ends, individual freedom."[1] To insulate liberalism from association with political coercion, its proponents distinguish the theory from its two presumable antecedents, Protestantism and the work of Thomas Hobbes. Thus, in Laski's view, "liberalism has usually, by reason of its origins, been hostile to the claims of churches." Hobbes he also dismisses as one of liberalism's many forerunners "hostile to its aims" and moreover "wholly free" of the liberal "passion for justice." Hobbes's defense of sovereign "omnicompetence" he regarded as an object lesson for Locke's creation of "a non-sovereign state."[2]

Theorists of modern socialism of course treat liberalism as a defense of property interests and its claims of freedom as the ideological support for capitalist distribution and control. But Tocqueville's contrary warning that its ubiquitous constraints (and even dangers of oppression) arise less from

111

inequities of ownership and distribution than from its unprecedented equality, while critical for the modern sociology of mass society, has been largely unheeded in considerations of the historical origins of liberalism. The routinization and liberal collectivism feared by Tocqueville are most often treated as recent, unanticipated complexities arising from modern industrial organization, marketing, and communications.

The study of the modern self and society has thus been fragmented by an implicit division of liberalism into periods: its coercive predecessors; a golden age of individual and personal freedom; and the subsequent decline of autonomy and the liberal self in modern organizational society.[3] These self-serving distinctions do not survive a more searching inquiry into the history of liberalism and its construction of social order. With regard to its early period, Locke's vision of a self-regulating citizenry on which the later "golden age" depends rests entirely on the institutionalization of his educational model. This early internalization of agency capacities and constraints was the very dynamic Hobbes imposed as the necessary grounding for a modernist self and society. And to complete the historical links, Hobbes's metapolitical reframing of political authority, societal organization, and human role derives from the Protestant insurgents. As for the modern period, to consider contemporary organizational liberalism as a deformation of the Lockean "free society" similarly ignores deeper theoretical continuities. English theory and American liberal society constitute stages in the larger adaptation of the agency character to structural necessities and opportunities in each phase. Restoring these links will establish liberalism's continuing reliance on the new Protestant paradigm in its own framing of social and self-formation and their joint contribution to and ultimate partnership in creating modern agency society.

The liberal claim of constituting a "free society" is, from the perspective of political theory and social formation, a perplexing one. Would not one expect the preeminently successful political system of modernity to be grounded in nonelective patterns of institutional and characterological formation? Its continuing and quite strident denial of such patterns is by no means accidental, but originates ironically in the thought of Hobbes. Long regarded as the major proponent of coercion in modern thought, Hobbes understood that the successful refounding of a polis in crisis involves a process of collective amnesia. Because "there is scarce a commonwealth in the world, whose beginnings can in conscience be justified,"[4] he expressed the "greatest objection" to raising questions of legitimacy after the fact, to the "practice; when men ask, where, and when, such [sovereign] power has by subjects been acknowledged." The only effective rejoinder to such questions is a warning about their consequences: "But one may ask them again, when, or where has there been a kingdom long free from sedition and civil war."[5] Given that people cannot "remember . . . nor after one generation past, so much as know in whom the sovereign power is placed," a "commonwealth," to be "long-lived," will need "subjects" who are continually reminded to "never . . . dispute of the sovereign power."[6]

One task of political theory, linking Hobbes to Plato, was to substitute an exemplary story of the founding, with its allocation of duties and prerogatives, for the murky and ambiguous reality of a collective's past. A free society, then, may be no more than a community that "remembers" an oft-told tale of a consensual foundation. In not only drafting such a voluntarist narrative but also relentlessly demanding its promulgation, Hobbes, who understood the costs of founding, would be himself ironically forgotten.

Hobbes and the Crisis of the English Revolution

Unlike either the traditionalists of his age who failed to grasp the changing world or subsequent liberals no longer forced to address their own problematic origins, Thomas Hobbes realized that the popular dynamic of rising individualism had precipitated a fundamental crisis of legitimacy. As the political consensus for stable monarchism collapsed with the English crown's failure to stem the tide, only the extremes remained—an increasingly ineffective defense of traditional authority and a call for an unprecedented society of individualists. Some blame for this situation was to be laid on "the better sort" who demanded "popular government" and those in the "city of London and other trading towns" who also wanted a government with favorable economic policies. Yet such quarrels remained among elites essentially pressing their own interests, the political insurgents for a new "oligarchy" in Parliament, the economic interests for government that "would to them produce . . . prosperity."[7] Hobbes in *Leviathan* distinguishes between such elites "taking pleasure in contemplating their own power in the acts of conquest" and commoners "glad to be at ease within modest bounds" wherever civil concord prevails.[8] The deeper political crisis arose when that latter group, the bedrock of political stability, became politicized contrary to all normal inclinations by promises of a new right to be free of alleged "oppression" by the "King" and "the bishops." That is to say, "the people were corrupted generally."[9]

The source of these popular expectations was laid by Hobbes to the religious insurgents: the Presbyterian "ministers, as they called themselves, of Christ" or "God's ambassadors; pretending to have a right from God to govern . . . the whole nation"; and the "Independents" and "sects" who preached "liberty in religion," "the private interpretation of the Scripture, exposed to every man's scanning." The "teaching, and preaching" of "the divines" and "so many preachers" disseminated a new view of human powers and capacities which undermined "the essential rights . . . of sovereignty." They exhorted "that men were to be assured of their salvation by the testimony of their own private spirit, meaning the Holy Ghost dwelling within them," and that "Christ's kingdom . . . [was] at this time to begin upon the earth," as well as other "peculiar doctrines I do not well remember."[10]

This preaching transformed the common view of political rights and public authority: "The people in general were so ignorant of their duty, as that not one perhaps of ten thousand knew what right any man had to command him, or what necessity there was of King or Commonwealth . . . but thought himself to be so much master of whatsoever he possessed, that it could not be taken from him upon any pretense of common safety without his consent."[11] This spreading sense of entitlement sapped the legitimacy of the traditional body politic: "In such a constitution of people, methinks, the King is already ousted of his government, so as they need not have taken arms for it." Thus, he asked sardonically, "had it not been much better that those seditious ministers . . . had all been killed before they had preached?" This "great massacre" would have killed "perhaps 1000" but "the killing of 100,000 is a greater" catastrophe.[12]

Hobbes's singular objective was to make a new human society "constant and lasting." The challenge was that the Protestant transformation of the human role had become too widespread and empowering to repress or retract. Hobbes had no wish to complete the goals of the English Reformation; rather, he was driven to repair the damage after having "seen by what causes and degrees a flourishing state hath first come into civil war, and then to ruin."[13] Moreover, he recognized tactically that the dangers of Protestant and sectarian agency, if not defused, would undercut all civil control of human conduct. And yet, since they could not be defeated, these forces had to be co-opted. Hobbes (paying them the ultimate if backhanded compliment) thus appropriated central elements of the insurgents' arguments in his project of containment, including their views of human capacity, societal role, and historical development. One aspect of his genius was to turn these arguments back on their proponents, pushing their claims to unsuspected political conclusions by thrusting the new psychological demands of the Protestant agent into the cauldron of liberal society. So began the ambiguous and dialectical relation between liberalism and Protestantism, an often unwitting, often ambivalent partnership generated by the Protestant inability to manage the political implications of its own transformative process.

The constitution of liberalism as the political response to this crisis arising at the onset of modernity begins from and builds on its precipitant—the triumph of Protestant individualism. The central question Hobbes poses, the starting point distinguishing modern politics, reflects its swift ascendancy and proliferation as a now "general inclination of mankind, a perpetual and restless desire of power after power that ceaseth only in death." The problem has suddenly become how a group of individuals with "their wills," their independent "power and strength," may be induced to "confer all their power and strength upon one man, or upon one assembly of men," creating or investing—in effect, by identifying with "praise and magnitude"—the requisite "one will" that produces the *"mortal god,"* the "great LEVIATHAN."[14] Thus, Hobbes distinguishes in *Leviathan* between "natural" states and modern society. In the former, "creatures . . . live sociably one with another" equating "the common good" with "the private." Notwithstanding Aristotle, this model no longer had human application, being feasible only for "bees and ants," given "that men are continually in competition for honour and dignity" and "private . . . benefit."[15]

Political theory had never before faced this question. Hobbes's extraordinary response was the work of his maturity, *Leviathan:* an epic narrative of political founding which appropriated the developmental realization of human agency for the establishment of an agency body politic. In ostensible form it is an exhaustive lexicon redefining every aspect of reality and human experience from the perspective of a radical individualism. Veiled within it is the story of how individuals, now active participants in forging their common destiny, collectively undertake the journey mandated by modern individualism from the illusions of personal certitude and effectuality through the valley of the terrors it necessarily unleashes, culminating in a reversal of motives which reaffirms a consensual civilization and coherence. The "education" attained by moving from a "childish disposition" governed by naive "desire" to the "capacity fit for what we desire," though egoistically deflating, will enable modern citizens to become "fit for society." Internalizing the requisite character, asocial individuals become equipped to sustain collective authority and the "bonds" and institutions of society.[16]

This epical journey led, given the novel challenge of individualism, to an originative grounding for political legitimacy: "In this time, that men call not only for peace, but also for truth . . . [I] offer new wine, to put into new casks, that both may be preserved together."[17] Hobbes wrote in *De Corpore* that "Civill Philosophy" is "no older . . . than my own book *De Cive*."[18] He further expected no ready reception of such new ideas: "In the revolution of states, there can be no very good constellation for truths of this nature to be born under, (as having an angry aspect from the dissolvers of an old government, and seeing but the backs of them that erect a new)."[19] And yet, it was in a time of such "disorders" perhaps more than any other that such a "way is opened to . . . travel" from a "beginning . . . in the dark" of "clouds," the "false and empty shadow" of moral and political chaos, "into the clearest light" along "the highway of peace."[20] The path was a narrow one with numerous pitfalls—"the close, dark and dangerous by-paths of faction and sedition," the "wanderings from . . . science" and "reason."[21] But with Hobbes as guide, proceeding "without partiality" on a path marked by "the known natural inclinations of mankind, and upon the articles of the law of nature," it would finally be possible, a "long time after men had begun to constitute commonwealths, imperfect," to construct a new "constitution, excepting by external violence, everlasting."[22]

Hobbes's Reconciliation with Agency

Hobbes understood the scope of the transformation taking place in the human role because he had followed this shift on his own intellectual journey. His sympathies lay with the monarchy his whole life, and he never fully recovered from the "prospect of all kinds of folly, and of all kinds of injustice" that brought it down. He wrote during the Restoration of the earlier disorders: "In the year 1640, the government of England was monarchical; and the King that reigned, Charles . . . holding the sovereignty, by right of a descent continued above six hundred years, and from a much longer descent King of Scotland . . . [was] a man that wanted no virtue, either of mind or body, nor endeavored anything more than to discharge his duty towards

God, in the well governing of his subjects."[23] Beyond this, as Leo Strauss has developed, Hobbes was an early believer in the preeminence of aristocratic virtue.[24] In the dedication to his 1629 translation of Thucydides, he recommended the *History* as "profitable instruction for noblemen, and such as may come to have the managing of great and weighty affairs" for it presented "plainly and distinctively" the "actions of *honour* and *dishonour*" which "in the present age . . . are so disguised" as to be unrecognizable.[25] In his study of rhetoric from 1637, his catalogue of what is good listed "honour" as superior to "money," for it transcends private interest, being "good of [itself]" rather than merely "that which we do . . . for our own sakes," and is thus more worthy of "glory."[26] The corresponding society, an aristocracy, is similarly the best: in democracy, the "people" want "liberty"; in "oligarchy" the "end . . . is *the riches of those that govern*"; a monarch pursues the *"conservation of his own authority"*; while "the end of *aristocracy,* is *good laws* and *good ordering* of the city."[27]

His grasp of the deeper shifts underlying the political turmoil led him in time to relinquish this model. The aristocratic belief in exclusive prerogative had not collapsed so much as expanded as many now claimed a superior entitlement: "That which may perhaps make . . . equality incredible, is but a vain conceit of one's own wisdom, which almost all men think they have in a greater degree, than the vulgar; that is, than all men but themselves, and a few others. . . . For such is the nature of men, that howsoever they may acknowledge many others to be more witty, or more eloquent, or more learned; yet they will hardly believe there be many so wise as themselves; for they see their own wit at hand, and other men's at a distance." This proliferating sense of precedence undermined the belief in inherent inequities which made elites possible. The universality of such claims, he strikingly reasoned, now "proveth rather that men are in that point equal, than unequal."[28]

In *De Cive,* his second work of political theory and direct predecessor of *Leviathan,* Hobbes still defended "inequality" in the form of monarchy as "the most commodious government" or "aristocracy" as "both better and more lasting than the rest."[29] Yet these defenses were now conditional, that of monarchy "not to be demonstrated, but only probably stated," while of aristocracy "we have said nothing." Since the multitudes now also demanded both liberty and glory, and "when private men or subjects demand liberty . . . they ask not for liberty, but *dominion,*" these regimes cannot adapt: "Glory is like honour; if all men have it no man hath it, for they consist in comparison and precellence."[30] Inequality was now quixotically defended only as a necessary bulwark against the "natural equality" of strength and desire still terrifying to Hobbes and whose reality he could not yet accept. Because equality as "the state of war" is in his view at the time still inherently unstable, the only secure basis of a "great and lasting society" is a system of status differentiation rooted in "mutual fear."[31]

By the writing of *Leviathan*, although Hobbes remained partial to monarchy, the issue was no longer the form of government.[32] Political structure must be determined not by abstract judgments external to the political process but by the capacity of a given society to establish consent for its own legitimacy. Each form of "commonwealth" to be viable requires such legitimacy for "the sovereign power," and it must be "indivisible, entire" for "*a kingdom divided in itself cannot stand.*"[33] Next to the limitation on sovereignty itself, the greatest "disease" for a commonwealth was "that every private man is *Judge of good and evil actions,*" leading all to "dispute the commands of the commonwealth; and afterwards to obey, or disobey them, as in their private judgments they shall think fit." But the very problem England faced was the fragmentation of legitimacy into alternative and competing conceptions, a condition "boiling hot with questions concerning the rights of dominion and the obedience due from subjects," in which "all men . . . even the vulgar" believe "civil knowledge" to be "a matter of ease . . . attained without any great care or study."[34] Under such conditions, equality, the great threat to previous systems of government, may if properly employed paradoxically become (as with freedom) its greatest strength.

The Discovery of Narrative

The epic of human agency culminating in agency political society came late to Hobbes, invested as he had been in establishing an irrefutable politics through "the true and only foundation of . . . science."[35] The problem, however, was that a "proof" in the body politic was determined not by its logic but by its reach. A theoretical demonstration was both "very difficult" and "understood by few."[36] Moreover, given "how subject" most individuals are "to equivocation, and how diversified by passion, (scarce two men agreeing what is to be called good, and what evil; what liberality, what prodigality; what valour, what temerity) and how subject men are to paralogism or fallacy in reasoning," some alternative from of argument was required. That is, it was likely "impossible to rectify so many errours . . . without beginning anew."[37] *De Cive*, which Bernard Gert calls "superior" to *Leviathan* "as philosophy,"[38] is structured as an argument "consonant to reason." Rather than activating the powerful motives of "fear" and "a care of one's self" as the origin of the state, Hobbes explained them cautiously and statically as "a certain impulsion of nature" and defended them apologetically as "not a matter so scornfully to be looked upon."[39] Resisting the bold narrativizing of human nature which began *Leviathan,* Hobbes merely asserted his new theory of politics rather than "telling" it.

And yet, as Quentin Skinner has argued, the sources for the epic in *Leviathan* were enduring.[40] Hobbes had long regarded stories as a primary way people made sense of their experience and were moved to act. His early work treated rhetoric, though inferior to "proofs," as a speaker's skill of "exhorting" to "stir up . . . anger, envy, fear, pity, or other affections." It also possessed the power to propound "*felicity* . . . to be obtained by the actors he exorteth unto" or to persuade the "contrary." Moreover, "proofs" in rhetoric were explicitly narratives, "either an example" of "some action past; or a *similitude,* which is also called a parable; or a *fable,* which contains some action feigned." The latter two were easier to "find out" than examples, being fictions constructed to meet the needs of the argument.[41] In *De Cive,* he noted disparagingly the predominance of "superstition" and "idolatry" stemming from "the violence" of "passions" and "the imperfect use" of "reason" among "the greatest part of men." At the same time, political "allegories" and "fables" in which were "wrapped up" the "science of justice," including "a most beautiful and allowed mystery of royal authority," enabled authority to be "reverenced" rather than "openly exposed to disputations" and "defiled" by "private men."[42] Similarly, in *Leviathan,* he indicated how the vast array of "different fancies, judgments, and passions" produced religions with "ceremonies so different" that "men" are "drawn to believe any thing." Regarding such stories and rituals of religion positively, he argued that they form "a part of" and an underpinning for "human politics." Their great strength was providing transcendent or other uncontestable support for the authority of political leaders, rituals of obedience, and sanctions for disobedience that make "men . . . the more apt to obedience, laws, peace, charity, and civil society." He drew distinction between "*Religion. Superstition. True Religion*" as "*fear* of power invisible, feigned by the mind, or imagined from tales publicly allowed, RELIGION; not allowed, SUPERSTITION. And when the power imagined, is truly such as we imagine, TRUE RELIGION." Yet both religion from "human invention" and that "by God's commandment" make "men . . . the more apt to obey."[43]

Collective narratives legitimize authority and instill obedience by offering "common people" a uniform, uncontradicted, and inclusive framework for both their "civil duty" and "their misfortunes." The dangerous diffusion of private values and judgments, "the contrariety of men's opinions," could thus be represented as a diffusion of narratives: "The secret thoughts of a man run over all things, holy, profane, clean, obscene, grave and light, without shame, or blame. . . . [T]herefore some men's thoughts run one way, some another; and are held to, and observe differently the things that pass through their imagination."[44] The result is a chaos of competing tales: "If it so happen, that . . . [men] pass their time in relating some stories, and one of them begins to tell one which concerns himself; instantly every one of the rest most greedily desires to speak of himself too; if one relate some wonder, the rest will tell you miracles, if they have them; if not, they will feign them."[45] As "divers men have written the history" diversely of "the late troubles," symbolizing the narratological fragmentation that caused the Civil War, public coherence—the product of a common narrative—would become the inevitable victim.[46]

Political consensus demanded a single narrative that could replace while admitting and incorporating the new condition of multivocality. Hobbes failed to provide this in *De Cive* because he was still torn between two opposing narratives—the very religious narratives of *Paradise Lost* contesting for dominance in his era. Thus, incommensurable historical origins are offered, one a political Eden in which men universally "reverenced the supreme power," the other a competitive nightmare "before the yoke of civil society" in which "all was equally every man's in common" and "no man had any *proper right.*" The political narrative was a story of decline, of "the mischiefs which have befallen mankind" since the time of "peace and a golden age" with the loss of "the benefit arising from . . . morality truly declared." Descending from "the beginning of affairs and nations," where "the decrees of princes, were held for laws" modeled on "that paternal government, instituted by God himself in the creation," each individual in time came to "have arrogated to [himself] the knowledge of *good* and *evil.*"[47] Once citizens were "taught" that it was "lawful" to form independent political judgments and "take up arms against kings," the golden age ended, leading "to the utter ruin" of the state.

In the economic variant, by contrast, the original "community of goods" without "security" is an "adversary" to peace because "there can be nothing *proper*" or discrete "to any man" which allows him to "use them alone."[48] The relentless drive for exclusive "inclosure," for "a *propriety* to which none

of [one's] fellow-citizens hath right," makes the original condition where individuals "can neither enjoy in common, nor yet divide" one beset by "contention" and "calamities." Collective ownership was a mere illusion of unity
whose shattering revealed the latent individualism and yet in so doing made
possible a realistic social distribution of "dominion and propriety."[49]

In positing the dynamic contention among equals as a new original condition to replace the traditional static model of hierarchical order, Hobbes
approached a new progressive metahistory. This new initial condition was
Milton's revisionist Eden, a state not of innocent obedience but of rampant wishes for individual "gain" and personal "glory"[50] simply not yet unleashed. The universality of such wishes rendered this an unstable condition
of maximum frustration: "For although any man might say of every thing,
this is mine, yet he could not enjoy it, by reason of his neighbour, who having
equal right and equal power, would pretend the same thing to be his." Offering an explanation with powerful developmental implications, Hobbes
explained this frustration, the gap between "desire" and being "in capacity
fit for what we desire," as a condition like the immature and necessarily outgrown period of childhood: "All men, because they are born in infancy, are
born unapt for society. . . . [F]rom their first birth, as they are merely sensible creatures, they . . . immediately as much as in them lies . . . desire and do
whatever is best pleasing to them." Children's "nature" would have them
"given . . . all they ask for" or "they are peevish and cry" and "strike their
parents." This new starting point while profoundly deficient is not morally
defective. It is neither intrinsically "wicked" nor a condition of disobedience
or violated "duty," for children cannot be expected from either natural instinct or the presence of positive laws to obey. The capacity to "know . . .
what society is" and to be "made fit" for it is not the product of nature but is
developed by "education." The task of harmonizing desire and attainment
only emerges over time, as "nature" is "better governed" through education
and experience.[51]

Hobbes was beginning to sense that individualism, while destroying traditional order, could also be harnessed to permit the "constitution" of a modern state. The story of the fall from political innocence was no longer useful,
given that the destruction to "ashes of monarchy" from "sedition" had occurred in the distant and therefore unrecoverable past when "the Roman
people" had "the name of *king* . . . rendered odious."[52] Return to an idyllic
prehistory was unthinkable, foreclosed by modernity. Treating individualism as the result of a fall, while refusing from fear to acknowledge its inevi-

tability, also undercut its potential role as a now stable (if dialectical) starting point for further statecraft. And yet, in *De Cive,* Hobbes remained unsettled by its legacy as the untamable destroyer of commonwealths, the irreparable fragmenter of common property into irreconcilable claims of exclusive "absolute dominion," of authority into multiple assertions of a personal right to "judge of good and evil," the "commonweal" into "factions," "the people" into "the multitude," the public "good" into "diverse . . . inclinations," and the "will of all" into "wills" which "differ so variously."[53]

Most enduring of the losses from individualism was the shattering of the common legibility of the world of appearances. In functionally separating what humans "inwardly believe" from what they "make an outward profession" of, individualism opened the vast and powerful, ultimately dispositive seat of personal judgment. Rendered inaccessible by all who "dissemble" their thoughts with "hypocritical sanctity" as "shall best suit" their "end,"[54] this realm lay beyond public control or even visibility. This metaphysical hypocrisy or disjunction between presentation and motive, so powerful that *Leviathan* refers to "the kingdom of darkness" as the *"confederacy of deceivers,"* defeated his hopes for restoring consensus as the visible deference to public hierarchies. Individualism, to be sure, opened the option of a politics based on "consent" deriving from each citizen's personal "understanding" of one's "hateful condition" that produced in turn a "desire . . . to be freed" from "misery" in order to "call anything rather his *own,* than *another man's.*"[55] Yet unable at this point to imagine the impetus for sufficient consent to ground a new society, he provided no narrative of political creation.

The Narrative of *Leviathan*

Hobbes was on the horns of the Protestant dilemma, stretched between a vision of shattered unity with no way back from irremediable fallenness and a still tentative progress from the delusions of harmony and personal gratification to a new form of order. *Leviathan* is the narrative that resolved that dilemma. The realization of his genius not simply as a "very able architect" but as a master rhetorician, the weaver of the "parable" and the "fable,"[56] it is the singular story of the human journey to the new society of agents. Tracing the movement from doubt to certitude, its underlying form resembles a Protestant conversion narrative, though as a liberal reframing it is to be undertaken by every citizen—not just believers—in every age. Mirroring the sinner's *extremis,* self-referentiality and the terrors of chaos were neither rendered philosophically coherent nor preemptively assuaged, but rather thrust to the heart of the work. With these as the guides, the sole resources, readers are borne on a radical journey of remorseless severance from all known reality toward its all-but-inevitable conclusion. The object is not to confirm convictions but to undermine them in a vast sea of doubt which dissolves all conviction. Readers are not asked to understand, but are rather deprived of all but the minimally necessary comprehension to constitute a bulwark against that incoherence. It is a tale of refashioning a fixed world in the very absence of certitude, of individual storytellers induced into a master narrative which they will henceforth offer as their own, of high-flying agents who turn in their individual warrants to work for a common author, divergent dreamers of intensely personal fantasies who would in time come to imagine a common narrative of their origin and history. It is a journey not of reason but of reasons, not of logic but of need, producing as its most enduring desire the demand for stability, which in the end constitutes the founding political myth of agency civilization, not of how humans became agents (that was no longer the issue), but how they came to construct and sustain an enduring order of individualists.[57]

Hobbes announced the resolution of his narratological confusion in the introduction with a pronounced developmental claim. While the creation of the new commonwealth is "the *art* of man," by which humans "imitate" the "art whereby God had made and governs the world" of nature, it is no mere repetition of the original condition of the world. This second creation, while it "resemble[s] that *fiat* or the *let us make man*, pronounced by God in the creation," is in Hobbes's startling assertion an *improvement* over God's original. For its product, "that great LEVIATHAN" which Hobbes likens to "an artificial man," is of "greater stature and strength than the natural, for whose protection and defense it was intended." Modern individualism necessitated a second and higher creation to supplement the defects of the original, a "King of the Proud" or *"king of all the children of pride."*[58] His proclamation or *fiat* announces that such a step of integration and consolidation is now feasible.

Leviathan is built on the distinction between the "prudence" of "experience" and the "sapience" of "science." Science offers the possibility of being more "certain and infallible" in the hands of "industrious men" who have "long studied" their subject: "The skill of making, and maintaining commonwealths, consisteth in certain rules, as doth arithmetic and geometry; not as tennis-play, on practice only; which rules, neither poor men have the leisure, nor men that have had the leisure, have hitherto had the curiosity, or the method to find out." But, unlike Milton, Hobbes refuses to privilege the perspective of knowledge, for few citizens are experts in statecraft: "They that have no *science* are in better, and nobler condition, with their natural prudence; than men, that by misreasoning, or by trusting them that reason wrong, fall upon false and absurd general rules." Prudential "ignorance" produces nowhere near the "folly" and likelihood of being killed or disgraced as occurs from "follow[ing] the blind blindly" in their erroneous conclusions drawn from "relying on false rules."[59] Reconstruction of the body politic is thus amenable to no discursive argument, nor to the reconstitution of knowledge itself, but only in the fashion of the early Puritans to a narrative addressed to the experience of the audience and responsive to its struggles and doubts. The vast cosmology of *Leviathan* is constructed to demonstrate the argument from experience.

The narrative proper begins with the profoundly radical assertion absent from the introduction (persuasion by demonstration rather than argument) of the narratological nature of experience. The discourse unfolds by developing two revolutionary claims: that *all reality is experiential,* and that *all experience is fictive.* Hobbes had in earlier discussions of human experience noted the prevalence of emotional distortions by "the *fiction*" of personal "glorying" or the "madness" of "excessive *vain glory, or vain dejection,*"[60] the perceptual distortions of *"great deceptions of sense,"* the mental "fictions" of composite images or of images retained after their "absence or destruction," even "dreams" which derive from the "imagination."[61] Yet, these were all just distortions that could be overcome, enabling reality to be fully distinguished and restored.

Leviathan opens with the assertion that in the beginning there was *only* experience. Chapter 1, "Of Sense," relates how all human internality derives from interactive collisions which "presseth the organ proper to each sense" and generate pressure "on the eyes, ears, and other parts of a man's body," without which "there is no conception in a man's mind" and no stimulus in the organs. All knowledge and understanding are derived from sense experience and are dependent on it for their claims to worldly correspondence. Thus, the reader is instructed to *"read thyself,"* and moreover the sovereign, "he that is to govern a whole nation," can do no better than consult his own experience, and "must read in himself, not this or that particular man, but mankind." For, Hobbes concludes, the truths of politics and the constitution of society "admitteth no other demonstration."[62]

Yet, on the first page of the book human experience is dramatically turned inside out by the fictional nature of encounters. The multiple universes that humans inhabit epistemologically are those of chimeras, fantasies, and dreams in which madness is simply another name for the predominance of imagination as the orienting human faculty. Sense experience, the only experience, while "every one" begins from "objects" which "press" our sense "organs" to stir "conceptions" in our "mind," in fact produces conceptions that do not—and can never be asserted to—correspond to the object. They are ever "a *representation* or *appearance,* of some quality, or other accident" of this object, that is, without any necessary or ascertainable relation to the object's true nature. Because we respond to the motion upon us without ever reaching or discerning the object or cause, we are left with "*seeming,* or *fancy*" only, "the same waking, that dreaming." We are, by extension, like "a man that is born blind" who tries to "imagine" the things "men call" by name or identify.[63]

A dagger has been deftly inserted at the heart of the "real," for every form of human knowing is constituted out of sense experience. Thus, "understanding" and "imagination," which are synonymous with "memory," are identical, each "nothing but *decaying sense,*" except imagination continues in "men . . . as well sleeping, as waking." Dreams are just such "imaginations" during sleep originating in "the sense." From the singular perspective of experience, however, they appear the most assuring "as if a man were waking," or more troubling but unavoidable, they seem "more clear," so that it is "a hard matter" and perhaps "impossible, to distinguish exactly between sense and dreaming." All comprehension of the world is thus fully interwoven with the work of the imagination, the future being a pure "fiction of the mind" amounting to "prophecy" or "guesses," while the past "has the same uncertainty almost with the conjecture of the future; both being grounded only upon experience." This leaves only two possibilities, equally imagined, equally fictive: "unguided" narratives which "wander . . . as in a dream . . . but without harmony," and directed narratives which are organized and "*regulated,* by some desire and design."[64]

Leviathan is the supreme example of a narrative directed by its ultimate goal. Its interim destination, the decomposing state of nature, is not real, for "there had never been any time, wherein particular men were in a condition of war one against another." Yet Hobbes does not hesitate to suggest that his final destination, the ahistorical myth of founding, could be "profitably taught in the Universities." Political "knowledge" is to emerge from the experience attained in the course of this journey, one neither more nor less real than others but more determined in its outcome. Given "the similitude of the thoughts and passions of one man, to the . . . thoughts and passions of all other men upon the like occasions," from this directed narrative, so long as undertaken by all, individuals will gather a fund of common experience leading all to subscribe to its results.[65]

A Narrative of Agency

The story was to be one about human beings no longer comparable to animals which "live sociably one with another."[66] The agency role with its new power was now synonymous with human nature: individuals unbound from all traditional constraints, whether transcendentally or politically mandated, could use every available means in the furtherance of their goals. *"The fundamental law of nature"* provides that "every man has a right to every thing," including anything "he can make use of, that may . . . be a help unto him . . . even to one another's body." All societal and cultural resources including life itself are defined as tools of personal power for creatures ever seeking to accumulate the "present means" to goals themselves provisional in an endless chain of accumulation: "The felicity of this life, consisteth not in the repose of a mind satisfied. For there is no such *finis ultimus,* utmost aim, nor *summum bonum,* greatest good. . . . Nor can a man any more live, whose desires are at an end, than he, whose senses and imagination are at a stand. Felicity is the continual progression of the desire, from one object to another; the attaining of the former, being still but the way to the latter."[67] This virtually definitional set of options regarding means together with an incapacity to define ends replicates in a more devious and canny fashion the Protestant view of the human role in God's plan.

The desire to establish agency as a cosmological principle led Hobbes to frame his politics within a science of physical motion that reinforced the instrumental limits on human capabilities. Defining reality, including human experience, as "so many motions of the matter" in which "motion produceth nothing but motion"[68] left only continual activity without access or reference to either first causes or final ends. The world consisted of continual collisions and intermediate causation: "Nothing taketh beginning from *itself,* but from the *action* of some other immediate *agent* without itself," in which life is "the production of effects," of "agents" having "other agents . . . working . . . upon them" such that they are "continually altered and changed."[69] In this world, *"the power of the agent"* is always "the *efficient cause,"* and "the END, or *final cause"* is the subsequent *"efficient cause"* of further motion, and any beginning prior to a specific cause, "a man cannot imagine it."[70]

This early proto-Newtonianism transformed traditional natural philosophy, which argued that bodies have an inherent "appetite to rest . . . in that place which is most proper for them." Reality, universal and endless motion, represented Hobbes's political acknowledgment of dramatic new human powers, including mobility and initiative.[71] Fearing this motion, however, Hobbes, clumsily replicating the equally problematic Puritan reconciliation of individualism with a divine plan through predestination, tried to contain it by asserting the claim of physical determinism. The goal was to situate nominally voluntary instrumental activity within a structure of scientized order: thus an "agent" can "work" with "nothing wanting of what is requisite to produce the action,"[72] yet an overarching cosmic or political plan (end) must result. Individuals are thus *"free* agents" in the sense that they undertake in a "VOLUNTARY" and "SPONTANEOUS" fashion the ends which are *"from necessitation"* determined elsewhere and not, ever, by themselves.[73] Just as "when a man willingly throws his goods into the sea to save himself, or submits to his enemy for fear of being killed," so the individual can either choose to follow the larger plan or "refuse to do it if he will," but must accept that the consequences or ends lie beyond one's own control. Hobbes himself equated the persuasiveness of absolute transhuman ends in religious predestination with his scientific determinism in motivating the will to order: "He therefore that thinketh that all things proceed from God's *eternal will,* and consequently are *necessary,* does he not think God *omnipotent?* Does he not esteem of his *power* as highly as is possible? which is to honor God as much as may be in his heart? . . . [I]s he not more apt by *external* acts and words to acknowledge it, than he that thinketh otherwise?"[74]

In his political cosmos, however, ordered motion was not cosmically given. In his critique of the original creation he made every effort to point out that the "natural condition of mankind" was one of maximum disorder, in his memorable depiction, "a time of war, where every man is enemy to every man . . . wherein men live without other security, than what their own strength, and own invention shall furnish them withal." Human nature had developed beyond "the beginning of affairs," without a corresponding advance of political order: "In such a condition, there is no place for industry; because the fruit thereof is uncertain: and consequently no culture of the earth; no navigation . . . no commodious building; no instruments of moving, and removing . . . no knowledge of the face of the earth; no account of time; no arts; no letters; no society; and which is worst of all, continual fear, and danger of violent death."[75] *Leviathan* admitted the indeterminacy of the second creation. A political incentive had to be established which turned a society riven by conduct lacking constraints into one of "determinist"—that is to say, predictable—behavior. The populace had to be provided with common ends reinforced by clear options—certain rewards for freely conforming action and equally certain costs for willingly refusing. But this required a single controlling narrative which could be utilized to bring order to a polity in disordered motion. How could agents all with diverse agendas and putative authors in a universe without design, different warrants in an omninarrational world, be brought together to subscribe to and act within a common story?

An Epic of Reversal

Leviathan, the great epic of liberalism, constitutes this common narrative. In *De Cive,* before grasping its narrative potential, Hobbes had described the formal structure of his philosophical "method." To understand the "generation and form" of "civil government," it was necessary first to dismantle it: "For everything is best understood by its constitutive causes. For as in a watch, or some such small engine, the matter, figure, and motion of the wheels cannot well be known, except it be taken insunder and viewed in parts; so to make a more curious search into the rights of states and duties of subjects, it is necessary, I say, not to take them insunder, but yet they be so considered as if they were dissolved."[76] He would later elaborate this as his "resolutive . . . compositive" methodology, first taking apart the given world of complex effects to find its "causes" or underlying "principles," then reconstituting a specific or certain "effect" from these causes or principles.[77]

   Leviathan precisely depicts the process of disassembling and reassembling the political universe. But the mechanical analogy is deceiving. By implying that restoration retraces the process of dismantling without tampering or creation, it suggests a substantial identity between what is taken apart and what is reconstituted. In fact, the first thirteen books of *Leviathan,* culminating in the "state of nature," radically and ruthlessly dismember the illusions and motives which sustain naive agency assumptions not to reproduce them but to substitute an entirely new and more realistic view of the world which will provoke the creation of a world of ordered agency. Hobbes revealed his ultimate method in a later work: "Philosophy, therefore, the child of the world and your own mind, is within yourself; perhaps not fashioned yet, but like the world its father, as it was in the beginning, a thing confused." Therefore, he advises, "imitate the creation: if you will be a philosopher in good earnest, let your reason move upon the deep of your own cogitations and experience; those things that lie in confusion must be set asunder, distinguished, and every one stamped with its own name and set in order; that is to say, your method must resemble that of the creation."[78]

This method contains within it a journey of education from the "dark" to "clearest light," an awakening from the initial illusion of order to its inevitable shattering to reveal a barely veiled tumult and division, to the necessity of constituting a humanly ordered reality.[79] To embrace this project of improving nature, Hobbes needed to relinquish his own illusions about humanity and the original condition of mankind. In *De Cive*, he had spoken of the dismantling phase as "a contra-natural dissolution." That is, if humans were primarily "rational," with a natural tendency toward the "constitution of government," then they would presumably resist any effort to "destroy the frame."[80] By *Leviathan*, the "laws of nature" are "contrary to our natural passions, that carry us to partiality, pride, revenge, and the like." For Hobbes, this meant giving up moral or rational directives for the pursuit of order, any inherent impulse toward the common. Conscience becomes not a clear beacon of virtue but "a thousand witnesses" brimming over with "secret facts, and secret thoughts." Similarly, "for want of a right reason constituted by nature," individuals identify it as being "no other men's reason but their own. . . . [T]hey will have every of their passions, as it comes to bear sway in them, to be taken for right reason."[81]

The sad truth is that "actions" once ascribed to "*children, fools, madmen, and beasts*" are indistinct from "actions *inconsiderate, rash,* and *spontaneous . . .* ordinarily found in those, that are by themselves and many more thought as *wise,* as wiser than ordinarily men are."[82] Now "the most part of men" have "the use of reasoning a little way," though "it serves them to little use in common life." Comparable to children, they are "called reasonable creatures" though "not endued with reason at all," because of "the possibility apparent of having the use of reason in time to come." But Hobbes's transvaluation is complete. Because individuals are by nature "wanting the free use of reason" and are moved only "by the lower parts of the soul," they are not to be held accountable but rather exonerated "from guilt" and "exempted from all duty" until they become "better governed through good education and experience." More cannot be expected where "men," including "the most sober," betray a "vanity and extravagance of their thoughts" and "passions unguided, are for the most part, mere madness." Even "beasts . . . at a year old observe more, and pursue that which is for their good, more prudently, than a child can do at ten."[83] Ironically, those for whom Hobbes had the greatest contempt, the religious and political "conjurers," now represented the typical or paradigmatic case confronting the political architect.

This rejection of a now "unintelligible" human morality and rationality transformed the function of politics in societal organization. The traditional conception of civil order as the product of a largely natural obedience to authority was now dangerously naive and irresponsible, leaving the commonwealth "mere words and of no strength."[84] The problem for political theory was without precedent: a populace empowered by modern individualism to demand a significant role in political life was precisely unequipped to play that role. Yet, even if overt political activism could be curtailed, the demand for political inclusion from the citizenry could not. This meant that the popular loyalty to the body politic could no longer be assumed, but rather had to be voluntarily generated.

Moreover, since social stability was no longer "natural" but imposed on the natural order of things, this willing integration had to be explicitly and continuously won. The founding and sustaining of commonwealths were equally the project of consensual agreements. Order had to be initially constituted, which meant that the body politic came into existence only as the result of a discrete founding. Because natural tendencies perdured, order had further to be sustained, requiring a continual rededication to established authority. Finally, insulation of society from the fatal diseases of factionalism and personal judgment necessitated the commitment of the entire populace. Hobbes's elitist conviction that "commonly truth is on the side of a few, rather than of the multitude" had to be relinquished. He now accepted the people as "the *makers,* and orderers" of the "commonwealth."[85]

The difficulties had compounded. Given this flawed human "matter" as the "stones brought together for building of an edifice," the modern commonwealth was henceforth artifice, a second-order human construction.[86] This same material had further to be universally induced to take responsibility for this political creation, to willingly enter and sustain these "artificial" structures and boundaries. The seemingly fatal specter of the modern body politic as a mere contingency, an "arbitrary . . . creation out of nothing by human wit,"[87] resting on the greatest contingency, popular consent, now appeared unavoidable.

Paradoxically, Hobbes's concession to the prevalence, even normalcy, of human irrationality, though a blow to human egoism, opened the path to an effective ordering role for political authority. Through a set of masterstrokes, Hobbes turned the Pandora's box of individual voluntarism into the foundation of modern regimes. The strategy, the underlying dynamic of liberalism ever since, was to provoke the citizen's political will into a *reversal*, into a voluntary renunciation of the implications of its own voluntarism. Because political order now required the continuing movement from nature to society, the contingencies surrounding the generation of consent could be reduced by framing nature as the greatest contingency. The consent to eliminate uncertainty could thus be turned against the unpredictability of consent by directing it toward universal integration within a society eliminating such dangers.

This structural solution might win individuals to social membership but not to a relinquishment of political activism, to authorship of the commonwealth but not to a common author. The deeper difficulty was that these empowered individuals did not—and could not without assistance—grasp their power, whether natural *or* in society, as the source of the crisis. The very task given to political citizens of rescuing society and their own fortunes from the natural condition involved in effect *a rescue from themselves*. Society was now attainable only as a developmental achievement transcending "childhood" because they—its very foundation—were the children needing development. The difficulties of insulating society from nature derived from their natures: they were that raw material that as shapers they could not without great difficulty subdue.

These very moderns who had just in this period discovered—and won Hobbes's recognition of—their new powers and capacities, which they insisted any subsequent state need accept, had to be let in on the more troubling implications. How could they in the midst of celebrating be convinced of such revisions to their role—not hero but danger, not potent but vulnerable, not knowing but impossibly ignorant? In embracing the modern project of constituting society from nature, liberal political theory in *Leviathan* recast human order as the two-part movement constituting a rigorous and unexpected political education for the shapers and subjects of the body politic: first, to render the material, themselves, workable; then, to frame it into an enduring order. The reversal from voluntarism to consensual order depended on this revised self-understanding, for only then would citizens seek the necessary assistance for the second stage: "For men, as they become at last weary of irregular jostling, and hewing one another, and desire with all their hearts, to conform themselves into one firm and lasting edifice: so for want, both of the art of making fit laws, to square their actions by, and also of humility, and patience, to suffer the rude and cumbersome points of their present greatness to be taken off, they cannot without the help of a very able architect, be compiled into any other than a crazy building."[88] The gradual grasp of their limits as agents alone enabled them to exercise the power of political creation according to the designated ends of the theorist-architect.

Leviathan, posing as the handbook for the constitution of modern political order, in fact narrates these two stages of political education for putative citizens. Beginning as did Milton by granting the now uncontestable sense of human power, Hobbes's originative strategy was thereby to unravel its intrinsic flaws, which would prepare individuals for its revaluation, reversal, and political founding. The goal, like Milton's as well, was to drive the characters who had eaten the apple of human empowerment and vastly inflated their powers and potentials into doubt of their real capacities, to identify the perception of self-advance as the very "childish" condition needing to be not extirpated but tamed and outgrown.

The dialectical ploy of the first stage was to provoke through exaggeration those very presumptions of advancement, fantasies of empowerment, and warrants of personal agency into a white noise of self-authorizing appetites, relentlessly expanding, inflaming, magnifying the self-referential and self-aggrandizing component of every motive and act. The goal in effect was to reconstitute Milton's garden brimming with emboldened and shameless Adams and Eves. The "childhood" of the species had become a myopic illusion of being safe to indulge one's extreme fantasy life by utterly failing to appreciate such tendencies in others. At the same time, the right to be agents was no longer in dispute. Hobbes moreover insisted that individuals regard themselves not as usurpers of preexisting authority, for in modernity such authority or haven did not any longer exist, but remarkably, necessarily, putative *authors themselves.* Every warrant of agency, like conscience, now betrayed the "secret thoughts" of self-authorization.[89] Once unveiled, Hobbes's narrative deprives the deluded species of a refuge or place of return. Stripped of both legitimacy and comfort, individuals are forced to realize their own inescapable drive toward narcissistic self-authorization.

The intent of the narrative was to provoke a crisis that would induce a *self-reversal,* that is, individuals in flight from the implications of their own claims in search of refuge, the self-repudiation of power seeming to originate voluntarily from the choices of empowered individuals. Hobbes's endgame strategy was to undercut and dismantle agency warrants by universalizing the very dangers which agency development had unleashed. If all human experience was now established as fictive, then all warrants of being retained as agents were—similar to all expressions of certitude—internal projections arising from personal delusion. Individuals were now unemployed agents. As such, they were now capable of being reemployed, but the question was how. With each step in the emergence of self-warranting comes an inexorable collapse of the power to act, the total frustration of all worldly goals. At the climax, the moment prior to reversal from the state of nature, full release has generated a world of howling, screaming self-warranters cowering helplessly before the enormity of their miscalculations. Every effort to establish one's credentials in order to exit the maelstrom replicates and reinforces its multivocality. With individuals ready to acknowledge their ignorance and impotence as their true warrant, the narrative can now offer the next stage in the education—the necessary umbrella of a single, common Author to manage the effects of individualism. New political structures would permit, even encourage, active, self-interested, and mobile members so long as the distinctive danger, the multiplying warrants of authorization with their diverse and divergent agendas, were defeated and their commitments abandoned. This acceptance of ignorance would not be a fall but in this new narrative, as in *Paradise Lost,* the first sign of knowledge and the wish to provide oneself with a remedy. For the many chastened who now doubted among other capacities their ability to forge such a remedy, *Leviathan* would provide a simple, immediately available, step-by-step guide of prescriptions and encouragement.

The Descent into Multivocality

The problem of individualism, Hobbes begins in *Leviathan,* was that by establishing the preeminence of the internal realm, it dissolved the world of common appearances and thereby destroyed the visible consensus regarding meaning. Most people in reading "men's actions" are forced to "decipher without a key, and be for the most part deceived," for "the constitution individual, and particular education, do so vary, and they are so easy to be kept from our knowledge." Thus, "the characters of man's heart, blotted and confounded as they are with dissembling, lying, counterfeiting, and erroneous doctrines, are legible only to him that searcheth hearts." The first thirteen books constitute the effort individuals take to restore consensus by themselves. The drive for certitude in a world where there is no longer a natural authority to rely on necessarily becomes pursuit of the power to restore consensus, but under conditions of individualism that pursuit turns with the unleashing of universal self-authorization into infinitely multiplied personal agendas. Aggrandizing efforts to monopolize power and proclaim self-validation reveal the loss of this common world and in turn precipitate the direct decomposition of all coherence and organizational legitimacy. As individuals, driven by the logic of self-referentiality to define reality in their own image and act as appetitive projectiles seeking "only the way to the thing desired," are forced ever deeper into this world, progressively isolated, fragmented, detached from one another, this dynamic propels a radical disinvestment from all previous structures of meaning.[90] Individuals are encased within a world of self-referential judgments and objectives. Each reader, blithely seeking to restore personal coherence, is brought into the drama in the designated role as putative author who becomes in fact an agent of this very collapse.

The narrative, as in the *Republic* before Plato's similar about-face to offer the new body politic in Book 2, is driven by doubt, what in *De Cive* Hobbes called "distrust and dread."[91] Deluded by blindness regarding external reality, and the passions internally which are but "notable magnifying glasses" distorting all experience, individuals grope about for the warrant they crave that would permit them to act with validity. Medieval knowledge is now a standing joke, consisting of "insignificant" and "unintelligible" doctrines.[92] Individuals will seek clarity and validation variously in experience, in God and religion, in knowledge and truth, and in moral certitude, only to have these presumptive foundations undercut and dashed.

Led initially by the loss of sense certainty to doubt their experience of the world, Hobbes's characters in their dreamlike condition reach out for the certainty of God, but can identify nothing stable or certain. In each person's "anxiety" to find coherence and direction in this impenetrable world, "to secure himself against the evil he fears, and procure the good he desireth, not to be in perpetual solicitude of the time to come," in the face of "his heart" being "all the day long, gnawed on by fear of death, poverty, or other calamity" without "repose," the individual posits for security "one God, eternal, infinite, and omnipotent." But this imagined being is beyond experience and therefore beyond communication or even comprehension: "When we say any thing is infinite, we signify only, that we are not able to conceive . . . [it]; having no conception of the thing, but of our own inability." God thus signifies what is "incomprehensible" and "unconceivable."[93]

Hobbes intensifies the agony. "Immediate revelation" should not legiti-mately be asserted "without the doing of miracles," yet God no longer acts in modern times by miracles: "Seeing therefore miracles now cease, we have no sign left, whereby to acknowledge the pretended revelations or inspira-tions of any private man." Individuals employ God to bolster their own wish for self-authorization and self-validation: "When Christian men, take not their Christian sovereign, for God's prophet; they . . . take their own dreams, for the prophecy they mean to be governed by, and the tumour of their own hearts for the Spirit of God."[94] The "pretense of inspiration" allows in-dividuals either to "stand in awe of their own imaginations" or to "admire themselves, as being in the special grace of God Almighty." They must be understood as pursuing the universal calculus of self-aggrandizement, using religion to further "the greatest use of their powers."[95]

A second way out of the self-referential conundrum is presumably through an accurate grasp of events. But where narratologically confusion and chaos proliferate precisely because individuals seek their own clarity, the project is self-defeating. Internal capacities are severed from contact with any reality beside the internal. Right reason fails for want of any exter-nal connection to "the real," leaving truth as an artificial construction like geometry, "attributes of speech, not of things," consisting of a "right order-ing of names in our affirmations" beginning from an agreement on the axioms or "definitions," the "settling the significations of their words."[96] Knowledge deriving from experience as the "very flawed" product of an in-evitably personal reading is simply another expression of the self-aggrandiz-ing motives of the subject. Thus individual "JUDGMENT" is merely an "opin-ion," the "last opinion" in a deliberative sequence based on the final and strongest "appetite." Reason, as well, is "nothing but *reckoning*," which is "to the desires, as scouts and spies, to range abroad, and find the way to the things desired."[97] But even a truth or understanding rooted in consensual language fails, for language too originates in private appetitive reckoning and is always subject to variations deriving from the "affections," the "na-ture, disposition, and interest of the speaker."[98]

The third presumably transindividual support is ethical. Hobbes surveys the diversity and confusion of moral claims and collapses this discourse into a claim for the validity of individual desires: "Whatsoever is the object of any man's appetite or desire" is what he "calleth *good:* and the object of his hate and aversion, *evil.*" The terms are instructive only "with relation to the per-son that useth them: there being nothing simply and absolutely so." But groups and individuals do not even use such terms with any consistency:

"Because the constitution of a man's body is in constant mutation, it is impossible that all the same things would always cause in him the same appetites, and aversions: much less can all men consent in the desire of almost any one and the same object." "*Good,* and *evil*" Hobbes calls "names that signify our appetites, and aversions; which in different tempers, customs, and doctrines of men, are different: and divers men, differ not only in their judgment, on the senses of what is pleasant, and unpleasant to the taste, smell, hearing, touch, and sight; but also of what is conformable, or disagreeable to reason, in the actions of common life."[99] Thus, even "the same man, in divers times, differs from himself; and one time praiseth, that is, calleth good, what another time he dispraiseth, and calleth evil." The terms merely signify the present "pleasure" and "pain," and even so are arbitrary, being only "the *apparent* or *seeming good*" or the "*apparent, or seeming evil,*" because subjects cannot comprehend the "consequences" or outcomes of their "action." Thus, individuals who would "*judge of good and evil actions*" in order to "dispute the commands of the commonwealth" would frivolously and in obvious folly raise their own momentary, apparent pleasure as the reference point for the collective.[100]

The objective of the narrative is to provide the freedom demanded by insurgents with a scope they never imagined, whereupon Hobbes invites them to consider the consequences. Liberation, in dissolving certitude, has unveiled the truth of human self-aggrandizing and self-referential appetites: the universal narcissistic wish of "every man" that others "should value him, at the same rate he sets upon himself." It has mobilized all resources, societal and personal, in the quest for "power after power" to support one's "*vain-glory;* which is commonly called *pride,* and self-conceit." Absent constraints of a common power or the censure of any moral code, individuals try to shape the world in their own image: "Where there is no common power, there is no law: where no law, no injustice. . . . [N]othing can be unjust. The notions of right and wrong, justice and injustice have there no place. . . . Justice and injustice are none of the qualities neither of the body nor mind. . . . They are qualities, that relate to men in society, not in solitude." Similarly, human "desires, and passions" are "in themselves no sin" nor "the actions, that proceed" from them. In this condition of total release, there is "no propriety, no dominion, no *mine* and *thine* distinct; but only that to be every man's, that he can get," with "force, and fraud" being "the two cardinal virtues."[101]

The equality also desired only exacerbates matters, simply expanding the dynamic so that everyone possesses this capacity for narcissistic release, what Hobbes calls the "equality of hope in the attaining of our ends." Because "nature hath made men so equal," or rather the follies of the English Revolution have, all individuals regardless of strength can demand that the world mirror their narrative and meanings, retaining "strength enough to kill the strongest" in pursuit of their agenda. Universal participation in the "competition of riches, honour, command, or other power"[102] makes every object in the world a field for disputes among the endless self-referential agendas.

Individuals fearing these consequences may seek to repudiate freedom or equality, or at least try to resist their extreme tendencies. But Hobbes, intending a rigorous inclusivity, holds moderns to their agenda. To disclaim the necessary consequences of the natural condition, the fact that this condition applies to them, or contend that they are free of self-referential aspirations and drives would of course be conclusive evidence of one's presumption, "for there are very few so foolish, that had not rather govern themselves, than be governed by others." The search for truth has led into a new realm underlying human nature, not into "the similitude of the *objects* of the passions, which are the things *desired, feared, hoped,* &c." because of human variance and internal inaccessibility, but to a "similitude of *passions*, which are the same in all men." Though few could have recognized it on their own because no one was willing to see, this journey to the center with Hobbes's guidance reveals the state of nature *within* as the core of human character, applicable to all. Except for perhaps in America and during civil war, there is not "such a time, nor condition of war."[103] But in every state, within every individual's impulse toward rebellion or selfhood, it is as real as the internal reticence to support established institutions and follow mandated conduct, which is to say, everywhere.

The narrative leads meticulously, methodically, and inescapably into the state of nature, each disclaimer only tightening the noose, to the verge of self-recognition. A modernist foundation has been posited from which states must henceforth arise, the divided cosmos of Milton writ as a political fable of universal narcissistic fragmentation and disintegration, a universal amoral childhood from which one must awaken. In a universe of dreams, the common metanarrative is that in which all actors are dreamers. A myth ahistorical and unproven, it is the collective fantasy or nightmare—of all that society eternally represses—which only stalks our wish for safety from the shadows. There it survives as a collective unconscious coextensive with every motive to reach beyond the societally given, engraved on the heart for each individual prey to modern drives to see. To this day, daily references abound in the newspapers to signs of Hobbes's lurking natural condition as reminders of the reason for institutions. In all the ways danger is warded off, with every locked door, Hobbes asks, "Do [we] not there as much accuse mankind by [our] actions, as I do by my words?"[104]

An untenable origin, of the undeniable fear and unspeakable terror, the absolute frustration of desires and the personal incapacity to correct the situation, has been established precisely to escape.[105] Traditional society, now inaccessible in an age before modern experience, remains only as a delusion of natural order. A dawning realization of being stranded in history produces the beginning of wisdom, the willing reversal of intent, one's guileless effort to substitute for the warlike competition of self-referential agendas the wish *"to endeavor peace, as far as he has hope of obtaining it."* With the preparation for individual consent, a modern state based on the emergence from the natural condition is now, finally, developmentally feasible. While there is as yet no clear way out, individuals are prepared to accept the most comprehensive guidance of Hobbes's "convenient articles of peace" to undertake the steps to the authorization and legitimation of agency society.[106]

The Self-Authorization of Agency

The stage of reconstituting legitimate authority could now go forward, using—only—the resources attained during the journey, proceeding as "the human mind proceeds in its reasoning from the known to the unknown."[107] Given the similar logic of human passions under similar circumstances, the shared experience of a dissolving common world evoked a collective willingness to shape the new insurgent values to the requirements of modern social order. In the reconstitutive process, Hobbes elaborated the path by which this was to be achieved. The equivalence of narcissistic agendas, having produced an equivalent frustration and "fear of death," generated in turn a comparable desire to seek peace in order to pursue "commodious living." Equality thereby becomes one cornerstone of the new commonwealth: "If nature . . . have made men equal, that equality is to be acknowledged: or if nature have made men unequal; yet because men that think themselves equal, will not enter into conditions of peace, but upon equal terms, such equality must be admitted." It is axiomatic, therefore, that *"every man acknowledge another for his equal by nature."* To frame this politically, the only antidote to wars over precedence was an equal commitment to the commonwealth and to the formal equality of all of its members thereafter.[108]

The demand for liberty, which in the science of motion is the "freedom" from "opposition" or "external impediments to motion" in pursuit of one's activity, also becomes a basis of the political re-creation. The specter of universal frustration was drawn in the knowledge that the newly active citizenry would reject this authorless condition just as they repudiated traditional confinements. If modern forms of activity could be secured within a new political framework, individuals would unhesitatingly embrace a liberty framed and ensured by civil order. At the center of Hobbes's architecture, as we shall see, was a novel assurance of the continuing freedom to move guaranteed paradoxically by the equally novel commitment to "voluntarily" sustaining the commonwealth.[109]

To achieve this modernist reframing, Hobbes counted above all on harnessing rather than repressing the explosive wish for self-warranting. By acknowledging the power of authorship or individually designated agency, he hoped ironically to rescue individuals who could not find an alternative to promoting their own narrative (even at a cost of descending collectively into a narrative void) through the collective power of narrative. This could be achieved if each and every one authorized and participated in a single narrative. But such consensus demanded one concession: the collective narrative to be authorized would henceforth constitute its founders as *agents*. Its resolution featured putative authors who in a foundational crisis resolved to cede all presumptive self-warrants and mandate their own agency, who willingly deauthorized themselves by establishing a common and distinct author to create and secure a regulatable agency society.

The climax would be a formal act of authorization to end delusions of self-authorship, creating a common author providing order for agents and their motion through a second and final creation. The transfer would be valid because legitimacy now flowed from self-consent and self-commitment. Access to prior personal authority would be precluded by the public narrative of founding, reminding citizens of their transaction. Access to present wishes for greater autonomy and self-authorization would equally be prohibited by the content of the agreement henceforth to relinquish such claims, by the elaborate socialization process requiring the renunciation of self-authorship Hobbes would put into operation, and by the equation of that wish with the state of chaos. Self-authorization, then, would be unleashed one time in order to institutionalize the reversal, the movement from nature to collectivity, and then isolated from ever returning to the common world. In a narrative of perfect circularity, any effort to break from the logic of systemic formation triggers the return to the crisis which led inexorably to the collective formation of common authorship.

In the neglected but pivotal Chapter 16, after laying forth the new axioms of equality and liberty and just preceding the climactic foundation scene in Chapter 17, Hobbes identified the new human power that would ground political legitimacy: the universal capacity for individual authorization.[110] He distinguished in effect between *principal* and *agent,* both contractually and characterologically. The "AUTHOR" is "he that owneth his words and actions" and has the preexisting "AUTHORITY" or "right of doing any action." To this he contrasted the "actor," who is the one who is delegated by "commission, or license" of the "author." The actor's "words and actions" are "*owned by those whom they represent.*" Characterologically, the actor is "a *feigned or artificial person,*" a "*persona*" or "*disguise, or outward appearance,*" in that the actor "acteth another, is said to bear his person, or act in his name."[111] In this initial position or natural condition where there is "not *one*" collective "but *many*" individuals, "every one" is an "author," which brings danger but also the equal and free power possessed by all to form states by establishing a social contract. As free individuals, they are instructed that contracts are inherently "voluntary acts," requiring from each a consensual "transferring" of "rights" in return for "some *good to himself,*" and are binding as a freely chosen obligation. Where reservations remain, individuals must withhold consent and remain in the condition of nature until personally satisfied.[112] Possessors equally of authorship, they will equally participate as signatories in the moment of founding, assuming responsibility by contractual obligation for all acts which follow from their warrant of legitimation.

The fantasy of authorship has come true, beyond the wildest imaginings of insurgent culture. By contract, these "authors" are presumably creating a common political actor or agent, "their common representer," to act on behalf of each and all. The contract, however, is rigged. For unlike other contracts, the social contract in Hobbes's ingenious formulation *reverses* the relation of principal and agent in the process of formation. The multitude of authors do not create an agent, but contractually each jointly and universally agrees to relinquish authority by "giving their common representer, authority from himself in particular," in effect authorizing a common Author. Each agrees in perpetuity to cede all originative power to define public rules or meanings for oneself. The exact words of transfer bear attention: "*I authorize and give up my right of governing myself . . . on this condition, that thou give up thy right to him, and authorize all his actions in like manner."* To "authorize" is to "give up" one's authorship, to "submit" one's will, "every one to his will," to produce the "one will" of a *"mortal god,"* to authorize this "SOVEREIGN" and turn oneself into a "SUBJECT"[113] henceforth acting by its imprimatur alone. The result of simultaneously self-authorizing one's own agency and self-limiting one's authority is a collectivity of self-authorizing agents.

The endemic difficulty in liberalism of determining whether the people authorize their representatives or representatives govern the people is systemic.[114] It points to a transfer which is not contractual at heart but—like the process of identification—psychodynamic. The transfer is a willing deferral of one's capacity to define ends, a consent to defer one's natural power of self-definition for the role as agent of the common will, subordinate to collective ends. To ensure this psychic foundation of the state, Hobbes cannily insisted on leaving the internal realm untouched: "There ought to be no power over the consciences of men." In fact, individuals are "bound . . . to obey" the law "but not bound to believe it: for men's belief, and interior cogitations, are not subject to the commands" of the state. Realistically, to monitor the realm of asocial "fiction" and "passion" which is "so inherent to the nature . . . of man" would "make sin of being a man."[115] Moreover, with human nature now unreadable, hypocrisy is inevitable, "simulation" and "play-acting" being "without fault," and "profession with the tongue . . . but an external thing."[116]

More important, the insistence on the radical distinction between "the internal court" and "the external court," in order to retain the realm of the internal author, and thus authorizing capacity, between untouchable "intention" and controllable "commission," is a stunning and calculated political move. The responsibility and thus public accountability for ceding underlying prerogatives, for turning the always dangerous and unreadable impulses into harmless readable ones, lay in modernity with the only one who could see within: each individual author.[117] Individuals can resist legitimately if at their peril all sovereign incursions, however valid, particularly in times of physical need, never ceding their ultimate judgment and authority.[118] Even in settled communities, the individual remains responsible to "own, and acknowledge himself to be the author" of all that the representative does.[119] The individual author, then, monitors its own reversal. Because projections which lapse always revert back to the subject, at every moment one must as actor in the world, the presentation, the ego, authorize the public Author and one's own subordination.

Hobbes has transformed human illegibility into a political virtue. Unable to see or "extend . . . to the very thoughts and consciences of men," the state—able only to "judge of matters . . . by external action"—is now concerned with the "conformity of their speech and actions" alone. It must ignore insincerity until the individual's "hypocrisy appear in his manners, that is, till his behaviour be contrary to the law of his sovereign."[120] It can insist only on manifestations or appearances with "an unfeigned and constant endeavor" which are "easy to be observed," that is, on the regularity of manifestations. Fear of internal discovery feeds the desire to perform conformably and to cede external control to the collective guidance system, the sovereign superego: "Whatsoever a subject . . . is compelled to do in obedience to his sovereign, and doth it not in order to his own mind, but in order to the laws of his country, that action is not his, but his sovereign's."[121]

Effectively, then, personal authority can manifest itself in the world only through the medium of its role, through the actor, one's presenting self, shaped and set in motion as the agent of the body politic. That is, it can be expressed only as a choice of motions and behavior within acceptable bounds, as personal preferences regarding the use of means under the given system of ends. There can be for agents no conceivable way to address the whole. To stand forth as an author is to madly allow the water to "spread" as a deluge with "no bounds."[122] The individual becomes finally not only the contractual agent in a flawed jurisprudence, but also, and more important, the psychological agent of collective values from a unified source, extrapolated from the transcendent author of Protestantism as a worldly constituter of ends. Now, however, the role is one that all citizens henceforth can and must play.

A Common Author in an Agency World

The institutional objective of this politics was to establish and empower an authoritative extension of the popular will, gaining people's identification with its determinations such that following its prescriptions constituted the willing fulfillment of one's self-authorizing power.[123] The new public Author which results is not "natural" but "artificial," a collective projection onto "an artificial man" run by "an artificial soul," a preeminently useful fiction in a world where all is fiction. The sovereign is as third-party beneficiary of popular agreement the recipient of the "power and strength conferred on him," a public identification with access to its collective "strength and means."[124] The citizenry become common investors merged in a "real unity of them all" under their single invested Author. In effect, private judgment and interpretation are replaced with a single collective "judge," individual conscience with "the public conscience," personal values with common "rules of propriety" regarding "*meum* and *tuum*" and "*good, evil, lawful and unlawful*,"[125] self-valuation with a "public rate of . . . worth," one's individual narrative with a single grand narrative provided for all.[126] The power to punish violations is ceded, permitting the common Author to scrutinize and punish even its constituters in their name when they become a danger to the collective.[127]

Within the liberal tradition, Hobbes's sovereign is commonly rendered as the return of an authoritarian politics of servitude. Though a profound misreading of his system, this is exactly the misreading he encouraged in order to "narrate" recalcitrant proto-authors into agency. To constitute an agency consensus, the personal transfer of authorization had to be absolute, decisive, and unambiguous. Certain and uncontradicted authority (no less than with servitude) was not a deformation of agency but rather its precondition, though liberalism's later ideological embrace of freedom has obscured its realities of sovereignty and collective warrant.

The crucial measure of agency distinguishing it from servitude is the extent of power given to citizens by the common Author for acting upon collective ends. Using this standard, Hobbes clearly acknowledges the agent as the sine qua non of the modern world. He insists that the sovereign adhere to the highest standards of public good: "The end, for which he was trusted with the sovereign power, [is] namely the procuration of *the safety of the people*." "Safety" is meant not as "a bare preservation, but also all other contentments of life, which every man by lawful industry, without danger, or hurt to the commonwealth, shall acquire to himself." Given the need for limits on political and religious agency, the rights of authority cannot be circumscribed by direct obligations to the citizenry: "Whatsoever he doth, it can be no injury to any of his subjects; nor ought to be by any of them accused of injustice."[128] Yet a legitimate authority, obligated instead to the "law of nature" and to "God, the author of that law,"[129] must now treat its citizens as *agents*.

In fact, the catalogue of sovereign responsibilities enumerated by Hobbes forms the metapolitical frame for the agency world and reveals his commitment to agency. Hobbes made initiative, the right to individual motion and activity, the center of the new society. Thus, "a FREEMAN" is defined as "*he, that in those things, which by his strength and will he is able to do, is not hindered to do what he has a will to."* This capacity to move "without hindrance" is the reason why individuals divest claims to *"all things"* and thus forms the subjective justification for political commitment: "It is necessary for a man's life, to retain . . . right to govern their own bodies; enjoy air, water, motion, ways to go from place to place; and all things else, without which a man cannot live, or not live well." Understood as motion, agency freedom was the universal right of the individual to choose among given paths, traversing at one's chosen speed, though in directions and toward ends set up by the system. Success and failure now depended on one's own capacities. The failure to utilize available motion rested entirely with the individual, and was due to solely internal causes, a lack not of "the liberty, but the power to move."[130]

With ordered motion, the paradox of freedom and political order was reconciled: "*Liberty* and *necessity* are consistent: as in the water, that hath not only *liberty,* but a necessity of descending by the channel; so likewise in the actions which men voluntarily do." It was a major design advance over the old system, in which the "water" was "inclosed on all hands with banks," it "stands still and corrupts," just as "subjects, if they might do nothing without the commands of the law, would grow dull and unwieldy."[131] A well-functioning modern system now featured secure channels of motion operating as the framework for individual activity: "The use of laws, which are but rules authorized, is not to bind the people from all voluntary actions, but to direct and keep them in such a motion, as not to hurt themselves by their own impetuous desires, rashness, or indiscretion; as hedges are set, not to stop travellers, but to keep them in their way."[132] This channeled motion, what Hobbes earlier had too dismissively called "a harmless liberty"[133] in order to distinguish it from dangerous license, now became "the *liberty* of *subjects* . . . of doing what their own reasons shall suggest, for the most profitable to themselves" in all permitted realms. These "praetermitted activities" encompassed the wide range of modern civil and personal pursuits, "such as the liberty to buy, and sell, and otherwise contract with one another; to choose their own abode, their own diet, their own trade of life, and institute their own children as they themselves think fit; and the like."[134]

Hobbes grasped the vast utility of directed motion to reconcile initiative and integration, enabling freedom to become for the first time a *requirement* of citizenship. Fearing individuals with the "most leisure to be idle,"[135] he insisted on "laws" to "encourage" both the "art and labour" of individuals and the "NUTRITION," the commerce and industry, of the commonwealth. All who are able must therefore be "forced to work" to ensure a *prevention of idleness.*"[136] Similarly, to safeguard popular commitment to the legitimacy of the patterns of motion and activity, the sovereign was also responsible for maintaining equality of access and an equitable regulation of conflict.[137] Hobbes realized that "complaints" about whether "public burthens" were "equally borne" were, if "just," a threat to "the public quiet."[138] The sovereign is directed to guarantee the equal application and administration of the law, not to produce equal outcomes but to "ensure a right application of punishments, and rewards." Further, for "the safety of the people" Hobbes "requireth" of the sovereign "that justice be equally administered to all degrees of people . . . rich and mighty, as poor and obscure." By promoting channels equally for individuals to "receive their motion" from the collective, all citizens would find their activity not in public matters but in the orderly motion of the commercial and civil realms.[139] As a network of orderly activity sustained by means of individual commitments to regulated action, the modern body politic achieves the integration of freedom with necessity, discretion regarding the means with unalterable ends, process with stability, motion and initiative with order, personal discretion with collective judgment.

Securing the Agency Cosmology

Hobbes understood the central task of the theorist as inducing people to direct their lives within this new system. To instill the requisite motion, to constitute the physio-political universe anew, he was certainly willing to use force, but realized that modern individuals could not be effectively governed on that basis: "And the grounds of these rights [of sovereignty], have the rather need to be truly taught; because they cannot be maintained by any civil law, or terror of legal punishment."[140] The vastly more effective strategy would instead preempt danger through the formation of proper "opinions and doctrines," "for the actions of men proceed from their opinions, and in the well-governing of opinions consisteth the well-governing of men's actions." The primary sovereign responsibility in this regard was political socialization, "public instruction" and "education," the effectiveness of which "wholly" depended on beginning from "youth."[141] The process was to reach the citizenry as a whole, including "the common people's minds," for "unless they be tainted with dependence on the potent, or scribbled over with the opinions of their doctors, are like clean paper, fit to receive whatsoever by public authority shall be imprinted in them." The formation of character was the sovereign's "duty" and "benefit," to be achieved by special public ceremonies and rituals on "days set apart" as well as the "right teaching" in "schools and universities." In this way alone could "men's opinions" and "civil amity" be "reconciled."[142]

The content of this "public instruction" consisted of public "doctrine, and example,"[143] that is, of Hobbes's political commandments and laws of nature illustrated by stories: biblical stories of sovereign obedience and God's order; cautionary tales of reform gone awry, like that of the "daughters of Peleus" who "cut him in pieces" to renew his youth but failed to make him "a new man";[144] historical narratives like that of the Civil War to engender prudence.[145] Above all, citizens would be taught the narrative of *Leviathan*, the terrifying natural condition and the story of founding with its awakening of prudence, reversal of desire, and willingness to enter society through the common creation and authorization of the "king of all the children of pride."[146] These stories, though subsequently identified with those of anti-liberal sentiments including Hobbes himself, have since been the basis of liberalism.

Hobbes foresaw that effective character formation was the fulcrum to bring order and a renaturalized cosmology to civilization. The primary virtues to be inculcated were no longer excellence which provokes envy, ambition which destroys states, or individuality which cannot be deciphered, but the common willingness to be adaptable, what Hobbes called "COMPLAISANCE; that is to say, *that every man strive to accommodate himself to the rest.*"[147] This internal regularization was continually reinforced by exploiting the need for inclusion, public confirmation, and validation, positing in effect an interactional marketplace of individual valuation.[148] By manifesting the universal signs of "mediocrity," comprehensibility, and adaptability, modern individuals can "conform themselves into one firm and lasting edifice." Although "there is in men's aptness to society, a diversity of nature, arising from their diversity of affections; not unlike to that we see in stones brought together for building of an edifice," now only uniform materials can be utilized:

For as that stone which by the asperity, and irregularity of figure, takes more room from others, than itself fills; and for the hardness, cannot easily be made plain, and thereby hindereth the building, is by the builders cast away as unprofitable, and troublesome: so also, a man that by asperity of nature, will strive to retain those things which to himself are superfluous, and to others necessary; and for the stubbornness of his passions, cannot be corrected, is to be left, or cast out of society, as cumbersome thereunto.

The warning to the recalcitrant was that they remained in the state of nature vis-à-vis the rest, to be either "cast out" to "perisheth" or "justly . . . destroyed."[149]

Though guardedly expressed lest it undercut the terror that propelled reversal, there emerges in Hobbes's work the vision of a new agency political cosmology, a dynamic architecture of universal activity within a vast and ordered process. He suggested in *De Homine* that a "real good" desired by an individual could where dangerous be "obstruct[ed]" and deflected to "the apparent and most immediate good." Motion deflected could be controlled, channeled into repetitive orbits which could be socially defined and ordered: "For life is perpetual motion that, when it cannot progress in a straight line, is converted into circular motion." Hobbes called this motion "habit," for it was not natural but precisely the triumph of an education in orderly activity producing a new or second nature: "From habit: because of this, that those things that offend when new (that is, those things that man's nature initially resists) more often than not whet that same appetite when repeated, and those things that at first are merely endured soon compel love." The constancy of the laws, of their interpretation and application, is dwelled on at length as the necessary notice citizens require to regularize their behavior: "Because ambition and greediness of honours cannot be rooted out of the minds of men, it is not the duty of rulers to endeavor it; but by constant application of rewards and punishments they may so order it, that men may know . . . the way to honour."[150]

Motion could be so regularized on two levels: "in the operations of the mind" or the ordering of internal motion; and "in the regulating of the body" or in societal conduct. The former would produce when "strengthened by habit" those "good dispositions . . . suitable for entering into civil society"; the latter would produce "manners" or suitable "actions with ease and with reason unresisting." The two results follow: a stable *"persona"* or "mask" for "play-acting," an adaptive character in other words which is artificial but "commanded by the will of the state"; and a stable social role or part for that actor equally commanded and responsive to external requirements.[151] At the level of social order, these social roles, the manners which follow directly from the renovated dispositions, would in turn be coordinated to constitute the dynamic system of ordered habits of modern liberalism, a universe of regularized activity demanding a greater initiative, self-reliance, and judgment than ever before but within clear paths of acceptable conduct.

Foreseeing the process of equivalent and conforming agents subject to a single authorizing governor in place, Hobbes pictured the result as an inclusive system, subject to laws "immutable and eternal" as if they were natural and to fixed "final causes."[152] In *De Cive*, he even dared to imagine the eventual outcome: a *self-regulating system* in which active sovereignty retreats as its injunctions are subsumed within the functioning process, such that "the government of the commonweal is like the ordinary government of the world; in which God, the mover of all things, produceth natural effects by the means of secondary causes."[153] With the establishment of functional regularity and conflict resolution now in the hands of internal administrative and judicial functionaries, the sovereign became like the seventeenth-century watchmaker God who had renounced miraculous intervention, stepping back to admire a creation more perfect than the original. This model of individual motion proceeding within patterns of universal order was of course to become the great Newtonian cosmology of modernity. Hobbes it seems imagined such a world. But, afraid to relax sovereign vigilance and the coercive rhetoric of foundation, he was unable to move beyond its creation to announce its consolidation, the point at which the awesome task of instilling and regularizing motion shifts to system maintenance.[154] At the same time, the outline of this vision approximated, once public power was referred to the state given its greater capacity to ensure universality, the participatory society to which the Protestant insurgents had aspired. With this concession, the way was open to the realization of agency in the world and personal salvation within.

As we will see, a Newtonian social science was to become a powerful model for post-organic order within a society of individuals. The new image of political order would be mechanical, a process whose order was contained within and sustained by the coequal parts now operating with only an internal(ized) principle of authorization. Adam Smith would express admiration for this "great system of government" in modern times, the "harmony and ease" of this "political machine" which combines the "invisible hand" of social order and the individually organized pursuit of "the means of gratifying . . . natural appetites, of procuring pleasure and avoiding pain." The resulting "regularity of its motions" produces "the perfection of so beautiful and grand a system" that its participants "seem to value the means more than the end . . . from a view to perfect and improve a certain beautiful and orderly system."[155] Among the less organized institutions of the young republic, Tocqueville was to express ever-growing amazement at the apparently mysterious regularity of individual behavior. By the turn of the twentieth century, the postbellum dream of an American science of social Newtonianism would be realized in the synthesis propounded by Dewey, Mead, Cooley, and many others of a coordinated "social process" embodying the "attitude of the engineer."[156]

There would be little realization among subsequent liberals that the roots of its regularity lay in the artifice generated by the Hobbesian transformation of an unwieldy original nature. The assumption would be made that each unit achieved its path, its direction and velocity, on its own without external coercion. Hobbes's understanding of the result as a curious unscientific mixture in which "*liberty,* and *necessity* are consistent" and freedom is possible only through "the act of our *submission*" would be lost. They would forget the terrors and concessions associated with the founding. They would even in time forget that voluntary motion was based on the "obligation" to "the end of the institution of sovereignty" leaving that "liberty which the civil law leaves us," a freedom of means to achieve authorized ends.[157] They would no longer need Thomas Hobbes.

The obscuring of Hobbes's role in the creation of liberal society is entirely consistent with the process of societal formation that he foresaw. Given that human order was now "artifice," a developmental attainment not to be presumed as a natural certainty, it would be highly subject to "internal diseases."[158] This natural weakness could be overcome only by the strength wrested from its citizens on a continuing basis. This required a constant pursuit of the reversal of the citizen's nature. Its very natural weakness, the looming specter of the "Hobbesian" initial state of nature, paradoxically drives the development of order, the citizen commitment to reversal, and the will to artifice, to make stronger than the natural what is without that determination unalterably fragile. Thus, as we shall see, the unprecedented danger of fragmentation, violence, and desocialized drift in the "wilderness" of American individualism produced in Hobbesian fashion—though never acknowledged—the almost renaturalized, preconscious devotion to a saving regularity which Tocqueville came to regard as the latent power of this new human order. Hobbes, in turn, came to be seen as the prophet of an innate disorder which he knew was necessary to turn the discretion individuals have regarding society into a "natural" wish to join and support, accommodate and conform. Institutional membership would henceforth be prudential rather than organic, calculated rather than instinctual, the price paid for our severance from the natural world—in Protestant terms a rebirth into agency superseding our natural birth.

By substituting a story of our imperfect and incomplete origins for Eden, which Protestants, given their reticence to admit our imperfect beginnings, could not do, Hobbes brought the drama of human development to the center of civilization. Through a myth in which all participate in the act of restoring order, Hobbes rescued modernity from sectarian fragmentation and self-authorization and gave permanence to the world which the agency character had brought about. By shamelessly bringing into history the power of self-authorization from the sects, Hobbes made it the paradoxical savior of agency through the foundational self-authorizing act to end individual authority, an act which moreover could not be undone. This enabled liberalism to enforce the prudential limits and reality constraints intrinsic to Protestant agency while inscribing as secular standards its equality (of opportunity) and (circumscribed) voluntarism. To this inclusive world of universal motion all could by its design—if with difficulty—demand access, as evident through the often torturous expansion of citizenship in the history of modern liberal reform. Similarly, freedom as the choice among mandated channels of participation according to preferences or interests—for values, convictions, absolutes amounting to structural alterations were no longer possible—and utilizing the capacity for selective motility without hindrances was celebrated. Accommodation to this more limited freedom, entailing the relinquishment of power over direction and ultimate ends to revel in the means, was a compromise Hobbes calculated would be unhesitatingly embraced by the early modern individual. This renunciation, as with Adam and Eve, of an empty—useless and destabilizing—self-warrant would be gratefully replaced by the mandated agency role which by the transformation of the political universe could now be fully employed. This heightened capacity, while not freedom, was the striking developmental achievement of that age.

Hobbes gambled that a theory of "natural" disorder would produce a "contra-natural" order. He believed that individuals would not dare risk retrieving their primordial self-author, the new deep and original sin, from the mechanisms of societal co-optation, or cutting the Gordian knot of authority and the sustaining projections of the liberal world. In time the specter of Hobbes's self-referential self who could only be contained—and of Hobbes himself—would recede before the triumph of liberal regularity. The state as a holding action would be superseded by its inscription as a renaturalized order, just as the state of nature receded from the origin story to the personal nightmare of an unsocialized instinctual core each individual would have to subdue privately. As its ends were collectively internalized and institutional-ized leaving only the means accessible to discretion, liberalism would come to regard itself as a system based on individual rights and personal virtue, with the rhetoric of voluntarism expanding into a consensual discourse. Such voluntarism signified a society in which agency was the given, its lim-its axiomatic and uncontroverted. This voluntarist emendation of the narra-tive, Hobbes understood, could be achieved only through post-founding socialization. The modern myth of the free liberal society and its necessary grounding in the education of the young for liberalism were equally the work of one man: John Locke.

John Locke and the Mythic Society of Free Agents

How to keep up a Child's Spirit, easy, active and free: and yet, to restrain him from many things he has a Mind to, and to draw him to things that are uneasy to him; he . . . that knows how to reconcile these seeming contradictions, has, in my Opinion, got the true Secret of Education.

—John Locke

Reading Locke's political, religious, and epistemological writings, one imagines oneself in the Enlightenment. Human reason surmounts its opposition as a powerful and even controlling internal presence, apprising this "rational creature" of the truths "common to us with all men."[1] With access both to the laws of nature which concern societal responsibilities and to the doctrines of faith which represent the certitudes of "divine revelation and authority," it brings ultimate political and religious knowledge "within the reach" of human "discovery."[2] Confusions stemming from sectarian diversity and political fragmentation have not entirely receded, but by hewing to the path of "light" and setting "bounds between the enlightened and dark parts of things," individuals achieve "*understanding* that sets man above the rest of sensible beings." Locke puts this new secular faith in the earlier religious language: "The Candle that is set up in us shines bright enough for all our purposes."[3] Moreover, under the guidance of reason as "judge" and guarantor, the truths of politics and religion are now at least compatible and often identical: the appropriate forms of conduct to ensure order within a highly individualistic society linked to the latitudinarian doctrines of a progressive consensual Protestantism. Locke had integrated liberalism and Protestantism and made that settlement accessible to every individual, each equipped to pursue his or her "conduct" in "this world" with "virtue."[4]

152

The development of human agency would appear complete. Under a single system of cosmic and worldly ends revealed internally, individuals are now free to seek their own "confortable provision for this life, and the way that leads to a better." Individuals, to be sure, are not born as effective agents, for reason, Locke insisted, derives from prerational individual experience. Neither truth, political wisdom, nor rational Christianity is innate; all are specific attainments arising from early experience. "But, alas, amongst children, idiots, savages, and the grossly illiterate, what general maxims are to be found? What universal principles of knowledge? Their notions are few and narrow." The child, who "first coming into the world" will have few ideas, "*by degrees* . . . comes to be furnished with them," principally from sense experience as Hobbes had developed it. Yet children inevitably "come to the use of reason," developing the capacity to attain clear and universal perceptions and norms.[5] Development also governs political reality, enabling liberal society to emerge from the state of nature and traditional political regimes. Kenneth Minogue writes of Locke's politics: "Individuals are found complete in nature; they can establish the laws of society by their reason, and the satisfaction of their desires by labour and enterprise. Society and State are created by them in the full knowledge of what each institution will involve. No fundamental change can occur in such individuals." Reason in adults now "stands as a solemn check on everything that is spontaneous, wild, enthusiastic, uncaring, disinterested, honourable or heroic—in a word, irrational."[6] Finally, the evolution of the Protestant covenant of faith from the earlier covenant of works and obedience entails the triumph of the rational religious agent. The rational order must be intuited and realized, but these developmental achievements are, if not natural, all but inevitable. This is truly the Locke who, for Voltaire, "has unfolded to man the nature of human reason."[7]

The traversal from pre-reflective and affective Hobbesian experience to guidance by reason, from "infants, weak and helpless, without knowledge or understanding" who need "rule and jurisdiction over them," to political "maturity" and a "non-sovereign state," from the "extravagent errors and miscarriages" of religious "enthusiasm" to the "true" which "*reason* warrants" suddenly appears effortless.[8] Yet Locke's confident movement from nature to culture, suggesting a species distinct from the previous inhabitants of England, raises unavoidable questions: How could the so recently dangerous beginning point of natural irrationality generate such a fully realized and integrated Protestant and liberal agency paradigm? And how could it do so seemingly without the two narratives of crisis resolution, Protestant and liberal, Milton and Hobbes, one internal and one social, demanding the un- avoidably contra-natural relinquishment of independent authorship? Given the always provisional effort to sustain the saving resolution of agency through self-vigilance, how, indeed, was an ordered individualist society suddenly so attainable?

Locke's Role in the Evolution of Liberalism

The seeming disappearance of the great conundrums involved in reconciling modern individualism with social order raises serious doubts about Locke's contribution to liberalism. More problematic even than the magical emer- gence of adult limits is the incompatible account of their origin and nature in his major writings on religion, politics, and metaphysics, leading Peter Laslett, though admiring, to call Locke "perhaps, the least consistent of all the great philosophers" with a corpus neither "integrated" nor "with a gen- eral philosophy at its center."[9] In Locke's philosophical *Essay Concerning Hu- man Understanding*, the certainty of reasoning emerges in the form of ideas from reflection upon "clear and distinct perceptions[s]" in experience.[10] In- dividuals thereby attain "the knowledge of their Maker, and the sight of their own duties" without either intuiting distinct laws of nature as the politics asserts or revelation, for "truth . . . from the knowledge and contem- plation of our own *ideas*, will always be certainer to us than . . . *traditional revelation*."[11] In *The Reasonableness of Christianity*, contrarily, Locke defends the primacy of revelation:

> It is too hard a task for unassisted reason to establish morality in all its parts upon its true foundation with a clear and convincing light. . . . [T]he knowl- edge of morality by mere natural light . . . makes but a slow progress and lit- tle advance in the world. And the reason of it is not hard to be found in men's necessities, passions, vices, and mistaken interests. . . . [H]uman rea- son unassisted . . . never from unquestionable principles, by clear deduc- tions, made out an entire body of the "law of nature."

Given that "a surer and clearer way" was necessary for "the vulgar and mass of mankind" than "the long and intricate deductions of reason," it required "one manifestly sent from God and coming with visible authority from him" to "as a king and lawmaker, tell them their duties and require their obedi- ence."[12] Finally in the politics, as we shall see, broadly apprehended "laws of nature" and universal but presumably chaotic "necessities" and "interests" now sustain the affirmation of societal norms.

The contradictory and fragmented picture of human nature in these discourses, within each individual and among the diverse sectors of the populace, reorients the search for the underlying consistency in the Lockean corpus. Its ground is to be found not in the rigor of his doctrinal formulations but in his assumptions regarding the liberal character. His writings uniformly emphasize consistent and acceptable adult conduct, the internalized behavior of the Protestant-liberal agent, over concern with its source. Individuals were expected to read appropriate agency "truths" about societal order, individual responsibility and initiative, and the value of religion to "concern our conduct" whether from laws of reason, revelation, or experience. Where faith provides the clearest light, as in the religious writings, faith should be "received" and "necessarily believed."[13] Where, as in the *Essay,* faith sometimes carries the individual away, then the other of the "two ways" of arriving at "truth," reason, must be called upon to achieve the full clarity of the same ends.[14] These convictions in turn serve a single end, the operation of dispositions and manners in the world: "To disobey God in any part of his commands (and it is he that commands what reason does) is direct rebellion, which, if dispensed with at any point, government and order are at an end, and there can be no bounds set to the lawless exorbitancy of unconfined man."[15] That is to say, these adult "inquiries" were in fact alternative or parallel teachings within the reconstructive or compositive phase of liberalism as Hobbes defined it. The uniformity and moral universalism of this phase, the ideological phase of Protestant-liberal institutionalization, could never be derived from the complex and disordered world of Hobbesian sense experience. They are instead read into experience as the path out of that world. The compelling issue, then, is how this normative universe can be assumed to inform the new character.

This interrogation suggests two of Locke's central—and intertwined—roles in the history of liberalism: as the mythologist of the free agent so crucial to its theoretical self-conception; and as the theorist who, far from dispensing with its two foundational narratives, transformed and condensed them from public strategies into pre-political directives for the socialization of the young. Regarding the second role first, Sheldon Wolin has detailed Locke's extensive doubts that human nature was amenable to reason.[16] To leave the critical truths directing politics and religion to the wisdom of adults was to forgo the only significant leverage that nature provided, that those who are "very little" are "as white Paper, or Wax, to be moulded and fashioned as one pleases." The very work of socialization suggested by Hobbes, of propelling into motion and channeling the human drives, could in Locke's judgment be undertaken effectively only with the young: "Of all the Men we meet with, Nine Parts of Ten are what they are, Good or Evil, useful or not, by their Education."[17] The early shaping of character was to be the bridge from nature to culture, infancy to adulthood, experience to reason, chaos to order, narcissism to conformity, setting up the pathways for all subsequent experience, understanding, and self-control.

Though moved up to the beginning of life, this developmental process virtually tracks the earlier transformational accounts. The creation of the agency character through defeat of self-authorization and the acceptance of universal norms and ends forms the very content of Locke's educational project. By locating the coercions which shape this formation of the Protestant-liberal character prior to the onset of personal memory in the life of the child, Locke hoped to render them inaccessible. Neither agency nor its ends would ever appear optional, yet the coercive foundation of this accommodation could not ever be located. Individuals would experience the motion and activity of their lives as the free exercise of resolutions long adhered to. They would consider themselves the agents only of their internalized personal reason, unaware of how reason itself had been formed as the repository and agent of Protestant and liberal institutional values. An early education would limit the task of disassembling error to the flaws of nature and natural pride without the complications of errant social reinforcement. The remaining work could then focus the individual on integrating agency norms and undertaking the worldly participation and commitments appropriate to the new society. The agency character, thus, was neither natural nor inevitable with growth, but a socialized self produced from a highly directed education. This self would move toward comfortable collective order, to realize internally and socially the rules of liberalism and the convictions of Protestantism.

In his other role, Locke originated what Hobbes might only have imagined with envy: the Protestant-liberal myth of the "free agent," the agent who, having forgotten the initial shaping, freely accommodates. Locke's vast influence in modernity suggests the immense power of this myth. Peter Laslett refers to Locke as a "post-Hobbesian" whose political theory is "of greater importance than *Leviathan*."[18] Nowhere was this evaluation more pronounced than in the United States. Jefferson called Locke's "little book on Government . . . perfect as far as it goes,"[19] while Louis Hartz characterized American society as a "Lockean settlement," that is, "a society which begins with Locke, and . . . stays with Locke."[20] His theory captured the national enthusiasm for the claim of a new developmental dispensation, a narrative that much more powerful if the compromises and costs associated with it were not evident. But unlike the narratives of Milton and Hobbes, Locke's myth is not a story which organizes the process of structuring the modern character. It is a fantasy that such a story is unnecessary, a denial of what is repressed and the act of repression itself. As Lockean education was woven into the Protestant-liberal world and the state of nature forgotten, its conclusions became self-evident. In this way, the developmental process would be recast as the growth not of agency but of freedom, leading in time to unwarranted claims about the nature of liberalism. Such falsifications would much later be remembered and recovered with the unsettling shock of a new discovery. Only then if unhappily would Americans recognize themselves as more agent than free, and seek to recover the prehistory of Lockean liberalism.

The Agency Foundation of Locke's Politics

Locke's political theory is frankly an idyll of "renaturalized" order. Its puzzling simplicity is explicable only when the politics is situated within his larger project: his state of nature is no Hobbesian original condition but a way station in the process of institutional formation. It has already normatively and institutionally evolved beyond "a state of license" as a functioning society. Natural freedom is constrained by a universally accessible law of nature mandating both liberal equality and voluntarism as absolute moral norms: "The state of nature has a law of nature to govern it, which obliges every one; and reason, which is the law, teaches all mankind who will but consult it that, being all equal and independent, no one ought to harm another in his life, health, liberty, or possessions." Further, there is "nothing more evident" than that all would "be equal one amongst another, without subordination or subjection." Human capacities and responsibilities all derive from the first and most self-evident of God's truths in the state of nature, that humans were put upon the world as his agents: "for men being all the workmanship of one omnipotent and infinitely wise Maker—all the servants of one sovereign master, sent into the world by his order, and about his business, they are his property . . . furnished with like faculties . . . [without] subordination . . . as if we were made for one another's uses."[21]

Institutional life, the movement toward society, is now presumed. "Man," having been "made . . . a creature" for whom "it was not good for him to be alone," is "under strong obligations of necessity, convenience, and inclination" that "drive him into society" and is "fitted with understanding and language to continue and enjoy it." God has "commanded" and given human beings the capacity "to labor" and "subdue the earth," and provided them through "the law of God and nature" the reason to discern and power to establish an appropriate political structure.[22] These motivations lead individuals inevitably into social institutions, the tightly organized nuclear family, the more extended working household of the age, and a quite informal "natural" association of these households "short of political society."[23] With "reason" and the "law of reason" teaching rights of ownership for "goods" which are "appropriated" through "labor" and limits to such accumulation,[24] "industry" flourishes in this natural condition, allowing individuals "out of bounds of society and without compact" to "continue and enlarge" their holdings, to set up "exchange" through market mechanisms of money, barter, and price, and to undertake "commerce" even "with other parts of the world."[25]

With complex society emerging absent coercive power, Locke's language conjures images of freedom verging on self-authorization: the "equal right that every man has to their natural freedom, without being subjected to the will or authority of any other man," and the right to be "master of himself and proprietor of his own persona and actions or labor of it."[26] This inflated rhetoric obscures the tight restraints on freedom, the preexisting directionality and fixed ends, bounds, and channels variously associated with "reason and conscience," "common equity" and "justice," "*right*" and "right rule," "preservation" and "revelation,"[27] which together constitute the rules, conduct, and role of agency: "The law of reason . . . in its true notion is not so much the limitation as the direction of a free and intelligent agent to his proper interest . . . which hedges us in only from bogs and precipices. . . . [F]reedom is not, as we are told: a liberty for every man to do what he lists . . . but a liberty to dispose and order as he lists his person, actions, possessions, and his whole property, within the allowance of those laws under which he is." Freedom is subject not only to moral strictures but also to a further set of affirmative obligations: one is "bound to preserve himself and not quit his station wilfully," to "preserve the rest of mankind . . . as much as he can," to carry out the "command" for "man . . . to labor" and "subdue the earth, i.e. improve it for the benefit of life," by being "industrious and rational," and "to preserve, nourish, and educate the children."[28]

Equality is equally confined within agency boundaries, as the abstract equivalence of rights within a framework of obligations. Inequality of outcome in a class society is presumed through the acceptable "inequality" of distribution, the differential reward due the different individual capacities: "Though I said . . . that all men by nature are equal, I cannot be supposed to understand all sorts of equality. Age or virtue may give men a just precedence; excellence of parts and merit may place others above the common level." Above all, "the different degrees of industry" or efficacy as an agent would "give men possession in different proportions."[29]

The Apparent Taming of the Natural Condition

With the new normative framework seemingly in place, Locke's use of social contract theory appears questionable. By preserving the "memory" of a collective founding, the theory risks undermining the increasing social regularity with a continuing right of individual authorization. Locke's retention of the original condition indicates his continuing need to ground agency principles through the process of social formation. Unlike later English theory, where the successful integration of agency by the mid-eighteenth century made access to individual options through the social contract expendable, Locke used the theory to insist on new political and economic principles.[30] At the same time, he sought to undercut its dangers by diminishing the original condition to one of individualism but not self-authority. Given that the norms and demands of agency are in place from the outset and all deviations are already "violations," self-authorization, now subordinated to the more dominant impulse to "execute" the "law of nature" and "punish" its "transgressors," is reduced from being a primal condition to being simply a personal misapplication of or failure to apply reigning values.

Politically, social contract theory established the consensual foundation for limited government still in dispute during the period of the Glorious Revolution. Locke's picture of a functioning natural condition justifies limits on the prerogatives of "political power," for "the end" of "civil government" is only "to avoid and remedy" the "inconveniences of the state of nature."[31] Government, though a late addition, can relieve individuals of the burden of remaining political judgments not by a reversal of fundamental commitments or inner nature but simply by enforcing the existing norms clearly in place. Thus, the preexisting "law of nature stands as an eternal rule to all men, legislators as well as others": "A man . . . having in the state of nature no arbitrary power over the life, liberty, or possession of another, but only so much as the law of nature gave him for the preservation of himself and the rest of mankind, this is all he does or can give up to the commonwealth . . . so that the legislative can have no more than this."

A viable state of nature also provided a safeguard against political tyranny, enabling society to dismantle unjust government and return to this condition. But once again foreclosing any extreme implications, Locke recast Hobbes's dynamic of rebellion by precluding the return not only to Hobbes's individual authorship but also even to his own condition of normatively bounded individualism. The right of the populace to dissolve government for "a long train of abuses, prevarications, and artifices," limited by agency principles now established in nature, produced a reversion of power "never . . . to the individuals" but one which "will always remain in the community."[32] In this way, the popular grant of consent to government is framed by its prior commitment to agency and its reclaiming of prerogatives subject to that commitment. Government power in turn is axiomatically conditioned by its furtherance of agency, and revocable with its failure to fulfill its mandate.[33]

Economically, the individualist original condition reaffirmed liberalism's commitment to a modern market society. In place of rewards from political privilege or social status, "the world" is to be given "to the use of the industrious and rational," utilizing personal "labor" to pursue "their lives, liberties, and estates."[34] Labor includes not only "the ploughman's pains" and "the reaper's and thresher's toil," direct contact with the earth as one "removes" goods "out of the state of nature" and creates value by having "mixed his labor with" it, but also secondary activities like "the baker's sweat" as well as more remote "exchange" which gains us "the bread we eat."[35] This regulating "the increase of land and the right employing" of it constitutes "the great art of government," and the main reason for leaving the "state of nature" which "disorder[s] men's properties" for "the power of society" which "is obliged to secure every one's property."[36]

The centrality of property in Locke's politics, such that those individual natural rights to be protected were identified by "the general name 'property,'"[37] illustrates the importance liberalism attached to establishing an individualist economics. Individual freedom could be reconciled with substantial obligations to preexisting ends so long as sufficient ordered spheres of initiatory, self-reliant activity were provided as channels to move within. Hobbes, starting from extreme dissensus about societal priorities, had emphasized political unanimity and could only suggest activity which was both initiatory yet harmless. By Locke's period, with greater political stability, the focus shifted from political control to release of individuals from the rigidities of caste and political regulation to pursue a structured self-interest, with political consent also offering freedom not as the choice of ends but as the implementation of those ends given. Thus he wrote that, in the formation of character, the effort *"to produce vertuous, useful, and able Men,"* the thing *"most to be taken Care of"* is one's "Calling."[38]

Economic activity directed to the building of a commercial society offered the best channel for sustainable individual and self-initiated activity. For all of its opportunity for initiative and release, it possessed the boundedness and orderliness of a highly directed activity. Organized by commercial regulations and societal procedures, "self-interested" activity pursued ends set by the community, the *"Welfare and Prosperity of the Nation."* It provided specific roles for the individual within a collective process and mandated the appropriate social virtues of being "Eminent and Useful in his Country according to his Station."[39] Success followed dedication to creating "value," which was defined as "useful" to others: "What would a man value ten thousand or a hundred thousand acres of excellect land, ready cultivated and well stocked too, with cattle in the middle of the inland parts of America where he had no hopes of commerce with other parts of the world to draw money to him by sale of the product?"[40] Moreover, exercising individual choices regarding productivity and commercial transactions made one personally responsible for one's economic condition and social status, and consensually obligated through property to the laws and procedures of the society.[41]

While necessary to ground liberal political and economic doctrine, the self-authorizing implications of social contract theory clearly troubled Locke. As a result, it was employed as a historical conceit whose normative benefits could be extracted while the remainder of the doctrine was discarded. Unlike Hobbes's state of nature, which bespoke a continuing psychological reality, Locke offered a sociological condition which no longer—if ever—applied. The original political condition, though sufficiently stable to undercut the necessity of unlimited government, was at the same time too unstable ever to have been realistically possible. Given that not only self-authority but also self-reliant individualism itself is untenable, "mankind" was in fact "quickly driven into society," where the consent to a "common measure" of "an established, settled, known law" becomes the obvious "remedy." Lacking resources, each individual now presumptively cedes the otherwise futile task of enforcing "preservation of himself and the rest of mankind" to a more effective power while relinquishing personal construction of lawful ends for a systemically structured individualism. The "tacit consent" to sovereignty could now be safely presumed from no more than "barely traveling freely on the highway," that is to say, universally. At the same time, with its claim that all government rests on "consent of the people," liberal society maintained an individual basis for the requirement of voluntary obligation on the part of every citizen, the mandated willingness of all "to give up all of the power necessary to the ends for which they unite into society to the majority of the community."[42]

The original economic condition, a myth of limitless opportunity where "as full as the world seems" now there is yet as "in the first ages of the world" a "vast wilderness of the earth," was equally untenable and beyond reach. The proprietor, the "natural" model of free personal productive activity with an independent connection to the land, turned out to be irrelevant in commercial England, which in order to cope with its "plenty of people," full enclosure, and "the invention of money," had long ago "introduced—by consent—larger possessions and a right to them."[43] With economic self-sufficiency foreclosed, the social contract now functioned primarily to produce the continuing obligation to labor. But the model had long since shifted from economic independence to the "Man of Business," the commercial leader in a complex society of "improved land" with "plenty of the conveniences."[44] Not in England but in the United States would the broader implications of Locke's social contract theory gradually emerge. In its self-reliant proprietary economy with rudimentary "truck"[45] run by independent households with a diffuse social network and weak political organization, immense credibility accrued to the narrative of a society rooting the individual in an original freedom.[46]

By historicizing the social contract, Locke hoped to free liberal society from self-warranting with a now deauthorized and institutionally integrated individualism. Thus relieving social contract theory of its inherent dangers, Locke's politics tried to create the impression that liberalism had been normalized. This impression was a profoundly misleading one: in fact, self-authority remained the paramount danger, and rather than disappearing, it had been removed from the public realm to the narrative of personal development.

The Emerging Perspective of
Individual Development

In his two other major discourses on what we might call the normative structure of adulthood, his metaphysical and religious writings, Locke admitted, as his politics could not, that the operation within the individual and in society of consensual natural laws was a mere construction. Focusing now on the personal development of normative clarity, we see that—while such norms are presumed to govern the universe—their individual internalization is deeply problematic. The goal of these discourses is to explain how the truths of liberal agency emerge from natural and religious experience. By means of the two experiential directives operating jointly, "reason," being "natural *revelation*" that "God has implanted," and "revelation," which is "natural *reason* enlarged,"[47] the individual will have self-evident if not innate access to the "*inclinations of the appetite* to good." These, which "never cease to be the constant springs and motives of all our actions, to which we perpetually feel them strongly impelling us," will direct them confidently toward the good.[48] These are the very *reconstructive* virtues now returning as "natural tendencies," the desire of individuals to achieve universal knowledge, moral certainty, and virtuous conduct,[49] to "keep their compacts," to "endeavor after a better state" and employ their "talents" in "their labours."[50]

This path to virtue, however, was by no means to be presumed. Given "many men's laziness, ignorance, and vanity," because of which "the greatest part" of them "cannot *know*," the claim that universal truth and moral certitude prevail is wholly tenuous. In religion, popular clarity required a self-evident consensus based on "plain, intelligible . . . articles" which "every laboring and illiterate man may comprehend" from "things familiar to their minds and nearly allied to their daily experience."[51] Yet, subjective religious "enthusiasm" that rises "from the conceits of a warmed or overweening brain" looms to undercut God's word. This enthusiasm, often working "more powerfully in the persuasions and actions of men than either . . . restraint of reason and check of reflection" in turn "carries all easily with it," becoming virtually "a divine authority" reflecting "our own temper and inclination."[52]

The parallel goal in the *Essay* is to demonstrate that the verities of agency derive epistemologically from the data of sense experience without the "obscurity and confusion" which lead to "mistakes" and "doubts and disputes," though unaided by revelation or the political imperatives of the original condition. To ground the account in sensation, Locke must explain how these normative "discoveries made by the use of reason, and truths that a rational creature may certainly come to know" evolve. "Moral principles," as with the emergence of a child's faculties, are not "innate," for children do not possess them, but must involve "a faculty to find out in time the moral difference in actions," or ideas which "*by degrees* [one] comes to be furnished with."[53] "All that are born into the world" encounter "bodies that perpetually and diversely affect them," producing a wide "variety of ideas," "great numbers of opinions," and a vast "difference . . . amongst men in their practical principles" and "moral rules."[54] This is further complicated by differences in "education, company, and customs" as well as "men's appetites," which can "carry" them "to the overturning of all morality" and coherence.[55]

Given these complexities, what accounts for the successful development of this faculty in children, who undertake an only gradual "search, and casting about," and find that its realization "requires pains and application"? What explains its final integration, given the prevalence in adults of "thoughts" which "wander" with "no sure footing" leading to "questions" and "disputes," their frequent loss of "clear resolution," and finally the incidence of "perfect scepticism" and the embrace of "fancies and natural superstition"?[56] "Reason," it turns out, is in fact "our dim candle,"[57] causing Locke to admit: "I DOUBT not but that my reader . . . think[s] that I have been all this while only building a castle in the air and be ready to say to me: To what purpose all this stir? . . . Is there anything so extravagant as the imaginations of men's brains? Where is the head that has no *chimeras* in it? Or if there be a sober and a wise man, what difference will there be by your rules between his knowledge and that of the most extravagant fancy in the world? . . . [T]he visions of an enthusiast and the reasonings of a sober man will be equally certain."[58]

This almost comically flawed internalization of agency threatens the philosophical reconstruction of normative liberalism. Regarding religion, Locke hopefully asserts that if reason is dim, the "light from heaven is strong, clear, and pure" as the sun, providing moreover "its own demonstration."[59] The teaching available to all from the development of a broad agency Christianity provides "a complete rule of life" in which "virtue" realizes "the perfection and excellency of our nature."[60] While no longer innate, yet because "we have been bred up in the belief from our cradles," Locke's religious teachings can become "familiar, and, as it were, natural *to us*,"[61] that is, universal and consensual. So, each taught personally to "set himself seriously on the courses of virtue and practice of true religion"[62] apart from any church doctrine or ecclesiastical structure, individuals can go forth, even to "the wild woods and uncultivated waste of America,"[63] secure in their moral precepts.

A similar bootstrap argument frames the reconstructive argument in the *Essay*. Despite the incessant opportunities for error,[64] "men, when they come to examine them, find their simple ideas all generally to agree" and in more complex matters "cannot differ much in thinking." Like Mr. Magoo, reason plows ahead, averting every pitfall to assert "*not fictions of our fancies*" and "not the bare empty vision of vain, insignificant *chimeras* of the brain," but "archetypes" or "essences" of "universal . . . knowledge" arising from certain standard mental operations.[65] Thus does the persevering individual come to do "his duty as a rational creature" on the basis of "that portion of truth" which "the eternal Father of light and fountain of all knowledge communicates to mankind" through "their rational faculties."[66]

While Locke's effort to wrest virtue from human waywardness was on its face implausible, the shift of the project of normative reconstruction from a collective project of contract formation to one of individual moral development entailed a powerful adjustment of liberal theory. The relinquishment of self-authority no longer had to be undertaken in the visible light of a consenting public where any might question or resist the outcome. It could now be relocated to a less noticeable and contentious pre-political space where adjustment and accommodation were generated by and responsive to private expectations. Locke in fact suggested an alternative political narrative in *The Second Treatise* by removing the social contract from the recent—and thus accessible—beginnings of modern liberal society to the early formation of human societies. The actual formation of states by social contract was in this account a viable option only "in the "first ages of the world," when individuals bestowed on "nursing fathers, tender and careful of the public weal," their unqualified and "scarce avoidable consent."[67] By this displacement, the shift from traditional servitude to liberal agency society could now be framed as the development from earlier—though less mature—established societies without a detour into the foreboding state of nature.

Political consent, still necessary because individuals are not born as rational and integrated citizens, was in long- and well-established societies no longer an original political act but the developmental subduing of each individual nature. Thus, in the *Second Treatise*, because of "the weakness of their infancy," children, like "lunatics and idiots" and "madmen," have not "such a degree of reason . . . capable of knowing the law and so living within the rules of it" as to be "capable of being a free man." These all require "the tuition and government of others," though with the young "it is but a temporary" condition, like "the swaddling clothes they are wrapped up in." As the child will grow up and achieve "age and reason," then he or she will attain "a state of maturity . . . capable to know . . . law . . . so he might keep his actions within the bounds of it."[68] This is in turn formalized by defining the "age of discretion" as the time when the child determines "what government he will put himself under." In this argument, Locke carefully distinguishes natural rights from the original capacity to utilize them, defining children as "not born in this state of equality, though they are born to it," thus limiting incapacity to childhood and undercutting any defense of traditional political authority.[69]

The revised account now frames consent as the voluntary overcoming of one's *individual* origins in willful desires and lack of self-mastery. Given the need for early and specific intervention, the key mechanism for applying pressure shifts from government to socialization. The "nourishment and education" of children become "a charge so incumbent on parents for their children's good" in order to achieve "the improvement of growth and age" that "nothing can absolve them from taking care of it," and parental failure severs their "power over them."[70] As the socialization process spread systematically, liberalism would in time derive its ascendancy from a firm grounding in the universal childhood shaping of an adaptive character. But, as Locke understood fully, that day had not arrived. For the task of producing an unshakable consent to one's new liberal nature in early life was, finally, the goal of his preeminent discourse, *Some Thoughts Concerning Education*.

The Narrative of Agency Education

What determines normative resolutions in Locke's adult discourses is a prior grounding discourse. That the individual, despite "a freedom of will and liberty of acting," has the "understanding to direct his actions" specifically "within the bounds of that law he is under"[71] can only be understood as the product of agency education. This transition from natural child to liberal adult was far from effortless. It was rather, we discover in the *Education,* a consuming conceptual and political task. Yet the *Education,* in which the illusions governing the other discourses that rationality, faith, and order came easily to the modern individual were unceremoniously dispensed with, has remained apart from the rest of Locke's corpus. Whether intentional or not, de-emphasizing the role of socialization, as of social contract theory, in modern liberal theory has served larger political ends: to have access to one's personal or collective ideological origins is to recall the possession and subsequent (reversible?) divestment of an otherwise long-abandoned capacity for authority.

The educational treatise fully lays out the process by which the liberal character is constructed in agency socialization: "The Difference to be found in the Manners and Abilities of Men, is owing more to their *Education* than to any thing else; we have Reason to conclude, that great Care is to be had in the forming Children's *Minds,* and giving them that seasoning early, which shall influence their Lives always after." Education constitutes the single indispensable political task:

> 'Tis [Education] which makes the great Difference in Mankind. The little, and almost insensible Impressions on our tender Infancies, have very important and lasting Consequences: And there 'tis, as in the Fountains of some Rivers, where a gentle Application of the Hand turns the flexible Waters into Chanels, that make them take quite contrary courses, and by this little Direction given them at first in the Source, they receive different Tendencies, and arrive at last, at very remote and distant Places. I imagine the Minds of Children as easily turned this or that way, as Water it self.

A proper, consistent socialization is the single source of normative clarity, without which "the Mind has not been made Obedient to Discipline, and pliant to reason."[72]

Locke frankly admits that the task is Hobbesian in scope, for the "original condition" of humankind is indeed a state of narcissism, anarchic desire, and normlessness. There are no "creatures . . . half so wilful and proud, or half so desirous to be Masters of themselves and others, as Man." Individuals are from "our first actions . . . guided more by Self-love, than Reason or Reflection." Humans without socialization, therefore, "before . . . brought to do the things are fit for them," above all else "love . . . Dominion." "This is the first Original of most vicious habits, that are ordinary and natural. This love of *Power* and Dominion shews it self very early. . . . Children would have their Desires submitted to by others; they contend for a ready compliance from all about them . . . [and] desire to have things to be theirs; they would have *Propriety* and Possession, pleasing themselves with the Power which that seems to give, and the Right they thereby have, to dispose of them, as they please." To prevent "almost all the Injustice and Contention, that so disturb Humane Life," therefore, one must ensure that these "two Roots" of power and dominion are "early to be weeded out."[73]

Locke's model of character affirmed the irreversible shift to modern individualism. This new type combined a deference to familial discipline and social norms which establish and maintain internal controls with the self-reliance required by liberal adulthood. Locke's reputation as an educational reformer derives from his insistence on producing self-dependent adults: "Every Man must some Time or other be Trusted to himself, and his own Conduct; and he that is a good, a vertuous and able Man must be made so within." Rejecting the character model of servitude, Locke understood that an authoritarian upbringing to "make them Slaves to your Estate" renders children useless in liberal commercial society: "If the *Mind* be curbed, and *humbled* too much in Children; if their *Spirits* be abased and *broken* much, by too strict an Hand over them, they lose all their Vigor and Industry. . . . *[D]ejected Minds,* timorous and tame, and *low Spirits* . . . very seldom attain to any thing. . . . *Severity* carried to the highest Pitch . . . often [brings] . . . a dangerous Disease, by breaking the Mind, and then in the place of a disorderly young Fellow, you have a *low spirited moap'd Creature.*" He concludes that a "*Slavish Discipline* makes a *Slavish Temper.*" Children now grow up to live on their own so "that Restraint will not last always." Suppression may make them ineffectual and bitter: "Imperiousness and Severity, is but an ill Way of Treating Men, who have Reason of their own to guide them, unless you have a mind to make your Children when grown up, weary of you, and secretly to say within themselves, *When will you die, Father?*"[74]

The other extreme, encouraging children's self-authorization by suggesting that "they must not be crossed . . . they must be permitted to have their Wills in all things," is also to be avoided. Children led to believe in their right to "Liberty and Indulgence" will be impulsive and unable "to *resist* the Importunity of *present Pleasure or Pain.*" Using ambiguous language that reflects the socializing goal of renaturalization, Locke writes that deference to "unguided Nature" will "corrupt the Principle of Nature in . . . Children." It will have "poisoned the Fountain," forcing parents "afterward to taste the bitter Water." Though opposed to corporal punishment as debilitating, Locke insists on its use for "one, and but one Fault," the least willfulness or imperiousness: "*Obstinacy,* or *Rebellion . . . Stubbornness,* and an *obstinate Disobedience,* must be master'd with Force and Blows: For this there is no other Remedy. Whatever particular Action you bid him do, or forbear, you must be sure to see your self obey'd: no Quarter in this case, no resistance."[75]

The project seems fatally inconsistent: to produce a child both obedient and independent. Locke grasped the dilemma: "how to keep up a Child's Spirit, easy, active and free: and yet, to restrain him from many things he has a Mind to, and to draw him to things that are uneasy to him; he . . . that knows how to reconcile these seeming contradictions, has, in my Opinion, got the true Secret of Education."[76] He has described the central project and inner complexity of the agency character from Hobbes's intuitive pursuit of both compliance and initiative to the very conundrums of the modern American self. Locke's educational strategy indeed reconciled these polarities, but not through a theory of obligation or by convictions about the moral universe or, for that matter, any set of ideas. It constructed an operational character capable of internalizing and adaptively synthesizing a fixed authority stipulating operational boundaries and limits with its own sphere of legitimated initiative and activity (only) within which it could regard itself as without restraint.

The task in his terms was to produce the "rational Creature" of his adult discourses. It is at times given an intellectual cast, "to set the *Mind* right," at others treated simply as learning to control one's inner nature: "The great Principle and Foundation of all Vertue and Worth is . . . [t]hat a Man is able to *deny himself* his own Desires, cross his own Inclinations, and purely follow what Reason directs as best, tho' the Appetite lean the other way." Yet unlike in his other discourses, the work of character formation is for the most part acknowledged as a contra-natural task: "The true Principle of Vertue and Industry, so contrary to unguided Nature is to be got betimes." The source of all evil, the natural "love of Dominion," must be "weeded out," and "Contrary Habits Introduced," which is in effect to lay new "Foundations," if necessary to "go deep to come at the Roots, and . . . cleanse the vitiated Seed-Plot overgrown with Weeds, and restore us the hopes of Fruit."[77]

Reason, then, whose "Rules and Restraints" form the channels for the new character which give individuals "the Power to govern" themselves and communities the capacity for order and consensus, is not itself natural, for "Reason comes to speak" in children. It comes, moreover, as an *imposition* from outside: "He that is not used to submit his Will to the Reason of others, *when* he is *Young*, will scarce hearken or submit to his own Reason, when he is of an Age to make use of it." Moreover, Locke admits, reason is not merely external to one's character, it is not even "reason": it is the *principle of parental authority*. The reason of others, in other words, is simply the will—the "Absolute Power and Restraint"—of others. Because parents "would like to be thought Rational Creatures," they insist their will serve children as reason's approximation: "The less Reason [children] have of their own, the more are they to be under . . . those, in whose Hands they are."[78]

The goal of education is to internalize this external authority in order to establish a transpersonal source for the continuing presence of normative standards. This imposition must be swift and unerring:

> Those therefore that intend ever to govern their Children, should begin it whilst they are *very little* and look that they perfectly comply with the Will of their Parents. Would you have your Son obedient to you when past a Child? Be sure then to establish the Authority of a Father, *as soon as* he is capable of Submission, and can understand in whose Power he is. If you would have him stand in Awe of you, imprint it *in his Infancy*. . . . I imagine every one will judge it reasonable, that their Children, *when little*, should look upon their Parents as their Lords, their Absolute Governors; and, as such stand in Awe of them.

The mechanism for internalization was identification, combining an affective Protestant embrace of idealized authority and Hobbesian identification with the aggressor. To "bend the Mind, and settle the Parent's Authority," to achieve "true *Reverence*," the parent must combine "*Love* and *Fear*," "Indulgence and Tenderness," and again "Fear and Awe . . . to give you the first Power over their Minds." The cultivation of apprehension "if rightly governed" has its use in generating the concern for "Self-preservation" that will "awaken their Reason."[79] This use of intimidation to ensure initial compliance, Hobbes's own recipe for the first phase of socialization, was now removed to a less controversial, pre-political period of life.

Once their authority is internalized, parents then methodically shift from fear to encouraging a positive emulation of authority: "Of all the Ways whereby Children are to be instructed, and their Manners formed, the plainest, easiest, and most efficacious, is, to set before their Eyes the *Examples* of those things you would have them do, or avoid." Such "Examples" of "the Practice" of others are "of more force to draw or deterr their Imitation, than any Discourses," and will "be better learnt, and make deeper Impressions on them . . . than from any Rules or Instructions." Given "how prone we all are, expecially Children, to imitation," both children and "Men" will "do most by Example. We are all a sort of Camelions, that still take a Tincture from things near us." The child, having come to identify the parent as the significant Author, now associates the parent's will with what "reason" will "authorize." Parents in turn are instructed to act as models: "You must do nothing before him, which you would not have him imitate." As these models "sink so gently, and so deep, into Men's Minds," the child should in time "be like our selves."[80]

Through an identificatory transaction, the personal reiteration of the Hobbesian social contract, the parent becomes author of the child's being. Once reversal occurs at infancy through the transfer of authorization and constitution of role, the parent has leverage as the sovereign to turn the child into an agent of parental will who carries out parental values: "By these Ways carefully pursued, a Child may be brought to desire to be taught any thing, you have a Mind he should learn."[81] From this point in the education, the development of an operational agency character is straightforward and on the surface unconflicted.

The Teaching of Liberal Voluntariness

To effect a modern agency character, which would direct rather than stifle individualism, Locke utilized pleasure as the lever for gaining individuals' consent to substitute acceptable objects for their desires. He explained: "I would [not] have Children kept from the Conveniences or Pleasures of Life, that are not injurious to their Health or Vertue. . . . I would have their Lives made as pleasant, and as agreeable, as may be in a plentiful Enjoyment of whatsoever might innocently delight them." The strategy was to encourage gratifications parents regarded as reasonably appropriate in place of the child's unsocialized whims, thus effacing self-oriented and self-referential impulses with "objective," socially referential, and collectively mandated desires: "The first thing [children] should learn to know should be, that they were not to have any thing, because it pleased them, but because it was thought *fit* for them." The goal, however, was not renunciation but redirection:

> If things suitable to their Wants were supplied to them, so that they were never suffered to have what they once cried for, they would learn to be content without it. . . . It is fit that they should have liberty to declare their Wants to their Parents, and that with all tenderness they should be hearken'd to, and supplied . . . but 'tis one thing to say, I am hungry; another to say, I would have Roast-Meat. Having declared their Wants, their natural Wants, the pain they feel from Hunger, Thirst, Cold, or other necesssity of Nature; 'tis the Duty of their Parents, and those about them, to relieve them: But Children must leave it to the choice and ordering of their Parents, what they think properest for them, and how much.[82]

Separated from self-referentiality and self-authorization, pleasure becomes both a sure and a safe path to voluntary accommodation. Shaped by attentiveness to the child's experience in "the favourable *Seasons of Aptitude and Inclination*" and, through respectful instruction, by filling their heads with "Suitable Ideas," it will lead children gently to "a Liking and Inclination to what you propose them to be learn'd." They will have in time "a good Disposition . . . talk'd into them" that will make them "in love" with those things that "will engage their Industry and Application." Children can now actively pursue their "fit pleasure," regarding "learning" and "Play" or "Recreation" as synonymous, such that "you may turn them as you please, and they will be in Love with all the ways of Vertue." Now possessing a "Mind rightly disposed," they will work harder, learning "three times as much when [they are] *in tune*." Once they are no longer disposed to refuse "the Government and Authority of the Father," their flaws can be—as with God's treatment of realized Protestant agents—treated as "but Mistakes" and "overlooked."[83]

Forming a stable character involved more than setting a child in motion toward appropriate satisfactions, for steady directionality was also unnatural: "The Natural Temper of Children disposes their Minds to wander. Novelty alone takes them." They "have almost their sole delight in Change and Variety. . . . Inadvertency, forgetfulness, unsteadiness, and wandring of Thought, are the natural Faults of Childhood." By Locke's own acknowledgment, very little to a child is "clear and distinct," at least until the educator intervenes with a steady application of demands and expectations: "Children are *not* to be *taught by Rules*, which will always be slipping out of their

Memories. What you think necessary for them to do, settle them by an indispensible Practice, as often as the Occasion returns; and if it be possible, make Occasions." Character, formed out of regularized conduct and fixed ideas, requires repetition, for "Order and Constancy" make "the great difference." "If it be some Action you would have done, or done otherwise; whenever they forget, or do it awkardly, make them do it over and over again, till they are perfect. . . . They . . . should be shewn what to do, and by reiterated Actions, be fashioned before-hand into the Practice of what is fit and becoming." Similarly in education, "accustom [the child] to order, and teach him *Method* in all the application of his thoughts" so as to provide him "distinct Notions" and "distinct and . . . clear ideas."[84]

Conduct will thereby achieve an admirable routinization: "By repeating the same Action, till it be grown habitual in them, the Performance will not depend on Memory or Reflection, the Concomitant of Prudence and Age, and not of Childhood; but will be natural in them . . . by constant use as natural to a well-bred Man, as breathing; it requires no Thought, no Reflection. Having this way cured in your Child any Fault, it is cured for ever: And thus one by one, you may weed them out all, and plant what Habits you please." Through this "forming of their Minds and Manners" by "constant Attention, and particular Application," with "nothing . . . over look'd and neglected" in the demand for "Mastery over [the child's] Inclination," "*his Appetite*" will by "constant practice settled into habit" submit to "reason." At this point, adults will find "the hardest part of the Task is over," for "Habit" effectively internalizes the "true Principle of Vertue and Industry," which is "the true Foundation of future Ability and Happiness." Similarly, by the parent's creating strong "intellectual habit," the child will gain the power of "right Reasoning," with its "right Notions, and a right Judgment of things," of "Truth and Falsehood, Right and Wrong."[85]

For Locke, the goal of internal organization is ultimately social adaptation, the integration of "Manners" or "good Breeding" for acting in society: "The tincture of Company sinks deeper than the out-side, and possibly, if a true estimate were made of the Morality, and Religions of the World, we should find that the far greater part of Mankind received even those Opinions and Ceremonies they would die for, rather from the Fashions of their Countries, and the constant Practice of those about them, than from any conviction of their Reasons." The child must be directed not toward normative clarity but toward behavioral accommodation: "Thus, the clear focus for the child must be upon "the Satisfaction or Disgust wherewith" conduct "is received," for "the manner of doing is of more Consequence, than the thing done." To "be acceptable" and "polish'd," to gain "a good Reception," children must be continually attuned to their social performance: "To bring a young Man to [settled . . . Habit], I know nothing which so much contributed, as the love of Praise and Commendation, which should therefore be instilled into him by all Arts imaginable. Make his Mind as sensible of Credit and Shame as may be." This will "put a principle into Him" which will "constantly work, and incline [him] to the right" by allowing the adult permanent access and control. Parents must dole out to their children "*Esteem* and *Disgrace*" as the "most powerful incentives" at every occasion. They must *"caress and commend them, when they do well; shew a cold and neglectful Countenance to them upon doing ill."*[86]

The child, now dependent on "being esteemed, and valued, especially by [its] Parents," wishing to "be beloved and cherished" and "have all other good Things," will "be in love with all the ways of Vertue" and have "a natural Abhorrence" of what brings "*Displeasure* in the Parents." Regarding "rational Creatures" as those in "Conformity" to parental expectations, children are then to be exposed to the need for the approbation of others. Taught that by "doing well" one gains "Esteem" and is "necessarily beloved and cherished by every Body," the child then willingly pursues the benefits of a good "Reputation": "Though it be not the true Principle and Measure of Virtue (for that is the Knowledge of a Man's Duty, and the Satisfaction it is to obey his Maker, in following the Dictates of that Light God has given him . . .) yet . . . the Testimony of Applause . . . [of] other People's Reason . . . comes nearest to it."[87]

In this way, the individual attains the social virtues of liberal agency society: those of "Vigour, Activity, and Industry"; the capacity for constant "Application"; the "*Foresight* and *Desire*" and "constant . . . Labour" to achieve; the "Wisdom" for "managing his Business ability"; the new worldly social skills that will "get him more Friends, and carry him farther in the world"; the capacity for "Civility" as "the very end and business of *Good*-breeding" to make oneself "bend to a compliance and accommodate" oneself to those one has "to do with" by "perform[ing] those Actions which are incumbent on, and expected"; and an unwavering belief in a benevolent and generous God. These virtues are to be understood as the essence of reason, whose "right improvement, and exercise" are "the highest Perfection, that a Man can attain to in this Life." By gradually replacing "their Parent's Reason" with "their own Reason" as the source of normative "advise," individuals achieve self-control and self-mastery. By "teach[ing] the Mind to get the mastery over it self," they become "accustomed . . . to consult, and make use of their Reason" and "master their Inclinations." In acceding to self-governance, for "every man can more easily bear a denial from himself, than from any body else," individuals achieve the vaunted self-reliance: "This will accustom them to seek for what they want in themselves, and in their endeavours."[88]

With parental authority and its conduct internalized, the new individual self is effectively renaturalized. Locke, who has shaped an individual "so contrary to unguided Nature," continually fashioning its "whole outward Demeanor," signals its success by confidently redefining the socialized self as the authentic self. Authenticity he now distinguishes from hypocrisy, the individual with "natural Coherences" from one with "counterfeit Carriage, and dissembled Out-side." The former, a triumph of educational artifice, has "Habits woven into the very Principles of his Nature":

> A Mind free, and Master of it self and all its Actions . . . is what every one is taken with. The Actions, which naturally flow from such a well-formed Mind, please us also, as the genuine Marks of it; and being as it were natural Emanations from the Spirit and Disposition within, cannot but be easy and unconstrain'd. . . . [W]hen by a constant Practice, they have fashion'd their Carriage, and made all those little Expressions of Civility and Respect, which Nature or Custom has established in conversation so easy to themselves . . . they seem not Artificial or Studied, but naturally to flow from a . . . well turn'd Disposition.

The "Counterfeit," which is "always Offensive," suffers from "Affectation," the "awkard and forced Imitation of what should be Genuine and Easie, wanting the Beauty that Accompanies what is Natural; because there is always a Disagreement between the Outward Action, and the Mind within." In the disharmonious self, self-consciousness hinders the "habitual and becoming Easiness" which socialization hopes to effect.[89]

With a consistent character, the individual can move at its own discretion, for it acts and thinks within the boundaries that have been established. One cannot "all his life" coop the young "up in a Closet." Each must "come abroad into open Day-light," and the "only Fence against the World is, a thorough Knowledge of it." One can "be trusted to himself, and his own Conduct" if one has the "inward Civility" and the "graceful Motions" to respect the "Fence and Guard" which protect people's activity so they do not "run themselves into the Briars." Now "the way [is] enough . . . open . . . for his own Industry to carry him as far, as his Fancy will prompt, or his Parts inable him to go."[90]

The Idyll of Free Agency

The product of Locke's socialization, individuals moving through the authorized channels of economic activity and social interaction, would—so long as that motion was voluntary—fulfill Hobbes's objective of bounded liberty. But how could the transparently coercive internalization and habituation shaping the "free individual," the economy of "Hope and Fear . . . *Reward and Punishment*" as the "Spur and Reins, whereby all Mankind are . . . guided,"[91] ever be consented to? Isn't this individual simply the extension of others' wills, shaped for "freedom" as routinized adaptation and "authenticity" as ingrained hypocrisy? Why should one relinquish one's initial authority absent the pressures attending political crisis to become the agent of larger societal ends? Isn't this a dangerously inconclusive transition from nature to society by which to ground modern social order?

Following Hobbes's advice on foundations, Locke relocated the dynamic of self-transformation to individual prehistory, preventing the liberal citizen from ever reconsidering its initial childhood grant of authority. Locke's remarkably effective strategy, which more than any other has shaped the misunderstanding of the liberal character, was to initiate the work of coercion "*from the first* Beginning," "*from their very cradles.*" The goal was to consolidate the internalization of authority before the advent of memory so that it becomes for the child as inevitable as life itself. "A Compliance, and Suppleness of their Wills, being by a steady Hand introduced by Parents, before Children have Memories, to retain the Beginnings of it, will seem natural to them, and work afterwards in them, as if it were so; preventing all Occasions of Strugling, or Repining. The only Care is, That it be begun early, and inflexibly kept to, till *Awe* and *Respect* be grown familiar, and there appears not the least Reluctancy in the Submission, and ready Obedience of their Minds." Unadaptive inclinations also could "all be weeded out, without any Signs or Memory that ever they had been there." Coercion, necessary to effect the process of subordination and accommodation, risked thereafter becoming a source of great contention. Locke's insight was that it was also expendable. His recommendation was that it be gradually reduced as the conscious life of the child emerged: "If you would have him stand in Awe of you, imprint it *in his Infancy;* and, as he approaches more to a Man, admit him nearer to your Familiarity: So shall you have him your obedient subject (as is fit) whilst he is a Child, and your affectionate Friend, when he is a Man." Once "Authority" has been "establish'd," and the child "is in your Power," the parent must "permit . . . him the full Liberty due to his Age" and induce him increasingly by means of "Tenderness, and "Affection." Childhood is thus consciously experienced as a progressive release from constraints and external demands which appear to have been part of the original natural condition rather than imposed at infancy: "As they grow up to the Use of Reason, the Rigour of Government [is to] be, as they deserve it, greatly relaxed, the Father's Brow more smooth'd to them, and the Distance by Degrees abated."[92] Not remembering the original pressure, the child makes the disingenuous inference that it is naturally or inevitably drawn to parental identification.

With a properly instituted socialization, the child will only experience an increasing confirmation of its urges for independence. As "Reason comes to speak in them," young people "may be allowed greater liberty," for "the Discipline and Government of Pupilage" is to be "relaxed as fast as their Age, Discretion, and Good Behaviour could allow it," as they are "allowed the liberties and freedom suitable to their Ages." By adapting to children's particular "Natures and Aptitudes," their "natural Genius and Constitution," parents will be seen as supportive of their "natural Freedom." This further bonds children to their parents as "their best, as their only sure Friends": "Love of you make them . . . obedient and dutiful." Children looking to their future will embrace and work to be worthy of their increasing range of discretion: "Children have as much a Mind to shew that they are free, that their own good Actions come from themselves, that they are absolute and independent, as any of the proudest of you grown men." Given broad areas where they are *"perfectly free and unrestrained,"* they will be "satisfied that they act . . . freely" and pursue available activities with great "Pleasure" and a "due and free composure."[93]

The secret of course is that control is already firmly in place in the inner recesses of the child's being: "if [parents] have established the Authority they should" and "the Awe . . . be once got," then "a Look or a Word from the Father or Mother" will "be sufficient in most cases." Thus, the child is in fact "in the State you . . . desire . . . whereby you will always have hold upon him."[94] The memory of coercion, the illegitimate, involuntary foundation of human society and personal character, is erased, too dangerous and unsettling to recall, replaced by the "memory" of a voluntary contract, a free and loving relation willingly entered into and abundantly reciprocated. This reconstituted past appears to be a vast improvement on Hobbes's pressured and flawed bargain. A deep attachment to and identification with authority, the desire to please it and be conformingly self-reliant, relief that one was never on one's own nor wished to be, reconciles liberal independence with societal order. The internal mechanism producing consent to future constraints is permanently in place, validated like the Protestant relation to God by the deep feeling of voluntarism now rather than any logical or contractual reality. As a result, the individual never grasps its own character as agent. It is content, its future defined as the smooth developmental accretion of reason and independence unimpeded by dangerous or rebellious wishes.

By constructing a narrative of developing freedom superimposed on a primordial, unremembered reversal into the parental orbit, Locke promulgated the myth of the free agent. Individuals experience their adaptive compliance as freedom, their unimpeded motion into established channels with a proper directionality as a willing movement. A deep anxiety exists about breaking step or altering direction, but it is easily avoidable. With socially constructed freedom replacing self-validation in the normal course of development, the crisis of self-referentiality is over. The child looking within no longer even imagines Eden, but thinks of its duty and its fear of shame and disgrace. Ultimately held to a self-obligation that it feels but neither it nor any logician can explain, it moves quickly forward, self-enforcing, self-demanding, self-initiating, to the markings of progress in the channels: "We ought to think so well of our selves, as to perform those Actions which are incumbent on, and expected of us, without discomposure, without disorder," without "shamfac'dness."[95] An unbroken narrative of development from nature to culture has been achieved, as the water, diverted at the source, before it could become politically contentious for adult society, now flows unimpeded along its given course.

The "free agent" was as Locke realized an original ideal. By no means universal within emergent liberal society, it would have to be disseminated and internalized. In England, with the power of civil, religious, and familial institutions to impose these new expectations, an internalized "moral sense"—the reason or conscience of liberal Protestantism—would soon become a central faculty of the naturally "self-directing" English character. This would in turn enable later English theorists to underestimate the developmental advance achieved by liberal socialization over the natural condition. In the New World, absent such institutions, consolidating the agency character sufficiently to affirm the self-reliant powers of individual reason or morality would be a far longer and more complicated process. The specter of social disorder amidst a diverse and tenuously socialized citizenry would propel novel institutions of consensual socialization, most notably popular religion, into the front rank of the nation-building process. Although the idyllic discourse of Lockean liberty in the United States would equally proclaim agency as a natural condition, the institutional constitution of a "rational," which is to say self-regulating, agency citizenry within a society of "self-evident" norms would take the entire nineteenth century.

As participation in consensual activities came in time to be seen as the product of unconstrained personal choice, Americans would become increasingly susceptible to the claims of "free agency." Regarding themselves as the land of *The Second Treatise,* they would be perplexed about the prevalence of conformity and mass accommodation, the increasing power of society and loss of moral and spiritual individualism. They would prefer to associate these images with Hobbes's bad (or anti-)liberalism rather than Locke's good liberalism. Trumpeting the "free individual" and "free society," they would not realize that the transfer of authority and construction of agency lay deep within their psychosocial development. The Declaration and Revolution, affirming the power to start anew without prior constraints, would seal the loss of historical memory upon the prior loss of personal memory. Agency society would be thereby left to emerge in silence.

Lacking the insights of Locke's *Education,* Americans would not recognize the Protestant and Hobbesian narratives condensed within the liberal rendering of a willing transfer of personal warrant and the consensual reconstitution of collective authority. They would celebrate the many variants of the free agent now prepared to step forward in their "naturalized" garb, from the free proprietor and free democratic citizen to the free market actor and entrepreneur to the now ubiquitous individual who presumably pursues rational choice. When Locke's resolution of a naturalized free agent was tested in contemporary times by the reemergence of instinctual individualism, new dangers of social fragmentation, and growth of organizational society, Lockean America would try to salvage the idyll of liberty. But as this rhetoric only fed the forces challenging liberal constraint, the underlying reliance on its predecessors for having shaped a deeper (and involuntary) reversal of anarchic passions and the constitution of normative authority by the always tenuous effort of the collective will was slowly retrieved from cultural amnesia. Relinquishing the Lockean idyll, the project of rescuing liberal society shifted to restoring the functionality of the agency character, even if that meant recalling from exile its two great narratives of integration.

II

*The Ascendancy of Agency
and the First New Nation*

6

The Great Awakening and the Emergent Culture of Agency

It is impossible to relate the convulsions into which the whole
Country is thrown by a set of Enthusiasts that strole about
harangueing the admiring Vulgar in *extempore* nonsense.

—Charles Brockwell

The Revolution was effected before the war commenced . . . in the
minds and hearts of the people; a change in their religious sentiments, of their duties and obligations.

—John Adams

The least controverted fact of American history is that "the
shot heard round the world" was fired on behalf of "liberty" and that, once
"the American Revolution . . . had succeeded," it produced a society
uniquely rooted in "these revolutionary ideals" of "freedom and equality."[1]
After all, Tom Paine, our most determined and effective advocate and Jefferson's inspiration for the Declaration, had indelibly characterized as our national project "to begin the world over again" as "an asylum" of "freedom,"
now "hunted round the globe" for "mankind."[2] For participants in that
struggle and later commentators, revolutionaries and Loyalists, English and
American, through the many variants of American civil religion even to our
own time, the revolutionary struggle unleashed a "contagion of liberty"
whose victory elevated the project of creating "a free society of free individuals" to the central place in American history.[3] Even the most skeptical of
scholars of that period, Charles Beard, noted approvingly the "prophecy"
of a revolutionary-era preacher who envisioned his land as a future "seat
of knowledge and freedom . . . for many millions of the human species,"
thereby becoming an "asylum for the injured and oppressed in all parts of
the globe" and fulfilling "everything that is excellent and happy to a greater
height of perfection and glory than the world has ever yet seen!"[4] The emi-

nent American historian John Higham more recently asserted that "the American creed lives on, but only one of its three pillars—the idea of human freedom—remains essentially unchallenged."[5]

The Importance of Colonial Religion

Because of its centrality in creating the national narrative and ensuing sense of identity, this conception of the American project is, I will suggest, the greatest of our national misunderstandings. The War of Independence, following upon the English Revolution and the evolution of colonial society, was one critical stage in the construction of agency civilization. While the agency character of the American Revolution will be the subject of the next chapter, any study of the period leading up to independence must contend with the long shadow on American historiography cast by its mythic character as a struggle for freedom. Nowhere is this more evident than in the study of colonial religion and the Great Awakening beginning in the 1730s, the pivotal event in the emergence of a distinctive American culture. It has been called by religious historians "the first . . . creation of indigenous religious cultures," a "turning point in the Christianization of the colonies," the "beginning of America's identity as a nation—the starting point of the Revolution," and if too boldly the "American declaration of independence from Europe" and the source of the "American tradition" of populist politics.[6]

And yet it has not surfaced as an event of the first magnitude in the larger historical account of the formation of the first new nation. Scholars have recognized at the center of eighteenth-century American culture the three parallel discourses which Locke had developed as the foundation of agency civilization: liberal political thought, Protestant religion, and Enlightenment rationalism.[7] The major histories of the Revolution and its causes until a generation ago, including those of Bailyn and Gordon Wood, routinely gave greatest weight to the secular discourses while according colonial religion little mention.[8] The periodic efflorescences of colonial religiosity including the Awakening were misinterpreted as returns to earlier colonial piety out of step with the progress toward liberal instantiation.[9] Recent broadly distributed scholarly accounts of the nation's history and founding values such as Pauline Maier's *American Scripture,* Eric Foner's *Story of American Freedom,* and Thomas Fleming's *Liberty! The American Revolution,* companion to the PBS series, continue either to ignore the religious role or to characterize it as the overmatched precursor to an emergent liberal ascendancy. The result is to reinforce the already widespread liberal narrative in the popular understanding.

This misunderstanding and neglect, once defensible, are no longer. Since the 1960s, a decisive role has increasingly been accorded to colonial religion by historians of the period. Beginning with Clarence C. Goen's *Revivalism and Separatism in New England, 1740–1800* (1962) and Alan Heimert's *Religion and the American Mind: From the Great Awakening to the Revolution* (1966), numerous scholars, including William G. McLoughlin, Sacvan Bercovitch, Harry S. Stout, Gary B. Nash, Rhys Isaac, Stephen A. Marini, Patricia U. Bonomi, Mark Noll, J. C. D. Clark, Nathan O. Hatch, and Ruth Bloch among others, have dramatically challenged the dominant national account.[10] It is clear now that the political and rationalist discourses had spread rather thinly in colonial society before the revolutionary ferment, primarily among the well-educated religious and social elites.

In his recent effort to redress the balance, Wood identifies the traditional oversight as a failure to consider "the prevailing beliefs of ordinary people in this premodern age," for whom Protestantism constituted "the principal means" by which they "ordered and explained the world and made it meaningful." This sharpens the problem with earlier historiography: "Could such a prevalent, popular, and powerful mode of understanding and fulfillment as religion have been so easily smothered by Whig political ideas and the reason of the Enlightenment?"[11] Perry Miller had revealed the fallacy of the dominant view long ago: "A pure rationalism . . . might have declared the independence of the folk, but it could never have inspired them to fight for it."[12] Regarding colonial culture as a whole, J. C. D. Clark writes of the religious underpinnings of the American Revolution: "American political discourse was preoccupied with its own issues. The idea of the existence of a universal secular idiom is difficult to reconcile with the richness, diversity and *sectarian* nature of colonial American publishing."[13] Furthermore, given the prevalence of "sermons by American clergymen and lay religious exhorters" in an active revival culture "delivered orally" to "an even wider public" of "the illiterate" and the other hardworking common people whose culture consisted of Bible study and Sunday worship, Ruth Bloch concludes that colonial "popular culture was particularly preoccupied with religious and domestic concerns."[14]

Pursuing the many levels of colonial culture, contemporary historians have established the continuing influence of religion and its impact on the Revolution. The second half of the eighteenth century, once framed as a transition from the religious orientation of early immigrants to the political focus of the revolutionary era, is now regarded as a time "of rising vitality in religious life, an era not of decline but the reverse—of proliferation and growth." The once prevailing view, what Bonomi calls "the dark theme of declension," resulted from a focus on the traditional elites, whose precipitous weakening during this period can now be explained by the dramatic rise of popular and sectarian religion after 1740 throughout colonial society.[15]

The failure of this work to make an impact on the American popular imagination stems from two conceptual problems addressed by the narrative of American agency. The first, taken up in this chapter, is to explain within the ferment and growing disorganization of colonial religion the major Protestant parties and their roles as well as the complex nature of their agreements and disagreements. The full dynamic of the period requires the inclusion of three internal groups: the traditional but increasingly worldly and rationalist Presbyterian and Congregational denominations of the seaboard elites; the intermittent revivalist wing of these denominations, seeking a return to early Puritan piety, whose greatest exponent was Jonathan Edwards; and the populist denominations (Separatists, Baptists, and later Methodists) and more radical sects propounding through revivals a democratic, egalitarian piety of immediate conversion and sanctification. The intense differences which drove the sectarian controversies and internal political struggles in the revolutionary period make it difficult without glossing over core disputes to access their common values. Recognizing that, even though the parties caught in the religious battles largely failed themselves to grasp shared elements, their own discourses led ultimately to the war against a common enemy enables us to search with Gordon Wood for "more deeply rooted determinants" and underlying historical commonalities.[16]

At the same time, with these parties routinely conflated, incompletely identified, or miscast, the crucial differences retreat from view. From the perspective of agency, the Edwardsian revivalists, typically grouped with the sectarians because of a similar commitment to revivalist piety, are much closer to the elites regarding their vision of social and characterological organization. With regard to their relative influence, the elite, once the heroes of revolutionary radicalism, are now seen as only one element of the colonial insurgency. The Edwardsian movement has in turn been pushed forward into this vacuum of cultural leadership by a vast scholarly process that exaggerates its influence on the radicalizing dynamic of popular society. The populist insurgents, the sectarian challengers of Puritan society and Puritan religious practice, are now receiving ever greater attention both as the force behind the second and unduly marginalized radical phase of the First Great Awakening and as the source of nineteenth-century religious consciousness and organization. Yet their larger role in transforming prerevolutionary society and culture requires further recognition of the Awakening as an event of the first magnitude. The failure to grasp this broader impact has led proponents of colonial "pluralism," what Charles L. Cohen calls a "post-Puritan paradigm," to question deeply the coherence of the period. Given "the perceived absence of a unifying thesis statement," the possibility of an "overarching scheme" or "distinctive shape," scholars have thus far wished for without locating "a new kind of historical language" providing a long overdue "synthetic history" of the period.[17]

The second conceptual problem, treated in Chapter 7, involves the relationship between the colonial religious dynamic and the national founding. Just as the first issue calls for a new understanding of colonial society, this one renders problematic the very meaning of the United States. For the popular and radical sectarians, who provided much of the personnel for the war against England, were hesitant supporters of that war and were locked in continuous political opposition against the other two parties whose cause it was. Recognizing their importance challenges the canonical understanding of the Revolution which embodies the perspective of the elites, and particularly their liberalizing, worldly outlook. Yet the important revisionist work emphasizing religious centrality in colonial life, the religious influence on and sectarian contribution to the Revolution, and the way "evangelical Protestantism" was to "dominate" antebellum "American culture" immediately afterward, hesitates before the received national founding. The Revolution remains either the consensual pursuit of the free liberal society or its achievement despite the revolutionaries' more complex agendas. The religious elements are in turn defined in terms not of their vision of postrevolutionary society but of their contribution to the liberal settlement. But the narrative of a liberal revolution does not accord with the new evidence. Wood thus acknowledges "the relation of religion to the American Revolution" to be an intractable "problem": "We sense that there should be a relationship, but we are not at all clear what it is or even ought to be."[18]

This scholarly disarray on both matters has impeded the formation of "a controlling narrative worth the name."[19] The underlying but unspoken agreements which shaped colonial society amidst its more visible conflicts and made a unified war against England possible can be understood only as the outgrowth and elaboration of the parties' common origin in English religious opposition. Given the narrow segment of English society which provided colonial immigrants, such that "while less than a tenth of Englishmen in 1776 were Dissenters, more than three quarters of Americans were," Clark has proposed that "American exceptionalism . . . be relocated on the territory of American religious experience."[20] That is to say, for the most part colonial Americans were partisans of a Protestant agency settlement. At the same time, the very controversies that rent colonial and revolutionary society concerned the ultimate shape of that settlement. The Puritan elite, defined by its English experience of opposition, imagined itself the consensual defenders of a radical new polity in the New World. They never understood that, within that thin band of settlers, they were a conservative party in power opposing English radical populism, insignificant in England but an ever greater force in the colonies. Within these poles of elite and egalitarian agency grew the dynamic and discourse of a distinctive American culture, and in evolving form the unique common ground within which its political struggles have henceforth been waged.

Reconsidering the Great Awakening

Central to the colonial formation of an indigenous discourse and identity and as the great popular movement preceding the Revolution, the Great Awakening looms as the critical event in our recovery of the Revolution and national narrative and paradoxically achieves coherence itself only with reference to its subsequent impact. As a result of its importance, its meaning has been hotly contested. Lost until recently by the focus on elites was its second stage. As the public emergence of sectarian consciousness whose direct outgrowths were the internal phase of the Revolution against domestic elites and following it Jeffersonian and Jacksonian populism, this movement, in short, represents the initial coalescence of those forces which most defined the character of the young republic. As such, it challenged the elites' religious and political control at the time as well as later readings of the period inscribing that dominance. The established denominations, which regarded themselves as the national religious establishment, were in both their ecclesiastical and Edwardsian revivalist wings shocked and permanently unsettled by the radical turn in the Awakening. Confronted by unsustainable contradictions in their doctrines and practice and their failure to reestablish institutional control, they gladly inflated the conservative phase with its renewal of piety challenged by "many inflammatory and revolutionary elements."[21] The popular insurgency has been treated as a continuation of this phase, asserting demands for institutional reforms—choice of membership, congregational independence, and denominational equality—to better achieve Calvinist goals.[22]

More controversially, the Great Awakening as a whole challenges the liberal narrative of a secular civilization emerging before the Revolution out of vestigial religious mists. Explaining the rise of a post-theocratic, inclusive liberal society has been at the center of the modernization agenda of "most American historians of recent times."[23] Finding the Awakening too close to the Revolution, the defining event of American liberalism to which the inevitable logic of colonial history presumably led, liberal historiography both minimized its influence while supporting the inflation of its Puritan character. In this way, the liberal triumph was ensured over either an obviously outmoded—rather than increasingly ascendant—religion taking its last gasp or Puritans now reinterpreted as proto-liberals waiting for a secular settlement.[24] The scholarly result was a "modern distinction between sacred and profane," a divorce between "the studies of religion and politics" in American culture and especially eighteenth-century America. Alternatives to the ascendant narrative have been precluded as these discourses now "go their own separate ways in virtual isolation," acting "like neighbors who are not on speaking terms."[25]

The sectarian proponents of the Awakening were themselves in no position then, and have not been since, to wrest the historical focus from the establishment chroniclers of the first phase. The surfacing of a "potent and permanent" sectarian role at this moment, while acknowledged by sectarian historians and even likened to the radicalizing dynamic of the English Revolution, was obscured by the origin of the radical phase of the Awakening out of its initial conservative impetus.[26] Furthermore, the confusion about the impact of a decentralized unleashing of long-veiled spiritual and institutional demands among disparate populations hindered any overview.[27] The divergent groups of emerging sectarians, the party of uncompromised agency, were focused on their own spiritual renewal and doctrinal struggles, on local rather than national goals. This precluded a central perspective from which to explain the larger process of sectarian emergence. Furthermore, despite their geometric growth, the sects turned ever more inward as the vision of a successful Awakening foundered in late colonial society. After the

Revolution, the focus of sectarian revivalism remained on personal and local community renovation together with a rejection of the increasing worldliness of the young republic. By the postbellum period the secularizing dynamic of American liberal culture was inhospitable to the notion of a sectarian American Revolution.

With a new skepticism about the liberal and denominational narratives, Wood concludes that "this neglect of religion and the American Revolution is about to end."[28] By searching once again behind elite institutional disputes and ideological debates, behind the claims of nominal "leaders" and their subsequent champions, one finds it possible to resurrect the role of ordinary colonial citizens and their explosive populist demands. Recent insights about the radical new convictions, practices, and organizations surfacing in the Awakening now enable us to identify it as a progressive rather than retrogressive force. Overcoming the anachronistic way even its "defenders often constructed continuities between older revivalism and the Awakening by cloaking itinerancy's market-related novelties in the rhetoric of tradition," we can identify how it sought to "transform the religious world." Responding to a "dynamic eighteenth century growth" in Atlantic culture, it generated an "openness in the religious sphere to an expanding array of choices for belief and behavior in an increasingly mobile, pluralistic world."[29]

By distinguishing the conservative and radical phases of the Awakening and reframing older theological disputes in terms of their cultural significance at the time, it is now possible from the perspective of larger Anglo-American developments to grasp the greater movement's transformative role. This was the time when full agency individualism burst the bonds of institutional containment and its own defensive posture to demand social legitimacy. Moderate and radical sectarianism had arrived with Winthrop and been fed continuously by the religious springs of colonial culture as well as by immigration, internal dissension, the freedom and inaccessibility of the frontier, and the dynamic of sectarianism and individualism within mainstream Protestantism. Stirred into action despite continuing repression by the Edwardsian call to spiritual renewal, sectarian insurgents invoked convictions and practices whose inspiration was the earlier English insurgency and *not* the more recent colonial governing wing of Protestant dissent.

Emerging from this earlier ferment, they resurrected the English dissenting logic of radical opposition and innovation, pursuing it toward the most extreme Commonwealth forms of universal sanctification. In reaching beyond denomination and parish structure, they hoped to engage peripatetic individuals no longer subject to parish boundaries and loyalties through personal, affective, and internal connections, supporting their adaptation to the realities of colonial life. Appealing to the absolute discretion of the individual will and conscience, they irreversibly transformed the locus of authorization for religious practice and belief. Defining the goal of spiritual faith as the sinless perfection of the "New Birth," becoming "regenerate souls . . . savingly renewed in the spirit of their minds," in shifting the theological emphasis they redirected American religious experience to living as realized agents on earth.[30]

What neither Awakeners nor anyone else ever expected was the receptivity of colonial society to this movement. In retrospect, the scarcely visible work of the 150 years after Plymouth and Jamestown leading to and including the Awakening was the steadily increasing integration of the agency character within the colonial citizen. Under conditions of economic and social mobility, vast available space, religious diversity, and individual proprietorship, the colonies were reproducing and accelerating the cultural dynamic of English individualism—the very seedbed of the religious shifts—in the prerevolutionary period. Allowed ever greater choice and self-reliance, immigrants similarly utilized expanding individualism to develop capacities for personal initiative and discretion as well as skepticism about institutional prerogatives. The first issue of *Poor Richard's Almanack* in 1733 observed: "Each Age of Man new Fashions doth invent; / Things which are old, young Men do not esteem: / What pleas'd our Fathers; doth not us content; / What flourish'd then, we out of fashion deem."[31]

With British institutions distant and unwatchful, the colonists—elites and populace alike—were consolidating this new individualism under the shadow of imperial order. The result was a burgeoning culture of agency in late colonial society. The religious and commercial elites, progressives in Britain and opponents of monarchic dominance, Anglican establishment and England's cultural hegemony, utilized the Reformation and Locke as the basis of their own liberal understanding of social order. The populace, while subject to internal religious, social, and commercial hierarchies, included the most progressive and resolute proponents of religious individualism. Though a fragmented minority, these activists continued to organize and proselytize within communities descended from religious dissidents and, even where now secularizing, were seeking greater independence, while impatient with institutional restraints. Local elites sought to contain the radicalization of agency values by linking them to institutional subordination and hierarchies of control (hence "proto-agent"). But the proliferation of radical doctrines and individual options, the absence of a traditionally entrenched establishment, and the limited reach of existing institutions made the dynamic virtually impossible to contain. In the colonial cultural marketplace created by this relative power vacuum, institutions both religious and secular in order to gain constituencies were forced to reshape themselves in response to popular demands. This required a continual adaptation to emerging if inchoate agency values.

As the principles and practices of individual agency spread throughout colonial America, the result was an ever-growing challenge to hierarchies. Once the elites accelerated the process of institutional and doctrinal fragmentation by sharply contesting among themselves and with the rising citizenry of the radical Awakening, a more thorough and universal agency emerged along with reduced constraints on individual conduct and belief. The whole society was quickly awash in personal religious choice. With a Hobbesian dynamic of multiplying interpretations, agendas, and claims of legitimacy again unleashed, the proto-agency and imperial strategies of containment were doomed. As the nonreligious agency discourses were in turn mobilized and radicalized, the colonies were set on a collision course with imperial and colonial opponents of uncompromised agency values. Together these discourses moved the nation into the struggle to realize an agency world. Given the distinctive features and progressive constituencies of colonial society, the result would be a different outcome from the English Revolution, that is, a radically modern form of nationhood and the transformation of internal institutions.

The Puritan Transition

In tracing the emergence of a new religious sensibility, by far the major component in laying the groundwork for the nascent agency character, the task is to explain how its doctrines and even more its practices emerged out of the Puritan establishment. New England was only one site of a sectarian revolt that in time reached all regions of colonial America, but given its unique character as a religious society, it was the locus of the most intense and self-conscious framing of the controversies. Colonial and particularly Great Awakening theological debates over infant baptism, the ministerial role, lay preaching, establishment, taxation, separation, and the certainty of personal godliness, uncomfortably contained within a Calvinist framework, are seething with the implicit conflict between the proto-agent constraints of orthodoxy and the free will individualism prefiguring the early-nineteenth-century Americanized religion of explicit personal agency. Religious practice is important to consider because the efforts of elites to retain doctrinal consistency and of sects to retain legitimacy belied profound shifts in religious behavior in which free will, individualism, self-confident sanctification, and egalitarianism increasingly infused dissenting religious life.

With clarification of the underlying dynamic of agency, the true "Puritan dilemma" is now apparent: the ill-suitedness of Puritanism to colonial America. Forged as an oppositional movement, the Puritans upon assuming local governance in the colonies were forced to take on the new role of political control. Containing "a mixed multitude" including "many unworthy persons"—"so many wicked persons and profane people"—which "the country" had become "pestered with" and subordinating them to "visible saints," to that limited number of "religious men" being "His people" in "outward as spiritual things," was an obvious necessity to retain the character of the nascent religious communities. Far more difficult, given the world-transforming expectation Puritans placed on their members to "be as a Citty upon a Hill" with "the eies of all people . . . uppon us," and their focus on personal salvation with its expansive possibilities, was containing the mobilized saints themselves.[32] Sustaining ordered and controlled communities required an authority to enforce collective limits. Janice Knight has described the resulting internal struggle in the Massachusetts colony as the optimistic millennialists who continued "presupposing a regenerate audience" lost control during an early and decisive conservative drift to the more realistic preparationists with their deep suspicions of human motives.[33] Reflecting ruefully on how "wickedness" and "sundry notorious sins" were still able to "grow and break forth here, in a land where the same was so much witnessed at and so narrowly looked into, and severely punished when it was known," William Bradford admitted that his community was led to "fear and tremble" at the specter of "our corrupt natures, which are so hardly bridled, subdued and mortified."[34] John Winthrop, who had on arrival spoken of the "bond" of "Love" and "brotherly affeccion" sustaining the colony, challenged in 1645 by his community, now spoke of "that wild beast" of "natural, corrupt liberties" which is "incompatible and inconsistent with authority, and cannot endure the least restraint of the most just authority."[35]

The result was what Harry S. Stout has called "the coercive and estab-
lishmentarian aspects of the New England Way," a corporate organization of
the community linking church and state in an ordered Bible commonwealth
under the leadership of ministers who "could and did enact unpopular legislation in accordance with scriptural precept." To ground these religious commonwealths, Puritans developed a new form of "sacred and exclusive covenant between themselves and God." Distinct from the individual believer's
covenant of grace, this bond established the collective foundation and special religious mission of the community and authorized the leadership and
regulations to sustain them.[36] Under trying conditions of unprecedented
mobility and voluntarism, these communities—as the English dissenters
could not—forged postmonarchic forms of worldly citizenship, collective
authority, and membership that made modern political order possible.[37] Religious and community leaders also preached and instructed young and old
on the paramount role of personal responsibility in maintaining community
cohesion absent external coercion, setting patterns of internalized norms essential to the rise of modern individualist society.

Yet the establishment of a corporate society with nonconsensual (proto-
agent) elites was to be fatally undermined by the agency dynamic intrinsic
to Puritan culture: its individualist legacy of personal faith; the tensions
between its hierarchic doctrines of governance and its religious values as
well as religious and secular practice in the new society; the incompatibility
of its commitment to faith over works with the worldly demands of community building; the relentless shift of social pressures in a situation of weakly
regulated individualism toward nontraditional incentives and expectations;
and the growing presence of cultural movements and values more adaptive
to these conditions. This was a fragile equilibrium ever under siege; "a mere
six years after landfall . . . Governor John Winthrop felt compelled to admit
the collapse of this 'holy experiment.'" The community was forced into significant repression in the struggle against voluntarism, but these belated and
ineffective efforts only compromised its doctrine and sense of direction, distorting the historical assessment of its project. Their pessimism only grew as
Puritans imagined an America very different from the one being formed.[38]

Having demanded individual discretion in England in one's religious
responsibility, and often themselves of sectarian and enthusiastic backgrounds, Puritans brought with them a theology replete with tendencies undermining predestinarian Calvinism. Their very emigration was framed as
the decision, in Thomas Shepard's words, to walk through "a wide doore . . .

of liberty" that was "set open."[39] Increase Mather told the colonists in 1670 how his father, Richard, a dissenter in England before the Civil War, demanded to "speak for himself, or declare the reasons which convinced his Conscience of the unlawfulness of that *Conformity* which they required." As Increase's son Cotton later wrote, they were *"to Leave their Native Country"* in order to "seek a Refuge for their Lives and Liberties, with Freedom, for the *Worship of God* . . . according to the Light of their Consciences."[40] Early colonists were continuously advised by such as John Winthrop to "ask thy conscience," to "satisfy" their "tender or good conscience in time of trial."[41] Thomas Hooker urged them to take personal responsibility, "look sin in the face, and discern it to the full," then go about "redressing of our hearts and ways." In pursuing *"the way of Salvation,"* believers must accept that *"their conscience now hath more scope, and the light of reason hath more liberty, and allowance to express that they know,"* which *"nothing now can withstand and hinder."*[42] The striving, as the early Puritan Michael Wigglesworth put it, was for the personal sanctity of "a new heart" and "for a paradise in this world." Even in the face of a "wretched backsliding heart" and the "prevailing corruptions in this world,"[43] the Puritans sought a "happy deliverance from all evil . . . in life" as well as "in death."[44] They sought to be *"the pure"* to whom *"all things are pure"*—in Cotton Mather's terms, "Patterns of *Holiness* and *Usefulness* upon Earth" and an "example" whether "but unto [one's] neighborhood . . . only on a ten-stringed instrument" or "upon a ten-thousand-stringed instrument" or "loud sounding organ, having as many millions of pipes as there be people under him."[45] In this way, they would achieve not only *"the Perfection of Christians"* but also *"the Perfection of Churches,"* what Edward Johnson called in his history "a new Heaven, and a new Earth . . . new Churches, and a new Common-wealth."[46]

The rhetoric of individualism affected every aspect of American Puritan culture. Freedom of personal faith meant that "servitude" under "tyrannicall Prelates" was intolerable, that to "submit" to false "ceremonies and become slaves to them" was "sin."[47] In fact, a legalistic orientation was *itself*—despite the move toward an increasingly formalistic governance—a sign of the servant mentality, a submission to "the yoke of bondage . . . the curse of the moral law," from which "Christ's gospel liberty" offered "deliverance."[48] The authority of conscience and Scripture superseded "the irrational or unscriptural traditions of the Elders": "It is foolishness for any man to pin his faith upon another man's sleeve, or take any man for a perfect pattern of faith." Individuals thus had the new "Covenant" equally accessible, for "the Good Lord" will "enlighten the minds of *all* those who seek for the truth" properly, and aims to "enlighten the *whole* world with His glory."[49] The new communities were "knit together" to "each other's good" and "the whole" by "mutual consent and covenant,"[50] based in "the People, in whom fundamentally all power lyes," and by their "free consent" the "foundation of authority is laid."[51] Personal discretion was crucial for men and women to "be able to govern themselves" both as responsible individuals and in society, since the people were responsible for "choosing such persons" who "will promote the common good" to lead them.[52] As Thomas Hooker preached in 1638, by "a free choice the hearts of the people will be more inclined to the love of the person [chosen] and more ready to yield [obedience]."[53]

The immense danger of this "open door" was that it might become "a broken wall" in the new land for those "many" wishing to have "crept out," a place continually through which "all ways were sought . . . to get out."[54] The covenant of community order was utilized to stem this individualism, but could do so only by embracing doctrinal claims of control that were either internally inconsistent or in conflict with Puritan religious commitments as well as with larger evolving social and religious tendencies. Within Puritan doctrine, the New World task of defending established governance led to the assertion of an "express biblical warrant" for the product of those human legislative efforts "set forth by civil and ecclesiastical 'fathers'" and a corresponding "duty of submission" to "our Superiours . . . both in church or commonwealth" never afforded by dissenters to the English regime.[55]

Problematically for theoretical consistency in a community where the people had originally been designated a buffer ensuring the godly society against the "great blasphemies" and "licentious abuse" to which human power was heir, and where the lessons of individualism and popular power were more palpable every day, they were now instructed unconditionally to obey human authorities: a legalistic order "to guide them and bind them to their good Behaviour";[56] magistrates who would serve as providers of those "bankes" or "wholesome laws" to ensure that the "raging Sea" of "Sins" did not "overwhelm all"; a hierarchy of "Superiours" and "Elders" to provide the order of "Places" and "Relations" in the community.[57] Godly legitimation was insisted on for the specific institutions and offices of worldly control, as implicitly for its holders and leaders, clergy, magistrates, social superiors, and parents, as bearers of "authority from God" and as God's "Viceroyes" who were "sent by God himself" and "set over us" to "Honour, Submit to, and Obey."[58]

Though deriving from personal conviction, this obedience at first estab-lished the consensual commitment to Puritan communal authority but, given the conditionality of God's worldly promises, ironically restored the individualizing tendencies by requiring one's continual performance of good works. The "two covenants" of Puritan life—personal faith and community cohesion—were thus pervaded by "separate and contradictory logics."[59] The insistence on tangible performance judged by the community, essential to enforce and organize the project of community building, undermined the supraworldly thrust of Puritan salvation. At the same time, it more subtly empowered individuals—relative to both God and the community—by au-thorizing far greater human capacity or agency than the theological cove-nant permitted. Individuals on this great mission, as Winthrop announced on the *Arbella,* were "Stewards" who "prosper shall that Sions building mind," what Urian Oakes, early president of Harvard, called "created Agents" or *"second causes"* in "partnership & fellowship with Himself," and further *"Co-workers* with Himself" with "all that is requisite on their parts" as "Means" to attain "His Ends" and "His own designs."[60] As participants in "providential history," they had been cast as "God's special instruments en-trusted with the task of preparing the way for messianic deliverance."[61]

The demands of forging an actual collective history *under their control* only strengthened the worldly dimensions embodied in the communal covenant. Particularly after the Commonwealth's collapse in 1660, the pressures upon this Protestant remnant sharply increased, as England was being "covered" once again in "darknesse," to be *"like a beacon upon the top of a mountaine"* and to survive as a model covenanted community.[62] Moreover, from King Philip's War to the flourishing of the colonies to the periodic revivals of pi-ety, each demonstration of human accomplishment reinforced the role of human capacity and importance and legitimacy of works. The further de-sire to stabilize the new communities in the face of severe uncertainties and forces for change brought greater legitimation to "ministers and magis-trates" acting "to root out heresy and preserve a pure orthodoxy" with their claim to "officially stand nearer to God than others do."[63]

The emphasis on works led to an increasing normalization of religious practice. From the Halfway Covenant to the early-eighteenth-century em-phasis on routinized virtuous conduct and a legalist orientation, a growing Anglicization and integration into the imperial system overtook even the dissenting colonies. The shift from piety created a wedge not only for the Edwardsians, who attempted to straddle the call to faith with the political project of nation building, but also the sects who could accept neither the de-emphasis on conviction nor the embrace of worldly hierarchy. The irony of this wedge—and evidence of a dynamic beyond Puritan control—was its origin in the Puritans themselves. This is emblematically revealed by the theological confusion and transparent hypocrisy of the ministers interrogating a resolute Anne Hutchinson at her heresy trial in 1638, shocked by her intimate knowledge of and reliance on their own principles of Puritan conviction.[64]

If the Puritans were initially pulled apart by their own theoretical tensions, the escalating dynamic of voluntarist individualism further undermined the efforts to retain dependence and hierarchy. The greatest unifying and defining experience of the larger collection of colonists who had to be governed was their common migration, a defining act of both severance and self-determination, "the best choice" despite "perpetuall banishment from their native soile," the "great enterprise" in Winthrop's own words, to "choose life, that wee, and our Seede, may live." The ever present opportunities for mobility rendered consent the de facto basis of town government.[65] Moreover, as settlers "forged new businesses, created new colleges, and carved new cities out of the woods," they garnered inexorably a new sense of personal worth and capacity as well as an increasing experience of power relative to community norms and practices, both social and religious.[66] Patricia Bonomi has emphasized the pervasive lay experience of leaving established communities to set up and govern new religious fellowships as the transforming education in democracy that prepared the colonists for a new kind of society.[67] Moreover, the religious conception of community elites dedicated to the public good was continuously eroded in the popular mind by their transparently personal pursuit of property, commerce, and speculation and their use of public authority to further it. Given that "the theory of government and the practice of politics was increasingly contradictory," the dynamic of separating into new communities and increasing pursuit of individual interests could not be stilled by claims of organic community or of submission to God's predestined will.[68]

The forces sweeping colonial culture swiftly punctured all elite pretentions and presumptions. Two stories will illustrate. Winthrop relates in his journal of a master who, having to sell his oxen to pay his servant his wages, decides to let him go. "The servant answered, he would serve him for more of his cattle. 'But how shall I do,' saith the master, 'when all my cattle are gone?' The servant replied, 'You shall then serve me, and so you may then have your cattle again.'" Bradford tells how in the early settlement goods were distributed by need. The reactions were symptomatic: the younger men who worked harder resisted working for others "without recompense"; the stronger refused in turn equal division with the weak; the old rejected being treated the same as "the meaner and younger sort"; and wives felt that helping other families was "a kind of slavery."[69]

Limits imposed neither by assertions of hierarchy nor by theological inability could withstand the multiplying claims of individual entitlement. Once set in motion in the new setting, the worldly support for and necessity of individual self-determination reinforced the corresponding religious values, creating resistance to presumptions of authority and preeminence. The internal colonial elites, convinced of the justness of their reformed society as well as their right to govern, responded with more of what was not working—a defense of their hierarchy while casting blame on the populace. But spiritual and social expectations were brimming over, expanding the diversity of cultural expressions. It was for all, religious and secular, "an unfamiliar world, a world for which by early training and normal expectation [individuals] had not been prepared," a world "open to question, concern, and decision." As "Poor Richard" put it, "Blind are the Sons of Men, few of the Kind / Know their *chief* Interest, or knowing, mind" that interest.[70]

The Puritan community collectively, and each individually, faced a heightened sense of drift and insecurity, the "serious disjunction between its ideal values . . . and its operational values."[71] Its determined efforts at mobilization in the face of a profoundly unsustainable vision fed fears of being a declining, unrealized experiment, "desolate and forsaken."[72] Puritanism was never able to overcome its own voluntarist wing let alone sectarianism, as the possibilities and powers expanding in everyday activities cried out to be clarified and consolidated rather than denounced. The individuals shaping this new land needed an understanding of their destiny more reflective of their emergent cultural values. No one foresaw that dissenting sects would in the name of piety draw upon the new voluntarism and sense of individual capacity, just as no one expected the resulting diversity to require the shift from a religious to a political settlement. Yet the Great Awakening would be the first full flowering of these processes.

Sectarian Antecedents of the Awakening

The sectarian roots of mid-eighteenth-century revivalism, and specifically the radical phase which transformed the Great Awakening, date from the colonies' origins. Beyond Roger Williams's struggle for a separated church and the founding of Rhode Island, the Antinomian Crisis of 1637–38, and the founding of activist Quaker and Baptist congregations in the colonies, radical English dissent, writes Philip F. Gura, was always present.

> The experiences of the Husbandmen and other radical Puritans in seven-teenth-century New England have not been studied with any completeness because of a prevailing disposition among historians of colonial America to regard American Puritanism as relatively homogeneous. . . . [Yet] Williams, Hutchinson, and the Quakers, as significant as were their challenges to the New England Way, offer only the most memorable examples of an inescap-able fact: between 1630 and 1660 the doctrinal and ecclesiastical, as well as the imaginative, development of American Puritanism was nurtured in soil thoroughly turned by radical elements in the New Englanders' midst.[73]

Plymouth Plantation was formed by English separatists, and supported the progressive revelation of God's light to common people through per-sonal prophesying. Gura notes the proliferating groups: "By the 1640's New England's congregationalists . . . complained that the colonies harbored self-declared (or scarcely disguised) separatists, antinomians, familists, Seekers, anabaptists, Ranters, Adamites, and Quakers, all implicitly aligned against the established church system because of their insistence that an individual's personal religious experience supersede the demands of ecclesiastical tradi-tion and civil law."[74] Charles Cohen writes as well of "the steady stream of Continental migrants . . . displaced by religious quarrels, sectarians alienated from state churches, as well as members of mainstream confessions unable to assume the majority faith . . . or put off by their orthodox clergy."[75] Throughout the colonies, into the middle and southern sections, and less visibly on the margins of settled colonial society, content to develop their communities without engaging the power structures, sectarians and the re-ligiously unorthodox gathered "like Wizards to peepe and mutter" their "blasphemies."[76] With this uncontrollable spread of religious diversity, toler-ation was a poorly concealed reality of colonial life by the end of the seven-teenth century.[77]

In their practices and beliefs, the sects developed the implications of Puri-tan religious individualism, pushing for voluntary churches and the priest-hood of all believers, the limited power of magistrates over religion, and the liberty of conscience and faith. As Baptist Thomas Goold said to Puritan Thomas Shepard in a debate in 1668, "Christ dwelleth in no temple but in the heart of the believer." They turned the rhetoric of the dissenting Puritans into a mirror to examine their more recent heavy-handed ways, driving these onetime insurgents into doctrinal incoherence and the contradictions of their own oppositional history. Baptist John Thrumble told the Congregational establishment: "We came for liberty of conscience as well as yourself. You had not a patent for such a form [i.e., to establish a Standing Order and require all to conform to it] and you are not perfect. We are daily exhorted to be growing in grace and knowledge, and if you be not perfect, we are to look for light as well as you." The elites were lectured: "You did withdraw from the corruption there [in the Church of England] and so we witness against your corruptions."[78]

Sectarians asserted the purity of voluntary adult faith and the Puritans' own covenant of faith by rejecting infant baptism and affirming the right of religious separation, and in the name of toleration rejected all forms of subservience to religious elites and establishments, whether Anglican or Puritan. In their bold assertion that "an infant is no more capable of Religion than a Parrot," they captured the invalidity of institutional claims on individual belief whose other side was the transformative role of adult sanctification. They were accused by Puritans of perfectionism, and in their zeal regarding the adult potential for sanctification they often were.[79] This was, of course, the perfectionism of the self fully and voluntarily dedicated to divine ends, an individual while, beyond both English and Puritan society, fully within the discourse of radical Protestant dissent.

This increasingly attractive claim of human capacity remained largely underground from 1660 until it reached the larger public in the Great Awakening. To be sure, sectarian activity as well as the dynamic of colonial life created an increasingly personal attitude toward religious worship in frontier settlements accommodating radical religiosity and anti-authority sentiments and amidst a growing populism and individualism in the cities.[80] Sporadic revivals with a sanctificationist orientation had broken out in the 1720s. Yet the sectarians themselves, struggling to remain attached to the core religious narrative of the colonies, did not grasp the true dimensions of their innovations. As in England, they regarded their task even into the radical phase of the Great Awakening and in their later separation and sectarianism as, following Edwards, one of restoration. They wished to "return," in Separating minister Ebenezer Frothingham's important work, to "the Order of the Gospel, and the Way of walking with God in practical Godliness."[81] The sectarians even claimed that "they were the real descendants of the Puritans . . .

now seeking to repurify churches" by "only returning" to their "more scriptural ways" of a pious life and spiritual community.[82]

To sustain this sense of continuity for their voluntarist individualism and egalitarianism, the sectarians had to rewrite Puritan history in America as a realization of their own beliefs in "Liberty of Consciance" and the individual's "just Rights."[83] Isaac Backus, the Baptist leader in the colonies, spoke of his movement's "faith and practice" as "the nearest to that of the first planters of New England, of any churches now in the land,"[84] that is, to "the tradition not of John Smyth and Roger Williams . . . but of John Robinson and the purest of the Pilgrims!"[85] By tracing the historical connections back even farther to link their spiritual agenda as a continuation of the radical English phase, if only understood by them in a "muted and ambiguous" way, we can from this new perspective better understand their achievement. We see how they were under the cover of "repurification" to shatter not only colonial religious institutions but the reigning assumptions of colonial Puritan faith and practice as well.[86]

The Great Awakening

The first phase of the Awakening began in 1734 under the leadership of Jonathan Edwards, a young Congregational minister, the grandson of the great mainstream minister Samuel Stoddard and in time the greatest Calvinist theologian in America. Mainstream revivalism had long been a means for calling the wayward back to the church, and Stoddard himself had been involved in such campaigns since 1679. Its focus, like that of the later Awakening, was on conversion or spiritual rebirth, but unlike for the radical Awakeners as for early sectarians, conversion—dependent on God's inscrutable will—was never assured.[87] Revivalism was thus understood as a periodic necessity, and Edwards, who had come to share his grandfather's pulpit in Northampton, Massachusetts, continued this tradition by stirring New England between 1734 and 1737 into a new religiosity. Responding to an increasing colonial worldliness with the call to revivify mainstream denominational practice, he boldly confronted the people with the terror of their own godlessness. After a period of retrenchment, the Great Awakening reemerged in 1740 as a vast decentralized movement under the influence of such preachers as the "Grand Itinerant" George Whitefield and other itinerant leaders such as Gilbert Tennent and James Davenport. Over the next six years, religious fervor spread to ministers, commoners, and whole congregations with an increasingly radical and individualizing impact. The result was a widespread separatist and sectarian challenge to religious orthodoxies, the first time the three major Protestant parties—that is, the establishment, mainstream revivalists, and sectarians—were explicitly contending for precedence. In 1744 one quite skeptical visitor from Scotland, Dr. Alexander Hamilton, found on his travels through the colonies that a "spirit of enthusiasm" and "great confusion" had "possessed the inhabitants" of the northern and middle colonies from "the preaching of some fanaticks and New Light teachers." Observing the shift of colonial sensibilities, he noted that "few Old Testament" or traditional Calvinists remained, "all having become *New Light* men" or participants in the radical Awakening.[88]

The early revival was begun to counteract the declining power of mainstream religion. Having embraced myriad new opportunities for shaping their lives, colonists within the older religious framework were increasingly adrift and dissatisfied by the attenuated impact of normalized doctrine and practice. Edwards sought to call this populace back once again to the Calvinist faith by generating a zeal and spiritual longing to restore the governing presence of the predestinarian Calvinist God in their daily lives. Toward this end, he attacked the two rising temptations: confident individualism on behalf of an overpowering and commanding deity; and commercial secularism in the name of a life of piety. When colonists heard Edwards's call of "having nothing to stand upon" or "take hold of," that they must repent and rejoin or face "the dreadful pit of the glowing flames of the wrath of God" and "hell's wide gaping mouth open," many were "seized . . . at once, with concern about the things of religion."[89] He wanted to stir a deep sense of individual worthlessness, of the sinner's depravity—what he often called "our own foolish, wicked, and treacherous hearts." Preaching that humans at all times "deserve to be cast" into "the flames" that "do now rage and glow," he hoped to restore "submission" not only to an "absolutely sovereign" God but also to the power and authority of a reformed ministry in a revitalized but traditional society.[90] Edwards described this world: "There is a beauty of order in society . . . [a]s, when the different members of society have all their appointed office, place and station, according to their several capacities and talents, and every one keeps his place, and continues in his proper business."[91] The institutions and laws, together with a zealous clergy, were to ensure this social and spiritual order.

Edwards has long been regarded as the central figure of late colonial religion, though in recent times his influence among contemporaries and on the subsequent development of American religion and culture has been seen as significantly reduced.[92] Edwards's conservative defense of religious and civil elites who shared with secularizing elites the rejection of uncontained popular religious enthusiasm and its empowerment of women and minorities,[93] and his increasingly marginal pessimism regarding American prospects,[94] represented desperate efforts to sustain the Puritan legacy. His support for the national covenant, particularly as expressed in the war against France, left him conflicted between piety and the importance of worldly works.[95] Yet where Edwards was at greatest remove from American developments was in his rejection of human ability. As Mark Noll has written: "Edwards lived before it grew fashionable to bestow great trust upon the self. . . . Where Edwards distrusted the self, the self became the originator of truth in the century after his death." Today he remains largely a cautionary voice, Melville's lonely prophet, improbably reminding a human-centered culture of the limits of human action.[96]

Edwards and his supporters in the early Awakening never grasped the popular resistance to being told that their guilt over individualism, independence, and self-reliance—which they surely were feeling—was an irremediable stain. Rather, people needed to hear, though were unable to ask for it directly, that this could be washed away, that for each the "eternal rays of light and love" of Jesus Christ might "shine down particularly on him, to remove his darkness, heal his wounds, and shed immortal blessing on his soul."[97] Individuals wanted, as minister Daniel Wadsworth grasped even before the radical phase of the revival emerged, to find certitude and validation for their new self-appointed role: "They want to know they shall be sure they believe, that they love God, that they are in the right way, are sincere and the like." They wanted to establish the "New Ground," the "Nature and Necessity of the *New-Birth*," though "but little known or thought of them," which would solidify "a real Change" in the self, a "thorough saving Change" involving "a saving Closure with Christ" and the ability to walk "in a right Gospel-Way."[98]

Thus, when Edwards began to call forth a return of the "full . . . presence of God" within the lives of colonial individuals, he was introducing untold dangers into a situation of declining authority.[99] These included personal criteria for belief amidst communities in which individualism was emerging as an alternative to institutional authority; popular mobilization where lay participation in religious organizations and church formation was challenging ministerial prerogative; choice in a culture of continuing "de facto voluntarism in religious and moral affairs;[100] enthusiasm amidst a dissatisfaction with elite trends toward worldliness and formalism. Above all, the call to "awakening" in effect asked individuals to act for their own salvation in a society where they were newly comfortable with exercising their own capacities. The directive to employ the means toward making God's revival a success, even as this activist culture was developing regional, national, and international ecclesiastical networks, organized religious campaigns and revival programs, narratives of personal faith, and mechanisms for distributing publications, only confirmed and made explicit the popular role as effective instruments promoting God's work.[101]

Edwards's call for return to a traditional order was lost amid the rush to move beyond existing constraints. His appeal to individual conscience triggered instead a surfacing of both religious sectarian individualism and the claims of elite rationalism in reaction to revivalism of all kinds. The former began the religious insurgency which transformed American culture in waves of spreading revivalism from 1740 to the 1850s. Those connected with the second process, to be considered later, evolved into the coalition of indigenous elites of moderate establishment Protestants, Lockean commercial interests, and Enlightenment rationalists who together organized the external revolution for national independence. The Edwardsian agenda was shunted to the margins as common people leaped over the existing boundaries to seek a frame for their New World experience.

The Radical Awakening

The second phase began in 1740, with barnstorming revivalist preaching initiated by George Whitefield's repeated campaigns and his innumerable followers throughout the northern and middle colonies stirring popular expectations outside of institutional frameworks. To recover this phase as a distinct entity is to realize how Whitefield—to many a hero, to some a dangerous instigator—rather than Edwards became the central figure of a vast popular movement, serving for several decades to "*Ministers, Rulers* and People" as an "*Angel of God,* or *Elias,* or *John the Baptist* risen from the Dead."[102] Moving quickly to the regions of historic English sectarian immigration and activity,[103] as well as to the vast unregulated frontiers "with a view of getting from under that yoke of bondage" from local elites,[104] gaining a foothold in urban areas, the radical Awakening over the next three decades expanded in these areas while spreading in a "torrent" further to the West and South.[105]

With the presence of dissenting "People of all societies," latent popular dissatisfaction with elite rule, and deep folk memories of the "internal call" against "authority" by "the first Reformers in *England*,"[106] the stirring of popular religious expression soon led "all classes of people" and especially rising groups to demand new adaptive forms of individual spirituality and institutional organization.[107]

The insistence on personal spiritual experience and inclusion as significant forces shaping religious institutional life reflecting their new capacities quickly made the elites expendable. The new test for activism of personal religiosity undercut the power of formalist ministers, for as Whitefield asked, "How can dead men" who are "preaching" of "an unknown and unfelt Christ" ever "beget living Children?" The long-standing use of "language of failure and declension" by ministers to castigate the populace was, ironically, turned back against these elites, "who came up short, not the people."[108] Cast as the "child" against "so great an army of learned men," the dissenters attacked the "Soul murdering tenets" of both Arminian elites and the Edwardsians, the latter for their notions of "a damning God" of "vindictive justice," their "*dark* and *gloomy*" theology, and their dependence on godless "bounds set by the traditions of men" established moreover by those who got "their gifts and abilities at college."[109]

Against this, they offered the power of a popular movement on the apostolic model utilizing "the *common* and *meaner* sort," for "the Work" is "more eminently" God's "the less probable . . . the Instruments used." The sectarian tradition of a "priesthood of all believers" opened the door to any believer's call to preach without "need of philosophers to see for them nor of princes to give them power."[110] Individuals in turn assumed the right to convene religious worship, participate within it, and continue their association without denominational sanction for the first time. Inspired by the Holy Spirit into a state of spiritual grace, ordinary people began preaching the Gospel themselves. Hamilton notes: "'Tis strange to see how this humour prevails, even among the lower class of the people. They will talk so pointedly about justification, sanctification, adoption, regeneration, repentance, free grace, reprobation, original sin, and a thousand other such pretty, chimerical knick knacks as if they had done nothing but study divinity all their life time."[111]

The call to personal experience brought a proliferation of itinerant ministries. Drawing multitudes in services in town squares and fields, in "barns[,] wigwams and private houses, and also in Meeting Houses of all Denominations, and upon almost all Ocations," they generated sustained religious fervor among the populace. Harvard professor Edward Wigglesworth spoke of "Itinerants and Exhorters, who have once and again overrun this, and the neighbouring Provinces and Colonies" seeking to "insinuate themselves into the Affections of other People and Churches."[112] A powerful and continuing feature of the revival initiating the permanent disruption of remaining traditional status demarcations was the class, racial, gender, age (including children), and ethnic diversity of the participants, including the itinerant ministers. One observer wrote in 1742: "It is impossible to relate the convulsions into which the whole Country is thrown by a set of Enthusiasts that strole about harangueing the admiring Vulgar in *extempore* nonsense, nor is it confined to these only, for Men, Women, Children, Servants, & Negros are now become (as they phrase it) Exhorters."[113] This popular explosion of lay activity and congregational participation, causing the proliferation of fellowships intermingling denominations, nationalities, and emerging heterodoxies created a confusing "Variety of Taylors who would pretend to know the best fashion in which Christ's Coat is to be worn."[114]

Amidst this "chaotic swirl of new choices and possibilities," participants and observers sensed "this new Thing in our Day," a "great Change on some of your Neighbors."[115] They further grasped that as a movement of the people and not theologians, these changes were not emerging doctrinally, that "it was no matter to us by what Means" or "profession as to Ceremonies or Forms" emerged "the Sanctifying Work," for "the different Opinions in . . . Doctrine . . . makes little odds to an honest Soul." Even opponents were credited with having "*truly experienced a call from the* SPIRIT *of* GOD." In this open marketplace of beliefs and gatherings, where "the power of the keyes" now "rested ultimately in the pew instead of in the pulpit, or even in an aggregate of pulpits," innovations arose as solicitous organizers and institutions shifted emphasis and practice to energize and mobilize this increasingly individualist society.[116] The result was a new kind of religious fellowship and the beginnings of a new American religion.

Institutionally, the "combination of itinerancy, emotional delivery, and cross-denominational preaching" was "better suited than the Edwardsian prototype to recruiting mobile, unaffiliated populations." Potential converts, attracted without regard to background or status, were now treated as "released from bonds of deference to local customs, family, and society to choose [one's] own community and shape [one's] own identity."[117] No longer constrained by ecclesiastical organization, such initiates in turn followed messengers with "*new* faces, *new* Voices, a new *Method*" virtually at will. The turn to lay and itinerant "exhorters" replacing "their old teachers" broke the existing order of parish churches and community discipline. As distressed critics watched "so much good" people "follow them" including "some of the chief clergy" who were "drawn away by these follies," the Awakening became an inclusive people's movement, the beginning of a social revolution.[118]

The Intensifying Dynamic

The logic of a new explicit choice of affiliation shifted the dynamic of religious life from community procedures and obligations to individuals. Rather than confront Calvinist doctrine directly regarding limited selection and ability, people demanding empowerment and validation through religious transformation simply sidestepped theology through the establishment of new practices. Pursuing once again "a new 'reformation without tarrying for anie,'" people sought a personal experience of spiritual grace within a community of sanctified believers. Common people everywhere were "elevated" by dramatic sermons into "a state of spiritual exaltation" and "spiritual fervor," the experience of election "to eternal sainthood," but given the weak and fraying social fabric the results were ever more individual. Absent ministerial and community oversight, within intermittent and unstructured revivals, "persuasion came to be the only practical means . . . to attract followers."[119] As the radical Awakener Hermon Husband argued, since "ministers . . . now . . . have no power," they must "softly sooth and in a Christian like maner entreat us," utilizing "good examples and an holy life and conversation" rather than "unnaturall or forcible means" as "the only means of promulgating the gosple."[120] Whitefield's accurate reading of the popular mood led him to center the movement's appeal on the individual's choice, offering his audiences what he called an "Invitation" to "take hold of" God's "Golden Scepter" and "Fly to him . . . by Faith."[121] In Stout's terms, "Whitefield's dramatic appeal to the passions encouraged individuals to become actors themselves and . . . enact roles of godliness."[122] This language of solicitation infused the calls as people were asked, "What will you render to the Lord?" and "[Who] will be perswaded to awake this day?" and told they must "either follow *God* or *Baal*."[123]

Individuals were challenged to assume personal responsibility over their religious destinies. Listeners were whipped up to believe that as the faithful they now had the power to determine their own religious fate: "The Holy Spirit in each man made him the agent of God, and, collected in a church, the saints were sovereign: 'all Power given by God, for the well-being of his Church' worked 'Instrumentally by the Members, according to the Grace and Gift of God given to each Member.'" They were told that they each had the potential for a personal relation with God, with Jesus, and particularly with the Holy Spirit, and were directed to develop that relationship. The preacher's message was that "salvation was within the grasp of all his hearers and that they might expect conversion under his preaching if they would only repent and turn from their sins."[124]

The critical ecclesiastical shift for believers was the validation of their "inward Experiences" over the "artificial" standards of "outward Duties" and directives of "skillful Guides," in Isaac Backus's terms to know "experimentally before . . . doctrinally."[125] Told that what was now determinative was the personal assurance of faith through the "direct 'Witness of God's Spirit,'" they were encouraged to become "certain of their gracious State," not to be "satisfied 'til they obtain" such "comfortable Perswasion."[126] One could now specifically ask God "to Direct me in the right way," to have the "truth . . . revealed to my Soul," to provide "the Glory" of "that Light . . . within my Soul."[127] God in turn would now respond, with "Heavenly Vision," with direct "Sight" of "my Redeemer," with a "gracious Voice full of Love, saying, '. . . only obey what I shall make known to thee'" and "trust your Soul with God."[128]

This "inward . . . Grace that speaks in your Heart" enabled the believer to discern right "in his own Conscience," making it possible "to bear [one's] Burden alone" with "no Trust" in "Men," without "the best saints that have ever lived, the Apostles, our forefathers, or any creature for our pattern and example," with even "the Scriptures . . . of but little Use." A reconstituted experience, enabling believers "to observe the divine will," in turn validated their powers of judgment, discretion, and will, their capacity to judge for themselves "out of the reach of all Curses from man," simply as one's "Conscience receives the Rule from God."[129] Individuals were given the "free liberty of examining their teachers and of acting according to their judgments" based on the power "to judge both of the doctrine and conduct of teachings." "In Christ's kingdom," Backus wrote, "each one has equal right to judge for himself."[130]

Commoners were in effect led out of the established church with its hier-

archy and controls to venture beyond the deferential basis of colonial society. They were encouraged to relinquish their dependence on social and religious elites: "The common people claim as good right to judge and act for
themselves in matters of religion as civil rulers or the learned clergy." Turning to "'feelings and impressions' from God's Spirit" made it impossible to
"submit to 'human Judicatures' who commanded" on the basis of "Rules
and good Order." The more the dynamic of revival intensified, in fact, the
more establishment denominations were condemned as the "great Curse
and Judgment" led by an "ungodly Ministry," by "Caterpillars" who "labour
to devour every green Thing."[131]

Increasingly self-reliant individuals flocked to the offer of a personal and
unconditional validation. They gained strength and resolution as God
"make(s) way . . . through all thy difficulties" and implored them "not . . .
Look back," but instead to take on "the Minister" and "the Clerk."[132] This
led them to challenge religious and secular authority at every turn, to demand the institutional reform of the churches and the elimination of civil
restraints. When met with resistance, they circumvented the existing laws
and institutions and transformed religious practice by separating to form
new churches of regenerate saints and then transforming old sects and creating new sects and doctrines. This split of congregations and proliferation
of sects accelerated the dynamic of choice, providing activist ministries in
many communities and a ready congregational "sanctuary to the contentious, refractory and ungovernable."[133]

Neither a repressive hierarchy nor the Edwardsian calls to a harsh self-abnegation would succeed in containing the impetus of the revivalists, instructed that "No Man lighteth a Candle, and putteth it under a Bushel.
Matt. 5. 15. Luke 8. 16." Defensive efforts at suppression only emboldened
the insurgents into new waves of separation and defiance. A conservative
preacher commented on the reaction: "One might as well expect to subdue
the Shrubs on yonder Plain, only by nipping off the Buds in the Spring as to
heal a vicious People of their mortal Diseases."[134] Where traditional cohesion had only been nostalgically imagined among the elites long after it began fraying, quickly their fears of fragmentation became consuming, of "the
divisions of families, neighbourhoods, and towns; the contrariety of husbands and wives; the undutifulness of children and servants; the quarrels
among the teachers; the disorders of the night." Individuals had been set
free to follow their own guides as they chose them. The populace, like the
elites, had become Yankees, though religious Yankees. The dynamic of sec-

tarian agency was producing as its logical outcome a society of individuals, of "members not classes."[135]

The Religion of the "New Birth"

The center of this dynamic driving colonial society beyond an ascriptive order, preparing the people for the individualist society evolving around them, was the most individualizing of all processes—the religion of the "New Birth." If "individual conscience" was the wedge in the English phase of the advent of agency civilization locating the warrant of authorization and mission within each individual, once conscience became a given the "new birth" became the foundation of the second phase in America. A major defense of itinerancy, the account of 1743–1745 of the Reverend Thomas Paine, Jr., asserted the "*absolute Necessity* of the NEW BIRTH" as the critical experience of colonial religion. Hamilton speaks during his travels of his landlady at an inn one night keeping him awake as "she abounded with tautologys and groaned very much in the spirit, praying again and again for the *fullness of grace*" and "the blessing of regeneration and the new birth." The center of this radical vision was the conviction that the individual could attain a regenerated character, becoming capable, willing, and dedicated to living out the realization of God's word. Whitefield described this dramatic shift as "the new life" which "imparts new principles, a new understanding, a new will, and new affections, a new conscience, a renewed memory, nay, a renewed body."[136] Stephen Marini defines the shift to the New Birth as "a new metaphysics of experience" whose essence was an "instantaneous conversion of the soul," produced when "the Holy Spirit implanted itself directly in the soul as indubitable evidence of divine grace" and resulting in "a total renovation of mind and body." William McLoughlin has written: "The essence of the New Light Calvinism or evangelical pietism that formed the central and driving force of popular action in the Awakening was to place the individual experience and judgment of the regenerated man, the New Adam, above the doctrines and practices, traditions and rituals of established civil and ecclesiastical authority."[137]

This conviction of personal transformation, spreading from Whitefield's campaigns and writings as well as others' into a culture of receptive sectarianism became "the grand Article of our Salvation." Building on the new validation of personal experience, theology gave way almost entirely to "a life-changing experience." Whereas salvation before had been "a process unfolding over a period of months" involving "successive stages," the radical Awakeners "compressed" the experience, raising expectations that "conversion" could occur "in a finite moment." As Whitefield exclaimed to audiences, "See that you receive the Holy Ghost before you go hence." For Andrew Croswell, the "long and gloomy accounts of the soul distresses requisite to faith," with their *"preparatory terrors,"* must give way to rebirth "in the *twinkling of an Eye.*"[138] This "direct partaking" of "divinity" with a "personal, immediate experience of the benefits of salvation" entirely undercut the existing institutional distribution of religious status. Now freely doled out by passing ministers regardless of community procedures, the immediate conviction of conversion left individuals to determine their religious state and even their warrant to preach.[139]

In centering on personal rebirth, the revivalists grasped the deeply felt need for empowerment. As the minister Jonathan Dickinson noted in a 1740 sermon, most individuals being reborn in the revival had never experienced God's terror.[140] Nor did they need or care to be driven into God's arms by "all the Terrors of Hell and Damnation." Devoted followers now saw the deity as "a benevolent God interested in the happiness of his children," very different from the frightening Puritan deity instilling "the Souls Danger, and Fear of divine Wrath." God was now "the Holy Spirit" bringing "great rejoycing" into lives by means of "sweet power" infusing "Liveliness and Liberty, Strength and Joy," the model of a dedicated mentor which would reshape authority in American culture.[141]

The goal now of this positive relation was to help seekers to achieve an ever-increasing personal intimacy with a loving God that would facilitate their identification with and internalization of the godly character. They were now to be attracted by their love of God and the reciprocal "Love and Kindness" of this "god of Joy," who showers "Oceans of Love, without any Bottom, and without any Shore" upon his intimate believers. They wanted to be "pierced . . . and overpowered with a sense of God's love," the "power" of "His all-constraining, free, and everlasting love flow[ing] in upon" their "soul." They moreover sought spiritual completion, to have "the lost Image of God . . . restored," to reshape themselves using "the image of God."[142] Whitefield sought that "all might be one, even as Thou Father and I are One . . . the inward union of the souls of believers with Jesus Christ, and not of the outward Church." Samuel Blair called the objective "a saving Closure with Christ . . . hardly known at all to the most."[143] Nathan Cole spoke of being "swallowed up in God," Elisha Paine of "the Union of the Christian to

God or Christ" which "was the same kind with the Union between the human Nature of Christ and the divine," Frothingham of a "Union to Christ by a living Faith."[144] The 1745 Confession of the Mansfield Separates spoke of overcoming the "full Sentence of Condemnation of our Original Sin, and . . . our actual Transgressions" once "GOD by his Spirit . . . has made us partakers of the Divine Nature" through "the Union between Christ and our Souls."[145]

This new appeal spoke directly to the power of individuals to seek personal change. Whitefield believed once ministers were "warmed with the Love of God themselves" and thus "like himself," "they cannot but be Instruments of diffusing that Love among others."[146] These preachers turned away from the use of threats: "I could urge many terrors of the Lord to persuade you; but if the Love of *Jesus Christ* will not constrain you, your Case is desperate."[147] They boldly offered God's unconditional love: "He wants to cover you with his Righteousness. . . . [H]e intends to *make you Saints* . . . to sanctify the Elect People of God." God intended to heal the souls of his believers: "He will sweetly guide you by his Wis[do]m on Earth, and afterwards take you up to partake of his Glory in Heaven." One need only accept the promise offered: "If you will not be drawn by the Cords of Infinite and everlasting Love, what will draw you."[148]

This "New-Birth" through "the power of godliness" was increasingly seen as a developmental advance to a completely new nature. Whitefield called it "a Marriage Feast" in which one is made by Jesus "Flesh of his Flesh, and Bone of his Bone." It was called "a real Change," a "thorough saving Change."[149] That change as described by Nathan Cole was dramatic:

Now my heart and Soul were filled as full as they Could hold with Joy and sorrow; now I perfectly felt truth: now my heart talked with God; now every thing praised God; the trees, the stone, the walls of the house and every thing. . . . And all the Air was love, now I saw that every thing that was sin was fled from the presence of God. . . . [W]here ever the Sun can be seen clear there is no Darkness. I saw that Darkness could as well be in the Clear light of the Sun, as well as Sin in the presence of God; who is so holy and Sovereign.

He further reflected on his own altered being: "Now I saw with new eyes; all things become new, A new God; new thoughts and new heart."[150] This "New Nature, which was implanted in every converted Soul, was as holy as GOD, and as perfect as God was," forming an individual capable of "a pure, spotless Righteousness." Isaac Backus spoke of becoming a "new man in Christ" with "new ideas and dispositions."[151]

Transformed individuals were now in effect new selves with a new character as the English insurgents had envisioned, for "their own rebirth [which] had been miraculous . . . had 'broken up old foundations' and provided a start *de novo* for them in this world." Frothingham suggested the individual grounding for this self:

> That Person that meets in any Place whatever, to worship God, because some godly Person meets in the same Place, and so takes that to be right; *mark:* That Person's Foundation of Action is upon the Sand. . . . Observe. That Person that has not his Foundation of Faith and Practice directly and intirely in and from the Word and Spirit of God, as much as if there was not another human Creature upon Earth, will assuredly suffer Loss sooner or later; for the Day is at hand, that will burn and consume all such Foundations.[152]

Individuals were now empowered directly by God through "his Glory, Power, Love, and All-sufficiency" and given by their personal relation "the Authority and Necessity of the inward and sensible Inspiration of the Holy Spirit."[153]

Its theological inevitability ignored, sin was now merely a condition to be remedied: "Do not say, you are miserable, and poor, and blind and naked, and therefore ashamed to come, for it is to such that this Invitation is now sent." It is "no Excuse" that God will "not call you because you are" not "already" saved, for this is precisely why he is calling you. Individuals were advised to "endeavor to moderate and bound their Passions," but "not so as to resist or stifle their Convictions" of being "Awakened."[154] The individual "Heart" and "Mind" were spoken of not as intrinsically evil, but as simply needing "the sudden, immediate Influences of the Spirit of God," which "always . . . leads the Heart towards God, and seizes the Mind with Reverence." The "Powers and Faculties of our Souls" are now intrinsically capable of being "seiz'd with Reverence and Awe of God's greatness." They need only "the Scene of the recovering Grace . . . open'd to their Understandings" for its "surprizing Beauty and Glory" to "enable" them "to believe in Christ with Joy unspeakable and full of Glory." In effect, God does no longer "*lay a Necessity on any of his Creatures to sin against him.*"[155] Congregants were now told that "*if thy Heart condemns thee not, then has thou confidence in God.*"[156]

The unregenerate world was sinful, to be sure, as were all who were not awakened, and even those seeking regeneration but not yet saved were nominally damned. Yet they were no longer to be treated as sinners but rather as sufferers asking for help, as "dead People" seeking to be "warmed with the love of GOD."[157] The preachers realized that "many souls" were already "under deep distress," afflicted with "inward Soul-concern."[158] Many participating were asking to be relieved of this burden of condemnation and incapacity—"We . . . do heartily wish, pray for, and willingly endeavor . . . Revival in the hearts of our selves and People"—and the preacher was under the "higher Employ" of "calling home Souls" to "Jesus Christ." Though "*some* affecting sense of our own very criminal Indolence in times past" was still present,[159] individuals wanted to be infused with "a renewed and warmer Zeal."[160]

The conviction spread that it was possible to have "that State of Perfection . . . in this Life,"[161] to have "Divine Light shining into the Understanding, and the Love of God . . . ruling in the Soul" so that "we don't judge by Man's Judgment, but by GOD in us" such that one can "know what I say to be true." Nathan Cole wrote of being "healed," being "lead both by the word and Spirit of God," of "a fountain springing up in my heart and Soul."[162] Hermon Husband spoke of "God within himself." Earthly regeneration in turn produced "a new World" with "the kingdom of heaven . . . within him," a condition "so much [like] being in Heaven, that *my Heart burned within me.*"[163] Had it ever been possible to turn back, it was no longer. The great issue now would be how to live in a transformed world.

Rediscovering the Agent

Though terrifying to the arbiters of social stability and unsettling to all others, the advent of the "born again" presaged not antinomian anarchy but new principles of internal and social ordering only barely discernible to most at the time. While most were not aware of its specific origins, proponents themselves understood that they were assuming a responsible new role in the world. The commitment to moral conduct would derive henceforth not from a "theology of limits" to full sanctity but from the *assurance of sanctity.* They referred repeatedly to "all true Converts" being "certain of their gracious State," to the "Assurance of Pardon," to having "no more Reason to doubt of God's good Will towards you, than if you'd never sinn'd," which Croswell even called *"full Assurance.*"[164] As one Separate church put this new certitude, "All doubting in a believer is sinful, being contrary to the command of God, and hurtful to the soul, and an hindrance to the performance of duty." Elisha Paine held that "all Christians have assurance, and those that think they have not are to be suspected of knowing nothing of Christ's beauty experimentally." This certitude was to be unyielding: "I knew my heart would never rise so against God as it had done."[165] When God "invites and requires us thus to do," he "has promised, that if we do, he will not *cast us out.*" God now offered "constant presence strength and assistance." It was by his "Faith and Light that we know ourselves to be Saints," which knowledge would henceforth "never lead a Person contrary to the Scriptures."[166] Whitefield, never in doubt of his own grace, preached the capacity to "be as certain, as though an Angel was to tell" you. To be "infallibly assured" meant in God's own words that "I will never leave thee."[167]

Predestination was being slowly excised theologically and experientially: "The evangelical doctrine of free grace and the evangelical practice of experiential religion were placing more and more emphasis upon the role of man in turning from sin, repenting of sin, and accepting Christ on faith. Backus might call it Arminianism to preach as though men were somehow capable of taking steps to save themselves, yet ever since the first tour of George Whitefield, more and more people had been construing New Light preaching in these terms."[168] Like their radical English forebears, they were to appropriate rather than submit to such Calvinist credos as original sin and predestination as means to sanctification.

The first was used to sharply pose the existential option between "salvation and damnation"; the certainty of God's control and direction now served as earlier to provide assurance for one's own choices from amidst the innumerable options posed by conscience, denominational creeds, and the paths to spiritual election. Hermon Husband talks of his troubling choice between his parish minister and "the New Lights." It was his "Desire" to go to the New Light meeting, but he was afraid "I should displease my Father" not to go to the parish church. He wrestles with the decision: "After some Reasoning in myself, I concluded to leave it entirely to God to enlighten me. Here I mounted on Horse-back, not yet knowing which way I should go . . . Right or Left." He was first "led" to his parish, where he found its absence of "true Worship in Spirit . . . did not suit my solid Condition." Realizing his mistake, he "walked out," with God's help, to join the New Lights.[169] This experiential role for God as ratifier and guarantor of individual choice is evident in Whitefield's dramatic sermons: "You are not your own; give Christ then your bodies and souls which are his!" Yet, he goes on: "Come then, do not send me sorrowful away. . . . Do not let me go weeping into my closet and say 'Lord, I have called them, and they will not answer.'"[170]

The sense of the capacity to exercise choice, of having "made great Resolutions" and "laboured . . . with all my heart might and Strength; and whole soul to seek God," of having the "Power and Light of Christ," infused popular discourse.[171] Experience Mayhew in 1744 articulated the practice of the radical phase: "What Kindness is it to any Sinner, that he has an Offer of Salvation made to him in the Gospel, if he have no Power given to him to accept of that Offer." Increasingly self-reliance, initiative, and personal responsibility were regarded not as enduring evils or flaws in the unregenerate, that is, threatening novelties needing to be stifled, but as capacities to be directed and utilized. Through their empowerment, believers had advanced to a new level of individualism, characterized by both an enhanced liberty and greater responsibility and by their mutual complementarity and indispensability. As God's will is increasingly integrated, the validity of spontaneity and inspiration is revived, permitting direct "revelation" among both the converted and those approaching conversion, in which they "knew it to be from heaven" to "shew them" of "the Lord's will."[172] Individuals could now be "set at liberty" with "freedom in [their] Soul" to "Judge" for themselves, becoming "the Lord's freemen" who "Freely . . . have received" and "freely give."[173]

Self-reliance was now possible because it was wholly contained by the structure of "Christian liberty," flowing from the willingness of individuals to embrace God "freely upon Gospel-terms," their commitment to being true within a voluntary, deep, and trusting relationship. Sin would now be mastered with "a new Obedience which flows freely from an immortal Principle of Holiness and Likeness to God." Ebenezer Frothingham wrote of "a great Tenderness upon our Spirits, lest we or some others should do something which would grieve God's Holy Spirit."[174] Husband admitted that "the Thoughts of bringing Dishonour to his Name has been a greater motive to restrain me [from "Sin"]; than all the Terrors of Hell and Damnation." Cole would "rather have my head cut off than brake Gods Law, knowingly and willingly." Once possessing "the *Love* and *Kindness* of God *his* Saviour," he knows that "all the Devils in Hell can't make him in Love with a wicked life any longer."[175] The believer now wanted to "prove my Love" in return. The personal ground of obligation was clear: "We all know that the greater confirmations an obedient child has of his father's love and the security of his favor, the more cheerful, active and diligent he will be in doing his father's will and careful not to do anything to offend him." The "Path-Way of Duty" was "Reverence," which "inclines the Person to Search, that he might know the Mind and Will of God."[176]

The great divisive issue of the First Awakening, adult versus infant baptism, posed in veiled theological terms this issue of full voluntary responsibility and propelled it to the center of the society's emergent discourse. Solomon Paine warned that the issue "runs through the body of Christians" and was capable of "rend[ing] all cords of union." The shattering of parish and even Separating congregations over the controversy and the dramatic rise of Baptist membership and then Methodist "free will" supporters following the Awakening testify to the growing power of adult voluntarism. These denominations rejected infant baptism as an imposition of institutional practice irrelevant to "the Renovation" of humanity's "corrupt nature," as moreover a "corrupt" practice "from the whore of Babilon," a "great sin" of "practical lying" about one's true condition.[177] While nominally consistent with older Calvinist theology, adult baptism in practice placed in the individual's own hands his or her effective religious destiny, undermining the very basis of colonial denominational membership.

By emphasizing the "New Birth" culminating in regeneration, the anti-paedobaptists made the specific experience of willing transformation the central event of religious life in place of formal belief and practice. Moreover, with the resulting personal faith and commitment treated as the primary requirements for entering the spiritual fellowship, the voluntary assumption of personal responsibility replaced institutional accommodation and deference as the basis of institutional practice. The contrast is thus starkly posed between a religion of "Bondedness" and a "Free" religion permitting a "freedom of approach to God." Free choice had become functionally essential, for "the personal confrontation between man and his Creator . . . depended largely on the liberty of the individual (both in body and mind). The individual had to be free in order to perceive and receive God's grace as well as to sustain the spiritual union with God." With adult baptism, the doctrinal or conceptual step was taken which would recast institutions as extensions of personal choice, and would in time lead to a voluntarist society.[178]

In this way, as the Awakening was "transformed" by its radicalizing dynamic—and was in turn transforming the culture—the sense reemerged of humans as "self-determining agents within the limits that God had chosen for them." The radical Awakeners grasped this new role. Experience

Mayhew stated that "God does neither in his Decree, nor in the execution of it, take away the Liberty of free Agents, such as Men and Angels are." A Philadelphia clergyman wrote that "mankind are free agents, capable of determining their own actions, and . . . God gives every man . . . a sufficient measure of light and the assistance of his Holy Spirit, to enable him both to see and perform his duty."[179] The New Birth was in effect, for believers, the achievement of a completed agency, of being "so sweetly conformed to Gods will that his will was theirs," the "Power from God" amounting to "a Commission in our own Wills." Whitefield asserted that God's "will" was to "chuse men who are vessels meet by the Operation of his blessed Spirit for his sacred Use."[180] Saints could in turn be trusted in their role of knowing and using "such Means as have the directest Tendency to answer the End designed" and further being "faithfull to improve all the gifts & graces that are bestowed on them in their proper place & to their right end."[181]

So commissioned, agents were expected to pursue God's "errand": to "keep not your Religion to your Selves" but rather "let your wives and families and neighbours and friends, have light from your Candle." Each was to work in his or her own way, achieving "Good . . . according to your Talent," exercising *"the fulness of help that is in himself,"* responsible to "improve the ability that He give."[182] In this way, the "true liberty . . . to know, obey, and enjoy his Creator and to do all the good unto" others would be the *"voluntary obedience"* of the self-perfecting, mobilized, and self-reliant agent, who realizes "both his duty and his liberty to regard the good of the whole in all his actions."[183]

The Emerging Culture of Voluntarist Agency

Out of this "psychological earthquake" came a "reshaped . . . human landscape" composed of "new men, with new attitudes toward themselves, their religion, their neighbors, and their rulers in church and state." William McLoughlin calls the Awakening the "conversion of a whole society from a burden of frustration, guilt, and anxiety to a buoyant assertion of self-assurance, self-confidence, and self-righteousness."[184] For those who would "give light unto all," the spread of Gospel liberty regarding convictions led inexorably to voluntary religious institutions. The institutional wedge as in England was individual "liberty of conscience." As the Connecticut Separates wrote in 1748, God, seeking to have individuals "taught by his unerring word and not by the precepts of men . . . hath given to Evry Man an unalianable Right, in matters of the worship of God, to Judge for himself as his Consciance receives the Rule from God." Any human institution, being "conditional," which refused to acknowledge this freedom violates the will of God, which requires the "perpetual" exercise of "obedience unto the *commands of Christ*" only and "no otherwise."[185] Gilbert Tennent preached that an individual "may *lawfully* go . . . where he gets most Good to his precious Soul. . . . To bind men to a particular Minister, against their Judgment and Inclinations, when they are more edified elsewhere, is carnal with a Witness; a cruel Oppression of tender Consciences, a Compelling of Men to Sin . . . an unscriptural Infringement on Christian liberty."

Individuals were now intent on creating churches reflecting their spiritual needs. Congregants demanded the independence—the "Inalienable Power within itself" and *"Right of private Judgment"*—of their individual congregations and the elimination of ecclesiastical hierarchies and consociational controls; governance of each congregation by a majority of the membership together with separate financing; and the lay power to ordain their own ministers and authorize speakers, including laity.[186] Christianity would "prevail gloriously" by "the power" of "the TRUTH" and "without the help of the sword." In this way, individuals would be led to religious fellowship by their own inspiration: "The Lord alone be praised for it was he alone who brought me out [with Separates] and not any Creature."[187]

Despite their challenge to traditional society, radical revivalists lacked the numbers, the clarity of direction, and the organization to transform the United States into a realized agency society, and to protect their own innovations most remained apart from the larger community until brought into politics by the Revolution. Yet, by making the willing assumption of agency the test of religious attainment, and by suggesting a voluntarist basis for institutions, they demonstrated how the structural change in individual character would necessitate a new order of society. Moreover, given their conviction that regeneration was not simply a peak experience but a "Change" both certain and continuing, it became possible to imagine orderly communities of "Harmony and Concord" within a society of sanctified individual agents: "There is a considerable Number who can afford all the Evidence . . . of their having been the Subjects of a thorough saving Change."[188]

The focus on individual sanctification was thus never separated from being "responsible for forming communities that fostered collective sacred experience and protected members from profanation," islands of "tight cohesive brotherhood."[189] More than saints living together, these communities represented the collective enactment of sanctification in the world in which "the Peace and Love of God has flow'd among the Saints like a living Stream, whereby their Hearts have been knit together in fervent Love or Charity." In settings of "close-knit, voluntary local expression" substituting for the unavoidable "loss of external boundaries," "every Sinner . . . may come to have his Nature renewed." The replacement of voluntarism for external coercion was not to accentuate individualism but to have it "mitigated" through "commitment to new forms of community," to contain "antinomian license" with "strict adherance to the rigorous terms of . . . church covenants," mutual accountability, and new internalized forms of conviction and conduct.[190]

Establishing "gathered churches" as a "communion of saints," the Awakeners pushed beyond ascriptive status and class subordination.[191] They opened the movement to all willing to move beyond traditional boundaries to embrace the new message, relying on individually determined levels of conviction and commitment. Whitefield admired the coming together in revival of "regenerate souls among the Baptists; among the Presbyterians, among the Independents, and among the Church folks,—all children of God," adding, "Who can tell which is the most evangelical?" Together they acted to remake the world in God's image: "We have left the House of dead Formality, and spiritual Idolatry, and meet where the sovereign Lord of Heavens and Earth grants his gracious Spirit, in its divine, quick'ning, and sanctifying Influences." In Frothingham's terms, "what makes a Place to be God's House, is his special, spiritual Presence; and where his Children meet, under the Divine Influence of his blessed Spirit . . . whether it be a public Meeting-House, or a private House, or the open Wilderness." The hope that "the Kingdom may be given to the saints of the moast high" required that they be prepared to act to that end: "A Dozen poor Illiterate fishermen Can Subdue Kingdoms, not with carnall weapons but with the Pure word of God. . . . He puts such Courage into his Dear Children that like the meek man Moses they Car not for Pharoh and all his Magicians."[192] Solomon Paine wrote: "The Saints must either be ashamed of Christ and his Word, or else they must be treated as Disturbers of the Peace (of that Community) who turn the World upside down; doing contrary to the Desires of Men, saying, there is another King."[193]

In imagining the project of societal reconstruction, the radical Awakeners were operating less from a social blueprint than from carrying through—as they were unable to do in England—the implications of radical Protestant convictions. They felt that sanctified individuals in a world overseen by a benevolent God could no longer operate by old institutional arrangements. Historians have debated over what specific institutional reforms were most central to the revolutionary agenda.[194] In fact, the radical Awakening was the harbinger of—made by and in turn forging—the voluntarist modern world, disrupting society at every level and within every institution. For saints undergoing a developmental step, all institutions would have to be fundamentally redevised to reflect individuals now capable of carrying out their own moral and spiritual convictions. New "American" religious and secular institutions would have to acknowledge and accommodate voluntary engagement and provide space for personal discretion and initiative for saints to fulfill their mandate as agents, to forge a new "connection between individualistic assent" and "communal order."[195] In organizing to create the institutions which accorded with this new agency character, these Awakeners, like their English forebears, again empowered agents to reshape the world. With this groundwork so laid, religious but increasingly challenging political assumptions and arrangements, the Revolution could not be long in coming, nor would the young republic be able to turn back the tide.

Institutional Challenges and Social Crisis

The radical Awakening by word and deed spread through the colonies the conviction that for religious renewal "the people would have to take the lead," to "be the central characters in the new religious history." Asserting the rights of "Going from Place to Place, to hear the word" and "get greater Good," and of resisting any "Law that is contrary to Gods Law" as having "no power in it," the "religious revival and prophetic theology" were as Eldon Eisenach suggests "intensely political from the very start" and quickly evolved into political protests revivalist in character.[196] Claiming that institutions were legitimate to the extent that they were voluntary and illegitimate otherwise, that conscience extended to the "Duty, as well as the Right, to see and examine whether . . . Rulers abuse [their] trust," it rejected all unnecessary interference by both secular and religious authority. Its proponents attacked and circumvented the efforts by ecclesiastical bodies to license or ordain pastors or otherwise determine who preached, to censure or control the affairs of individual congregations through larger organizational structures, to tax community residents for the established church, its projects, and its ministers, or to direct or allow ministers to circumvent the will of the congregational membership. The secular authorities, who by law mandated religious establishment and enforced its decrees, stepped in to bolster the crumbling order. They acted to suppress dissent by fining and imprisoning those engaging in or leading illegal worship and breaking up "illegal" congregating, as well as through more rigorous enforcement of establishment policy. The Separates and sectarians resisted, fighting within the established procedures for toleration and voluntarism and ultimately venturing toward a "Duty to withdraw" and pursue "the cause of a just Separation" though it might lead to "defending every one of different sects, in their sacred rights of conscience."[197]

Imperial and domestic institutions which constrained liberty were cast once again as opponents of Reformation, remnants of earlier forms of bondage. For Solomon Paine, being jailed for refusing to pay a religious tax was simply an exercise of the "power" placed "unjustly" in the "hands" of the state. Illegal constraints were by the formidable rhetorical tradition of Anglo-American religious radicalism soon characterized as the work of "a fierce and Dominearing Golia[t]h" and of a "Pharoh," as "the abominable Oppression and Persecution"[198] of "religious tyranny" from "the second beast of Revelation,"[199] as "this Image" of Caesar imposing "tyranny, persecution, and suppression."[200] Frothingham asked: "If that Beast which hath two Horns like a Lamb, and speaks as a Dragon, has no rule in this Land . . . whence it is that the Saints of God have been so imprisoned of late Years . . . contrary to the plain Letter of the Word of God?" It was, he suggested, the work of "the Priest and the Ruler, the Great and Learned" become "wicked Oppressors . . . even against the Sovereignty of God": *"for the Wicked doth compass about the Righteous, therefore wrong Judgment proceedeth."*[201]

This increasingly strident language was being disseminated among a populace with long religious roots in dissent and where many of the more secularized settlers had long been happily independent of and suspicious of state control. It was, moreover, a rhetoric which, as we shall see, the commercial and political elites were beginning to use in their quarrels with England. Its application as a lingua franca against all exercises of authority undermined the presumptions of the local elites to control and threatened to divide colonial society. With each group asserting its own belief and conduct without regard for the systemic consequences, divisions proliferated, creating a market dynamic of unfettered individualism altering the face of American religion, a "rise of rampant sectarian pluralism among a people no longer satisfied with the parish church and its official religion" which "destroyed the homogeneity" of the "territorial parish system." Amidst "such a flood of confusion" emerged as well religious radicals "disputing the Personality of the Godhead, and denying the Lord that brought them; others are ridiculing . . . important Doctrine" and "perverting the Designs of the Gospel."[202] At the margins were the fragmentation of sects into personal religions and the most serious claims of personal "perfectionism" and self-authorization to date in the United States. Some saw that religious diversity might be the logical and perhaps optimal result of voluntarism: "These Scriptures shew, that the most eminent Saints have been divided; and *Paul's* Epistles to the Churches, shew that there were Contentions often amongst them; and yet not withstanding God did a great Work amongst them . . . so also, God is doing a great Work amongst us in this Land . . . [despite] such Contention." Others foresaw greater and inevitable "Opposition and Division" arising from the "Sword" of "the Gospel," causing "implacable enmity" between "converted and unconverted."[203]

Even the opponents of revival were afflicted by "this dividing Spirit," affirming their right to a "separate Congregation" despite having "made the loudest Complaints of the like Disposition in Others." The traditionalist Puritans were qualified defenders of revival so long as it was in their control and its "extraordinary influence" was utilized to lead individuals to an authorized faith "from the Spirit of God."[204] The moderate Old Light establishment, once it began losing institutional dominance to radical revivalists in the 1750s, shifted its commitment from centralized institutions to the protection of (its own) minority liberty, after all not so distant in its history: it stressed the "essential rights and liberties of particular churches" and the "natural and unalienable Rights" of individuals "to search, examine, and judge for themselves," obtainable through personal faith and individual reason. Gary Nash has shown how the urban Awakening was most popular among social groups seeking communal protection from growing entrepreneurial individualism. But the net effect of calling these sectors away from established commercial institutions was to mobilize them as claimants seeking liberation.[205] All of the Lockean discourses—including a new theology of freedom throughout a fragmenting predestinarian Calvinism—were gradually pushed toward anti-institutional implications as control slipped away from group after group. It was easier to gain popular support against institutional intrusions than to justify institutional interventions on behalf of collective agendas.

The proto-agency religious elites, employing the premise that some

"men" could "force" others "to do their duty if *they* were in error" by demanding "a complyance with their Duty as it is pointed out by the Laws
of God or the good and wholesome Laws of the Land,"[206] wilted and collapsed under the onslaught of the second phase of the revival. Efforts to
restore uniformity by reestablishing church hierarchy, outlawing lay itinerants, withdrawing licenses for dissenting churches, punishing insurgent
pastors and congregations with censure, ordering confiscation of property
and jail sentences, and enforcing the structure of and taxation for the established church had ironically become counterproductive, "founded in *partiality* and *caus[ing] divisions and offenses*" perhaps "bringing ruin . . . to the
state."[207]

Their only effective hope, denying assurance of present sanctification
which elevated individuals into effective equality and beyond the reach of
proto-agency hierarchies, was no longer available. Backus noted the "surprising event" that "'illiterate, bold, itinerant preachers' should prevail so far
as to vanquish all the learned teachers and lawyers." The establishment
minister Isaac Stiles wrote in 1745: "Many Churches and Societies are broken and divided;—Pernicious and unjustifiable Separations are set up and
continued. . . . Numbers of illiterate Exhorters swarm about as Locusts from
the Bottomless Pit."[208] Stiles, like many in the established church, asked if
something might "be done to heal our unhappy divisions? To put a stop to
and prevent Unscriptural Separations & Disorderly Practices . . . subversive
of Peace, Discipline & Government."[209] The established churches were powerless because the insurgent language was their own. The Preston, Connecticut, Separate Church expressed the dilemma, addressing those members in
1757 withdrawing to become Baptists: "Nor Dare we bid you God Speed . . .
yet in as much as you plead Conscience: And we would by No means Pretend to Govern any mans Conscience for God and his word ondly are Lord
of the Conscience: therefore we leave you to Stand or fall to your own Master."[210]

Edwards and his followers, like the moderate English Puritans, eventually
broke with the radical movement of "that wild enthusiastical sort of people"[211] who showed no great affection for "Mr. *Edward's* Scheme."[212] They
rejected its validation of the individual believer, no longer "infinitely sinful" but now "appear[ing] righteous in their own eyes, and look[ing] upon
themselves as deserving well at the hands of God."[213] The resulting shifts
were also rejected: the elimination of ministerial oversight of a congregant's
spiritual condition; the demand for absolute assurance of holiness and puri-

fied churches over the ambiguities of Calvinist faith; the willingness to separate and join sects; the radical antinomianism and belief in an infallible inner witness and spiritual union. The Edwardsian Awakening following the Puritans held that "the inscrutability of God's electing will made certainty of sainthood unattainable." They demanded that "a people under affliction & public calamities . . . cry . . . for deliverance," couching regeneration "in terms of 'reasonable hope' and 'evidence of grace' rather than experiential surety . . . [a] lifelong process of growth in grace. . . . In principle, the Puritans never knew they were saved."[214]

Above all, Edwards rejected the greatest single indicator of the emerging voluntarist religion: adult believers' baptism. His inclusion of children as members in the church, leavening true faith with the demand of integration into existing hierarchies, reveals his proto-agent fear of individualism. Edwards's followers in following years became ever more opposed to those "subjects" who "despise the Deity and contemn all authority, are full of discontentment and murmuring, divided into angry parties."[215] The Edwardsian answer as a reform movement was theological rather than simply political: "the greatest" personal and collective "strictness and watchfulness," an emphasis on the continuing capacity to sin which made life on earth no indulgence in glory but a profound battle with self that would be resolved only at the day of Judgment.[216] Its failure, even nonresponsiveness, is emblematic of the "Puritan dilemma" in America.

The emergence of the discourse of freedom in the Great Awakening, while the clear sign of an approaching crisis, represents a process distinct from the narrative later consolidated as the revolutionary idyll. Many scholars of this period acknowledge that the drift toward liberty was a decidedly *unintended* consequence of the struggle for institutional control. In *The Myth of Democratic Individualism,* Barry Shain shows that all three of the colonial Lockean discourses—and religion more than any—repudiated the freedom of "autonomous individual liberty" for "liberty characterized by a voluntary submission to a life of righteousness that accorded with objective moral standards as understood by family, by congregation, and by local communal institutions." Thus, "for reformed Protestants, the ability of the saved individual (saint) to live voluntarily in accordance with the laws of God was an important indication . . . that he or she was indeed truly reborn in Christ."[217] Freedom was understood in effect as agency, not "negative liberty *from* authority" but "positive liberty *toward* the goals of a dedicated Christian life."[218] The early political struggle for toleration and later disestablishment was as in England simply regarded as a necessary precondition to gather together as spiritual agents within religious communities.

And yet, the logic of Protestant sectarianism was propelling participants beyond their intended outcome. Seen by many as a "revival of the spirit and principles of *Separation* and *Anabaptism*," the "fatal Contagion" of religious "Libertines" and "Antinomianism," it recalled the uncontrollable "controversy of the 1630's."[219] In this way, the contest for preeminence again devolved into particularist claims of privileged or aristocratic agency. Every effort to contain freedom through hierarchy in fact extended it, the very situation Hobbes identified as the condition requiring equality and choice: "The immediate effect" on religious unity of "the Awakening was . . . rather an ever-widening divorce than a temporary alienation." No insurgents "believed that total religious laissez-faire, or even Calvinist pluralism was desirable," nor did they believe in extreme individual voluntarism absent religious commitment. Yet the result of "question[ing] everything," of Backus's injunction—"Be entreated no longer to take things by tradition"—was an all-too-predictable "surprise," which is to say, the eventuation of a "laissez-faire outlook which maintained that the well-being of the whole was best attained by the freedom of each to pursue his own self-interest."[220]

Richard Bushman has most fully expressed this dynamic:

> While ecclesiastical liberty was not the chief aim of Old or New Lights, it was the salient result of their dispute. . . . The truly revolutionary aspect of the Awakening was the dilution of divine sanction in traditional institutions and the investiture of authority in some inward experience. Thereby the church lost power, and individuals gained it, using it to reform the old order both in principle and in practice. The final outcome, though largely unintentional, was to enlarge religious liberty.[221]

Of course, as Shain himself recognizes, "a certain degree of unintended freedom for the individual paradoxically grew . . . not the result of 'an overall ideology of freedom—but of the existence of many communities within the society each with its own canons of orthodoxy.'" In seeking the space from control to exercise that right of conscience which in turn presumed the restructuring of all authority, the sectarians made freedom from external institutional interference the cultural expectation. In order to mobilize these disparate groups for the Revolution, this discourse—though religious at core—would in time shape the rhetoric of political insurgency.[222]

Left to its own dynamic, Protestantism was threatening the very cohesion of colonial society. Universal agency seemingly precluded any exercise of power by one agent over another, and the liberty to pursue agency threatened to become liberty regardless of agency constraints. The remedy of institutional schism for any failure to facilitate individual spiritual realization established expectations that no worldly organization could fulfill. Yet the emerging Protestant response to proliferating religious views was greater "liberty by defending every one of different sects, in their sacred rights of conscience, not allowing one sect to disturb another."[223] Ezra Stiles wrote: "Such are the circumstances of our churches, so intermixt with sects of various communion, that it is impolitic to use extreme and coercive measures—since universal liberty permits the oppressed to form into voluntary coalitions for religious worship." Toleration was indispensable both to personal belief, for "no action is religious Action without Understanding and Choice in the Agent,"[224] and to social order, for the involvement of government in one sect's "suppressing and persecuting another" produced only "animosities and Quarrels." Equal treatment made people "most likely to act the Part of good Subjects toward their Rulers, and that of good Neighbors toward one another."[225]

The problem with toleration for a theocratic society was that the priority given to religious values made it impossible to establish political control. Even though claims of religious autonomy were becoming ever more open-ended, efforts at state control were identified as intrusions within the framework of religious dissent. Government was powerless to reverse the dynamic: "The civil Magistrates . . . have no Right to touch that which does Infringe upon Conscience." Where conscience touched more and more matters, the state's primary function was being constricted to "Protecting and Defending" particularist "civil Rights and Privileges." Although few could admit it, toleration in fact signified the collapse of the godly nation. Popular religion could be neither directed from a single source nor even controlled in its spiritual manifestations.[226] The fear grew among insurgents as well as opponents that claims of false assurance would bring a spirit of "rebellion" and the "arrogance" of "deluded souls," including *"false Christs and false prophets"* who "fancy themselves called of God" and *"shall* DECEIVE.*"* With the emergence of so many sects and renovated spirits unwilling to consider the systemic implications of their views, "a wide door to Licentiousness" was open.[227] If many voices could not be made one and prevented from political opposition only by a policy of continual accommodation, the great Protestant dilemma emerged once again: how to establish governance amidst the diversity of uncompromising transcendent views? In the end it would require a reframing of the underpinnings of the American polity.

The Need for a Liberal Resolution?

The crisis which evolved from the Great Awakening was both political and spiritual: if the insurgent religious sector eschewed collective ecclesiastical organization and treated the state merely as a profane concession to order, it flirted with the failure to establish the political base by which its society of true agents was to be constituted and maintained. Diversity would mandate the eclipse of a religious orientation. As. J. C. D. Clark has written: "One reason why the nature and purpose of the Revolution could be interpreted in merely secular terms was that the diverse sectarian components of the colonies dictated the search for common denominators."[228] That is, the religious community had again left for the state—and nascent liberalism—the problem of creating, implementing, and ensuring order. In this view, the dominance of the secular realm during the Revolution does not reflect an enduring cultural shift. Rather, the political arm of agency culture was called upon to resolve the matters of national independence and internal rule. Once these were achieved, the religious dynamic reemerged.

As in England, then, liberalism was to rescue Protestantism—at a cost. The political discourse would appropriate its rhetoric of individualism, voluntarism, and resistance to authority, and above all collective mission for the "liberal" American Revolution and nation building. To effect this transition, the state as defined by insurgent Protestantism would have to be recast. Government was clearly necessary if only to mediate the conflicting religious visions and demands as well as to control "the greatest part of the inhabitants of the commonwealth . . . destitute of piety or true heart religion." Yet the reason "men enter into a state of civil society" could no longer be framed in terms of "piety and religion" but henceforth "to promote their common interest."[229] Specifically, the colonists were being confronted with the reality that "the civil authority was the sole institution binding society. The state was the symbol of social coherence, as once the Established churches had been. Group solidarity depended on loyalty to the government."[230]

At the same time, the state could not revert to being a mere imposer of external force. As Hobbes had realized long before, to consolidate the radical individualism of the Reformation and replace the churches as the defender of agency, it would have to be transformed into a "Protestant" institution. Political control would depend henceforth on a recognition of new "individualistic and egalitarian assumptions . . . about social order and authority" derived from "popular foci of authority."[231] Put in the language of religious dissent, the question was to establish an inclusive society of saints however they claimed warrants, an authority—for authority would surely still exist—capable of controlling universal presumptions of sanctification, of bringing order to "the Children of the Proud."

Thus, amidst the internecine organizational disputes and intricate theological contentions of the period, we can miss that agency principles spread so rapidly that their victory was assured *before* the Revolution. The "rebellion" was in this sense "accelerating a movement *already in progress*" among "the lower rather than the upper strata of colonial society."[232] The incendiary issue now was *whose* agency doctrine, supported by *which* institutional powers and limits on others, would authorize and define community membership. The colonists did not have a blueprint for this development of a cohesive agency society. The brief period before the Revolution was not adequate to crystallize the characterological step being taken, and the dynamic of revolutionary insurgency further complicated matters for an already confused populace. But the people increasingly sensed that this new experience of collective power and individual initiative made America different from Europe, first France and then England, and that their traditional status as colony no longer reflected their new internal capacities. As the indigenous political elite after 1755 gradually developed its own identity as the defender of this distinct society, the elites and the radical Awakeners alike began to conceptualize institutions that could be the protector of both religious differences and agency values. The revolutionary period would be a learning process of applying the lessons growing out of the Great Awakening to the creation of such popular institutions.

To recover the process leading to revolution, we must acknowledge the radical dynamic of the Awakening with its insistent demand for a renovated world. This surely formed the basis for the resolute optimism and fervent commitment of the revolutionary masses, which was then extended as liberal rhetoric focused the demands of inclusion upon the more universal call for a newly conceived nation. Crossing the "Rubicon"[233] to a culture of voluntarist individualism and the sectarian proliferation of the 1750s, 1760s, and 1770s, the radical Awakening overleaped the Puritan anxiety about decline and cautious millennialism. By claiming the collective advent of sainthood, it spread a transformative fervor to the developing national popular culture it was creating. As Ruth Bloch has written, "It was the Great Awakening that spread the millennial tradition of New England Puritanism into the rest of the colonies" and "diffused among an exceptionally large and committed population" its "visionary ideas."[234] Transformed individuals were now prepared to remake the world, "to take root and bear fruit, and fill the land." Seeing regeneration within and around them, they understood history again as the steady increase of God's "further light."[235]

The heirs of English Puritan millennialism, they reclaimed the belief that God was offering to his faithful enhanced insight into and more favorable conditions for the realization of the Word. They believed that they could "excel our Predecessors in Virtue, much more to come even." To "rest in the Light that they now have" was to fail in the task of achieving "further Reformation" in "the present." They must be "duly pressing forwards for further Attainments,"[236] for the transformation of self and society which they were promised and to which they were pledged. The revivalist preachers spoke of the coming of the new age, of "the Kingdom of God . . . come unto us at this Day."[237] This in turn prepared the populace of the colonies to hear the demands for political transformation.

The Revolution, then, was to be neither wholly Protestant nor wholly liberal. The religious expectations aroused by the Awakening could find a powerful outlet in the political rhetoric of national independence and new domestic institutions because both were part of a larger agenda—forming a new human role in relation to authority. Given the inability of the denominations and sects even to frame a common project of independence and a new society, the turn toward a liberal polity was necessary for the realization of underlying shared aspirations. The upcoming political conflict would fit into and build on this progress toward perfected agency, as colonial citizens understood "the meaning of human action" anew. They realized that "purposeful endeavor was instrumental in achieving millennial happiness," and that one must choose to side either with "the forces of Christ or those of the Antichrist" in that project.[238]

Modern scholars cite John Adams approvingly on the origin of the Revolution:

What do we mean by the American Revolution? Do we mean the American War? The Revolution was effected before the war commenced. The Revolution was in the minds and hearts of the people; a change in their religious sentiments, of their duties and obligations. . . . *This radical change in the principles, opinions, sentiments, and affections of the people was the real American Revolution.*[239]

Adams, of course, with his focus on national independence and his hostility to religious insurgents, did not understand the half of it, how the revolution in the "minds" of the colonists took wing long before 1760 in the demand for a new relationship to authority of every kind. The exposure in the revivals of the extent to which the new character had been realized highlighted the inadequacy of existing institutions. At the same time, their sharpening of religious conviction made the search for new institutions sustainable despite the difficult course of revolution ahead and the lack of clarity about the shape of the future society.

7

The Revolutionary Triumph
of Agency

Liberty of conscience, the great and most important article of liberty,
is evidently not allowed as it ought to be in this country, not even by
the very men who are now making loud complaints of encroachments upon their own liberties.

—Isaac Backus

The American dream, as the nineteenth and twentieth centuries . . .
came to understand it, was [not] the dream of the American Revolution. . . . This has given rise to a great deal of confusion.

—Hannah Arendt

Perhaps one helpful way of breaking out of the difficulty . . . is to see
both religious and political developments as consequences of more
deeply rooted determinants.

—Gordon Wood

This nation's identity as a free society of free individuals was
the legacy of the American Revolution, the foundational act—we have been
taught—of modern secular liberal society. Rooted in radical Lockean values, the Revolution in this understanding was fought to create a republic
based on self-government (the "free society") and personal liberty (the "free
individual"). Jefferson's stirring words in the Declaration have ever since
its writing been an inspiration to the world and a framework for national
self-definition. The nation has in turn measured itself by these words: it
has judged itself harshly when it failed to live up to their vision; so has it
proclaimed itself the model society either for imagining its fulfillment of
their noble prescriptions or at times merely for believing in them. Rarely
have Americans turned back to the Revolution to reconsider the viability or

historical accuracy of its message. Treating it as a sacred story, they have thereby created an American idyll.

The American Revolution Reconsidered

We have misunderstood the Revolution, and therefore the republic on which it stands. The interpretive crisis surrounding the freedom narrative and belated efforts by historians to restore it suggest deep confusion regarding the nation's original principles. Accumulating evidence from the colonial period confirms that the new republic was the first post-traditional society, but also that liberty was neither the central goal nor the major achievement of the Revolution. It was not liberty but agency which united the disparate forces of the Revolution. Agency brought together denominations and sects, interests and regions, to fight the British Empire, the bastion of servitude and long-standing enemy of Protestant dissent. It was the impact on the revolutionary actors of this enduring tradition, its resistance to external intrusions and its collective obedience to transcendent ends, that we must examine—not the stunning anomalies of Jefferson's Declaration and the subsequent myths that it spawned. In the end, we must therefore reconstruct the original meaning of the role that Jefferson and the Declaration played in framing the Revolution. This will in turn enable us to see how that discourse has risen to such eminence that the great movements of the age have been all but unrecoverable.

I will treat the Revolution as two distinct movements for agency: an insurgency provoked by increasingly confident elites for national control against the British effort to retain its empire; and a popular struggle undertaken in the vast areas affected by sectarian consciousness and ideals for internal reform and universal prerogatives against these domestic proto-agency hierarchies. Rhys Isaac has written in a groundbreaking work on the prerevolutionary period, *The Transformation of Virginia, 1740–1790,* of a "double revolution in religious and political thought and feeling that took place in the second half of the eighteenth century." One, the "gentry-led patriot movement," was constituting "new expectations concerning authority" as a feature of the movement for independence. The second, which resulted in time in "revolutions in church and state," was the product of "intense popular movements" spurred by an "evangelical movement" which had for some time "been effecting radical cultural changes." Together, Isaac asserts, they produced "the transformations of community ethos" that constituted the

new nation.¹ Both movements were rooted in agency principles, and utilized to different degrees the cultural discourses which dominated colonial
society—the Protestant, liberal, and rationalist agency discourses.

The leaders of the War of Independence, the commercial, political, and religious elites including the signers of the Declaration, were merchants, legislators, and professional men, prominent members of the mainstream clergy,
and among the more progressive southern plantation owners. Descendants
in a number of cases of insurgent Puritan divines, they were educated men
who, with the more recent emergence of cosmopolitan attitudes, had begun
to incorporate the political and rationalist discourses developed by their
ministers and by the educated laity. Contrary to later understandings, these
elites resisted not only radical religious developments but also the more individualist and universalist revisions of the secular doctrines emerging in
England after Locke. Instead, they exploited these doctrines' defense of differential personal qualifications of virtue, reason, and ability to support a
hierarchical republic of agents. Finally pushed despite their reticence to the
struggle for independence, they eventually—but only temporarily—acceded
to a more radical understanding in the Declaration. Their primary goal
throughout, however, was to mobilize and co-opt the popular revolution on
behalf of a moderate revolution for separation—not universal liberty—that
would legitimate their political leadership and buttress their commercial position in society.

There was another popular revolution whose meaning and even relevance have languished since the midcentury decline of Progressive historiography. It was made by a mobilized populace in the villages and on the
farms and frontiers of largely agrarian America as well as in several major
cities. These people, we shall see, fought against domination by the internal
elites very much as against British rule. Throughout the colonies, this group
refrained from the elite cause and its agenda before the war while pursuing
their own local demands. In the framing of early state constitutions, they resisted the elites with a more egalitarian and antistatist agenda, and later became anti-Federalists demanding bills of rights and full self-government.
This struggle finally coalesced in efforts to forge a populist society and government freed from ascriptive class precedence which became Jeffersonian
and Jacksonian America.

Was it the makers of this second revolution perhaps who sought to establish "a free society of free individuals," thus saving the timeliness of the Jeffersonian peroration? The weight of the evidence suggests otherwise. This

group was neither familiar with nor motivated by radical Lockean conceptions of a liberal republic of "free" or rational citizens. Their inspiration was the momentous sectarian transformation of American culture and spiritual life beginning from the Great Awakening. In region after region, underlying their political and economic claims in the emerging internal struggle over institutional power was the defense of their distinct religious destinies against all forms of elite control. The theoretical roots of this mobilization, of course, lay in the one enduring antihierarchical, egalitarian, activist tradition in American life, the two-hundred-year legacy of dissenting principles. Their dream was to create communities of voluntary believers under a single transcendent Author. These proponents hoped, in other words, to create a society of voluntary *agents*.

By recovering the American Revolution as a historical movement rooted in and achieving agency principles, we are able to move beyond the conventional conception of the three Lockean discourses as fierce contestants for the shaping of the nation's identity, and to demonstrate their deeper consensus.[2] Each of these discourses was invoked and pushed in an ever more radical direction to frame the nation's distinctive culture and values during the insurgency. That proponents of each were able finally in crisis to overlook their considerable differences and, unlike in England, unite in a single movement suggests their common underlying commitment to agency principles and, moreover, to new institutional structures. Both revolutions, the one for independence and the domestic insurgency, were thus fought in the name of agency.

How, then, did American society come so quickly to misconceive its own work as a revolution not for agency but for freedom? The genius of the Declaration is that it incorporated in universal language both the elite discourse and the popular agenda, forging a unified movement for independence. At the same time, these sweeping claims, which involved a set of pragmatic decisions by the internal elite directed toward mobilizing quite recalcitrant domestic opponents, provided rhetoric which fatefully overstepped its immediate conceptual task. This in turn thrust into the center of the national culture an expansive—and quite impracticable—conception of personal rights and their harmony with social order that not only was unattainable, but that enabled ordinary citizens to utilize its radical implications to validate their own agendas. This led in time to the demise of the elites which announced it—and to a nineteenth-century agency nation.

This rhetoric of the Declaration fixed in the national consciousness the idyll of liberty to which American society to this day remains hostage. The immediate result in the early republic was a massive disorientation from previous cultural moorings for the overcoming of which proclamations of freedom offered little assistance. In the longer run, this idyllic formulation has repeatedly prevented an accurate appraisal of the nature of American institutions. It has also led to tortured and polarized readings of American history and of the Revolution itself.[3] By looking beneath the liberal meta-narrative by which this era was "reinterpreted in retrospect"[4] and to the factions which made the Revolution and their agendas, I propose to recast the formation of the American national experience. This involves placing the Revolution back into its context as the fulcrum of a new civilization: on one side, with its roots in the great Anglo-American Protestant movement which gave birth to the agency ideal in England and to the foundation for a new society in colonial America; on the other side, with its legacy in the Protestant-liberal society coalescing in the nineteenth-century United States on the basis of agency principles. The American Revolution is the bridge between the formulation and implementation of this modern worldview, the point at which its cultural aspirations become operational principles.

The Complex Situation of the Colonial Elites

To understand the agenda of the elites which would propel their involvement in the Revolution, it is crucial to recognize their complicated social position as leaders of a colonial opposition and the constraints this placed on the articulation of that agenda. As religious dissenters and proponents of colonial economic prerogatives, even the elite governing classes located their validation in the nontraditional discourses of agency. Unlike popular colonial culture, which was slow to separate from an exclusively religious orientation, the educated sectors in touch with the ideas of the British opposition gradually supplemented indigenous religion with the increasingly modern variants of Lockean liberalism and rationalism.[5]

Yet, paradoxically, their use of these discourses was distinctly less radical than among the British oppositional heirs of the Commonwealth legacy.[6] While the social contractualist and rationalist discourses in the colonies resisted entrenched British privilege and set limits for traditional regimes, they—together with the orthodox Puritan theory of the "Good Ruler"—provided a defense of ordered society governed by agency hierarchies on the basis of differential virtue, reason, and merit.[7] The very thrust of Lockean liberalism as we have seen was to posit the state of nature as a prior, no longer existing condition from which the impetus toward social integration and the consensual constitution of legitimate institutions arose. For citizens thereafter, this prior consent produced not participation but only the continuing expectation of tacit, quiescent support. The indigenous structure of power and authority in the colonies had evolved from such a communal founding, and there was in Locke no place for subsequent individual contestation of this settlement or for explicitly political "rights" within it. The social role of rationality was also understood to take the form of governance by the few on the basis of unequally distributed and unalterable abilities. Countering the atomistic tendencies of colonial life as well as an increasingly revivalist and sectarian individualism, the evident implication of Lockean agency was rule by the best. When combined with the establishment dissenting principles of the elect and limited grace, it further suggested a coherent basis for determining those "best."

The political and ideological bind of the colonial elites, which would by the early days of the Revolution undermine their position, was that their contests with Britain for power and reduced imperial control and their growing resentment of British encroachments forced ever more radical and populist expressions of agency values. The historical accounts which identify the remarkable outpouring of secular oppositional discourse date its effective beginning in the early 1760s. Until then and even later most moderates derived their political identity from "the glorious fabrick of Britain's liberty" within a community "born under the most perfect form of government."[8] As the conflict escalated, the commercial and cultural elites felt greater pressure to locate a basis distinct from British nationalism and British principles of governance by virtual representation to define the distinctive achievement of colonial society and set it off against English practices.

The oppositional English discourses of secular agency had survived since the Civil War, if in attenuated form and only at the margins of a society marked, in the words of the historian J. H. Plumb, by "an almost monolithic stability" which "made it an almost impregnable citadel . . . impervious to change."[9] Seeking relaxed social constraints and increased spheres of self-regulation within an operational commercial society virtually inscribed and self-evident, religious dissenters, oppositional political writers, and proponents of self-sufficient reason had evolved abstract agency principles as a substitute for British institutional claims. While propounding a Lockean freedom to operate more self-reliantly, these moderates located their critiques fully within the established boundaries of English society. These discourses, whose expansive rhetoric was later utilized for colonial rebellion and further inflated as the basis of the revolutionary idyll, were a restatement of—not an alternative to—existing practice and in no sense a defense of individually pursued ends.

Thus, Algernon Sidney as well as John Trenchard and Thomas Gordon, writing as Cato, developed the radical rhetorical implications of freedom in Locke's political thought within an unqualified defense of British government. By identifying extreme statements of liberty with existing institutions, they in effect produced an idyll of a society without coercion.[10] A similar development in British moral theory after Locke asserted that norms transcending the individual whether cosmological or social and apprehended within practical "motives" and "rational deliberation" now exerted "the pull or bindingness of obligation." That is, individuals were now intrinsically *agents*, "deliberating moral agents" independently able to apprehend and act on "the good." Despite significant differences, Shaftesbury, Hutcheson, Butler, Hume, and others replaced Locke's valiant but struggling reason with an intrinsic moral sense or conscience that eliminated ethical ambiguity.[11] The result variously stated was the assertion of a normative consensus which opened the personal idyll of an individual "free"—that is, fully adapted—to act by "natural stint and bound" in socially appropriate ways.[12]

The English culmination of the idyll of a "free agent" without visible institutional coercion was dissenter Daniel Defoe's myth of a self-regulating individual in his 1719 novel *Robinson Crusoe*. Stranded on a seemingly barren Caribbean island for nearly thirty years—no Miltonian garden of abundant servitude—by discovering God, employing "reason" and "rational judgment" to order his life and "master . . . any mechanical act" or worldly process, and independently directing his "infinite labor" to cultivate his Lockean homestead, Crusoe is able to turn himself into a religious, rational, liberal agent.[13] With this transformation, "my very desires altered, my affections changed," my "delights . . . perfectly new" with "a different knowledge" and "different notions of things," he is now equipped to turn his "Island of Despair," his "prison," into a new "planted garden" of agency.[14] For Defoe, unlike Locke, even the state of nature was a condition of self-directed, self-reliant, and fully functioning agency which need not be abandoned for civil order. With reason, conscience, and political liberty operating compatibly within the agency self, the individual could presumably navigate the shoals of an independent life. Societal institutions as well as external expectations seemed to exist only at the margins to moderate occasional interactions.

Defoe could not have imagined that in writing this extraordinary personal adventure he was, half a world away, virtually shaping a social myth. Nor would he have countenanced an individualism which denied any interference by others. For Defoe was a strong believer in the shaping role of adult authority in preparing the individual for a life of duty to God and community. In his immense work *The Family Instructor,* he unveils the mystery of Crusoe's conversion and self-discipline.[15] It is a tract designed to fortify parents in their shaping of their children's character. The idyll of Crusoe's adult voluntarism had to be read as a shift of the burden of character formation from extraneous adult institutions to legitimate socializing processes, in which parental values of agency would in Lockean fashion be effectively instilled early in life as the precondition of release. That part of Crusoe's story, however, never made it to the colonies.

Thus, when the elites imported the oppositional rhetorics with their implications of inalienable rights and popular consent, they provided a discourse far more radical than they intended. They in effect imported into the colonies the idyll, or at least its language, which would undo their own privileged status. Because they never grasped the extent of popular disaffection, they were unleashing a set of extreme formulations containable in England into an emerging society without established institutional restraints or effective social controls or indeed any consensus regarding the meaning or limits of agency. In this way the populist legacy of the English Reformation, which had been cast into the English political wilderness by the Restoration, was ironically in the wilderness of colonial America to find its way to the center of political discourse.[16]

Early Elite Discourses

The ultimately untenable tensions within elite doctrine, though only implicit at the outset, are evident in the efforts of the moderate, often socially prominent clergy early in the eighteenth century to apply Lockean political and rationalist principles. Defending local prerogatives against imperial constraints and denominational control, they quite ingenuously expressed their grievances in the dissenting language of liberty of conscience and the explosive rhetoric of secular agency while assuming them to be fully compatible with existing social distinctions and rule by "the best." Although scholars such as Alan Heimert and Henry May have persuasively demonstrated how the mainstream New England clergy developed the Lockean discourses to support colonial opposition with a framework of social conservatism, this role of American Lockeanism, which challenges the central national narrative, has never been adequately grasped. Seeking to assert local claims in forceful terms within a larger defense of constituted government and internal hierarchy, the moderates grasped the integrative and elitist logic within the secular discourses of agency: "They preached Locke almost as a justification for the *status quo* . . . deploring and seeking to subdue the revolutionary enthusiasm that was, despite their hopes and efforts, arising in the American populace."[17] Lockean liberalism afforded for the local elites a necessary rejection of monarchical absolutism in favor of a ruler committed to "the good work of advancing the public welfare," while at the same time a defense of the legitimacy of a government committed to the *"general good"* without need for "public participation or control."[18]

In his 1717 writing on government, *A Vindication of the Government of New England Churches,* and other important pamphlets, John Wise, a Congregational minister and Lockean, challenged both British colonial policy and Massachusetts Presbyterian demands in the name of congregational independence. Asserting the abstract individual rights of both political liberalism and rationalism, Wise claimed that individuals are "all Naturally free and equal," with each "perfectly in his own Power and disposal, and not to be controuled by the Authority of any other." With each using the "Preroggative to Judge for himself," thus either "to subside into a State of Natural Being . . . without a Civil Head" or to enter into society "voluntarily," commonwealths are legitimate when founded by the "Covenant" of "each Man" to "joyn in one Lasting Society."[19] Similarly, the individual is to be "Guided and Restrained by the Tyes of Reason," which is "Congenate with his Nature": "God has provided a Rule for Men in all their Actions; obligating each one to the performance of that which is Right, not only as to Justice, but likewise to all other Moral Vertues."[20] Yet Wise quickly rejected the anti-institutional implications of these discourses. The natural state of "unbounded License" and "ungovernable Freedom" is "a very bloody Condition," requiring every individual to "Divest . . . himself of his Natural Freedom" and exercise a preeminently "Sociable Disposition" to at all costs "unite" with "his own species" and embrace "the necessity" of "publick Rule and Order."[21] Now "under Government" with its powerful "Authority," the individual is "obliged to Sacrifice his Private, for the Public Good."[22] This "Sovereign Power," neither democratic nor egalitarian, is modeled on "Mixt Governments" as in Venice or Britain, combining monarchy, aristocracy, and democracy. The "People" as "Subjects" possess significantly limited rights within a social order honoring "all *just Distinctions* amongst Men of Honor."[23]

Elisha Williams, the longtime rector at Yale and a Connecticut judge from a leading family, distressed by establishment restrictions on dissenters' religious practice, penned *The essential Rights and Liberties of Protestants* in their defense. Citing "the celebrated Mr. *Lock*" on natural right, individual reason, and the consensual foundations of government, Williams limited the power of established government over individuals' property rights, free speech, and particularly matters of conscience and religious practice, asserting a "*natural Liberty or Right* of *judging for themselves in Matters of Religion.*"[24] Any "civil Government" which seeks by "*Unity of Faith* and *Uniformity of Practice* in Religion" to place citizens in "a State of *Slavery*" and "a Yoke of Bondage" is a "spiritual Tyranny" and "one of the greatest Plagues that can be sent upon the World."[25] Yet, he assured his readers, individuals by "*Reason*" inevitably "*join in Society*" and "institute one common Power" to remedy the natural condition. Moreover, the "*Exercise of private Reason, and free Enquiry*" should be consistent with "Uniformity in the essential Principles of Christianity as well as Practice," as well as with "the most sure Method of procuring Peace in the State," to be ensured by admitting only Protestants. Given the English and Puritan experience, such a demand for consistency indicates the lack of mainstream realism prior to the radical Awakening.[26]

With the growing power of separatism and sectarianism toward midcentury, at the same time that establishment denominations were threatened by efforts to impose an Anglican settlement,[27] the doctrinal tensions in the elite use of the secular discourses dramatically sharpened. Leading ministers such as Charles Chauncy and Jonathan Mayhew, socially well positioned as the clergy for seaboard commercial elites and strong supporters of local civil authority, used oppositional populist contractualism and individual reason to promote their own concepts of domestic political legitimacy while at the same time castigating insurgents. Forced by their polarized situation toward a bifurcated application of Lockean doctrine, they showed little awareness of the popular exploitability of their concepts. Chauncy contested British authority as based on "*meerly* . . . birth and fortune," particularly the "restraint . . . of religious rights" by authorities without allowing each "freely to choose . . . profess and practice" religion. Where a "sovereign" promoted "slavery and misery" or abrogated "the common good and safety of society," doing not *"God's"* but *"satan's"* work, Mayhew, too, defended the Lockean right to "resist" and deny "obedience" to "lawless, unreasonable power" acting "contrary to the will of God."[28] Given the "Right and Duty of Private Judgment" enabling each "to make the best use he can of his own intellectual faculties,"[29] a *"legal establishment of religion"* was a "gross perversion and corruption," making disobedience "lawful and glorious." Noting Cromwell's resistance to Charles I, he offered a "warning to all corrupt *councellors* and *ministers*": *"Britons* will not be *slaves."*[30]

Despite these strong statements of dissenter prerogatives, the moderate clergy were within internal politics ardent defenders of indigenous elites, reacting stridently to the radical Awakening attack on authority and the order of society. Arminian Lemuel Briant of Braintree, Massachusetts, wrote in 1749: "The unthinking Multitude may be best pleased with that they understand least, and be carried away into any scheme, that generously allows them the Practice of their Vices, tho' every Article be a down right Affront to common Sense . . . [and] be ready to die in the Defense of Stupidity and Nonsense."[31] As Chauncy put it, "Some are entrusted with [power] over others" and are "distinguished from, and set above vulgar people."[32] "Rulers" who are "just," with "suitableness" for "this service," who are not "men of low natural capacities" or "small acquired accomplishments," must protect the "people's liberties" from those "who strike in with the popular cry of liberty and priviledge," exploiting the "fears and jealousies of the people" as "uneasy, turbulent and mobbish spirits" acting as "fomenters of animosities, feuds and factions."[33] Those who "behave ill in their respective stations" must be "narrowly watched,"[34] by those "checking the first outbreakings" by "lusts of men, insurrection or rebellion."[35] Chauncy affirmed his fealty to Britain by offering his "respect" to his *"civil Fathers"* and by suggesting that the English monarch, subject in the past to *"arbitrary* reign," should now be "continued in his royal house forever! . . . so long as the sun and moon shall endure."[36]

Mayhew similarly asserted his contempt for "vassals to the lawless pleasure of any man on earth," who *"use our liberty for a cloak of maliciousness"* and "strike at *liberty* under the term *licentiousness"* and *"popularity* under the disguise of *patriotism."* These *"few desperadoes"* form "a private *junto,"* a "small seditious party" to "embroil the state."[37] All "reasonable and just authority"[38] must "be aware," while citizens must be *"loyal"* and "pay due Regard to the government over us; to the KING and all in authority,"[39] realizing that "government is sacred" and "not to be *trifled* with": "It is our happiness to live under the government of a PRINCE who is satisfied with ruling according to law; as every good prince will." The ultimate public values were "peace and good order" and a "spirit of union,"[40] best furthered by the "rule and superiority" of the able and the "subjection and inferiority" of the less able as "contented and dutiful subjects."[41] In this defense of colonial elites, "the secure Enjoyment of our Rights and Property" was to be "obtained" only where "the various Ranks and Offices, carefully perform their respective Duties."[42]

Their reading of Locke argued for "Obedience to those who are appointed to command" based on the willingness of the people to consent to be ruled by "an equitable and paternal authority over them."[43] Thus, "a great deal of *implicit confidence*, must now unavoidably be placed in those that bear rule: this is implied in the very notion of authority's being originally a *trust*, committed by the people, to those who are vested with it."[44] With the state of nature in this integrative view intolerable, a "state of general disorder, approaching so near to anarchy," the social contract to found government was inevitable, necessary, and prudent. Even inalienable rights were, because of their incendiary impact on the populace, rejected in favor of the people's constitutional rights as British subjects.[45]

The belief in human reason and its universals which the moderates claimed against British arbitrariness also had to be distinguished from popular irrationality. As an antidote to popular enthusiasm, the powers of rationality and the "moral sense," a power to "distinguish between good and evil" in order to learn from God's "works, what is good, and what is required," were most potent instruments in God's "just and *rational*" world.[46] But by no means do "all men"—as was evident, they argued, in revivalist irrationalism and ignorance—have "*equal abilities* for judging what is true and right,"[47] distinct from those "few" with "Sense eno'" to "trust their own Faculties so far, as to *judge in themselves what is right*."[48] Thus, magistrates and elites generally, including this moderate establishment itself, were "*ordained of God*" as "*God's ministers* for good" by virtue of their understanding and carrying out "Magistracy duly exercised, and authority rightly applied," and being able to "refine, improve, and exalt" the "rational powers" of others. To the populace, reason by contrast would dictate their "reasonable allegiance to 'all persons in authority,'" the want of which was "ignorance, or weakness of the understanding,"[49] or worse, depravity requiring societal discipline and correction.

The two secular discourses thus merged in establishment thinking with the proto-agent defense of religious elites empowered to enforce societal order.[50] The "dictate of nature," the "good of society," the "voice of reason," and the "voice of God" all offered the same wisdom, given "the nature and constitution of things," that "rational liberty" entailed respecting one's "duty to God and man, as agreeable to the sacred oracles, to the dictates of sober reason, and adapted to the occasion." God clearly worked through the "instrumentality or agency of men," but did not choose or utilize those "means or instruments" equally.[51]

The moderate dilemma was that these abstract discourses, Mayhew's "natural rights of mankind," kindled a belief that institutions were subject to preexisting limits beyond those already embodied in the British system.[52] At a time when hierarchies were stable, as in England or the colonies before the full impact of the Awakening, the original liberal strategy of outflanking the radical Reformation by appropriating its individualist and universalist formulations in order to motivate and legitimate political reintegration and the rational embrace of universal norms while at the same time offering a populist alternative to English control worked effectively. But as deference to claims by domestic elites to have achieved a consensual and transcendental mandate unlike the empire for social integration and normative accommodation dissipated after 1760, the Lockean accretion of radical inferences, as with the religious rhetoric of conscience, provided weapons to be sharpened and used in the hands of the people. The moderates' language—that "the essence of slavery consists in being subjected to the arbitrary pleasure of others"—set up an expanding aversion to all dependence and deference. Their distinction between the "rational" and the "obedient" was destined to collapse before universal claims of agency.[53]

How was the line between "arbitrary" and "reasonable" subjection to be determined? Tyranny versus authority? License or reason? Godless versus godly? The language, becoming ever more fluid and expansive, could not distinguish one "*Reason, Will* and *Conscience*"[54] from another. Elites had taken the Hobbesian gambit of presuming universal agency only in order to assert their popular social mandate, never grasping that in America it might backfire, given that such universalism was becoming an actual entitlement enabling individuals to speak for themselves. When the colonial elites, already fighting off their own marginalization by both enthusiasts and Anglicans, embraced extreme inferences themselves against the British, the match was struck. Once they signed and disseminated the Declaration of Independence, the fire was lit that would spread universal rights across the land.

Radicalization of the Elite Discourses

The colonial leaders in the 1750s were in an anomalous situation. Though with a strong dissenting background and an emerging unease with British assumptions of empire, they were overtly contented with their status as British subjects. What turned the elites from their allegiance, to expand in turn the radical inferences of their discourses, transforming incipient agency into a distinct agency culture, ultimately proclaiming liberty and bringing even radical enthusiasts to embrace the consensual idyll of freedom? The shift began with the period of the French and Indian Wars. The early colonists had, particularly after the defeat of the Commonwealth, understood their project in transnational terms. But the continuing crises and failures in establishing a cohesive model society had led colonists to withdraw to their own regional and denominational fates. The growing accession to British power and influence in the eighteenth century weakened earlier historical antagonisms and brought into leadership interests supportive of and dependent on stronger imperial ties. It was in the crucible of foreign affairs after 1755, first with France and then Britain, that the internal elites began to reassess the distinctive character of their society. Faced with challenges requiring them to mobilize as a collectivity, these elites gradually sensed a growing disjunction of interests, which led them to question their assumption about being like England. Seeking a common framework to explain perceived differences, they crafted in the absence of religious unity an inclusive political language laced with dissenting principles. Through this process, the common beliefs that led to their initial migration, and divergent historical development and identity thereafter, reemerged with the underlying implications for a principled separation.

The first war between the British and French (1745–1748) led with further French and Indian activity on the frontier to the Seven Years' War (1755–1762). The earlier warfare, largely ignored by the radical Awakeners as ancillary to revival, had been pushed by the moderate leadership in support of Britain and colonial commercial expansion. These leaders had for the first time employed dissenting rhetoric to nationalize a secular struggle, casting the enemy as "the merciless Rage of *Popish* power." The language was designed to garner popular support: "Cruel *Papists* would quickly fill the *British Colonies*, seize our Estates, abuse our Wifes and Daughters, and barbarously murder us; as they have done the like in *France* and *Ireland*."[55] The language, lacking a sense of the colonies' distinctiveness, was a general plea for Protestant England and its way of life.

By the French and Indian Wars, a much greater popular effort was needed to gain control of the frontier. Instigated by local leaders including Washington and Franklin, it became over time an expanding contest to secure the future of the colonies. Stirred by its intractability to an ideological campaign for popular mobilization, the elites sought a common language beyond internal divisions that would tap the growing sense of colonial power. They found it in the deep common religious roots, making this a war to save "the *Protestant Lamb*" from being "extinguish[ed]" by the Antichrist composed of "the *Devil*, the *Pope*, and the *French King*."[56] The repeated vilification of "the Romish Antichristian Power" in turn mobilized some radical Awakeners who had seen the revival subside and their influence wane. Pressured to join the war effort, insurgent leaders with modest success recast it as a struggle to save the Protestant cause and the Awakening itself, calling on the people to rise "in the name of the Lord of Hosts" to defend their "evangelical ministry."[57]

A partial coalition was thus forged to fight a "grand decisive conflict between the Lamb and the beast."[58] The moderates gained some popular enthusiasm for the cause, in the process shifting their immediate antagonism from the revivalists to the war enemies, though clearly in retrospect mobilizing their own internal opposition. Sectarian leaders in some regions in turn regained the evangelical initiative, though by recasting their millenarian project in national terms they opened "the popular mind" to "the possibility of confusion, or even substitution" of secular patriotism for a Protestant polity.[59] The result was an early form of the later national revolutionary millennialism: "More concerned with the common struggle than with divisive questions many clergy found remarkable solidarity in a renewed sense of apocalyptic history," except that now "the American republic" was becoming "the primary agent of redemptive history."[60] The moderates, to frame their cause in bold terms, further utilized the uncompromising rhetorics of Protestant millennialism and Lockean political legitimation. Though carefully defending colonial class prerogatives against populist inferences, the discourses grounded society on radical bases which could not in the end support those prerogatives. Thus proclaiming what they as Britons believed were the principles of British society, they provided instead, given a vastly more radical colonial experience, definitions applicable only to American society.

In a 1756 sermon on the French and Indian Wars, the prominent Presbyterian minister Samuel Davies addressed the "encroachments, depredations, barbarities, and all the terrors of war" by which "France, that plague of Europe . . . has of late stretched her murderous arm across the wide ocean." Part of a larger spiritual campaign for "the kingdom of Christ," the "glorious scheme for the recovery of man," this project required all God's soldiers to turn "the kingdom of the earth" into *the kingdoms of our Lord* so that it "shall yet shine like lightning, or like the sun, through all the dark regions of the earth."[61] Even more explicitly, the noted minister Samuel Dunbar spoke in a 1760 address of a holy war against "the enemies of God's people," using "[ourselves] the Lord's people, in this land" who "have had . . . the happiness of engaging and enjoying the presence of God with our armies."[62] In a 1762 election address, "A Sermon Preach'd at Boston," pastor Abraham Williams utilized Lockean rhetoric to defend royal authority in a local Massachusetts dispute. Praising the "Wisdom, Virtue and Fortitude" of those leaders "whose Business it is to secure the Society against foreign Enemies," Williams justified the formation of governments from a state of nature by naturally free and equal individuals in order to provide "the secure Enjoyment of our Rights and Properties."[63]

These universalizing rhetorics were strictly circumscribed by their understandings of English social and political differentiations and inequalities, which though truncated at top and bottom in colonial society were considered both natural and inevitable. For Davies, God's "ministers are "appointed to preach his word, to administer his ordinances, and to manage the affairs of his kingdom." Because God's work "requires superior intellectual and moral endowments," those "that shall rule his people" only "such as God will approve" must for Dunbar be "men of virtue and piety . . . of fidelity, generosity and a public spirit."[64] Williams regarded existing *Magistrates* as *God's Ministers,* as "Persons of Penetration, Attention and Uprightness," of "Courage, Prudence and Fidelity," of "Wisdom, Virtue and Fortitude," that is, "the fittest for their respective Posts" and *out of all the People, able Men,* who could best carry out *Good to the People.*[65] He would permit *Liberty of Conscience* and worship, so long as individual liberty was strictly limited by "social Virtues" maintained by "Rules of Righteousness" and "Obedience, Honour and Tribute" to political and religious authority by all "the various Ranks and Offices" who "carefully perform their respective Duties" without "Private Views, selfish Lusts, and haughty Passions."[66]

And yet, without intending it, these discourses were opening a Pandora's box. Davies contrasted "human governments," worldly "kingdoms" including not only "France" but also "Great-Britain," which are often "defective and unrighteous" and ultimately come to "declension and ruin," with the perfect "kingdom of Christ," which "shall never have an end."[67] Dunbar, calling to "his peculiar people" who in *"keeping covenant with God,"* by "owning his cause, pursuing his interest, doing his will, and advancing his glory," uniquely come into the "presence of God," inadvertently spoke directly to the emerging radical Awakeners.[68] In a different way, Williams's defense of the *"Rights and Liberties of British subjects,"* his requirement of a higher level of "due Performance" in public business by "those intrusted with public Affairs," his assertion that any "person of *common Sense*" might *"honestly perform any Part* Providence may assign," was pregnant with incendiary implications.[69]

Moreover, the moderates drew upon the dissenting and secular discourses to establish the polarity between the "Tyranny" and "Slavery" of France and the British "Love of Liberty." Their injunction to "Fight for Liberty and against Slavery," their secular reframing of "evil" as "oppressive and arbitrary civil governments" rather than "papal Rome" more specifically, of Britain as the land of freedom and its liberty as their great legacy, and the decisive struggle as occurring in "the arena of politics and nations," set the rhetorical groundwork for a radically different kind of polity.[70] It was as Gordon Wood reflects a quite unstable hierarchy into which this message was sent forth, a "society in tension, torn between contradictory monarchical and republican tendencies," in which the "capacity to bind one person to another" had become "exceedingly fragile and vulnerable to challenge."[71] By repeated inferences of the "free society" and the "free individual," they diffused a political vision very different from Britain which could offer an increasingly self-conscious populace the means to articulate more radical agendas.

Sharpening Divisions and the Search for Distinctiveness

The irrevocable phase for the emerging indigenous culture and identity was the period from the Stamp Act controversy of 1763 to the temporary lull in 1772 before the final conflict. During this period, the colonial elites came to appreciate the divergence of their commercial interests and by extension their political and legislative agenda from English interests. Their objective in controversies over taxation and trade restrictions was to defend colonial economic claims within the ordered system of British governmental authority and economic supremacy. The results were clumsy, combining extreme oppositional rhetoric amounting to "symbolic assaults" that were "far outside the context of British constitutional debate and into the realm of sacred history"[72] and a sharpening sense of polarity with promises of loyalty and deference to the "*earthly* power which *must* exist in and preside over every society."[73] Insistence on representation in "some proportion" and actively expressed "consent" as the basis of a "civil government" of "free men" were conjoined with the recognition of George III as "rightful king and sovereign," Parliament as "supreme legislative," and the "*British* constitution" as "perfection."[74] The "natural, essential, inherent and inseparable rights" of "free born British," particularly to full control over one's property and to "a right of private judgment" regarding one's government, were placed beside the desire to be "good, loyal and useful subjects" merely asserting standard claims which "all British subjects are intitled to."[75] These demands for electoral participation and rights as citizens, whose denial would be "a state of slavery," a "most unsupportable Oppression and Tyranny,"[76] were asserted as properties of a presumptively free British system with little realization that the British people did not in fact possess them.

Commitment to "untainted Loyalty and chearful Obedience," even "Submission" to Britain's "Superiority,"[77] was undercut as the rhetoric of an "inestimable Right" of "Consent" over laws affecting "internal Polity and Taxation," of "Liberties" and "Freedom" allegedly "possessed by the people of *Great Britain*" and "constantly recognized by its Kings," was invoked to legitimate colonial interests at every disagreement.[78] The strings of loyalty frayed as the colonists realized that compromise, the adequate colonial representation in Parliament, was impossible. Underlying Lockean inferences of independent judgment and self-governance were for the first time emerging as *prospective* possibilities. The sharp rhetoric available within a dissenting culture labeling unwanted authority as submission to "Discord, Poverty and Slavery,"[79] which was turned against the continual interferences with colonial legislative prerogatives and individual property rights, sharpened the divergence: "We are therefore—SLAVES" intolerably subjected to "A NEW SERVITUDE."[80] The appeals brimmed with the alternative: "*We cannot be* HAPPY, WITHOUT *being* FREE. . . . YOU indeed DESERVE liberty, who so *well understand* it, so *passionately love* it, so *temperately enjoy* it, and so *wisely, bravely,* and *virtuously assert, maintain, and defend* it."[81] That this cause included leaders such as John Dickinson of Pennsylvania, Richard Bland of Virginia, and the minister John Tucker of Massachusetts, men of quite conservative bent who balked before independence (let alone inalienable personal rights), is evidence of elite naïveté.

During this period, the moderate bind sharpened, for resisting English incursions increasingly required popular support for a united and mobilized front. The moderates needed, in John Adams's words, to begin "cultivating the sensations of freedom" at all levels of colonial society, with organized protests and economic boycotts as well as public rallies and celebrations toasting "the patriotic Supporters of the Bill of Rights," "the Liberty of the Press, in its utmost Extent," "the Sons of Liberty" with "Confusion and Disgrace to all their Enemies," "the uncorrupted Minority" in Parliament, the spread of the "glorious cause of Liberty." And some people responded, not only to join in the protest against commercial restraints, but with what one colonial agent called a "general Discontent" and "an almost universal Clamor," producing a "Gloomy" situation in which "the People are distracted and Liberty mad, and the Enthusiasm is spreading fast over the . . . Colonies."[82]

For the most part, however, there was, except where directed by the elite on the seaboard, little popular interest. In fact, a much more important popular discontent was emerging directed toward elite control at the colony and local levels. Using the same language of "Free-Men" seeking to resist "Factions" that wished to "tyrannize" their fellows and the "oppressive, unreasonable and unjust" condition of *"Slaves,"* frontier insurgents from Massachusetts to North Carolina rose to protest against inequitable legislative representation, unfair taxation, suffrage restraints, and monetary, judicial, and land policies on behalf of equitable justice and local control. The elite discourse, a demand for "a Purer Air of Freedom" and "the *utmost Enjoyment of Liberty,* and *Independency,*"[83] was slowly catching on. Similarly, in the cities, common people were increasingly mobilizing with an ever clearer sense of their grievances against the depredations of local economic interests and repressive political authority.[84] At the same time, the insurgent religious movement was expanding with revivals in every region, and continuing protests and petitions against fiscal inequities and legal restraints on their activity. Despite ridicule by establishment members such as John Adams, its leaders were beginning to apply the prevailing discourse of religious liberty.

Some moderates were starting to worry that they were losing control of their own movement. They "began to be terrified at the Spirit they had raised" and "to perceive that popular Fury was not to be guided." Gary Nash has written: "Their central problem after 1765 was to lead the movement to resist British policies, employing those below them as necessary to create mass protest without losing control of the popular assembly parties which they dominated."[85] They had to resist not only "the slavery and distress of a despotic state" but the "riotous tumult, confusion, and uproar of a democratic" populace as well,[86] what James Otis called "private tumults and disorders" tolerable under "no possible circumstances, tho' ever so oppressive." Sam Adams was already intoning, "NO MOBS—NO CONFUSIONS—NO TUMULTS."[87] The focus of their worry was their very rallying ideal—the "Rights" of "free men & Subjects." Though wedded in their minds to claims of property and elite representation in Parliament, its reach expanded to incorporate the inferences of universal government by "consent" and of "unalterable Right in nature."[88]

The moderates struggled to limit power to the "virtuous." They asserted that colonial society might more capably direct its internal affairs when led by the worthy. This claim, that they could more responsibly and fully exercise British liberty than even England, was a nearly impossible one.[89] It expressed less a cynical desire to contain and control the contagion of liberty than a wish to establish a legitimate basis for domestic control—though not yet independence. They hoped to affirm loyalty to *"Country"* and "King" through the use of British principles of legitimacy while at the same time employing them against British prerogative.[90] Demands for English constitutional liberty were even less effective against Britain's duly constituted processes. Thus, insofar as arguments for a "free society" inconsistent with British rule were risks not to be taken yet, the rhetoric of virtue, part assertion, part exhortation, was necessary to establish a domestic warrant.

Asserting that the "claim to FREEDOM is on *Virtue* built," they proposed a society of *"Law, Truth,* and *Justice, Liberty* and *Right"* without *"Compulsion,"* unlike Britain, which could ensure more legitimate and defensible standards of "What you *ought not to do,* and what you *ought.*"[91]

> The prevailing principle of our government is, *virtue.* . . . By that only can liberty be preserved. . . . By *virtue,* I here mean a love for our country, which makes us pursue with alacrity . . . its preservation, and cheerfully resist the temptations of ease and luxury, with which liberty is incompatible. For lux-

ury and idleness bring on a general depravation of manners, which sets us loose from all the restraints of both private and public virtue . . . [permitting] the behaviour and politics of artful and designing men, who meditate our ruin. . . . From immorality and excesses we fall into necessity, and this leads us to a servile dependence on power, and fits us for the chains prepared for us.[92]

Virtue ensured that every interest was submerged by "public virtue" to the "public good" by acting in turn as "agents" of that good.[93] Any immorality or "corruption" undermined the capacity to govern and revealed instead a need for subordination to governance by others.[94]

To withstand British class presumptions, the moderates rejected virtue as an ascriptively hierarchical ethic, defending their view of differential "*orders of the society*" regarding social position and public role as based on and reflecting individual merit: "The superiority of *the higher orders,* or the authority with which the state has invested them, entitle them . . . to the obedience and submission of the *lower.* . . . [T]he subordination of the lower ranks claim protection, defense, and security from the higher."[95] The requirement of virtue was universal: each in the society from top to bottom, from minister to artisan, was expected to perform his or her role appropriately, to offer "public veneration, public obedience, a public and inviolable attachment . . . to contribute all he can to promote its good by his reason, his ingenuity, his strength, and every other ability."[96]

Never foreseeing the democratic thrust of merit, the moderates assumed the entitlement to rule. They imagined themselves the "wise and just Ruler" under the Lockean principle that the settlers in the colonies, possessing "freedom" and "equal claim," as the theory designated, had made a "compact." This established the legitimacy of "their Authority" in modern terms as coming "originally and solely from the people." The resulting structure of differential authority also reflected a popular agreement that the best leaders rule and made the *"people"* the *"viceregents"* and united supporters of the rulers.[97] The "liberties and privileges of the people" were thereby circumscribed, subject to "those rules which arise from the moral fitness of things productive of the general good which they are ever bound invariably to obey"[98] and requiring their "correspondent and uniform submission." Although they presumed this political system to flow from British laws,[99] it was despite its faults an early form of the unique self-government which had been created in the colonies. Because obedience was "free," given the assumption of present political consent and an earlier consent to transcendent principles both divine and political, it could be legitimately defended in their view as "a matter of choice, and not of force," the optimal "medium" between "slavish subjection" and "a lawless license."[100]

Despite protestations of loyalty by colonial elites to imperial Britain and British principles and by popular insurgents to established domestic authority, the logic of demands for self-government was uncontainable. The principle of parliamentary sovereignty could not be made consistent with colonial home rule. New commercial duties and restraints beginning in 1773, and the predictable but repressive effort to enforce English authority, would make that evident to the colonists. A few colonial thinkers had already begun developing the implications of a theory of consent: if obligation is derived from consent as "a Principle of the Law of Nature, true, certain, and universal," and this consent must be through explicit and not "*virtual* Representation," then Americans "could never be represented in the *British* parliament" and must be at least internally or even fully self-governing.[101]

These early radical formulations still cautiously sought to limit participation to British "Freeholders" or to those "having . . . property, especially a landed estate," to distinguish in effect between the elite model of a self-governing society and a fully "free society." Yet there was increasing awareness that England's failing regarding representation was rather the colony's distinctiveness, its practices regarding popular participation the sign of political evolution rather than a legacy from Britain. For with "nine Tenths of the People of Britain . . . deprived of . . . being Electors," there was "a great Defect" in the "original Purity" of England's "present Constitution."[102] The moderate rhetoric grew ever more universal: "Our fathers fought and found freedom in the wilderness. . . . We cannot, we will not, betray the trust reposed in us by our ancestors, by giving up the least of our liberties.—We will be freemen, or we will die."[103] This was provocative rhetoric, overshadowing all implied franchise qualifications for those so inclined.

And many were so inclined: ordinary people in the cities, products of the evangelical movement, were moved neither by the agenda of the commercial and political elites nor by their "society of virtue"; the insurgent Awakeners in the rural and frontier areas garnering popular support to protest the local powers and the ecclesiastical establishment spurred localist mobilization in many areas. They wanted a government responsive to their interests and fully subject to popular rule, and freedom from establishment to practice their religion and from a repressive "public good" to pursue their own economic interests.[104] In place of established institutional authority, they defended "fundamental rights" derived from the "duty to God and religion" and directed to the goals of the Awakening. As the elites more widely promoted home rule in order to protect their own interests from "Grievous tribute" and "an American Episcopate," they increasingly after 1772 framed their demands in terms of the "necessary . . . consent of the inhabitants" and full "Civil *and* Religeoous rights."[105] This rhetoric in service of elite claims both frustrated the populace and emboldened their own assertions, complicating efforts to gain their support for domestic commercial interests and, in time, to fight the war.

The Elite Drive for Independence

The final phase in the elite movement toward independence culminating in Jefferson's effort to frame a unified agenda for war was the rejection of parliamentary sovereignty. There remained strong sentiments as evident in the First Continental Congress to restore "a happy connection with Great-Britain."[106] Yet the two societies' interests were being increasingly regarded as fundamentally incompatible. The British government it was believed might very well find it "popular and reputable at home to repress us" and by "inventing schemes to serve the mother country at the expense of the colonies."[107] As confidence in the presence of a systemic balance of interests or of checks on "arbitrary government" dissipated, such rising leaders as John Adams and Jefferson sharpened the rhetorical divisions and political differences.[108] They distinguished the acts of legitimate government from the "iron hand of oppression" by "despotic masters" acting "with all the rapaciousness of Roman publicans" to "subjugate and bear down the inhabitants" under "abject slavery."[109] Adams in 1773 expressed the view for the Massachusetts colony that, as "the right of representation in the English Parliament could not have been exercised by the people of this colony," then Parliament by constitutional principles "never had such authority" over it. Jefferson in his bold way argued "from the nature of things" that "every society must at all times possess within itself the sovereign power of legislation."[110]

The fervor of these rhetorical assertions, the perplexing, opportunistic, and disingenuous claim that Parliament's monopoly power had never been constitutionally mandated, as well as the claims of oppression now regarded as vastly inflated if not contrived, together suggest an internal push toward revolution. Gordon Wood has concluded in this regard that "the white colonists were not an oppressed people. . . . In fact, the colonists knew they were freer, more equal, more prosperous, and less burdened with cumbersome feudal and monarchic restraints than any other part of mankind in the eighteenth century."[111] The otherwise puzzling reaction to a rather unexceptional British rule is explained in retrospect by a growing sense among moderates that the colonies were at least an equal and quite likely a fundamentally different (and better) society. James Wilson wrote: "The original and true ground of the superiority of Great Britain over the colonies is . . . unaccounted for" and "cannot be accounted for."[112] The colonies with their "*free* constitution" that were "such nurseries of freemen" had already before independence surpassed England, where only "160,000 electors" ruled undemocratically not only that society but also "four millions in the states of America, every individual of whom is equal to every individual of them, in virtue, in understanding, and in bodily strength."[113] The social and characterological advance underlying colonial experience had over time generated sharply divergent social expectations regarding legitimacy and local prerogative and revived old historical antagonisms to servitude.

As the conceptual barriers to a distinct colonial reality retreated, arguments for independence mushroomed.[114] Adams offered the "conclusion" that "the colonies" were to be "thus independent" and "distinct states." James Wilson counseled that "the superiority of Great Britain over the colonies" and their "dependence" both "be rejected." Simeon Howard argued that "laying unreasonable burdens and restraints upon a people" by "an encroaching power" must be countered by "the right and duty of a people to engage in war" to save "public liberty."[115] Daniel Leonard, a later Tory writing as Massachusettensis, saw "no doubt but it is fit, and perfectly consistent with the principles of all laws human and divine, to resist robbers, murderers, subverters of the government of free states." So it was with ministers Nathaniel Hale, Gad Hitchcock, and Samuel Sherwood.[116] Jefferson in 1774 proclaimed by "the God who gave us life" and "liberty" that under no circumstances shall "our properties within our own territories . . . be taxed or regulated by any power on earth but our own."[117]

The language was uncompromising. Civil authority was to be strictly limited, for "the madness and folly of oppressive rulers" will, "if they are submitted to" by a people, "debase their minds, break their spirits, enervate their courage." The "caprice" of "arbitrary will" cannot be "*lawful government.*" Rulers as "trustees of society" must exercise "their authority . . . for, and to no other purpose than, the common benefit."[118] As for those rulers, including the British, who "act in an arbitrary, tyrannical manner, to oppress and enslave their subjects; they do the highest injustice and wrong, and the greatest mischief and evil of any men in the world; and are the biggest plagues." Being in their "high and elevated stations," they bear the "heaviest judgments."[119] The right to participate in government was in turn expressed in universal terms. Adams called it "one of the liberties of free and natural subjects . . . to be governed 'by laws made by persons, in whose election they, from time to time, have a voice.'" The Continental Congress subscribed to the view that "in a free state, every man, who is supposed to be a free agent, *ought to be concerned in his own government.*" Jefferson argued that "the great principles of right and wrong" underlying "the whole art of government" are "legible to every reader."[120]

Liberty itself was now praised in extreme fashion. Howard regarded all "power granted to rulers" to be "limited" by a continuing "natural liberty." Leonard asserted the continuation in established society of the people's original "right to life, liberty, and the possession and disposal of their property." The Continental Congress spoke of "the invaluable rights . . . without which a people cannot be free and happy," which "*you* are entitled to."[121] Nathaniel Niles celebrated this "land of liberty" in which "we have boasted of our liberty, and free spirit." Hitchcock asserted that we "hold our liberties sacred," Levi Hart that "this [is a] land of liberty where the spirit of freedom glows with such ardor," Samuel Sherwood "our precious liberties and privileges."[122] The less cautious though no more radical went so far as to claim that tyranny dissolved all government, which in Leonard's terms "naturally throws us back into a state of nature." Sherwood asserted that "when rulers . . . will not comply with . . . a reasonable and equitable demand from the subject; the society is dissolved . . . and the relation between the ruler and the subject ceases." Thus he defended the British in "deposing king James the second, that tyrannical oppressive prince."[123]

Despite a clear radical trajectory in hindsight, these discourses served the cause of internal elite succession and not the restructuring of internal society unimagined before Paine's fireball and resisted thereafter. As the colonial leaders, the moderates regarded independence as the full agenda of the insurgency. They lacked interest in political or economic reform as well as any social agenda beyond the "repudiation" of British "hereditary status and the privilege derived from it."[124] For them, the rules of a hierarchical agency society were fixed and enduring. The individual was a "moral agent, and accountable creature" ruled by the ends of God and society as they had become institutionalized in the colonies. This meant a world governed by the "practice of religion and virtue" and by "our superiors" whose "religion and virtue," "superior wisdom and conduct" made them "the guardians of our common interest." Society would thus achieve "good order and regularity" in which "all ranks of men move in strait lines, and within their own proper spheres."[125] As the "leaders," including Sam and John Adams, James Otis, and Elbridge Gerry, "were quite content to see a continuation of existing social and political relationships," they believed that the Revolution was completed with "the abolition of the prerogative and the reestablishment of the traditional institutions of the colony."[126] They assumed colonial unanimity in which "the individuals are of one mind" and "unite" for "the highest good of the whole." "Persons of rank and fortune" were to possess "great influence" and popular sway by promoting virtuous, responsible rebellion through "their example."[127]

They were in no way prepared for the force and duration of the popular mobilization over internal policies and the domestic distribution of power:

> All of these developments were to become somewhat disquieting to the Whig leaders who had so lavishly used the vocabulary of freedom before 1776. It had apparently not occurred to them that anyone besides Tories could question their right to represent the whole people in all cases whatsoever, or that their own doctrine might be used as a platform for reform of the very government through which they exercised power. . . . [I]ndeed, they considered restrictions on the people to be just as necessary for the preservation of freedom as restrictions on a political despot.[128]

Only "dimly at first," Carl Becker writes, "but with growing clearness, the privileged" realized that proto-agent hierarchies were being fundamentally contested. This left a "most difficult problem," that of "maintaining their privileges" and view of society "against royal encroachment from above without losing them by popular encroachment from below."[129]

The Second Revolution

The concept of a second or internal revolution central to the Progressive school of historiography collapsed after World War II as the effort to identify it in economic and class terms faltered: there was neither sufficient economic deprivation in the areas of greatest resistance nor anything approaching an ideology or understanding of economic mobilization (for the people accepted material disparities) to explain an interest-based movement from below. That second revolution, however, has refused to disappear before the onslaught of consensual models. Ronald Hoffman, a leading historian of the period, echoes concerns of other modern scholars who find the "lesser sorts' challenge" to "privileged status and notions of proper social order" an indispensable element of the Revolution. He elaborates: "The turmoil of war and its attendant social dislocation unleashed resentments long suppressed by the structural framework of colonial society, and when invigorated by the 'leveling' tendencies inherent in the 'contagion' of Revolutionary rhetoric, this rancor threatened the leadership's social and political position."[130] Hoffman's provisional class analysis, however, risks reviving a no longer convincing Progressive paradigm.

Because historians with few exceptions have been unable to explain this dynamic central to the forging of the nation, the internal revolution remains a challenge to the foundations of national identity. The failure, which involves the inability to link the Revolution to the great popular awakenings before and after it, to the continuing revivals that fed it, or to the two-hundred-year discourses against authority, privilege, and external intrusion that framed popular attitudes, has left us unable to explain either the fierce contests over state constitutions and bills of rights and the federal Constitution, or the swift (magical?) decline of the Federalists, or the popular construction of a new nation through Jeffersonian and Jacksonian populism. It is now an unavoidable conclusion that the trajectory of the Revolution derived from the conjunction of two rebellions, the elite and the popular revolt. The former alone would have led to a self-governing society in the hands of a proto-agency hierarchy. The latter, as we shall see, was fueled by the dramatic emergence and spread of universal agency in the radical revivals, and demanded release from colonial elites and their control over "state and church." Combining "this popular spirit of pietistic self-righteousness with a new commitment to inalienable natural rights"—new because it only really emerged with the influence of the Declaration—this insurgency fought and ultimately undid the colonial hierarchy.[131]

The perennial issue whether the Revolution was a conservative defense of an already post-traditional colonial society or a radical transformation of society is thus to be resolved by noting the presence of both. Although the two movements shared a deep historical grounding in dissenting values and were to ally temporarily in the struggle against "servitude," their distinctive agendas cannot be neglected. The moderate project drove the imperial struggle and culminated in the Federalist constitutional effort to found a centralized nation which protected elite minorities from popular rule if it could not reinstate them. While the impetus for this movement came from political and economic differences, British claims of authority—including, but not only, ecclesiastical claims—tapped deep and "ancient hatreds, often sectarian," of an imperiousness which had shaped the histories of the moderates.[132] And the moderate clergy further drew upon the communal religious covenant to frame the justice and necessity of independence. The popular revolution sought the ending of all ascriptive differences through principles of political, economic, and religious equality and a society freed from external controls on local governance. That the victory of the latter in the early nineteenth century would only portend the formation of new democratic elites few at the time grasped.

The difficulty in acknowledging the full importance and character of this second revolution beyond the liberal and denominational biases of historians lies—as with the Great Awakening—in the nature of its movements. The revivalists since the 1740s had migrated toward areas beyond institutional control, where their communities of worship could operate without constraint. Awakening spread from eastern New England and the middle colonies toward the West and Southwest beyond the glaring eye of dominant institutions. For this reason, only quite recently have historians such as Patricia Bonomi, Stephen Marini, and Thomas J. Curry made a strong case for the "proliferation and growth" of "rival denominations" in the revolutionary period.[133] Marini suggests that the "image of religion as weakened and confused, its institutions languishing and its resources depleted" during the age of the Revolution itself is "inaccurate," that "far from suffering decline, religion experienced vigorous growth and luxuriant development during the Revolutionary period." In particular, "the religious world of America's backcountry from Maine to the Carolinas" had "substantially altered" as "the colonial configuration of religions had largely been replaced by a new and long-lasting pattern of evangelical dominance." Marini argues that "evangelicals there had swiftly and unexpectedly moved from the periphery to the center of religio-political influence," even gaining "their first glimpse of majoritarian power and the possibility that the new nation's government could embody their agenda."[134]

Yet the Awakeners continued to define themselves in apolitical terms: "The confrontation between evangelism and the traditional order . . . was not over the distribution of political power or of economic wealth, but over the ways of men and the ways of God." They believed in "the separateness of true religion from the world," regarding themselves as "called out of the world . . . to live together, and execute gospel discipline among them." To the extent that they mobilized, it was "to advance the gospel 'against all the Powers of the Earth.'"[135] Until the period of the Revolution, all but a few leaders like Isaac Backus were confined to winning souls in their own community. Moreover, the religious reformers long doubted their capacity to influence the larger political agenda. To the degree that they were political, in Wood's terms, "they confined themselves to local issues" in their aspirations and expectations. Their structures were local and their denominational role, in large part depending on its stance toward popular revivalism, varied by region.[136] None of these groups, according to Curry, "theorized about, much less fought for, causes that did not directly involve themselves . . . neither did they concern themselves . . . with practical implications for society." They viewed organized government with suspicion and "tended to identify centralization with tyranny."[137]

What mobilized the internal revolution ironically was increasing and organized elite efforts to take over domestic politics. The radical Awakeners' fear and dislike of internal elites had been building since the Awakening and before, as this group consistently utilized legislative power at every level of the colonial structure to enforce its political, economic, and religious will. Elites attacked the insurgents as akin to "the madness of Munster" and "persons of a gloomy, ghostly, and mystic cast, absorbed in visionary scenes" while proposing "innovations" out of "the most foaming zeal," making them "enemies to our country."[138]

Robert Taylor observed that the populists in western Massachusetts between 1740 and the mid-1770s showed "indifference and even hostility to the views of the Boston Whigs," with votes in opposition to the latter's policies "often unanimous."[139] The western revivalists were convinced that "the established Congregationalism of the colony constituted a greater danger to freedom than the distant threat of an established Anglicanism." In New York there were sentiments that the local elite would "subject the people 'to a tyranny and oppression . . . not much better' than the British."[140] In Virginia and North Carolina, the evangelists challenged gentry life and social order at every chance, "overturning . . . deference and respect" with their vision of a reformed, egalitarian spiritual order.[141] Backus, fearful of elite "self-love" and "religious pretense," cited a friend's reservations: "Formerly there was a check on the licentiousness of power in America by an appeal to the Crown; but where shall the persecuted Americans appeal now? They can only appeal to their oppressors and accusers."[142] In Pennsylvania and New Hampshire, populists feared with the political mobilization of the local "men of fortune" for "independence" that "a minority of rich men" would "govern the majority of virtuous freeholders of the province."[143] At points, populist regions supported Britain as a lesser evil and even considered secession.

As the moderates mobilized to gain control of state legislatures and the conventions being called to draft new state constitutions, the populace was forced to respond in self-defense. The future of domestic power arrangements lay in the balance, and of particular concern was the role of religion in the new society. These issues had already been contested in several colonies with fractious internal politics, including Connecticut, Pennsylvania, and North Carolina, since the 1760s. Now with every colony being restructured, "thousands of provincials from every rank and section . . . became embroiled in political activity as a consequence of their religious loyalties. . . . Lay members, and in a number of cases clergymen themselves, provided the leadership for movements whose initial religious aims rapidly became indistinguishable from political ones."[144] The growing mobilization of "the patriot movement" in the name of "traditional deferential social order" was, to everyone's surprise, "unleashing forces" that "undermined" the colonial way of life and established decisively "new political conditions."[145]

The populist forces were profoundly handicapped in that, far from being Lockeans, they had always regarded themselves as being in religious opposition and lacked any secular theory of governance. They drew not from applicable models of governance such as "classical republicanism or British constitutional theory, but rather from the Bible."[146] Moreover, these beliefs were inconsistent with radical Lockeanism, which made "a dangerous error" with the view that "true government" was inconsistent in any way with one's "true and full liberty" as a Christian. They were largely members of an oral culture with a primitive education that extended only to the Bible and the sermons of local preachers.[147] Because "radical Protestantism privileges the spoken word," writes Robert Ferguson, "the closer we get to the Revolution, the less satisfactory the printed text becomes as a barometer of thought."

Their movements also suffered from "primitive political conceptions," being "visionary, impractical, and marred by localism" as well as "vague and confused" regarding institutional practicalities.[148] Their traditional acceptance of structural inequalities and power relations was in direct—and unre-solved—conflict with the "conviction that the Bible revealed an alternative, far more decentralized structure of government that would establish the ba-sis for the millennial New Jerusalem in America." For the most part, "com-mon people" did not perceive "government as a means by which economic and social power might be distributed or the problems of their lives re-solved." David Thomas in 1771 justified the sectarian stance in which "we concern not ourselves with government . . . nor make any attempt to alter the constitution of the kingdom to which as men we belong."[149] It was only with *Common Sense* and then the Declaration that the people began to grasp systematically that the structure of society itself was capable of being con-tested. They would then begin to appropriate the available discourses of elite politics, in the process transforming their meaning and scope.

Given their lack of indigenous ideas about governance and a further in-ability to mount intercolonial political organizations, it is a wonder that this movement had such reach and impact. One curious reaction by local and regional historians studying the prerevolutionary and early revolutionary period is their consistent surprise at uncovering vibrant local opposition, which they tend to treat as atypical, given the larger picture of the period. The resulting neglect has led, as Rhys Isaac notes, to the "rich records of popular religious upsurge" being "left as the preserve of denominational historians" and never "given the same importance as the records of the struggle for independence."[150] Yet Awakener insurgencies within the po-litical arena appeared in every colony, emerging from the areas of strong sectarian agitation. Despite their localism, moreover, they focused their pri-mary discontent on a common range of domestic issues with similar ob-jectives for reforming and restructuring government. Their long common roots, their shared history and vision of the human order, and their patterns of continual intermigration account for these parallels.

The issues taken on by the second revolution are by no means only reli-gious in nature. To be sure, in the internal struggle between 1775 and 1789 the issues of toleration and disestablishment, discriminatory taxation on be-half of established denominations, and sanctions on religious diversity were the most comprehensively put forward by the legions of radical Awakeners. In every colony where toleration and disestablishment had not already been won and dissent accepted as in Pennsylvania, Rhode Island, Connecticut, New Jersey, New York, and Delaware—that is, in Massachusetts, North Carolina, Virginia, South Carolina, Maryland, Vermont and New Hampshire, and Georgia—the religious clauses in the state constitutions and bills of rights were fiercely contested. As Marc Kruman notes in his 1997 book *Between Authority and Liberty: State Constitution Making in Revolutionary America,* "of all the rights enumerated in the declarations and constitutions, the one that appeared in all and received the most treatment was freedom of religion."[151] In the later mobilization over federal ratification and the federal Bill of Rights, fears over the possible linkage of church and state, as Madison realized, stirred sectarians throughout the colonies.[152]

At the same time, there is ample evidence to claim that the moving force in the wide range of other political, economic, and juridical issues was in the same areas and among the same groups that led the fight on religion. Popular contestations over the franchise, specifically suffrage requirements and equitable districting, over the power and staffing of the judiciary, over popular ratification of state constitutions, over patronage issues and qualifications for office, over the very inclusion of broader guarantees in state bills of rights, all stemmed from the strongholds of religious dissidents. Here the vision was articulated of "a simple Democracy" absent "everything that leans to aristocracy or power in the hands of the rich and chief men exercised to the oppression of the poor."[153] It was in these regions that the call went out to resist the imposition of "a yoke of oppression we are no longer able to bear." From the West came the cries for "popular sovereignty as the right of the people," that "just as all men are equal in the sight of God, so all men are equal in the creation of fundamental law."[154] Issues such as franchise restrictions were framed as a violation of the cause "under God" of "working out the great salvation in our land." Elite rule, "for the Majority to consent to be governed by the Minority," was called "down right popery in politicks."[155]

The decades-long religious insurgency in Bonomi's terms "forms the bridge between the Great Awakening and the American Revolution" in that it transformed "patterns of leadership" and "popular participation in organized opposition to authority." It further established a growing connection between the ways the populace "framed political and religious issues," and led to the development of "new ways of thinking about authority." One consequence was that "the church congregations" became, in her analysis, the "school of democracy," now extending alike "to rich and poor, men and women, the schooled and the unschooled."[156] Similarly, as Stephen Marini and Robert Rutland have pointed out, the later anti-Federalist agitation on nonreligious issues was directly associated with the radical Awakeners.

In colony after colony, these groups exploded in numbers during the war years. Out of their "consensual, covenantal, and localist religious dissent" grew the anti-Federalist vision: "a national federation of the several state republics that was minimal in structure, strictly limited in authority by the guaranteed, enumerated rights of the people, and animated by a spirit of consensus and a virtuous regard for the common good."[157] These insurgents organized across the country for a more just Constitution and the inclusion of a Bill of Rights.

Despite their oppositional and democratic leanings, it would as I have suggested be a mistake to regard the popular upsurge as the locus of the American idyll. The central issue regarding the internal distribution of power was not ensuring liberty but providing dissenters space from elite and state intrusion to pursue their very different but fully constrained vision of the agency community: "The fundamental aim of their political action, institutional design, and economic program was to preserve their traditional communitarian society."[158] Individuals were expected to lead pious and ordered lives within "a close, supportive, and orderly community, 'a congregation of faithful persons, called out of the world by divine grace, who mutually agree to live together, and execute gospel discipline among them.'" Even as the influence of the Declaration infused their public writings with the rhetoric of the idyll, Awakeners throughout the land proceeded locally ever more consciously for the next seventy-five years to "facilitate the proliferation of gathered churches."[159] This commitment to agency, while by no means an embrace of freedom, would soon make them supporters of independence from external controls.

The "Mobilization"

Given a populace very different from the one ordinarily portrayed, the colonial elites—if they were to mount an effective war for independence—could not take its support for granted. Even well into 1776, after Ticonderoga, Bunker Hill, and the Prohibitory Acts, ordinary colonists had not rallied in great numbers to their cause. As moderates promoted their agenda throughout the colonies, they grew worried. John Jay seriously questioned New York's popular support for the Whig cause, and rural districts revealed particular disinterest. In Massachusetts, the eastern leaders were upset by the western preoccupation with the internal revolution as well as by urban discontent, and Rhode Island was equally disinclined. The town of Pittsfield declared in 1775 that "if the right of nominating to office is not invested in the people, we are indifferent who assumes it whether any particular persons on this or the other side of the [wa]ter." In Virginia, among lower gentry and common people, their attention was "very little taken up with the war."[160] Ronald Hoffman acknowledges "the perilous position of the patriot cause within a disordered society so rent with economic and social divisions that its members had little incentive to swear allegiance to it."[161] Throughout the backcountry, in North and South Carolina, in Massachusetts, and in Virginia, substantial support was offered for a time to the British in protest of internal elites. Some used the growing rift between the British and Whigs as an exploitable division to press internal concerns.

There is a propensity regardless of the evidence to treat the mobilization for independence as a popular cause and the gradual emergence of public support as a "'ripening' of opinion." This is captured in Pauline Maier's unintended irony when she refers to elite strategy as "the effort to build an Independence movement 'from the bottom up.'"[162] The truth is that the elites simply could not depend on popular support. As Isaac writes, "it was imperative for the patriot gentry to communicate to the populace not only their fearful view of what awaited . . . should they remain supine, but also the vision of the good life that inspired the struggle."[163] The moderates had learned over many years the "technique of mobilizing the people" at the local level, and moderate clergy throughout the colonies were encouraged to turn "colonial resistance into a righteous cause."[164] Representatives were dispatched to the dissenting areas to "woo settlers to the patriot cause." Before Jefferson's Declaration, local declarations would be drafted across the land by leadership but attributed to—and intended to stir—"popular sentiment."[165] The press was mobilized and committees and conferences were called to push independence. Public events were staged as "important ceremonial means of mobilizing the populace," including "dramatizing to freeholders the awful menace of British power and the noble solidarity of Americans. A glow of virtue was combined with the exhilarating sense of brave defiance gestured on a world stage."[166]

The difficulty of mobilizing the populace was crystallized by the publication of *Common Sense*. With Tom Paine, a British political exile of Quaker origins, the Commonwealth vision achieved its fullest expression. It set the land afire with radical dissenting ideals and made a national Declaration of Independence as a statement of common purpose which also addressed the internal revolution virtually inevitable. Advertised everywhere, this statement quickly sold 150,000 copies and galvanized the colonies for independence. This reception of Paine's call in early 1776 for an "open and determined DECLARATION FOR INDEPENDENCE" to announce to the world the fact and legitimacy of separation, that "the last cord is now broken" and "the Rubicon is crossed" such that "'TIS TIME TO PART,"[167] testifies to the vast distance the American colonies had traversed.

Paine's great innovation as harbinger of a "new aera of politics" based on "a new method of political thinkings" was to reframe the question of internal political legitimacy. For the first time the moderate Lockean discourse was turned inside out, linked to a populist agenda. The state of nature is no longer a mere theoretical support to pressure an existing government to redirect its priorities but a normative standard deriving from a viable if temporary condition. By its terms not merely foreign rule but monarchy itself is unnatural and, given the feasibility of actually returning to nature and starting over—"We have it in our power to begin the world again"—unnecessary. With *Common Sense,* a language once limited to elites is employed against all existing institutions. Irreducible limits on sovereignty, inalienable claims of equality, and self-government through participation of "every part of the community" become requirements of founding as well as ongoing conditions of legitimacy. Society needs political authority to contain individual license, but only if both inclusive and severely limited in its interference with the voluntarist operation of society. The question of authority poses a simple choice: "Whether we shall make our own laws, or whether the king, the greatest enemy this continent hath, or can have, shall tell us *there shall be no laws but such as I like.*"[168]

Behind this stark shift in the grounds of political legitimacy lay Paine's appeal to the Americans' new agency natures. This young colonial people were capable of forming a society on new internal principles because they had grown up, they had developmentally "come of age." All forms of servitude to internal *or* external masters, "the distinction of men into KINGS and SUBJECTS" arising in "dark and slavish times," are with "no truly natural or religious reason."[169] Individuals are now naturally agents who willingly seek to constitute "the reciprocal blessings" of society and collective life on terms of *"the happiness of the governed,"* and the protection of that condition is to be thenceforth the only legitimate function of politics. Human development cannot be stopped: "Nothing can be more fallacious than . . . [to] assert . . . that the first twenty years of our lives is to become a precedent for the next twenty." The colonies are "a youth who is nearly out of his time"; in fact, urged Paine, we are "parents" already who "should take our children in our hand."[170]

Paine most fully articulated the vision of a universal, voluntary human agency and America's unique destiny as its bearer to be the "asylum for mankind" where all others have failed.[171] As a defender of the popular agenda yet adept at liberal theory, he revealed the theory's great and flexible capacity for inclusion. His statement, as Henry May has pointed out, is not as radical as the Declaration: it is a defense not of individual freedom but of a new equality both of individuals and of nations.[172] At the same time, by expressing the case for universal agency in rhetoric that carried him toward the Lockean idyll, Paine prepared the way for the more extreme formulation of the Declaration. If "oppression" and "tyranny" "overrun . . . [e]very spot of the old world," then it is "freedom" which "America alone can save": "The birthday of a new world is at hand, and a race of men . . . are to receive their portion of freedom."[173] While Paine did not explore the possibility of individual rights apart from society, the enthusiasm for his driving rhetoric galvanized popular sentiments and helped persuade Jefferson, fearing the divisions and recognizing the stakes, to take the final step.

The populace was now beginning to grasp more clearly the grounds of their national distinctiveness. *Common Sense* was being talked about everywhere. It was read by insurgents at public meetings, used in populist pamphlets, and cited in legislative struggles. One New York publisher wrote, "It is certain, that there never was anything published here within these thirty years . . . that has been more universally approved and admired."[174] The incongruousness of the moderates' effort to monopolize domestic political control while embracing an ever more uncompromisingly populist agenda and rhetoric on their own behalf was exposed by the new radical discourse. This led Awakeners toward a further rejection of all hierarchical political authority. If, as one opponent put it, combining religious and the new liberal rhetoric, "CHRIST *hath made all his People Kings*," then political inequity was by definition an unwarranted infringement on equal "Freedom and Liberty."[175] The Baptists, having already begun a broad campaign of civil disobedience, now modeled their public appeals ironically yet aptly after the Sons of Liberty and "eagerly used" the Revolution's "slogans and the spirit it generated to aid their own cause."[176]

The moderates were caught in the contradictions, not to say hypocrisies, of their own assertions. The anomalies within the elite cause were readily apparent to Backus: "Liberty of conscience, the great and most important article of liberty, is evidently not allowed as it ought to be in this country, not even by the very men who are now making loud complaints of encroachments upon their own liberties" by the British. He warned Sam Adams about governing bodies that would "deny to their fellow servants that liberty which they so earnestly insist upon for themselves. A word to the wise is sufficient."[177] Virginia radicals asserted that "the Sons of Liberty" of all people ought not to "carry on unjust oppression in our own province."[178] Patriot leaders were seen as "very noisy about liberty but . . . aiming at nothing more than personal power and grandeur." Those recently "on an equality with some of the meanest of us" were condemned for seeking dominance.[179] Paine's manifesto allowed the populace to demand "to see realized . . . the Revolutionary principles which the patriots had urged against British oppression."[180]

Among the moderates, *Common Sense* produced their gravest crisis to date. It revealed that the elite "mobilization" was not working, or was working contrary to expectations, and many hated it. John Adams "dreaded the effect so popular a pamphlet might have among the people, and determined to do all in his power to counteract the effect of it."[181] He feared the "rude and insolent rabble" which Paine, with his "absurd democratical notions," wanted to empower to "confound and destroy all distinctions, and prostrate all ranks to one common level."[182] The result was his influential "Thoughts on Government," a defense of the moderate hierarchical agency society which influenced numerous state constitutions. James Allen wrote: "All may bid adieu to our old happy constitution and peace. . . . I love the cause of liberty; but cannot heartily join in the prosecution of measures totally foreign to the original plan of resistance. The madness of the multitude is but one degree better than submission to the Tea-Act." Some asked that publishers "would not reprint 'Common Sense'; the peoples minds not being prepared."[183]

The surfacing of the internal revolution and the seemingly irresistible logic of inclusion and expansion led to deep foreboding. John Adams wrote, "Such a leveling spirit prevails . . . that I fear we shall be obliged to call in a military force to do that which our civil government was originally designed for."[184] John Jay was "disturbed by the lack of 'good and well ordered Governments' to counteract 'that Anarchy which already too much prevails.'" William Smith asked, "Why raise a military spirit that may furnish unmanageable adventurers on this side of the water unfriendly to a province in which you and I have something else to lose?" Expanded suffrage, he believed, would lead to "all sorts of Rapine and Plunder!"[185] The rise of "new men" pressing new ideals created in Sam Adams's view a "danger of errors on the side of the people" whose political and religious aspirations he ridiculed. Gouverneur Morris warned that as "the mob begin to think and reason," he imagined "with fear and trembling, we will be under the worst of all possible dominions . . .—a riotous mob."[186] Samuel West referred to the political opposition as "a monster in nature, and an enemy to his own species. James Otis proclaimed, "When the pot boils, the scum will rise."[187]

The strategy of stigmatizing popular government as the anarchic and moblike acts of "poor ignorant Creatures" when it pursued its own agenda while affirming the glorious "voice of the people" only when it rallied to the moderate cause was not working.[188] Many members of the internal elite reflected seriously on backing out of the campaign.[189] A Tory reflected on the Whig leadership that "those of prosperity are afraid of their estates, and are coming about fast. They say they have gone too far." The people were now, according to the British general Thomas Gage, following the example of those leaders "who first sowed the seeds of Sedition amongst the People and taught them to rise in Opposition to the Laws," creating results that were "easily foreseen."[190] But it was too late to back out. The deep historical divisions within the British world were now fully apparent, and the military contest for colonial control had begun. The populace still possessed no unified organization and no coherent theory of government. As far as their potential to lead was concerned, *Common Sense* had after all been a set of wholly unrealistic assertions. The people could still presumably be won, as they always had, to the moderate cause if the right case was made. That was to be the task of Jefferson's Declaration.

A Revolutionary Idyll

The unity to make common cause was clearly absent: there were in the colonies two movements but no revolution, two theories of agency quite different from England's but with radically distinct agendas—independence without reform, and reform regardless of independence. Each agenda was moreover a red flag before its opponents. The language of being "oppressed in this land" either religiously or politically and needing a "liberty" with which "no human authority can intermeddle" to pursue "the kingdom of Christ," of refusing to "take Directions . . . from any Body" regarding "the Cause of the People," sent the colonial moderates into a rage.[191] Equally, the directive to "MAGISTRATES AND MINISTERS" to "inculcate the knowledge and practice of true religion and virtue" in "the people committed to their charge" by using "their influence and authority" reeked of Old World tyranny.[192]

It was up to the moderates, as the dominant party with more immediate goals, to forge a consensus. The colonial cause had to be defined in a way which muted if it did not reconcile basic differences, and in some ninety local declarations of independence in the months preceding the national Declaration the elites developed a discourse of greater popular appeal as a basis of national mobilization.[193] They increasingly moderated their punishment of insurgent activity, recognizing that "concessions" were essential for "colonial harmony." In place of the divisive language of virtue or of economic or property rights, there was increasingly a defense of collective "lives, liberties, and properties" and a litany of common complaints against British tyranny. The latter, including impressment, stirring of Indians and slaves on the frontier, and recent British heavy-handedness, was geared toward popular grievances.[194] The primary right, also weighted toward popular approval, was a new form of government based on the "Influence and Controul of the People."[195]

As they learned the power of voluntarist rhetoric to stir popular enthusiasm, the elites increasingly turned the campaign of ideas over to those leaders who could articulate it.[196] While Jefferson was to seal the centrality of this discourse by announcing its most extreme case, in evaluating his document we must be clear that individual voluntarism was at the core of neither revolution: for the elites it was politically incendiary, for the populace incidental to other substantive goals. To understand the Declaration, then, we must dispense with the ritual belief, as stated by Pauline Maier, that "by the late eighteenth century, 'Lockean' ideas on government were accepted everywhere in America" and thus the Declaration "restated what virtually all Americans—patriot and Loyalist alike—thought and said."[197] As David Freeman Hawke has developed at length, this idea is "a half-truth at best," for the Declaration "evoked, a private vision of America's past and present," offering a "liberty, equality, and government by consent of the governed" incommensurable with the elite commitment to "wealth, property, and class as the basis of political power."[198] Instead, we must ask first how the Declaration, far from stating "absolutely conventional" popular views, aimed to mobilize vast populations indifferent or hostile to Lockean ideals and to those promoting them.[199] Second, we must ask how these advocates of class society with deep anxieties about social change put their stamp of approval on Jefferson's and the drafting committee's work. Those who organized the external revolution were canny politicians, in Merrill Jensen's words "superb organizers" and "propagandists with a touch of genius" and a clear sense of their own interests.[200] Yet what the Declaration expressed, far from being accepted or even desired among the Lockean moderates, opened up not only fundamental claims of egalitarianism but also, more drastically yet, individual rights against government and finally an uncompromising statement of the most dangerous idea in modernity: the idea of self-authorization.

The overriding need to mobilize the internal revolution on behalf of the war and its elite proponents explains one aspect of the Declaration, Jefferson's deft synthesis of the elite agenda and popular demands. In fact, three of the four claims are unexceptional, and reveal the striving for consensus. The elites clearly demanded the "separate and equal station" of independence. "Deriving their just powers from the consent of the governed" they believed they had already attained as the consensual leaders of validly established Lockean polities arising from the state of nature. As they wanted internal self-government but not a universal "free society," the assertion of "all men" being "equal" appears to be an affront to virtuous government. The populist movement, rising such that Jefferson was seeing that "two-thirds of the people had become dissenters at the commencement of the present revolution," accounts for the unequivocal equality and an expansive view of the consent of the governed as enunciated by Paine.[201] The document weaves together the views of the two movements and frames likely terms for the emerging nation's political discourse—an agreement to be agents of a common polity and to debate as fellow citizens how equal is equal enough and how broad a consent bestows legitimacy.

It is the last claim, of "unalienable rights" of all individuals against established internal governments, that appears anomalous, unthinkable to those contesting the doctrine in every state. By his simple words, Jefferson announced a new vision of the human polity in a language uprooted from its Lockean task of validating existing society and social relations and framed in its oppositional purity. The natural right, now affirmed by a national leader, is to be a "free individual," or one who personally defines the purpose of life, the extent of liberty, and the meaning of happiness. This in turn becomes a continuing precondition for maintaining any future polity, the abrogation of which justifies dissolution. Moreover, not only was Jefferson affirming as doctrine the free society and the free individual, but he was doing so from *within the state of nature*.[202] For at the signing of this document government was dissolved, transporting the country at once into the terrifying setting where individualism was its most dangerous and all elite claims were effectively abrogated.

For the first time, the state of nature with its enduring nonnegotiable conditions—conditions that were anathema even within functioning society to its very signers and Jefferson's appointers—becomes an *existing* barrier to all political reconstitution. No longer limited to a set of past aspirations that inform, however imperfectly, an existing settlement, the doctrine now constitutes an underlying and permanent set of truths. In this way two unprecedented principles are graven into modernity. The free individual and the free society of equal and self-governing citizens become, despite their incompatibility, equivalent primordial claims. Furthermore, liberal civilization is to dwell henceforth within two (contrary?) realities simultaneously—nature *and* society. In this way, the idyll was given life.

Jefferson, of Protestant background and a liberal, thus reinserts Hobbes's free individual and self-authorizer into the foundation of the American project, the very wishes that would drive individuals to inflate their powers and reject the accommodations necessary for consensual society. Worse yet, they are attached to the collective power of sovereign dissolution and reconstitution no less than the personal right to frame one's life in one's own terms. Jefferson thereby reopens that very set of fundamental challenges to the agency formulations underlying Protestant individualism and liberal contractualism whose subduing and banishing had alone made modernity possible. Placed within the national mission statement, claims of individualism are moved to the center of the American cause and of its subsequent history.

Though an uncomfortable truth, not only does this statement vastly exceed any contemporary sense of what was at stake, but there was scarcely anyone alive who would have understood let alone supported the prospective political application of these ideas. Not Paine. Nor Crèvecoeur, who had resisted independence. What was the Declaration seeking to achieve, and why did it take the form it did? What possessed Jefferson to pursue this line of thinking? And if he was thinking what he indicates he was thinking, what could have possessed the elites in turn to designate him spokesman to deliver their message?[203]

Jefferson was an unlikely candidate to articulate the collective Whig cause. His prewar views on independence were regarded as "far too radical" to be accepted by his associates either in Virginia or in the First Continental Congress.[204] Though he was an accomplished writer with a populist flair, his initial draft of the Declaration was also quite extreme in its "unremitting" vituperation, a "flood of words . . . full of passion . . . heaping one denunciation on another."[205] John Adams regarded "the expression too passionate, and too much like scolding." Several of Jefferson's specific claims against the king had to be either moderated or deleted.[206] Finally, although Maier finds no complaint about the initial statement of general principles, many Whigs became quickly skeptical of the document and its implications. This was only another instance of Jefferson's "radical proposals," which were later to include efforts to dramatically restructure Virginia's laws on the franchise, the state constitution, education, and religious freedom. On the first three he was soundly defeated by his colleagues, and the last achieved only belated approval after much popular lobbying.[207]

The choice of Jefferson was a measure of the Whigs' perceived sense of crisis and need for unity. The Declaration was frankly meant as a document of mobilization "for domestic consumption," playing into the "unmistakably oral orientation to patriot 'propaganda,'" and was officially ordered set into print and read aloud throughout the colonies: "Congress ordered that copies 'be sent to the several assemblies, conventions and committees, or counsels of safety, and to the several commanding officers of the continental troops, that it be proclaimed in each of the United States, and at the head of the army.'"[208] Given the importance of "the spoken word" for "radical Protestantism," Jay Fliegelman's argument that "the Declaration was written to be read aloud," constituting it as "an event rather than a document," strongly suggests the audience Jefferson had in mind.[209] It was filled with a train of British abuses framed to incense all sectors of the populace and specifically westerners and common people. Its larger goal was to "provide . . . a vehicle for announcing Independence to the American people" and thus to "evoke a deeply felt and widespread commitment to the cause of nationhood and, above all, inspire the soldiers who would have to win the Independence that Congress proclaimed."[210]

Jefferson was responding not only to the intellectual challenge of *Common Sense* but to the political context as well. The populist agenda was being stridently put forward in state assemblies, conventions, petitions, and urban protests and in the outpouring for Paine. Jefferson's substitution and highlighting of the general "happiness" for the more exclusive "property" was intended to reach deep within colonial society: it "bound together the pietist and the rationalist, the deist and the dissenter, the Congregationalist and the Baptist more surely than any concept of constitutional liberty or of the rights of Englishmen, for each could define happiness in his own way."[211] A similar analysis applies to the inclusion of inalienable rights generally. Jefferson had watched the rising dissent and the intense, paralyzing controversies in Pennsylvania and Virginia. In both fledgling states the moderates, including his esteemed colleague George Mason, had gradually given way to more extreme statements of individual rights in an effort to ensure the passage of new constitutions as well as civil concord.

Jefferson's inclusion of the idyllic formulation, then, came into being as a judgment about the depth of the elite dilemma and the necessity of creating an alliance, a judgment which at the time his colleagues supported. It was a pragmatic effort to assimilate two disparate agendas not by means of forging a liberty that transcended the existence of states and institutional authority, but through the rhetorical olive branch of mutual toleration and "letting alone." The populace would not fight for hierarchy or property or elite virtue. Even equality was an inadequate concession, for it portended no end of political wrangling and a likely continuance of elite legislative manipulations. Through the idyllic formulation, the moderates were deferring symbolically to the radicals by backing off claims of hierarchy and virtue, suggesting that individuals and communities would be allowed to pursue their own internal agendas in exchange for immediate support for the only basis on which either agenda could be exercised, a successful fight for independence. As fellow dissenters, so they offered, they unlike the British could accommodate such self-determination among the populace. They in effect agreed to withdraw from their internal demands for the duration, enabling and encouraging the populace to frame the war in their own terms. On the basis of this inclusive language of reconciliation, this temporary retreat from their conception of responsible governance, the colonists could now imagine themselves—long enough to go forth—as Jefferson's "one people."

Agency: The Hidden Premise

Jefferson's strategic offer of maximum individual voluntarism obscured the agency foundations of that voluntarism: "The American Revolution cannot be ascribed to some prior colonial invention of a modern and newly-powerful language of liberty: none such emerged." He had in an earlier draft specifically noted the developmental step that America was taking from "subordination" to an "equal & independent station."[212] In the final draft, the transformation is not mentioned but is assumed as a "self-evident" conclusion from "the laws of nature and of nature's God." More important, those overarching "laws" which govern ends making the human world one of agents are conspicuously absent from the section asserting the existence of rights, leaving an inference of individual determination. The two forms of agency, indeed agency itself, are now swept up in a rhetoric which presumes it to be natural, inevitable, indisputable, and unenforceable in any particularity by one group against another. Any sense of tension between the two has been dissolved for the sake of revolutionary harmony. In its place is the American idyll, a free individual in a free society, for which Americans will be told in ceremonies and celebrations everywhere they are going to war.[213] After the war and henceforth, it will constitute the meaning to be given to our "dissolv[ing] the political bands" and "institut[ing] new government." This construction of an immaculate transformation to an at once free and natural individuality would overshadow all subsequent explanations, providing one anchor of certitude if not clarity for a nation in seemingly perpetual change.[214]

That such an alliance was possible even briefly reflected the deep common commitment to agency in some form which had always separated the colonies from Britain and now made the colonists a distinct people. Neither the beleaguered moderates, wanting—as the ratification struggles and the Framing evince—to preserve colonial hierarchies or at least protect elites from the leveling of a "free society," nor the ever-growing populists by contrast seeking the flexibility to establish a new society with collective authorship, nor anyone else in revolutionary America believed in the Declaration's full claims. What their "fathers and brethren" shared to make possible "a general union" for "the preservation of our liberties," insurgents realized, was common "ancestors" who "fled for religious liberty." As Ruth Bloch has pointed out, the perplexing irreconcilability of classical republican and liberal formulations of revolutionary ideology stems from treating them as alternatives or even mutually exclusive ideas. What is striking to her in this period among populace and elites is the intermingling of "communitarianism and individualism . . . as compatible . . . themes within American Revolutionary ideology" which have been too "misleadingly torn asunder." The "individualism" of the period "surely upheld the freedom of individual choice, but the choices described within these religious and sentimental frameworks were not those of individual autonomy but of identification with the communal groups of church and family."[215]

In developing this line of argument, Mark Noll traces it to the dissenting religious framework: "If the American revivalist tradition effortlessly joined together these kinds of individualism and communalism, it illustrates, or maybe even explains, why the communal and individualistic elements of the republican tradition which modern historians regard as so contrary may have been able to function together with a similar absence of strain."[216] This was precisely the equilibrium of agency and the agency world, the common ground to which Isaac suggests both groups equally subscribed: "A deeply-lying connection between popular evangelism and patriot republicanism can be more certainly established if we consider certain shared orientations. . . . The two ideologies struck common chords. Certainly both called for positive individual acts of affirmation as the basis for a new moral order. The patriots attested their participation in revitalized community by signing self-denying 'Associations.' The evangelists did so by bringing to meeting the humble testimony of hearts being regenerated by God's grace."[217]

Patricia Bonomi makes a related case for a new national enterprise by grounding a sense of "American exceptionalism" in the prominent role of dissenting religions traditions. She refers specifically to the continuing colonial practices of constituting voluntary churches, reliance on lay leadership, the proto-democratic process of breaking away and forming new congregations, and majoritarian control which characterized the dissenting denominations of American religious life. The communities, while acting separately, often at odds, together produced new, powerful, and long-evolving expectations about the character of acceptable institutions which emerged at the Revolution as "very clearly" a "separate culture."[218]

At the same time, with religious ideals infusing the popular understanding of the revolutionary struggle, the role of human effort had now moved to the center of the process of collective formation. Providing a powerful model of human action that would easily eclipse the remains of predestinarian theology, the rhetoric of the Revolution, largely promoted by the clergy, "elevated the idea of individual agency" to a cultural truth.[219] This "new 'idiom' of religion"—its original combination of "Individualism and elective community"—can now be regarded as generating the distinctive "national character in the nineteenth century." This was the "peculiar mixture of antistatist individualism and social communitarianism" which

Tocqueville saw as America's paradoxical "libertarian and conformistic" synthesis,[220] the mixture whose struggle for integration and whose unrelieved tensions framed the first agency nation.

The Immediate Aftermath of the Declaration

Why did the "Religious . . . Awakening" join the "political Revolution"?[221] Many commoners saw that "their pull to the left [had] been so strong that it forced the center into drastic modifications" and responded to the Declaration and the campaign it anchored. They were told "many clever things" about "our future glory," which "induced" them "to put to sea without a compass."[222] Urban working people, who were mobilizing economically and politically against the business interests right up to the Revolution, joined the war effort. Many sectarians similarly embraced the Revolution thereafter, not as a fulfillment of a "bible Commonwealth" but as one step in their larger agenda. The elite struggle for a "free society" without imperial domination offered to eliminate the top layer of external interference with the people's religious practices, local self-government, and property and constitutional rights. With the Declaration promoting one political aspect of their cause, they would, despite different agendas, rather support the defenders of national independence. Natural rights they now understood as their protection from state intrusion in establishing voluntary agency communities: "Natural rights, social contract, the protection of property, provided the best milieu for the reception, distribution, and expansion of God's grace."[223] Political insurgents, secular and religious, seeking state and local democratization, saw in the new statement of purpose the "unequivocal principles" of "a government of our own choice" and the recognition of individual "liberty" as "the direct end of . . . Government."[224]

The revolutionary coalition succeeded in the short run among moderates as well because they convinced themselves that colonial unity under their leadership reaffirmed their republic of hierarchical virtue. Gordon Wood writes of the post-Declaration period: "Enlightened men could believe . . . that new habitual principles, 'the constant authoritative guardians of virtue,' could be created and nurtured by republican laws, and that these principles . . . could give man's 'ideas and motives a new direction.' . . . Only this faith in the regenerative effects of republican government on the character of the people can explain the idealistic fervor of the Revolutionary leaders in 1776."[225] The religious leadership, like the insurgents, deferred to the political leadership, recognizing that the national cause required a far broader base of inclusion. By framing "the cause of liberty, united with that of truth and righteousness, [as] the cause of God" in their own terms, they presumed that control over the communal covenant and providential history rested as always in their hands.[226]

Moreover, the moderate elites, while extolling their cause in extreme populist terms, never for a minute believed that it would be picked up by the uneducated, decentralized, and disorganized populace. The rhetoric of universal liberty was, after all, only words, while the cause of fighting for elite interests was tangible. The delegates to the Continental Congress "considered these paragraphs little more than attractive, if necessary, generalities to build the case against Great Britain," which "they took no more literally . . . than the Virginia Convention did Mason's version." They believed that these words would be symbolic, retractable, not realizing that the people had been well prepared by their dissenting cultural tradition to apply them to their own situation. They had been "compelled by the logic of their argument for rebellion" to reinforce "an egalitarian vocabulary," whose unintended effect was to link in the national mind in perpetuity "the cause of liberty and the federal covenant."[227] The people for their part heard the Declaration and liked what they heard. In this way the elite, to win the Revolution, had given the people their greatest weapon, not realizing until too late that these words were themselves the Revolution. In shock, they quickly tried to contain the damage, but the barn door was off the hinges and a new national lexicon had been established. By these words, a developmental right to individual agency two centuries in the making had been confirmed, a dynamic that would make agency the birthright of all Americans equally, the framework for the national self and society and the basis of its social experiment.

The power of the idyll notwithstanding, the pragmatic unity was most temporary and began fraying virtually before the ink had dried. The nation was quickly split again explicitly by the state and national constitutional debates into the two preexisting revolutionary agendas. The extraordinary radicalism Gordon Wood attributes to the Revolution seems premised on the secular surfacing of claims articulated for centuries among religious dissenters. What is truly "revolutionary" was the necessity for public institutions to adopt marginalized principles of dissent as the foundation of civil order. The success of the idyll ironically made the populists in the early republic its heirs: it articulated most expansively and powerfully their rights *as insurgents* even though, despite their political success, they would never achieve undisputed political control to shape the society according to their principles. At the same time, the idyll would provide secular liberal protection—through broad representation and limited government—against intrusions upon their transpolitical agenda. The moderates for their part, fearful of the popular thrust of the idyll, abandoned its call after the breakup of revolutionary unity. Still in charge during the war, they returned forcefully to their traditional "republic of virtue." They hoped with the solidarity resulting from the war to engender a commitment to "the Public Good" for which individuals would willingly and virtuously sacrifice their personal interests as well as accept the leadership, the "Respect, and Veneration . . . for Persons in Authority."[228]

Wood is puzzled by this embrace of "a vision so divorced from the realities of American society, so contrary to the previous century of American experience."[229] The colonial elites had been able before independence to have their cake of post-traditional Lockean individualism and eat it with their social distinctiveness under the wing of British class society. With independence and Jefferson's expansive statement, liberal rhetoric was being taken from them, leaving no authorization for a rigid societal elite. The classical republicanism of the Revolution, a de-liberalized version of their long-standing views, stemmed from the elites' failure at the time—Madison aside—to grasp the compatibility of radical liberalism with social stratification. Afraid of open-ended liberty, eager to incorporate the masses in their revolutionary project, and stymied by the oppositional revision of Locke, they turned to the language of classical republicanism for a theory of political authorship which was both inclusive and elitist. Older class-based republics combined stratification with popular consent without giving way to universal governance. The goal was to make a virtue of willing compliance again, in John Adams's terms, such that "love and fear will become the spring of their obedience" to "disinterested men" of capacity who "would employ them whole time for the public good."[230] This would again combine agency with hierarchical deference in a proto-agency compromise.

The moderates may for a moment during the early "remarkable and unexpected union . . . throughout all the colonies" have fantasized that the nation possessed "virtue enough" or that the cause would "inspire Us with many Virtues, which We have not."[231] But they were anxious and with great reason: with scarcely a pause for the onset of the Revolution, in Pennsylvania, in Virginia, in New York and Massachusetts, in state after state people mobilized against public officials, legislatures, and courts for a role in forming new governments and drafting state constitutions. They organized against entrenched power, demanding religious freedom and religious equality as well as disestablishment, for political equality and popular government, against wealth and status, against economic consolidation and on behalf of more favorable fiscal policies, against the fiction of virtual representation and in favor of an explicit right to vote and popular representation. With the debate over suffrage requirements and bills of rights in the new constitutions, matters came to a head. Throughout the country, the people organized in town meetings to press for self-government and a constitutional statement of individual rights. Wood writes: "The Revolution became something more than a move for home rule. In 1776 and more intensely in the coming years in different times and places . . . it broadened into a struggle among Americans themselves for the fruits of independence, becoming in truth a multifaceted affair, with layers below layers."[232]

The alliance was not to last long, for in this newly constituted "state of nature" the people accepted Jefferson's incautious invitation to join on their own terms. And their terms, as myriad scholars have noted, propelled them toward an egalitarian vision of society which the moderates, unmindful of the extent of political and spiritual ferment, never adequately gauged. The people, mobilized by the war and war rhetoric appealing to the popular principles of the new nation, increasingly circumvented existing political structures by convening public assemblies to express their will. Merrill Jensen observes that "the Declaration of Independence was taken seriously by many Americans, or at least they found its basic philosophy useful in battling for change in the new states." The language spread as "all segments of discontent . . . rushed to apply these arguments to their own needs and ambitions," including "dissenters," who "were among the most zealous," for liberty was applied "as easily against habits and traditions *within* American society as it was against outside threats."[233] As John Mecklin writes, "The Baptist separatist had but to substitute the fictions of the philosophy of natural rights for his theological fictions to find himself at one with . . . Jefferson." Backus quickly prepared a Declaration of Rights oriented to dissenter principles.[234] Democratic populists like the laborer William Manning were able to reframe in "the ideas of liberty and free government" their older defense of "a Christian life" and "profession of faith" and to use this broader and more inclusive currency after the Revolution to support the "Many" against the "Few," those "leading men" who were turning from "republican principles" to "arbitrary government."[235] Awakened communities were able to merge "the privileges which God and nature had given" with "that power . . . which ought forever to remain with the people inviolate who consider themselves free and independent." A Massachusetts radical editor argued, "Nor can any man who acknowledges the being of God be justly deprived of any civil rights as a citizen."[236]

Again and again, the moderates found themselves confronted by their own language, appropriated by the local populace in their dawning understanding of secular society. These principles made the obvious disparities between elite rhetoric and behavior transparent and indefensible: "The Declaration of Independence stripped the government of its fictional legitimacy. . . . 'The fund of revolutionary theory . . . supplied an insurmountable obstacle: here was no consent of the governed, only a relic of the tyranny Massachusetts was fighting.'" Everywhere people now spoke the language of rights, demanding complementary institutions, for "liberty, to great numbers . . . meant more than independence from Great Britain."[237] As Hawke explains: "Even plain people of the eighteenth century did not push the idea of equality to the point where they argued that common men with common understanding could or should lead. This, the basic ingredient of the Age of Paine that infuriated John Adams, came . . . in part because the Declaration was there as a guide." In the instructions provided by many towns to state convention representatives were now "the manifest desire of the citizens for some statement of personal rights."[238] Robert J. Taylor writes, "Once the Western farmers had grasped the principles advocated by the Whigs and enshrined in the Declaration of Independence, they insisted that these principles apply at home as well as against Great Britain." The American Revolution in this sense "exerted . . . a profound educative force" on the American people, producing in Bernard Bailyn's phrase a "contagion of liberty."[239]

The moderates could not effectively resist this tidal wave of popular empowerment. They were horrified by the collapse of the "republic of virtue," but given the emerging premise of popular government that virtue is a matter of consensus, they were shorn even of a language in which to express that horror. They could only repudiate the idyll, and turned against the people in the name of exclusive virtue and popular sin, "reactionary social and political expectations," hastening their final marginalization and collapse.[240] The "people," they alleged, had been taken over by "their private views and separate interests," led by unscrupulous *"demagogues"* from "the bottom" taking the "power" which is "the property of their rulers" to pursue "dark, ambitious, or (not likely) speculative purposes" leading to "anarchy and confusion." Through the 1780s they fell into deeper crisis and disillusionment as they saw the nation overwhelmed by "the intolerable burden of . . . accumulated evil."[241]

The cruel irony for moderates was that they had unleashed the idyll and it had succeeded: "The people had turned against their teachers the doctrines which were inculcated in order to effect the late revolution." Deference had disappeared: "Every man wants to be a judge, a justice, a sheriff, a deputy, or something else which will bring him a little money, or what is better, a little authority." All preestablished distinctions were rejected, *"authority"* was held in *"settled and habitual contempt"* through a *"defect of obedience* in the subjects" and liberty made "a popular *idol."* Populist interests had taken over the new states, and the moderates saw the end of the orderly society they had known before the war and wished to continue.[242] As moderates worried about "where it would all end," many in the dissenting communities broke through "their apolitical shells" to become political citizens shaping the new republic.[243]

Realizing that the cause of liberty was out of their control, moderates pursued a common strategy in the negotiations over the state and later the federal constitutions. They would exploit populist support for the idyll and their localism by permitting community self-rule while firmly securing hold of the new central institutions. Elisha Douglass has written:

> Democrats probably considered the Bill of Rights a victory. . . . Actually, however, the document did little to advance the cause of democracy. The bills of rights in the first state constitutions were valuable as the basis for restricting the sphere of governmental authority and as expressions of liberal political philosophy, but they did little to make government more responsive to the people. The attainment of democracy required political equality and majority rule; theoretical restrictions on governmental authority and assertions of popular sovereignty, while salutary, could not accomplish the objective alone.[244]

Thus were bills of rights, appended to conservative constitutions to gain popular support, "measures that the conservatives could accept, if not with enthusiasm, at least without serious concern."[245] Similarly, at the national level, Federalists believed they could retain power with little threat by supporting the Bill of Rights. Madison clearly realized that it would not "endanger the beauty of the Constitution in any one important feature" nor contribute to "weakening its frame or abridging its usefulness," yet it would make it "better in the opinion of those who are opposed to it."[246]

An Idyllic Nation?

The moderates achieved their legislative goals but misjudged their importance in framing the aspirations and directing the energies of the new nation. The idyll in contrast transformed the nation by giving a new language and empowering legitimacy to the people: "Republicanism had . . . been turned around. Launched at first by the gentry as a means of regenerating traditional authority, it had become a vehicle of popular assertion . . . for dismantling such institutions and for resisting attempts to revive a system that legitimated forms of deference."[247] The people thus found in the Revolution and then in Jefferson's victory in 1800 the enthusiasm and dream of the Great Awakening in the triumph of a free and popular society. They understood their own triumph, as Jefferson put it himself in his First Inaugural, as the combined "transcendent" achievement of "election by the people" through "the decisions of the majority" and "our equal right to use of our own faculties," leaving us "free to regulate [our] own pursuits."[248]

Although born of two very different conceptions—neither idyllic—of the American project, the idyll regardless of its historical incongruence has endured as the strongest expression of national identity ever since. For the revolutionary historian Jack P. Greene, the idyll provided an almost magical healing of self and society with the realization that being "free" meant that "unrestrained individualism was not necessarily or even usually antisocial." This allowed the citizenry to "comprehend the character they had assumed, to come to terms with themselves and their environment, to appreciate themselves and their societies for what they were and had become," to in effect develop "a new conception of American identity" which was to "close in one heroic effort the chasm" between reality and their ideals.[249] Gordon Wood more recently points to the achievement of "a prosperous free society belong[ing] to obscure people . . . free and equal with the right to pursue their happiness."[250] Despite or perhaps because of its effectiveness as a popular rallying cry, its vacuity as a theory has been less attended to, although it bequeathed deep inherent contradictions to the new nation: the unresolvable tension between the "free society" placing authority in the majority and the "free individual" which contests all forms of authority was not to be bridged during the long course of the nation's history.

Was a Declaration of Independence necessary from the elite perspective? Surely the demands of mobilization were imperative and pressing. Was the rhetoric of the idyll also necessary? With regard to matters of conscience, it was clear that no worldly authority could be interposed between the dissenter and his or her God. Further, as we have learned from the English Revolution and from Hobbes's "artificial" commonwealth, Jefferson's natural self-authorization lurking behind agency civilization was a force that dissenting religion could not contain and for which it required liberalism. This distinction between Protestantism and liberalism, in which the latter achieves order through Hobbes's distinction between the unenforceable internal and enforceable external realms, was abrogated by the Declaration. In the Hobbesian and Lockean settlement, religion may well push for a maximum right of internal freedom, but the saving power of liberalism was to isolate that right from the secular requirements of behavioral consensus. Protestant freedom would then be compatible with liberal controls, individualism with collective order, divine warrant with political agency. By placing those rights not in a revival tract but in a *foundational liberal document*, Jefferson shattered the delicate equilibrium of the agency framework.

For the next century and more, though Americans being agents, as we shall see, would make their way toward a new agency nation, the prominence of the revolutionary idyll led them to imagine themselves constituting a nation of the idyll. Its success in framing the national sense of project reflects a sudden and unprecedented independence. There was, as Bailyn, Wood, and others have pointed out, a significant lag between the fundamentally novel social, political, and economic conditions of late colonial life and the lingering popular commitment to social hierarchy, governing elites, religious establishment, and personal deference. The colonists were in no position to comprehend fully the larger political and cultural implications of the systemic shift.

Moreover, the ever-increasing social flexibility in the colonies, further expanded and made explicit after independence, made liberty a plausible substitute for the less perceptible emergence of an agency society. The confusion within the three agency discourses and their radicalized rhetoric conflated claims of individual liberty with larger systemic obligations to the colonial and then national cause. The extreme case of the attraction of idyllic rhetoric was the importation of the "free agent" under the belief that it more accurately reflected the open colonial reality than the English one. While this genre's importance has been vastly inflated to buttress the liberal narrative of the Revolution, it was present in works such as Crèvecoeur's *Letters from an American Farmer.* Written in the late 1760s, Crèvecoeur's reflections on the power of the American setting to remake the individual into a natural agent reveal how easily the language of the idyll could be employed to describe this condition. The inevitable contrast of a world suddenly with "no aristocratical families, no courts, no kings, no bishops, no ecclesiastical domination, no invisible power giving to a few a very visible one,"[251] led Crèvecoeur to an extreme formulation of the idyll of freedom: "From nothing to start into being; from a servant to the rank of a master; from being the slave of some despotic prince, to become a freeman. . . . What a change!" Yet he was keenly aware that the case for liberty could be overstated, noting that those who give up habits of "subordination" and "servility" are only too "often passing from one extreme to the other." The true American embraced a Crusoe-like commitment that freedom was clearly to be exercised subject to larger ends by using "sobriety, rigid parsimony, and the most persevering industry" as an independent proprietor to build family, community, and love of country. Yet, this unprecedented condition of an individual fulfilling those ends on the basis of "my own land," from *"self-interest,"* from "independence," led Crèvecoeur to equate agency with "the most perfect" freedom.[252] Thus, even before the revolutionary struggles crystallized the national idyll, before they made Crusoe a national best-seller, the colonists were Americanizing (and radicalizing) Crusoe in fact.[253]

In this way, the "antithesis" of "slavery" came to be "liberty" in the United States as it had evolved in the British opposition.[254] Freedom was regarded not as an ultimate goal distinct from the positive commitment as agent to the transcendent ends of God, liberal society, or reason, but—in growing opposition to external and domestic controls—as the ever more indispensable means. Voluntarism at the level of individual choice and a consensual community was required for the personal apprehension and integration of such ends and for harmony among the many variants of agency. Thus, the unfolding logic of agency in a decontrolled setting once again made liberty to pursue a personal faith in, social contract with, or rational comprehension of the authorial mandate the necessary condition for agency and for the effective individual discretion to fulfill its conditions. Where the dynamic of radical individualism had been set in motion, eliminating the validity of any worldly constraints or institutional mediations authorizing the power of one (mere) agent over another, then the protected realm of individual discretion became an absolute requirement, more certain than any common feature of the many variations of the agency role itself. With no consensus or even clarity regarding agency, and moreover no common author (unlike in the late-nineteenth-century Protestant-liberal synthesis) yet emerging out of the myriad cultures of colonial America, liberty was elevated programmatically. The effective result, in other words, was a concept of personal responsibility grounded in an individualism so pronounced that voluntarism became the sole basis for consensus. When the revolt against foreign domination, hierarchy, and constraint, framed as freedom against servitude, was added to this accelerating internal dynamic, the national narrative of freedom was complete.

The swift success of the Revolution further exaggerated the potency of the idyll. By producing an unprecedentedly clean institutional slate, with the proponents of coercion both internal and external seriously disabled, the postrevolutionary society believed itself to be in a position, so unlike in England, to implement the opportunities which had inspired the struggle for a new human possibility. The openness of American life socially, economically, and spatially was to reinforce its mythic understanding. Moreover, the revolutionary triumph validated the voluntarist institutional innovations by which colonial society had adapted to its novel populace and situation, and gave by its language and principles conscious impetus to the belief that society was a malleable entity to be shaped by the choices of its members. It crystallized a sense that an unprecedented break with the past was possible, that it was possible to "dissolve the political bands" of constraint in the "free air" of American life and, as Jefferson put it in his First Inaugural, leave individuals "free to regulate their own pursuits of industry and improvement."[255] The process was virtually irresistible. In Tocqueville's more fearful European words, this "movement which impels [us] . . . is already so strong that it cannot be stopped, but it is not yet so rapid that it cannot be guided."[256]

Of the three discourses of Lockean agency, only the political and not the religious or rational discourse would survive—transformed by the idyll—as the basis for a common rhetoric. The dream of a Protestant commonwealth was being fragmented as in England amidst the multiplying alternatives, leaving the religious communities to discover again, as we shall see after the Second Awakening, their need to seek refuge in the secular state. The Revolution would find the discourse of political liberalism also eclipsing the rationalist discourse. Enlightenment rationalism, never widespread, failed to take hold in this unconstrained and illegible new world. Of the three agency discourses, rationalism is the one least confined and directed by institutional boundaries and necessities. "Eternal reason," lacking any consensual arbiter, could most easily become the dangerous self-authorizing reason of the individual, particularly where, as in the United States, there were no common truths or realities for it to intuit.[257] The faith in reason, or the innate moral sense which informs it, is most socially adaptive and integratable by individuals where a preexisting agreement on transcendent norms and appropriate means directs its conclusions. Hence the eighteenth-century English conviction reflects the growing consensus within that society. Similarly, in the Indian summer of colonial society, this faith existed for a time in some quarters. As the tumultuous colonial society slid toward opposition, insurgency, internal conflict, and populist demands, the breakdown of clear normative and adaptive guidelines left instrumental reason without any guidance as to the identity of common transcendent values and procedures. The centrifugal, individualizing discourse of reason gave way to the centripetal, integrative emphasis on political and religious virtue. Despite its momentary efflorescence with Paine and Jefferson, the radical Enlightenment and its liberating belief in a rational natural agency played a relatively small role in the American Revolution.

The consensual rationalism of mainstream agency would only appear prominently when the full elaboration of the Protestant-liberal consensus we are tracing brought orderly guidelines once again to American culture after the Civil War. At this point, pragmatism would emerge as a doctrine celebrating the power of instrumental reason rooted in the now "transcendent" clarities of the Protestant-liberal moral-theological universe and its public good. The freedom of this "rational agent" would of course expand with the increasing dominance of this consensual framework in the twentieth century, becoming in modern "rational choice" ideology and case law the merger of the real and the rational in its influential conception of the perfectly adapted or "consistent" autonomy of its "rational" agents.[258] In this way, the "self-evident" consensus of discourses in this later period, foreclosing all other possibilities, is embodied in the notion of the *free* (i.e., liberal) *rational* (i.e., possessed of transcendent reason) *agent* (i.e., Protestant).

The Lockean political discourse of social contractualism and natural rights, severed ideologically in America from any consciousness of agency constraints, fit with and fueled the popular commitment to the idyll. It accorded with the evident features of late colonial experience: collective authority at the level of local institutions increasingly constituted by popular mandate; ever-increasing personal discretion for individuals in matters of property rights, conscience, and social conduct. As the young republic remained in many areas suspended in a virtual state of nature, the limits within this model were being eliminated on the collective level by the increased popular role in forming new representative national and state governments and at the individual level by the growing importance of natural rights, bills of rights, and the Jeffersonian cult of the free natural agent. The discourse of rights was of course fully explicable within liberalism as the capacity to carry out duties without worldly interference by others.[259] Yet with remaining constraints disappearing, the rhetorics of individual rights and popular government were joining to become the free society of free individuals in the young republic.

A national myth of adult liberty was being created ironically from liberalism's strategic use of voluntarism in the "civilizing" of agency. The strategy was employed by the domestic elites in uncanny reflection of the Hobbesian tactic, but the emergent republic possessed no societal framework to enforce reversal and reintegration: not only stably functioning adult institutions and adult socialization in normative regularity but also the early formation of the young for social accommodation were nonexistent. Nowhere in reality or in the revolutionary version of the liberal narrative were there constraints to direct the popular formation of a new society in the lives of the citizenry. What was to hold this new society together? Although "'order' somehow seemed to 'grow out of chaos,' there was no answer since 'it was increasingly clear that no one was in charge.'"[260]

What Is to Be Done?

The revolutionary idyll was a double-edged sword. It had boldly led the American people out of the house of servitude, of quasi-agency and hierarchy and deference. Yet in its very boldness, it had overstepped the causes for which it had been constituted, stimulating unreal and unfathomable fantasies of human and societal possibility. What did it mean to be free? Without institutional demands or expectations? Did that mean one could or should want to live in an established society? Develop an economy? Participate in politics? Socialize one's children? Listen to the advice of others? What if one didn't want freedom and needed authority? What if others did not act properly and this new world became dangerous and illegible? What would hold us together? Can one be free and have authority at the same time? If not, which does one choose? Gordon Wood reflects the endless series of troubling questions posed at the time about the crisis of authority: "By what right did authority claim obedience? was the question being asked of every institution, every organization, every individual. . . . If everyone in the society was interested, who was to assume the role of neutral umpire? Who was to reconcile and harmonize all those clashing interests and promote the good of the whole?"[261]

The initial result of being thrust precipitously into this new condition without preparation was far less the national creation of ordered liberty, far more a sense of shock and disorientation. Bailyn suggests that the dramatic modernization of ideas during the Revolution brought the thinking in the young republic into line with the conditions of American life.[262] In fact, the Revolution's radical break with colonial culture produced a profound new disjunction between the idyllic language of the Revolution and the agency values which formed the basis of the culture, a "hiatus in American politics between ideology and motives that was never again closed."[263] The post-revolutionary society as a result was left to figure out its fate with neither a sense of its past nor any—except misleading—guidance on the institutions, structures, or behaviors now required. The Declaration, then, in substituting a collective idyll for the historical development of an agency society paradoxically fulfilled for the nation the Lockean injunction that the conviction of freedom is achieved through the forgetting of previously imposed restraints. The pursuit of liberty, so cogent in response to internal hierarchy and external coercion, was an empty container in the young republic, a battle cry with no principle of authority or consensus, devoid of direction, a logic of reactiveness rather than construction.

The novelty of the developmental step to a full agency character led to a vacuum of authority and a crisis of culture and direction in the young republic so troubling that it was to shape the preoccupations of the republic for the next century. Tocqueville, one of the greatest observers of American society, was never able to grasp it fully. Ordinary citizens did not have a chance. Wasn't this, wrote Charles Nisbet in 1787, "a new world . . . unfortunately composed . . . of discordant atoms, jumbled together by chance, and tossed by inconstancy in an immense vacuum," a "very diffused state of society?"[264] As the millennial fervor cooled for a time with the dampening of intense revolutionary expectations in the 1780s, the American populace began to confront a new society far less realized religiously, morally, and institutionally than they had dreamed. Moreover, the reverberations of the popular revolution spread across the land in waves that were to continue unabated for seventy-five years. Everywhere, "respect for authority, tradition, station, and education eroded. . . . Political convulsions seemed cataclysmic; the cement of an ordered society seemed to be dissolving." No institution was safe from "challenges to any authority that did not spring from volitional allegiance."[265] Americans, it seems, were better at dismantling the old world than in suggesting the new. The revolutionary fiction of "independence" as "the only bond" to "tie and keep us together" was just that, useful in the war, myopic and debilitating ever after.[266]

The great emblem of the age intimating a problematic idyll is Rip Van Winkle. A representative of the postrevolutionary loss of bearings, Rip is, as we shall see in the next part, only one of many cultural expressions of anxiety and panic in the new republic. Though he is fatefully asleep in the countryside during the Revolution, it is the sleep of historical symbolism. With his upbringing in an earlier traditional backwater of class, hierarchy, deference, and servitude, Rip on waking and returning to his village has no chance of reading or comprehending the new signs and symbols that had everywhere replaced the old ways. The Revolution had brought about an utterly discontinuous reality: "All this was strange and incomprehensible. . . . [E]verything was strange. His mind now misgave him; he began to doubt whether he and the world around him were not bewitched." The people too were unreadable: "The very character of the people seemed changed. There was a busy, bustling, disputatious tone about it, instead of the accustomed phlegm and drowsy tranquillity." Rip is told he is no longer "a subject of his Majesty" but "now a free citizen of the United States," and hears about the glories of the Revolution, but it is "a perfect Babylonish jargon to the bewildered Rip Van Winkle." A recently freed traditionalist, he can appreciate only his release from his own "yoke" of "tyranny," that of his now deceased wife's "petticoat government." Beyond that, he is lost: "Everything's changed, and I'm changed, and I can't tell what's my name, or who I am!"[267]

One might surmise that Rip is in an unusually unfavorable position, having undergone the vast shift as a trauma, unlike the hustling young Americans in his town who experienced the years of change. They are to be sure better able to adapt to the new society than Rip, who escapes into nostalgia, but with their collective amnesia regarding the past and loss of any point of reference perhaps they understand it even less. This dynamic new society is the one Tocqueville visits, the one that comes to frighten him deeply as he reflects years later on his visit. What had seemed at first to be an "immense spectacle" of "freedom . . . unrestrained" has become in reflection a "longer, more secret, but more certain road to servitude," and *no one realizes it:* "Thus, they become more alike, even without having imitated each other . . . though they seek not, though they see not and know not each other."[268] The new American was moving at a prodigious rate, but in what direction no one had any idea. Tocqueville became terrified that the endlessly repeated idyll of freedom was, in the bewilderment about directionality and the processes of societal formation, obscuring the ability to see and respond to a new and terrifying kind of order.

In these uncharted waters, the moderates before they fell silent were provided by the confusion attending the multiplicity of local agendas under the decentralized Articles of Confederation one last opportunity with the federal Constitution to fulfill their dream of a free society ruled by "the worthy against the licentious."[269] But a measure of the effective shift of the national discourse to the revolutionary idyll is the extent to which it had become the unavoidable basis—alternatively legitimation and cover—for Madison's efforts to contain it. That is, remarkably, Madison is left only with the brilliant and devious strategy which he brilliantly and deviously employs of reversal, of trying to turn the idyll against itself. No hint of inherited virtue or entrenched prerogative remains, and what virtue remains is parsimoniously distributed. The capable will now be those who can master the immense new demands of broad popular appeal and the rigors of intricate constitutional infighting, the populist lion and the elitist fox in one. To be sure, the complex system of checks and balances, direct and indirect voting, the very size of the nation may allow those with "the most attractive merit and . . . established characters," that is to say, the most inclusive views, a disproportionate opportunity to succeed. But in a world of individuals who have the "liberty" which is now by consensus "essential to political life," factious popular republics with their "unjust and interested majority" are a fact of political life. The only limits will be those that can be framed within the idyll, which is to say, there is only "a republican remedy for the diseases most incident to republican government."[270]

The issue, then, is now not so much whether entrenched elites will have the mantle of governance, but whether their sense of "public good and private rights," their "personal security" and "rights of property," can be "secure" against the "danger" of the "majority." Madison's solution, his only successful option, was to engineer a trick, but it was an agency trick commensurate with the underlying principles and limits available in the New World: to "preserve the spirit and the form of popular government" while in fact dispensing with the idyll of a free society of free individuals.[271] That is, he designed a system which appeared to be in popular control, but in fact directed the people's participation into structures that would contain their kinetic activity. In this process, individual authority is consensually displaced onto a collective author by the memory of the participatory Founding ratified by every election vote, which in turn transforms those "free" authors into voluntary yet "conforming" agents who must obey "their" representatives. The scheme is of course a constitutional reformulation of Hobbes's great structural foundation for liberal society. Madison also achieved structural limits on freedom, but only by embracing the more universal and radically participatory agency principles of his populist opposition.

Madison's prescient reading of the new political landscape would make the federal structure one of the ultimate triumphs of the agency civilization evolving in the United States, an eventual governor on the self-authorizing propensities unleashed by the idyll. For the revolutionary moderates, however, it was if not too little yet too late. Unlike in England, where there were modernizing societal elites equipped to commandeer the state and recompose it, the limited reach of this elite in the young republic allowed it to control the Constitutional Convention and ratification, but not the nation. The federal constitutional structure, remote from the immense unleashed initiative and societal formation occurring throughout the country, could not contain, direct, or even significantly affect this new activity. The rising populist forces in the local economy, politics, and society were sweeping away the internal elites.[272] Jefferson's and then Jackson's election, the decisive defeat of the Federalists, suggested that there was no going back. John Adams, fearing "all decorum, discipline, and subordination . . . destroyed and universal Pyrrhonism, anarchy, and insecurity of property . . . introduced," even entertained the wish to *"give us again our popes and hierarchies, Benedictines and Jesuits, with all their superstition and fanaticism, impostures and tyranny."*[273] These would remain, in Hawthorne, Henry Adams, and others, cautionary voices issuing warnings primarily to themselves about the fate of the popular voyage.

For the populists, the dilemma was much deeper: it was the problem of success. As the imperial structure was overthrown and colonial hierarchies overturned, with overt restraints eliminated on all forms of activity and individuals now released to pursue their interests, the idyll spread to the distant corners of the new republic, framing what seemed like a free society of free individuals. The Anti-Federalists, for example, with "great confidence ... in the voluntary exertions of individuals," could not understand the Federalist panic, and attributed it to scare tactics.[274] The democratic populists embraced the Declaration and its promises as the impetus for their electoral triumphs every bit as much as the Federalists relinquished it, for it had been the great proclamation which brought them into the center of national life. Quickly, however, the reality of an open-ended situation would set in, as well as the need—if inchoate and unarticulated—to distinguish the idyll from the serious tasks at hand.

The Burden of the Idyll

The Lockean mythos of an adult voluntarist society filled the vacuum only by confusing the young republic about its own achievements, giving "the people an unrealistic view of politics and power. . . . Freedom for the eighteenth century had carried with it obligations to society that restricted the right. . . . Now liberty, or *laissez-faire* as it came to be called, carried no duty to act only in the best interests of society."[275] That the two axioms, "free individual" and "free society," were reconcilable—so the English forebears had grasped—only as a Protestant agent in liberal society, few Americans at the time wanted to know, being "blocked" from "any deeper understanding" of their history, ancient and recent, by "the Jeffersonian perspective." The idyll preserved a common society but at the expense of denying the agency character being established and of validating resistance to efforts to construct a new agency society.[276] The project of realizing the idyll obscured for two centuries the underlying agendas that were at work, leaving the true development of the republic to occur below the level of systemic comprehension. Yet no sooner was the idyll created than Rip's children would seek to reorient themselves in this untutored space by developing the institutions of agency civilization. Under the guise of freedom and choice, they would proceed by mass revivals and institution building and consensual societal conformity to establish new forms of a common Author, religious and societal, to guide them. Driven by a largely internal, psychocultural dynamic and their need for societal cohesion and role certitude rather than any clear agenda (hence the secretiveness and subsequent confusion about this process), they would remake the world as an agency world.

The struggle for self-realization in the nineteenth century was therefore also a struggle for self-recognition, to surmount the weight of illusions and idylls. For every advance from a proprietary society toward societal development and institutional integration, every inevitable movement away from the Crusoe-like condition of extreme self-reliant individualism, every acknowledgment that for agents overarching structure was needed, was to haunt Americans as the looming failure of the revolutionary promise. At every point the rhetoric of Jefferson, the myth of the founding fathers and the sacred Declaration, Tocqueville's early euphoria, the idyllic misreading of *Crusoe* and Franklin, the Jacksonians and Gettysburg, the "free market" and the modern culture of "rights" sustained a disjunction with the web of institutional reality to which we nominally "consent" and within which we in fact live. Even those few who saw the agency nature of the American enterprise—Melville, Emerson, Thoreau, Tocqueville—were themselves victims of the power of the idyll. For compared to the "free self," the agent fell far short of the nobility of the revolutionary promise. With their focus on its weaknesses but not its strengths, it appeared a compromised figure highly susceptible to authority and dependence, willing to trade—or give—away a meaningful self-direction and self-authorization for a circumscribed individualism within the rules.

In this way, the idyll has cast its long and continuing spell over the republic's history, diminishing throughout the sense of what has been achieved. The Revolution was a millennial achievement, transforming the world through human growth rather than fall as the early Protestants in England had divined. It had made the developmental step to universal agency character irreversible, and had fittingly made ordinary citizens the *means* for its achievement in history.[277] Despite the loss of the godly nation, a nation under God, the new nation of agents would be constituted by moderates and populists alike. By coalescing the nation as an inclusive new society, the integrative dynamic of liberalism, proceeding by means of the Declaration, national struggle, and founding, rescued dissenting religious culture and established a common political destiny: "It was the Revolution, and only the Revolution, that made them one people."[278] This newly conceived society, Richard Price said in 1784, "opens a new prospect in human affairs and begins . . . a new aera in the history of mankind" as a "most important step" vindicating "the progressive course of human improvement."[279]

Despite the many severe tests which this young nation was to face, it never seriously considered retreating to Rip's nostalgia, to servitude, or even to proto-agency. Guided by the felt reality of its new operational social character, it would to the contrary pursue innovation across the many sectors of society to create the institutions of agency civilization to complement that character. Because as agents Americans would need authors so long as of their own making, they would turn to the great Anglo-American visions of consensual authority, not to an active memory which had been erased (leaving it to those who came after to reconstitute the record) but to the internal patterns which had been there all along: to the willing quest within for individual validation from a personal Author using the Protestant epic and to a willing engagement externally in social roles and systemic behaviors derived from the collective liberal process of societal formation. Proclaiming their freedom, they would nevertheless create in the nineteenth century a voluntarist agency society, to be sure not "a free society of free individuals," but the first modern nation.

III

The Dilemma of Nationhood

8

The Liberal Idyll amidst Republican Realities

A vast and concentrated interest and influence has grown up among us. . . . The remedy is easy. . . . It is to give freedom.

—William Leggett

Surely individuality is ruinous to an age of standardization. . . . Had men but escaped out of the prisons of the Old World into the more horrid prisons of the New?

—Sherwood Anderson

If the conceptual legacy of the Revolution was the Lockean idyll in its most radical form, the effort of the first century of nationhood would be to reconcile the ideals of American liberalism with the emerging realities of a new post-traditional society. The classic dissenting Protestant and Federalist discourses struggled to direct the new republic toward a less individualist form of society. But given a vast, thinly organized world from which all societal authority had presumably been lifted, the vision of a primordial individual and community defined and limited only by nature was to capture the public imagination. Ironically, this very condition of openness which defeated all competitors to individualism was to bring the eventual demise of the idyll itself. English liberal theory had confined its test of the logic of agency to a conceptual withdrawal of authority, thus ensuring reversal into society by means of functioning institutions of societal and characterological formation. Postrevolutionary America, the ultimate and unplanned test of the logic, imagined itself beyond institutional demands for compromise. Presuming this increasing attainment of the mythic voluntary republic, Americans instead discovered in the project of social formation a chastening and unintended lesson: the dynamic by which freedom qualified by their needs as agents produced its opposite, the necessity for overarching institutions and practices. For the formation of viable institutions to proceed, Americans would have to acknowledge—if only indirectly—the unsustainability of their idyll. Social organization, institutional authority, and the human collectivity itself, even if rooted in new understandings based on their originative individualism, would have to be established.

The relentless dispersal of Jeffersonian principles has long led us to locate the dynamic of the new "polity" in its commitment to "personal autonomy."[1] The emergence of a newer and higher individualism, either in democratic society or as often in spaces of Edenic openness, has shaped our understanding of this "huge bustling, boundless nation."[2] With the growing constraints of urban and organizational society, Americans from the end of the nineteenth century increasingly displaced the viability of individual freedom back onto the antebellum period. It was the once vast spaces of the "ever retreating frontier," Frederick Jackson Turner proclaimed in 1893, that had been "a gate of escape from the bondage of the past" and "the bonds of custom" by establishing "that dominant individualism" that "comes with freedom" and a "triumphant . . . unrestraint." For the noted literary historian F. O. Matthiessen, the American Renaissance created the vision of a realized democratic hero, often westward leaning, impatient of restraint, the triumph of personal character and spirit.[3] With the Revolution providing "the freedom to be left alone," Gordon Wood writes in our time, "only the self-restraint of individuals—their moral 'character'—now remained, it seemed, to hold this burgeoning, unruly society together." Eric Foner defines freedom in this period as "an unending process of self-realization by which individuals could remake themselves and their lives."[4] The historian Robert Wiebe has defined the early national period as one of "self-rule: people ruled themselves collectively, people ruled themselves individually. . . . Free individuals formed democratic communities; democratic communities sustained free individuals."[5]

This view, while by no means universal, does highlight the central conundrum for the discourse of American freedom: how institutions and social consensus arose from the idyllic culture. Were they merely unintended? I suggest in place of inadvertence an underlying process of cultural retrieval in the early republic. It occurred on two levels: through the overt crisis caused by the incompatability of Jeffersonian individualism with expanding institutional formation; in turn, through a collective psychosocial reversal from the dislocation and directionlessness of the new setting, sharpened by the failure of revolutionary ideals, prompting a largely veiled return to agency values and institutions. Together, these prepared the citizenry for the post–Civil War reconstitution of liberalism as a modern theory and practice of societal organization, the unprecedented nexus of a nation of agents.

Liberation and Revolutionary Expectations

Nowhere was the expectation to affirm the public narrative of liberation greater than among those living in the shadow of the Revolution. In ante-bellum America, long before skepticism intruded upon the faith, many held deeply to the ideals of the Declaration. A vision of the world, otherwise implausible, gained credibility as Americans replaced their colonial history with the state of nature which they imagined around them, and from which institutions were regarded as emerging. Shaped by the Revolution, which by its "very success" swept away traditional hierarchies, the young republic constituted "a different world, that required new thoughts and new behavior."[6] Paine had regarded the elimination of serious political, social, and economic constraints as an unparalleled opportunity for a nation and its people to achieve a "natural . . . maturity." Edward Everett framed it as a decisive test of human potential: "There are no more continents or worlds to be revealed; Atlantis hath arisen from the ocean, the farthest Thule is reached, there are no more retreats beyond the sea, no more discoveries, no more hopes. Here then a mighty work is to be fulfilled, or never, by the race of mortals."[7]

Henry James, assessing the challenge for a writer of Hawthorne's era, recounted being "struck by a large number of elements that were absent . . . from the texture of American life." He enumerated:

No state, in the European sense of the word, and indeed barely a specific national name. No sovereign, no court, no personal loyalty, no aristocracy, no church, no clergy, no army, no diplomatic service, no country gentlemen, no palaces, no castles, nor manors, nor old country-houses, nor parsonages, nor thatched cottages, nor ivied ruins; no cathedrals, nor abbeys, nor little Norman churches; no great Universities or public schools . . . no literature, no novels, no museums, no pictures, no political society, no sporting class.

For Americans at this time, James suggested, "it should become a wonder to know what was left."[8] In Hawthorne's story "Earth's Holocaust," the citizens of a western town gather to set fire to and consume in a final conflagration all of history's "outworn" and repressive past.[9]

Broadly understood as a contest between fundamentally different conceptions of authority, victory in the revolutionary struggle was seen as a developmental advance over the prior organization of society. The deep and growing popular resolve to hunt out every last vestige of servitude represented an unwillingness, in the words of the laborer William Manning, of "the Many," emboldened by the promise of "true liberty, and the rights of man," to submit to "views and schemes of the Few" who "work to destroy free government." As Tocqueville described it, by 1831, the "principle . . . that the interests of the many are to be preferred to those of the few" had become "so absolute and irresistible," so "reign[ing] . . . as the Deity does in the universe" that to challenge it, as no one dared or even wished to any longer, would be to "give up one's rights as a citizen and almost abjure one's qualities as a man."[10] In the great social contract scene of *Moby-Dick,* Ahab, calling a public meeting with the crew, realizes that to mobilize them with the initiative necessary to undertake his heroic quest as a collective project, he must turn them from servants in a shipboard monarchy working for their stratified percentage shares into "parties to this indissoluble league." Now, Melville suggests, after all including Starbuck and Ishmael have drunk from the common cup, the new experiment in popular society had truly begun, for henceforth Ahab will be able to remind the "citizens" as authorizing members of their commitment to the collective—that "I do not order ye; ye will it."[11]

Tocqueville, most cognizant of the social forms being displaced, experienced the new society as the release of a tidal wave, "having thrown off the yoke of the mother country" and "aspired to independence of every kind"; the result was a "movement . . . so strong that it cannot be stopped" toward "a new world." With all possibilities thrust open, "political principles, laws, and human institutions seem malleable, capable of being shaped and combined at will."[12] More than a particular experiment in nation building or even, as he first believed, simply the quintessential modern national project, this new community he came to conceive as arising from within the self as the ultimate expression of human nature: "All the nations which take, not any particular man, but Man himself" will, following the experiment of the United States, "arrive at something nearer to the constitution of man, which is everywhere the same."[13]

Amidst a "society without roots, without memories, without prejudices, without habits, without common ideas, without national character,"[14] many sought direction in Jefferson's radical statement and welded it into a narrative reassuring the new nation about its mission. Jefferson himself, the prophet of popular virtue and agrarian independence, set the tone in his First Inaugural: "a wise and frugal government" is one "which shall restrain men from injuring one another" and "shall leave them otherwise free to regulate their own pursuits of industry and improvement."[15] The South Carolina statesman Hugh S. Legaré referred to the Revolution in an 1823 July Fourth address as a unique *"work of principle"* defining the "whole history of the colonies" and "our declaration of independence" as the story of "how to be free and great."[16] Lincoln, who was to learn how crucial Madison's work was for preserving Jefferson's ideals, defended his profoundly interventionist state as an adjunct to the "free society of free individuals."[17] Even Tocqueville was at first caught up in the euphoric claims of liberty: "The sight before my eyes is none the less an immense spectacle. Never before has a people found for itself such a happy and fruitful basis of life. Here freedom is unrestrained. . . . [T]he American . . . ends by regarding it as the natural state of man. He feels the need of it, more, he loves it; for the instability, instead of meaning disaster to him, seems to give birth only to miracles all about him."[18]

Expectations were heightened that the United States could find release from its collective past. Everett called on Americans to "dwell not on a distant, uncertain, an almost forgotten past but on an impending future, teeming with life and action, toward which we are rapidly and daily swept forward, and with which we stand in the dearest connexion."[19] For the *Democratic Review*, "Our national birth was the beginning of a new history . . . which separates us from the past and connects us with the future only."[20] Similarly, the belief in Americans as "free individuals" encouraged citizens of the young republic to imagine themselves unbound from all vestiges of their own histories, such that "the tie that unites one generation to another is relaxed or broken; every man . . . readily loses all trace of the ideas of his forefathers or takes no care of them." Each seeks "to evade the bondage of system and habit, of family maxims, class opinions, and . . . national prejudices; to accept tradition only as a means of information, and existing facts only as a lesson to be used in doing otherwise and doing better."[21] Emerson in his essay "Experience" instructs us to resist, of all things, past experience itself: "Distrust the facts and the inference . . . [for] the anchorage is quicksand. . . . If we will be strong with [Nature's] strength, we must not harbor

. . . disconsolate consciences, borrowed . . . from the consciences of other na-tions. We must set up the strong present tense against all the rumors of wrath, past or to come."[22]

Imagining themselves set down full-blown into "the perfection of the world," citizens were to "shun father and mother and wife and brother" and "write on the lintels of the door-post, *Whim*."[23] The early models of secu-lar individualism, *Robinson Crusoe,* Franklin's *Autobiography,* and Crèvecoeur, promised an uncomplicated release from Old World constraints. Under-taking the self-parenting "project" to achieve one's own "perfection," one could even at "thirty-seven years old," as Whitman exclaimed, "begin / Hoping to cease not till death."[24] Wellingborough Redburn on his trip to Liv-erpool, seeking his bearings with his father's prized old guidebook, has the uncanny experience of personal release: "The bare thought of there being any discrepancy, never entered my mind . . . [b]ut [the place] bore not the slightest resemblance. . . . Then, indeed, a new light broke in me concerning my guide-book. . . . It was nearly half a century behind the age! and no more fit to guide me about the town, than the map of Pompeii. . . . [T]his precious book was next to useless. Yes, the thing that had guided the father, could not guide the son." Redburn is forced to reassess his place in the world: "This world, my boy, is a moving world. . . . Guide-books, Wellingborough, are the least reliable books in all literature; and nearly all literature, in one sense, is made up of guide-books." He concludes that "every age makes its own guide-books, and the old ones are used for waste paper."[25]

Triumphant Individualism and Institutional Viability

With institutions arising to threaten the idyll, antebellum Americans were forced toward a selective perception of developments. Acknowledging only "the assumption of free choice," they regarded institutions as deriving from natural individualism: "the most successful of the new institutions operated as if their immutable principles . . . arose in spontaneous generation" by "enunciating the people's will," the result of "an uncomplicated line run-ning from individual wills to public results."[26] This stringent view of legiti-macy as requiring informality, uncoerciveness, and inclusivity dramatically constricted the scope of viable institutions. Religious institutions were, de-spite their prevalence, far too contentious and divisive to serve widely as a model for natural social organization. The idyll was centered in the economic and social realms, defined in Lockean theory as intrinsically able to function without coercion or interference. English liberal theory had posited an antecedent proprietary condition not to promote an idyllic individualism but in order to assert the continuance of that initial "freedom" within emerging market structures. So too it had ignored the existence of entangling social relations not to dismantle the social realm but to separate its constraints as personal and civil arenas beyond state intervention. Yet this strategic argument, imported into a very mobile proprietary economy with its fluid social relations, created expectations that the initial theory resisted in its use of the national condition only as a prehistorical point of departure. Because of this coincidence of fiction and reality, Americans were emboldened to embrace the liberal myth of origins seriously as the description of these sectors.

The political sector, the state, played a more complicated role. For while liberalism from Locke to Madison had accepted that political space was to be radically circumscribed in favor of less threatening activities, the state was both necessary and inclusive. But its intrinsic dependence on overt coercion disqualified it as an explicit organizer of a voluntarist society: "Forms of government have been, for the most part, only so many various forms of tyranny."[27] The resolution had been to accord it a secondary status as protector of an otherwise natural condition, which coincided with the view of the early republic as a liberal "original condition." This was bolstered by its early ineffectiveness in the direct integration of individuals into society.[28] The federal government remained remote from the daily lives of citizens; local governments either were just being formed or were unable to enforce their authority on a mobile and resistant population. Of the two political models, the Whigs and the Jeffersonian-Jacksonians, the latter more closely fit antebellum cultural demands. Though both were "firmly fixed on the past,"[29] these were different pasts. The Whigs, seeking to contain the democratic forces with a conception of natural elites as stewards of a moral nation, found little popular support. Lacking any "counter-symbol to Jefferson," whom they eventually appropriated, and forced into a "mystical" nationalism amidst sectional and party divisions, Whigs succumbed to middle-class populism and Democratic Party organization to secure electoral appeal.[30]

For Democrats, so Andrew Jackson reasoned, political institutions were largely unnecessary: "The planter, the farmer, the mechanic, and the laborer" who "form the great body of the people of the United States . . . all know that their success depends upon their own industry and economy."[31]

Given the "perfection of the polity, when it rests on a natural basis," Charles Ingersoll concluded that the political realm could be all but dispensed with: "It is the perfection of civilized society, as far as respects the happiness of its members, when its ends are accomplished with the least pressure from government. . . . [T]he American federation is the natural offspring of commerce and liberty, whose correlative interests will bind it together in principle, even after its formal dissolution. . . . The states, as now organized, may be consolidated or dismembered, may fall asunder by the weight and weakness of the union, or may separate in a convulsion."[32] Perhaps, in Everett's idyllic articulation, politics was required only for founding: "Government . . . is the first thing to be provided for. Some persons must be employed in making and administering the laws before any other interest can receive attention. . . . Society must be preserved in its constituted forms or there is no safety for life, no security for property, no permanence for any institution civil, moral, or religious. The first efforts then of social men are of necessity political." Yet stability might lead, remarkably, to the state's eventual withering away: "Though . . . we have not wholly left them . . . *we* are constantly receding from these stages."[33] The enduring dream was of a society that had found its principle of order without coercion.

The fear was that while the state persisted it would, by unleashing individual and group ambitions, deform the malleable new characters of the republican citizenry. Charles Grandison Finney expressed the fear: "Christians seem to act as if they thought God did not see what they do in politics. But I tell you, he does see it, and he will bless or curse this nation, according to the course they take."[34] The influential midcentury minister Henry Ward Beecher concurred:

> Political dishonesty in voters runs into general dishonesty, as the rotten speck taints the whole apple. A community whose politics are conducted by a perpetual breach of honesty on both sides will be tainted by immorality throughout. . . . The guile, the crafty vigilance, the dishonest advantage, the cunning sharpness, the tricks and traps and sly evasions, the equivocal promises and unequivocal neglect of them, which characterize political action, will equally characterize private action.[35]

The formation of a new republican character would have to counteract the compromises and inflamed appetites of politics: "The genius of our government directs the attention of every citizen to politics. . . . If its channels are slimy with corruption, what limit can be set to its malign influence? The turbulence of elections, the virulence of the press, the desperation of bad men, the hopelessness of efforts which are not cunning but only honest, have driven many conscientious men from any concern with politics."[36]

Emerson, prefiguring his student's more famous statement on civil disobedience, was equally sharp-edged: "Every actual State is corrupt. Good men must not obey the law too well. What satire on government can equal the severity of censure conveyed in the word *politic,* which now for ages has signified *cunning,* intimating that the State is a trick."[37] William Sprague, a revival leader, warned young men about "the lion's den" and "Nebuchadnezzer's furnace": "Let such men as [Washington and Jay and Rush] be your models; and when you reach the point where you can no longer remain in political life, and exemplify the character which adorned them in respect to integrity, let that be the point that shall mark your withdrawal into some other sphere of publick or private usefulness."[38]

The turn from politics was a matter not only of idealism but of practical anxiety. For many, populists and elites alike, politics in this contentious and divided society could too easily be harnessed to the agenda of one's opponents, increasing their leverage and even ensuring their dominance: "In the exercise of this power of intermeddling with the private pursuits and individual occupations of the citizen, a government may at pleasure elevate one class and depress another."[39] Jackson spoke of the people's being "in constant danger of losing their fair influence in the Government" from "the power" of "the moneyed interest" and the need to "detect and defeat every effort to gain unfair advantages over them."[40] William Leggett, a Jacksonian newspaper editor, discussed the rising threat of new elites: "The tyrant is changed from a steel-clad feudal baron or a minor despot . . . to a mighty civil gentleman who comes mincing and bowing to the people . . . at the head of countless millions of magnificent *promises.*" James Fenimore Cooper was equally outraged from the other side by the ascendance of popular government, the new "public—all-powerful, omnipotent, overruling, law-making, law-breaking public": "The grossest enormities are constantly committed in this good Republic of ours, under the pretence of being done by the public, and for the public. . . . Men will have idols, and the Americans have merely set up themselves. . . . Resisting the popular will, on the part of the individual, they consider . . . arrogance and aristocracy *per se.*"[41]

Since politics could not be dispensed with, optimally it could be treated defensively as a barrier to the opposition's encroachments, in Jefferson's terms, as "a mild and safe corrective of abuses."[42] It would maintain "untrammeled by human devices the just and natural relations of man to man" in the original condition so that social life might "flow in those channels to which individual enterprise, always its surest guide, might direct it."[43] In this way, the evasion of political realities led to an—equally evasive—emphasis on those realms defined as voluntarist to guide early national formation and to serve as the conceptual basis for liberal institutions in the early republic.

The Liberal Economic and Social Idylls

Although American society underwent its formal elimination of traditional class and status demarcations with the expulsion of England, imperial controls on land, labor, and internal trade had been declining for generations. Absent national regulatory institutions, the end of colonial status produced the unique condition overnight of a virtually unregulated economy. This reified a naturalist framework from the outset in American practice.[44] As "a race of cultivators" in Crèvecoeur's terms, Americans by nature work and consume, pursuing market rewards pre-politically from individual biological and psychological motivations; their "labour is founded on the basis of nature, *self-interest;* can it want any stronger allurement?"[45] Personal fulfillment was thus also intrinsic to economic activity. Writing in 1834, William Leggett asserted that "as a general rule, the prosperity of rational men depends on themselves. . . . They are therefore the best judges of their own affairs and should be permitted to seek their own happiness in their own way . . . [through] the free exercise of their talents and industry."[46]

Absent external constraints, the liberal individual is axiomatically free— "man . . . free as he ought to be."[47] As the visitor Michel Chevalier observed, "The English and their children in America call a decent standard of living *independence.*"[48] Freedom was primarily conceived economically: "The lien of this 'mighty continental nation' is commercial liberty . . . geographical absolution from all but the slightest restraints; the inherent and inalienable birthright . . . a heritage as natural as the air they breathe . . . of commerce and liberty."[49] In the Jeffersonian canon, the self-sufficient proprietor was the center of this republican experiment.[50] Whitman made it the "substrata" of his entire "Democratic Vista."[51]

Antebellum Lockean liberal economic theory grounded the natural inalienable rights of individuals to life, liberty, and happiness as to individuality and citizenship in the universal right to acquire property.[52] Property provided freedom by ensuring both economic self-sufficiency and individual discretion whether and to what extent to participate in market exchange. Paul Conkin notes the reigning ideology of early American economic theory: "The glory of the American economy was not so much prosperity as freedom. The idealized American producer was free and independent, without an economic master. He owned his own land or shop or tools, commanded his own labor, reaped his own returns, all without any obligation to anyone else. The idealized American was always a proprietor, whether a farmer, mechanic, or merchant." For the economist Leummi Baldwin, the liberal economy was "remedial," with the power to shape the new citizenry. It promoted *"perfect freedom"* and thus elevated all citizens, "free[d] them from dependence," overcame "stupid torpor" and "listless apathy" by "promoting the general industry of the people" through "securing" to all individuals the power to benefit themselves and rely on themselves by "working for their own behoof."[53] The economy was thus the natural foundation for the new republic, a "political order" which is "the result of the passions and wants of man . . . in other words the wisdom of nature; all acting in such beautiful subserviency to her suggestions as to raise the idea of original arrangement."[54]

The message which was to "direct" our nation "as long as we pretend to constitute a republic" and hoped to validate the revolution was clear: "Make every member of the community a proprietor of the soil, and he shares in the sovereignty of the state; the jurisdiction and the right of property will exist in the same person, and . . . the former will never be prostituted to the aggrandizement of the latter."[55] Available to many, this option was widely selected: "The prevailing ambition of the greatest portion of the people is to acquire and enjoy an estate in land. To favour this strong and natural desire, no government or country can offer more propitious circumstances. This passion prevails over all others, and surmounts all obstacles."[56] Jefferson's own faith in the unique "vigour" of the American republic, constituted by "husbandmen . . . who labour in the earth . . . the chosen people of God," imbued with virtue and independence, was henceforth to be contrasted to the "mobs" of Europe characterized by "subservience and venality," "corruption," and "degeneracy."[57]

The success of popular opportunity in its decentralized economy explains the extraordinary hold on the mind of nineteenth-century America of its self-image as an agrarian republic, an endless expanse of self-sufficient proprietors. The result was in Henry Nash Smith's terms the myth of a "virgin land" or "Garden of the World," of a "vast and constantly growing agricultural society in the interior of the continent," the "collective representation, a poetic idea . . . that defined the promise of American life."[58] Even as market structures emerged, the prevailing belief in a proprietary economy persisted. While a few economists and politicians including Matthew Carey, Francis Wayland, Henry Clay, and Whig manufacturers defended Hamilton's program for a national manufacturing sector,[59] this Federalist view was marginalized by the "new-truisms" of the "day."[60]

Order in this vision derived from individual economic activities. The economist Erick Bollman wrote: "All human institutions being conducted by men, and nations at large being only a society of individuals, they . . . must proceed after the same manner as individuals . . . each pursuing their own interests for their own sake." The apparent regularity in turn suggested a natural, pre-political cohesion to the new republic: the "correlative interests" of the "American federation" are to "bind it" in "mutual commercial dependence"; and a "reciprocity of interests" creates "strong bonds of union."[61] The "cultivators of the earth" were the "most valuable citizens," for in addition to being "the most vigorous, the most independent, the most virtuous," they were for Jefferson "tied to their country, and wedded to its interests, by the most lasting bonds."[62] While *"l'intérêt"* was the "only . . . tie" in this unregulated society,[63] it organized the "floating atoms . . . into a far more perfect and harmonious result than if government . . . disturb . . . the process."[64] Tocqueville believed that "new wants are not to be feared there, since they can be satisfied without difficulty; the growth of human passions need not be dreaded, since all passions may find an easy and legitimate object, nor can men there be made too free, since they are scarcely ever tempted to misuse their liberties."[65] The "celebrated economic interest itself" was in Samuel Blodget's view "the best adhesive a society could have . . . 'the most to be depended on of all.'"[66] In their strength and seeming lack of constraint, pecuniary ties were seen as *"golden chains"* effortlessly constituting "incorporated monied commonwealth associations" most compatible with the "golden" future of the American idyll. Thus, "we hope . . . the United States, and all our associations shall be linked in these golden, social chains . . . even if . . . extended over all North America."[67]

The fluidity and voluntarism of life in the early republic with extreme role and geographic mobility reinforced an idyllic denial of the continuing power of social networks with their authority and constraints. The rhetoric of a new societal experiment without fixed class, civic, or social groupings further supported a denial of collective pressures toward integration. Because

Americans expected the social sector to look as it had in their European past, they did not recognize or realize its novel constitution until it had been largely completed and was already established as a system of popular social integration. It was thus possible well into the post–Civil War period to deny a social process, and to insist that claims of uniformity were the fantasies of social critics and outcasts. To this very day, no politician in America could acknowledge in Turnerian language the closing of the "social" frontier.

This image of a world free of social entanglements emerged during the revolutionary age. The recently settled American interior was a world without society, without "the bonds of custom" recently left in Europe through "a gate of escape from the bondage of the past."[68] This along with the "migratory habits of the American people" opened the sense of an almost uncontrollable fluidity. As the novelist Caroline Kirkland put it, "The habit of selling out so frequently, makes that *home*-feeling, which is so large an ingredient in happiness elsewhere, almost a non-entity."[69] The many agricultural regions offered not community but emptiness, a "prairie home" starkly alone on a spacious "homestead," "farm wives . . . driven crazy . . . by the isolation of farm life."[70] In her 1845 novel *Western Clearings,* Kirkland captured the underlying sensibility of settler life: "We have no days consecrated to innocent hilarity . . . and strengthening the links of human sympathy. But this is a work-a-day world, and we are a working people. . . . [O]ur family-friends, where are they? With our joy there would mingle a touch of sadness. We could not rejoice in thinking of the absent."[71]

From early on, "society," with its obligations of ritual, behavior, and belief associated with stultifying confinement and servitude, was to be resisted. The model of course was Crusoe, read and cited everywhere, with his society of one. Jeremy Belknap, in his 1792 allegorical novel *The Foresters,* treating America's history to the time of independence, described the social constraints of English and Puritan society: "She had taken it into her head that every one of the family [society] must hold knife and fork and spoon exactly alike; that they must all wash their hands and face precisely in the same manner; that they must sit, walk, kneel, spit, blow their noses, and perform every other animal function by the exact rule of *uniformity* . . . from which they were not allowed to vary one hair's breadth. . . . Such was the logic of the family in those days!" This in turn caused many colonists to "quit the house."[72] For them, the new society was no more than a collection of individuals, each operating according to their own priorities. This "modern society," having dispensed with all elements of the coercive past, as Crèvecoeur observed, having "no aristocratical families," no courts or kings, no bishops, and no "ecclesiastical dominion," no "all invisible power giving to a few a very visible one," was "different" from everything "hitherto seen."[73]

For Paine, America was the "only spot" formed on the "principle of society," that is, "natural liberty."[74] Tocqueville spoke of the "novel spectacle" of a society "able to spread in perfect freedom" without any "hierarchy of rank," where overt subordination or even deference to the community was regarded as a personal failing. The individual was in fact encouraged to resist entangling connections and commitments, typically having "tried ten different estates . . . lived in twenty different places and nowhere found ties to detain him . . . placed in the middle of an always moving scene, himself drawn by the irresistible torrent which draws all . . . accustomed only to change."[75] E. W. Howe in the realist novel *The Story of a Country Town* portrayed the frontier settler: "When he came to a place that suited him, he picked out the land he wanted—which any man was free to do at that time."[76] The continuing sense of unlimited openness, of a "continent" of "vacant spaces" there for the "filling up," produced an enduring sense of being without society, in an "anti-social" or "atomic" condition in which "the individual was exalted and given free play . . . out of the freedom of his opportunities." The chance to outrun every restraint or pressure, to remain only if one chose the constraints presented, produced a mindset of "antipathy to control, and particularly to any direct control."[77]

The Self-Socializing Economy

This picture of chains which were not chains because everyone agreed to be bound and could untie themselves at will was illusory, the exception made into the rule. Structural transformation was organizing the economy in two phases: the first, our present concern, entailed the antebellum emergence of an extended market economy; the second, occurring after the Civil War, involved growing control by massive industrial and commercial organizations. The former shift was the stimulus for the development of laissez-faire economic theory (Chapter 12), the latter for the subsuming of the economy within an integrated liberal society (Chapter 13).

Through the first half of the century, regional and national markets were burgeoning as production shifted from self-sufficient agricultural holdings with secondary surplus and home manufacture for local markets and small artisan trade to specialized agricultural production and growing commercial and manufacturing entities. Despite market exchange being treated by the terms of the idyll as secondary and incidental, most families from early on engaged in simple interdependent production and distribution systems. The development of internal transportation and communication, the increasing wealth producing a demand for machinery, transport, and consumer goods, and ever more specialized trade led many either to focus their agricultural or industrial production or to forgo self-employment for work in larger companies. Although the size of industrial units before the war, except in the last decades in cotton textile and arms manufacturing, iron rolling mills, and a few other areas, remained small-scale, as did commercial enterprises, farmers and artisans were nevertheless becoming increasingly dependent on commercial suppliers and marketers and squeezed by larger producers. It was still possible in this period to believe in an economy of individual actors, if now increasingly rooted in interdependent exchange rather than self-production. Yet the market increasingly shaped individual incentives and priorities, weakening the idyllic claim of independent economic actors, equal leverage, and noncoercive exchange.

The process of economic integration, though largely obscured by revolutionary ideology, was paradoxically intended by liberal theory. Given the liberal claim of constituting a formally noncoercive society, voluntary membership required some realm in which all individuals continuously and willingly transferred their authority to institutions signifying an at least tacit acceptance of inclusion. To provide the requisite universality, this realm had to feature sustained and significant activity (beyond mere residence) undertaken by the whole populace without visible systemic force. From this, a dynamic of universal and unfailing transfer—of integration and accommodation—could be inferred. The idyll of a free natural economy was clearly a superior basis for "voluntary" systemic commitment. With social relations, the far greater personal discretion and inaccessibility to effective systemic controls insulated them from consistently applied leverage.

The economy by contrast, as evident in the *Second Treatise,* though mythically conceived as an arena of precommunal initiative presumed continuous universal involvement. Absent a social safety net, as Jeremy Bentham had understood, "the great masses of citizens will most probably possess few other resources than their daily labor, and consequently will always be near to indigence." Thus, he argued, "the force of physical sanction being sufficient, the employment of the political sanction would be superfluous."[78] The pursuit of subsistence and comfort, while framed as voluntary activity, entailed the unceasing activation of natural necessity by all toward consensual ends evidently independent of political coercion. Its source could thus be imagined not in the intensifying economic pressures but in self-reliant productive activity driven by personal need in a pre-political world of self-motivated units. At the same time, this activity in reality entailed an unavoidable commitment to interpersonal procedures.[79] Few lived outside either economic exchange or its requirements regarding participation. This in turn enabled the market to be regarded as a natural construction by individuals to facilitate their own economic ends and its network of regulations intrinsically voluntarist and self-subscribed.

In the early republic, the informal incentives toward economic integration were so powerful that Americans could easily believe themselves to be "free participants in a free economy." The opportunity for engagement from its inception in the establishment of a national economy drove individuals to identify with and subsume their own interests within the collective creation of wealth. David Ramsay wrote in 1778:

> May we not hope, as soon as this contest is ended, that the exalted spirits of our politicians and warriors will engage in the enlargement of public happiness, by cultivating the arts of peace, and promoting useful knowledge, with an ardor equal to that which first roused them to bleed in the cause of liberty and their country? . . . teach[ing] mankind to plough, sow, plant, build, and improve the rough face of nature. . . . Such will be the fruits of our glorious revolution. . . . The face of our interior country will be changed from a barren wilderness into the hospitable abodes of peace and plenty.[80]

Joel Barlow brought Columbus into the future to witness "a new creation. . . . Great cities grow and empires claim their sway." Charles Ingersoll joined the chorus: "Universality of successful employment diffuses alacrity and happiness throughout the community. . . . Each individual feels himself rising in his fortunes; and the nation, rising with the concentration of all this elasticity, rejoices in its growing greatness."[81] Each person could provide "a service which conduces to the wealth and happiness of individuals and to the community."[82]

The ubiquitous "air of industry" which they "breathe . . . under the paternal roof, in public meetings, everywhere, at all times and in every act of life"[83] generated palpable but unidentifiable pressure on the individual: "The notion of labor is presented . . . on every side, as the necessary, natural, and honest condition of human existence. . . . Public opinion forbade [idleness], too imperiously to be disobeyed." An individual who resisted was "in bad repute if he employed his life solely in living," and was led to believe that "there was something wrong with him."[84] Yet such pressures were regarded as entirely tangential. With the unprecedented opportunities to shape careers, businesses, professions, and trading networks, Americans were convinced that their economic lives grew out of their individual activity, maximizing personal goals even as they followed the emerging institutional priorities and guidelines. With no choice but to work, given the relatively undeveloped economy, the intense pressure of biological deprivation made the liberal economy ideally situated to extract willing participation and rendered explicit social pressure unnecessary.

Moreover, the euphoria of release from the shackles of the past, in "the first essays of an industry, which hitherto had been suppressed," obscured even informal pressures. A new sense of shaping one's own role and place emerged as they "cut down the first trees, erect their new buildings, till their first fields, reap their first crops, and say for the first time in their lives, 'This is our own . . . raised from American soil.'"[85] Americans were "readily discover[ing] that they are not confined and fixed by any limits which force them to accept their present fortune."[86] Seemingly without precedent, the central moral requirement was conduct so apparently liberating, dazzlingly energizing, and unconflictedly self-gratifying that the institutional engagement in material well-being was easily won.

In the economy as nowhere else in young republican society, each "actor introduced upon a new scene" in America learned "the part he was to perform."[87] Gradually, most caught on by "attentively consider[ing] the prosperous industry of others, which imprints in their minds a strong desire of possessing the same advantages." They experienced "a powerful spur" to undertake "progressive steps" to "partake of our great labours" by "dint of sobriety, rigid parsimony, and the most persevering industry."[88] Chevalier spoke of "this ardent and entire devotion to business," a "constant direction of the energies of the mind to useful enterprise . . . [and] indifference to pleasure."[89] This unique condition in which "everybody works," in which "everything . . . draws" the "human spirit" toward "industry," the "only road open" toward which "all energetic passions are directed," was regarded as the essential attribute of American society.[90] The opportunities were available to great numbers on a scale previously undreamed of: "Subsistence is so easy, and competency so common, that . . . [n]ative Americans are very seldom to be met with in menial or the laborious occupations. . . .

[W]ages are very high, and hard labour is altogether optional. Three days work out of seven yields a support."[91] Frances Trollope referred to a land "flowing with milk and honey."[92]

The exuberant, unreflective embrace of economic participation directed freedom effortlessly into agency, making the economy the institutional linchpin of idyllic liberalism with its conflation of individual and collective ends intrinsic to neoclassical and rational choice theory. The individual's "utmost exertions" for personal rewards became, in Ramsay's terms, "active virtues" in constructing this new economic system which the "necessities of our country require."[93] Where "the whole community is engaged in the task . . . to improve the state of society," embracing "all those quiet virtues that tend to give a regular movement to the community,"[94] the result was "that fine union of public with private feelings," the "unison" of "all the true interests of society," of "public happiness," and the "masses['] . . . own interests."[95]

Given "a physical condition so happy that the interest of the individual is never opposed to the interest of the whole,"[96] independence and self-sufficiency were quickly relinquished for systemic engagement. In a development that confounded Tocqueville, individuals were actually seeking their own socialization: "They cannot prosper without strictly regular habits and a long routine of petty uniform acts. The stronger the passion is, the more regular are these habits and the more uniform are these acts. . . . [I]t is the vehemence of their desires that makes the Americans so methodical. . . . Commerce is naturally averse to all the violent passions; it loves to temporize, takes delight in compromise. . . . It is patient, insinuating, flexible . . . [with] habits of prudence and restraint."[97] Wealth led not to four days off but contrarily to increased devotion to material improvement: "The lassitude and dissipation, which might be expected" from the opportunity for "so much leisure, are provided against by . . . inexhaustible fields of adventure and opulence. The inducement to labour, the recompense is so great, that the Americans, with the utmost facilities of subsistence, are a most industrious people."[98] With even "wealthy persons" now "intoxicated," the "love of well-being has now become the predominant taste of the nation . . . sweep[ing] everything along in its course."[99]

It took foreign visitors to recognize the regimentation hidden from Americans. Tocqueville more than any other observer came to understand the depths of the relentless commitment to work and its obsession with regularity and order: "The love of wealth is therefore to be traced, as either a principal or an accessory motive, at the bottom of all that the Americans do; this gives all their passions a sort of family likeness and soon renders . . . them exceedingly wearisome. This perpetual recurrence of the same passion is monotonous."[100] Mrs. Trollope found that the obsession with wealth produced the "sordid tone" of "an ant's nest." Chevalier spoke of Americans' "ardent and entire devotion to business" as a kind of "fanaticism" amounting to "intolerance, inquisition," yet strangely "it is submitted to without a murmur, and few persons are really annoyed by it, or show that they are."[101]

This almost magical routinization in which "minds naturally tend to similar conclusions" and "involuntarily and unconsciously concur"[102] was the internalization of the market agency role as the operational equivalent of economic freedom. Within the emerging market system, "the idealized figure of the independent republican producer almost imperceptibly changed shape into the striving self-made man," fueled not by "individual 'independence'" but by its liberal substitute, market "self-interest."[103] Work for reward replaced proprietorship as the arena for shaping one's own identity and destiny, prolonging indefinitely the vision of inwardly motivated economic actors. As a most unstable proprietary economy quickly gave way to economic consolidation and interdependence, participants raced to establish and pursue consensual ends and designated means through directed motion within a single universal system. Presumably natural impulses in a presumptively noncoercive setting were in fact creating the very structure that would undo the "natural" economy.[104] Nor could it be otherwise. Basic market rules could not be altered by individuals; nor was there permission or economic support for them to refrain from engagement. Faced with the biological imperative to labor and the social desire to participate in collective development in an unformed, insecure new society with no resources but labor and no social value but exchange value, individuals ineluctably chose integration in the acquisitive process which confirmed their agency status. Desires and goals while motivated individually had to be framed interdependently, conceived in terms of exchange and satisfied in an arena beyond individual control within which collectively mandated "procedural" regulations or instrumental "facilitations" were easily embedded.[105]

With voluntary universal engagement, freedom became an attribute of systemic membership synonymous with participation. The only question for individuals was their effectiveness in this pursuit of systemic ends, one's capacity for using the "freedom" given. For the world after traditionalism, individual participation in a commercial society was an incalculable advance of liberty. That it was the activity of agency par excellence never occurred to those recently arrived from economic and social subservience. In a static world, or one of infinite expanse, this combination of individual freedom and collective purpose might have endured with its contradictions undiscovered. But as those chains grew ever tighter in the form of developed institutions, they became, despite great resolve to sustain the idyll, impossible to neglect. What is intriguing is that it was not until after the Civil War that such institutional development was plausible even to some, and that it is to this day still unthinkable to many.

The Slowly Spinning Web of Social Relations

The formation of the social realm is a matter of intense controversy in the history of liberalism because of its ambiguous relationship to the original liberal project. As a political reordering of medieval society based on the principle of voluntary integration, liberalism found problematic the secondary and informal associations located between the individual and the state. To be brought within the ambit of voluntarism, social roles, networks, and associations were now reframed as informal fields of choice rather than pre-existing institutional systems of designated place, class, and function with inflexible demands, expectations, and structures external to the adult individual. At the same time, early liberal theory betrays an ultimate reliance on the power of involuntary integration. Its objective was not to achieve autonomy but to replace the multiple closed organizations of traditional society with an inclusive associational reality integrating all members through a common socialization and behavioral code. Though presented simply as an adjunct to voluntary adult activity, this realm would in fact incorporate citizens from infancy within a universal web of meanings and activities, preexisting ends and legitimated means. The goal was to ensure social cohesion for an active, individualist populace without benefit of established hierarchy and overt subordination.

A social realm providing interconnection in a society founded on liberal values presented a novel problem. The English theorists could minimize this realm, informally relying on their society's existing web of preliberal social and class institutions. Integrating a vast, disparate populace in the United States as traditional relations of family and local community frayed with assimilation and geographic mobility made the constitution of an effective social authority ensuring adaptive conduct problematic. What was a social realm, a realm of secure status and stable place, to be in a fluid and "free" society? How could social institutions now needing contradictorily to be both voluntary and integrative be constituted and maintained? To be "free," as with the originative constitution of other emerging sectors, they had to eschew all fixed hierarchies and innate inequalities while acknowledging the formal equivalence (regardless of actual disparities) of all members, the equal option to step forward before God, the universal political access to vote or participate in governance, the opportunity for all to pursue economic rewards. Authority and leadership thus had to be popular and temporary, and pressures informal and even invisible in order to ensure the sense of voluntarism. Yet some predictable and unavoidable basis for integration within institutions composed of formally equal members was necessary.

As each sector reconstituted itself on the basis of equivalent agents, Americans willingly reconceived freedom as participatory motion within complementary institutional processes. The social realm presented the most considerable structural and conceptual challenge, for it was initially tied to no specific individual or public goal acknowledged as a common end in liberal society. Its informal relations and associations provided the rich connectedness of daily life, but only through variants of status, place, and affiliation within the community. Given the liberal conceit that integration was natural and that liberal society constituted a single social class, social customs and symbols constituting nonliberal markers of distinction had to be ignored or taken for granted. One measure of antebellum avoidance was the appropriation by early social theory of the contractual framework from liberal economics. In a major work of the period, *The Elements of Moral Science*, Francis Wayland, president of Brown University and professor of moral philosophy, used the voluntarist language of liberal contractual exchange to frame community institutions as voluntary "societies and associations" subject to individual discretion.[106]

In time, as cohesion was recognized to be the product of institutional pressures, the social realm was to evolve its function: to facilitate the process of universal integration. The liberal mandate to avoid fragmentation while resisting inflexible hierarchy would require a common language of visibility and presentation, impersonal enough to overcome or fit on top of deeper differences and disparities, sufficiently accessible to mute those differences, fluid enough for availability to all and responsiveness to popular shifts. Without distinct ends beyond the suspect one of belonging, means and ends became circular, the goal of universal equivalence becoming the demonstrable pursuit of universal equivalence, supported by a social authority itself displaced into intangible communal pressures to sustain that pursuit. Treated as a mere adjunct to and facilitator of—a highway of interpersonal communication serving—the "real" functional sectors as they expanded in complexity, this realm of visible commonality, so evanescent and so ubiquitous, was allowed to grow unobserved.

The early evidence of such a realm, then, is indirect. Occasional insights from the margins by those beyond the reach of or rejecting pressures for inclusion—foreigners, the excluded, the rebellious—complement our understanding of liberal institutional formation more explicitly under way in other sectors. The nearly invisible phenomenon these early commentators were trying to grasp was actually two contrary—and seemingly self-canceling—drives: the wish to remain free of entangling communities and the equally powerful need to constitute a single society of consistent behaviors. The result of this tension was vocal individual voluntarism combined with a camouflaged but unrelenting network being spun of majoritarian deference in matters of opinion, taste, conduct, and goals. Only the most acute observers could see beneath the alleged voluntarism new forms of authority through the informal realms of American life reflecting the wish for agency integration: foreigners such as Tocqueville and Martineau; Federalist virtual exiles like Cooper and Brackenridge; individualist outsiders such as Emerson, Thoreau, and even Melville; Kirkland, perhaps uniquely observant of emerging social networks as a woman in a society controlled overtly by men.[107]

These "outsiders" intuited beneath the "firm reliance on their own opinions" the pressures on individuals to adapt to a common set of attitudes, to "defer" to "the public, as sacred and paramount."[108] Thus the Irish immigrant William Simpson wrote of the public sphere, "It is round you like the air and you cannot even feel it."[109] Michel Chevalier, who came to America for two years in 1833, elaborated: "The Unites States constitutes a society which moves by instinct, rather than by any premeditated plan; it does not know itself. It rejects the tyranny . . . of [the] past, yet it is deeply imbued with the sentiment of order. . . . [A] feeling of the need for self-restraint runs through its veins. It is divided between . . . its thirst after freedom and its hunger for social order."[110] In an essay on his Kansas childhood, the historian Carl Becker remembered the pioneers "forever tugging at the leashes of ordered life, eager to venture into the unknown. Forsaking beaten paths, they plunge into the wilderness . . . where new forms of life, whether of in-stitutions or types of thought, are germinated." Yet this was an "individual-ism" of "achievement, not of eccentricity." In other words, "however eccen-tric frontiersmen may appear to the tenderfoot, among themselves there is little variation from type in any essential matter. In the new community, in-dividualism means the ability of the individual to succeed, not by submitting to some external formal authority, still less by following the bent of an un-schooled will, but by recognizing and voluntarily adapting himself to neces-sary conditions." He concluded, "What strikes one is that . . . native Kansans are all so much alike."[111]

Tocqueville, as developed in the next chapter, most fully grasped the very power and ubiquity of this invisible psychological web of commonality be-ing woven beneath the rhetoric of a free society. Cooper, in a brilliant ex-tended synopsis of societal formation in the young republic, also captured the combination of novelty, informality, and necessity that made the very real social realm appear a mere extension of individual choice:

> The progress of society . . . in what has been termed a "new country," is a little anomalous. At the commencement of a settlement, there is much of that sort of kind feeling and mutual interest which men are apt to manifest towards each other when they are embarked in an enterprise of common hazards. The distance that is unavoidably inseparable from education, hab-its, and manners, is lessened by mutual wants and mutual efforts. . . . Men, and even women, break bread together, and otherwise commingle, that, in different circumstances, would be strangers. . . .
>
> This period may be termed, perhaps, the happiest of the first century of a settlement. The great cares of life are so engrossing and serious that small vexations are overlooked, and the petty grievances that would make us se-riously uncomfortable in a more regular state of society, are taken as mat-ters of course. . . . Good will abounds; neighbor comes cheerfully to the aid of neighbor; and life has much of the reckless gaiety, careless association, and buoyant merriment of childhood. It is found that they who have passed through this probation, usually look back to it with regret.

In the second period,

> society begins to marshal itself, and the ordinary passions have sway. Now it is that we see the struggle for place, the heart-burnings and jealousies of contending families, and the influence of mere money. Circumstances have

probably established the local superiority of a few beyond all question, and the condition of these serves as a goal for the rest to aim at. . . . Then commence those gradations of social station that set institutions at defiance. . . . The struggle is only so much more the severe . . . for, as men usually defer to a superiority that is long established . . . here [it] is the subject of strife. . . . This is perhaps the least inviting condition of society that belongs to any country that can claim to be free.

The third and last condition of society in a "new country," is that in which the influence of the particular causes enumerated above ceases, and men and things come within the control of more general and regular laws. The effect, of course, is to leave the community in possession of a civilization that conforms to that of the whole region . . . and with the division into castes that are more or less rigidly maintained.

The vicissitudes of American life, however, obscure this process:

In some places, the pastoral age, or that of good fellowship, continues for a whole life. . . . The second period is usually of longer duration, the migratory habits of the American people keeping society more unsettled than might otherwise prove to be the case. It may be said never to cease entirely, until the great majority of the living generation are natives of that region. . . . Even when this is the case, there is commonly so large an infusion of the birds of passage, men who are adventurers in quest of advancement, and who live without the charities of a neighborhood . . . a numerous and restless class, that of themselves are almost sufficient to destroy whatever there is of . . . local attachment in any region where they resort. . . . [A]s they may be said almost to live without a home . . . there is to be found for a long time a middle state of society, during which it may well be questioned whether a community belongs to a second or to the third of the periods named.[112]

Because of the tenuous and provisional character of American social institutions, the lack of enforceable membership and discipline, the refusal to acknowledge societal formation and stratification together with a practical resistance to settling down, the voluntarist conception of the social realm veiling the formation of community has persisted in classical liberal doctrine until our own time, in Walter Lippmann, John Rawls, the libertarians, and others. This persistence partially explains the cultural shock as Americans are rudely reminded that they are living in society and acting out its patterns of socialization and prescribed conduct and have moreover been doing so all along. It is often more disheartening to realize that what seemed like a betrayal of liberalism was in reality liberalism itself finally being recognized.

The Economic Idyll in Crisis

The dynamic of institutional formation was producing by the late antebellum period a society of unexpected complexity and organization. As Americans discovered that overarching institutions were not to be eliminated, that the idyll in effect never had a chance, their fantasy of natural order quite dramatically turned into panic that freedom was disappearing, defeated by the rising collective. Caroline Kirkland wrote: "After one has changed one's whole plan of life, and crossed the wide ocean to find a Utopia [of . . . unbounded freedom], the waking to reality [of "heavy restraints"] is attended to with feelings of no slight bitterness. In some instances within my knowledge these feelings of disappointment have been so severe as to neutralize all that was good in American life, and to produce a degree of sour discontent which increased every real evil."[113] The notion that community is rooted primarily in human failure haunts the American experience of society from conservatives like Hawthorne in "Young Goodman Brown" to radical individualists like Thoreau and reflects mainstream cultural sentiment. As committed as Americans to freedom as "a holy thing,"[114] Tocqueville recognized that the "free society of free individuals" had given way to new forms of institutional authority and deference, and was left similarly disillusioned.

Antebellum disappointment spread. Given its bifurcation between individuals whose extensive pre-political and preinstitutional—including pre-market—rights and options made interdependence optional and institutions whose primary function was constraint, revolutionary liberalism could only record the emergence of markets, social networks, and other formal institutions with dismay. In its late Jeffersonian and Jacksonian formulations, every accumulation of disproportionate economic leverage, wealth, or government privilege was regarded as a coercive and thus illegitimate imposition on the natural economy. The decline of self-sufficient proprietorship and rudimentary local markets became a deformation of the liberal polity undermining the foundation of the free republic. The agricultural proprietor, no longer the sole prototype for economic independence, remained the backbone of the economic order: "So fixed in their mind was the Jeffersonian equation of republican virtue and agricultural vocation that radical Jacksonians . . . saw no prospect of elevating the poor workers except by making each one an independent proprietor, preferably a farmer."[115] With the growing imbalance of leverage, the economy risked becoming, like liberal politics, a realm of institutionalized coercion, in which preinstitutional freedom was sacrificed to the ends of the institutional process as determined by its dominant participants. Later Jacksonian economists, no longer able to ignore the increasing division of labor which was undercutting self-sufficiency and rendering market distribution and exchange necessary, prophesied the decline rather than adaptation of liberalism.

In the face of these threats, the proponents of Jacksonian economics— despite insurmountable contradictions—reaffirmed Lockean independence. With ownership no longer the viable yardstick and their constituency entering commerce and production, productive labor was substituted as the common denominator. Their theory was expanded to include "journeymen and laborers," "mechanics," and "operatives,"[116] with labor made *"the source of wealth."* A just society provided the right to labor, leaving "all to the free exercise of their talents and industry" unhindered by legal restraints, and required "the *distribution of property on the principle of the worth of labor.*"[117] But how could the capacity to participate in production be the guarantor of an individualist freedom within a set of increasingly organized, consolidated, and thus dispositive market processes? Rejecting the spreading values of Protestant agency, the Jacksonian answer, though differing from the earlier Jeffersonian one, was equally idyllic and unrealistic: it was to posit a simplified world of ideal(ized) exchange relations reflecting a local market economy. Market interdependence was now acknowledged, but within a society of small, predominantly independent producers, freedom could be sustained by the relatively equal power and leverage of each member.

In this system of "equal rights" and "free competition,"[118] the driving force was individual enterprise, "unrestrained competition, one man with another": "[T]he prosperity of rational men depends on themselves. Their talents and their virtues shape their fortunes. They are therefore the best judges of their own affairs and should be permitted to seek their own happiness in their own way, untrammeled by the capricious interference of legislative bungling." This economy of equals, "on the true basis of merit and labor," would tend "by its own weight, to equalize property on a scale of equity and comfort and to adjust the wages of labor in a manner conducive to the general happiness."[119] Where no one was able to procure unfair political, extramarket advantages, this "unprecedented activity on equitable principles would . . . pervade all occupations, and, instead of a few becoming rich at the expense of the many, the advances of society would be comparatively uniform and in mass." Given the extreme decentralization posited, there would be neither coercion nor even unfair leverage. Everyone, laborers included, would have the right to "fix [one's] own price" and participate in the market voluntarily with a "freedom to trade" or "leave enterprise."[120]

Despite the alarming disappearance of this simple market with its roots in proprietary independence before concentrations of wealth, "the encroachments and usurpations of power" by the "aristocracy" of "the consumers, the rich, the proud, the privileged" who steal "from the many" on behalf of "the few,"[121] Jacksonians refused to acknowledge these developments as a "natural" or inevitable stage of economic formation. "Nature" as framed by the Declaration would never condone a descent into dependence and servitude.[122] The causes, therefore, had to be located elsewhere, either in pseudo-populist trickery or in political machinations, that is, in the desire of institutions to form themselves over and at the expense of the people. They fantasized that a return to revolutionary values and to popular government by abolishing special privileges and government intervention would re-create the freedom of a level and competitive playing field and "happiness, simplicity, and independence."[123]

Joseph Blau calls their views "scientifically unsound," the product of nostalgic sentiment.[124] They were worse: they were a deluded, if honorable, effort to resist the inevitable logic of national formation. To acknowledge economic growth as natural would be to admit that revolutionary liberalism had been unsustainable, that "what we gained in *principle*, we lost in *practice*," that "we voluntarily became *dependent* in fact while we proclaimed ourselves to be independent in theory." Americans would have to acknowledge that while "establish[ing] the principle of *equality* and the fact of *nominal political independence*," they were submitting to a very different reality, even perhaps "to all the forms, usages, and trappings of the old gothic monarchies."[125] The alternative to facing the situation, widely adopted, including by the economic thinkers of the period, was shock, rage, and ultimately despair:

> Our first generation of economists wrote during the infancy of associated modes of production in America . . . [which] suggested an irreversible trend toward larger productive units, more centralized management, greater eco-

nomic interdependence, and more wage labor. . . . [T]he move from farm to factory was a very painful grudging surrender to economic necessity . . . [requiring one] to alter his self-image, give up earlier fortifications of self-respect, and confess the failure of a noble American dream—that all men could be free.

These early theorists thus became alternately "prophets in the Hebraic sense" for whom "precautionary warnings, often tinged with laments over a lost innocence, dominated their analysis,"[126] and proponents of "impossibly Quixotic schemes," economies without accumulation, manufacturing, or speculation, that is, without economic or political institutional formation.[127]

Unlike Jacksonian liberals, for whom the benefits of market exchange, its goods, transport, and communications advances, were still available without vertical and horizontal integration or a dominant national market, traditional economic liberals after the Civil War faced a more dire situation. The elimination of local competition with increasing organizational size and market share signified the systemic irrelevance of proprietorship, while even production itself—regardless of the scale—was becoming one modest aspect of a vast system of leveraged exchange. It was no longer meaningful to suggest that individuals had a viable choice regarding market participation or even the terms of that involvement.

The shock waves expanded. Reflected in the literature of the age, serious and popular, muckraking and reformist, was a nation losing contact with its formative condition: Henry Adams's "new universe" of the "dynamo"; Frank Norris's "galloping monster, the terror of steel and steam," which represented "vast power, huge, terrible, flinging echo of its thunder over the reaches of the valley, leaving blood and destruction in its path; the leviathan, with tentacles of steel clutching into the soil, the soulless Force, the iron-heated Power, the monster, the Colossus, the Octopus."[128] Many echoed Jack London's plaint of a citizenry being "bound upon the wheel" as "slaves of the machine." Sherwood Anderson gave vent to the nation's fears of a "land . . . filled with gods but they were new gods and their images, standing on every street of every town and city, were cast in iron and steel" and "feeding on the old dying individualistic life."[129] If all systems were enslaving as revolutionary liberalism presumed, then the servitude of the modern liberal individual and the collapse of the national identity was a foregone conclusion. To save the liberal project, a new economic theory preserving market voluntarism but within a framework of organizational structures was needed. That was to be the task of postbellum laissez-faire theory.

The Social Idyll in Crisis

We can uncover the emerging social realm in nineteenth-century America as a feature of the pragmatic tasks of building functional political, economic, and religious institutions in order "to provide for the wants of this world," such as schools, meeting halls, and roads, and for running fairs and administering the courts.[130] This process in time produced a web of civil associations and informal networks, the emerging social institutions of village life, what Kirkland described as "the magic circle of . . . our cherished exclusiveness, the strong hold of *caste*, the test of gentility, the temple of emulation, the hive of industry, the mart of fashion," what Sinclair Lewis was to refer to as the village "aristocracy" of "Good Influence" and his character Carol Kennicott the "Village Virus," the "blank wall" of village orthodoxy.[131]

As the social infrastructure expanded its influence and the reach of its values in city, town, and village, the pressure to join and the psychic costs of a failure to belong also increased. Kirkland wrote with rare early perceptivity of the pressures in her Michigan town:

> The principle of "let-a-be for let-a-be" hold not with us. Whoever exhibits any desire for privacy is set down as "proud," or something worse; no matter how inoffensive, or even how benevolent he may be. . . . The better classes of English settlers seem to have left their own country with high-wrought notions of the unbounded freedom to be enjoyed in this; and it is with feelings of angry surprise that they learn after a short residence here, that this very universal freedom abridges their own liberty to do as they please in their individual capacity; that the absolute democracy which prevails in country places, imposes as heavy restraints upon one's free-will in some particulars, as do the over-bearing pride and haughty distinctions of the old world in others.[132]

But the image of a tightly constraining society exercising powerful social pressures, judging, excluding, and isolating, emerged into general visibility only at the end of the century and thereafter in the novels of Cather and Lewis, *The Damnation of Theron Ware, Tiverton Tales, Pembroke, Spoon River Anthology*, and *Winesburg, Ohio*, among others.

Nevertheless, between the Civil War and the turn of the century, though often expressed retrospectively, Americans began to experience the presence of a unitary community through the haze of denial, idealization, and mobility both in the village and in the city. Identified primarily in light of the revolutionary idyll as a realm threatening the free ways of American life, this blanket of social expectations and pressures to comply is increasingly recast, not as a remnant of remaining traditional institutions which can be escaped by moving to a less constructed and more modern setting, but rather as a characteristic of the new society, the future, from which there is no escape.

Two remarkable early portrayals of this emerging social realm, at once ubiquitous and all-powerful and yet *invisible,* haunt two late-century short stories, "A Point at Issue!" by Kate Chopin and "The Monster" by Stephen Crane. Written in 1889, Chopin's story is a psychological investigation of the internal pressures on a freethinking young couple to conform. Eleanor and Charles seek to wed without traditional constraints. This entails marrying privately, traveling widely, and living for periods separately. The intense jealousy that follows and the decision to live in a more conventional marriage are portrayed partly as a product of internal insecurities, but their retreat is also attributed to the pressure of social stigmatization. The sources of that pressure are never identified, only alluded to, and characterized by the presence of a disembodied voice which ever more stridently asserts communal norms: "That two people should presume to introduce such innovations into matrimony! It was uncalled for! It was improper! It was indecent! He must have already tired of her idiosyncrasies, since he had left her in Paris. And in Paris, of all places, to leave a young woman alone! Why not at once in Hades?"[133] Their inability to identify the locus of this sense of collective judgment as well as their confusion as it intermingles with their own voices and fears of exile and stigma make them incapable of defending themselves against it. In the end, they gratefully succumb to its strictures.

"The Monster," published in 1899, is one of Crane's Whilomville stories. It is an emblematic study of the very birth of the social will of the community which is coming to subtly infuse and inarticulately coordinate its seemingly fragmented movements. Dr. Trescott is a respected physician whose son Jim is befriended by the family horse groom, the young black man Henry Johnson. When Henry rescues Jimmie from the burning Trescott house and saves his life, his face is allegorically mangled beyond repair: "He now had no face. His face had been burned away." Dr. Trescott in gratitude arranges support for the now deformed and brain-damaged Henry to live in Whilomville. Henry's frightening presence around the community, however, that of "a monster, a perfect monster," when added to a pervasive racial antipathy, leads to ever greater terror and loathing among local inhabitants.[134] Dr. Trescott is told by a friend that he is "restoring" Henry to life ("You are making him. . . . He is purely your creation"); but ironically, what he is actually bringing to life is a collective sensibility beginning to realize its own existence. As people begin talking, and a common revulsion grows whenever Henry appears around town, a sense of solidarity emerges. Talk starts about boycotting the doctor's practice. The community becomes aware of itself as "the whole town" in which "everybody says."[135] Emboldened, three prominent friends come to warn Dr. Trescott that his practice may fail if he continues to flout the collective will. Continuing to defend Henry, he comes home one afternoon to find his wife sobbing. Fifteen women from their circle had visited her earlier, a pervasive yet faceless monster of polite community sensibility infiltrating their lives. There was nowhere to turn.

With communities tightening and urban realities expanding at the end of the century to produce an interdependent social nexus demanding adaptation incompatible with liberal freedom, disillusionment spread. The idyllic dream these writers had grown up with of a land without the "social," a collective without set connections or expectations, was disappearing. Sherwood Anderson wondered if "something went wrong in the beginning. We pretended to so much and were going to do such great things here. This vast land was to be a refuge for all the outlawed and brave foolish folk of the world. The declaration of the rights of man was to have a new hearing in a new place. The devil! We did get ourselves into a bad hole." Seeking "to be superhuman," instead we were weaving ever thicker chains, "the whole absurd business of building bigger and bigger towns, bigger and bigger factories, bigger and bigger houses . . . creating our great industrial system, growing always more huge."[136] Was America simply becoming a "dreary commercial and material . . . Empire?" "Had men but escaped out of the prisons of the Old World into the more horrid prisons of the New?" In the new age will we "all have houses alike, all men and women clad alike . . . all food alike, all the streets in all of our cities alike? Surely individuality is ruinous to an age of standardization. It should be at once and without mercy crushed out." How, beyond irony, could one recall the promise? "Was I free? Did any man ever achieve freedom?" The nightmare of entrapment intensified: "Can nothing stop the descending iron bell? It stops and hangs for a moment and now it drops suddenly and I am a prisoner." Perhaps liberalism was itself to blame, perhaps it "promised too much, wanted too much."[137]

Social norms, practices, and expectations were no more going to disappear than the organizations that propelled and sustained them, for they were precisely what made complex civilization possible. Revolutionary liberal culture had no answer beyond the now wistful—and deluded—frontier fantasy, of trying to "blow all factories away with a breath of my fancy." Beyond that lay oblivion: "You cannot blame us that we are somewhat reluctant about finding out the very human things concerning ourselves. One does so hate to come down off the perch."[138] Chopin's story ends with the characters forgetting "the point at issue" regarding their goals (which is precisely the point at issue!) in the haze of domestic ritual; Crane's ends in the stunned silence of a slowly disappearing last note of selfhood. Carol Kennicott's final effort to gain praise for her failed revolt from Main Street fades in the face of her husband's quotidian rejoinder: "Say, did you notice whether the girl put that screwdriver back?"[139] Life ahead will be rescued only by a refusal to think about the consequences of integration.

The idyll of a proprietary Eden with its fluid society would spread westward with the pioneers, from the yeoman ideal of the Middle West to the disastrous, politically driven postwar rush for arid homesteads in the West.[140] Even as the market economy and social organizations solidified, the culture of voluntarism, supported by unprecedented individual discretion, mobility, and opportunity, sustained the image of a "free economy" and "free social arrangements" within a "free society." The mere presence of less developed areas portrayed as a "gate of escape to the free conditions of the frontier," though ever contracting, reinforced the idyll by sustaining the viability of the option to remove oneself from economic constraints and entangling social connections to begin anew:

> Americans had a safety-value for social danger. . . . This was the vast unoccupied domain that stretched from the borders of the settled area to the Pacific Ocean. . . . No grave social problems could exist while the wilderness at the edge of civilizations opened wide its portal to all who with strong arms and stout heart desired to hew out a home and a career for themselves. Here was an opportunity for social development continually to begin over again, wherever society gave signs of breaking into classes. Here was a magic fountain of youth in which America was continually bathed and rejuvenated.[141]

Proponents of industrial combination later in the century continued to promote the idyll to justify growing poverty, unemployment, and inequality as choices within the individual's domain. Thus Edward Atkinson addressed the Boston Labor Lyceum in 1887: "Why do you work for wages here if you don't want to? Why do you work more than eight hours a day if you don't want to? . . . Nobody can compel you . . . [Y]ou'd quit if you dared to, and go somewhere else. There is plenty of room in this world and in this country."[142]

So long as the frontier stayed a theoretical option, the American imagination remained suspended at the moment of voluntary social formation. Turner's thesis then represents not the point at which the natural condition was lost, but the moment at which Americans were shocked into facing almost a century of prior societal development. Even so, Herbert Croly and Vernon Parrington among others well into the twentieth century bemoaned the continuing streak of romantic individualism, with its "unrestricted individual aggrandizement and collective irresponsibility,"[143] which failed to acknowledge—and thus needlessly delayed the conscious shaping of—modern institutions. The idyll, with its emphasis on negative rights and self-sufficiency, remained without a substitute as the nation's common language.[144]

Nevertheless, beneath the denials Americans were producing a national experience not in freedom but in popular institutional formation. Hidden by the idyll lay the psychosocial dynamic driving this movement toward integration, the elusive truth which displaces the liberty narrative as the central explanation of national development. Retreating from the terrors of release toward the security of institutional connection, Americans were slowly constituting an unprecedented new society: more free than anyone had ever before imagined, and yet less boundless and unstructured than the fantasy had led them to expect. Slowly they were coming to produce—if not to understand—a nation of agents.

9

From Liberation to Reversal in a World without Bounds

It is difficult to read the literature. . . . produced by the young nation. . . . without being struck by how antithetical it is to our modern
rendition of the American Dream.

    —Toni Morrison

Thus, they become more alike, even without having imitated each
other.

    —Alexis de Tocqueville

       The culture of the early republic has long been regarded as an
affirmation of the liberating dynamic of the revolutionary project. In this
view, the powerful national literature emerging during this period provides
in D. H. Lawrence's terms the deepest expression of the culture's wish for
"liberty," which "in America has meant so far the breaking away from *all*
dominion," to "do away with the old thing . . . with masters," finally with
"everything." For F. O. Matthiessen, the writers of the American Renaissance "felt it was incumbent upon their generation to give fulfillment to the
potentialities freed by the Revolution, to provide a culture commensurate
with America's political opportunities."[1] This retrospective elaboration portrayed the new "free society of free individuals" as presumably stable but for
the external institutional forces which led to its undoing.

    In fact, the literary culture of the early republic reveals anything but a
verification of revolutionary expectations. The reexamination of representative fiction strikingly reveals a pervading sense of bewilderment and panic at
the loss of all moorings, a largely inexplicit recognition of the untenably
boundless and normless conditions attending the release from traditional

society, producing a consistent pattern of retreat to collective security, that is to say, *reversal*. Writers of the period, obsessed as many Americans were with the promise of becoming a free individual in a free society, did consistently propose in their fiction the new paradigmatic journey beyond the constraints of authority. But what protagonists encounter in the unbounded space is not freedom but a nightmare world of personal fragmentation and social disorder.[2] Realizing the danger of liberation without controls, they return to society, in effect establishing a neglected pattern for American fiction I call the *narrative of reversal*. Yet in undertaking this personal journey of experience and education, they achieve through the collapse of the idyll a new self-reliance and understanding of place and selfhood within post-traditional society. The community they return to participate in building will thus be quite different from the one they fled. By framing the experience of release as a learning process, the narratives of reversal, while rejecting freedom as an end, prepared their readers for embracing the new majoritarian and individualist society. Through this work and the writings of Tocqueville, it is possible to understand the deeper dynamic by which citizens moved forward to constitute, out of their own voluntary action, not the idyll but the institutions of post-traditional society.

The Crisis of Boundlessness

The early republic, according to American historian Robert H. Wiebe, faced two simultaneous and unprecedented tasks, the "movement from the security of the 18th century into the chaos of the 19th" by relinquishing the past, and the subsequent, often parallel "creation of a national society" and "new ways of life." The suddenness of the former magnified the role of "democracy" in this period as a ubiquitous "destroyer, leaving by the 1840's almost nothing of the revolutionary gentry's venture except the shell of the Constitution." The uncomfortable truth framing this period is that the swift and unpredicted dismantling of previous institutions left little clear direction for the future. The result was a "formless . . . society" amidst a "centrifugal whirl," a "release" in John Higham's terms from "material and institutional confinements," a "disastrous loss of cohesion and erosion of institutional authority," into "boundlessness," producing "an age of anxiety," of "agitation and instability . . . spreading everywhere."[3] William McLoughlin locates beneath the "deceptive . . . harmonies" of the "ideals of the Revolution" multiplying "indecisions, inconsistencies, and contradictions." The fear of "collapse" in this new "uncertain world" lay just beneath the surface of early republican culture.[4]

Corresponding to a now markerless external world was the opening of an individual inner world without clear patterns of thought and behavior. Even thoughtful celebrants of the nation found it "infinitely . . . difficult" to locate the "springs of national character," particularly for a new country "where many stars are waning and many have set," which would "require time to be freed," moreover, from "the empire of habit and of prejudice" resulting "from European pupilage."[5] Individual release to an ultimate but indecipherable presocial fate infused the powerful and original literary expressions of the period. In the most powerful depiction, Melville cast *Moby-Dick* explicitly as a journey of near-hallucinatory inwardness to the center of the human soul, to locate "not so much predictions from without, as verifications of . . . things within." As Starbuck fearfully muses, "For with little external to constrain us, the innermost necessities in our being, these still drive us on." Thus, the project is to "fly all hospitality" by seeking "all the lashed sea's landlessness," for "in landlessness alone resides the highest truth, shoreless, indefinite as God. . . . [A]ll deep, earnest thinking is but the intrepid effort of the soul to keep the open independence of her sea" by resisting "the wildest winds of heaven and earth," which "conspire to cast her on the treacherous, slavish shore." The voyage of the *Pequod* will assail all constraints until we, like "Narcissus," finally come face-to-face with "the tormenting, mild image he saw in the fountain" and which "we ourselves see in all rivers and oceans." This ultimate internal destination, "the key to it all," we are told, is, alas, an "image of the ungraspable phantom of life."[6]

Abandoning oneself or being abandoned to the forces of inner and external nature could be simplistically equated with being free only at the great cost of coherence. In its "feverish"[7] frenzy to release individuals from the past, with its "iron law of servitude," the American embrace of the idyll erased every vestige of orientation by which individuals could grasp the specific nature of their achievement. On the collective level, an idyllic formation of "free," self-governing communities from a (colonial) state of nature replaced the *actual* historical creation of agency from imperial servitude. The conception of the free individual similarly led citizens to imagine themselves possessed of mythic origins. The result of this liberation into boundlessness with little evident guidance beyond the superficial rhetoric of revolutionary possibility was not measured freedom but a trauma of release into chaotic disorientation.

Stranded out of a history and personal narrative to which they could return, poised between heightened, untested expectations and the realistic need to organize society, individuals were now remarkably in the nearly perfectly replicated condition of Hobbes's natural state. The genius of his formulation of a condition of universally inflated wishes was its impossibility. He had expanded the free and equal access to self-authorization and self-fulfillment to ensure the certainty of its absolute frustration. Faced with the specter of this overdrawn condition, individuals would willingly undertake the saving reversal of directionality to self-authorize the abrogation of personal authority, the creation of consensual authority, and willing integration. The paradox of the American abandonment to this perilous situation was that the idyll, serving as their new guidebook, legitimated and gave permission for the continuation of that very "natural" condition. The strategy of Jefferson and the moderates had in effect circumvented the Hobbesian calculus. It placed before the American people validation of that most dangerous naturalism and personal self-authorization against which liberal society was first formed to save agency. It further presumed to derive agency society less from a past lesson of failed self-authorization (the contract) than from an ongoing popular authorization of its institutions. In effect, it dared Americans to constitute the new body politic.

From Freedom to Voluntary Reversal

The overriding question posed by nineteenth-century America is how agency values came to form its basis not only absent theoretical guidance but moreover in direct defiance of its own idyll. We must discount those few, like Madison, who understood the role of agency but who had only a marginal impact on events. The agency society came about because, as the great English theorists of Protestantism and liberalism had uncannily realized, the internal logic of the individual abandoned to its own resources without guidance and the logic of release into an interactive condition of multiple unconstrained individuals would, even without a theoretical blueprint, generate the reversal into agency integration. Milton had shown how the new agent, even in innocence, released into the wilderness of its most expansive wishes, would have to confront and retreat before its characterological limits. Hobbes had demonstrated that many such agents, released into a collective setting of their most expansive wishes, would similarly be forced to acknowledge and submit to necessary institutional constraints to contain those wishes.

As Melville had surmised, the new American had in the very openness of the new setting been released from history into not freedom but character. Despite the Declaration, though the new republican citizens could never have imagined it or admitted it, they were led by its demands not to fulfill the revolutionary idyll but to *mitigate its extremity*. In *From Boundlessness to Consolidation*, John Higham identifies a critical antebellum shift associated previously with later periods in which "the predominant direction changed, when the emphasis in American culture shifted significantly from diffusion to concentration, from spontaneity to order."[8] Because this directional shift or reversal which initiated nineteenth-century American societal formation was inarticulate, rooted in needs obscured by and contrary to the reigning ideology and undertaken in the absence of any external force, even our most perceptive observers of the period are perplexed when they notice it.

And yet, the reversal is the key to constituting new internalized and institutional authority. The inarticulate longing for clear, stable personal characters and social roles within functional institutions which accommodated Americans' evident strengths—their burgeoning initiative, self-discretion, and participation—produced a trial-and-error struggle to forge agency selves and society. An intuitive approach-avoidance system warned citizens away from the reefs of too great deference and back from those of too great independence. The reversal involving always a personal decision to forgo personal ends for collective place in effect reinterpreted the national idyll by substituting *voluntarism* for *freedom*. The very willing relinquishment of freedom enabled the movement toward integration to be regarded as a natural impulse itself, one fully consistent with the idyll. It also rendered all institutions and authorities that resulted equally voluntary, tangential, erasable— hence by definition unauthoritative and uncoercive.

In this way, individualism was turned into a consensual search for integration, the drive toward assimilation into a project of *self-socialization*, and agency into the fulfillment of American freedom. The power of the reversal would be evident in the revivalist fervor to direct participants into lives within institutions. But as an already institutional phase of the dynamic, these organized revivals in the early republic raise a possible specter of centralized coercion and manipulation. By examining the literature of the early republic, we find the dynamic of reversal to be a pervasive preoccupation preceding any thoughts of institutional engagement. Thus, long before the emergence of organizational America and its theoretical framework, its citizens were seeking a way out of disorientation by telling a new story—a story ringed with disappointment and veiled in denial, but a story that would lead to a new model of society and collective authority. The extent of the national preoccupation with the tension between voluntarism and institutional life accounts for the powerful continuing role of this literary pattern.

The Narrative of Reversal

Framed in terms of the paradigmatic narrative of freedom, the journey of release eventuating in a glorious escape from social confinement came to be regarded as the ritual center of the American literary form. R. W. B. Lewis wrote in *The American Adam,* a seminal study of antebellum culture, that "the valid rite of initiation for the individual in the new world is not an initiation *into* society, but, given the character of society, an initiation *away from it,*" which he called "*de*initiation."[9] Henry Nash Smith discussed the growing body of nineteenth-century fiction in which individuals flee in "hatred of the dull life of settled communities" to "anarchic freedom and self-sufficiency." The hero of this new saga is identified as "a radically new personality," what Smith called "completely autonomous, isolated, and self-contained," in Lewis's terms "an individual emancipated from history, happily bereft of ancestry, untouched and undefiled by the usual inheritances of family and race; an individual standing alone, self-reliant and self-propelling, ready to confront whatever awaited him with the aid of his own unique and inherent resources."[10] Leslie Fiedler, though aware of the dark pressures shaping liberation, argued that the American protagonist was forever in flight toward "the last horizon of an endlessly retreating vision of innocence—on the 'frontier'" where "he is forever *beginning,* saying for the first time . . . what it is to stand alone, before nature or in a city as appallingly lonely."[11]

The problem for these efforts to vindicate the experience of release is that freedom was never the result. What is remarkable is that these accounts invariably portray the break with history toward freedom as a *failed* narrative, eventuating not in liberation but in a "tragedy" brought on by "the illusion of freedom," now felt as "more and more inaccessible" and even "quite irrelevant for a society committed to the ideals of . . . progress." Resisting—

or challenging—the reigning cultural expectations, the fiction of the period highlights characters who have lost their bearings amidst disordered liberation and boundless individualism. "The American dream" of "breaking through all limits and restraints" into "total freedom" ends in Fiedler's terms as a "Faustian nightmare."[12]

More recent critics have noted the integrative resolution in the fiction of the early republic, suggesting that its role was to guide readers into the new "America" that was fitfully emerging, "different from the official one,"[13] and "offer a blueprint for survival under a specific set of political, economic, social, or religious conditions."[14] Cathy N. Davidson argues that the novels of the period encourage increasingly literate common citizens to assert themselves against elites as women and men worthy of power, education, and opportunity in a potentially inclusive democratic community. For Jane Tompkins, this literature frames as an alternative to a questionable Jeffersonian freedom the codes of conduct and institutional commitments necessary to order this heterogeneous new society. In *The Land before Her,* Annette Kolodny turns to women's writing to discover that, in contrast to "male assertions of a rediscovered Eden," women ventured—usually with their families—into the West to reconstitute home and community life within new "cultivated gardens . . . in the wilderness."[15] In *Writing and Postcolonialism in the Early Republic,* Edward Watts perceives an emerging resistance to internal elite "recolonization" with strategies of literary and social "decolonization." The goal was to alert the public to the illegitimacy of traditional authority and to catalyze an inclusive and egalitarian agenda.[16]

The effect of this social reconstructionist perspective has been either to reinscribe the revolutionary discourse or to displace it entirely. In one view, early texts extend the discourse of "freedom of the individual" to all members of a reframed America "not as some stable, traditional, premodern community . . . but as a vital, dynamic society that flourishes in originality or heterogeneity."[17] In the other view, the dynamic of individual freedom is subsumed by the deeper need to construct order and civilization out of the untamed wilderness or chaotic urban milieu. Both accounts neglect the dialectical journey beyond settled order in which the experience beyond boundaries triggers the lessons for life in the new republic.

The narrative of reversal is a profoundly American account of personal experience, for—though derived from *Crusoe*—it centers on and structures both tasks of modernity, liberation and reconstitution, that individuals now faced. It begins with liberating oneself from entangling constraints and definitions: having as Americans left already their societies of origin in defiance of traditional authority relations, individuals must once again strike out, obsessively, even ritually, for freedom by leaving the settled community, representative of continuing pressures for domination and confinement, for a space beyond societal authority and predetermined institutional structure. Just as the nation was determined because of its new developmental capacities to find its own identity in "our own character, our own actions, our own principles" by "flying westward from civil and religious thralldom . . . far from foreign corruption," so too was its prototypical individual now impelled to undertake the same break from all preexisting authority relations, the symbolic world of servitude.[18]

This break in turn presents the most crucial and troubling of all questions for the new American: What fate, what realistic options (for this journey was no mere metaphor), await those who have definitively forsaken their earlier way of life? The experiential lesson of these narratives is that these questions can be answered not by continuing the journey toward openness indefinitely but only by in time relinquishing it. The "failure" to sustain an impossible freedom is indeed the true heart of this narrative, the necessary and inevitable second stage in which the character is forced to confront the impossibility of perpetual release. One can no longer indulge, like Defoe in comfortable London, in fables of remaining indefinitely on an island. The experience following liberation never measures up to the initial—often vague—expectations, nor could it, for it is the fantasied escape of those still in constraints. Because of the extreme disjunction between vague idyllic expectations and the realities of social disorganization, these narratives starkly delineate the problematic of the freedom narrative.

In this fiction, the crisis which release typically provokes is a gradual, accumulating, but ultimately decisive confrontation with a terrifyingly structureless reality. In the wilderness, the individual encounters a void beyond meaning which can be neither inhabited nor faced. As Toni Morrison has written, "The flight from the Old World to the New is generally seen to be a flight from oppression and limitation to freedom and possibility." And yet, she notes, "how antithetical" the "literature produced by the young nation" is "to our modern rendition of the American Dream. How pronounced in it is the absence of that term's elusive mixture of hope, realism, materialism, and promise. For a people who made much of their 'newness'—their potential, freedom, and innocence—it is striking how dour, how troubled, how frightened and haunted our early and founding literature is." It is characterized by quite specific "fears" and "demons": "Americans' fears of being out-cast, of failing, of powerlessness; their fear of boundarylessness, of Nature unbridled and crouched for attack; their fear of the absence of so-called civilization; their fear of loneliness, of aggression both external and internal."[19] The larger theme within this "head-on encounter with very real, pressing historical forces and the contradictions inherent in them" is "in short, the terror of human freedom—the thing they coveted most of all."[20] In different forms, the individual is left with the choice of either finding the way back to society or facing the terror of unknown conditions and the madness of an isolated inner world abandoned to chaos, silence, dangerous self-authorization, projective incoherence.

Given the power of the idyll, the return after such a determined and defining leave-taking is widely regarded as a tragic failure, the foreclosing of options rather than the resolution to begin life in society. And yet this collapse, in effect, of the idyll, though admittedly unsustainable, is by no means tragic. It is the very experience of reversal that defines the journey to a novel popular society: from the bonds of servitude through the nightmare of unboundedness to the harbor of a new community. Most crucially, neither the world one returns to nor the selfhood one achieves along the way is available at the beginning. Both have been developmentally transformed by the journey. In the act of recomposition, though authority and obedience again result, they must be established on new foundations. There must henceforth be an unyielding recognition on the part of society of the individual's initiative, interests, and self-reliance as the forces which drive the social order and of collective judgment as the coagulant which holds it together.

The journey of reversal, then, is a journey of self-education—or, if you will, self-socialization—from destruction to reconstitution, leading citizens to shape new communities that reflect their greater initiative, self-discretion, and popular responsibility. Although the theme of reversal never achieves self-consciousness, for this would be to admit that the nation could reexamine its idyll, this pattern, with its overwhelming and often inarticulate needs, its profoundly unexpected shifts and conclusions, haunts where it does not dominate the course of many—including some of the greatest—American novels. This inarticulate process accounts for the disorder of these novels, mirroring the social and psychic confusion of the time. And in being so unself-conscious and so unwished for, I would suggest, lies the authenticity of the story it tells.

The themes and patterns of the American narrative of reversal are first set forth in fiction at the very outset of the young republic. The step into history and "open" space, which Milton allowed only at the end of his "education for character," for Americans initiated the process of education. The fact of a frontier vaster than the imagination could embrace and early institutions could contain turned the wilderness into the primal scene for the American development of character. In the novels of the first sixty years after the founding, those of William Hill Brown, Hannah Foster, Royall Tyler, Charles Brockden Brown, James Fenimore Cooper, Caroline Kirkland, Robert Montgomery Bird, Bayard Taylor, Hawthorne, Poe, and Melville, I will suggest the pattern of release, confrontation with the unbounded inner and external worlds, and return as a response to the conditions in the new society. This pattern by which the liberty narrative is quietly transformed into a narrative of "refounding" in turn ranges through subsequent American fiction. Although this reversal is universally regarded as a collapse of ideals, I will argue from these narratives and from the work of Tocqueville that it propels the effort to locate and ground oneself within the new society. This fiction is thus part of the larger story of the consolidation of a novel society of individuals.

The Journey into the Wilderness

The impulse toward release from the confining structures of one's community forms the common beginning for many of the pre–Civil War narratives, including the first American novels. In *The Power of Sympathy* (1789), the prototypical new Americans with their resistance to society are represented by two beautiful young women, Harriot and Ophelia, one an orphan lacking all parental guidance, the other the daughter of a domineering and vindictive father. Harriot, the main character, eager to be released from her youthful "dependence" to pursue the teachings of "experience," finds the lessons of tradition to be the empty moralizing of those sheltered from new opportunities. In both cases, they follow the "flame" of love that, Harriot declares, "fired my reason and my senses" with "visionary prospects" into the "wilderness" of "irresistible impulse."[21] In *The Coquette* (1797), Eliza Wharton, a young woman—"a dutiful child"—in whom "both nature and education had instilled into my mind an implicit obedience to the will and desires of my parents," suddenly decides "to gratify my natural dispositions in a participation of those pleasures which youth and innocence afford" by "leaving my paternal roof."[22] Determined to innocently grasp "the charms of youth and freedom," she embraces the "independence of a single state" over the "tomb" of marriage.[23] In *The Algerine Captive* (1797), Updike Underhill, of radical Protestant background, a reader of *Crusoe* and Bunyan, decides to leave his home and family on the ship *Freedom* for fortune and worldly adventure. Classically educated but of the middling class, he has been dissatisfied with and comically unfit for the rude, rustic, uneducated society created by the Revolution.

The great early novelist Charles Brockden Brown tells in *Arthur Mervyn* (1799) the story of a young man, a rustic and inexperienced child who "preferred to ramble in the forest and loiter on the hill. . . . to obey the impulse of the moment . . . just as my humor prompted me" and was indifferent to the judgment of others. Arthur, who now "lived merely for the sake of pleasure" and seeking "to go free," runs away from a violent and abusive father and domineering stepmother, who had "degraded" him "to the rank" of "servant," to find his fortune in the city.[24] In the first great American novel, his *Wieland* (1798), a prophetic elaboration of the new American psyche, the family of a radical Protestant sectarian and mystic withdraw "from the society of others" to dwell in the woods of Pennsylvania. Here they seek to live "by no religious understanding" but by personal inspiration and individual reason, all subject to "the guidance of our own understanding" and the "present enjoyment" of "lively feelings, excited by reflection on our own happiness" and "the grandeur of external nature."[25]

Cooper's Leatherstocking Tales (1823–1841) portray the epic character Natty Bumppo, a man "without kith or kin in the wide world" who "love[s] the woods" and is "formed for the wilderness," where he can "eat when hungry, and drink when adry." Having become fenced in with the development of the New York frontier after living there his whole life and becoming enmeshed in its petty legalities, Natty, "weary of living in clearings and where the hammer is sounding in my ears from sunrise to sunset" and all "keep stated hours and rules," heads in the ultimate tale "towards the setting sun" in the West and its "endless forests."[26] In Caroline Kirkland's fictional journal of Michigan frontier life, *A New Home—Who'll Follow?* (1839), she acknowledges the "power" of "freedom from the restraints of pride and ceremony" in "a new country," the "instinct, dulled by civilization . . . of nature that scorns boundary and chain; that yearns to the free desert; that would have the earth like the sky, unappropriated and open." In the journal she tells the story of Evarard and Cora, two well-to-do cousins from

New York with "a taste for the wilderness" and a "yearning common to those who have lived in the free woods," who fall in love and elope against their parents' wishes to "a forest home" of "highland solitude," which was "wild and mountainous and woody."[27] Robert Montgomery Bird's major novel of the Kentucky frontier, *Nick of the Woods* (1837), is the story of Nathan Slaughter, a pioneer who has taken to living in the forest: "No, friends, my lot is cast in the woods, and thee must not ask me again to leave them." Among his companions on his forest adventures are the cousins Roland and Edith Forrester, who have left their esteemed Virginia family, apparently disowned and under a cloud, to "plunge into the forest" and begin again like Milton's Adam and Eve with "the world . . . before us."[28]

Maxwell Woodbury in *Hannah Thurston* (1864), a story of antebellum life, has run from domesticity to the adventures of a life in India, now returning in retirement to "the certain repose and seclusion which he craved" in the "isolation from the world" in the upper New York woods.[29] In two of Hawthorne's greatest stories, *The Scarlet Letter* (1850) and "Young Goodman Brown" (1847), the "dark inscrutable forest" calls individuals away from the community of "the law" and its rigid application to an experience of "the wildness" of their "nature."[30] Edgar Allan Poe's sole novel, *The Narrative of Arthur Gordon Pym* (1838), shows the reach of this new pattern. It follows Arthur, the son of a successful Nantucket family who is consumed by "the greatest desire to go to sea . . . at all hazards," the "wild and burning expectation with which I looked forward to the fulfillment of my long-cherished visions of travel," despite his family's determination to disown him and his mother's "hysterics at the bare mention of the design."[31]

The master of the narrative of release is, of course, Melville, who often returns to it over the course of his career. Redburn in the 1849 novel, inclined as a child to "long reveries about distant voyages and travels," resolves in "a vague prophetic thought, that I was fated . . . to be a great voyager." These "demoniac feelings" unceasing, he gives in to the typical demand of American "boyhood," says good-bye to his uncomprehending family, and undertakes to "begin life" on a boat bound for Europe.[32] In the greatest of these narratives, young Ishmael, who "abominate[s] all honorable and respectable toils, trials, and tribulations," and unbound by any land obligations, "tormented with an everlasting itch for things remote" and "crazy to go to sea" like "almost every other robust healthy boy," signs on to an extended whaling excursion on "the watery part of the world."[33]

The Confrontation with Emptiness

If one did not understand the profound internal issues and adjustments that citizens of this new society were confronting, it would be most puzzling to consider the world into which these protagonists are released. Far indeed from the quotidian realm of pragmatic Yankee toil, writer after writer draws a murky, indecipherable world of hallucinatory chaos, a world of unfathomable wildernesses and unreadable cities, of sleepwalkers, projected voices, underground palaces of sin, plagues and delirium, of masks, shifting identities, and endless frauds and deceivers. In this world the unconscious reigns without challenge, provoking characters to every possible obsession—to incest, debauchery, torture, murder, rape, suicide, addiction, domination, massacre, self-divinity—rarely provoked from without, always driven from within. In fact, these tales are written explicitly as dream narratives, as if the experience of revolutionary release without external constraint had opened the possibility of pursuing every untrammeled, undeflected wish lurking within, and the narrative structures follow the logic of freely emerging impulse life.

The stories in *The Power of Sympathy* are driven by the "voluntary" immersion in the "irresistible impulse" of "nature—helpless, debilitated nature" leading to "transports of . . . dear delusion" beyond "reason" and "every social duty."[34] Harriot and Ophelia are caught in a "dream of insensibility . . . deluded by an *ignis fatuus* to the brink of a precipice," thus "drifting upon a sea of inconsistency . . . like a ship without a rudder, buffeted on the bosom of the ocean." Both characters are led by deep emotional and narcissistic wishes into incestuous relations, to, as Harriot's lover puts it, "fall in love with the offspring of our brain" as the "imagination dresses up a phantom to impose on our reason."[35] The naive and newly independent Eliza Wharton, "tenacious" of her "freedom," follows her "imagination abroad in quest of new treasures."[36] She rejects a stable life with a staid cleric to follow "the delusions of fancy" and ends up in a relation with a known seducer, a "Proteus" who "can assume any shape that will best answer [his] purpose."[37] The result is "a disordered mind" lost in a "deceptive mist," in the "desert" of a "fixed melancholy" resulting from "the delusive dream of sensual gratification."[38] Updike Underhill is captured and made a slave for seven years among Algerian Muslims, fulfilling his mother's recurring "dream" when he was a child that "he would one day suffer among savages."[39] To the "learned reader" who would "smile contemptuously" about the power of "dreams in this enlightened age," he cautions that human motives and the events that befall us are subject to deeper forces, reminding us that the "forewarning of future events" is exercised "by Providence through the intervention of dreams."[40]

Arthur Mervyn after leaving his home wanders into Philadelphia, a dangerous, crime-ridden place of rootless individuals on the make like himself suffering from a plague both physical and spiritual. The story is in fact a series of narratives within narratives mirroring in their many perspectives the shifting identities, wanderers, transformations, and coincidences of a society prey to every schemer and evil plan. Arthur can locate no coherent or identifiable features, given the city's "absolute . . . novelty," and feels a "loneliness" greater than ever experienced "in the depth of caverns or forests." His quixotic aimlessness—he is "alone in the world" with no anchoring "traces of the past," propelled by "abundant . . . unforeseen occurrences" through a "world of revolutions and perils"—is at moments recognized as "no more than—a *dream!*" the "insanity" of his senses operating as "the sport of dreams."[41]

Charles Brockden Brown's *Edgar Huntly* (1799) is a perversely complicated story of a man who wanders into the "deepest" wilderness, a man addicted to "the spirit that breathes its inspiration in the gloom of forests and on the verge of streams," to "wandering into dark and untried paths" as the "the first who had deviated thus remotely from the customary paths of men" since "the birth of this continent."[42] In the obsessive search for his best friend's murderer, Edgar traverses unprecedented "vicissitudes of peril and wonder . . . [p]assage into new forms, overleaping the bars of time and space, reversal of the laws of inanimate and intelligent existence." This precipitates a psychological break in which he encounters a sleepwalker, murderers, subterranean caverns, mistaken identities, and marauding Indians as well as his own sleepwalking and the emergence of his own inner "tribe of ugly phantoms," his "spirit vengeful, unrelenting and ferocious" in "the silence and darkness of the night."[43] His actions lead needlessly to many deaths in a narrative "incompatible with order and coherence" shaped as "a nocturnal journey in districts so remote and wild" into "the recesses" of the "soul."[44]

In the unthreatening forest, the Wieland family, raised with the sectarian belief in an immediate accessibility to God's word, having "shut out every species of society" and bound by no "social worship," is led into a nightmarish "reverie" of "fancy."[45] Manipulated by a ventriloquist who emits voices

with godlike authority, the grown children are led to confuse divine commandments with the depraved suggestions of the deceiver as he weaves a
"dream" world, a "mist" of commands around them that shatters their capacity for "distinguishing between sleep and wakefulness."[46] In the 1844
bestseller *The Monks of Monk Hall,* George Leppard depicts an urban nightmare world in an underground mansion beneath Philadelphia in which every form of brutal and bestial behavior is endlessly indulged in by the city's
elite. It is a journey into "the Theater of Hell," a gothic "dream" world in
which these debauchers prey on rootless runaways in a setting where all impulses are to be expressed without restraint.[47]

Cooper's epic entails a nostalgic worship of the idyllic quest "to enter into
the world unshackled and free." In the West, Natty and others "turning"
their "back" on "civilization" to seek an "out-breaking" from "restraint"
have "no other guide than the sun" in a land "not unlike the ocean" with its
"endless and unexplored regions." Yet this "bleak and solitary place" is one
of "fancied as well as real advantages" to which "none but the strong should
come." For the present frontier, unlike that of colonial nostalgia, is a terrifying and chaotic realm of marauders and misfits, self-aggrandizers and petty
despots, each acting out the "following of his own wishes." With his realistic
sense of national development, Cooper acknowledges that the apparition of
a freely roving Natty as the "end of my race" is in fact an elegy to the
"blessed Prairies" overwhelmed by modern social forces.[48]

> There never was any fairy known in Otsego; but the time has been when
> we could boast of a Natty Bumppo. . . . Some people maintain that there is
> no echo at all, and that the sounds we hear come from the spirit of the
> Leatherstocking, which keeps about its old haunts, and repeats everything
> we say, in mockery of our invasion of the woods. . . . Alas! . . . the days of
> the "Leatherstocking" have passed away. . . . I see few remains of his char-
> acter in a region where speculation is more rife that moralizing, and emi-
> grants are plentier than hunters.[49]

In their "forest sanctuary," the "very home of her dreams," in which "all of
bliss the poet ever painted" would "be realized," Everard and Cora begin to
suffer the effects of the isolation and guilt resulting from their "undutiful
conduct."[50] Nathan Slaughter has with his Virginia companions taken to the
impenetrable forest, a realm of "solitude in which vague and shadowy prospects . . . stirred the imagination," producing "strange things, dreams,—
thoughts in freedom, loosed from the chain of association, temporary mad-

fits undoubtedly: marvelous impressions they produce on the organs of sense: see, hear, smell, taste, touch, more exquisitely *without* the organs than *with* them." Driven by the loss of his family to Indians, his retreat to the forest enables him to unleash his vengeance on the Indians "as from a dream." He becomes a mythic killer known as Jibbenainosay or "the Spirit-that-walks." Roland and Edith in turn are kidnapped and threatened with untold violence by Indians and scheming settlers.⁵¹

The narrator in *The Scarlet Letter* speaks of his detachment from his present-day Salem, and enters the story of its "by-gone days" in which "my old native town will loom upon me through the haze of memory, a mist brooding over and around it; as if it were no portion of the real earth, but an overgrown village in cloud-land, with only imaginary inhabitants to people its wooden houses, and walk its homely lanes."⁵² The story itself is a "legend" or "shadow of a dream" of "the heart's native language."⁵³ The Puritans' "Utopian" journey to the woods is mirrored by Hester and Dimmesdale's more extreme entry into "the moral wilderness" through sexual abandon and young Pearl's yet more radically internal woodland life far from restraint: she "flirted fancifully with her own image in a pool of water beckoning the phantom forth," trying to reconcile "impalpable earth and unattainable sky."⁵⁴ The increasing incapacity to control impulse life, where vast spaces beyond societal control exist, renders the American setting inherently amoral. Goodman Brown's journey into the wilderness "solitude" where all horrors and "an unseen multitude" lurk is presaged by his wife's "dream" which "warned her what work is to be done tonight."⁵⁵ It may well be, the narrator tells us at the end, that Goodman Brown had "fallen asleep in the forest and only dreamed a wild dream of a witch-meeting." In the "heart" of the "dark wilderness," Goodman is brought to witness a "heathen" ceremony involving all of his fellow townspeople, and discovers the root internal "instinct that guides mortal man to evil." By this deeply interior transvaluation, the confrontation in the woods reveals the true and evil "nature of mankind," while the visible community dedicated to "virtue" now appears "all a dream."⁵⁶

In Poe's novel, Arthur's voyage to sea is a fantastical tale of mutiny, cannibalism, slaughter, savage island natives, starvation, long confinement in the bowels of the boat, and repeated flights from enemies. The narrative commences with Arthur's entrapment in the hold, where he experiences "dreams" in which "every species of calamity and horror befall me," which become "as prophetic glimpses" of the course of the story. The journey of the mutineers, who seek in the "delirium" of their "ardent imaginations" to gain "the perfect security and freedom from all restraint to be enjoyed" in the Pacific islands, from "the deliciousness of the climate . . . the abundant means of good living, and . . . the voluptuous beauty of the women," brings the naive Arthur and the crew to the brutal outcome of this "frightful dream."[57]

Redburn likens his shipboard voyage to "all a dream" of "estranged children" left "without father or mother." He gradually realizes that he and his shipmates are in "a dream" of "some new, fairy world," destined "to follow our own pleasures, regardless of their pains."[58] This journey without guidance leads him from the "strange and new . . . barbarous world" of the "endless sea" into the "house of the dead," the "sodomlike" depths of urban Liverpool, to an intoxicated visit to the gaudy decadence of a fantastical Oriental palace of sin in London, and finally back to America.[59] *Moby-Dick*, incapable of adequate summary, involves the turning of a routine whaling expedition into the mobilization of communal "violence and revenge" to exorcise Ahab's "delirium," his "demoniac" projective universe constituted in "madness maddened" through a "fancy pregnant with . . . a mighty birth."[60] Melville slices through to the internal character of the voyage. Since his injury incurred from hunting a white whale on an earlier voyage,

> Ahab had cherished a wild vindictiveness against the whale. . . . [I]n his frantic morbidness he at last came to identify with him, not only all his bodily woes, but all his intellectual and spiritual exasperations. The White Whale swam before him as the monomaniac incarnation of all those malicious agencies which some deep men feel eating in them. . . . [D]eliriously transferring its idea to the abhorred white whale, he pitted himself, all mutilated, against it. All that most maddens and torments; all that stirs up the lies of things; all truth with malice in it; all that cracks the sinews and cakes the brain; all the subtle demonisms of life and thought; all evil, to crazy Ahab, were visibly personified, and made practically assailable in Moby Dick. He piled upon the whale's white hump the sum of all the general rage and hate felt by his whole race from Adam down; and then . . . *he burst his hot heart's shell upon it.*

Ishmael, who must report this delusional reconstruction of the world by a human soul released from all bounds, is able to carry it out because he shares a "wild, mystical, sympathetical feeling" with Ahab's psychic quest, himself also yearning as a young man to open "the great-floodgates" of "my inmost soul" from "an everlasting itch for things remote . . . to sail forbidden seas."[61]

Education and Return

If these dream narratives typify early American stories, they together chart out in many variants the American experience of reversal. Given that these narratives involve a collapse of the dream of freedom amidst unexpected and nightmarish consequences, they are cautionary tales. That is, the outcome demonstrates to the character or associates and ultimately to the reader the folly of the original expectations. Yet by this very flight and the realizations that it produces, understanding is clutched from "failure." In some cases the experience of loss is leavened by an explicit recognition that the journey was essential despite the failure to achieve its initial goals.

The collapse of the idyll has many variants. In *The Power of Sympathy,* as the women venture further and further into resisting obedience or an unregulated life, they become "lost in a wilderness." Though they "strive to oppose the *link of nature*" that draws them on, their "feeble . . . reason" will not allow them to reverse course. Being "no nearer to escape," they "still . . . travel on," a "prey to warring passions,"[62] to their deaths. Readers, however, are to behold the story "like a sailor escaped from shipwreck, who sits safely on the shore and views the horrors of the shipwreck." They are cautioned to "contemplate well" the dangers of an untrammeled *"independency of spirits,"* to choose instead an "education" with "experience" as the "tutor." By gaining a new "prudence and fortitude," individuals will activate a moral *"internal monitor"* allowing them to see their "character" and its "deformities" in "its proper light." This recognition will in turn "govern" them "without extorting obedience, and . . . reclaim them without exercising severity," enabling them to "be happy in the state in which we are placed."[63]

In *The Coquette,* the inevitability of leaving a too burdensome "constraint and confinement" is acknowledged. Yet for Eliza, the vulnerability of being newly freed from dependence, with much "yet to learn," having "looked but little into my own heart" and its "future wishes and views," is also unavoidable given her previous "situations in life" and unstable emotional response to her new release. The combination destines her to a life of catastrophic errors.[64] Unwilling to trust any inclination or advice but her own, and rejecting all social conventions, she allows the fashionable seducer to entrap her by praising her "wish" for "freedom and independence." Winning her heart only to abandon her, he precipitates a deep depression in Eliza, who, after his marriage to another, nevertheless becomes pregnant by him. Having forgone all parental involvement, she flees, "a wretched wanderer from my paternal roof," a "fugitive" in shame and despondency, who—unwilling to relent—ends up taking her life, "dying among strangers."[65] The story of her death "at the shrine of *libertinism*," however, is to "serve as a beacon" to Americans that the "choice" is theirs and they must consider the "dangerous tendency and destructive consequences" of rejecting all forms of institutional control.[66] Eliza's friends repeatedly advise her about protecting her "virtue and innocence": "We are dependent beings. . . . When stripped of one dependence, the mind naturally collects and rests itself in another. . . . Are we not all links in the great chain of society . . . each upheld by others, through the confederated whole?"[67] The revolution, then, must produce not an idyll of freedom but new forms of authority.

Underhill's boat, *Freedom*, leads not to release but to seven years' captivity, during which he experiences the cruelty of the slave trade as well as being "degraded to a beast" and "despoiled of all the honors of the free" himself. His experiences, however, turn him into a serious young man, accepting of the hardships of common people, curious about other societies, questioning of his own society's practices and moral failings. At the same time, he becomes ever more appreciative "as one risen from the dead" of the joys of the life he left: "How *naturally* did the emaciated prodigal in the Scripture think upon the bread in his father's house. . . . It was amidst the parched sands and flinty rocks of Africa that thou taughtest me that the bread was indeed pleasant, and the water sweet."[68] Updike dreams of "being surrounded by congratulating friends and faithful domestics . . . pressed by the embraces of a father, and with the holy joy [of] . . . a mother's tears." Above all, he understands how America has broken with the slavery of imperial societies to secure "the blessings of liberty," and that it can and should not return to the past. He returns home, seeking nothing more now than to "secure" the "enviable character of a useful physician, a good father, and worthy FEDERAL citizen," realizing, moreover, after his enslavement that America even with its constraints was by contrast "the freest country in the universe."[69] The message he offers is "to know how [one] loves his country, let him go far from home; if to know how he loves his countrymen, let him be with them in misery in a strange land." His final act of integration is to offer his book that "my fellow citizens may profit by my misfortunes" to learn the value of a new "union among ourselves."[70]

Unlike the cautionary tales of the frontier *(Edgar Huntly)* and the urban wilderness *(The Monks of Monks Hall)*, which warn us "never" to "sleep but with candle burning" to avoid "darkness" and its "signals to summon up a tribe of ugly phantoms,"[71] *Arthur Mervyn*, like *The Algerine Captive*, offers a reversal. Arthur is forced to undergo an education vastly more complicated than Franklin's own Philadelphia story and in turn to offer "a disclosure of the truth" of "the delay and toil which the removal of my ignorance . . . cost."[72] Simple virtue will not ensure survival in a world where crafty individuals prey on all who are desperate. No individual, however well meaning, can avoid either risks or compromises. Amidst anonymous others, one is "walking in the dark," in an unreadable situation where the motives of others, which one "could not interpret," are often "contrary to appearances." To avoid naively "drop[ping] into pits before . . . [being] aware of [the] danger," one can neither retain innocence, avoid suspicion, tell the truth upon demand, follow the simple dictates of virtue, resist some dissimulation, avoid some dependence on others, nor fail to exert one's own interests.[73] Arthur's education is a "revolution in my mind" in which he charts a course between psychic dissolution or regression to a life of failure and abandoning himself to the "deceitful and flagitious world." After experiencing repeated evil in the city, he comes to believe that "competence, fixed property and a settled abode, rural occupations and conjugal pleasures, were justly to be prized." He marries a matronly older woman of means, whom he appropriately calls "mamma." Despite regrets about his hard path to maturity, he understands that his later resolutions "could be known, and their benefits fully enjoyed only by those who have tried all scenes . . . who have partaken of all conditions." The republic's new "school" of "fortitude and independence" was essential to creating modern individuals and communities.[74]

Kirkland's tale also involves a reversal as the two lovers, faced with despair and a dying child, are visited in the Michigan woods by Cora's parents. Overwhelmed with gratitude and relieved by the child's recovery, these "undutiful children" undergo a transformative "atonement" for their "disregard" of the "feelings" of others and "the common obligations": "Cora was a new creature, a rational being, a mother, a matron, full of sorrow for the past and of sage pleasure for the future."[75] Together the couple reestablishes family ties and becomes connected with the agricultural development of the once virgin land. The message of the journal is that to get "schooling" one must "come away from the conveniences and refined indulgences of civilized life," for "many a sour-faced grumbler . . . would be marvelously transformed by a year's residence in the woods." In joining a new democratic community, people learn about the importance of mutual dependence, the contributions of ordinary individuals to the group, the need to organize social institutions, and the impossibility of "unbounded freedom . . . to do as they please."[76]

In Bird's story and Cooper's narratives, the examples of Jibbenainosay and Leatherstocking, both incorrigible loners, have a chastening impact on others. Roland and Edith, who came to the frontier to start over, after their disturbing adventures with Nathan in the "boundless West" turn back from danger and madness "towards the East and Virginia,—towards . . . home: to enjoy a fortune of happiness to which the memory of the few weeks of anguish and gloom passed in the desert only served to impart additional zest."[77] Leatherstocking comes to represent an impulse submerged in the poorly understood but powerful American appetite for economic advance and societal development. He is thus not only the "end of my race" but unwittingly the very leading edge of that development, "the foremost in that band of pioneers who are opening the way for the march of the nation across the continent."[78] Cooper is suggesting that the "new race" of individuals cannot help "socializing" the wilderness, given the terror of the "illimitable and dreary solitude" which rushes through the empty western expanse "like the whispering of the dead." Natty himself comes to learn that "yes, the law is needed, when such as have not the gifts of strength and wisdom are to be taken care of," and two of the young adventurers return to society to careers in the burgeoning state government.[79] In *Hannah Thurston*, Woodbury falls in love with an ardent feminist, who is determined to keep her independence as well. As they marry and have a child, they must each, particularly the woman, come to terms with their "almost forgotten sensation of *home*," and renounce "freedom" and "independence" once "ignorantly claimed" in order to achieve "the fulfillment" of an "ideal union" with its "joy of sacrifice."[80]

In Hawthorne's work, his fear of the declining possibility of reversal without the community discipline of the Puritan elders leads to his later social— as opposed to continual moral—pessimism. Hester, banished to the forest but psychologically tied to the village, achieves a partial break with its values, while Pearl, an "elf-child" of the woods, will be freed from its grip entirely.[81] On the moral level, however, escape is impossible, for as "Young Goodman Brown" powerfully expresses, the woods are uninhabitable, its fantasies destined to fail before the rough truths of our natures. The individual cannot withstand the onslaught of projections, wishes, and fantasies, so must quickly retreat into town, to the safety of willing self-repression before the watchful, shaming eyes of others, tortured but saved by the failure of release. For Poe, there is no ultimate relief from the horror of freedom, which leaves us "floating about at the mercy of every wind and wave," both internal and external, "on the merest wreck in the world." Yet there is no doubt that, lost and often "cruelly" ignored on the vast, empty expanse, voyagers are in desperate need of rescue and repatriation, to be "happily awakened" from their "frightful dream" and "most happily deceived" when help comes.[82] Redburn, in contrast with a shipboard friend who "like rootless sea-weed" cannot settle down but takes to sea quickly to be "tossed to and fro" and ultimately killed, ends his maiden voyage "at home" surrounded by "embraces, long and loving."[83]

It is Melville and Brockden Brown who reveal the deeper dilemma of the new society. The impulse to break away contains with it now, partly as wish and in part as unavoidable consequence, the propensity—ever growing—toward self-authorization. Where all earthly authorities are relativized and divine ones turned into personal extensions of each individual's nature, the substitution of one's own will as the "cogged circle" around which all reality "revolve[s]" is inevitable.[84] *Wieland* is a cautionary tale for "the benefit of mankind" of the dangerous extent to which the individual can go in "solitude" with "erroneous or imperfect discipline" and "no religious standard," that is, with neither external society nor internal socialization as a check.[85] Dependent solely on "the guidance of our own understanding," the brother and his family, prone to extreme introspective religiosity, stimulated by the evil suggestions of the ventriloquist, begin to associate "phantoms" of their "own creation" with "a sensible discourse with the Author of nature."[86] Led into greater and greater delusions, with no stable reality to serve as a counterweight to "the testimony" of the "senses" and "disentangle the maze,"[87] indeed no Deity to "check" the extreme subjectivism of the religious dynamic, the brother, following the projected suggestions, slays his wife and children and later himself. They were to be a religious sacrifice "to fulfill a divine command" out of "the supreme delight of knowing thy will, and of performing it." This "abyss" to which the remaining characters are brought is explained as the tendency to form independent "notions of moral duty and of the divine attributes."[88] There can be no permanent safeguard from these impulses and their secret wishes. There is only continuing vigilance:

fearing the uncontainability of self-authorization and admitting that its power alone might enable one to retreat from its danger.

Moby-Dick is the reversal of reversals, similarly a voyage out to "the heartless voids and immensities of the universe," but now fully unveiled as internal wish, as the "fixed purpose" which has the power to drive psychic life. Ahab, by "thrusting through the wall," will find out the accuracy of his surmise that all reality is "but as pasteboard masks" which humans place upon it to hide the cosmic emptiness.[89] By defining the whale—already heretically—as both deity and projective surface and then striking through it, Ahab will pose the defining question of the New World: "Who's over me?" Is reality the truly existing Other which harnesses humans to its purposes, or is it merely "the very creature" one "creates," making humans indeed self-authors of a world that is their agent? Ahab's interrogation penetrates to the very center of the American conundrum: "That inscrutable thing is chiefly what I hate . . . be the white whale agent, or be the white whale principal." Ishmael, "quick to perceive a horror, and . . . still be social with it," must as an Everyman in agency America untangle the mixture of terror, disgust, and fascination which accompanies the emergence of this dangerous, illicit wish for self-authorization.[90] He comes to understand well before the voyage is over what is at stake, and it is his very internal reversal, his retreat to *"the margin of the ensuing scene,"* that saves him: "I forgot all about our horrible oath . . . I washed my hand and my heart of it . . . I felt divinely free from all ill-will, or petulance, or malice." He realizes the saving power of reversal, that "in all cases man must eventually lower, or at least shift, his conceit of attainable felicity; not placing it in the intellect or the fancy; but in the wife, the heart, the bed, the table, the saddle, the fire-side, the country."[91]

Tocqueville's Search for the Principle of Order

There is one final illustration of the experience of reversal in the young republic: Tocqueville's uncanny analysis of American society in *Democracy in America*.[92] The dynamic of reversal is the center of and key to Tocqueville's insight into American society, for what he is describing—and increasingly recognizes—is a society *in mass reversal*. His perplexity in Volume 1 emerges with the receding of his initial awe at encountering the "spectacle" of a truly free society. Absent traditional bonds, this society seemingly permitted unlimited autonomy. He wrote in his notes at the time of the journey that the "development of individual power" from the "absence of government" is an ever present reality in this new society: "Each man learns to think, to act for himself," becoming "accustomed to seeking for his well-being only from his own efforts . . . without counting on the aid of an outside power." He puts it even more forcefully five years later in Volume 1: "The citizen of the United States is taught from infancy to rely upon his own exertions . . . he looks upon the social authority with an eye of mistrust and anxiety."[93]

And yet to his surprise, seemingly without standard sources of cohesion and with an ethos of unprecedented equality and independence, American society appeared to hold together better than the troubled new popular societies of Europe. He is ever more perplexed upon realizing the extent of social order: "It's really an incredible thing, I assure you, to see how this people keeps itself in order . . . with such perfect regularity."[94] This sense that "the community" was "at once regulated and free," that one "is free, and responsible to God alone, for all that concerns himself . . . the best and sole judge of his own private interest" and yet "society in all its branches proceeds with the greatest uniformity," required a serious revision of his thinking: "The appearance of disorder which prevails on the surface leads one at first to imagine that society is in a state of anarchy; nor does one perceive one's mistake till one has gone deeper into the subject."[95]

Social stability is by no means natural, yet he can locate no power which produces it: "There is, or appears to be, no government . . . no central idea seems to govern the movement of the machine." It is, incomprehensibly, "a mass of general results defying enumeration."[96] Thus, he concludes, "although everything moves regularly, the mover can nowhere be discovered. The hand that directs the social machine is invisible." In his confusion, he faces the ultimate theoretical question regarding this new world: "Why, then, does [one] obey society?"[97] He wonders "what serves as a tie to these diverse elements? What makes of them a people?" As he uncovers the extraordinary extent of that order, his focus and the objective of his work shift: no longer needing to seek an antidote to the "perpetual instability in the men and in the laws" in a "*démocratie* without limits," he must now attempt to locate and explain the sources of that order which succeeds not only more effectively than narrowly political forms of order but also virtually in their absence.[98]

Tocqueville's inquiry, then, his quest for "a new science of politics," involves a searching examination of the social and psychological elements producing the thrust toward integration in American society.[99] He realizes that he has encountered the laboratory of a new institutional foundation, the "most singular state of affairs that has doubtless existed under the sun." Americans constitute "a people absolutely without precedents, without habits, without dominating ideas even, opening for itself without hesitation a new path in civil, political, and criminal legislation; never casting its eyes about to consult the wisdom of other peoples or the memory of the past; but cutting out its institutions, like its roads, in the midst of the forests it has come to inhabit."[100] He realizes that the mystery of cohesion must also be unraveled with a novel investigation. Thus, he sets off on this new course: "I should say that the physical circumstances are less efficient than the laws, and the laws infinitely less so than the customs of the people . . . the peculiar cause which renders that people the only one of the American nations that is able to support a democratic government." The theme of the work is set: "So seriously do I insist upon . . . the important influence of the practical experience, the habits, the opinions, in short, of the customs of the Americans upon the maintenance of their institutions" that to leave it unclear would mean "I have failed in the principal object of my work."[101] As he goes deeper into the subject to uncover the psychopolitical dynamic of American cohesion, his gradual appreciation of its deeper and less rational sources emerges. As a believer in the idyll's premise of rational voluntarism, he eventually becomes alarmed that individuals are willingly—if unknowingly—succumbing to the pressures to belong. His late view, a dark view indeed of the human potential for freedom with American society as a closed cage of voluntarism gone awry, is the direct product of this conviction.

Thus, his analysis begins with a most voluntarist reading of individual integration. During his trip he affirms the liberal vision of a community requiring no greater bond than the self-interest so evident in all activity in this new society. Given that "the whole world here seems a malleable substance that man turns and fashions to his pleasure," "l'intérêt" can be "the only tie which unites the different parts of this vast body."[102] Reflecting on this early in his first volume, however, he realizes that pure self-interest would be fatal even in American society, for it would produce "a course almost without limits, a field without horizon," a fragmenting dynamic in which "the human spirit rushes forward and traverses . . . in every direction."[103] Some countervailing force is required, some principle or motivation opposing fragmenting individualism, and for this he would henceforth search.

His early explanation is a "voluntary obedience" to religious controls. Collectives can only be directed by "the free union of their will; and patriotism and religion" alone "can long urge all the people towards the same end." The older social basis in the traditional world, the "period of disinterested patriotism" rooted in an unquestioned commitment to the collective, the "instinctive, disinterested, and undefinable . . . reverence for traditions of the past," he announces, is "gone by forever." This leaves religion as the handmaiden of liberty, which he surmises Americans choose from their own conscious judgment regarding the need for limits: "The human spirit stops of itself . . . it bows with respect before truths it accepts without discussion. . . . [R]eligion . . . reigns in the hearts of men unsupported by aught beside its native strength." Yet, upon further analysis, he concludes that religion, given its diversity as well as the often secular basis of American social beliefs, was insufficient to regulate such a complex popular society. Americans, it now appears, believe not in God but in themselves: "The people reign in the political world as the Deity does in the universe. They are the cause and the aim of all things." Religion remains important in combating individualism, by "impos[ing] on man some duties toward his kind . . . [which] draw him at times from the contemplation of himself," but its greatest influence seems to be less its unique transcendental power than its role in disseminating the more quotidian and universal values of "this world."[104]

The inquiry thus turns again to a common basis for America's social attitudes and practice, and to its modernist understanding of patriotism as a voluntarist and rationalist connection to the community. Tocqueville's working model at this point, one he never entirely relinquishes, is that of a person who astutely distinguishes the scope of his or her individual freedom from legitimate social expectations and effectively balances and satisfies these divergent demands: "He obeys society because he acknowledges the utility of an association with his fellow men and he knows that no such association can exist without a regulating force. He is a subject in all that concerns the duties of citizens to each other; he is free . . . for all that concerns himself." The source of social commitment, then, is "a mature and reflecting preference for freedom" which incorporates, even features, "a love of order and law." This responsible, independent calculus of utility would become in Volume 2 the universalizing principle behind liberal individualism he called "self-interest rightly understood," which subsumes through the concern about one's fate in the afterlife even religious motivations. By this principle, individuals express "an enlightened regard for themselves [which] constantly prompts them to assist one another and inclines them willingly to sacrifice a portion of their time and property to the welfare of the state. . . . Each American knows when to sacrifice some of his private interests to save the rest."[105]

This grounding in an expansive yet prudential self-interest establishes not the "disinterested patriotism" from the age of implicit "self-sacrifice" which is "already flitting far away from us," but "another species of attachment . . . more rational . . . less general and less ardent . . . it springs from knowledge . . . it is confounded with the personal interests of the citizen. A man comprehends the influence which the well-being of his country has upon his own . . . he labors to promote it, first because it benefits him, and secondly because it is in part his own work." This new patriotism was, he noted on several occasions, the "chief remaining security" for modern states.[106]

While central to Volume 1, Tocqueville's rational voluntarism is challenged by two reservations which grow stronger with reflection. First, individuals are often not so "rational and intelligent" as he postulates, but driven by "private interest," the "only immutable point in the human heart." While the result is "an all-pervading and restless activity," his fears about its tendency toward "narrow selfishness" are quelled for the moment by the extent of local participation and its role in generating a sense of the collective good. His second worry arises as he comes to sense America's extraordinary, even intransigent and inflexible cohesion: "In my opinion, the main evil of the present democratic institutions . . . does not arise, as is often asserted in Europe, from their weakness, but from their irresistible strength."[107]

He thus acknowledges late in Volume 1 the sudden new specter of a "majority" which seems to act with a single will in shaping the societal landscape, with its "prodigious" and "irresistible" authority for which "no obstacles exist which can impede or even retard its progress." Confused for a time by the multiplicity of parties, governments, newspapers, and associations, he slowly notices its recurring presence, "the perpetual influence," and the power of even its "idlest cravings" in the public area to produce an underlying consensus regarding "certain principles" and institutional legitimation "to which everyone must then conform."[108] The original premise of a rational citizen balancing personal and community interests now increasingly gives way to a quite striking vision of self-abnegation: "Freedom of opinion does not exist in America. The Inquisition has never been able to prevent a vast number of anti-religious beliefs from circulating in Spain. The empire of the majority succeeds much better in the United States, since it actually removes any wish to publish them. . . . Attempts have been made by some governments to protect morality by prohibiting licentious books. In the United States no one is punished for this sort of book, but no one is induced to write them." Such restraint, apparent neither to others nor to the individual, strangely suggests a society that operates with the appearance of rational voluntarism by predetermining what it is possible to be "free" and "rational" about, that is, a society of invisible channels and bounds. In such a society, he fears, "the body is left free, and the soul is enslaved."[109]

These two disturbing trends do not lead Tocqueville at this point to rethink the basis of his science. He offers only a cursory, largely formal consideration of how to prevent them from prevailing, placing his trust in the American *"habits of the heart,"* the combination of social custom, historical preparation, political institutions, and favorable physical circumstances. The strong inclination of Americans to "take a part in the public business" would counteract privatism, while the "habits that freedom has formed" and "the love of freedom itself" would contain majoritarian pressures. Thus he concludes without worry that "nor can men there be made too free, since they are scarcely ever tempted to misuse their liberties." Each individual in America, with sufficient resources "to be happy and to be free . . . has only to determine that he will be so."[110]

Tocqueville's "Reversal"

By Volume 2, the seemingly unlimited power of the majority and the pervasiveness of self-interest, ever more pronounced in Tocqueville's analysis, were to become the basis of a revised conception of American individualism. Initially, these two forces seemed to cancel each other out, for if group pressures point toward the primacy of collective integration, self-interest suggests a priority for individual ends, or what he would call "individualism." The shift in Tocqueville's thinking is a fateful insight: what appeared as a rational equilibrium of divergent but integratable tendencies now emerges as the surging dynamic of two deeply affective, even blind forces which, instead of being irreconcilable, actually feed on and grow from each other and their opposition. Increasing self-interest ought to raise a danger of collective fragmentation if individuals are shifting away from a sense of common project. Yet not only is the majority strong, but by Volume 2 it is also on its way toward achieving an "extremely great" power, a sense of "omnipotence and sole authority" with "no limits," an "immense and tutelary power . . . absolute, minute, regular, provident, and mild," which "presses with enormous weight upon the minds of each individual" and "surrounds, directs, and oppresses him." The majority in fact exploits individualism: "Despotism . . . sees in the separation among men the surest guarantee of its continuance, and it usually makes every effort to keep them separate. No vice of the human heart is so acceptable to it as selfishness. . . . [It] applauds as good citizens those who have no sympathy for any but themselves." Clearly, individuals were being held together not by their political participation, nor by an enlightened commitment to the collective, but by some deeper set of forces or pressures, neither rational nor overtly associational, not even visible, which somehow strengthened the commitment to both narrow, unenlightened self-interest *and* to an equally unenlightened "common dependence" on and "strict uniformity" within society.[111] This dynamic not of rational balance but of mutually escalating polarities called for a deeper understanding of the individual's relation to the collective and, as both the individual and the government were novel, ultimately to a rethinking of the new psychopolitical dynamic of liberal societies.

The growing importance of self-interest now dwarfed the role of political and civil associations. What he previously heralded as an essential education for democracy was now seen as forms of activity designed to further individuals' "comfort," "well being," and "prosperity" just like all other forms of activity. In place of associational enthusiasm he now saw an "excessive taste" for "those physical enjoyments for which they are always longing." This "individualism" leads to a concentration on private affairs; it "disposes each member of the community to sever himself from the mass of his fellows." Political involvement is now irrelevant: "The discharge of political duties appears to them to be a troublesome impediment which diverts them from their occupations and business. . . . [T]hey cannot waste their precious hours in such useless engagement." The individual "willingly leaves society at large to itself." The values gained by associational involvement are lost: "Individualism . . . saps the virtues of public life. . . . In their intense and exclusive anxiety to make a fortune they lose sight of the close connection that exists between the private fortune of each and the prosperity of all." The individual retreats into "selfishness," which "throws him back forever upon himself alone and threatens in the end to confine him entirely within the solitude of his own heart."[112]

At the same time, Tocqueville was gradually becoming aware that what he had during his visit called the diverse and dizzying "spectacle" of freedom was regrettably, he writes late in the second volume, a "continual motion" not toward individual ends but rather toward a new form of dynamic routinization: "As nothing urges or guides it forward, it oscillates to and fro without progressive motion" such that "society" is "invariably fixed" and "mankind" is "stopped and circumscribed." Thus he concludes: "It would seem that nothing could be more adapted to stimulate and to feed curiosity than . . . the United States. Fortunes, opinions and laws are there in ceaseless variation. . . . Yet in the end the spectacle of this excited community becomes monotonous, and after having watched the moving pageant for a time, the spectator is tired of it." The constant changes were predictable, even "wearisome," because "all these changes are alike." That is, "all that Americans do" can be "traced . . . at the bottom" to the "love of wealth." "This perpetual recurrence of the same passion is monotonous; the particular methods by which this passion seeks its own gratification are no less so." Even worse, it was leading to a centralized social power devised by the people themselves out of a potent popular wish "to be led," a desire "to shape their souls" to that "great and imposing image of the people at large." Thus "they devise a sole, tutelary, and all-powerful form of government, but elected by the people. They combine the principle of centralization and that of popular sovereignty; this gives them a respite; they console themselves for being in tutelage by the reflection that they have chosen their own guardians. Every man allows himself to be put in leading-strings, because he sees that it is not a person or a class of persons, but the people at large who hold the end of his chain."[113]

To explain this powerful and complementary relationship between extreme individualism and encompassing collectivism, Tocqueville sought a new theory of society. This was not in any way a traditional imposition of authority and institutional regimentation from above: "The old words *despotism* and *tyranny* are inappropriate; the thing itself is new." He never found the word—"since I cannot name, I must attempt to define it."[114] What he describes is a process by which individual freedom in effect dynamically turned into a pursuit of dependence. Individuals wishing to leave the group en masse were somehow turned about to join it en masse, and, not recognizing it, continued to assert their freedom and autonomy. What he describes of course is the *reversal*.

This mysterious process of collective reversal with its momentous implications for understanding popular society needed to be explained. Its strange paradox of compliance which was voluntary and yet so powerful accounts for his irresolution in Volume 1 and at least in part for his determination to return to the subject five years later. The problem was obviously central to his reflections between volumes, for he begins Volume 2 with an analytical bombshell. The very first two chapters detail the process by which voluntarism becomes adaptation and individual judgments are turned into consensual norms: it is the internal psychosocial dynamic of reversal which accounts for the larger societal dynamic. It is moreover, he now understands, likely to be more powerful and ubiquitous, more hidden and less admitted, the more free and individualist the society, for it is fed by those very conditions.

In those chapters he details the deeply preinstitutional process by which "the minds of all the citizens" come to be "rallied and held together by certain predominant ideas." The American is, without the influence of or respect for "the ideas of his forefathers," without "the bondage of system and habit, of family maxims, class opinions, and, in some degree, of national prejudices" or "traditions," left "to seek the reason of things for oneself, and in oneself alone." Social equality and cultural voluntarism further ensure an extreme individualism in which "everyone shuts himself up tightly within himself and insists upon judging the world from there."[115]

But as this process unfolds, it breaks down in a way no one could suspect. For the individual's desire "to seek for truth by isolated paths struck out by himself alone" is untenable, not only for society by undercutting "common belief" and the possibility of "common action," but more so for the individual:

> If I consider man in his isolated capacity, I find that dogmatic belief is not the less indispensable to him in order to live alone than it is to enable him to co-operate with his fellows. If man were forced to demonstrate for himself all the truths of which he makes daily use, his task would never end. . . . As . . . he has not the time, nor, from the limits of his intelligence, the capacity, to act in this way, he is reduced to take on trust a host of facts and opinions which he has not had either the time or the power to verify for himself, but which men of greater ability have found out, or which the crowd adopts.

Tocqueville is now prepared to recognize that there must "always occur, under all circumstances . . . [a] principle of authority," a source of "moral and intellectual" certitude in every society: "Thus the question is, not to know whether any intellectual authority exists in an age of democracy, but simply where it resides and by what standard it is to be measured." In a popular democracy, where no individual or group can stand out given the strength of the belief in equality, the sole overarching presence for the individual is the collective itself, the aggregate of all, the indisputable "common opinion" of the "multitude": "His readiness to believe the multitude increases. . . . At periods of equality men have no faith in one another; but this very resemblance gives them almost unbounded confidence in the judgment of the public. . . . [A]s they are all endowed with equal means of judging, the greater truth should go with the greater number."[116]

Most important, however, the source of individual reliance is by no means merely one of rational calculation or even utility. To leave people entirely to their own devices like Crusoe as liberalism purports to do would create an individual "at once independent and powerless," at "perpetual unrest," without any clarity or stability. The individual seeks refuge in the collective judgment which it cannot, will not, and does not want to resist because isolation to a confused, ungrounded, and undefined personal subjectivity is unbearable. There are neither formal nor informal supports to turn to, and without them, meaningful autonomy is impossible: "When he comes to survey the totality of his fellows and to place himself in contrast with so huge a body, he is instantly overwhelmed by the sense of his own powerlessness and insignificance," exposed "alone and unprotected to the influence of the greater number." Tocqueville elaborates the agonized internal dynamic: "His debility makes him feel from time to time the want of outward assistance, which he cannot expect from any of . . . [his equals], because they are all impotent and unsympathizing. In this predicament he *naturally turns his eyes* to that imposing power which alone rises above the level of universal depression."[117] The individual finds support, validation, and security by willingly acceding before the collective will, but in a process so deeply veiled that the transfer is never recognized.

While Tocqueville initially gave a qualified endorsement to this new dynamic, calling reversal "a salutary servitude, which allows [one] to make a good use of freedom" in remaining areas, he was increasingly terrified by the prospect that this "free society" was in reality a society of voluntary subservience. For reversal involves a shift of legitimacy and ultimately of *authority*—from the individual to the public, which is now firmly, if invisibly, in place: "Of that [imposing] power his wants and especially his desires continually remind him, until he ultimately views it as the sole and necessary support of his own weakness." Tocqueville recognizes how, in their powerlessness to generate knowledge or certainty, Americans turn toward what he calls "equality" in preference to freedom. Finding one's own path and asserting one's values in public discourse, that is, true individual and social freedom, requires "sacrifices" and "great exertions." Equality, now read as equivalence whereby individuals will not "differ much" and will "naturally stand so near that they may all at any time be fused in one general mass," comes easily, in all the "small enjoyments . . . at every instant felt" by which they assert a desperate need to belong.[118]

Equality is made to look like freedom in that it releases individual initiative, self-reliance, and discretion, so that Americans resolutely believe that they have the full measure of both. Thus is "equality . . . confounded with freedom," for the choices in fact exercised are those which are socially authorized and laid out: in public life Americans are "circumscribed within the narrow space that politics leaves them"; they voluntarily and gladly take "the only road open to them" in the economic realm, the prescribed ends of commercial activity and material improvement; and they willingly pursue the full coloration of society, its "multitude of ready-made opinions," in order to be part of "the general will" in the social realm. In this way, pursuit of the "free individual" is transformed into the ironic triumph of the "free" or popular society in which the individual in effect chooses its own powerlessness. This produces the anomaly of a society in which "none are forced by their condition to obey" and each is nominally empowered to "choose his own path and proceed apart from all his fellow men," but "to live at variance with the multitude is, as it were, not to live." It is a society which "prompts desires" but then immediately "restrains" them "within necessary limits," which "gives men more liberty of changing, and less interest in change," not by coercion but by popular sentiment: "The multitude requires no laws to coerce those who do not think like themselves: public disapprobation is enough; a sense of their loneliness and impotence overtakes them and drives them to despair."[119]

In this way, the poles are united: the path of individual release to pursue personal interest is indelibly linked to the growth of the collective. The specter of despotism now arises from a public willing to relinquish all public responsibility in exchange for a "crude" conception of "self-interest," though for "the better to look after what they call their own business, they neglect their chief business, which is to remain their own masters." The result is a community where individuals have "chosen their own guardians" and "leading-strings," and "love the power" which they have created to shape their "will," "secure their gratification," and "watch over their fate."[120] Initiative and self-reliance have found a circuitous path by which they become the support for social integration. Free individuals now freely conform, electing deference (as in Locke's childhood) without recognition or memory like mass sleepwalkers, constituting by their own personal judgment the hidden omnicompetence of the collective: "Thus, they become more alike, even without having imitated each other. Like travelers scattered about some large wood, intersected by paths converging to one point, if all of them keep their eyes fixed upon that point, and advance towards it, they insensibly draw nearer together,—though they seek not, though they see not and know not each other; and they will be surprised at length to find themselves all collected on the same spot." Tocqueville's persistence leads him to grasp first the originative *agency* quality of American society, a synchronized network of agency institutions and roles seemingly flexible and voluntary. Consensus is "maintained without effort because no one attacks it," for the "force that restrains" individuals and "unites" them to society is "hidden." The result is a society with prodigious levels of initiative and self-reliance—"all are perpetually striving"—but within the "settled order of things," with an acceptance of ends such that there is a complete resistance to challenge or even question "general principles," which "do not vary."[121]

The denial that society was necessary only sustained the indispensability of reversal as the basis of social formation, which explains its continuing presence throughout subsequent American fiction: in *Babbitt, The Great Gatsby,* the works of Dreiser, Edgar Lee Masters, and Sherwood Anderson, *Humboldt's Gift,* Updike's Rabbit novels, and *On the Road,* to suggest just a few. Its ubiquity underscores how the revolutionary project complicated the process of constituting order and limits in a voluntarist society. The willing reversal, elemental and foundational yet unacknowledged and unmentionable, could alone assist institutions in the struggle against fragmentation in a society that proclaimed its freedom. At the same time, because post-idyllic life was anticlimax, individuals would undergo integration with a kind of psychological amnesia, either denying the existence of institutions (and demonizing them as betrayers of the idyll) or magically reconstituting them as conservers and guarantors of freedom despite significant indications to the contrary. Both options foreclosed the possibility of democratic engagement and cast an air of unreal expectation and denial over nineteenth-century American society.

The constitution of agency society, its complex formation of initiative without autonomy, self-reliance without self-authorizing selfhood, the power to move but not to direct the movement, would require the full mobilization of institutions. To wrest order finally from chaos, citizens would have to be led from their reversal into functional collectivities. Although

Tocqueville cannot name this new reality, he chronicles the popular society emerging from the needs of newly liberated individuals. Unlike most citizens of the new republic, Tocqueville could, yearning for an authority both rational and limited, sidestep the crisis of release and reversal by leaving. Those many citizens without this option would have their work before them: to gather in that clearing and constitute institutions that would provide them with the stable characters and societal roles of which, even if they in no way realized, they were in need.

IV

The Creation of an Agency Civilization

10

National Revival as the Crucible of Agency Character

God will soon call you to give an account. . . . To-night it will be told in hell, and told in heaven, and echoed from the ends of the universe, what you decide to do. . . . Are you ready?

    —Charles G. Finney

All my observations are directed [to] the union of these two doctrines of *activity* and *dependence*, which are so commonly felt to be subversive of each other; the bringing of both to bear with undiminished force on the minds of the impenitent.

    —Robert Baird

With the swift erosion of the proprietary ideal and the looming specter of an untamed and untameable wilderness, the idyll of a "free society of free individuals" could remain plausible only by restoring within its meaning a community of shared ends and common institutions. Fortuitously, as English Protestantism and liberalism had foreseen, citizens of the new society released as agents into a setting unstructured by traditional institutions and values would find their way out of the idyll. Driven by deep psychosocial needs, they were enacting the dynamic of reversal, what David M. Potter has called "a voluntary drawing together."[1] The structural problem for the young republic with its revolutionary legacy of voluntarism and antitraditionalism, now expanded to include political populism and functional self-reliance, was to devise a collective framework to complement—to both employ and contain—this new individualism. Voluntarism had been accepted as a birthright, unleashing what Tocqueville called a "feverish ardor" and the leading antebellum revivalist Charles G. Finney referred to as "torrents of worldliness" from "great political, and other worldly excitements" which was the marvel of the nineteenth century.[2] The growing need for order and place, institutions and values, would have to be met in a way

369

previously unknown in the history of Western society: by structures consistent under the terms of the new culture with idyllic voluntarism. The constitution of an ordered society would be led by that sector most capable of mobilizing the experience of reversal to form voluntarist institutions—the religion of American Protestantism.

The Logic of American Institutional Development

The more extended process of American societal formation would be undertaken in stages: initially, by a populist Protestantism which was the crucible through a sustained national revival for forming and stabilizing the agency character and preparing individuals for institutions of common authority; thereafter, by a majoritarian liberalism which evolved functional structures of economic, social, and ultimately political integration grounded in and demanding agency adaptation to create a coherent national society. The American Protestant revivalists and secular liberal modernists, to be sure, had distinctive agendas deriving from their different historical origins, and regarded each other as competitors for the direction of American life. In the experiential field of the early republic, however, as the Protestant and liberal movements evolved their distinctive societal visions, each failed increasingly over the course of the century to produce societal cohesion independently. Each was stymied by the limits of its own strategies and priorities and by the popular expectations of the revolutionary idyll. Over the course of time, they were each to turn in crisis to a reconfiguration of their own agendas and ultimately to the other in a common effort. This cultural synthesis, featuring the institutional triumph of its characterological framework, was to this extant the well-known liberalization of American Protestantism. At the same time, as a synthesis equally reconciling American liberalism with its Protestant origins, the result suggests a national formation dramatically distinct from that portrayed by the dominant thesis of an increasingly triumphant secular modernism.

The synthesis evolved as these two movements realized their need for each other. Liberalism, wedded as we have seen to its idyllic formulation and thus to marginal, narrowly instrumental institutions largely furthering individual rights and ends, found itself unable to cope with the rise of institutional society. Faced with ever-expanding institutions, it could—given its avowed voluntarism—neither overtly direct self-interest into prescribed forms of institutional integration nor provide for the shaping of a social character that affirmed the necessary socialization of self-interest for institutional participation. American liberalism consequently was in turmoil throughout the nineteenth century. In its quandary, it would turn to the Protestant model from which its classical theory had ambivalently derived. This model explicitly framed voluntarist individualism as the personal commitment to undergo characterological socialization and pursue institutional inclusion. In postbellum American society, the influential theorists of (free) market integration, social interdependence, and political incorporation utilized Protestant formulations to establish a "free agency" basis for the individual role in the economy, society, and political system. In this way liberalism, even while claiming its continuing fealty to individual freedom, initiative, and self-reliance, was reconceiving individualism as institutionally constituted, bounded, and channeled.

Protestantism at the same time was to be in crisis by midcentury. By insisting on a voluntary but rigorous fulfillment of its way of life, it was of such strenuosity as to be rejected by many, particularly in a society where it was denied effective control over nonmembers. Operating through decentralized revivals and multiple denominations, it also produced variant and mutually incompatible beliefs among adherents. As a result, it generated divergent and conflicting sects, unleashed extremes of sectarian exclusivity and societal withdrawal, and created a vast unaffiliated population beyond religious regulation. Revivalism, a powerful source of the reemerging significance of Protestantism in American life, further fanned the flames of individualism, doctrinal diversity, and social militancy. Protestantism lacked in its search for characterological and behavioral rigor a capacity for promoting adaptation to pragmatic rules of conduct as well as inclusive secular and nondenominational institutional goals. It found in liberalism a system of universal and less conflictual forms of institutional behavior and constraint anchored by an adaptive character type, and by midcentury began turning toward liberalism as its ally and guarantor.

After the Civil War, then, a dynamic partnership evolved from the mutual strengths of the two movements to create the American social character, the "Protestant agent in liberal society." By the 1890s, John Dewey was framing the synthesis being suggested by a "liberal" Protestantism increasingly committed to social and civil religion and a Protestantizing liberalism which was recasting liberal theory as an account of institutional practice. This new synthesis, the "wider and fuller union of individual efforts in accomplishment of common ends," was framed as the historic triumph over the "earlier *laissez faire* phase" of liberalism "with its opposition of society and the individual."[3] Behind the rhetoric of the idyll, of a mutually compatible individual and collective freedom, was its decisive transformation into the completed *society of agents.*

The formation of republican institutions will be treated here in terms of specific sectors because of the peculiar organizational dynamic of liberalism within the American setting. These various sectors were of course engaged in the common project of shaping a coherent and cohesive society. But the liberal insistence on voluntarism severely limited the employment of overt coercion to establish collective norms and to direct individual conduct within institutions. Religious, economic, and social activities were therefore insulated to an unprecedented degree from the political sector to follow their internal priorities, in the words of Roger Friedland and Robert Alford, their "internal logics."[4] Political coercion was not eliminated but veiled—as by shifting it to the judicial process—to immunize it from public contention.[5] Nor did the sectors constitute entirely autonomous arenas of activity, subject as they were to the presence of "secondary logics" from coexisting sectors, though in their rudimentary form they exerted little direct leverage over one another.[6] Thus, during this period, the emerging forms of integration and internalized discipline were shaped to a large extent by the nonstatist incentives and disincentives within each sector reinforced by subtle influences and pressures mobilized by the other, nominally distinct sectors and coordinated primarily by the underlying cultural dynamic which framed common goals for the populace.

To establish functioning processes—including both common superseding ends and the designated arenas for achieving them—without traditional powers of control, each of these sectors would be called upon to reconstitute effective systems of governance within a voluntarist framework. Authority and freedom could be reconciled only if the framing of ends and means were derived from the popular will and guided by the priority of individual initiative, including sufficient incentives to define pursuit of the designated ends within set directions and limits as arising from the will and desires of individual participants. The shaping of sector activity had to be driven not by social rank or inequality or by a leadership cadre but by the emerging collective experience of formally equal members. Boundaries and procedures were to be generated from and attentive to the wills of the participants, managed by those who had achieved and accumulated rewards within the given activities.

As classical liberal theory had recognized, continual explicit opportunities to shape common ends would open society to dangerous expressions of self-authorization. Voluntary commitment could be safely obtained only if framed in behavioral terms: by inducing participatory motion toward systemic goals within contained processes. If the opportunity for such motion could be provided on a universal and formally equal basis with sufficient rewards for participation, then most members would be willing to join of their own will. If the available means required steady and stable activity, individuals would be encouraged to regularize their integrative motion and directionality. And so long as the rewards continued, participants would regard themselves as moving without restraint. In this way, the "free" exercise of legitimated means toward provided ends would produce a voluntary and yet self-regulating system. The project of shaping institutional channels and socializing adults to act within them could then be organized behind the veil of voluntarism as the encouragement of "free activity" and supported indirectly by informal, consensual, and juridical pressures within the process.

As these sectors emerged with specific forms of authority, adaptive conduct, and incentives, each with its unique attractions and dangers played a distinct role within a complex division of societal labor to define and reward appropriate behavior in national formation. Beginning shortly after the founding, the religious, economic, and social sectors were each to become at different times the principal arena for shaping the larger experience of integration in the community. While these sectors were all evolving in line with the new criteria, this shifting preeminence is explained by their distinctive capacity to build on the momentum of reversal. In the early republic, this process would be dominated by religious institutions, followed in turn by the postbellum ascendancy of economic processes and from the end of the century by the growing reach of the social realm.

This chapter and the next develop how the religious sector, with its unparalleled power to mobilize popular anxieties to shape individual characters into social roles and disciplined behavior within a system of authoritative ends, served institutionally as the entry point for assimilation into the new society. Its greatest effectiveness was in the early period before the inevitable sectarian fragmentation recurred, at which point the religious sector relinquished its central role to sectors with greater means of operational verification of both conformability and reward. The economic and social sectors, by contrast, defined in Lockean fashion as noncoercive, were unable to undertake the initial shaping of the agency character in the early republic. For each, the "free economy" and the "free society," was under the sway of idyllic voluntarism and dared not assert explicit institutional demands or the necessity for individual deference to authority. Furthermore, the economic arena, with its insistent, acquisitive motion, was frightening to an antebellum society which had never experienced such an intensive and widespread pursuit of worldly wealth, while the social realm was not even acknowledged to exist for several generations. Only as the agency character was crystallized and the economic and social realms informally evolved from below were their major roles to emerge: to provide strong incentives within increasingly formal systemic channels in order to induce a pursuit of consensual worldly ends. Universal movement toward structured incentives prepared by the prior process of national character formation completed agency adaptation to institutional life by validating the conflation of regulated systemic striving with the perception of unlimited choice.

After midcentury, the economic sector, structured and bounded by legislative and judicial initiatives and its actors disciplined by religious socialization, became the prominent arena. With the prod of vast incentives and anxieties that produced participation seemingly without a trace of external compulsion, the economic system with ever clearer channels and procedures of market participation became a space more universal, more uniform, and less contentious than the religious arena. With its merger of personal success and community benefit, its demand for participation only on an individual basis, economic activity became the great inclusive path for integration in the national society. With economic development, however, as large-scale production and discretionary consumption weakened the linchpin of economic necessity, survivalist accommodation to the market with its predictability and inevitability severely weakened. It became evident that the motivations to institutional engagement in economic production and consumption, particularly in an increasingly organizational economy, were social pursuits of status, place, inclusion, and success.[7] This emergence of the social basis of liberal accommodation characterologically and institutionally shifted the primary source of cohesion. The social realm, the least acknowledged in the early republic, was in the end the strongest definer of motivation and directionality, constraint and place, absorbing the others as the principal locus of engagement. Individuals had evolved with organizational society from Tocqueville's wanting-to-belong to George Herbert Mead's belongers (Mead being in effect the third volume of *Democracy in America*), beings who now rarely imagined freedom apart from institutional options.

The Challenge for American Religion

In the rudimentary new society, religious institutions resurfaced quickly after the founding and, surprisingly to many, as the primary locus for the popular search for order and direction. Offering a language of character organized in terms of deference, social duty, and individual responsibility, religious reformers and evangelists uniquely framed an authoritative context for personal accommodation and structured participation. Driven by remarkably voluntarist sects and processes, the religious movement laid the groundwork for a new human order rooted no longer in traditional fear, exclusion, and hierarchy but in modern forms of popular engagement. In this first of the two phases in the development of agency society, the agency character was made into a common social expectation and procedures were established and disseminated for its attainment universally.

Before the Revolution, this movement had suffered from an inconsistent and irregular reach. In a now freed and anchorless society for the first time in the hands of common people with its stream of immigrants and absence of effective childhood socialization, the problem of constraining adults took on new urgency. The pressures for providing a common adaptive character committed to the consensual framing of attitudes, values, and goals sharpened. Recognizing this crisis, populist Protestantism, which had already been operating as a school of personal integration reaching deeper into the new society than any other formal institution, responded. Evolving a radically more voluntarist, individualist theology and developing powerful new participatory forms of community revival, it became the institutional setting to initiate the construction of a fixed foundation in stable identities and worldly roles.

The remarkable success of popular religion in the early republic, eclipsing both liberal values and traditional denominations, has never been adequately taken into account in explaining national formation.[8] Because mythical Jacksonian yeomen and artisans were more than likely sectarian Protestants, the Age of Jackson was equally the Age of Finney.[9] The campaign of mobilization and outreach, revival and conversion, by denominations and interdenominational programs alike reaching into every corner of the new society produced a sixty-year upsurge before the Civil War, what

Perry Miller has called "an internal convulsion," a "volcano . . . sometimes smouldering, now blazing into flame, never quite extinguished," which emerges as the "dominant theme in America from 1800 to 1860."[10]

Max Weber, reflecting on American society after his 1904 visit, noted that "nobody who visited the United States" in the past "could overlook the very intense church-mindedness which then prevailed."[11] Early visitors routinely remarked that without "doubt . . . the Americans as a whole seemed to be a distinctly religious people. . . . The churches were filled . . . public profession . . . was nowhere else more conspicuous. . . . [T]he person who went so far as to openly avow himself an atheist or a deist was exceedingly rare." Karl T. Griesinger, a German who lived in America in the 1840s and 1850s, observed: "Nowhere in the wide world . . . are you more likely to be asked whether you belong to a congregation, and to which. Nowhere in the whole world is more done for the conversion of the heathen, nowhere more Bibles distributed, more money collected for missions. Churches and chapels are legion, and nowhere are they more heavily frequented than in this land of tolerance and freedom."[12] Philip Schaff, a Swiss clergyman visiting America, noted "more awakened souls and more individual effort and self-sacrifice for religious purposes, proportionately, than [in] any other country." One British visitor "swore that nowhere had he seen a single person working at a trade, nor a single store open on sunday. In city and countryside alike, the churches were filled."[13]

Such observations suggested a deeper pattern, what Robert Baird, a Protestant believer who undertook an immense study of American religion during the 1840s and 1850s, called "an all-powerful influence . . . in every direction."[14] Charles Ingersoll noted the "phrensy of fanaticism," with "the number of persons devoted to pious exercises" being "greater in the United States, than in any other part of the world."[15] Francis Grund, a learned visitor in the 1830s, saw a way of life permeated with religion as the "basis of the most important American settlements . . . their revolutionary struggle . . . their rights . . . their liberties . . . their councils . . . the laws. . . . It is to religion they have recourse whenever they wish to impress the popular feeling with anything relative to their country; and it is religion which assists them in all their national undertakings."[16]

Given such voluntarist conditions, the extreme popularity of religion with its message of absolute authority and the need for individual subordination was confusing. This intensity surprised Moritz Busch, traveling through the eastern United States in 1851 and 1852, in light of the American "hostility toward all authority" and "aversion toward everything old."

> Not since the fire of the Reformation was extinguished by dogmatism has the religious spirit expressed itself in any part of the Christian world as powerfully as among the peoples of the United States. . . . Compared to our conditions, the life of the Christian church in America seems almost like a remnant of the fantastically fluid primeval world alongside the solid regularity and rational dryness of present-day nature . . . a volcanic wonder-fire. At times it runs through the land in the form of will-o'-wisps, so that rational people, confused, shake their heads about it; and at other times it flames up in intense revivals. . . . The spirit which once descended upon the disciples in flaming tongues is still dispensed here in abundance, and every year thousands do not merely celebrate but actually experience Pentecost.[17]

Frances Trollope expressed fear that despite "the great blessings of its constitution," a "religious tyranny may be exerted very effectually" with its demand for "unqualified obedience." Emerson spoke of sects as "Unthinking corporations" which were "devised to save a man from the vexation of thinking."[18]

The enigma was more sharply drawn by religious commentators at the time, who attributed the success to the very *absence* of external coercion. Lyman Beecher's moderate Congregational journal embraced this unique condition in 1831: "The government of God is the only government which will hold society, against depravity within and temptation without; and this it must do by the force of its own law written upon the heart."[19] The voluntary principle was, according to Baird, responsible for the system of religious institutions reaching people "from one end of the country to the other": "Upon the mere unconstrained good-will of the people . . . does this vast superstructure rest. Those may tremble for the result who do not know what the human heart is capable of when left to its own energies, moved and sustained by the grace and love of God." This "very activity, energy, and self-reliance it calls forth," by its "cultivation of an independent, energetic, and benevolent spirit," enabled individuals to become "co-workers with God in promoting His glory, and the true welfare of their fellow-men."[20]

This institutional vigor demonstrated the very possibility of an effective voluntarist order. Freed from religious constraints since the First Awakening, individuals were surprisingly utilizing this opportunity to affirm their commitment to collective beliefs and institutional engagement. Even with the Second Great Awakening turn from Calvinist proto-agency controls to a religion of full individual agency responsibility for one's spiritual fate, institutional compliance seemed to be self-regulating, rendering superfluous the compulsive power of government. Charles Finney wrote: "The first condition of moral obligation is the possession of the requisite powers of moral agency . . . intelligence enough . . . sensibility to good sought, and evil shunned . . . and . . . the power of choice between possible courses to be chosen. . . . Supposing the individual to know what he ought to choose it does not grow out of the fact of God's requiring it, but lies in the value of the end to be chosen . . . subjectively present to his mind."[21]

Individual choice, according to Robert Baird, became the anchor for the unique "voluntary system" of organization, "the 'American plan' of supporting religion, by relying, under God's blessing, upon the help of the people, rather than upon the help of the government."[22] He continued: "The voluntary system rests on the grand basis of perfect religious freedom. I mean a freedom of conscience for all; for those who believe in Christianity to be true, and for those who do not; for those who prefer one form of worship, and for those who prefer another."[23] In a religion whose basis was the true state of the believer's will, constraints were incompatible with legitimate authority, responsibility, and commitment. Baird thus denied any attribution of social pressure: "M. de Tocqueville . . . does forget for the moment what sort of religion it was; that it was not a religion that repels investigation, or that would have men receive any thing as Truth, where such momentous concerns are involved, upon mere trust in public opinion. Such has never been the character of Protestantism, rightly so called, in any age."[24] Even outsiders, including secular observers such as William Leggett, praised the extraordinary success of Christianity in America, attributing "the auspicious results" to *"perfect free trade in religion—*of leaving it to manage its own concerns in its own way, without government protection, regulation, or interference of any kind or degree whatever." This was a model for the sustainability of a natural, noncoercive order, operating by the *"voluntary principle"* which is the "fundamental principle" of "democracy."[25]

This enigmatic embrace of authority, a restatement of Tocqueville's paradox, affords another perspective on the deeper dynamic of American culture. Vast changes had Americans uncertain of their spiritual supply lines, of their links with their traditions and narratives of meaning, with one another, with the ways to integrate the unceasing demands for innovation as the political, economic, and social systems themselves tried to adapt and find new forms of stability. The religious sector was the obvious crucible in which to structure and disseminate a new collective framework for adults seeking identity and order within the new society. Though it had been abandoned by many in the revolutionary embrace of a national, worldly future,[26] where else with the waning of revolutionary enthusiasm could people locate the larger implications of the place they had forged for themselves and their nation?

Religion possessed a unique power as the deepest continuous narrative of the popular experience of the journey to America and of the larger task to be achieved there. It alone offered an encompassing structure of unambiguous ends deriving from the past. Through its (as yet incomplete) evolution of the agency paradigm, it had worked to forge an equilibrium between liberty and constraint at the cosmic, institutional, and characterological levels. Even in its more voluntarist forms, the religious project had as its center the continuing commitment to authority and its ends, a "true submission . . . in the whole government of God," a "perfect acquiescence in all the providential dealings and dispensations of God; whether relating to ourselves, or to others, or to the universe. . . . It is vain for a child to pretend a real acquiescence in his father's commands, unless he actually obeys them." A personal resolve regarding internal self-discipline, behavioral self-restraint, and institutional deference was, after all, its aim: "The first idea of submission . . . [is] that you should make your own happiness subordinate to the glory of God and the . . . public good."[27]

Recognizing that "all is in a ferment there," in this "land of the future," religious leaders compared "the character of the nation" to "an unripe youth" or an "idea only half-developed in the minds of those who were to live under it."[28] To harness that potential, the religious sector would finally have to incorporate the two central additions to popular experience emerging from the revolutionary and early republican age: freedom as the right to personal voluntarism and the experience of reversal. The two were linked. The social and psychic dislocations of a voluntarist culture provided the evolving populist religions unique opportunities to organize. The responsibility demanded by spiritual individualism and radical personal choice amidst a vacuum of community expectations only sharpened the yearning for connection, integration, and guidance. Religious leaders were discovering how individuals made to confront this reality in extremis would of their own free and trembling will embrace God's authority and purpose. Once the movement found a process which incorporated reversal to establish a voluntarist basis for its institutions, the great challenge of the republic—to merge the revolutionary idyll and a dispositive authority—would be achieved. As the historian Donald G. Mathews asserted in a seminal 1969 essay, the evolving revival techniques of the Second Awakening provided the first great "organizing process" of the new society, which succeeded by "giv[ing] meaning and direction to people suffering in various degrees from the social strains of a nation on the move into new political, economic and geographical areas." Marshaling the deep-seated desire to "impose order" in response to the "fears," "uneasiness," and "vague anxiety" caused by "independence and intellectual turmoil," this "vast mobilization of the people" established a national pattern of "voluntary associations for common goals."[29]

Constituted by reversal, the dynamic of the Awakening was never fully understood: "People seldom spoke of why they or their neighbors participated in it. Many people were unaware of its dimensions" and "took it for granted that God's hand lay behind the work."[30] Yet this grasp among individuals for a common authority, with its sense of being "commissioned" and the determination "to reform or reshape themselves" and their "characters," resulted, for Daniel Walker Howe, in a new "identity" integrating both "freedom and discipline." This "voluntary embrace" of "self-discipline" operated to ground "personal identity" and "social order" absent "strong social or political institutions."[31] In this way, the nation was bound to God, to "His principles of free agency," to produce the model citizen as "free moral agent."[32] Shaped first by new revival techniques among the sects which were then extended throughout mainstream denominations, the agency character was institutionalized as the American model of selfhood within a new popular agency civilization.

The unprecedented success of revivalist waves in antebellum America emboldened many to foresee a realization of the Reformation dream of a godly nation and some abolitionists to believe that "the growth of the 'pure spirit' of Christianity would be more effective against the extension of the institution [of slavery] than a hundred legislative prohibitions."[33] Yet the sectarian dynamic of a liberated Protestantism would in the long run again fragment religious life in the society and defeat the possibility of a Protestant polity. This awakened society would, like earlier ones, be forced to replace its aspirations toward national spiritual coalescence with liberal culture and a liberal "civil religion" reconstituting "virtue" as patterns of behavioral uniformity. Before religion relinquished its leadership, however, as Perry Miller has written, in the "magnificent result" of ecclesiastical outreach the American churches "had found the soul of the nation."[34]

The Emergent Mainstream and Its Oppositions

As a fluid, decentralized popular movement, the Second Great Awakening is difficult to grasp in its entirety, particularly as it changed in response to the evolving needs and expectations of the citizenry. The focus in this inquiry will be on the psychosocial shifts driving the religious movement as it employed theological innovations and practical experimentation in the formation of a republican character. This emphasis on a new "ideal character type" does not presume it to be either morally exemplary or universal in that age. To the contrary, the very claim of a widespread drive for a common identity explains the many responses of refusal, exclusion, and victimization wrought by the surging dominant culture and provides a point of contrast for understanding the values and narratives of the marginalized.

In fact, the project of forming a mainstream value system was highly contested. In restoring the Awakening from a secondary religious movement to the center of national formation, I offer neither the dominant view historically of a religious consensus for protestantizing America[35] nor a more recent conflictual view that emphasizes differences within and among denominations on issues such as democratization, religious practice, regional variations, social class, and doctrine.[36] A third, more subtle and expansive view treats the religious sector not in terms of specifically religious goals, which accounts in part for the pervasive underestimation of the Awakening in our national history, but as a dynamic social movement seeking to forge new unities, "a new synthesis," out of cultural conflict and fragmentation.[37] Precipitated by crises in the credibility and functioning of existing norms and values, periods of revival play a key role of "transformation or regeneration"[38] in which new norms and values are dialectically framed and internalized. This understanding can explain shifts in the mode of characterological organization, including the embrace of the agency character in the pre–Civil War revivals. At the same time, the result of such a new integration is not a simple reestablishment of consensus; rather it provokes a corresponding relocation of cultural divisions around this reconstituted center as a comprehensive readjustment to the precipitating social and cultural shifts.

From this dialectical perspective, the quest in the Second Awakening for a common Protestant character was fueled and crystallized by the drive to overcome internal disorientation and external dislocations within post-revolutionary society through a cohesive characterological adaptation to the new society. The model of agency, only inchoate at the outset of the Awakening, had achieved initial clarification of its own principles of institutional formation and internal coherence in opposition to an already existing mainstream which located it at the margin of a spectrum operating since the inception of the colonies. With its subsequent coalescence and dominance, new cleavages of historic proportions emerged producing both denominational schisms and a proliferation of new sects which generated distinctive divisions and fault lines. Thus, its emergence was framed in opposition to the traditional Calvinism of the religious orthodoxy at the outset of the revival. Its eventual limits in turn were clarified in reaction to the increasingly emboldened religious radicalism called by Sydney Ahlstrom a "sectarian heyday" spawned by the spiritual ferment itself. This vast religious experimentation with its "strong reassertion of sectarian distinctions" producing perfectionism, millennialism, universalism, illuminism, and communitarianism Whitney Cross identifies as "a natural consequence of the revival cycle."[39] As older options realigned with new ones, the evolving mainstream model of universal agency became the center of a new spectrum flanked by its two primary variants, the traditional neo-Puritan model of proto-agency and the emerging model of self-authorization.

The new divisions emerging within American Protestantism provide a psychocultural Rorschach test of the power of worldly human potential to shape this formless and undefined new setting. The theological splits among and within denominations, while loosely linked to class or economic differences, were, given the similar backgrounds among many participants, more a reflection of beliefs about the human ability to direct the enormous changes and order the profound uncertainties in the new republic. By overcoming Calvinist proto-agent limits on human initiative and then resisting the expansive individualism of sectarian self-authorization, the dominant popular movement was able to clarify and consolidate the dynamic integration of its agency values: a voluntarist privileging of individual human initiative with absolute constraint rooted in God's unqualified authority. By examining the cleavages this produced, we can better discern the project of the Awakening, the premises of the mainstream synthesis that emerged, and the reasons for its success.

The emergent mainstream will be identified as what Roger Finke and

Rodney Stark call "the upstart sects" that "win America," whose "meteoric rise" of individualizing populist Protestantism radiated from the Methodist movement and the Baptists throughout the denominations together with the increasingly free will and Arminian wing of New England theology reshaped by the Awakening.[40] Scholars have noted how the radical post-Calvinist voluntarism, emotionalism, universalism, and spiritual optimism of Methodism, propelled by its vigorous methods of populist outreach through circuit riders and camp meetings, defined the age.[41] Richard Carwardine has called American Methodism "both a perfect metaphor for the emergent capitalist market of the early republic, and indeed the principal beneficiary of the free spiritual market that superseded the colonial system." Its success as the most powerful and influential denomination of the period transformed American theology and practice, forcing American Protestantism to "keep up with the times" in the religious marketplace by embracing voluntarism, shedding the Calvinist intransigence of sin, and making popular revivals the center of religious experience.[42]

Agency, with its precise combination of voluntarist empowerment and authoritative limits, offered an optimistic and highly individualized social and spiritual message that reflected its increasingly successful economic and social proponents. Typically this upwardly mobile cohort who flocked to the new movement were the rising new entrepreneurs, merchants, traders, professionals, public officials, and master artisans who were leading the commercial transformation in towns and cities.[43] Amidst their prosperity and faith in individual enterprise and choice, these groups were slowly stepping forward from denominational hierarchy and theology to undertake full individual responsibility for their religious lives. They were increasingly convinced of the beneficent role for human and specifically individual effort as reflected in progressive theology with its "resolution to escape from the trammels of 'inability,'"[44] and in "energetic schemes of social and economic improvement."[45] A theology was wanted that not only vindicated their successes to date but also legitimated their continued striving in all facets of life. Such a theology of empowerment would sweep like wildfire across this new cohort, as amidst the rising urban commercial sector during the urban phase of the revival (1840–1865), among the vast opponents of slavery leading to the Civil War, and finally within that postwar Protestantism that identified human progress with a rising, successful America.

The Calvinists, who controlled traditional mainstream Presbyterianism and Congregationalism at the outset of the Second Awakening, continued to believe that human sinfulness, original sin, and limited grace demanded containment of worldly initiative through divine omnipotence, human predestination, and ecclesiastical control. Despite their revivalist and reformist activism, they insisted on human powerlessness in the face of God's will: "All human efforts to salvation were sinful and insulting denials of God's sovereignty. If God wanted to save the world He could and would." Waiting patiently for God's guidance and blessing, individuals were to live and work for God's Kingdom under the shadow of uncertainty. Because most were not expected to achieve grace or to thrive amidst such ambiguity, the Calvinist communities limited full membership to that modest number who had achieved complete conversion.[46]

The rejection of Calvinism in the Awakening is one of the great instances of the power of popular culture. In the early phase after the turn of the century, "New Birth" transformationism and the possibility of immediate conversion spread through mass revivals as itinerant preachers sought to craft public rituals and doctrines for "the multitudes" seeking "a hope of deliverance" from sin and "a manifestation of the *heavenly state*."[47] Predestinarian forbearance toward a divinity that had *"foreordained whatsoever comes in to pass"* and lengthy procedures for admission collapsed before claims of "answered . . . prayer" and the immediate presence of the "spirit" within, "flow[ing] like many waters." Calvinist exclusiveness was no match for "those who had laboured and travailed upon the covenant of promise, and felt the living zeal of eternal love." Ministers seeking to reach the populace "could not dare preach that salvation was restricted to a certain *definite number*." Congregants trusted their experience of witnessing whole communities reborn: "God was no respecter of persons—willeth the salvation of all souls—has opened a door of salvation, through Christ, for all—will have invited all to enter." Original sin was rejected, for enthusiasts "could not, dare . . . insinuate that any being which God had made, was, by the Creator, laid under the dire necessity, of being damned forever." The aspiration to fundamental self-transformation, where "every thing" might be "new" and without "relation to the old bed of sand upon which they had been building" from an "old foundation," became "like a dead fly in the ointment of . . . the Calvinist."[48] Now in Joseph Haroutunian's view "a cultural anachronism," "all creeds, confessions, forms of worship, and rules of government . . . especially the distinguishing doctrines of Calvin" were rejected as a "soul stupifying creed" to be "laid aside," as William Ellery Channing believed, "sinking to rise no more" and "giving place to better views."[49]

As the new view of human ability within agency limits consolidated beginning in the 1830s, the two primary forms of subsequent opposition regarding the limits of human efficacy, what Cross has called the right and left paths, "one fundamentalist and the other modernist," emerged.[50] Traditional denominations tried in the 1820s to accommodate the shifts with the "New School" of New England theology under the leadership of Nathaniel Taylor, Lyman Beecher, and the younger Charles Finney. Taylor developed a modified Calvinism that placed the responsibility for achieving God's grace upon the will of the individual, but within a system of traditional theology. Following Methodist successes, proponents were driven to popular revivalist voluntarism and theological trimming. A journalist for the *Christian Advocate and Journal* wrote in 1831 that "'the good old doctrines of Methodism' were being 'proclaimed zealously by Presbyterians and Baptists.' Instead of 'talking in the dry old style, about "waiting God's own good time . . ."' they now insisted that 'christ tasted death for *every* man,' 'All may come,' 'If you are damned it is your own fault,' and 'All things are *now* ready.'"[51] While Congregationals effectively liberalized, though without popular success, and redirected their efforts to moral reform, these shifts produced schisms elsewhere. The "Old School" Presbyterians and rural and southern Baptists rejected the trend toward human voluntarism, bolstering the claim of human limitation with a fundamentalist adherence to Scripture, a renewed affirmation of predestination, and a retreat from humanly organized political reform, economic market initiative, and even religious educational and missionary activity—in a word, a reaction "against 'human effort.'"[52]

One antebellum outcome of this reaction was apocalyptic offshoots such as the Millerite millenarian movement which aroused the Northeast about God's advent to come in 1844. Heated to a fever pitch in the enthusiasm of the age, this conservative millennialism was pushed into a scenario of instantaneous godly intervention and fulfillment to outflank mainstream optimism. Entirely bypassing the gradual results of human effort, these movements embodied what Cross has called "an escapist's short cut to the millennium, looking to supernatural forces for miraculous change."

William Miller was in the beginning . . . entirely unsympathetic toward the enthusiastic crusades of the twenties and thirties. He thought "these fire-skulled, vissionary [*sic*], fanatical, treasonable, suicidal, demoralizing, hot headed set of *abolitionists*, are worse if possible than anti-Masonry—and if they go on this way they will set the world on fire before the time." He disliked the "Birchard stile" evangelism. "Negro's, drunkards and brothels, together with Magazines, Newspapers and tracts" were distracting the ministry. If they had "their Bibles and *concordance*, with a common English education . . . they would feed more sheep . . . tell more truth and learn more their dependence on God." . . . [In the movement], [t]he breaking and scattering of churches; reluctance to imbibe sound doctrine; the spread of seducing beliefs like Shakerism, Catholicism and free thought; false prophets and teachers; and the "scattering of holy people:—such occurrences received increased attention. . . . [T]hey found the world beyond reason, legislatures corrupt, and infidelity, idolatry, Romanism, sectarianism, seduction, fraud . . . all waxing stronger. . . . Church and state alike had filled "the cup of iniquity" and were "now fitted for destruction."[53]

While this resistance retained a proto-agency mixture of individual responsibility and personal transformation within God's overarching control over individual fate, the spread of an increasingly voluntarist culture and religiosity and the collapse of the millenarian campaign were the Millerites' undoing. The surfacing of their underlying worldly pessimism led to sectarian withdrawal and to a sense of the impending Civil War as a final divine judgment on human progress.

Finney's response to the Millerites that "the world is not growing worse but better" reflected the significant psychocultural divide: the "free grace and popular democracy suited to the rising lower-middle class optimistic about achieving appreciable worldly success and more fully imbued with middle-class outlook" opposing an "extreme predestinarianism with revivalist assurance" in which "culture, wealth, and worldly honors were deemed secondary" for those "without such expectations of material achievement."[54] The latter were in turn resentful of "the Finneyites' wealth, their education, their aptitude for organization, and their self-assured role as the cultural vanguard of market society and moral reform," in effect, their worldly activism.[55]

As the revival expanded, a radical opposition emerged in the form of an extreme perfectionism with a vision of individual empowerment and liberation from worldly authority. Embracing the optimistic dynamic of spiritual transformation even as revivalism waned, this offshoot, to be considered later, was a major precipitant of the mainstream turn from the dangers of religious enthusiasm. This perfectionist dynamic, by forcing the hand of the new religious mainstream, became a defining moment in the formation of

American culture. Through this confrontation the mainstream awoke to the dangers of a populace remaining in a constant state of religious, even millennial, expectation, deferring all worldly matters. Religious sector energies had to be refocused and the new synthesis consolidated and turned to practical tasks of individual—and community—realization in a world now recast according to agency principles.

The mainstream movement, which had begun its own perfectionist revision against the lingering Calvinism of eastern Protestant orthodoxy, now found itself retreating in response to its own radical wings: "For the radicalism of the reform movements and the heresy of perfectionism turned moderates into conservatives and prepared a substantial portion of each major denomination for a contest to determine . . . orthodoxy." Ever bolder claims of radical self-authorization crystallized for the party of agency its ultimate grounding in divine sovereignty and community practices and its consolidation of institutional controls and behavioral limits on individual and worldly change. The declining "faith in the goodness and automatic accomplishments of the regenerate man and more faith in measures calculated to make men behave aright" resulted in an increasing focus, as we shall see, on spiritual stability, regularization, predictability, and gradualism.[56] Thus the national revival, which succeeded in transforming the American character and with the Civil War triumph of agency institutions, the nation itself, would give way later in the century to the stabilization of that new synthesis. The seeds of the later Protestant turn toward civil religion and a liberal polity lay in its success in this period in securing a clear progressive center, surmounting the conservative rejection of agency as an unwarranted release from God's governance over a sinful world and repelling in turn the radical perfectionist impetus.

To Make a Nation of Agents

The project of creating a common social character for the nation and complementary institutions required less the redirection of a revolutionary liberal society toward Protestant values than the continued expansion of the sectarian dynamic to a receptive Protestant nation. At the same time, that liberty now presumed as a cultural birthright had to be conceptually and organizationally reconciled with the options provided to individuals within a community of believers. The conceptual task was quickly accomplished in the popular mind as the revolutionary discourse of Jeffersonian individualism and Jacksonian populism was folded within the tradition of "Gospel liberty," rendered "official" though in the late-century transformation of liberal ideology into the agency discourse. In villages, towns, and cities alike, the political call to universal empowerment and individualism was redirected by the people to the desire for spiritual sanctification and religious membership. John Leland, the "Jeffersonian Itinerant," defended the "democratical genius" of "congregational" autonomy, each being "a complete republic of itself," against all forms of political and social authority. The radical Methodist minister Lorenzo Dow supported the right to "think, and judge, and act" individually "in the matters of religion, opinion, and private judgment" as incontestable since "all men are 'BORN EQUAL,' and endowed with unalienable RIGHTS by their CREATOR, in the blessings of life, liberty, and the pursuit of happiness."[57]

Not only religious radicals like Elias Smith conjoined the "traditional Christian concept" of "liberty from sin gained through faith in Christ as Savior" to "political and personal liberty derived from the Revolution and enshrined in the Declaration of Independence and the Federal Constitution."[58] The great movements of Methodism, Baptism, and other populist sects drew, in the words of the Methodist minister C. C. Goss, from "the immortal Declaration" to support the vision that "as his sun shines on all, as Christ died for all, and as heaven is free to all, so the Church on earth should be the living exemplification of God's universal love."[59] Rural Jacksonians rose on the platform of "Christian and egalitarian ideals"; townspeople were told that "as Jehovah . . . broke the chains and secured the liberty of his ancient people," so he precipitated "the establishment of our Independence."[60] Urban residents heard that "the cause of liberty was the cause of God" and "the triumph of liberty as realized in America would accompany the coming kingdom."[61] Movements of common people, workers and artisans, women and blacks, "subsumed" their ideals within the "language of Christianity" to "realize . . . the 'good time coming,'" the freedom and equality of the Declaration becoming the "light which nature's God has revealed to us" as "gifts" to be "dispensed to all mankind." For the religious radical Alexander Campbell, the Revolution, beginning a new age of "political regeneration," heralded a corresponding time of "ecclesiastical renovation."[62]

The constitution of this radical Protestant experiment, however, as populist leaders understood from the outset, was not simply a matter of theoretical elision. The very inclusion of the common people within the new religious settlement itself represented the triumph of revolutionary ideals and, of necessity, shattered proto-agency controls. The more serious problem was organizational—how to bring the new religious consciousness to this populace disaffected from traditional elitism but unsure of both its prerogatives and its capacity to provide institutional alternatives. To a nation yearning for new structure, the religious mobilization brought a new sense of personal identity and the direction to forge responsive institutions. Religious leaders—ministers, revivalists, circuit riders, believers—became its midwives. They sensed the desire for more consistent behaviors, values, and roles, and understood the unique part religion could play. They also realized that in an individualist culture their message had to be brought to every individual in the land, and organized campaigns to reach them over and over, to work upon them unrelentingly, by encouraging, imploring, demanding, accusing, threatening, welcoming, marginalizing, until very many of them took heed and "turned themselves" toward the new dispensation.

The awesome task of quickly transforming both "a raw and uncouth frontier society" and heterogeneous urban centers into "orderly and well-regulated communities" involved the full mobilization of a nation. It required a vast array of denominational institutions working independently and through interdenominational organizations to "evangelize the world" and, above all, through an increasingly systematic revival process that blanketed the land.[63] With little preexisting structure, they quickly produced missionary ministers and circuit preachers to reach far-flung communities, then in turn missionary districts, congregations, Sunday schools, Bible classes, maternal societies, primary schools, grammar schools, academies, colleges and universities, education societies and seminaries for ministerial training, and religious societies. They printed and distributed many millions of Bibles, spelling books, primers, catechisms, maps, and reference books for the whole country, and published newspapers, magazines, pamphlets, and works of moral and religious teachings and advice by the hundreds to distribute to parents, children, prisoners, and the community generally. Church employees and volunteers went systematically door-to-door from urban centers to the deepest frontiers as often as once a month selling or giving away religious materials and encouraging individuals into the fold. "Society mad" Americans set up organizations for communities to deal with temperance, sabbatarianism, indigence, women, vice, the aged, and the disabled.[64] While some campaigns were coordinated by umbrella organizations such as the American Home Missionary Society and the American Bible Society, equally powerful were the denominational organizations which sought to win over these vast new populations for themselves. The result was a feverish competition among denominations to gain converts and found churches, if necessary pulling from other denominations, with continual new entrants in the field, producing unceasing innovation, democratization, and market pressure in organization, societal outreach, community participation, preaching, and service.

For all the organizational developments, the key within the new cultural order was winning individual conviction. The genius of revivalist Protestantism was its recognition that behind the obsession with freedom lay the vulnerability from intense anxieties over boundarylessness and normlessness, confusion over place and role, fear of self and others, a longing for a certitude that only authoritative structures and ends could provide. Freed citizens could not acknowledge that there was "everywhere a search for community," but they could be led to accept an authority that they willingly chose.[65] Integration thus required effective techniques that accepted their individual power to decide these matters for themselves. While some have explained the profound grip of religious institutions and religious authority as a matter primarily of institutional strategizing and efforts at social control, the demand for a new "way to conceptualize . . . both social control and personal identity" must "take account," in Howe's understanding, of "political *psychology*."[66]

Although the willingness to adapt could of course be sharpened by increasing institutional pressures, this view denies the real need for spiritual and societal integration. Far from leading compliant citizens into their arms, the religious institutions were constantly adjusting their religious practice and theological values, racing to keep pace in response to popular congregational initiatives and demands for greater individual choice. This populist dynamic drove organized religion, despite strong resistance by the leadership, toward an American theology and religion of the individual will and ultimately to an embrace of spiritual perfection and worldly success. And at the center of "one of the greatest moral achievements of the past century," designated by a God who "raises up systems, as well as men," was the Methodist contribution of revivals, from which "its life-power has been drawn."[67] In revivals, as sectarian Protestantism drew upon the dynamic of reversal, individuals were transformed—and transformed themselves—into community members, common people became full citizens, freedom emerged as societally bounded voluntarism.

The Revival: A Model of Institutional Voluntarism

The greatest and most powerful of all the innovations stemming from the fervid quest for souls, at once symbolic of the religious frenzy of this age and its most extreme expression, was the religious revival, expounded on, defended, explained, and attacked at great length throughout the period. Finney, the greatest revivalist and model for the age who drew upon the emerging innovations in popular outreach, argued that nearly "all the religion in the world has been produced by revivals," which were in his time the "only possible" means to "restore religion," to break "the power of the world and of sin" and provide "a new foretaste of heaven, and new desires after union with God."[68] William Sprague in his book on revivals called them the great manifestation of the age, incomparable "evidence that *there* has been the agency of the Spirit of God" during which "far the greater number of those who are turned from darkness to light . . . experience this change."[69] Robert Baird called them "the greatest and most desirable blessings that can be bestowed upon the church," "indispensable to all successful Christian effort," approved of by all "evangelical Christians throughout our country."[70]

The experience of revival was to enter the very heart of a blazing fire:

> Let any church, in its ordinary state of feeling, hear that the Holy Spirit is poured out in a neighboring town, let some of its members visit the spot, and bring back a report of what is passing there; that the people are animated with all the zeal of their first love, fervent in prayers and labors for the salvation of sinners, full of joy and hope; let them tell of the crowded assemblies, the deathlike stillness, the solemnity and awe depicted on every countenance; of some who but a few days before were thoughtless and even abandoned to sin, now bowed down under a sense of guilt, and of others rejoicing in the hope of having found the Saviour, and reconciliation through His blood; let it appear that there is nothing . . . but the natural and appropriate effect of *Divine truth* applied to the conscience by the Spirit of God; and what is there that can appeal more strongly to all the sensibilities of a Christian heart?[71]

The quintessential democratic form in a society without rigid social hierarchies, the revival became the inclusive communal undertaking: "A distinction of names was laid aside, and it was no matter what any one had been called before, if now he stood in the present light, and felt his heart glow with love to the souls of men; he was welcome to sing, pray, or call sinners to repentance. Neither was there any distinction as to age, sex, color, or any thing of a temporary nature: old and young, male and female, black and white had equal privilege to minister the light which they received, in whatever way the spirit directed."[72]

The religious innovators realized the depths of spiritual suffering and confusion, for as "there prevails a spirit of deep religious anxiety . . . many are just forming the purpose to set their faces toward heaven, and . . . multitudes are heard simultaneously requiring what they shall do to be saved." Horace Bushnell spoke of our religious nature as "an orphan, out in the broad world alone . . . longing and hungering" for a relationship with God though "alienated" within "solitary worlds of vacancy and cold." The old way only made matters worse, as it cast the individual "writhing under the conviction of sin, crushed by a sense of his utterly helpless condition in himself considered, tempted, under repeated failure," and confused, leaving traditional believers with "their minds so wandering . . . so entirely in the dark . . . that most of the time they give to contemplation is wasted in chaotic thought."[73] Finney argued that "revivals do not, and cannot prevail" so long as the "crippling errors" of traditional belief "paralyze the influence of a good portion of the church."[74]

Unable to sustain flight, people were turning toward the church. Sprague reviewed "the history of our American church," noting that "within the last half century a wonderful change has taken place in the order of God's providence towards it" as communities were aroused: "The young man, and the old man, and the middle aged man; the exemplary and orthodox moralist, the haughty pharisees, the downright infidel, the profane scoffer; the dissipated sensualist, may sometimes all be seen collected with the same spirit in their hearts—the spirit of deep anxiety. . . . Those who once would have disdained . . . the least concern for their salvation, hesitate not to ask and receive instruction. . . . All the shame which they once felt on this subject they have given to the winds."[75] Spreading religious enthusiasm made communities "easy targets" for revival, and for the new certitude of place, identity, consequences, and direction within a universe certain, legible, and ordered because—and who was to doubt this?—it was under "the moral government of God."[76]

At the same time, revivals were a potentially serious intrusion on and even a threat to established religious institutions in the community. Some like Baird were critical of their "subversive" tendency, and others like Bushnell and Orville Dewey attacked the inevitably transient religiosity and unrealistic expectations produced by revivalist stimulations.[77] But many including Finney and the successful Methodists felt that in "most churches there are probably more or less hypocrites," including ministers, in their "carnal slumbers," who needed continual awakening by such unprecedented methods.[78] If ever more universally embraced, anticipating the future liberal-Protestant synthesis, the church would perhaps not have to utilize such extreme measures to tame the wayward and recalcitrant adult spirit: "As the millennium advances, it is probable that these periodic excitements will be unknown. Then the church will be enlightened, and the counteracting causes removed, and the entire church will be in a state of habitual and steady obedience to God." But in the current "state of the world," with "so little *principle* in the church, so little firmness and stability of purpose . . . so little knowledge, and . . . principles . . . so weak," the work of founding and disciplining a new society, establishing a stable character and societal behavior, required more dramatic means.[79]

The profound challenge for religious institutions was to "get the public ear" and "the attention, of men to the gospel of Christ," by "meet[ing] the character and wants of the age" so that "character" is "changed." Old ways were failing; "such ministers as our fathers would have been glad to hear, now cannot be heard, cannot get a settlement, nor collect an audience." More adaptive groups like the Methodists "have gathered congregations" and "will run away from us," requiring major institutional shifts: "It is impossible for God himself to bring about reformation but by new measures. . . . When he has found that a certain mode has lost its influence by having become a form, he brings up some new measure, which will BREAK IN upon their lazy habits and WAKE UP a slumbering church. And great good has resulted."[80] While Finney put the initiative with God and the church, the test of successful innovation driving the Methodists and all who followed, the "only way of determining," was "results" or popular effectiveness.[81] Given the competitive, client-driven, often decentralized state of denominational activity in a society of generally localized institutions, the process of institutional integration had to reflect popular expectations: Americans to an unprecedented degree were finding, or creating, the religions they wished for.[82] As individuals seeking a place in this new community rushed forward, the secret would be less to get them in than to frame a revival experience that could keep them.

The Fulcrum of Individual Conviction

Underlying this movement's new techniques of community outreach and informal pressure was its focus on the individual. Institutions were to arise from individual commitments as facilitators of personal agendas. Prior beliefs were no barrier, as one revival leader described in 1808: "As to worship, they allowed each one to worship God agreeably to their own feelings, whatever impressions or consciousness of duty they were under; believing the true wisdom, which 'lives through all life,' to be a safer guide than human forms, which can only affect the outer man: and hence, so wide a door was opened, and such a variety of exercises were exhibited at their public meetings."[83] Describing in evocative terms the benefits of inclusion and the costs of refusal, preachers evoked the vivid picture of a people marching together to a millennium just ahead. Within the soul raged the cosmic battle to restore the light of heaven from the reign of darkness, affirming its central role in an unfolding transcendent narrative bringing order and clarity to a world in disarray.

Offering a cultural mirror which reflected the people's newfound freedom and self-reliance, their newly experienced achievements, capacities, and prospects, revivals laid before each individual the decision over one's personal fate: "The law of God is a true standard by which to try our character. . . . It is nothing less than a positive command that we should ascertain our own true character, and settle the question definitely for ourselves, whether we are saints or sinners, heirs of heaven or heirs of hell."[84] To the continuing amazement of traditionalists with their "incessant cry of 'new Lights,' 'New Divinity,' 'New Measures,'" and "Innovation,"[85] the continually expanding capacity for effective and constructive worldly action catalyzed nothing less than a theological transformation. Its culmination was the supreme and unprecedented power to decisively shape one's own character.

The theological watershed crossed by this new message, evident in the title of Finney's sermon "Sinners Bound to Change Their Own Hearts" in an 1836 book *Sermons on Important Subjects,* was an explicit assertion of human ability:

> Does God . . . require us to make ourselves a new heart, on pain of eternal death, when at the same time he knows we have no power to obey? . . . All holiness, in God, angels, or men, must be *voluntary,* or it is not holiness . . . voluntary obedience to the principles of eternal righteousness. The neces-

sary adaptation of the outward motive to the mind, and of the mind to the motive, lies in the powers of moral agency, which every human being possesses. He has understanding to perceive and weigh; he has conscience to decide upon the nature of moral opposites; he has the power and liberty of choice.

Those affirming radical voluntarism rejected any locus for sin or conversion outside the will, as in the "constitution," for that would "destroy personal identity" and the "powers of moral agency."[86]

All depended on how individuals "are disposed to use, and actually do employ, their moral and physical powers," on "that abiding preference of our minds" "over which we have control," by which we determine "the supreme object of our pursuit . . . the choice of an *end*." Sin, dependent given universal capacity on state of mind alone, is to be "able" but "unwilling," for the sinner's "preference for sin is the" individual's "own voluntary act." Regardless of aid or encouragement by the Holy Spirit, "cannot" is merely "will not."[87] David Reynolds, studying the religious literature of the young republic, points out that protagonists were increasingly being offered moral and allegorical options. As in the aptly titled story "The Choice of Abdala" (1796), the author's new "confidence in an innate ability to choose between right and wrong" signified "a repudiation of orthodoxy's firm stand on God's ineffability and man's incapability."[88] The popular hymn of the period "The Freedom of the Human Will" put it best: "Know then that every soul is free / To choose his life and what he'll be / For this eternal truth has giv'n / That God will force no man to heav'n."[89]

The more establishment denominations, while resisting complete theological voluntarism, were led in practice by the denominational competition for successful revivals and conversions, toward the decisive role for the participant's will, as "revivalism and Arminianism went hand in hand." The leading Methodist minister Peter Cartwright observed how Presbyterian ministers "in this revival . . . almost to a man, gave up . . . high Calvinism" to "preach Methodist doctrine."[90] Relying more heavily on the active spirit of God, Methodists, Lutherans, Freewill Baptists, some Presbyterians, Congregationalists, Disciples of Christ, and others incorporated "Arminian doctrines of free will, free grace, and unlimited hope for the conversion of all men."[91] The result was a broad cultural movement in which the practices of individual members, though framed as the difference in "the meanings of the formulas" between ability and the role of the "Holy Spirit," was never "as divergent as the words."[92] Methodists argued strenuously that "the moral power of choice" by free will was "the great point of division between Arminianism and Calvinism," which had "for a century been embodied in Wesleyan theology," and the great source of their "strength in demolishing Calvinism, antinomianism, and sin."[93] Finney with his Congregational teachers had in fact developed the doctrine of "natural ability" from the Methodist view of "a free salvation to all mankind" who come "as a free agent to Christ."[94]

Revivals succeeded by putting the choice to the individual directly and sharply: "God is renewing the hearts of many others, why may He not renew mine?"[95] The goal of the experience, of which Finney was master, was to make the power of self-determination palpable: to bring each individual to the point of choice and to make a successful self-transformation available to every individual who had chosen. Each sermon built toward a challenge: "What is your character, and what has been your conduct? God will soon call you to give an account. . . . Are you ready to have your accounts examined, your conduct scrutinized, and your life weighed in the balance of the sanctuary? . . . If not, repent, *repent now* . . . To-night it will be told in hell, and told in heaven, and echoed from the ends of the universe, what you decide to do."[96]

Those stressing the Holy Spirit's influence on the individual will also proclaimed the efficacy of individual choice. Baird spoke of the revivalist fervor sweeping communities:

> Nothing is more calculated to fill the hearts of Christians with courage, and expectation, and hope than the feeling that God is in the midst of them with the peculiar dispensation of His grace. . . . "God is *here* with the effusions of His Spirit!" Who does not feel the thrill of joy, of hope, of confidence, which pervades the heart of every spiritually-minded Christian? What can be more suited to . . . bring the whole Church to harmonious action, to fervent prayers, and strenuous effort? Where the confidence thus inspired has been high . . . resting on the mighty power of the Spirit and the efficacy of Divine truth, when has God ever failed to bestow a signal blessing?[97]

Methodism, in particular, proclaiming the coming of the Holy Spirit, experienced camp meetings as great visitations of the "awakening and converting power" of the "immediate superintending agency of the Divine Spirit of God."[98] Methodists preached that "the divine grace or energy of the Holy Ghost begins and perfects every thing that can be called good in man, and consequently, all good works are to be attributed to God alone." Yet "this grace," which was universally available, "does not force men to act against their inclinations, but may be resisted and rendered ineffectual by [the] perverse will of the impenitent sinner."[99] Thus were conversions described as an infusion by the Holy Spirit and the love of God: "God was with us, owned his word in power. . . . [S]o powerful was the work of God on the hearts of sinners and saints that some were crying aloud for mercy, and other[s] shouting for joy. . . . My own soul overflowed with the love of God incessantly day and night."[100] Perfectionist Methodists simply extended the role of the Spirit to providing a "perpetual . . . uninterrupted influence of the love of Christ" with its "highest possible efficacy over the heart."[101]

That individuals' entry into the Kingdom of God hung by their own will, "suspended upon your own choice," or even more spiritually empowering (if less precisely voluntarist) by their will aided by intense effusions of the divine spirit, was an awesome assertion of human potential. What was not now possible? Posed this way, the voluntarist reformulation of American religion became the defining moment for American Protestantism, and for the future of American culture. For in the elimination of all supervening restraints, all external situational and institutional barriers, and all cosmic-theological objections at the moment of decision, before the redeemable promise secured in the very enunciation and for some the facilitation of God's offer, individuals came to regard themselves as the independent, dispositive force regarding their spiritual destinies and ultimately "the salvation of the whole world."[102]

The Religion of the Reversal

The consuming task of the revivalists as institution builders was to generate not only personal sanctification but permanent institutional integration as well out of the individual's voluntarism. As they discovered and built upon the powerful wish for inclusion that the people were manifesting through their participation, they located the core dynamic: that every increase in the encouragement of unsupported voluntarism in the name of freedom sharply increased its burden and made reversal into the arms of responsive institutions that much more likely. The moment of reversal was recognized as the critical point in the transformative process: "The will is, in a sense, enslaved by the carnal and worldly desires. Hence it is necessary to awaken men to a sense of guilt and danger, and thus produce an excitement of *counter-feeling* and desire which will break the power of carnal and worldly desire and leave the will free to obey God."[103] Given this dynamic, moreover, every subsequent act of integration—arising from voluntarism—could be characterized as the *fulfillment of freedom*.

To a remarkable extent, the revivalists grasped the process. To expand their movement, they explained quite graphically the techniques for mobilizing the individual will. Experiential logic dictated to them that the free embrace of authority would come more decisively through sharpening the burden of freedom with its unmanageable responsibilities. They strategized how to prolong and heighten the sense of disconnection until its untenable internal tensions produced incorporation without any cloud of external coercion or internal resistance. Finney, like Sprague and others, carefully distinguished possible converts by the degrees of their religious anxiety, as careless or awakened or convicted sinners, and laid out distinctive techniques of approach and argument to win the souls of each. They constructed in effect a ladder of preparation delineating the process of bringing the will to the moment of decision and reshaping its priorities into a new self. At each stage lay indecisions and doubts which had to be addressed, and greater resistance to being told that one's refusal constituted a personal failure. While affirming the desire for sanctification and entry into the religious community, the strategy was not to ameliorate the anxiety attending resistance, but contrarily to exacerbate and sharpen the sense of failure before the individual's weakening and ever more desperate willfulness. In this way the crisis prompting reversal was made the very center of the sinner's agony and the means for the final embrace of God's preeminence.

This crisis became the center of the new agency self because it was structured to force the individual to turn back from both comforts of servitude and illusions of autonomy. It was precipitated by hammering at the two polar truths of the new Protestant: one's absolute choice, here and now, and God's absolute sovereignty. Every individual must be pushed to realize that he or she is "possessed of all the powers of moral agency, *capable* of turning to God, and *on this account,* and no other, inexcusable for not doing so." Sin was no longer either original or perpetual but simply the present failure to acknowledge God's authorship and one's own agency. The minister was urged to stress sharply to each that "the actual turning, exchange, is the sinner's own act,"[104] while at the same time "bear[ing] down on . . . the nature and extent of the Divine law, and . . . of entire submission to God," to press these together, repeatedly, without letting up: "Do not turn off upon any thing else." Do not fear unsettling the listener: "Do not fear to press that, for fear of driving him to distraction." Do not fear repetition: "Turn an important point over and over . . . till even the children understand it perfectly."[105]

The crisis must be sharpened: "In dealing with a convicted sinner, be sure to drive him away from every refuge, and not leave him an inch of ground to stand on." Individuals seeking a new character must "first be persuaded of its absolute *necessity* . . . that they are on the brink of ruin . . . alienated from God . . . as a starving man feels the necessity of immediately applying to the search for food."[106] Baird described the revival process as forcing individuals to "look at their condition and ponder it deeply" in order to "feel the extremity of their wretchedness and guilt." Continually press the gap, he instructed, between their free will and their divine commitment, because individuals in their weakness cannot withstand that disparity and the terror of misusing their freedom: "Place [the individual] under pressure of both these doctrines," of freedom and dependence, and "the necessity of action on his part in coming to God, the weighty obligations which urge him to do it, the crushing sense of guilt every moment he delays, the momentous interests . . . the fearful doom."[107] The crisis under proper handling will grow:

> And do not be too anxious at once to abate this feeling. The abasement of will; for no one can feel guilt too strongly, nor abhor sin too deeply. The time will come, when he will learn to follow the direction of the Apostle, and think of himself soberly, as he ought to think! But at this first fair inspection of the deformities of his character it is not to be expected that he should make his estimate with perfect sobriety. Only let every thing be done to guide, and soothe, and encourage him, and nothing to exasperate his self-condemnation, or drive him to insanity or despair.[108]

In a plain, practical, and common style, the minister must reach into the soul of every congregant and revival participant, making them experience this deeply and personally, uprooting every hiding place, defeating every excuse, until the immediacy of spiritual crisis is provoked.

On the bubble, before God and the world, with the awesome responsibility for their destiny in their own hands, individuals will seek to be relieved. They will want to claim inability, that they cannot change. They will struggle—by giving up freedom or distancing themselves from God—to reject one of the poles of the authoritative relation. Do not let them. Call it a slander to God, an act of rebellion, a lie against the God who makes us free. *It is no longer possible not to be free.* Take up each again, one at a time; work through their objections, their fears, their resistances, their mistaken ideas. Learn every form of false comfort, "the endless fooleries and falsehoods" to relieve their distress; resist applying any palliative, alternative, excuse, weakness, or encouragement at the cost of their souls: "Never tell a sinner any thing, or give him any direction, that will lead him to stop short, or that does not include absolute submission to God."[109] Do not even convey that they are making progress, for the gap between sin and obedience is always infinite, and the will often most desperate and recalcitrant when submission is closest.

The revivalists catalogued endless public evasions: "Sinners often cling with a death grasp to their false dependencies. . . . They had rather make any sacrifice, go to any expense, or endure any suffering, than just throw themselves as guilty and lost rebels upon Christ alone for salvation."[110] They will want to place other matters before religion. Get them alone, arrange an appointment when they are more "tender" or vulnerable, acknowledge their sins and their rebellion, and tell them that God's absolute dominion will not and cannot be avoided. Above all, do not let them off, do not reduce the tension, do not "*make any compromise* with them on any point where they have a difficulty." In short, "Do not yield an inch," for "what is all his distress but rebellion itself?"[111] The agony is justified; it is the path to a willing self-reversal into God's embrace. The minister must recognize each excuse, confront the individual with it, and insistently push the one unavoidable outcome: free submission to God as agent.

It was a remarkable endgame of spiritual extremis:

> To do this often requires nerve. I have often . . . found myself surrounded by anxious sinners, in such distress, as to make every nerve tremble, some overcome with emotion and lying on the floor, some applying camphor to prevent them fainting, others shrieking out as if they were just going to hell. Now, suppose anyone should give false comfort in such a case as this. Suppose he had not nerve enough to bring them right up to the point of infinite and absolute submission. How unfit is such a man to be trusted in a case like this. . . . Better suppress your false sympathy, and let the naked truth cleave them asunder, joints and marrow.[112]

Individuals were hopelessly caught between "salvation or damnation . . . absolutely suspended upon [their] own choice." There was "no chance for them to remain at ease."[113] Driven by the whole weight of the revival experience, all avenues of escape cut off, the resolution was inevitable: "Now the object of instructing an anxious sinner should be to lead him by the shortest possible way . . . by the shortest rout, to this practical conclusion, that there is, in fact, no other way in which he can be relieved and saved." Over and again, individuals must be exhorted to "come forth promptly": "Don't wait for feeling, DO IT." This process "calls men to instant decision,"[114] to "repent *now*. . . . It gives not the sinner a moment's time to wait; it presses upon him with all the weight of Jehovah's authority." For "the floor" underneath is "just ready to give way," the "roof" is "beginning to give way, and ready to fall in upon you. . . . Your little ones . . . are shrieking. . . . You see no way of escape."[115] The pressure "of *obligation* to immediate right action" was irresistible: "*Press him down*, and tell him he must submit to God, and generally he will." They *"will be compelled to yield"*; for "they can not stand before it."[116]

The Gate of Voluntary Surrender

This moment of decision was understood as the willing constitution of a new relation to authority and of one's role in a universe of authoritative ends. With remarkable acuity, Baird identified this unique synthesis, "the union of these two doctrines of *activity* and *dependence*," calling it "the point to which all my observations are directed." Though these were "so commonly felt to be subversive of each other," the key to revivalism was

> the bringing of both to bear with undiminished force on the minds of the impenitent. Establish just one of these doctrines to the exclusion or weakening of the other, and just to the same extent is the Gospel robbed of its power. Inculcate dependence without pressing to the act of instantly giving up the heart to Christ, and the sinner sits down quietly to "wait God's time." Urge him to duty on the grounds of his possessing all the requisite power, while . . . you do away with his dependence, and his reluctant heart will lead him to take his *own* time.[117]

Revivals became the crucible for Protestant character and community formation by resolving the deepest psychosocial tensions between authority and self-direction, coercion and voluntarism, agency and selfhood: "Some persons think of obedience as if it . . . could be nothing else, than servitude. And it must be admitted, that *constrained* obedience is so . . . who obeys by compulsion, and not freely. . . . On the contrary, true obedience . . . which flows out like the gushing of water, may be said . . . to possess not only the nature, but the very essence of freedom."[118] Through the process an individualism emerged by which servitude was impossible, followed by a reconciliation with authority which precluded self-authorization.

The culminating step was thus often referred to—by using the two polar components of agency—as a "free surrender" or "voluntary surrender," a freely given identification and subordination.[119] This duality was captured in the very depiction of the act. On the one hand, potential converts needed to know that the barriers to salvation were "as low as they possibly can be,"[120] and the way is accessible to all who inquire: "The gate of heaven stands open, and . . . beckons you to come. . . . The spirit and the bride say Come, let him that heareth say Come. . . . God is clear, angels are clear. To your own master you stand or fall; mercy waits, the Spirit strives; Jesus stands at the door."[121] The people must believe regardless of their preexisting situation that "all creeds, confessions, forms of worship, and rules of government invented by man, ought to be laid aside . . . [and] so wide a gate . . . opened."[122]

On the other hand, out of a "free choice" was to come at the same time a decision bound by the most unrelenting and irresistible necessity and authority: "Cherish therefore the conviction of this necessity." This was not a resolution one could stumble on by accident, nor a doorway so low and so wide one could merely happen across: *"Not only are the conditions of salvation necessary in their own nature"* but furthermore one must *"comply with them."*[123] Faced with two paths for the soul, one must be chosen. The Methodist Reverend W. H. Poole saw it clearly in a dream:

> Open to every eye was a hall, or gallery of judgments, through which every one must pass on his way to his reward. On the right, and above, this hall or gallery was connected with the celestial home or heavenly country, while on the left and beneath it was connected with darkness and woe. . . .
> [T]hose of pure motive and holy life went over . . . with a buoyant step and a bounding heart, as if gravitation had lost its power over them; while the disobedient and unholy disappeared quickly in the darkness below.[124]

The literature of the period often posed the choice for the traveler or seeker: an apparently more accessible path along the landscape which is in reality fraught with temptation and spiritual failings; and the seemingly more arduous journey climbing up a mountainside in wild natural settings, flying into space, ascending by a "visionary ladder," all symbolizing spiritual transformation.[125] The forces of gravity and nature pull the will and the heart down;

there were no free rides, no accidental ascensions. These forces had to be transcended by choosing the ascendant path in one's nature.

It is important not to treat this transition from hindsight simply as a loss or retreat. Weighing in the balance formless independence against voluntary inclusion, idyllic illusions versus rootedness in an underlying Protestant universe, newly liberated Americans found that release from the burden of freedom in the great and empowering offer to be God's earthly actors was not coercive or diminishing but a step upward, hardly to be refused. Believers must yield *"obedience of heart to God"* and *"to God's authority"* only that they might be "better," "stronger and stronger."[126] Reverend Hill testified that the moment of yielding to God "does not destroy *individuality"* but is an experience of holiness and *"an endowment of power."* Reverend Neff experienced "a power which I never felt before," which was at the same time "a conviction of duty." Henry Ware referred to the "yoke" and "burden" as "heaven . . . already begun."[127] William Boardman defined the nature of the journey toward sanctification as one which will "accumulate power as it progresses from stage to stage" by "perfecting obedience in love."[128]

In a "few moments" one could be "joyful in God," voluntarily entering the divine order as part of the divine plan, overcoming isolation and rolelessness to be a moral actor in a moral universe, operating "like the gravitational motion of bodies" through "the force of moral governance" in "the orbit of his obedience."[129] The revivalists contrasted failure and success, the confusions of sin with the clarity of conversion, the chaos of "riot and drink" versus "the perfection of Christian sobriety," the "waverings and flickerings, and gleamings forth of the struggling mind" against "the great truths of revelation."[130] Presbyterian Barton W. Stone recognized this growth process: "We order upon the sinner to believe *now*, and receive salvation . . . that no previous qualification was required, or necessary in order to believe in Jesus, and come to him. . . . When we began first to preach these things, the people appeared as just awakened from the sleep of ages—they seemed to see for the first time that they were responsible beings."[131]

This powerful juxtaposition of unlimited access and stringent conditionality, contrasted with the apparently easy path of the unstructured idyll leading to a spiritual dead end, was best captured in a metaphor of Bushnell's: "There is a way for dissolving any and all doubts,—a way that opens at a very small gate, but widens wonderfully after you pass."[132] For individuals to walk through this gate, they had to trust the revivalists' vision of ascension to a new self and society. They needed to be shown "the path of the just, growing brighter and brighter to the perfect day," and made to "SEE CLEARLY what God wishes to have them do," what Reynolds increasingly finds in the religious literature of the period portrayed as "well-lighted paths to heaven."[133] Baird spoke of the power of revivals to "remove obstacles out of the way, and throw a light on the path before them" by providing "witness" to many "still wholly skeptical of any inward principle of spiritual life" of the "amazing change produced in the character of many around them."[134] Bushnell's image of a widening road addressed the simultaneous wish to belong. The gate with its conditions of entrance posted, while narrow, was open to all, for "every human soul . . . has a key given to it."[135] Just beyond the fence, accessible with a moment's willing, lay for all who found the key the broad path opening, the revivalists promised, to a new relation, place, and identity in the sight of an awaiting God as an empowered—even perfectible—member in a spiritually engaged community of the saved with its national and cosmic project. As images of this distinctly American reality were made palpable, very many walked through to their rewards quickly and ecstatically.

From New Birth to New Character

The focus of personal transformation was itself evolving and sharpening. In the early phase of the Second Awakening, the influence of First Awakening radicalism was evident in the declining reliance on damnation and the focus on "New Birth." Amidst a public that was "generally Calvinist," the early revivals after 1800 stressed the immediacy of spiritual transformation, "a near prospect of the true kingdom of God": "The late revival was not sent to RE-FORM the churches. It did not come with a piece of new cloth to patch the old garment, to mend up the old hope with some new experience; but to prepare the way for that kingdom of God, in which all things are new." The means were spiritual empowerment of the individual:

> While irresistible beams of light presented objects to the view which persons could not avoid seeing, and they were rushed into exercises of body by a force of operation which they could not withstand, the continuance of the work in this fashion, was precarious. . . . Therefore in order to [allow?] the continuance of the work, a number of its subjects have found it necessary to receive this extraordinary power as an in-dwelling treasure, to unite with this supernatural agent, to dwell in him and he in them, and become work-

ers together with him, and without force or violence, believe and practice whatever he teaches.

This was the "pivot" on which "the revival turns," that "with each individual . . . [t]he power or light of God, continues with those who continue in it, his spirit abid[ing] only with those who abide in him, and do continually the things that please him." This "new and strange doctrine of receiving Christ, and walking in him," by "feeling how freely his love and goodness flowed to them," was available to "each individual who honestly sought after it." It allowed individuals to "forsake their sins" and "testify a full and free salvation in Christ," enabling their "heart" to "glow with love to the souls of men." This "direct manifestation of spiritual light from God to the soul," whose followers were increasingly known as *"New-Lights,"* was "a new birth" into "a sinless life."[136]

As the Awakening spread from early spontaneous camp meetings to organized efforts to convert whole communities and in effect reshape the society, its leaders gradually realized that the goal was not simply a "new birth" but a "new life." That is, there was a necessity of regularizing the energies and motivations of this more highly developed individual beyond the sudden inspiration of "inward light." As Methodism spread its *"sine qua non,"* a "higher experience" of "sanctification through the spirit" leading to a "higher and divine inward life" thereafter,[137] this self-integration of the new life was increasingly framed as the creation of a new *character.* The requirement now was, in Finney's words, our "positive command" to "understand our own hearts . . . to make proof of our real characters, as they appear in the sight of God . . . not . . . our strength, or knowledge, but our moral character . . . our own true character . . . definitively for ourselves."[138]

Personal choice thus culminated in the power to effect the "radical moral transformation of human nature."[139] In dispensing with all forms of proto-agency, it placed before individuals the extraordinary new power to realize a novel internal character. Finney's view of "actual *ability* and *free agency*" meant that individuals possessed "*all* the powers of moral agency" to "make themselves a new heart," to "change our moral character."[140] "To say [God] has commanded them to do it, without telling them they are able," is "a libel upon Almighty God." If humans were ready and willing to convert only to be barred by God, the failure would be God's own: "If we are under an obligation to do what we have no power to do, then sin is unavoidable." Such a view is "absurd," for as "God required men to make themselves a new heart, on pain of eternal death, it is the strongest possible evidence that they are able to do it." As a result, no external force could be saddled with the responsibility, including the Holy Spirit: "*A sinner, under the influence of the Spirit of God, is just as free as a jury under the arguments of an advocate. . . .* It is not the appropriate work of God to do what he requires of you. . . . It must be your own voluntary act."[141]

Henry Ware, a Unitarian, advised his listeners that "to form . . . the Christian character . . . is the very work for which you were sent into the world," a task which is "arduous" but either "done" or "you do nothing." According to Asa Mahan, the Congregational leader, one must seek "the perfect assimilation of our entire character to that of Christ" by placing "the action of all our voluntary powers . . . every choice, every preference, and every volition . . . in entire conformity to the will of God."[142] The revival leader William Sprague pushed this remarkable power over shaping one's character toward the very capacity for an agency separate from others:

> Let me say, if your parents err . . . you are still moral agents, and you have no right to be misled by them. . . . [I]n weakness sometimes incident to parental affection, they may leave you to choose your own course, and may seem to take for granted that whatever you do, is . . . right; you are to regard this as a snare. . . . If you are permitted to choose between idleness and activity, be active. If between the culture and the neglect of your intellect, be studious. . . . Remember that you are to form a character for yourselves; and that you have no right to suffer even a misguided parental affection to stand between you and a virtuous, honest, useful life.[143]

Bushnell wrote that "a man is never in religious character till he has found God; and . . . he will never find him, till his whole voluntary nature goes after him, and . . . communes knowingly with God, receives of God, walks with God." Unlike in the teachings of Calvinism, "His point" is no longer "to crush our will, or reduce it" but rather "to gain our will."[144]

Bushnell described "the new type of character" for which "the world is waiting": "Before the great day of Christ shall come there must be [this] new development of the Christian life." He goes on: "I wish to produce an impression that God has not held us responsible for the effect only of what we do, or teach . . . but quite as much for the effect of *being what we are . . .* our *spirit,* one whose character is shaping in the molds of our own. . . . If a man were to be set before a mirror, with the feeling that the exact image of what he *is* . . . is there to be produced and left as a permanent and fixed image forever, to what carefulness, what delicate sincerity of spirit would he be moved."[145] Sprague addressed in his book "the general formation" of "character," for "in this life, happiness has chiefly to do with the world within: it is just in proportion as the faculties are kept in harmony with each other and the will of God."[146] Henry Ware, writing *The Formation of Christian Character* in 1831, found "a work on character . . . needed," that individuals must "above all things be anxious about their own characters." There is "nothing to be more earnestly desired," he declared, and "about every other result I am indifferent," for "he is but poorly fitted to honor the cause of Christ, who has not first subjected his own soul to his holy government . . . for its own sake . . . not simply because it is respectable in the eyes of the world and favorable to the decency of the commonwealth."[147]

Awakeners were convinced that their historical and social achievement demanded this new religious consolidation. Finney, for example, cast the "traditions of the elders" as "the grand sources of most of the fatal errors of the present day." Indeed, "for many centuries, but little of the real gospel has been preached," being "so mixed with the traditions of men, so . . . false" with their effect as "to break its power." Americans needed to let go of past "prohibitory applications" of God's commandments in order to embrace the "absolute, positive perfection" they offered.[148] Asa Mahan believed that an evolving perfectionism required a "new covenant" which promised a "confirmed state of pure and perfect holiness."[149] Methodists like Peter Cartwright referred to the early circuit riders as "the pioneer messengers of salvation in these ends of the earth," ignited by a novel "religious flame" of revival that "spread . . . through all the land, and it excited great wonder and surprise."[150] Horace Bushnell extolled a "new type of character" emerging "in our day," based in a "heroic life of faith." This more realized individual for which "the world is waiting" would replace "all the pietistic, artificial, dogmatically enfeebled and emasculated forms of piety."[151] William Boardman asked the troubling question, "Why have eighteen centuries been allowed to roll away" before the "true principles were embraced?" The response: "Until now the time has never come for it. Now is the time" of "new life begun in the Church," the time for the "millennial *type* of *Christian character* and life."[152]

This willing integration of agency polarities, a voluntarism which was obedient, a self empowered and individuated through self-deferral, was achieved through the attraction of the godly relation, forming character through identification. Submission was precisely to the God who empowers, a God who, for the first time, asked personally for obedience to the mandate of voluntarism, individualism, and perfection, a God who allowed and encouraged rising ever so far and yet is ever above, who insisted on both nothing more and nothing less than full agency. For that reason, little emphasis was placed in revivals on the harshness of God's rule, the likelihood of evil, or the onerousness of human obedience. Ministers learned that "preaching terror *alone* is not calculated to effect the conversion of sinners," and detracted from the ultimate intimate relation that God and humans were creating. More effective was laying out the infinite benefits of a loving God irresistibly drawn to humankind, which only increased the burden of the promise and the need for a trusting authority. Such "weighty considerations" of divine connection produced the "natural tendency . . . to influence" the individual "to obey his maker," the "tremendous power as to induce him to turn." In accepting the intimate call, individuals were shaping themselves in God's presence as they would "be to all eternity"[153] through *"the giving your heart a permanent bias."*[154]

Without coercion, then, individuals could be led to this higher acceptance and confirmation: "Their Christ was the Good Shepherd who sought out even the last, lost sheep; their God, the loving Father who welcomed every returning prodigal to a life of holiness and love."[155] The community was in turn advised to instruct the wayward with "the best of motives," out of "kindness and tenderness." The goal was to act "for their benefit, because you wish them to be good, and not because you are angry." A "severe and critical . . . manner," even "a single unkind look," may "harden the heart" and "confirm" the "wrong courses," or "close the mind against . . . influence." The preacher must now on behalf of the loving God "win their confidence, and attach them to you, and give an influence to your brotherly instructions and counsels, so that you can mould them into finished Christians." Individuals must be offered a place within the "family of Jesus Christ, as members in full. . . . They are embarked with him, they have gone on board, and taken their all."[156]

Identification with the author who shared its own power, prerogative, and sanctity through the intimate relationship defined the process of internal growth. Bushnell framed the complex theological mix of power and deference as the new union with Christ's "power over you and in you," a new sense of being "endued with power . . . in every direction" through "the leading of God's spirit."[157] For Finney, converts had to "break . . . down into a child-like spirit . . . so that they can be moulded into proper form," which was to "bear the image of Christ," or for Bushnell, "to be empowered as sons of God."[158] Ware regarded Jesus as "the model which you are to imitate" to "become spiritually the child of God," while Boardman affirmed that "submission" which provided "the affections, and the position, and the interest of a son, in the house and the kingdom of his father."[159] While available to all equally, this new dispensation at the same time protected one's individuality, for God attended to each personally: "Having direct access to the mind, and knowing infinitely well the whole history and state of each individual sinner, he employs that truth which is best adapted to his particular case, and thus sets it home with Divine power."[160]

In this rising into an identifying sonship, the appropriating of one's highest divine potential through a loving personal apprenticeship, came the promised certitude of the new realized character. By the "break up of the old foundations," one became "a new man"[161] with the "durable and ceaseless character" such as "really and truly to be" shaped "in the form or likeness of God."[162] In fact, certitude was now possible as never before. In the healing fire, before the "pure moral mirror that reflects the exact moral character," the individual was conclusively recast as a new human type. All who sought would find a "conscious positive assurance," the "inward conviction" that "the world had long needed" of "sins forgiven, and love and joy abiding," stable identities as "the children of God."[163] This certitude was a "true resting place" for the soul with one's "heavenly Father," the "entering of God . . . by the soul's open window."[164] In return for one's "strong and abiding preference" for "God and his service," converts were offered unambiguous clarity regarding the new life: "God's moral government . . . lays down a definite, and perfect rule of feeling and action. Its precept marks, with the clear light of sunbeams, the exact course of duty."[165]

This empowering discipleship, with its higher responsibility in the divine plan, both grounded and demanded much greater mastery over worldly independence and initiative. This reinforced the role of agent, the "steward" as "one who is employed to transact the business of another, as his agent or representative in the business in which he is employed."[166] This role was not in "the mere channels of a divine agency, but always . . . [as] agents ourselves in a more complete and free sense than before, 'co-workers with God.'"[167] In walking through the open gate, one relinquished the old will and was "refitted," one's fallow ground replanted, one's self remade.[168] It was the "critical moment in the history of [one's] character,"[169] when it was "moulded into proper form." Freely embraced, transcendental authority restored order, clear obligation, and eternal promise, giving religion a uniquely American grounding as "an engine of prodigious power," leverage with which to shape the novel forms of American life, all through "a new man" coming "into a new world."[170]

To Be an Agent in the World

The transformation of the individual will was for all but the most radical Protestants only the first step in realizing the "new world." This new character freely affirming common institutional authority and common ends could not rest until those institutions and ends were constituted. By formalizing the dynamic of reversal, the religious sector enabled the individual to relinquish disordering autonomy and self-referential authority while integrating the agency capacities for choice, self-discretion, personal regard, and a sense of individual power. Now the path would as promised open wide, but . . . to what? As agents of what? The end of Awakeners, the core attribute of the full agent, was of course the continued and ever more effective implementation of God's purpose in the world. Those individuals who became "workers together with him" had to be counted on to fashion this new world,[171] which accounted for the reformist ferment and ultimately the moral intransigence of antebellum populist Protestantism.

From conversion, individuals were strongly directed toward moral activity as the locus of the realized life. "And if you teach them thoroughly what religion is," advised Bushnell, "and make them SEE CLEARLY what God wishes to have them do, and lead these to do it promptly and decidedly, ordinarily they will not be harrassed with doubts and fears, but will be clear, open-hearted, cheerful and growing Christians . . . a blessing to the church and the world."[172] Finney put it boldly: "Faith without works is dead."[173] Hence his injunction: "If duty calls, DO IT. Don't wait for feeling, but DO IT."[174] Sprague advised "the young convert" to "begin the Christian life with such resolutions and principles, as will be likely to secure the greatest amount of activity and usefulness."[175] For Ware, the realization of a Christian character was precisely "to prepare us for the right conduct of actual life." He continued: "We must come down from the mount. We must enter the crowds and distractions of common life. We must engage in common and secular affairs." The world was the test of conviction. "It is but partially that character is formed which is formed only by thinking, musing, and purposing. It wants the completeness of active habits. It wants the test which is to be found only in life. It wants the principle of growth which can be found only in action. . . . [A]*ction is an essential and all-important means of religious growth*."[176] T. C. Upham defined "man" in "very obvious" terms as "a rational and voluntary being . . . designed for action." Humans were "co-workers, with God," endeavoring constantly to strive for "maximum co-operation with God," the fullest realization of God's ends. Individuals were to be discouraged from a preoccupation with doctrinal issues or sectarian disputes, the state of their religiosity, or even a continuing celebration of religious experience.[177]

Now equipped with a personal and self-reliant moral system and internalized role to act in the world, individuals were resolutely prepared for engagement. What was the nature and extent of the engagement to be? The divine mirror producing and reflecting the new agency self did not yet extend to "the true images of things" in the world,[178] for the world as the convert was alerted constantly did not yet reflect the new dispensation: "The whole frame-work of society, almost, is hostile to religion. Nearly all the influences which surround a man, from cradle to his grave, in the present state of society, are calculated to defeat the design of the ministry." Reflecting its historic transformative fervor and unbending determination (whose obverse side was to render Protestantism unequipped to coalesce national consensus), the renovated individual remained in a state of heightened distinctness if no longer antagonism with the world, with an obligation to both resist and transform it: "He has something more to do than merely to contend with enemies, he has to labor directly for the advancement of Christ's cause. His lot is cast in a world lying in darkness and nakedness; and it is for him to lend his aid to enlighten and reform it."[179]

For modernizing Protestantism, the disparity between the religious individual and the world did not lead, as with the conservative wing and with the Puritans earlier, to a closed and protected community of believers. The objective of the movement was to prepare an individual of requisite strength to be engaged in but not entirely of the world, to channel religious voluntarism into shaping lives and institutions in consonance with its agenda. For this emerging mainstream, including even its revivalists, the energies of enthusiasm had to be redirected from the transitional experience of conversion into a religious ethic of steady, predictable conduct that would solidify engagement, ensure self-discipline, and stabilize the new path. Finney thus rejected as an end point a religion of "zeal": "Teach them that religion does not consist in raptures, or ecstasies, or high flights of feeling." Emotionalism, though a part of religion, was unpredictable, in his term "involuntary,"[180] and therefore a dangerous, unstable basis for enduring religious community. Nowhere more than in revivals, Sprague acknowledged in his defense of them, is there "greater danger of . . . being misled. There is in the minds of most men a tendency to extremes; and that tendency is never so likely to discover itself as in a season of general excitement," for this is "when men . . . are in far more danger of forming erroneous judgments, and in adopting improper courses, than when they are in . . . sober reflection."[181]

For the new agent, the transformation of society began with the world as a field of spiritual testing to develop its self-definition and confidence in its character integration and operational efficacy through action that fulfilled mandated responsibilities. In a culture of self-reliant, mobile individualism, the onus for maintaining steadiness of purpose lay heavily upon each individual. The internal demands for sustaining appropriate perseverance in the practices and attitudes of an effective religious life after conversion were thus made the constant preoccupation. This was rooted in "the firm determination to act out duty and to obey the will of God" regardless of one's "feeling" or "state of mind"; for "whether he feels any lively religious emotion at the time or not, he will do his duty cheerfully, and readily, and heartily, whatever may be the state of his feelings."[182] Character in action was simply the continual fulfillment of religious responsibility, which was based on "fixed principles for the regulation of [one's] whole conduct" begun in "firm resolution" not to "yield," a sturdiness of will "strengthened *only* by experience,"[183] a "rigid self-discipline" designed "to keep the spirit habitually right." Then "add to the authority of principle the vigor and steadfastness of confirmed habit, and your religious character becomes almost impregnable to assault. . . . Habit is a thing of tremendous power: it is sometimes omnipotent in men."[184]

Francis Wayland also called the goal "habit," "the repetition of a virtuous act [which] produces a *tendency* to continued repetition" in which "the power of the will over passion is more decided: and the act is accomplished with less moral effect."[185] Ware called it "a calm and composed state of the affections, an equanimity of spirit, a serenity of temper . . . not excited to ecstasy" or fearing "occasional dullness or darkness."[186] The object of meeting the spiritual challenges of everyday life contrasted

religion which is occasionally and transiently felt in the heart, but which does not constitute the character of a man; and . . . religion which dwells there habitually, and is the predominating disposition and mind of the man. . . . It is a tremendous thing to consider . . . fine sentiments . . . [and] passions . . . [b]ut the world is not essentially changed. . . . There are occasional splendours of thought . . . and rich gleams of fancy, and transient corruscations that kindle the whole heaven of his imagination; but . . . [h]e does nothing; he gains no victories over himself; he makes no progress.

In place of these "visions; ever in the distance, never approached, never made realities" of religious heroism and instant transcendence Orville Dewey offered "the hard and beaten path of daily care, full of uncelebrated sacrifice," framed by "not the ordinary virtues of an extraordinary life, but the more extraordinary virtue of ordinary life."[187]

As mobile individuals who answered to no one else, believers were to maintain constant vigilance over themselves: "Young converts should be taught to keep their conscience just as tender as the apple of the eye. They should watch their conduct and their motives. . . . They should maintain such a habit of listening to conscience, that it will be always ready to give forth a stern verdict on all occasions." Sprague insisted that individuals in order to maintain their character "should be impressed, from the beginning, with the importance of habitual self-examination," to "inspect narrowly their motives from day to day" and with regard to larger religious ends. Ware demanded "constant . . . watchfulness" whereby the individual was "to be ever on the alert."[188] Self-examination was necessary to maintain steady control over one's selfish and self-aggrandizing propensities. In a world of novel, powerful, and unremitting temptations, the disciplined denial of such motives required ongoing inner control, the ability to "*turn your thoughts away instantly* which are impure," the "responsibility, the will" to sustain a life of active "self-denial" through the "exercise over yourself" of "unremitting and ever-wakeful discipline."[189] Franklinesque lists of qualities and conduct to be exercised and avoided[190] were to produce steady conduct and ultimately self-imposed directionality, "a fixed purpose, and a steady course of endeavors," a "course" which does not "wander,"[191] the capacity to "*maintain singleness of motive*," to be a "consistent man."[192] This pursuit of characterological regularity would distinguish the mainstream revival from sectarian enthusiasms. In its intentions, however, the insistence on steady habits in performing mandated activity was on behalf not of normalcy but of transformation, for this movement had no less an objective than to remake all selves in a remade America.

The Emerging Voluntary Community

To produce a society transcending existing limitations, religious institutions of the antebellum revival organized their mission around ecclesiastical communities. These collectives formed the effective frame for sanctioned activity, at once shaping individual integration and forming a mechanism for remaking the larger society. Scholars now understand how revivalism appealed to those seeking a "greater individual freedom . . . still rooted in communal values" through the "communal ideal" of "a well-ordered, egalitarian community."[193] The "millennium" would result by "God freeing 'America' from the deadness of state churches to voluntarily choose true obedience and moral reform and thereby establish a sanctified community."[194] The Reverend C. C. Goss spoke of his awakened Methodist church as a community of mutual aid, "a spiritual workshop, where persons who enter are expected to work for Christ." The decentralized movement worked to include individuals as "members of small, local, and . . . autonomous groups."[195] While revivals and even religious institutions, unable to generate from localism the necessary cohesiveness for modern society, would be quickly supplanted by more inclusive institutions, they provided the original voluntary agency communities within which the new character would be nurtured. They further established the vision of "an ideal Christian society," which was now also "an ideal republican society," providing the early model of a transformed America during the war against slavery.[196]

Revivals taught Americans that institutions could survive and prosper though formed directly by the will of individuals. As Donald Mathews has suggested, though made suddenly "responsible for ordering a new holy community . . . many Americans found it relatively easy to participate in the only organization which sought them out" within a movement "built . . . upon their own experience."[197] Offered the opportunity to enact as true participants the dynamic of Hobbes's mythical social contract, individuals were easily induced by the importance of their roles to undertake and sustain communal engagement. At the same time, with the dynamic of reversal and its needs for order, security, and community pervading individual motivations, the churches could deflect any claims of reimposing "servitude," casting their function quite legitimately as a response to popular psychological distress and dislocation. The individual in the New World, Baird explained, had undergone

the separation of himself and his family . . . from old associations and influences; and the removal, if not from abundant means of grace, at least from
that force of public opinion which often powerfully restrains from the commission of open sin. . . . Then, there is the entering into new and untried situations; the forming of new acquaintances, not always of the best kind; and
even that engrossment with the cares and labors attending a man's removal
into a new country, especially in the case of the many who have to earn
their bread by their own strenuous exertions.[198]

By recognizing people's sense of dislocation, cultivating their underlying
needs, and directing them toward community formation, reversal was institutionalized even as the primacy of individual choice was stressed. In this
way, paradoxically, the churches secured their indispensable place in the
new society.

Revivals, often lasting up to several weeks, were thus more than mobilizations of individual piety. Creating intense, inclusive communities, they
formed a "social environment" offering "order and continuity." Amounting
to "temporary cities," the "camp meetings provided the ideal religious and
social solution to the isolated circumstances" of local life.[199] Individuals,
asked explicitly to lay down the burden of their sins before God, were effectively being asked at the same time to lay down the weight of their individuality to join in communal "resurrection" or integration. The private "praying, preaching, singing, and lamentation" preceeding revival, followed by
public exhortations, convulsions, and witnessing at camp meetings before
the group, were steps constituting entry into the community. Continually
aroused by "frequent . . . meetings" with "at every step, the assistance of
an experienced mind," individuals were continuously coming together, at
times "all lying upon the ground" with their limbs in "incessant and violent
motion," then giving way to "a multitude joined in chorus . . . the combined
voices . . . heard at the dead of night, from the depths of their eternal forest,
the many fair young faces turned upward, and looking paler and lovelier as
they met the moon-beams."[200]

Dominating community life for an extended period in which little else
was done, revivals enabled their leaders to single out and address each citizen and particularly resisters. Preachers and community members would often meet and press conversion with individuals seeking direction in gatherings after services or in private homes. Churches increasingly incorporated

revival techniques and practices, as many utilized the public service to focus community expectations on the struggling participant. By a procedure known as the "anxious seat," derived from early Methodist revival practice, individuals worried about the state of their soul would be asked to come forward to a place near the pulpit where they could be directly prayed for and instructed. Preachers howled and implored: "Come, then! . . . Come to us. . . . [W]e will make way for you; we will clear the bench for anxious sinners to sit upon. Come, then! come to the anxious bench. . . . Come! Come! Come!" If the public service or revival was inconclusive, participants would be called off one at a time to meet with ministers and sometimes elders. Providing a "more familiar and direct instruction suited to their case," reinforcing their anxiety of "separation" from loved ones who were quite likely converting, the effect was to "bring them at once to the point; to anticipate and remove objections; to draw them off from resting in any mere preparatory work." It was then possible to *"call them to do it,"* to call them "completely under the power of Divine truth" and to a reconciliation with the community of believers.[201]

In a sense, the community was the subject of revivals, for all about were "crowded assemblies," transformed individuals recently "abandoned to sin," intimates everywhere "rejoicing" and praying for the recalcitrant: "How do we see parents pleading for their children, wives for their husbands, friend for friend, with all the importunity of the patriarch of old, 'I will not let Thee go, except Thou bless me.'" With others quickly drawn into the circle, the undecided were overwhelmed by their "strong tendency . . . to be moved and excited because we see others excited around us."[202] This dynamic encouraged individuals to thrust off their isolation and move toward a place in the community. The rhetoric of the religious experience even suggested this wish to belong, "to unite with this supernatural agent," to "cling to the cross for safety."[203] With the call at first to "each individual," for "on this pivot the revival turns," these gatherings became "a crowd of awakened souls" which "gradually spread" to "still greater multitudes" as "the people flocked in hundreds and thousands" to become "convened in one vast multitude":

> How striking to see hundreds who never saw each other in the face before,
> moving uniformly into action, without any preconcerted plan, and each,
> without intruding upon another, taking that part assigned for him by a con-
> scious feeling, and in this manner, dividing into bands over a large extent of

ground. . . . How persons, so different in their education, manners and natural dispositions, without any visible commander, could enter upon such a
scene, and continue in it for days and nights in perfect harmony, has been
one of the greatest wonders that ever the world beheld.[204]

These communities spontaneously arising without any presence of institutional coercion, while fragile and transient, appeared models of free institutions.

In fact, foreshadowing the process of American institutional development
generally, revivals were constituted as exercises in collective pressure. The
mandate regarding those who avoided these gatherings was to "hunt them
up, find out the cause of their absence, pray with them and urge them to the
all-important duty of attending." The failure to join, the refusal to be a part
of the community, was itself made the focus of vulnerability:

> The *sense of shame*, the *reluctance to be singular.*—one of the strongest im-
> pediments (especially with the young) to entering on a religious course—
> loses, at such times, almost all its power. In an extensive revival, the singu-
> larity lies on the other side. . . . Everything, at such a time, presses upon
> them with united force to make them decide at once, and decide right. The
> well-known shortness of such a season . . . the uncommon clearness and
> pungency with which the truth is preached—the solicitude of Christian
> friends—the importunity of young converts who have just "tasted that the
> Lord is gracious"—the impulse of *the mass of mind* around them, moving in
> one direction, with all the multiplied influences that concentrate in a re-
> vival, unite to impress the truth with irresistible force.[205]

The pressure was unabating to maintain the burden of marginalization: "If
there was one so stubborn that he would not yield from worldly pride . . .
the meetings were continued from Sunday until Monday, and kept up every
night of the week at the house where the owner of the obdurate heart lived,
so that he finally gave in: for peace and quiet, if for nothing else."[206]

The institutionalized anxious seat highlighted this pressure on the resister
to belong. Finney wrote: "If you say to him, 'There is the anxious seat, come
out and avow your determination to be on the Lord's side,' and he is not
willing to do so small a thing as that, then he is not willing to do *any thing*."
"Brought out before his *own conscience*," this individual has failed to be
"pressed by the truth." The ministers fully grasped the public effect: "When
a person is seriously troubled in mind, every body knows that there is a

powerful tendency to try to keep it private that he is so, and it is a great thing to get the individual willing to have the fact known to others." Conversion of such individuals was a public declaration, a response to "their fellow-men," and the community indicated its stake through messages "not only" in "language, but by their looks, their tears, their daily deportment" as well.[207]

Revivalism promoted the popular formation of churches sustained by the willing vocation of the converted. Moved by "a missionary spirit" to universal outreach, believers were expected to "labor zealously" to bring others to God. "They will feel grieved that others do not love God, when they love him so much. And they will set themselves feelingly to persuade their neighbors to give him their hearts . . . their friends, relations, enemies."[208] The organization of community religious experience for both believers and novices through camp meetings, prayer meetings, classes, and family prayers created shared activities by which "the weak have been made strong; the bowed have been raised up; the tempted have found delivering grace; the doubting mind has had all its doubts and fears removed; and the whole class have found that this was 'none other than the house of God, and the gate of heaven.'"[209] Reaching families on a regular basis, providing ministerial visits into all communities, churches were established as popular institutions.

In this way, societal formation proceeded through "a vast mobilization of people," through "the relevance, power and similarity of thousands of local organizations," what Ellen Eslinger has called "a quilt of local communities."[210] As co-participants in a common project defined by collective means as well as ends, individuals discovered voluntarism not as abandonment to self-direction or even the later economic agency self-interest, but as personal responsibility in a consensual institutional project. The institutional management of reversal had supported the shift of operative values from remaining singular to joining regardless of reservations. Yet, framed as a journey from the Hobbesian nightmare to community, it became as Hobbes had envisioned a profound gain in effective capacity and opportunity.

By pioneering the constitution of voluntary institutional authority, the antebellum churches formed the bridge to the institutionalization of American society. Through stages begun with revival and conversion, they were able to locate the necessary attributes of "free institutions": to define their creation as a product of the individual wills of the members; to harness the power of common needs and community pressures to direct the motion of individual reversal toward collective cohesion; and to sustain their cohesion by shaping theological priorities to the new conditions and opportunities faced by the membership. With institutional ends and authorized activities now extensions of individual goals, freedom was equated with institutional voluntarism and voluntarism with ordered conduct. This provided the ideological opening for institutions, though defined as ancillary "supports" for an order defined as individual in essence, to grow untrammeled. The channels of liberal behavior could now be characterized as "innate," "natural," preinstitutional, traceable if at all—through the midwifery of religion—to no institutional hand but to God. As voluntarism was directed into choices which were routinized and socialized, societal integration involved seemingly no loss of options. Similarly, reconciling voluntarism and obedience, adult liberal institutions were able to manage rigorously the consequences of reversal while avoiding culpability for the movement into collective life. This process, by which American society moved beyond its ideological commitment to the idyll, would have as its eventual result the "free organizational society." The culmination of reversal in the moment of religious and institutional entry, this "change" in "the entire current of the soul," was the mechanism through which Americans would be induced to drive themselves—"freely surrender"—to a society of voluntarist agents.[211] All that remained was to realize such a society.

To Remake the World—for Keeps

The mobilization to reshape the self and local community life would surge into collective activism in the 1830s with the success of revivalism. The quest for "personal moral perfection" would not rest content until the perfectionist aspirations for "social" reconstruction were also fulfilled.[212] As Robert H. Abzug writes: "What would the tests be of this individual sacred order beyond the first, quickly achieved step of conversion? How would one live, by what signposts, in a world that supplied an ever-changing and evanescent offering of wants and needs? . . . Reform began to answer such questions."[213] The religious emphasis was on spreading the new personal dispensation to all who had been bypassed, with the expectation that appropriate institutional forms would necessarily follow. This was its great strength and its weakness. As the great progressive force of the age, the "engine driving" both "change" and "modernization," the unyielding insistence on the power and responsibility of every individual fueled social reform movements that guaranteed the triumph of an agency nation.[214] It further promoted this apotheosis while resisting during this period worldly liberal economic and social priorities.[215] At the same time, its inability to address structural and institutional matters sealed its eventual eclipse and capitulation to the priorities of the nation it had forged.

The mission of collective transformation ranged from participation in new forms of collective worship to directed efforts to organize society into a millennial religious body. For less proselytizing groups, Unitarians like Ware and some perfectionists, a life of personal piety and discipline through meditation and action was to be confirmed by common religious practice and the fellowship of rituals such as the Lord's Supper. The rigors involved in shaping one's life to higher religious ends might also form a model of how to "mould and rule the character" for all "to imitate." Ultimately, if slowly, this process might change the world. "Indeed, its desirable influence upon the state of society can be gained only through this deep devotion to it of individuals; because none but this is genuine religion, and the genuine only can exhibit the genuine power."[216] This was the goal of individual perfectionist testimony, "to show others who would ascend, the foot-marks by which you have ascended." For those faltering in "the horrible pit," stuck in "miry? clay," "your Forerunner has caused the eyes of the multitude to be fixed on you" to "illustrate the way by which you have *experimentally tested* the solidity of those foot-marks by which you have thus far ascended."[217] These personal testimonies themselves offered the power and inspiration to change hearts.

The most prevalent and middle position, adopted by Finney and most Methodists among others, framed societal transformation in terms of revivalism, denominational outreach, and conversion. Believers were to be "*trained to labour,* just as carefully as young recruits in an army are trained for war. . . . Heaven calls from above, 'go preach the Gospel to every creature.' Hell groans from beneath, and ten thousand voices cry out from heaven, earth and hell *'Do something to save the world!' 'Do it now!'* O, Now, or millions more are in hell through your neglect." Their role involved stringent responsibility: "If God calls on them to employ any thing they have, their money, or their time, or to give their children, or to dedicate themselves, in advancing his kingdom, and they refuse . . . it is vastly more blameable than for a clerk or an agent to go and embezzle the money that is entrusted to him."[218] Methodist ministers and circuit riders, called "to 'go and preach the Gospel to every creature' . . . whether invited or not" as a "godly example" for the "perishing millions of our fallen race dying in their sins," believed themselves responsible "for the moral order in a great and good degree that prevails in . . . this vast wilderness."[219]

The participants of the Awakening, like the older denominations pursuing religious benevolence, understood that religious outreach was closely linked to the moral reclamation of the downtrodden. They organized and engaged in widespread movements to promote temperance, antislavery, educational reform, and women's rights as well as campaigns for dietary changes and on behalf of Indians and against prostitution and Masonry. Finney, defending "the great business of the Church . . . to reform the world—to rub away every kind of sin," supported "aggressive movements in every direction . . . to reform individuals, communities, and governments."[220] At the same time, both groups defined this moral "benevolence" by its religious objectives as an "'appendage' of spiritual regeneration."[221] The older denominations had more moderate objectives of universal moral and character reform,[222] while revivalists believed that a disciplined church would create a universal society of Protestant agents carrying out divine ends: "If the Church will do all her duty, the millennium may come in this country in three years." This meant avoiding divisive controversies from "any other subject" including political reform. "It is THE CHURCH that God has chiefly in view. How shall we avoid the curse of war? Only by a reformation in the Church. It is in vain to look to politics."[223] All moral reformation must issue from religious objectives: "GO FORWARD. Who could leave such a work, and go to writing letters, and go down into the plain of Ono, and see if all these petty disputes can't be adjusted, and let the work cease. Let us mind our work, and let the Lord take care of the rest."[224] This view demanded that the society be brought entirely to religious fellowship.

The third approach also involved the Christian transformation of the world, but focused on the larger society through taking responsibility as God's agents to explicitly remake national institutions. For such movements growing most strongly in revival regions,[225] involving many who had begun in the awakened church and those socially disenfranchised who had gained a public role in the Awakening, the task was collective reform. From humanitarian reform movements for the disadvantaged to worker associations of self-help to the more intransigent forms of abolitionism, individuals joined together in voluntary organizations to raise all as empowered agents within a Christianized nation. Particularly in the cities, national temperance and ecumenical benevolent work on behalf of the poor, convicts, and orphans in the decades before the Civil War, involving not only religious out-reach but also practical assistance with living conditions and employment training, sought an ultimate spiritual regeneration of society. As the least fortunate were brought to reform their character, they would see the wisdom of God's ways, "of Jesus, his love, his sacrifice, his readiness to pardon, his perfect righteousness—all, all the sinner's own by simple faith."[226]

Such institutions, while nominally secular and ever more inclusive, brought to the larger populace, in the words of the reform activist Thomas Gallaudet, "the great system of good" anticipating "the millennium."[227] Methodist William Arthur explained the effort:

> Nothing short of the general renewal of society ought to satisfy any soldiers of Christ. . . . Much as Satan glosses in his power over an individual, how much greater must be his glorying over a nation embodying, in its laws and usages, disobedience to God, wrong to man, and contamination to morals? To destroy all national holds of evil; to root sin out of institutions; to hold up to view the gospel ideal of a righteous nation . . . is one of the first duties. . . . [T]he gospel is come to renew the face of the earth.[228]

The forces of renewal and transformation reached their peak in the anti-slavery movement. Its great power stemmed from uniting the religiously mobilized northern populace and social reformers representing the two more engaged approaches to worldly activism.[229] By confirming the primal and horrific incommensurability of human slavery with the new dispensation of humankind as godly agents, it defined the cause as a test for the larger public of the identities they had forged in the revivals.[230] Further linking these strains of "moral energy" and "the moral imperatives" of "evangelical Protestantism" with the political call to "free labor," itself an agency euphemism for a new systemic individualism, the Republican Party—shedding Federalist and Whig elitism—galvanized the nation behind this new dispensation.[231]

The movement toward armed struggle in defense of religious and political principle was a fateful turning in the national formation, an acknowledging that "to purify the church alone would not sanctify the nation." Accepting that even war might be required to fulfill God's promise of a morally trans-formed world, the religious leadership shaped the Civil War as the coming of God's governance of American society, the fulfillment of its plan whereby "the kingdom of heaven is at hand."[232] Called to war, the American citizenry became "active agents" in the ultimate national revival fulfilling the inclusivist and democratic logic of awakened religiosity, a logic vindicated as principles of universal agency were established with the northern victory.[233] Affirming that "we are all agents and instruments of Divine Providence," Lincoln himself confirmed this apotheosis.[234]

At the same time, the irony of the "millennium" as a political cause with its principles enunciated by a political leader, one for whom the Union itself was paramount, could not be avoided. The price of affirming agency as the societal foundation was the inevitable ascendance of the liberal polity. The religious sector, "incapable" of a "peaceful solution" to "the problem of slavery," failed in Protestant fashion even to avoid further fragmentation with its massive schisms.[235] Having "launched evangelical crusades to make the United States a fit millennial instrument . . . after seven decades . . . their efforts had not prevented moral confusion and political disorder.[236] As an "armed prophet" became necessary, not only social reformers but also those committed to transformation within the churches had to eschew Protestant "voluntarist means" for "a new and unprecedented recourse to coercion" to achieve "the unity, order, morality, and homogeneity deemed essential to a Christian republic."[237] Once again, the godly nation theologically understood would have to give way to the cohesive instrument of modernity, a religiously informed liberalism.

11

From Sectarian Discord to Civil Religion

It was not necessary that Christ should be visible to our fleshly eyes, in order that he should reign in the world. . . . Who cannot see + feel that we have entered upon a new era.

    —Angelina Grimké Weld

But these fires [of revival] are less splendid only because they are more potent. . . . They traverse and permeate society in every direction.

    —William M. Evarts

The reconsecration of the project of creating a nation of agents as one of liberal universalism, now irreversibly with the movement toward a single principled collective during the Civil War in the hands of national civil institutions, was an outgrowth of the very dynamic of the Second Awakening. Under way long before the commencement of the conflict, this shift was far from a usurpation by an ambitious secularism turning religion into a "captive" to "the world" the revivalists had tried to "capture." Nor, despite the crisis caused by the "centrifugal" tendencies of an "organizationally fragmented" religious governance, was civil ascendancy simply the "failure to transform America into the promised land."[1] Rather, underlying revivalist intransigence itself was the impetus to produce a nation on agency principles. The very success of the Awakening in broadly establishing this character organized to manage modern individualism mandated a turn from personal religious empowerment to institutional consolidation.

Many participants in the movement had realized the dangers of a continual escalation of religious individualism as early as the late 1830s. Given a decentralized and institutionally uncontainable process, the voluntarist energies of individual transformation released by the force of missionary zeal generated manifold versions of the "millennium" and fiercely divisive strategies for achieving it. Religious leaders watched as the lengthening specter of sectarian and societal perfectionism gave rise to populist mobilizations and unrealistic expectations threatening a young nation straining for cohesion and stability. Beginning before the Civil War and increasing thereafter, they sought to harness these energies to shape national institutions reflecting the evolving internal capacities of the citizenry. As the antebellum generations moved beyond the boundaries of denominational life and applied the initiative and skills developed in the Awakening to shaping the new society, localist ecclesiastical structures no longer sufficed. Driven by its own dynamic of national formation, the religious community gradually evolved into a more comprehensive liberalism.

The Perfection of Agency

The logic of the cultural expectation that Americans would shape their new character before the world as empowered agents finally answerable only to God and God's mission propelled antebellum revivalism toward a radical new individualism. New Light Presbyterian free will and the universal possibility of grace gave way to Finney's universal "natural ability," then to Methodism's increasingly popular belief in "the premise of man's immediate perfectibility . . . through the operation of the spirit of God" in a "'second blessing,' called entire sanctification, which would cleanse away the moral depravity" of the soul.[2] Absent institutional controls on voluntarism, the uncompromising commitment of believers to godliness as "finished Christians" continually pushed the logic of spiritual possibility and fanned the flames of sectarian expectation. It was, as Timothy L. Smith puts it, "only one step" from an acceptable "radical transformation of human character" to Christian perfectionism, a release from sin and works with the doctrine that "salvation was also subjectively real, that divine grace might heal the sinfulness of the soul."[3] Just beyond lay the even more radical perfection of the self emerging under its own authorization.

Both voluntarists and proponents of the indwelling Spirit hoped to secure the developmental integration of agency powers while containing the dynamic of perfectionism and self-validation. For Finney and the radical voluntarists, the individual was, despite options as "the agent who exercises choice," constrained to act as "the Spirit of God plies him with motives to make him willing" to fulfill larger divine purposes. While the Spirit cannot will human actions or substitute itself for individual determination, transcendent leverage operated to "induce" generated conduct.[4] At the same time, the believer was empowered by this direct relation: through "silent communings of the soul with God" the "believer . . . gathers strength and grace" by which, after conversion, the Spirit by its "direct agency" will "prepare him for heaven." Through this abiding and empowering divine presence the believer, "amidst the various duties and trials which meet him in the world," is "sustained and carried forward"[5] to fulfill one's role in the divine plan with "strength, stability, firmness, and perpetuity." Remarkably, this process eliminates for believers "the need" to "backslide" or even *"having or expressing doubts as to their conversion."*[6]

The result was an individual approaching perfect sanctification. Believers, declared Finney, "should *aim at being perfect.* Every young convert should be taught, that . . . his *purpose* [is] to live without sin. . . . [I]t is the duty of all to *aim* at being perfect. It should be their constant purpose, to live wholly to God, and obey all his commandments. They should live so, that if they should sin, it would be an inconstancy, an exception, an individual case, in which they act contrary to the fixed and general purpose and tenor of their lives." The transformed will in turn transforms the character: "It is astonishing to see how much the conscience may be cultivated by a proper course. If rightly attended to, it may be made so pure, and so powerful, that it will always respond exactly to the word of God. . . . [T]his new preference needs only to become deep and energetic enough in its influences to stamp the perfection of heaven upon the whole character."[7] One's place in the divine pattern of ends was achieved: "All the various powers of the soul . . . are to be brought into exercise, according to the particular end which the Spirit may design to accomplish. . . . And thus the whole man becomes more and more pure, until he reaches at last the fulness of the stature of a perfect person in Christ." Now accepting that "they *ought not* to sin at all," believers will become "as holy as God is" and go forth to *"exhibit their light"* to the world.[8]

The proponents of the indwelling spirit found in its abiding presence the possibility of a similar transformation. One Methodist minister foresaw "the destruction of sin," which would provide for "universal brotherhood—& purity . . . [a] world redeemed from sin & ignorance etc."[9] For this growing Arminian movement, God's healing love, "purifying their hearts by faith,"[10] would "give to the truly faithfull who are regenerated by his grace the means of preserving themselves in this state."[11] This active integration with God, by which "we may be free from sin & folly," created a recast nature "perfecting holiness."[12] As the Awakening intensified, the cautious approach to a fully realized spiritual transformation shifted for many, including an evolving Finney, to increasingly confident convictions of spiritual perfection. "'Perfection' meant perfect trust and consecration, the experience of the fullness of the love of Christ. . . . [The preachers] varied . . . in their terminology. Finney preferred the phrase, 'entire sanctification'; Henry Cowles, 'holiness'; Asa Mahan, 'Christian perfection'; and John Morgan, 'the baptism of the Holy Ghost.'"[13] For Asa Mahan, "perfection in holiness is attainable in this life" as the "declared object for which the Holy Spirit dwells in the hearts of God's people." It entails an "entire freedom from all sin, and the transformation of our entire character into a likeness to [Christ's] own."[14]

This movement continued to grow in the years before the Civil War, spreading through the Methodist world to mainstream revivals into the radical theology of Thomas Upham, William Boardman, and the Oberlin perfectionists, among whom Finney became a prominent figure. Phoebe Palmer, a leader of perfectionist organizing, collected testimonies of individuals cleansed and "perfected" under the influence of "Perfect Love."[15] In such testimony the Reverend R. W. Hawkins spoke of having "felt the witness of the Spirit that I had believed unto the saving of the soul," becoming "blameless" and convinced of his "own righteousness." Converts spoke of their "great baptism of fire and power," "fervid waves of divine influence . . . through my entire being, leaving a delightful consciousness of moral refinement and elevation," followed by an "increasing delightful consciousness of inward purity . . . of perfect harmony with the whole unfallen, unstained, or renewed, and restored universe."[16]

Horace Bushnell, a major influence on post–Civil War liberal theology, was profoundly influenced by this movement. He regarded as being shaped through the Spirit and participation in the divine nature a psychological perfection of character approaching modernist self-empowerment:

> Instead of seeking to reduce our individuality or the assertion of our will-force in religion, God rather designs to intensify it and bring it into greater power. . . . [N]o man is required in coming to Christ, to make any sacrifice that will at all diminish or infringe on the distinctive will-force of his personality. He will be just so much more of a man as he is more of a Christian. His unregulated force, becomes regulated force, will be weakness raised into power. His will . . . now all-dominant, will yet be manifold stronger than it is now. His command of himself will be greater, his thoughts higher,

his vision clearer, his affections broader and more full, and there will be a certain divine inspiration in him that will lift him into a higher range of consciousness, and empower him for greater works and undertakings.[17]

By "knowing God," one "knows how to be more completely; boldly himself . . . able to assert himself in a higher, nobler key." Being "lifted," one is "made positive and heroic," "great . . . loftier and stronger in every thing desirable—in capacity, and power, and all personal majesty . . . great in being raised to such common council, and such intimate unity with him in his ends, that we do, in fact, reign with him."[18]

The increasing godliness of a self intimate with God and infused with divine love was producing, in Perry Miller's terms, "so complete an uprooting of the historic conception of American Protestantism, so profound a reading of new meanings."[19] Christian transcendence of self was giving way to a heightened experience of self-worth. Finney, despite condemning the sin of selfishness, acknowledged the "self-love" of the redeemed individual as "not in itself sinful," and the desire to "gratify" it likewise "not sinful."[20] For Upham, self-love is "implanted in man" and thus "conceded . . . by theologians" to be "in its subordinated and legitimate exercise . . . right" when appropriately "in the pursuit of our own happiness."[21] Bushnell attacked the theological "error" of traditional religion, which prefers us "having or daring to have no desires," instead of seeking to "complete and glorify" our being as "a distinct centre of choice, feeling, and life."[22]

This spreading sense of human power emboldened many revivalists to project an unlimited spiritual advance, the "millennium" in "three years," "*the complete moral renovation of the world* . . . the wilderness . . . everywhere . . . as a garden of the Lord."[23] They predicted at a "time . . . near . . . upon the earth 'a holy generation, a royal priesthood, and a peculiar people.'" Bushnell asserted that with "this power . . . developed in you . . . [a]ll things are possible." This power would manifest itself in "individual life and action" and in what each would "do for the world."[24] For "partakers of the DIVINE NATURE," this nature would "be unfolded in their history" and made "powerful," enabling them to fulfill the covenant on earth and "absorb all the human races in its dominion."[25] Andrew Jackson himself in his first inaugural address expressed the belief "that man can be elevated; man can become more and more endowed with divinity; and as he does he becomes more God-like in his character and capable of governing himself." This universal dispensation was to give direction and common purpose to the new, "liberal" nation: "Let us go on elevating our people, perfecting our institutions, until democracy shall reach such a point of perfection that we can acclaim with truth that the voice of the people is the voice of God."[26]

The Sectarian Crisis Replayed

Inevitably, the spreading belief in individual transcendence and societal transformation was stirring spiritual and social experimentation. The revivalists realized the danger of their own exhortations. At the height of his ministry, Finney cautioned "the church" to "go on steadily in a course of obedience without" such "powerful excitement," which, "if long continued, injures our health and unfits us for our duty."[27] William Sprague from the outset warned against the "prominent evil" of "a revival," which is *the cherishing of false hopes,*" for amidst the enthusiasm many people will "mistake some accidental and joyous, yet temporary, commotion of the animal feelings, for the exercise of a principle of true piety."[28] And yet, while the details of this story are beyond the scope of this work, the promotion of an intense, personal sanctified relation—even union—with God unleashed a dynamic of millennial expectation, extravagent promises made, choices offered, and empowerment supported. Embracing an empowerment independent of any established institutions or procedures, sanctified groups and communities spread across the land: from "middle-class evangelical reformers" who "sought to transform society as they had transformed themselves" advocating "the millenium—the thousand years of Christian social perfection," to a "brave and uncompromising minority" who "followed Finneyism to its furthest anarchistic and perfectionist conclusions. If perfection began in individual autonomy, they reasoned, then *all* coercive human relations were sinful."[29]

This search for sanctification and the godly nation, unchecked in its expression and uncontainable in its results, grew in both numbers and scope throughout the 1820s and 1830s from perfectionist offshoots of mainstream denominations to more radical groups demanding a polity of realized saints—in varieties of perfectionism, sectarianism with its extreme of spiritual individualism, and often merely aberrational behavior. The increasing sense of worth, virtue, and fitness through an indwelling sanctification undermined demands for gradualist spiritual improvement under socially mandated regimens. The religious visitor Moritz Busch noted the "unusual intensity" of American religion—most evident in extreme revivalists who "among all peoples have the most self-confidence, and so they behave like heaven-stormers."[30] Roving ministers, competing through ever longer periods and more comprehensive methods, were thrusting communities into a state of continual spiritual arousal:

> An exaggerated dependence on revivalist measures . . . helped establish the notion that special efforts under a person of particular talents would create a keener spirituality than the ordinary course of events could achieve. Its rapid spread after 1830 made many a person echo the thoughts of a Lockport clergyman: "by the by—before the millenium comes will not Christians hold 365-day meetings every year? . . ." The revival engineers had to exercise increasing ingenuity to find even more sensational means to replace those worn out by overuse . . . [which] helped the measures themselves grow ever more intense, until the increasing zeal, built up inside of orthodoxy, overflowed into heresy.[31]

The religious zeal knew no bounds: "Who would accept as the truth . . . that not two miles from the capital of New York there exists a settlement of . . . otherwise quite reasonable and worthy people—who believe in all seriousness that . . . the second coming of Christ has already taken place in the form of a woman?"[32]

The validation of personal choice at its extreme shifted spiritual life from institutions toward religious autonomy. That "a change of mighty import— nothing less than a new creation—old things passing away, and all things becoming new" was arising from a popular movement stirred hopes that "it may be accomplished independently of a divine influence; or that a man has nothing to do but to wish himself a Christian in order to become one." Personal certitude and the reliance on human initiative during revivals were becoming the evil of *"self-confidence."*[33] Finney warned that "whenever Christians get strong in their own strength, God curses their blessings."[34] The perfectionists were particularly aware of how dangerously close their sense of an animated inner Spirit was to personal license. Mahan wrote "to guard the reader" from "considering impulses and impressions as the teachings of the Spirit," but the distinction was subtle if not unclear: "The man who is led by the Spirit, is filled, not with impressions and impulses, but with light."[35]

Despite such warnings, calls to personal conviction reinforced the centrality of personal understanding, certitude, and control regarding one's spiritual life. Nathan Hatch details how this dynamic expanded the evolving mainstream appeal to individual choice into a virtual theology of personal transcendence. According to the influential radical Methodist preacher Lorenzo Dow, "if all men are 'BORN EQUAL,' and endowed with unalienable RIGHTS by their CREATOR, in the blessings of life, liberty, and the pursuit of happiness—then there can be no just reason, as a cause, why he may or should not think, and judge, and act for himself in matters of religion, opinion, and private judgment." Others elaborated this into personal interpretations of Scripture, private councils with and revelations from God, individual prophecy, and finally the denomination of oneself, "alone, unconnected to or with any one."[36] The extreme individualism arising out of the mainstream spiritual logic pushed not only into a replication of radical English sectarianism but also toward Unitarianism, Emerson, utopian secularism, and the emergence of a new American progressive countertradition, rooted in the individual's self-commissioned and self-authorized power to enter heaven or achieve earthly paradise without regard for God's will. One emblem of this proliferating personal validation is the prophet Matthias's report of his troubled meeting with the Mormon prophet Joseph Smith in 1835: "I told him that my God told me that his God is the Devil."[37]

Institutional fragmentation was an unavoidable consequence of heightened cultural voluntarism. Spiritual individualism multiplied sects and denominational schisms as prophets, revivalists, and itinerants roamed the land seeking inspired followers for their unique message from God. Driven by personal visions, insurgents relentlessly attacked institutional hierarchy, elite ministerial monopoly, and coercion in all its forms in their pursuit of a free and revolutionary religiosity. Many called, Nathan O. Hatch writes, "for the abolition of all organizational restraints of any kind. . . . Only by renouncing all institutional forms could 'the oppressed . . . go free, and taste the sweets of gospel liberty.'" Alexander Campbell, rejecting "church government," wanted "'no system of our own, or of others, to substitute in lieu of the reigning system. We only aim at substituting the New Testament.' . . . [Others] declared that the attempt 'to impose any form of government upon the church' . . . would be 'like binding two or more dead bodies together' and coercing people 'like parts of a machine.'"[38] While some ministers and movements such as the Disciples of Christ directly promoted personal understanding and belief, the major denominations also contributed to a situation of unlimited spiritual options. They could not hold on to members, who moved and switched with alarming if not incomprehensible rapidity, nor could they effectively control the direction of individual churches or doctrines. Violations of church discipline or disagreements with local church doctrine thus led not to permanent exile but simply to membership in or creation of another church or denomination.

Revivalism itself was creating an authority crisis for mainstream religion, diminishing the importance of religious institutions and denominational messages. Denominational rivalry weakened the credibility and drawing power of individual congregations and strengthened the role of innovators and initiators. Personal conviction undermined ministerial authority and promoted "the universal priesthood and kingship of Christians." Busch identified the dynamic of constant challenges to existing doctrines and institutions, this "continual change in all affairs" as one in which for the innovator "his house, his books, even his churches must always be new," feeding in turn the popular "hostility toward all authority." Questioning everything was leading to "an absolute lack of respect, which not infrequently becomes impiety."[39] Relying on the "Lord alone" easily evolved into an emphasis on the "taking of a *bold stand* for *stigmatized truths* and unpopular *reforms*."[40]

Americans of this period were increasingly shaping religious institutions as a direct expression of their own spiritual agendas. Able to "find an amenable group no matter what his or her preference in belief, practice, or institutional structure,"[41] they were forcing institutions "to meet the folk on their own terms."[42] This fearsome range of alternatives, referred to by one missionary at the time as "a realm of confusion and anarchy," a "sea of sectarian rivalries," threatened not only a consensus on values and appropriate societal behavior but also the very idea of organized religion and even a single society.[43] Philip Schaff called the "SECT SYSTEM" a "great evil" which "contradicts the very idea of the unity of the church." Christianity's goal "to leaven and sanctify all spheres of human life" was thwarted by "the religious subjectivity and individuality of the sect system" and its ultimate, inevitable consequence, "that religious fanaticism, to which" Americans "are much inclined." Busch found this "land of heresies and sects," of "confessional confusion," with its "continual ebb and flow" of contradictory beliefs and institutions, ever more dangerously fragmented. The "hundreds of little churches and chapels in which Americans now worship" precluded a single "holy temple" for all the people: no one had "as yet to draw the plans" for its construction, and "not even the foundation stone has been laid."[44] Charles Ingersoll believed that the greatest threat to the young republic, the "evils of faction and fanatacism" driven by "enthusiasm" and "the lust for novelty," was "fomented by freedom,"[45] that is, by the revolutionary idyll itself.

The Turn from Enthusiasm

By the late 1830s, continuing religious fervor had itself become the problem. The path to the millennium was threatening the authority and cohesion, even the functionality, of the religious sector. Many in the now dominant sects were revising their spiritual time line, demanding a more orderly— if much longer—journey to collective redemption. This extension of the earthly passage clouded the role of spiritual enthusiasm and expanded that of organizational controls on religious practice. At the same time, an increasingly successful and socially integrated membership was becoming less tolerant of the disregard for responsibility and respectability among religious dissidents and individualists. The sector which had first organized individual reversal was also to pioneer the institutional response to bring containment to the excesses of "liberty." While other institutional sectors were required—if disingenuously—to proclaim the sanctity of self-interest and self-governance, religion alone was able to highlight a voluntarism whose outcome was the subordination of individual ends to the authoritative ends of the collective.

Even partisans of the Awakening were beginning to realize that sharpening the dialectic of reversal, magnifying individual voluntarism in order to provoke spiritual commitment and congregational solidarity, highlighted the sense of empowerment with its unpredictable consequences. The religious groups emerging into dominance were increasingly "eager to clamp a lid on the box of youthful enthusiasm," to "bring discipline and consolidation to a culture marked by experimentation and novelty."[46] In the Connecticut Valley of Vermont, erupting political, social, and religious conflict as religious crusades "excited unreliable emotions, unleashed charges of religious tyranny and fanaticism, and raised questions about a Christian's duty toward others," prompted a widespread desire to "bring moral order to the valley."[47] Similarly, in upstate New York, the "acrimony, rebellion and strife" from proliferating religious individualism led congregations to seek the return of "the unity of the spirit" and the "union and harmony of the Church."[48] In the nascent labor movement, "sectarianism in religion and politics" was repudiated in favor of a "call" for individuals to "end all divisions—religious, political, social" through "solidarity preached by their religion, to bring order out of disorder, unity out of discord."[49]

Continual intense activity also provoked increasing fears of declension as each wave of enthusiasm resulted in a declining receptivity to renewal: "Enthusiasm could not be perpetually sustained, and the increasingly sensational efforts to defy this religious law of gravity only generated reaction. Hastily made converts 'returned to their wallowing,' and churches threatened with poverty grasped the harder to fill their own pews."[50] One Methodist minister mused: "In seeing the people rejoiceing, this thought was impressed on men, that there is an impropriety in wishing always to be in such extacies as it would prevent men from answering the end of [God's] creation in many things."[51] Bushnell was an outspoken opponent of centering religious experience on revivals. Far from renewing faith, it had the effect of eroding it: "Having made every thing of a revival of religion, and little or nothing of religiosity itself, we spend the intervening times in mourning over ourselves because we cannot live in the extraordinary as an ordinary thing!" The result is the feeling that "God, because he does not help us to realize an impossibility, is withdrawn, and since the revival is gone by, what conclusion have we left, but that 'Zion languishes,' and that life is to no Christian purpose any longer?"[52]

The minister Orville Dewey writing in 1847 decried the dependence of the church on emotional bonds: "Christian brethren! We hear much in these days, about excitement. Why, every prayer—of a Christian at once perfectly rational, and perfectly devoted—every prayer is an excitement; and every religious service, every sermon, is an excitement as great as he can well bear. . . . Is a man never to be moved by his religion but when some flood of emotion is sweeping through society; when agitation and disorder and confusion are on every side of him?"[53] Employing diverse fellowships to realize a Christian republic, revivalism was further failing to universalize its mission and even repelling some. Amidst competition for members, many involved for a time "fell away into sin or indifference,"[54] while everywhere—particularly in urban areas—revivals were failing to attract vast segments of an increasingly heterogeneous society. The inability of the enthusiast spirit to stabilize religious institutions would require new forms of cohesion, processes of integration and accommodation offering a straightforward path to religious membership.

Most problematically, the churches were losing touch with evolving membership needs. In these years, opportunities for participating in the political, economic, and social formation of the new society abounded, releasing and redirecting vast popular energy into new institutional developments. Despite a surprised leadership, it was no accident that the members were becoming the leaders in forging the emerging political, social, and economic sectors. Under their very leadership, citizens in religious communities had achieved both inner discipline and the experience of community governance, economic responsibility and the skills of sociability and accommodation which the increasingly democratic, populist, and entrepreneurial age demanded.

The awakened citizenry were becoming less rural as well as "wealthier and higher-status," unable given their discipline to "avoid worldly success"[55] as they moved from being "cultural outsiders to insiders," from "alienation to influence."[56] Experiences of worldly success and the pleasures of worldly rewards "broadened the outlook,"[57] as a result of which they "compromised more and more with the world."[58] As they increasingly sought the "respectability" attached to "middle-class propriety and urbane congeniality," their goals shifted to finding more broadly communal and orderly "means to defend their town from evil . . . to build and judge the character of townspeople, and to defend the prestige and the economic position of 'respectable' citizens."[59] The pressure imposed by the discipline and strenuosity of a world-transforming religion was becoming too burdensome. The stark choices, the "all-or-nothing" demands for spiritual intensity posed by religious reversal, could no longer guarantee commitment where individuals had other, less onerous spiritual and worldly options. It risked driving individuals into other sectors for measures and expressions of their success, sectors which offered a voluntarism and a range of lifestyles without the intensity demanded by the churches, without constantly testing the depth of their internal commitment. For this expanding cohort, if the goal of intensifying reversal was merely principled institutional commitment, it was no longer necessary, for they were leading proponents of societal integration. If more, it would fail.

The turn from religious revival, given its centrality to national formation, amounted to a crisis of authority for the republic recalling that which had prepared the way for revolution seventy-five years earlier. This time, however, was different: the issue was no longer the nature of the new authority but its *mode of institutionalization*. Where the entire weight of spirituality was on individual agents, how was popular authority to be exercised, its presence insisted upon, its expectations enforced? Given a populace which no longer understood by tradition or instinct the place of religion and responsibility in a vastly different spiritual economy, how was the religious community that was vital to successful societal integration and still deeply committed to spiritual progress to be sustained? With ubiquitous inducements to hyperindividualism, what demands could be exercised by a God of "Perfect Love" who operated to restore, heal, and sanctify rather than to threaten using sin, damnation, and destruction? Was agency, now in place characterologically, to mean institutionally whatever individuals wanted it to mean, sectarian or mainstream, religious or secular, Bushnell's world proselytizer or isolationist, Emersonian or Presbyterian, northerner or southerner? Why should an "agent" rest with being merely one agent among others, or an agent at all?

American Protestantism, which had given agency to the nation, was struggling to render that sense of identity, role, and authority workable. A culture needing a counterweight to voluntarism and anti-institutionalism, so mobilized for world-transforming activity, had to find its restraining center in a set of institutions and disciplined behaviors applicable to all. The Puritans had failed to achieve institutional cohesion, and had lost not only power but also influence in a modernizing world. The Protestantism of the young republic also risked losing power and the consolidation of agency society before the very self-empowerment which the new society appeared to offer. The first alternative to revivalism through the structures of local religious community, though still necessary for backsliders, failed to contain the broader dynamic. As a result, the religious sector ultimately endorsed the shift of socialization and regulation to secular sectors more effective in structuring worldly practice. Thus did the impulse toward a proto-liberal regularization of conduct emerge in the Protestant community and contribute to the "liberalization" of American society.

The Consolidation of Religious Institutions

The aim of popular religious mobilization, a Protestant commonwealth, required winning people who would forge a permanent religious community by involving themselves in the ongoing life of the church. Revivalists hoped to overcome the vicissitudes of the conversion experience by insisting that the believer "obey the will of God . . . always . . . [w]hether he feels any lively religious emotion at the time or not . . . whatever may be the state of his emotions." Finney at this early juncture resisted the more self-empowering implications:

> Multitudes . . . speak of sanctification as if it were a sort of washing off of some defilement, or a purging out of some physical impurity. Or they will

speak of it as if the faculties were steeped in sin, and sanctification is taking out the stains . . . supposing that sanctification is something that precedes *obedience*. . . . [I]t is not something that precedes obedience, some change in the nature or the constitution of the soul. But sanctification *is obedience*, and, as a progressive thing, consists of obeying God more and more perfectly.[60]

All "powers and susceptibilities" were under "the control of one principle— 'faith in the Son of God'" with the goal of a "complete, entire, unreserved, unconditional devotement of self to God."[61]

There was also an effort to bring order to revivalism itself by adopting "a regularly organized plan" which reduced its "exertions" to a "system."[62] Finney worked to "train up a new race of pastors" with the "special knowledge and special skills . . . needed to promote revivals."[63] But as its dangers became more apparent, churches began to regard themselves as the only source of continual direction and pressure for the self-discipline lacking elsewhere in society: "Thus you see that young converts are thrown into the hands of the church, and it depends on the church to mould them, and form them into Christians of the right stamp."[64] This increasingly involved the need for institutional controls to bring structure to religious practices. The priority shifted to holding individuals within emerging institutional structures through continuing participation in religious community.[65] The fears and anxieties about separateness stirred by revival were redirected to fellowship attachment. Backsliders were labeled "rebels" and "sinners," blamed for destroying "all benevolence" and wishing to "introduce universal selfishness and rebellion against God."[66] Such individuals even if prominent in the church were to be shunned: "Christians" must "naturally avoid the society of those that abuse God."[67] Mere association with such a person was to "go with him and adopt his principles." The goal was marginalization and isolation through "the ill will of . . . friends" and associates alike: "Who can trust such a character? Who can help despising him. The ungodly despise him. . . . The church distrusted him and set him aside as a broken reed."[68] The doubter was forced to confront that "one shall be taken and another left."[69] John Godfrey, the protagonist of Bayard Taylor's novel *John Godfrey's Fortune*, by refusing to join his family and village in conversion had "cut off the last bridge to reconciliation," making life in the village "unsupportable" and forcing him to leave for the city.[70]

Within the religious fellowships, the fragile emotional threads holding revivalists together were replaced by regular religious practice and moral codes enforced by communal discipline. There were schisms in sect after sect as the organizational noose was tightened around perfectionist popular agitation. The popular "revulsion against extreme revival manners and practice" led to the replacement of reformers who defined institutions as a means to further religious or social causes with "a new order" of ministers and leaders committed to the interests of organizational unity who "stressed orthodox doctrines and kept enthusiasm within strict limits."[71] Established churches within communities now focused on membership, broad doctrinal consensus, and the importance of service over dogma. Worldly distinctions were allowed into the church, standards of membership reduced, and spiritual preparation de-emphasized. The goal was to provide stability for parishioners who could be gently guided but no longer pushed toward the millennium.

The regularization of practices signified a commitment to community stability in place of continual demonstrations of religious fervor, "less faith in the goodness and automatic accomplishments of the regenerate man and more faith in measures calculated to make men behave aright."[72] Each denomination thus developed during this period internal rules of conduct and mechanisms for ensuring compliance. Community norms applied to misconduct in the family or business, religious practice, social and interpersonal relations, and personal rectitude. As the primary institution promoting general moral and behavioral standards, particularly in less settled areas, the churches influenced not just their members but others who attended and, as members became social leaders, the communities themselves:

> Though the membership of the churches constituted but a small proportion of the population in any given frontier community, they set the moral standards and patterns of conduct. . . . But why did the individual church member submit to the extra-legal action of the churches in their attempts to regulate his life and conduct? One reason, undoubtedly, was because he considered the voice of the church the voice of God, and feared divine retribution. Also, to be condemned by the church was to be condemned by the whole community, and therefore, to maintain his position among his neighbors, whether church-members or not, he needed the approval of the church. To be expelled was to be disgraced in the eyes of all.[73]

In some denominations such as the early Methodists, whose members were expected to discuss their personal lives in detail, the regulations involved comprehensive rules governing all areas of behavior.

The institutional oversight in small communities of believers could be quite encompassing: "They should be watched over, by the church, and warned of their dangers, just as a tender mother watches over her young children . . . in this great city, for fear that the carts may run over them, or they may stray away and be lost; or as they watch them while growing up, for fear they may be drawn into the whirlpools of iniquity. . . . The church should . . . know where they are, and what are their habits, temptations, dangers, privileges, state of religion in their hearts, spirit of prayer." Vigilance ranged from probationary periods during which potential members were scrutinized to the ongoing regulation of members' conduct. Typically, those who were alleged by a fellow member or by reputation to have violated community norms were investigated and, if believed warranted, tried by church disciplinary bodies. Denominational punishments ranged from censure to public denunciation to suspension and expulsion for serious or repeated offenses.[74]

The increasing struggle to maintain religious ascendancy, given the growing comfort of the membership with economic success and social advance, gradually centered on the question of what activities to allow beyond church boundaries. The institutional church by no means simply praised such activity before the war, which is to say that liberal and Protestant values at this point clearly diverged. Yet a modernizing Protestantism which systemically demanded work, productivity, initiative, and leadership could not merely reject worldly ambitions or condemn their growing rewards. Enforcement of artificial distinctions would not contain that worldly involvement and, worse, would split the religious sector. The early-nineteenth-century resolution, temporary at best, was to circumscribe economic and social activity conceptually within the religious mission.

The ambivalence toward worldly success in this period is striking. The revivalists continually reminded their audiences to resist the temptations of material success and political ambition, to *"beware of the world"* as a "deadly enemy to the believer's growth in grace":[75] "If you are worldly *minded*, you are a backslider." The truly religious individual "has less relish for the world . . . less and less desire for its wealth, its honors, its pleasures." One struggling with temptation, "in danger of being carried away by the love of the world," must "shut down the gate, and determine . . . [not to] add to your wealth."[76] Peter Cartwright idealized the early ministers who "would brook the hardships and undergo the privations that must necessarily be endured in preaching the Gospel" to "plain people" focused on "the unsearchable riches of Christ,"[77] in contrast to "the unnecessary thousands expended" in later times for "ornamental churches, to make a vain show and gratify pampered pride."[78] Yet worldly success was inevitable. The older generation of Methodists grudgingly came to realize the new role of economic success as the church "has risen in numerical strength, and become wealthy."[79] Finney, too, recognized that his audiences were both deeply engaged as well as ambitious in such matters: "God has so constituted us, that a certain amount, and certain kinds of worldly objects, are indispensable to our existence."[80] Individuals have a duty "*suitably* to provide" for themselves and their family, and may "desire . . . to be rich," to "seek . . . wealth and honor."[81]

Worldly motivations "to be rich," or "to get some office," or to gain "friends"[82] were as yet without particular virtuousness or educational value or intrinsic worth attached to the activities themselves. Commerce in particular was not regarded as godly work: "Business principles, or the principles of commercial justice, are the principles of supreme selfishness. . . . Upon these principles it is neither demanded, nor expected that any one should seek another's wealth, but that every one should take care of himself, purchase as low and sell as high as he can. . . . Can a man love God supremely, and his neighbors as himself, who daily and habitually transacts business on [these] principles?"[83] It is simply a "duty which God requires, to be busy, always usefully employed in some way," subject to the stricture that "men are God's stewards, and HE never employs them so they cannot have time to commune with him." Their morality and purpose derived from their ultimate religious uses, following the command to "*be religious in every thing*," "to have just as *much religion in all their business*, as they have in prayer."[84] Piety focused on the use to which resources were put: "*Sanctified* wealth will always provide a blessing to the Church of God. . . . If our wealthy people will come themselves and bring their wealth . . . it is almost incalculable to tell the instrumental good that can . . . result to the cause of religion."[85]

Commercial activity, political involvement, and social relations were to be framed to utilize one's constant participation to further the ministry and one's agency in it: "The only way in which money can be used for the glory of God and the good of men, is to promote the spirituality and holiness of men." To those who complained about the impact of moral strictures on successful commerce, Finney defended ethical practice: "Suppose all Christians did so. . . . Christians would run away with the business of the city. The Christians would soon do the business of the world. . . . Only make it your invariable rule to do right . . . and you control the market." Similarly, moral rectitude in politics would allow the religious to "sway the destinies of nations, without involving themselves at all in the base and corrupting strife of politics."[86] Every business decision, vote, act of friendship, contribution, or expenditure of money must reflect that "a man loves supremely the kingdom of Christ, and longs exceedingly for its coming and extension."[87]

The Failure of Success

It is tempting to regard the ultimate inability of the religious sector to contain worldly impulses within a godly American society as a failure. It is harder to appreciate how the Awakening was destined to be undone by its very success. This Protestant mission would not be like the Puritans' failure, for it offered rather than a transitional doctrine a grounded theory of operational selfhood and a framework for institutional formation. Yet the paradoxical outcome by which religious values were relocated within a broader society suggests the dilemmas it faced. In generating a fervor for and confidence in worldly transformation, the movement emboldened its members to remake the larger society beyond denominational limits. By giving discipline and shape to individual character and empowering, equipping, and stabilizing members in their new worldly tasks both as individuals and as cooperating citizens in the community, the church also prepared its constituents to further their ambitions beyond the bounds of the religious sector within the complex new terrain of voluntarism, consent, and deference in the larger majoritarian society.

This turn toward the world was in a profound way the fulfillment of the religious mission. From the outset, the logic and deeper impetus of agency made the world the arena for testing one's fulfillment of God's responsibilities. Humans, confined as they are to the temporal realm, can vindicate God's delegation only within—by transforming—that realm. Though many were disheartened by the shift, by preparing individuals with the internal resources and institutional skills for this worldly project, the age of revivals succeeded admirably. As a profoundly transforming religion, awakened Protestantism directly secured the developmental advance to agency for vast numbers, while many more Americans of this age not directly involved—embracing the message if not the messenger—looked to the religious formulation of character and self-discipline as the clearest guidance for identity and social role in this uncharted world. Even on the institutional level, its experimental, evolving efforts to contain and direct voluntarism, to bring it within—as a building block of—the collective, of turning voluntarism as freedom into the active and responsible self-discipline that so surprised Tocqueville with its effectiveness, pointed the way in the utter absence of traditional hierarchies and regulating authorities toward a new liberal model of authority.

Its mechanisms—the societalization of spiritual goals, retention through group solidarity, limitation on worldly impulses, and enforcement of church discipline—represented the first effort in the new society to evolve effective authority from *within*. Theological authority, by mandating agency, prepared individuals for deference to subsequent secular authority. Participating in collective education, supervision, and discipline amidst their equals from disparate backgrounds, Americans learned to build communities by mutually assimilating into the goals, larger processes, and daily rituals that were being developed. In this training process, individuals were being turned—turning themselves—into proto-liberal Americans, establishing the foundation and stability liberal institutions would so deeply need. This great process propelled the United States into a uniquely modernizing society with a liberal center both institutionally and at the foundational level of citizen character structure.

As members of the religious community, exhorted to engage and shape the new society, overflowed its containing walls while turning from religious strenuousity and discipline to the less spiritually consuming demands of secular society, the religious sector faced a crisis. Its strategy, the necessary organizational competition for new converts, only exacerbated the problems. Multiplying the number of "vendors" escalated the need to create marginal product differentiation in order to reap a competitive advantage. But how could the actors in the religious market—in any decentralized market—counter this centrifugal dynamic? By selling harder, making the remedy for overdose, alas, another dose. This inevitable dynamic destabilizing church life mandated "that people have to be won over and over again as they move geographically and as they change their class orientations and find different aspirations for themselves."[88] The church needed some way to protect its gains: "A revival will decline and cease, unless *Christians are frequently re-converted.* . . . Christians, in order to keep in the spirit of a revival, commonly need to be frequently convicted, and humbled, and broken down before God, and re-converted."[89] Robert Baird insisted that revivals continue: "Whatever abuses, notwithstanding . . . it can not be disputed that our truly zealous, intelligent, and devoted Christians believe firmly in the reality of revivals . . . [as] the greatest and most desirable blessings that can be bestowed upon the churches."[90]

Neither "persuasion" and "informal pressure" on the one hand nor "formal, coercive methods" on the other could prevent the exhaustion of the religious dynamic.[91] Institutionally, organization of the nation's energies and ambitions could not be contained within the ecclesiastical framework. The localist strategy of keeping individuals within small islands of preexisting purpose failed to address the vast structural and institutional demands of a modern society with its unimaginable sprawl of diverse immigrants, nonbelievers, the worldly ambitious, and scions of religious communities determined to move on. On the level of conviction, local pursuit of a "millennial community" offered little guidance for the larger national project, leaving people "increasingly skeptical of the capacity of Christianity to provide an answer."[92] At the same time, having adapted their message to the culture of voluntarism to reach the broader public, the religious institutions had forsworn any mechanism or discourse for overtly excluding from the nation individuals with divergent priorities.

From a larger perspective, sectarian religious preoccupations no longer addressed the nation's critical concerns. Many Americans, internally adapted to the new societal realities, now needed validation and direction for the engagement of their developing powers of productive agency. The gradual redefinition of freedom as responsible institutional agency within "wider activities" with "additional possibilities for self-realization," namely, the economic, political, and social arenas emerging in the Jacksonian period, represented the realistic organizational response to those needs.[93] Religious institutions still largely shaped the constitution of character and the motion toward and values informing institutional society, but collective order would come only from comprehensive, "nonpartisan" rules within an inclusive agency society. The task confronting the religious sector was to identify this more specific role for itself and to situate it within the larger consolidation and implementation of the new psychohistorical reality.

Toward an Inclusive and Worldly Church

This gradual assumption of the church's modern function within the process of national formation represented yet another instance of the Protestant turn to liberalism as the carrier and guarantor of its mission. Despite earlier caution about identifying with any secular enterprise, the dominant tendency after the Civil War toward reconciliation with the liberal polity in fact began in the antebellum period. Protestant leaders slowly reframed the project of societal transformation as creation of an overarching community under church guidance if not control. Given the growth of church membership and increasing prominence of religious constituents, the nation's emergence out of the postrevolutionary "wilderness" could easily suggest the triumph of religious purpose within a national "community." Busch imagined a future "reconciliation" of religious "contradictions," when "an American church will be formed upon the ruins of present-day sectarianism" and "the nation will proceed to the realization of its great national idea."[94] Schaff envisioned America as "the land" of the "grandest future," which has gained "the favor of Providence" to fulfill "the destiny of mankind" and "a new leaf in the history of the world and of the church."[95]

Even Finney, with increasing doubts about the effectiveness of revivals, began to imagine a national religious society, while Cartwright eventually noted "how changed was the whole face of the country" now distinguished by "rising glory and strength."[96] Hatch, persuasively resisting the traditional view of a unified, cohesive age of revivals in this "most centrifugal epoch in American church history," acknowledges nevertheless its common project: "For all this fragmentation, one could not have designed a system more capable of Christianizing a people in all of its social, geographic, and ethnic diversity."[97] Bushnell, reaching the highest millennial pitch at this time, spoke of "a great nation here to arise and come into the public history of the world, possibly as a leading member," a "Spiritual Colony" that will "unfold more of wealth and talent" than anywhere before, become a "mighty power to win over and assimilate the nations," and "overspread and fill the world" as the "Heavenly Colony."[98] More prosaically, Baird noted the practice "now common, in almost all parts of the Unites States for Sabbath-schools to assemble on the Fourth of July . . . for the purpose of hearing appropriate addresses, more religious than political; of uniting in prayer for the blessing of God upon the country . . . and of praising Him from whom all our privileges, civil and religious, have been renewed."[99]

The early social, political, and moral reform movements, treated from an earlier perspective as millennial enterprises, must also be understood as in part a concession to the growing engagement of both populace and leadership with civil society. Angelina Grimké Weld wrote in 1845: "*I have felt great sympathy with all true hearted Second Advent believers in their great disappointment at the non appearance of their Lord + Master . . . [but] it was not necessary that Christ should be visible to our fleshly eyes, in order that he should reign in the world. . . . Who cannot see + feel that* we have entered upon a new era."[100] Revivalists noted the shift toward public action and social reform in their own audiences, "so occupied with political issues that they could admit to no religious consideration."[101] Just as the establishment Congregational and Presbyterian denominations had with their declining religious influence gone "outside the framework of organized religion" in efforts to shape the larger society,[102] so the newer sects similarly turned from an "earlier preoccupation with salvation from personal sin and the life hereafter" to movements of "community improvement" through work with "poor and needy sinners" everywhere.[103]

The establishment reform and tract societies and the Sunday school movement aimed to restore the basis for "moral order" by establishing a "transformation of character" with its *"safe and permanent principles of conduct"* that would promote "respectability and usefulness" within a diverse, weakly restrained populace.[104] To counteract their own growing divisions, the newer branches turned as well to national benevolent activities. The objective was to forge a "better weapon against disorder" by emphasizing broad community standards of morality rather than "spiritual commitment," "character" as expressed in "temperate behavior and proper conduct" rather than salvation. "Nonreligious movements . . . could also unite evangelicals and nonevangelicals, church members and nonmembers, in a common cause without offending particular religious principles. By making people think of their reputations rather than their souls, they could spread more quickly a compulsive concern for personal rectitude, and they could demand some token of commitment from everyone, even those who felt no call to membership in a church."[105] The increasing prominence of these reform societies signaled a declining role for the church: "They made respectability, not church membership, society's password. . . . [T]hey assumed that the churches would no longer play the most important role in defending society and the family."[106]

This promotion of consensual civil morality independent of the church established the larger polity as the arena for the expression and elaboration of the new character. Religion would now concern itself with the gap between "what is felt at church, and what is done abroad in the world," between weekly professions of abstract morality and the daily struggle for practical virtue. Spiritual strenuousity had to be replaced with consistent rules of practical behavior and a religion "steady and constant . . . deep, sober, strong, and habitual . . . not periodical, but perpetual; not transient, but enduring."[107] This emphasis on worldly action, practical ethics, and moral responsibility was reflected in shifting themes among religious authors by the mid-1830s. In place of spiritual searches, religious visions, and consorting with angels that dominated earlier fiction, the characters of subsequent novels cultivated the virtuous self-discipline for social and family engagement and for productive careers. Bessie Lee in Catherine Maria Sedgwick's novel *The Linwoods* (1835), having learned that "we must 'come down' to humanity and 'adapt ourselves to things as they are,'" dedicates herself to "active virtue" through a career in social work. Sedgwick's novels increasingly defined religion in terms of "nurture, social concern, and domestic morality," suggesting that "secular affairs have been elevated to a level of sanctity, while religion had been divested of its visionary idealism." The preoccupation was now with obligation to the world. The novelist Lydia Maria Child underwent a long journey during this period from religious themes to "a church of deeds, not of doctrines of any sort."[108] In his late novel *Richard Edney* (1850), Sylvester Judd replaced the religious quest with a concern for virtuous conduct and social amelioration, "TO BE GOOD, AND TO DO GOOD." Spiritual vision needed to be rigorously contained, reduced to "palpable bounds," and "the actual and the real," including "social problems like poverty, war and slavery," made the concern of "honest moral endeavor."[109]

This shift made possible the eastern urban and suburban revivals between 1840 and 1860, where established religious leaders successfully preached a progressive gospel of human worth, religious toleration, social progress, material well-being, and spiritual comfort to equally established audiences. People flocked to hear this accommodating message, to be told that wealth too had a role, secure that "a combination of the Revival with business could be managed without the loss of liberty—without businessmen having to submit to impracticable or utopian dictates of evangelists."[110] At the same time, the increasing emphasis on worldly morality "not only undercut the possibility of a unique evangelical culture, it also blurred the distinction between church members and the world. How different could a church member be from a nonmember when both contributed to the same charities, served with the same fire department, and supported the same political candidates?" Civil activity, now providing "other ways to allay the anxieties that fueled the revival," was beginning to subsume the church.[111]

This incipient effort to come to terms with a society more divisive, heterogeneous, and intransigent to local spiritual discipline than the early revival movement had pictured revealed how far Protestantism had evolved. The refusal to withdraw from—indeed, the increasing preoccupation with—the agency mission *in the world* suggests a deep Anglo-American Protestant commitment to society as the ultimate site of spiritual attainment. But the Protestant leadership could not produce the integrative phase of nation building, a comprehensive consolidation of the vast numbers fashioned by the very preparation for a religiously transformed society. The religious sector would discover with the Civil War that its agency values could be secured by the inclusive national project, and only by institutions capable of advancing that project. In return, its place within the larger community would be served by forming values and goals affirming the worldly mission of that community. The result would be American civil religion.

The Religion of National Immanence

Ironically, religion's vast success as abettor in the crusade to end slavery in America was the culmination of its transformational role. Recognizing the danger of unsocialized voluntarism, the religious sector broadened the basis for integrating agency values and activities. With voluntarism nonnegotiable in a liberal culture, discipline, order, and purpose would have to be brought to the community at large by more universally applicable "free institutions." Reframing the missionary sense of ends and the pursuit of worldly means within a more inclusive, less divisive setting, begun before the Civil War, accelerated thereafter. The authoritative setting would be the nation itself, both as representative of divine ends and carrier of popular ends. With religious bodies lending their considerable authority to that reframing of nation as church, they provided legitimacy to the institutional sectors of civil society. These sectors—organized around inclusive criteria and procedures—could then shape worldly activity as the means toward the transcendent and collective mission, enabling the society to realize Protestant-liberal agency.

There were costs to ceding control to the secular sectors of liberal society as they appropriated the religious framework of institutional authority and individual integration and applied them to the task of nation building. Despite the rhetoric of the Protestant nation, the creation of a "universal church" necessarily inattentive to spiritual priorities and nuances and with an emphasis on worldly conduct would end the dream of a religious commonwealth. The progress of societal transformation would now be effectively measured in liberal terms, by the incidence of the agency character structure and its institutional development rather than by its transcendent fulfillment of godly spirituality and values. The primary role of religion in the national project would thenceforth be to lend its moral legitimacy to the creed of civic liberalism—republican nationalism, market economic participation, and social integration—and to the efforts undertaken by these secular sectors to institutionalize agency.

Religion by no means retreated entirely from its missionary leadership. Though framed largely as resistance to the dominant liberalization of American Protestantism, "fundamentalists" and "social gospellers," each "preserving one or the other half of the old evangelical equation," argued variously for the godly sect and the godly nation. Revivalism was left primarily to those who resisted the Protestant turn to civil religion and the decline of religious life, withdrawing from liberal society to defend congregational and denominational purity.[112] For others, the merger of religion with the liberal polis was resisted by holding secular society to more uncompromisingly spiritual principles of service, community, and virtue.[113] Given the practical bent of post–Civil War America and popular retreat from spiritual enthusiasm, however, these proponents of the social gospel only found their outlet in the Progressive reform movement of the late nineteenth and early twentieth centuries. Unwilling to expand the (common) agency vision beyond restricted institutional settings, both insurgencies posed a divisive challenge to liberal accommodation that paradoxically strengthened the liberal demand for a secular settlement on inclusive and enforceable terms.

The antislavery and northern triumph in the Civil War thus set the stage for the instantiation of the nation as both object and carrier of the mission and for the validation of worldly activity within its redeemed community as the morally optimal means for individual participation. The *political* victory of God's spiritual legions meant that God had chosen to locate ultimate truth in the world, reveal it progressively *to humans* through a gradual unveiling in the world according to the divine plan, and render human action in the world the means of its achievement. This responsibility to bring the divine into the world was an extraordinary strengthening of the role of agency, making humans the *exclusive agents* in their domain. Authorized to shape the worldly mission, they had made the divine *dependent* on their work. As Lincoln had proclaimed, "with firmness in the right, as God gives us to see the right, let us strive on to finish the work we are in . . . [and] achieve . . . a just . . . peace."[114] Humans operating to shape history "have by the use of our human powers, under divine guidance as we trust" gained the capacity to form sacred characters, values, and institutions, and thus in effect to render God more fully immanent in the world.[115] Lyman Beecher's son Edward wrote in 1865 that the kingdom "can only be effected by the *universal indwelling of God in the individuals* of whom human society is composed, inclining and enabling them to act on his principles . . . in all departments of life."[116] So empowered, one now legitimately "feels the glow of progress and finds himself . . . eager to carry on the grand historic march of his own day and generation."[117]

This transcendent shaping of the world, utilizing America as God's first full Kingdom, made the nation rather than any congregation or community the locus of the agency vision. If prewar religious activists burned with "the gospel ideal of a righteous nation," fashioning the new society as a single moral enterprise in the Civil War made that view a widespread conviction. By God's vindication of the power of human action to sanctify and cleanse the world "for God," the war became the ultimate test of the nation's religious destiny, of God's blessing upon the land as a whole. The defeat of the powers of servitude, though at great human cost, reinforced and made explicit the more inchoate prewar sense that America was becoming the Protestant nation prophesied about, "that divine order and conduct of human society which Jesus Christ called the Kingdom of God." It was in the words of Gilbert Haven, earlier a leading Methodist abolitionist, speaking at Grant's inauguration, a "land . . . renew[ed] in holiness and love."[118]

The nation's goals were to be regarded as sacred goals, its successes sacred accomplishments: "Men in all walks of life believed that the sovereign Holy Spirit was endowing the nation with resources sufficient to convert and civilize the globe, to purge human society of all its evils, and to usher in Christ's reign on earth."[119] The nation's governance and direction would henceforth replace the fate of the churches as the strategic center of the mission. The loss of control, though increasingly felt with the passage of time, was muted by church enthusiasm toward the American role in the world. The churches' objective, then, was not to withdraw but to become guardians of the national mission, guiding the nation in its promise "to renew the face of the earth."[120]

An Agency Made Worldly

With the sanctification of the nation, secular institutions now participated in God's immanence, that is, as full participants in the worldly realization of an ideal agency world. Designated sector agendas in turn took on a new—now transcendent—legitimacy: "Protestant optimism extended outside the strictly religious sphere into a prophetic vision of the future greatness of the nation, now purged of its deepest sin. The swift opening of the Far West, the disclosure of vast new wealth, the bustling energy of industrialization all were cited as further evidence that 'Our political and social mission may be sublime beyond that of any other contemporary people.'"[121] Moral agency was thus reshaped as worldly sector activity by this "secularization of the eschatological vision," as "perfecting the world" was now "an achievement of human evolution with only tenuous ties to a transcendent deity," its goal "a transformed earthly city" brought about by "Anglo-Saxon culture, Christian morality and organizational genius."[122]

With the worldly sectors of liberal society legitimated by their own "portion" of potential—and realizable—divinity, it became possible to openly affirm and encourage economic, social, and political engagement independent of a specific religious focus. Pressure could be redirected from the dangerous, uncontainable, and even unmonitorable realm of spiritual rigor toward "voluntary" belonging in those other sectors: "As Protestants ceased to devote themselves to an intensive examination of their own spiritual state, the habit of extreme religious individualism weakened. . . . As intricacies of theological debate ceased to command clerical energies, as an unquestioning surrender to Christ in a mystical experience grew to be a less all-compelling goal, a new outlet for Christian energy became necessary."[123] Directing one's energies within these sectors now constituted action toward the fulfillment—and embodying—of divine ends: "The Christian life is to be an incarnation, a realization of divine purpose, presence, communion in our everyday occupations" which will "raise the commonplace to a sublime level by making it the abode of God."[124]

As these sectors took on this fuller, more distinctively religious character of their own, their very operation was now regarded as independently and intrinsically embodying religious values. Sector-discrete principles of transcendent ends within the larger national project and religiously virtuous conduct at the individual level were formalized as theologies of the agency market, agency society, and participatory politics, in effect branches of the national theology. And where such principles were incompletely realized, these sectors were now charged with effectuating them. Secular authority would, in keeping with the idyll, of course be derived from participating individuals, but with the increasing presumption that individuals ceded their authority to institutions through reversal.

This shift in validation and emphasis in fact freed the other sectors from religious control and foreshadowed the ultimate ascendance of concrete worldly priorities over abstract, intangible measures of spiritual success: "It would not be strange if some eyes should blink and some feet stumble in the rapid readjustment. But . . . the secularization that is complained of is of the same kind that Jesus exhibits when, by living a human life, he shows us what God is."[125] This process also gave the secular sectors the capacity for integration of individual freedom with collective purpose that liberalism on its own lacked. Individual freedom could be recast as responsible and moral voluntarism and institutional coercion as transcendentally authorized common purpose.

The religious constitution of secular theologies of ends and means began during the middle third of the century. The legitimation of worldly success later predominant after the Civil War had already begun, particularly in affluent communities on the eastern seaboard where congregants were already resistant to enthusiasm as well as austere religiosity.[126] This generation influenced by Timothy Dwight, the conservative Congregational and Federalist president of Yale—including the young ministers Horace Bushnell and Henry Ward Beecher (through his father, the influential minister Lyman Beecher) as well as Orville Dewey, Thomas P. Hunt, and Francis Wayland—was by the late 1830s shifting the theological focus from work to the rewards of work, from motivation to result. Bushnell assured his Hartford congregants "that, by divine ordinance, virtue created riches. God tempted men to industry by lavish rewards and benevolently assured the conjunction of virtue and prosperity. . . . Wealth was the index to virtue, 'a reward and honor which God delights to bestow upon an upright people.'"[127] Beecher, struggling to reconcile the sharpening "conflict between the ethic of work, thrift, and asceticism and the urge to utilize newly earned wealth for leisure, improved social status, and a more refined and luxurious way of life," lightened the spiritual burden for his Brooklyn congregation: "The very way to feed the community is to feed the family. . . . Money contributed there is contributed to the whole." Thus, there is no "selfishness" in the "generous expenditure in building up a home and enriching it with all that shall make it beautiful." This is an act of benevolence "for the whole neighborhood, not for [oneself] alone."[128]

Cartwright surveyed in the 1850s an almost unrecognizable Methodism composed of a "great many worldly-minded, proud, fashionable members of our Church," including "many of our preachers."[129] The Reverend Thomas P. Hunt declared in 1836 that "[no] man can be obedient to God's will . . .

without becoming wealthy." A Reverend Wainwright of New York called "the unequal distribution of wealth" the "only system by which . . . happiness and improvement can be promoted."[130] The Reverend Orville Dewey expressed admiration for the American "spectacle of active, absorbing, and prosperous business" driven by an "honourable" devotion to "business and accumulation . . . universal and unprecedented activity among all the classes of society, in all the departments of human industry."[131] Congregants had often pushed even beyond their ecclesiastical leadership, creating the anomaly of "a striving, rising, middle-class oriented people among whom were many wealthy and influential community members" who were typically addressed "as if they were still small persecuted or withdrawn groups of regenerates."[132] Congregations everywhere were moving toward distinctions among the membership, such as pew rents, based on economic differences.

By linking the ultimate end of worldly transformation to secular activity, the church provided the door through which Americans walked with enthusiasm—*religious* enthusiasm—to embrace the world as a necessary extension of the religious life: "Commerce has always been an instrument in the hands of Providence for accomplishing nobler ends than promoting the wealth of nations. It has been the grand civilizer of nations . . . the active principle in all civilization" spreading to the world "the principles of humanity; the natural desire of knowledge, liberty and refinement." Now "public welfare" or public good meant worldly well-being. The secular means themselves, the sanction to pursue and enjoy economic well-being and social inclusion within the civil community, had become intrinsically legitimate independent of religion: "The Scriptures, like conscience . . . do not lay down any specific moral laws of trade. They command us to be upright and honest; but they leave us to consider what particular actions are required by these principles." This sector was to be governed by distinct nontheological principles: "It is said that we ought to treat all men as brethren," but "there cannot be a brotherly identity of interests between the members of society. . . . We are not to break down the principle of individuality, of individual interest, of individual aims." The maximization of one's market advantages through "power acquired by a large property, or by a monopoly . . . should be used." Moral judgments in the economic sector must be left to economic calculations: "You may, in a fit of generosity, or a scruple of conscience, sell [some things] for less; but the moment they are out of your hands, they will rise to the level of the market; you have lost the difference, and gained nothing for your generous principle. In fine *the value of a thing is the market price of it.*"[133]

By this logic, business activity became the test and its success the fulfillment of moral and religious enterprise, "lawful and laudable, an appointment of God to accomplish good purposes in this world and better for the next." Its rewards were—unless applied to overtly un-Christian or, now its secular equivalent, unproductive ends—equally moral: "I hold it to be an advantage to the world, that restrictions . . . are thrown off; and that a greater number of competitors can enter the lists, and run the race for the comforts and luxuries of life. . . . I do not say . . . that it is wrong to desire wealth, and even, with a favourable and safe opportunity, to seek the rapid accumulation of it."[134] The obvious outcome was a system that by its very operation embodies and thus promotes both secular and divine justice: "Thus spiritual, in its design, is nature. . . . [N]o merely wearisome, uncompensated toil, or perplexing business; but a ministration to purposes of infinite greatness and sublimity. . . . In fine, I look upon business as one vast scene of moral action. 'The thousand wheels of commerce' . . . I regard as an immense moral machinery. . . . The aspirings of youth, the ambition of manhood, could receive no loftier moral direction than may be found in the sphere of business." In this just process, the outcomes must themselves be just: "There is no being in the world for whom I feel a higher moral respect and admiration, than for the upright man of business; no, not for the philanthropist, the missionary, or the martyr."[135]

By the postwar period, the striking affluence uncontainable within religious boundaries together with the infusion of civil institutions with agency values required the mainstream church to adjust its views on worldly achievement. The legal restructuring of the marketplace was quieting remaining antebellum reservations about transcendent justice in the economy: "The best legislation in the industrial and commercial sphere of human activity has long since been enacted by the Supreme Lawgiver; and every interposition by human government is both impertinent and harmful."[136] While the political system (as distinct from the "nation") acting as a unity was never regarded as sufficiently transcendent, the government was effectively reshaping the social realm by mandating Christian values: laws authorizing public Protestant worship and the support and maintenance of its teachers, recognizing and enforcing the Sabbath, setting aside religious days, granting land for religious institutions, stipulating religious oaths as a condition of legislative services and judicial testimony, appointing military chaplains, criminalizing intemperance, polygamy, and blasphemous, licentious behavior, and promoting religious-based education at all levels as well as religious education in public schools.[137] These religious-based efforts to Christianize society continued throughout the century into Prohibition the push for legislation against immigrants including outlawing their private schools, and so forth.

The result, led by Protestant ministers, was a religion of social respectability and regularity, personal conformity, doctrinal consensus, and theological inoffensiveness centered on a theology of wealth and what the Baptist minister Russell Conwell called the "gospel of success": "To make money honestly is to preach the gospel . . . the foundation principle of godliness and the foundation principle of success in business are both the same precisely."[138] The gate to heaven had become "the gates to wisdom, to love, to wealth, and to happiness."[139] With worldly progress the immanent fulfillment of the divine mission, earthly achievement came to represent independent evidence of higher ends. Affirming its own ancillary status and desire for inclusion in the liberal project, the postwar Protestant mainstream undertook the redefinition of society as a Christian enterprise. The determination "to make our Christian civilization secure and permanent, and to perfect its beauty" through "education, virtue and religion," required a denominational flexibility regarding traditional theological divisions through a nonsectarian message and strategy of integration.[140] To these ends, educational leaders in 1884 demanded "a *religious* basis to our educational system; an acknowledgement of our religious obligations, and the natural and common presentation of incentives to piety . . . in the common school, or it utterly fails of its mission, and will soon go the way of all effete institutions. . . . This *does not* involve either cant or sectarianism."[141] Denominations joined in outreach, through nondenominational Sunday schools, interdenominational agencies, the introduction of religious education into the public schools, and a united public voice. Religious dissent was by no means quieted, but social gospellers and fundamentalist revivalists—like their latter-day Progressive, New Deal, Great Society, reform Democrat, and contemporary Christian right descendants—would be debating within a common framework about the moral requirements of a now consensual agency polity.

The Religious Role in the Liberal Synthesis

While the task of directing and channeling voluntarism would now fall to more inclusive institutions, thereby assuring their eventual ascendancy, the religious sector retained a major role: to instruct the other sectors on the nature and operation of agency and to assist them in its promotion and enforcement. Religion found moral discipline and universal standards more easily applied within and through the social and particularly the economic realms, which were uniquely able to reach, shape, and channel the characters of a vast membership, provide tangible and universal measures of adaptation and success, offer space for universal inclusion, and promulgate and enforce consistent standards of membership. They could be far less easily—if at all—evaded, for they brought their own intrinsic pressures for participation (added to religious strictures) rooted in economic survival and accumulation or social inclusion and status. Their rewards were tangible, offering—unlike salvation or sanctification—visible criteria for pious action and universally recognizable models of "virtue." Furthermore, they operated under more generalized, less sectarian or divisive rules applicable to all, enabling religion to reduce the spiritual intensity in order to serve as an integrative force in the national task of assimilation and normalization.

This was achieved by redefining the liberal idyll, utilizing the religious imprimatur to transform freedom into voluntary integration with universal standards of character and conduct, interpersonal integration, and institutional deference in the secular world. The theology of the free market emerged as the religious orthodoxy: "Nowhere . . . did the business spirit find greater favor than in the Protestant church. . . . The Protestant minister . . . gave his support to laissez-faire and the *status quo*. . . . The general well-being and progress of society were declared to be in proportion to the freedom of the individual to acquire property and to be secure in its possessions."[142] But the freedom to produce quickly became a requirement of behavioral regularity, for "it was meant that all men . . . should work. . . . God has made a law against idleness, which no human power could ever annul, nor human ingenuity evade." Evasion was to be morally condemned as "an inborn, entailed evil,"[143] and "any attempt to escape from this law" must draw the condemnatory "eye of the moral observer" as a violation of "the public welfare."[144] Unconstrained activity in the secular sphere, once anathema to the revivalist church, was now validated as the gateway to membership in the new national community.

By moving ever steadily from matters of inner life and faith to performance according to liberal rules of behavior, and ultimately toward the nontransformational test of visible congruity to societal norms, the religious sector as the educator of the nation in effect prepared individuals for their participation in the larger community. As the institution most capable of instilling valid limits, the "influence of the pulpit" was heavily responsible for inculcating the "general good order, tranquillity, and happiness" of society, its "conservative character . . . obedience to law, respect for magistracy, and the maintenance of civil government," while "resist[ing] the anarchical principles of self-styled reformers, both religious and political."[145] The "unregulated force" of worldly energies with their specter of an "all-dominant . . . will" was to be tamed by religious morality or else "the universe is a moral chaos without . . . design, and . . . a moral desolation."[146] This adoption of more accessible and measurable criteria of self-realization, the morality of "ordinary life" through behavior "ordered, rationalized, and regularized to guarantee predictable results,"[147] ensured the successful adaptation of Protestant agency to the requirement of liberal integration.

The match would be completed as revolutionary liberalism in the postbellum period turned to—and was reshaped by—Protestantism with its conception of social character, institutional integration, and institutional authority which entailed a voluntary deference to institutional imprimaturs. A Protestantized liberal society was now within reach which would "concern itself as much with the social as the spiritual condition of sinners . . . and set new standards for mutual obligation and civic restraint among civic-minded citizens." This "helped" the new citizenry "reshape family, community, and class relationships, revive their sense of moral community and political purpose, and achieve social stability."[148] Thus, along lines first intuited by Hobbes, a modern order in the form of predictable motion was to rescue agency from transformational religion.

The religious dynamic culminating in the Civil War had validated the dream of an institutional America even as it dashed the lingering memories alike of the godly nation and the Jeffersonian republic. By formulating characterological and institutional constraints which encompassed the valid agency of all in both formulation and operation, by establishing a new authority cleansed of traditional ascriptive hierarchies and external impositions, these theologians and popular movements made voluntary integration to societal authority the fulfillment rather than the frustration of selfhood. Limitations through steady patterns of self-direction and self-constraint could now be acknowledged as the acceptable concomitant of new potential, not requiring as revolutionary liberalism would have it a loss of rights and naked subordination to the collective will, but affording a positive realization of self and institutions. As participants in the tasks of divine mission and societal formation, Americans were equipped to enter the self-regulating world of the young republic. The specter of self-authorization had been defeated with the reestablishment of institutional authority, just as proto-agency had been transcended in the developmental consolidation. Agents, resolved with their place in the order of things, could now act purposively and self-reliantly in the world as they had forcefully acted to shape themselves and their intentional communities.

The narrow view echoing the revivalists' "sore disillusionment" that increasingly worldly priorities meant facing the fact that "slight, if any, progress" had been made "along the wearisome road toward Utopia"[149] suggests that the failure of transformational movements is inevitable. It further posits that the institutional consolidation of such movements is necessarily a corruption of their original intent. Yet this great movement with its "compelling vision" had with "thundering legions stormed the hinterland of the nation" to shape and order the intense aspirations moving Americans toward a belief in their own power of and readiness for agency.[150] Turning the open but undefined opportunity for freedom into a set of internal and institutional norms, it had pushed their vision beyond the limited voluntary agent of Puritan Protestantism and the small radical wing of the First Awakening to the full voluntary agent at the center of the emerging culture. In so doing, it had fulfilled the developmental aspirations of Anglo-American modernity.

A decade beyond the Civil War, Americans could after a full century of independence observe a nation vastly different from the one produced by the Revolution, a nation not merely promised but to a significant degree achieved. Formed in the crucible of revival, they now saw an authoritative Protestant self and institutional order (re)emerging from the ingenuous liberal talk of freedom. They could sing the glories of a revolutionary *and religious* republic composed of free yet ever-integrating members. Speaking at the centennial of the Declaration of Independence at Independence Square in Philadelphia on July 4, 1876, in a national ceremony modeled as such ceremonies increasingly were on a Protestant church service, the noted lawyer and orator William M. Evarts highlighted the synthesis of the liberal-revolutionary and Protestant traditions. He asked whether Americans had answered the unprecedented challenge of founding a stable post-traditional nation:

> Has the free suffrage, as a quicksand, loosened the foundations of power and undermined the pillars of the State? Has the free press, with illimitable sweep, blown down the props and buttresses of order and authority in gov-

ernment . . . ? Has freedom of religion ended in freedom from religion? and independence by law run into independence of law? Have free schools, by too much learning, made the people mad? . . . The chief concern in this regard, to us and to the rest of the world, is whether the proud trust, the profound radicalism, the wide benevolence which spoke in the "Declaration," and were infused into the "Constitution," at the first, have been in good faith adhered to by the people, and whether now these principles supply the living forces which sustain and direct government and society.[151]

He answered by explaining how the young nation was recast by the "marvelous and wide system of vehement religious zeal, and practical good works, in the early part of the nineteenth century." Though less observable recently as a distinct movement, this revivalist spirit was in fact more powerful for having become the source of national meaning and cohesion:

> But these fires are less splendid only because they are more potent, and diffuse their heat in well-formed habits and manifold agencies of beneficent activity. They traverse and permeate society in every direction. They travel with the outposts of civilization and outrun the caucus, the convention, and the suffrage. . . . The great mass of our countrymen to-day find in the Bible—the Bible in their worship, the Bible in their schools, the Bible in their households—the sufficient lessons of the fear of God and the love of man, which make them obedient servants to the free Constitution of their country . . . the home of liberty, the abode of justice, the stronghold of faith among men, "which holds the moral elements of the world together," and of faith in God, which binds that world to His throne.

Liberty and Protestant agency had been seamlessly meshed in "the national religion, a religion of civilization" in which "conflict between church and world seemed to be disappearing," constituting a "continuum of Christ and culture."[152]

12

The Protestant Agent in Liberal Economics

In American treatises . . . theology becomes the backbone of economic science.

—T. E. C. Leslie

The economic sector was at the center of the validation of postbellum liberalism: its opportunities for wealth generation offered an unparalleled inducement to participation in a single universal system framed by authoritative ends and a circumscribed range of acceptable means. The great problem for economic theory, facing the decline not only of the proprietary but also the self-sufficient economy and the emerging integrated market system of industrial America, was to preserve its historic commitment to revolutionary liberal values. Laissez-faire or free market theory has claimed since the Civil War to preserve individual freedom against the "tyrannies" of organizational society and a regulated economy. Even when criticized as an impractical or ideological defense of market options amidst increasing integration, this claim has been conceded as an accurate account of its values.

The emergence of laissez-faire theory during this period of dramatic institutional consolidation, however, should raise questions about its historical function. For its status as the theory of the free economy represents a fundamental misreading of its conceptual origins, normative framework, systemic agenda, and theoretical legacy. In a remarkable irony, the historical project of this paradigm was to effect the repudiation of antebellum Jeffersonian society rooted in proprietary independence and self-reliance. Instead of preserving freedom, American market theory emerged in the late nineteenth century to explain and justify the rise of an institutional economy, an interdependent, inclusive, unavoidable (the frontier was closed) system driven by institutional priorities, rewards, and coercions. Rooted in a crucial "discovery" of old cultural verities by its first generation of theorists, freedom

459

emerged as structured systemic participation, voluntary only in the sense that one could refuse to function as an economic being. Paradoxically this truth, though pushed as a modern idea, derived from the only available source in revolutionary liberal culture for a conception of freedom compatible with institutional society. Though largely lost to memory, American laissez-faire theory explicitly appropriated the traditional Protestant liberty to serve God willingly to establish the systemic market and mandated participation by its "free" market agents.

The Universal Economy

The "brave spirit" of "commercial liberty" that was "pervading the republic, and binding it together" was gradually emerging as the "firm foundation (a chief foundation) of human society."[1] After the divisive religious discourse of sin and salvation, with its impractical goal of universal conversion and impossible task of separating sinners from believers, the economic sector offered the desired universality. Though Emerson complained of his fellow citizens' unquestioned "reliance on Property," on "what each has, and not . . . what each is," and Thoreau of the "fool's life . . . so occupied with the factitious cares and superfluously coarse labors of life," it was this universal striving which throughout the century defined the American citizenry.[2] As the prominent late-century economist and religious reformer John R. Commons wrote, religion had failed in that it "worked on the principle that it can do nothing for the unjust, that is, non church-members. It can build up Christian character only in those who have already come into the fold."[3] In the economy, "all could join the fray," and, while they were "duty-bound to do so," the rewards of success were "within the reach of the many rather than the few."[4]

Because of its very worldliness, the economy's operational rules, goals, and outcomes were observable and inherently accessible to all. No exclusive conversion was necessary to join or selective transcendent set of principles required to comprehend. All could participate responsibly by understanding their role and the operational rules if not the process as a whole. Further, if membership was universal, it was also lifelong. Tocqueville wrote, "A native of the United States clings to this world's goods . . . so hasty in grasping at all within his reach," insatiably engaging in a "bootless chase of that complete felicity which forever escapes him."[5] The economy demanded unrelenting work and production while seemingly deriving from pressures self-generated without visible institutional coercion. Unending commitment became a truism of economic popularizers after the Civil War. William Mathews of the University of Chicago insisted that "to do anything perfectly, there should be an exclusiveness, a bigotry, a blindness of attachment to that one object, which shall make all others . . . seem worthless."[6] As Orison Swett Marden counseled, "Successful men . . . owe more to their perseverance than to their natural powers, their friends, or . . . favorable circumstances. . . . Genius will falter by the side of labor, great powers will yield to great industry."[7]

In a brilliant study of the culture of work in the United States, *The Work Ethic in Industrial America, 1850–1920,* Daniel T. Rodgers probed this single-minded and unceasing commitment to labor, ironically in the period of industrial expansion when such dedication was increasingly unwarranted: "As rhetorical commonplace, as political invective, or as moral shibboleth, the equation of work and virtue continued to pervade the nation's thinking long after the context in which it had taken root had been all but obliterated. . . . What was it that made work the aim of life? As industrialization gutted the old answers, leaving only the rationale of discipline, and in its ever greater flow of consumer goods undermining even that, it became increasingly harder to say."[8] And yet, induced by a continuing, increasing supply of rewards, a supply unavailable to religion, the images of a treadmill of endless work and a bottomless basket of goods merged into a lifelong preoccupation.[9] To the relief of liberalism, the individual could henceforth be relied on to sustain economic participation.

The Protestant Turn of Liberal Economic Theory

Increasingly grounded in economic activity, liberalism could not entertain the loss of economic "freedom." Yet with established economic institutions now preexisting the entry of individual actors and further structuring viable participation, loss of the option whether or how to participate in the market raised the invalidating specter of "enslavement" or servitude. Given the incapacity of Lockean liberalism to locate freedom within the context of institutional participation, the national commitment was in greater jeopardy with each economic advance. As with the other sectors, the formidable task of liberal economic theory became to generate a plausible conception of economic options compatible with societal integration. The stakes were high because the United States, believed to be the ideal liberal society, was the great proving ground of liberal theory and of its economic theory in particular.

The possibility of "free individuals" maintaining a "free economy" into first the market and then the organizational age, so English economist T. E. C. Leslie suggested in 1880, would be determined here:

> America . . . is the country above all others to which we might naturally look for original and considerable contributions to the science of wealth through the inductive study of new facts. The diversity of some of the economic phenomena of this new world from those of the old; the unparalleled rapidity of its material progress, and the novel conditions, physical and political, under which it has taken place; the freedom from the limitations by which the populations of European countries are restricted; the absence of monarchy, aristocracy, and the military element, and of the peculiar direction which they give to production and distribution, seem to open a most promising field of observation.

Given the importance of American economic thought for the future of liberal economics and its theory, it was not "unreasonable to expect that in a country the most important of whose economic developments had taken place within living memory, some important discoveries might have been reached with respect to the laws of social evolution under which this gigantic growth has been attained."[10]

Beginning in the 1860s, a rising group of academics from other fields including Amasa Walker, Arthur L. Perry, Simon Newcomb, W. D. Wilson, and Francis Bowen founded the new field of academic economics. Together with the myriad popularizers turning out a torrent of self-help literature promoting financial success in the new economy, they explained and justified the postwar industrial market economy. They calmed and redirected public anxieties with ever-increasing self-confidence by extolling the opportunities and setting forth the behavioral guidelines within this vastly restructured system.[11] A *transvaluation* of economic freedom, this new model required a series of theoretical shifts which amounted to a relinquishment of revolutionary liberalism for a model of interdependent integration. Despite its grand claims as an ideological Maginot Line for freedom, post–Civil War laissez-faire theory abruptly and unceremoniously dispensed with the model of proprietary independence central to revolutionary liberty in the name of market agents in a coordinated economy. That is, its historical role was not to defend (an increasingly marginal) economic independence but to explain and assuage the loss of that independence in industrializing America. It "softened the blow of the failure of Jefferson's agrarian democracy while providing the rationale to maintain faith in self and in the efficacy of the new social order."[12] Deceptively called "laissez-faire," this reframed version of classical Smithian economics substituted a theory of unalterable institutional integration and subordination to its ends. Dramatically relocating individuals within a preexisting institutional process—the market, with its preinscribed and inflexible rules, laws, and procedures—this theory offered a "freedom" that was neither autonomy nor even a power to reform systemic rules, but only the ability to use systemic means to act toward the ends therein established and given.

How could individuals steeped in Lockean rights and proprietary independence be persuaded to embrace employment for another, an overarching market, the loss of landedness, and corporate consolidation? Was this not a return of economic interdependence associated with the constraining hierarchies of the Old World? How could the pervading, highly skewed market which before the Civil War had posed such a dire threat to freedom be trusted to ensure it, and moreover, to ensure it increasingly just as individuals were becoming more subsumed and defenseless in a coalescing commercial network and amidst geometrically expanding inequalities? Where lay the necessary justice of unprecedented social stratification in a society recently defined by its equality of conditions? Did this new system not represent a broken promise of the Revolution and the early republic? How would Americans regather from the loss of their proprietary republic and be induced willingly to enter the very institutions that foreshadowed the end of their dream of natural autonomy and equality?

The market system was widely questioned. In this crisis, the sudden emergence in postwar economic theory of an explicitly religious grounding and frame underlying the dislocating shift to an interdependent economic system recast American economic thought. Before its later retreat behind the veil of descriptive scientism, laissez-faire theory defended the new economy by framing it as a harmonious process which guaranteed individual choice and systemic justice by transcendent authority. Utilizing the Protestant understanding of institutional freedom and morality for its conceptual base, it defined the market and the laws of its operation as the embodiment of God's transcendent and unalterable plan within which individuals operated as voluntary and yet integrated members. Given the universal and unwaning participation in economic pursuits, integration could be comfortably defined in agency terms as commitment to systemic participation, that is, as both voluntary and deferential to collective structures and purposes transcending individual wills. Freedom could in turn be construed systemically as an attribute of inscribed activity arising from the voluntary will of individual actors. The only open question would be the individual's capacity for using the given freedom in the pursuit of authorized ends. The agency discourse could now be used to validate the authority of nontranscendent institutions, the internalization of its procedures within the citizenry and their moral enforcement against recalcitrant individuals, all in furtherance of "individual freedom," while any human authority that might alter that plan became coercive (and heretical) tampering to be rigorously excluded.

The story of this Protestant turn and the larger significance of the theoretical shift to interdependence for American economics is little known. Evidence of this historical amnesia is the continuing identification of post–Civil War market economics with William Graham Sumner. Robert H. Wiebe refers to Sumner as "a giant" among the American originators of the central "theory within which men would maneuver for the balance of the century."[13] Henry Steele Commager identified Sumner as the one who "elevated laissez-faire into a social and economic law and assigned to it the same standing as the law of gravity," while James T. Kloppenberg more recently called him together with Stephen J. Field the major "spokesmen" for post–Civil War "American liberalism," responsible for "the replacement of ethics by economics."[14] Even Sidney Fine in an otherwise masterly study of postbellum economic and social thought regards Sumner as the thinker in this period by whom "the laissez-faire theme was most cogently expressed."[15] In fact, Sumner's grotesque naturalistic Darwinian war of attrition, the result of candidly applying idyllic individualist principles to an economy capable of mobilizing great institutional power, only revealed to mainstream laissez-faire economists the desperate need for an alternative theoretical foundation. To justify the unpalatable result of his own unregulated version, Sumner disingenuously used as his reference point to distinguish the freedom of the market system the feudal command economies of Europe. This contrast successfully drew attention away from charges that the emerging national market was betraying the revolutionary promise of a "free society of free individuals." It also enhanced public receptiveness to the freedom offered within a modern institutionalized economy.

Sumner's campaign was therefore entirely ancillary to the early theorists' main concern of justifying the evolving economy in the terms of classical liberalism. At the same time, they fully understood that the new framework they required of overarching ends and mandated integration, while deeply embedded in the culture, undercut the popular view of liberty as unconstrained choice. Hoping to obscure the theological origins, they worked to embed their theological reassurance into cultural and theoretical practice. As the transition to market agency was effected, its procedures internalized by adult socialization and externalized in economic behavior, and freedom confined to institutional action, most Americans willingly substituted affluence for self-reliance, interdependence for onerous labor, market voluntarism and "rational choice" for structural choice, and the available opportunities for work and reward for freedom itself. With this regularization, these theorists quickly withdrew the telltale theological framework from their writings. Extrinsic divine governance gave way to the modern behavioral and scientific system which purported only to describe presumably free economic behavior. The secret of the field's "mystical" origins disappeared, leaving a system without a trace of external design or coercion.

These clouded origins have insulated the theory of the "free economy" ever since. The classic histories of American economic thought, Joseph Schumpeter's *History of Economic Analysis* (1954) and Joseph Dorfman's *Economic Mind in American Civilization* (1959), passingly treat its founders in Sumner's shadow while ignoring issues of theoretical transition. More recently, the dominant scientific paradigm has erased all sense of the field's American origins. The early theological arguments are remembered only in rare intellectual histories such as Fine's work. Even here, however, religion is understood as being used to justify the morality of the market. Taking at face value their claim that this theory is noncoercive, giving its participants "utmost freedom" because a role for the state is denied, ignores how theology provides a systemic response to the structural crisis of organizational interdependence.[16] In this way, the powerful informal religious, social, and cultural pressures that were mobilized to demand godly behavior in institutionalizing the market system as well as systemic coercions preventing disengagement or institutional restructuring are ignored. As a result, market "freedom," though a euphemism for market integration, remains securely divorced from its theoretical underpinnings.

Crossing from Individualism to Systemic Liberalism

The task of the new postwar economics was to undercut the legitimacy of the antebellum economic model. To do so, its self-sufficient, small-scale, and decentralized framework had to be discredited as outmoded and no longer viable. In the span of a few years, proprietorship was recast by liberals and conservatives alike, according to Simon Newcomb of Johns Hopkins University, as a primitive condition of minimal options rendering individuals "as good as helpless."[17] It was to be found, in the words of W. D. Wilson of Cornell University, only among "a savage population on some island." Richard T. Ely, a professor at Johns Hopkins and later at the University of Wisconsin and a strong reformer, identified a proprietary economy with "the earliest stages of human development" in which the "lowest of the human race resemble most closely beasts in the individualism of their economic life."[18]

In one of the earliest textbooks in the field, Arthur Lathan Perry in 1866 suggested the shift from the prewar perspective: "The hermit, who neither buys nor sells, who neither gives nor receives anything in exchange, is not amenable to the laws of Political Economy. So far as men satisfy their own wants by their own efforts without exchange, they stand outside the pale of this science. . . . Robinson Crusoe came to lead a very tolerable life upon his desolate island by means of his own industry. He did everything for himself. . . . The whole course of such a life could never have developed the idea of value."[19] The proprietary model was now synonymous with unlivable deprivation. Francis Bowen, a professor of religion and economics at Harvard, advanced the general "proposition" that "a country" devoted to agriculture "cannot become wealthy, whatever may be the fertility of its soil or the favorableness of its situation." An economy in which "each man must provide by his own toil for all his bodily wants" is indication of "low capacity . . . want of education and general intelligence," for without "wealth" there is "no progress, no refinement, no liberal art," no "civilization." The once liberating independence of the struggle with nature was now "the stern necessity of daily brutish toil on the most repulsive tasks," lacking any amenities of culture or enlightenment. Ely implored readers not to look back: "Yet how wretched this independence! How illusory! For the chief and most trying dependence of man is brought about by physical laws."[20] For Edward Atkinson, the old model of freedom was beneath consideration: "If you don't want to pay Mr. Vanderbilt for bringing your barrel of flour from Chicago to Boston, you needn't; you can wheel it yourself."[21]

The problem with self-sufficient production was that it represented a rudimentary level of economic organization: "The great difference between civilized and savage communities is that in the latter each individual for the most part works for himself, while in the former each one labors for all the others."[22] The defining "feature of modern civilization" is "the extensive cooperation of employments, produced by the minute subdivision of labor." Atkinson asked whether in the last few years "this country . . . has not . . . become one great neighborhood in which all men serve each other." The paradigm was a network or "great co-operative association, extending over the whole country, nay over the civilized world."[23] Capital is "one blade of the shears" and labor is "the other blade," and "it takes both blades to cut."[24] Individuals no longer can or ought to live separately from institutions: "The first man . . . was indeed a wonderful structure. . . . But it was not good that the man should be alone." The new model thus posed universal, inevitable inclusion within a market economy. For Amasa Walker, professor of public economy at Amherst College, "Since men have different capacities and tastes—since they are placed in a variety of circumstances . . . their products will be various; and yet, since all men desire really the same objects, an interchange of their respective commodities will become a necessity."[25]

In Newcomb's view the "helpless" self-dependent individual, by "exchanging services with his fellow-man," can acquire "the great mass of objects of desire." But, Perry explained, one "cannot, in a state of isolation, with all his efforts, procure for himself one thousandth part of the comforts which he easily procures for himself by less efforts, through exchange. Society and exchange are . . . matters of necessity."[26] For Atkinson, "We are members one of another, and the very existence of society rests upon the interdependence of its members." The "success" of each individual depends on "the services which you are capable of rendering to your fellow-men."[27] Wilson identified the process of "exchange" as originating "at the very inception of civilization." Perry found exchange "going on in a thousand directions, at once," and "reaching everywhere and permeating everything . . . in every department of life."[28]

With this shift, an ontological divide had been crossed: institutions structuring production and distribution now preexisted the individual and formed the unalterable context for economic participation. Economic "differentiation" required that "every part of the social organism" undergo "increasing adaptation" to become "more closely connected with every other part." This is highlighted by the theoretical revision of the concept of value, precisely the foundation of economics, what Perry called "the one word that marks and circumscribes the field of economy." Economics could no longer even entertain individuals' acting independently: one "able to satisfy his own particular desire by his own unassisted efforts" has "no relation to Political Economy."[29] The new undisputed measure of value was now "purchasing-power," lying firmly within the market as a systemic product. Value itself is neither an "inherent and invariable attribute" of anything, nor is it accessible to individuals to determine what is valuable for themselves.

Value, it was admitted at the time with surprising candor, was not like desire, a measure of what people truly need or even want: "Desirableness is not value. Utility is not value." Such things "are personal to individuals. There is no common standard with which they may be compared. They are not exchangeable."[30] It exists only relative to "some other thing" through a "transaction" establishing "its power of purchasing other things" in a collective process, what communities systemically or collectively—rather than individually—agree on pursuing.[31] It is simply the constructed result based on "an arbitrary definition of a Man," abstracting "every other human passion or motive" unrelated to "the desire for wealth,"[32] determined not by individual desire or collective need but by options for transferability within the boundaries of that process. Economists had found a new theoretical foundation. "Political Economy . . . has to do from beginning to end with a relation,"[33] and that relation was the market: "Value is the exchange power which one commodity has in relation to another."[34]

The meaning of production was also transformed, from an individual activity extracting an intrinsic wealth from nature to an interpersonal process preparing objects to become wealth, "recognized and compensated as such by the community."[35] Production for oneself or by one's own judgment was now extraneous, for definitionally "goods are produced not for use but for exchange."[36] What is being rewarded is the ability to satisfy others: "What is ultimate, therefore, in all exchange, is not commodities but services," for "what is really sold is the service, and not the matter." This requires the ability to "adapt" objects "to satisfy, either directly or indirectly, some natural want or artificial desire of men."[37] Labor and production, the very creation of economic goods, had suddenly become incidental stages in generating wealth, displaced to a nonessential pre-market realm.

The conclusion was inescapable. The economy, and by implication society, now existed as collective realities, "composed," in Ely's terms, "of interdependent parts performing functions essential to the life of the whole." They were now a "bond of union" or "community of interest" whose parts were inseparably "bound" within "one vast hive of buyers and sellers."[38] Bowen wrote, "We are all co-operating with each other as busily and effectively as bees in a hive, and most of us with as little perception as the bees have, that each individual effort is essential to the common defense and general prosperity."[39] Newcomb summarized this as a new "social organism," whose "operations" composed "a single harmonious system" the "object" of which was "to supply each individual man with certain objects brought to him from all parts of the world and necessary to his existence, health, and pleasure." While suggesting "one great piece of mechanism," this system had "no directing head to move it," establishing its harmony by balancing "an infinity of internal forces, each of which operates only within a very limited sphere." This structure of supervening forces within which individuals necessarily acted was at the same time too extensive for them ever to grasp, let alone alter.[40]

In asserting the nature of an encompassing institutional framework reminiscent of Hobbes's "bees and ants," these economists perilously approached, in metaphor at least, the principle behind those traditional hierarchical communities in which "the common good differeth not from the private . . . by nature." Intending as defenders of American liberalism no such retreat, the theorists searched for an alternative systemic model. Newcomb suggested the problem: "Although we may consider society as an organism, we must not carry the analogy with living organisms too far. . . . We think of every plant and animal as having an individuality of its own, distinct from the conglomeration of organs which form it. Moreover, we cannot add or subtract from the parts of a plant or animal without detracting from its character." Societies are different: "There is no such completeness in the social organism. We can add new men to any extent, or we may divide the country into two without changing the character of the organism." In other words, it has "no such attribute as *individuality*." Ely likewise asserted the distinctiveness of the social organism in that "the separate parts are themselves organisms," and it is thus "composed of individuals."[41]

Therefore, in the nontraditional social system the components, while functionally interdependent, are ontologically distinct. The ends of participation and forms of activity are defined by the process, and to avoid ascribed hierarchies are constituted independent of control or influence by particular members: "No man could ever have contrived such a system; and . . . no man or combination of men could direct its work, any more than they could send the blood through the body of an individual." "Individuality" for the parts does exist, though its "degree . . . depends on the degree of association, each advancing hand in hand with the other."[42]

The model in modern liberalism for a nontraditional system was Newtonian mechanics. In it, the constituent units are distinctively individual, yet their activity is defined as the pursuit of ends within the structural channels of the process. This was applied to the new economic theory as the operation of proto-Newtonian laws of interdependence, exchange, and division of labor by adaptive market actors. In this "mechanism" or "social machine," component "molecules are individual men" driven by "forces" which are "individual desires."[43] Society is "a complex and delicate machine," the parts of which are "wheels of a machine."[44] Though each part is driven by "forces that propel" it into "motion or movement," the "perfection" of "various parts combines into a single harmonious whole."[45] A systemic order fixed and capable of "clear demonstration" with nothing "hypothetical or problematic," nothing "whimsical or accidental," this derives from and corresponds to the systemic behavior of individuals, that is, to "laws of human activity" or the "general laws" of "the habits and dispositions of men . . . manifested in their efforts for the acquisition of wealth" akin to "the laws of nature."[46] Atkinson spoke of "a law of harmony in the universe, ultimately controlling the relations of men to each other . . . as truly as the planets in their course are bound by the supreme law." The model of natural law was in turn applied to each aspect of the new system. Interdependence is now a "higher law" of "mutual service on which modern society is founded."[47] Exchange as a feature of that system "obeys laws as certain and immutable as . . . any of the great forces of nature," and the "division" of labor is equally to be "determined by natural laws."[48] Humans as components equally possess fixed natures, "ready-made as it were," with "a constitution . . . fixed in the constancy of nature" to "satisfy" their "want[s]" with "labor" in the market.[49]

Within a liberal system of motion, it was axiomatic since Hobbes that freedom was not the deviant wish to refrain from or alter mandated participation but a capacity to move willingly as mandated so long as the activity was defined as the product of the individual's own impulses. This became the axiom of "interest," the "universal" law of the process "without exception": "In Political Economy all persons are assumed to be actuated by self-interest, or possibly, pure selfishness." They are further entitled even to pursue those interests to "only . . . their own credit and advantage."[50] Even if "sordid and covetous" in their full range of "good and evil tendencies," market initiatives were not to be judged, for "all wants" which "impel men to exertion" are treated as valid "forces."[51] The voluntary drives toward economic rewards become the axiomatic and unavoidable foundation of the larger system as required by the liberal model: "There is no social force stronger than interest, and interest is driving society continually to exchange, and to . . . a higher and higher degree of association."[52]

"Self"-Interest as "Voluntary" Directional Activity

Freedom, then, was rhetorically asserted as a full choice of individual motivations amounting to a self-determination regarding directionality. And yet, this was merely rhetoric. Motivations as directed participation toward market ends through available market means had already been established axiomatically: the universe of desires had been radically circumscribed leaving only those impulses which strove to create value for and extract value from the interpersonal exchange process. This limitation exclusively defined and contained the human role in the liberal economy: "The one force which keeps every part of the social organism in activity is the desire of each individual man to enjoy certain results of the labor of others, which he can command only by himself laboring for others."[53] Because value could be determined only by the transindividual market's judgment and obtained only in the market, the ends of motion and forms of participation were also systemically predetermined. The independent capacity to move became the exclusive activation of *relevant* desires—henceforth known as "interest": the market process "compels" the individual "to work for the material welfare of his fellow men," defining "those efforts of man directed to the satisfaction of his desires" as legitimate "labor," and "every effort that is not so directed is thrown away."[54]

Drawing on the cultural attraction of its theory, postbellum liberal economics pursued a dual strategy to extend the dominance of interest-based activity. The theoretical wing spoke in reasoned terms about the universality of market labor and exchange: "Wealth . . . must be perpetually renewed, or it quickly disappears. . . . Let labor universally cease, let every man, woman, and child rest with folded arms, or do nothing but eat, drink, and be merry,—and those riches would melt and waste like snow under a July sun." Thus labor must be systemically inscribed: "Human labor is the only motive power . . . for the production of wealth." Wilson elaborates, insisting that "*all persons [be] considered as laborers* . . . all persons need to work." Those who do not "are so few . . . that we need not take them into account for the discussion of the general principles of Political Economy." The theorists acknowledged that "man is averse to labor and privation,"[55] making it by no means universal or inevitable: "Man has no natural instinct for saving, no natural propensity for labor. . . . The hardest lesson for children and savages to learn is that of economy,—the necessity of bridling the inclination or appetite of the moment, with a view toward some prospective benefit."[56] But without it the inclusive system collapsed, so they resorted in this early period to cultural pressure, "a thorough training in correct principles of action" aided by "laws and institutions," even "repression," enabling "the acquired inclination" to replace "the original impulse," resulting in "self-control" and internalized liberal norms. They were encouraged that the universal scramble for wealth would instill constant directional incentives to motivate "even the Irish immigrant . . . [who] here soon loses his careless, lazy, and turbulent disposition, and becomes as sober, prudent, industrious, and frugal as the rest."[57]

Within popular liberal culture, greater doubts about the inevitable embrace of systemic ends led to the new commercial genre of mass-market exhortatory self-help books.[58] Beginning before the war, by the 1870s a torrent of books inundated the public, typically offering large doses of advice on effective personal, business, and later employee behavior interlarded with pocket biographies of successful businessmen, politicians, military heroes, and historical figures as well as quotations from religion and literature. The themes, endlessly repeated with little divergence, inevitably located success in the individual virtue activating all other talents: perseverance—patient dedication to one's "chosen" task amounting to unyielding directionality using available means in the pursuit of designated market goals. Edwin Freedley set the tone in his *Practical Treatise on Business* in 1853: "The tendency of matter is to rest, and it requires an exercise of force or of will to overcome the *vis inertiae*. When a thing should be done, it must be done immediately, without parleying or delay. A repeated exercise of the will, in this way will soon form the habit of industry."[59] It is evident from the early emphasis that directionality, by no means assumed as later, was the product of a campaign of "edification." This virtue was exemplified in "that great quality which Lucan ascribes to Caesar. . . . [W]ho first consults wisely, then resolves firmly, and then executes his purposes with inflexible perseverance . . . can advance to eminence in any line."[60]

Freeman Hunt in 1856, "arranging and digesting" the as yet unorganized popular literature on business conduct, echoed and re-echoed Freedley: "Success in life mainly depends upon perseverance." Again: "The history of every great success in business is the history of great perseverance." And in case the point was missed: "To every man of business, perseverance should be the motto." The images were of mechanics and directionality: "Fixed and steady aim, in short, steadiness of purpose and steady consistent effort are the conditions of success," producing the capacity for pressing forward which is "momentum," according to "a fundamental law of mechanics" and of "spiritual dynamics." Strivers must realize that in mechanics, distance is not speed but speed times duration. Those moving slowly "have abundant reasons for rejoicing," for "all great, grand, and most durable things are of slow growth." The ultimate message? "Keep moving!"[61]

After the Civil War, the message of persevering participation became the cultural drumbeat: "Go-at-it-iveness is the first requisite for success. Stick-to-it-iveness is the second." The message, shifting slightly, was more self-confidently driving and even immoderate, as if motion was now safe at any speed.[62] The heightened push for unqualified success—to "reach 'acres of diamonds,'" to "win" and to "have conquered life"—reflected the increasing cultural consensus regarding economic ends, that "you ought to get rich, and it is your duty to get rich."[63] The key to perseverance was to presume the given ends, now laid out and self-evident. Thinking, with its dangerous capacity for imagining alternative ends, interfered with the capacity to act, to move with the societal flow:

> The sum of the matter is, that life is *action*. Thoughts and schemes, while they remain such, will avail you nothing. . . . A man who sees limitedly and clearly is both more sure of himself, and is more direct in dealing with circumstances and with others, than a man with a large horizon of thought. . . . It is passion which is the moving, vitalizing power; and a minimum of brains will often achieve more, when fired by a strong will, than a vastly large portion with no energy to set it in motion. . . . Men of genius . . . are tempted to waste time in meditating and comparing, when they should act instantaneously and with power. . . . In short, they theorize too much. A loaf baked is better than a harvest contemplated.[64]

With directionality secured, "self-motivation" and self-assertion could be intemperately encouraged and "power" unambiguously asserted as "what you want": "The man of real power does not wait for favorable conditions. His own inherent force radiates power which enables him to plow his way through obstacles, instead of being the victim of them."[65]

Despite the rhetoric of freedom, the deeper sense of an established systemic directionality was reflected in the recurrent images of ordered individual motion now used to describe individual participation. Such metaphors had been used earlier with extreme caution: "Search with a keen, sharpened inspection into the world's experience. . . . [T]o be more successful . . . trace out accurately the bounds within which [to] go safely, and beyond which there is danger" for one "traveling the thorny path of business."[66] By the late 1870s, images of hacking through an unreceptive wilderness had been domesticated into those of traversing society's "natural and self-chosen channels" along "that path which society instinctively chooses for itself."[67] Growing up in this period, Sherwood Anderson writes: "In America there seemed at that time but one direction, one channel, into which all . . . young fellows could pour their energies. All must give themselves wholeheartedly to material and industrial progress."[68]

Traveling along roads which are now built and well graded, the individual becomes like "a horse with blinkers" who "chooses his path more surely and is less likely to shy," even in Ely's terms "the modern trotter . . . developed in the race-course."[69] The emphasis was no longer on risk but on the safe and cautious route. While "wretchedness, starvation, and death by suicide" awaited those pursuing dreams of wealth "in a strange land," to the one who "remained at home and dug his own cellar, or underneath his own wheat fields, or in his own garden" went the "acres of diamonds." With external disorder subdued and systemic motion fully established, the only feasible option was to move accordingly: "Harmony is within our power, is not dependent upon chance or forces outside of us. We produce harmony or discord."[70]

Agents in a "Science of Exchanges"

With the market structure in place, the theorists and self-help promoters sought to clarify the individual role to citizens struggling to find their place within the evolving economy. And the role was in every sense that of an agent. As Bowen put it, individuals were now "agents, co-operating in systems not less manifestly indicating design, but no design of theirs."[71] The human role is to act "simply as an adapter of means to ends" without "inquir[ing] how these ends arise, nor whether they are really the ends toward which men should strive." Freedom was identified with integrative and system-sustaining behavior and precluded opportunities for personal or collective influence over the process. The economy was a system of "rational free agents" who operated nonetheless "as regularly . . . as if they were merely the passive wheels of the machine" moving within "channels" simultaneously "natural" and "self-chosen." "Individual freedom," though the basis on which "the whole fabric of modern society is erected," directed ever "more closely connected" constituents toward a necessary *"integration,"* and "increasing adaptation of the parts of the organism."[72]

While the economy was for Walker a set of "voluntary . . . relations" which "grows spontaneously," nevertheless "all of its parts are calculable," that is, fixed, because uncompromised by "the caprice of individuals."[73] Ely spoke of it as a set of "interdependent parts performing functions essential to the life of the whole" and punishing "those who offend it and violate its well-known desires," though "each of these parts" was still accorded "a purpose and destiny of its own." Reflecting this ambiguity, "free exchange" for Perry became a "matter . . . of necessity," as free—*and as unfree*—as "breathing."[74] Atkinson roots this "age of freedom" in "Individual Liberty," which operates yet according to "a law of harmony in the universe ultimately controlling the relations of men to each other . . . as truly as the planets in their courses are bound."[75]

With freedom now localized as a property of individual units and utterly predictable, its choices woven in systemic patterns, it was possible to assert systemic order as a predictive science charting certain and repetitive phenomena: "Political Economy is not, as many suppose, the art of moneymaking, any more than meteorology is the art of predicting the weather. It is no *art* at all, but a *science*."[76] It now met the primary requirement of science—consistency: "Nothing in its fundamental principles is hypothetical or problematic. . . . Each thing is susceptible of clear demonstration. . . . The wants of man . . . are a certain and constantly-operating force." This science would "investigate the laws of human activity."[77] Scientists could in turn "reduce to general laws the habits and dispositions of men . . . manifested in their efforts for the acquisition of wealth." These general laws, in effect propositions of policy and program, could then be restated as "calculable" laws utilizing the certitude of "mathematical equations,"[78] shorn of all ambiguity and veiled from all assumptions and external pressures.

This new science, rooted in the presumption that conduct was directed exclusively to interactions within the market, was called "the science of exchanges."[79] Its findings were to arise, as in the physical sciences, only from the observation and analysis of objects whose initiative and resulting actions were prior to, independent of, and unaffected by the observer. To this end, the once proprietary American was "renatured" as "the only trading animal on earth,"[80] in turn reified as the "animal that makes exchanges,"[81] driven by "no social force stronger than interest . . . continually to exchange."[82] This system of natural traders "the operation of natural laws" as was thus capable of being formalized as a "comprehensive and impartial science," just like all other "laws of nature."[83]

With the construction of a "natural science," the theoretical framework should have been complete, the only task remaining to observe and describe the phenomena as given. But the establishment of a self-ordering process was not for the purpose of scientific clarity. Rather it was meant to separate economic behavior from all other societal processes as a natural transhuman system beyond individual authorship or collective intervention, to protect the market through the cover of science from public intervention on behalf of progressive distributional adjustments and other social policy objectives. The ends—the goal of "the great social machine" as "the production of wealth"—were now "scientifically" embodied in the economic institutions.[84] The market's means and values were equally beyond debate: "If it favors morality, it does so because morality favors production. It favors honesty, because honesty favors exchange. It puts the seal of the market upon all the virtues." The argument from nature safeguarded the systemic authority of the market economy much like Madisonian constitutionalism in the political sector, by reinforcing the wisdom—and necessity—of leaving the market mechanism to operate itself without societal intrusions or "deformations": "As a science, it does and must discuss and decide all questions upon economical grounds alone."[85]

The basis for the defense of the economy's isolation was its great benefit to society: "Wealth is that element of civilization which supports all the others, and . . . without it no progress, no refinement, no liberal art would be possible." Modernity is "the day of the merchant," upon whom "greatly we depend" as the "motive power . . . in the social system" for "our means of social progress and religious effort." Economic motivation was the *"one force which keeps every part of the social organism in activity,"* enabling "reciprocal wants" to "draw men together locally and bind them together socially . . . [forming] a firm foundation (a chief foundation) of human Society."[86] Virtue was an intrinsic feature of a market society. By its "benevolent design," "the prosperity of each depends on the welfare of all." The "social and moral aspects" of commerce promoted "moral progress, for it is what industry tends to." The economists affirmed that "the best physical condition of mankind" would with certainty emerge from "the natural order of things" so long as "human laws and institutions do not interfere."[87] They attacked "the assumption that there is not enough for all, that a few must fight desperately, selfishly, for what there is" as "fatal to all individual and race betterment." The "scientific" policy consistent with such benefits was of course "*Laissez faire;* 'these things regulate themselves.' . . . Let the course of trade . . . alone."[88]

In their tolerance—and defense—of unequal levels of motivation and distribution, the laissez-faire economists tried to downplay specific market outcomes: "The idea of obligation, on which the science of morals is founded, and the idea of value on which the science of economy is founded, are totally distinct. . . . As a science, [Political Economy] has no concern with questions of moral right." Social results were irrelevant to production and consumption: "If men are so foolish as to prize highly many articles which answer no purpose but of vain ostentation or gross and sensual enjoyment, it is not for the political economist, who views things as they are,—not as they ought to be,—to censure their folly. He leaves this office to the moralist or the preacher."[89] Even with societal problems such as alcoholism, the economist should not "be expressing any opinion upon the good or evil of the drunkard's desires. It is his sole business to trace cause to effect, and in so doing to accept things as they exist."[90] For "they are all wants," even "vicious indulgence and debauchery," which "will impel men to . . . the kind of exertion that creates value."[91]

At the same time, a societal process which claimed to optimize production and distribution could not ignore results. Claims of market utility only emboldened reformers to open the issue of optimal social outcomes. Market proponents stigmatized policy tampering: we must leave things "to the operation of natural laws . . . confident that a better state of things will result than can be brought by man's wisdom." Yet they were clearly troubled by ever-increasing attacks on the market's legitimacy for producing sharpening distributional inequities as well as for requiring institutional integration incommensurate with the American revolutionary promise of freedom. The excesses of an unconstrained market had to be admitted even by its defenders: "extravagent indulgence" in "luxurious consumption," unproductive and amoral choices to pursue "vain ostentation or gross and sensual enjoyment," "unrestrained competition" unleashing and inflaming "the inherent selfishness" and acquisitive *"egoism"* of individuals,[92] producing through an unremitting "struggle for life and the survival of the fittest" conditions for many of "wretchedness and misery" at "the lowest form of existence."[93]

Similarly, for many nominal choice was being subsumed by a vast process that Social Darwinism might call nature, but critics could point to as the second structural transformation, from an economy centered on market exchange to an organizational economy. Large-scale manufacture integrating all aspects of production and distribution on an economic scale of national and international proportions was increasingly immune from the normal rules and controls of decentralized exchange mechanisms. Farmers and artisans were now engulfed by commercial, transport, and industrial combines that either absorbed employment or dictated terms to remaining independents. Given the vast size differentials, the self-sufficient, let alone proprietary, economy was disappearing as market leverage replaced production as the controlling factor. Defenders were forced to acknowledge that "let alone" does not mean "that every man should always be at liberty to do as he pleases. . . . His liberty is necessarily limited by the conditions which surround him." Humans in fact "are all servants of one another without wishing it, and even without knowing it."[94]

The freedom and justice of the market had to be addressed directly. The Social Darwinist view that "a drunkard in the gutter is just where he ought to be," for "nature is working at him to get him out of the way, just as she sets up her processes of dissolution to remove whatever is a failure,"[95] only undercut the virtue of nature, strengthening the argument that societies have a responsibility to intervene even against nature (if nature it is) as they invariably do when faced with its undesirable consequences.[96] Moreover, these economists knew that the market was neither natural nor inevitable, for they had witnessed and recorded its rise and foreclosure of other possibilities. They had seen how communities in which "each individual for the most part works for himself" were replaced by those in which "each one labors for all the others."[97]

Lockean liberalism was not, like planetary orbits, beyond the claim of artifice. If the market represented one possible stage of economic development, dominant in some places and times while far less so in others, then its consequences could be debated. To fail at the task of legitimation was to cede the decision to reformers who argued that human systems having been created could therefore be altered or abolished. The debate against Darwinism was in a sense a sideshow. The economists feared that for the populace the argument of a natural system would not be dispositive. For most people, the claim that the market was beyond intervention, that neither moral purpose nor incentives could or should be imposed on it, would be convincing only if the outcomes were acceptable. But outcomes were invariably open to dispute, and such disputes would inevitably open the process to human—that is, political—tampering. The fear was that in a majoritarian society, where human control becomes majority control, distributional results, however equal and open the opportunity, would not satisfy popular demands. In this context, any moral challenge to market legitimacy undermined its autonomy and rendered it vulnerable. Following Madison's constitutional provisions in the political sector, the insulation of specific outcomes from popular disposition and the market's transcendental status from the perception of its malleability required a comprehensive structural defense. The Newtonian analogy, partly successful as a "naturalistic" response to claims of inequity, raised further anxieties about the future of freedom. For in asserting the predictability of market conduct, even if individually motivated, the theory bordered on determinism. But absent scientific naturalism, how could the human control over ends and means be prevented?

The Theology of the Free Market

The theoretical and political dilemmas were sharply posed: to defend a system of human interdependency as a condition of optimal freedom; to accept an ethical concern with outcomes as legitimate and yet defend the sharp inequities of an unregulated market as indisputably just. To place systemic ends safely beyond human alteration, the market would have to be defended as a universal system maximizing both freedom and equity. An active though deferential role utilizing available means without any power over ends within the process had to be reframed as producing not simply harmonious integration but freedom itself. Narrow perceptions that participation with different possibilities of success within that same process constituted injustice had to be recontextualized within a moral frame promising consistent equity.

As theologians and philosophers raised in the evangelical culture of the early republic and its great nation-transforming revivals, the early economists turned to the distinctive conceptions of liberty and opportunity evolved in the nation's central cultural tradition: the revivalist God's governance of the world of modern individualism reconciling the great paradoxes of moral order and personal choice. Sidney Fine emphasizes how "many of the American economists, whether clergymen or laymen, were prone to associate the natural laws that they elucidated with the laws of God and to assume, partly as a consequence of this association . . . that these laws operated in a beneficial manner."[98] In his 1880 survey of American political economy, T. E. C. Leslie observed that "in American treatises . . . theology becomes the backbone of economic science": "Assumptions respecting the divine will and designs are employed by both protectionists and free-traders in support of their theories. . . . Children used to have a way of classing books as 'Sunday' or 'week-day' books by looking over the leaves for sacred names. According to this criterion several American treatises on political economy would be set apart as Sunday books."[99]

It is possible to observe in its principal texts the astonishing turn of postwar economic theory—this new "science"—to a religious foundation. At its inception as a field, God is employed to set forth its principles of formation and operation. Controversial demands for an institutional integration which cannot be justified as natural (not at this point either consensual or observable) or framed within secular liberalism (either the now irrelevant idyll or unpalatable Hobbesian conformable motion) have become the working of God's master plan. The natural market is recast as the principled construction of a transcendent agenda: free because initiated and sustained by a Prime Mover who—as a "higher" paradox of faith—both oversees and respects the voluntarism of the participating members, equitable because its laws embody that agenda. As a construction which is suddenly no longer arbitrary, the market becomes insulated from the "heresy" of political restructuring. Its emergence from earlier primitive disorganization now achieved the sanctity of both the social contract creation of the liberal state from nature and the original transcendent ordering of the natural world from chaos.

The God of the Newtonian cosmos thus reappears as the God of the Smithian economy. The "permanence" of the economy's "foundation," "the perfection of its working," is one which "no man could ever have contrived."[100] The "natural and self-chosen channels" of market activity derive from their "real Author and Governor" who "is divine." Economic laws by which "God regulates" the market" are "as constant and uniform as those which bind the material universe together." As "consonant with the providential structure of the world and of society," they "evince the wisdom and goodness of the Creator quite as clearly as any of his arrangements in the organic kingdom."[101] Why has proprietary individualism lost its viability? It is self-evident "at the very first glance that the Creator has not made men thus. Society is God's handiwork . . . the most wonderful . . . final, work of his hands," and "God impressed upon that organization, as upon all others, its own proper and peculiar laws." By "clear design," "God has so ordered" the "organization" of a market economy that "interdependence" becomes a "higher law." Thus, "labor . . . for the good of others" that "increases the grand aggregate of means to supply human wants" is "our Lord's require-ment,"[102] for "God designed man to be a producer." The "laws of exchange" are in turn "the will of God," for "God has made men" to "procure . . . through exchange" and "the divisions of employment."[103]

Because such a system offered the "choice" of means to pursue preestab-lished moral ends, the willing performance of one's role in pursuit of these ends represented "moral liberty." All "matters of necessity" now being "un-der God's ordination," God's necessity is by divine plan participation auto-matically in a system designed for (agency) freedom.[104] Thus do "the forces by which human action is guided and controlled" ensure "an age of freedom . . . personal liberty, freedom of thought . . . action . . . commerce." Economic relations become axiomatically "voluntary," marked by "individual free-dom" and "freedom of intercourse," "free exchange" and "free competi-tion," and divisions of "capitalists and laborers" yet "both free."[105] Individ-uals are definitionally "rational free agents" who can choose or "prize" whatever "articles" they want, even those which "answer no purpose," and "nobody can compel you to work for wages" or "more than eight hours a day" or "to buy factory cloth if you don't want." The "rights of man" now involve "the exclusive right to the use of his own faculties," which means "to make such bargains" in one's "interest," even to "be obliged to work" with "the right . . . to employ his own efforts for the gratification of his wants."[106] The systemic pursuit of "self-interest" is equated with the full "free development" of "capacities," the "continually freer development of individuality."[107] Structured channels even increase freedom by forcing po-tentially "useless and discontented drones" to self-fulfilling extremes of "en-ergy and activity," creating through wealth and luxury consumption options which make people "rich, prosperous, and independent."[108]

Similarly, regarding equity, some apparent injustices will appear in the short run, from "a portion [of wealth] that will not receive its best applica-tion, either morally or economically." But to question a system "designed by God for the welfare of man" is to doubt how "rain falls" in the "natural or-der of things."[109] By "a wise and benevolent arrangement of Providence . . . even those who are thinking only of their own credit and advantage are led, unconsciously but surely, to benefit others."[110] Protestantism provided the ontological premise of equal opportunity, the equal potential for all souls, justifying in turn differential levels of effective agency corresponding to divergent levels of character integration and contribution. Newcomb drew on the spirit of frontier founding to explain such differences by likening society to "a great party of men who are trying to make their way over a rough untrodden road, in some wilderness of the West. Such a party gets along most successfully when every man in it is allowed . . . to get along as fast as he can. Every man who is ahead of another has to make a better road . . . for all who are to follow, and thus while . . . [they] enjoy an advantage over their fellows, those who are behind have the advantage of a better road." The "accumulation of the largest possible wealth" and consumption by the "complex, far-reaching, and intricate" plan of "the benevolent . . . Designer" propels every "element of civilization."[111] Inequality follows from "the unequal distribution" of capacities and the role given to "the fear of poverty and the hope of rising" in "the dispensations of Providence," of whose "purpose" humans are largely "ignorant."[112]

Since market economics "accepts our Lord's method" and "the assurance he gave" of divine justice, humans must "let alone! and do not attempt to amend the ways of Providence!" trusting instead "his general laws, which always, in the long run, work to good."[113] We must "leave to the operation of natural laws, when undisturbed by legislation and prescription, confident that a better state of things will result than can be brought about by man's wisdom." Atkinson wrote: "To him who has faith in a higher power which is both supreme and wholly beneficent . . . the conditions of this life are the best conditions that could have been established for the development of mankind; and . . . the struggle for existence, hard and severe as it seems to us, must be the necessary school by which man could have been elevated above the beasts of the field. If there could have been a better world or a better method for the development of mankind, man would have the right to ask his Creator why it had not been established."[114] Human intervention amounts to "caprice," for "man cannot interfere with His work without marring it,"[115] either through "false social and political opinions," the reform efforts of the "busybody," or the "evil" of misguided "indiscriminate charity."[116] The only systemic initiative acceptable in a godly plan is to undo any (necessarily flawed) revisions of divine legislation, to "remove such stumbling blocks" as legislative intrusions and prevent "interference with the natural order of things."[117]

Triumph of Immanence

Appealing simultaneously to principles of transcendent morality and the natural, divine necessity and freedom, teleological purpose and human responsibility, religion endowed the market with full "normative" validation. These economists, in fact, were candid that their project was prescriptive, that economic laws describe not human economic conduct but rather religious norms that individuals should—and thus might not—follow. Wilson wrote: "I look to science—and to Political Economy more than any other science—to teach men that the laws of health and happiness in this world, are a part of God's laws also, and that the recognition of, and submission and obedience to, these laws" are crucial for earthly "morality," for the "masses of men, and preparing them for the life that is to come." Yet the norm will exist only after people "submit to law" out of a "hearty acceptance of Christianity" and "an acknowledged submission to God as the One Supreme Being and moral Governor of the Universe." The poor and working peoples of America may very well refuse to regard these prescriptions as binding. To them, it was advised, "let us preach the Gospel. To the poor say with our Lord, 'Be content with your wages,' work for what you get, but work: go to work now, work always and constantly. . . . Be quiet. . . . God will take care of the rest." If individuals resist acting to change society and "leave the matter to free competition," the result will conform to "science . . . under the law of supply and demand." Science, then, exists only when the populace "accepts our Lord's method."[118]

And yet, despite the evident need for its normative absolutes, the laissez-faire economists approached theology with trepidation. They feared turning the economy into a sector riven by the pursuit of religious ends and values. They needed the larger characterological and systemic premises of agency while resolutely separating the economy from the excesses of antebellum religion with its worldly suspicions, political and theological controversies, and moralizing activism. They intended only to derive legitimation from God's great power to initiate a cosmological system and then so infuse it with moral principles and a clear and desirable human role that it becomes self-operational once individuals embrace their "chosen" place. With God's further intervention no longer needed in the process except to bless its continued functioning, the emerging moral regularity could then be attributed to the natural order of the economy.

As a result, the theological framework never made it into their later work.

As laissez-faire mechanisms and procedures were integrated into the economy and freedom was rendered axiomatic, market principles were reframed according to the scientific models treated as objective today. The declining role of religion as this new Protestantized science became more firmly established is illustrated in the work of Arthur Lathan Perry. In his innovative 1866 work *Elements of Political Economy,* Perry suggests a virtually theological cast to laissez-faire theory, finding God's will in every facet of the evolving society. It is interesting to contrast this early elaboration, where God essentially guides humans through each stage of institutional formation, with Perry's 1891 work *Principles of Political Economy.* Reliance on religion lasted only as long as it took to implement the new system, and so long as its operating principles were in doubt. What was previously self-intuitively religious is now self-evidently observable. The narrator stands on a bridge in London and muses about the nature of the visible human world. It is now "inductive" that what we "observe" is "men's Buying and Selling": "Wherever there is a street there is some exchange of commodities upon it." Its roots remain "unseen," as the true nature of an eclipse is to be explained "from the wholly hidden and ever enduring forces of gravitation." Yet the power of economics is that it makes the "inward and invisible" capable of being "seen and known" and in turn calculable and predictable. Economic laws are to be intuited from "the market-place," the phenomenal product itself, from "the wants and labors and fashions and projects of men," producing an increasingly "objective" science of "exact definitions" and "sound principles," an ever more perfect "construction," "more compact, more robust, and more beautiful as the decades and centuries roll by."[119] The transcendent world is now immanent and, if hard for the untutored eye to discern, achieving the full realization of ultimate plans and purposes through the activity of its secular—including economic, technological, and scientific—sectors.[120]

As observable behavior achieved ascendant status, religion in turn, with its dangerous power to transcend a given reality, was radically severed from daily activity. In the late prewar pioneers of the self-help genre like Freedley and Hunt can already be seen—if tentatively and transitionally—a growing resistance to religious intrusions.[121] The postwar writers on success, intending to replace religious values, no longer displayed such temperateness: "The theory that we are poor, miserable worms of the dust, victims of limitation, of weakness, of darkness, and of discord," must undergo "persistent denial."[122] Religion was now extraneous to people's daily lives: "Born in an age and country in which knowledge and opportunity abound as never before, how can you sit with folded hands, asking God's aid in work for which He has already given you the necessary faculties and strength?" Suffering "waning interest" because its "old dead creeds" failed to comprehend "the true purpose" of the "necessary work which must be done so long as man dwells . . . upon the earth," religion was merely a refuge for the economically maladjusted, "pale, ghostly looking, over-read, over-fed, intellectually *blasé specters*" that ministers—so lacking in "animal power"—"often are." Religious ideals often betray a wish to escape from life: "It is therefore a great saying that 'heaven is probably a place for those who have failed on earth.'" Or worse, remarkably, the religious are egotistical in a way economic activity can no longer be, because of which "the world is condemned" in favor of one "devoted to a little, petty, selfish undertaking in saving his own soul."[123]

Even ministers such as Wilbur Crafts, F. E. Clark, and Russell Conwell were impatient with religion's insularity from modern priorities. Clark and Crafts wrote books on "true success" from interviews with wealthy businessmen, not with clergy, typified as "a recluse, who shuts himself up with his books, and knows little of the temptations and struggles of real life."[124] Religion was now to be regarded as merely "the guide and helper of busy men" for its disciplined cultivation of "character," "integrity," and "virtues," that is, for its characterological message.[125] Ministering itself was to be seen as a form of commerce, one career path among many to the primary goal of success in this life. Jesus in this way becomes the model for a successful career: "The first published words of Jesus were, 'I must be about my Father's business.' His last words on the cross were, 'It is finished.' During the twenty-one years that intervened between these sentences, Jesus made religion the chief business of his life. But let it not be forgotten that during eighteen of those years he served God as a layman and a carpenter, and during only three as a preacher." Religious institutions and commitments were to be evaluated by the standards of commercial enterprise: "The church, like Brooklyn under the best of mayors, ought to be managed as a great business corporation, in which men are junior partners with God."[126] In Conwell's legendary story, it is a priest who is given a stone by an owner of property whose original possessor tragically and futilely searched the world for riches. This modern, obviously quite worldly priest informs the man that it is no mere stone he has brought: "I tell you I know a diamond when I see it. I know positively."[127] The most extreme account was Bruce Barton's biography of Jesus, *The Man Nobody Knows*, in which Jesus has become the prototype for the great corporate magnate: "A failure! He picked up twelve men from the bottom ranks of business and forged them into an organization that conquered the world."[128]

Belief in the market system was now its own "great faith" to which individuals must turn, its power evident in bringing "the ideal" and "the real" into "identity."[129] In this divinely realized world, the "Potato Gospel" of economic development becomes the "fulcrum" on which to "rest the lever" of the "spiritual gospel." Its prodigious output is to be cast as "the modern miracle of the loaf." Individuals, seekers included, must and can find their "mission" in "this world," for its channels of productive engagement embody godly ends: "'Blessed is he who has found his work,' says Carlyle. . . . 'He has a work—a life purpose; he has found it, and will follow it.'"[130] In a remarkable revision of history, Newcomb offered a story of time travel in which a New England deacon from the early eighteenth century visits a farmer's dwelling in 1886. Overwhelmed by the material bounty in people's lives and the evidence of modern industrial output, the deacon believes he has seen a Second Coming where people "will no longer believe in the fall of man nor in total depravity, and will indeed be so well satisfied with this world as never to want another."[131] The path to salvation now lies in a divinely immanent world.

By rendering secular institutional authority theologically and morally compelling, liberal Protestantism made individuals' subordination to secular institutions as fully transcendent agents possible. Economics was in fact the new school—and universal expression—of this modern moral character: life is a probation, and business may be designated as a means for perfecting the moral nature. Therefore, "let him who desires to test the strength of his principles, or improve his moral nature by wholesome discipline, embark in trade."[132] With religion relying on worldly measures, the state of one's character need no longer be deferred to subsequent transcendental determination but was ascertainable by observable material success. By the postwar period, the secret was out: character is wealth, wealth is character.[133] As Conwell put it in *Acres of Diamonds*, the classic statement of the age, "Introduce me to the people who own their homes around this great city, those beautiful . . . [and] magnificent homes . . . and I will introduce you to the very best people in character." The advice for all was "to get rich" as "your Christian and godly duty."[134] Character was visible to all.

The "free market" was thus composed of "free agents" of equal status within a system affording individual choice as a property of engagement and a divine assurance of systemic harmony and justice. As God's "engineer," each individual has the task to "guide the forces of nature" toward divine ends,[135] for "labor" as a means to each given "end" is "good" whether or not it is possible to discern those ends. One must play one's part with an even greater conviction of being God's agent than previously, for modern "Political Economy" was "removing and extollating the very evils which Christianity aims to help us to bear with patience."[136] Wilbur Crafts suggested, with the hyperbole common to the self-help treatises, that "we are partners with GOD, 'co-workers' and 'co-witnesses' with him. It is the firm of '*God and sons*' that is to save the world." It was an agency made exclusive by the maturation of the human role, likened by Marden to "the Chosen People [who] supposed their progress checked by the Red Sea and their leader paused for Divine help, [whereupon] the Lord said, 'Wherefore criest thou unto me? Speak unto the children of Israel, *that they go forward.*'"[137] The institutionalization of secular immanentism made an agency role ever more available, "so that all men needed to do was 'fall into [God's] plans intentionally and to co-operate with him intelligently for the perfecting of mankind.'"[138]

Americans were reinforced in this new activist role—"Men who succeed have great life plans and they build to their plans"[139]—by a mobilized cultural apparatus from erudite theorists to the most crass of popularizers: "New institutions, spokesmen, and forms of self-help literature expressed a new philosophy of success. . . . [T]he philosophers of success projected their message to a wide and devoted audience through books, magazines, and speeches, and helped to shape the attitudes of a generation of Americans."[140] Embracing this message, they went forward into the industrial, entrepreneurial society of the late nineteenth century with little question that they were doing God's work in the market. As the popularizer Marden wrote, "The man who is working with God is working the most effective way for himself."[141] With market directionality increasingly "naturalized" and further given the power of the market to discipline participants, individuality could now be promoted without fear of self-authorizing conduct. But it was the carefully circumscribed and directed individualism of "competitive life," the "fair and free competition of intelligence and ability" in the pursuit of "opportunity" and "reward," the individualism of the resolved economic agent.[142]

Toward the Social Economy

The theoretical transformation to an agency economy, to a collectivity achieving its ends by each person working in a differential place to create "one great neighborhood in which all men serve each other" whether "rich or poor,"[143] established the ideal of the self-regulating economy. Yet with the growing wealth and more sharply increasing disparities produced by the emergent organizational economy,[144] laissez-faire economic theory would fail, as liberal religion did previously, to protect the insularity and preeminence of its own sector. Its freedom even redefined as market interchange could not be effectively defended as promoting choice, given the vast accumulations of economic power and the resulting *social* disparities that were spilling over from its demand for functional autonomy. To circumvent ludicrous, cruel, ultimately Darwinian consequences, the economy was gradually recast by social reformers as one sector within a larger societal process to be subject to—and to be altered as necessary to realize—societal priorities. The result, despite the laissez-faire fiction of freedom which persists to this day, was the gradual emergence of the social economy and of the social realm as the integrative sector of the completed liberal society. In this way, the economic claim of sector autonomy central to revolutionary liberalism was gradually defeated through the integration of its operation within the great Protestant-liberal settlement in the forming of American nationhood.

In fact, it was the very solving of the riddle of production by the economic sector, such that *"while our consumption is limited the power of production is practically unlimited,"* that accounted for the growing pressures to socialize distribution.[145] The movement for the social reform of the market which emerged toward the end of the century was equally an outgrowth of modernizing Protestantism and as such rooted in agency.[146] These reformers insisted that a religious concern for individuals went beyond mere assurances of initial inclusion in the economy and society. They treated the economy as a central institution in "a society which embraces all men," as an "organism . . . composed of interdependent parts" derived from the understanding which "Christianity offers us." The realization of universal agency as mandated by the "brotherhood of man" is possible only if "individual development," the concrete fulfillment of one's agency nature, is available to all.[147] Charles Clark wrote: "Is it not evident that our economic system is diametrically opposed to Christian teaching? . . . Christianity means co-operation and the up-lifting of the lowliest; business means competition and the survival of the strongest."[148]

Agency entails in its nature an equal place under a common author— "Brotherhood cannot be real and genuine without fatherhood"—in a community of "social solidarity," "unity," and mutual "dependence."[149] The language used was that of personal development and differentiation, but it was clearly an agency idea, "self-development for the sake of others," in which "self and others, the individual and society, are thus united in one purpose."[150] Agency required that individuals "subordinate their own inclinations and interests to the well-being of society" and take responsibility as "stewards" of the divine community for "the welfare of our fellow-men."[151] Those who were disempowered to act as agents by societal conditions were in effect being driven from the divine order. The "distinctive teaching of Christianity" was in their view "the maintenance and increase of efficiency in men and the general productive power of men."[152]

Reformers were able thus to gain the Protestant high ground. As believers they understood that "nature" was neither a finished nor an autonomous entity; it was the mere material of God's justice, always subject to the goals of God's greater good and thus to human reform as a bearer of God's will. Human agency in the world was of greater scope than simply market activity:

> We are suffering today from that habit of traditional economic theorizing, unduly to sunder economics and general sociology. This is unscientific. It hampers right analysis. . . . Can you so sharply separate our economic from our other life . . .? [N]o men always, few ever, act in the sole character of economic agent. . . . [T]o grapple with any of society's greatest latter-day problems, you will be forced to go outside of your economics. It is to the credit of our chief industrial reformers that they place man and not wealth at the centre of their systems.[153]

The laissez-faire insistence on the preservation of the "natural" market was a form of hubris codifying in mere human theories the final state of God's plan.

This challenge put late-nineteenth-century liberalism in a predicament. In a way understood by ordinary people, true agency and real freedom—not the arbitrary conditions required by the theory—would actually be enhanced by employing the "regulation" that laissez-faire had demonized as authoritarian statism:

> Law makes it possible for us to live our lives in security. Do we own a house? That implies law. Do we go to business every day in a street-car? The construction of street-car lines is always made possible by laws. . . . Do we send and receive letters? It is through an institution, the creature of law, owned and operated by the government. But, after all, this is not felt to be a

limitation of freedom. It is only in this state that freedom can be realized. . . . Their aim as a whole is to prevent an abuse of liberty; to keep the strong and cunning from injuring others, thus to increase real liberty.[154]

Government intervention could "increase the average net freedom of all men who come within the scope of its power."[155] Laissez-faire theory had in fact manufactured this dilemma by claiming sector autonomy for a product of systematic legislation and adjudication, and vilifying all subsequent, indeed inevitable, developments. The mendacity of its theory of freedom, in fact, lay deeper: by prioritizing interpersonal exchange, demanding learned behavior under systemic rules, and making all ends not achievable by exchange unreal, it had already socialized economic conduct.[156]

The decline of the decentralized market—given the importance of market theory in preserving the liberal values of voluntarism, above all, and equity—boded ill for liberalism. Though the laissez-faire theorists had accepted the necessity of internal discipline and the emergence of rudimentary channels and procedures, they had not addressed the role of personal initiative, given industrial consolidation and social stratification. The reformers' search for a new systemic perspective fully embraced human agency as the basis of greater opportunity and distributional equity, but risked eliminating (as was henceforth charged) the voluntarism at the heart of agency. How would voluntarism be preserved without a market of independent competitive actors? Without "the terms of competition" to render it "equal, free, and intense"?[157] What if the laissez-faire solution of saving the horizontal market, through rendering syndicates illegal and breaking up trusts so that "mighty combinations" might "pass away," was a "delusion"? "The age of competition as we have known it is gone forever. Recall it? As well try to waken the dead."[158] As Lester Ward and many others pointed out, "society" needed structural "agents to transmit its common business" in both industrial and governmental spheres, and that agent was "*organization*."[159] An "eighteenth-century" theory of economic decentralization simply ignored how society "has steadily been taking the initiative, assuming responsibilities, undertaking various enterprises, and taking in to its own control one after another a great array of industries and functions that had hitherto been entrusted to individuals."[160]

To sustain agency, a reform model would be needed that retained market motivations and differential rewards to willingly undertake and continue directed motion now that Americans were irredeemably "*in*" society."[161] The issue for reformers was to answer how initiative—the very basis of agency directionality particularly but not only in the economy, the "self-reliance and self-exertion," the "inducements" which "cause men to perform the acts beneficial to society"[162]—was to be preserved in a system of coordination and cooperation. Socialism was anathema because it dispensed with competition as the main incentive, laissez-faire because self-defeatingly it could include no other. Given the inability of the economic realm to resolve the nature of agency in an organizational society within the narrow arena of exchange, American society would have to reconstitute the inquiry within the more wholistic and inclusive domain of "society." This was a most difficult admission for a people reared on revolutionary liberalism, who regarded the community as one of the disposable institutions associated with the tight constraints and hierarchies of the traditional world. This shift to a "societal agent," as we shall see in Chapter 13, would represent a triumph of liberal order within institutional reality—Newtonian institutions to be sure, but within a system in which the ordered operation of the individual parts now described societal cosmology.

This consolidation of the liberal vision would propel it to its period of confident ascendance in the twentieth century. Though beyond the scope of this project, once the principle became established during the first half of the century that the economy was to operate as one integrated component within a process organized around societal ends, it remained for subsequent economic theory to locate a "social physics" that would preserve maximum incentives for directional motion within a late industrial and postindustrial framework. Forms of voluntarism had to be established *within organizations* which sustained the socialized will's endeavor toward economic motion and directionality. Within organizations, incentive would be framed to promote vertical competition and differential rewards within the transcorporate organizational structure, producing a system now known as the meritocracy. Within the entire nexus of societal priorities, regulatory structures, and distributional mandates, liberal character would continue to be assessed as it had in the past by a complex calculus of talent, initiative, and utility amounting to vertical liberal motion within organizational hierarchies. Voluntarism would be preserved within an institutional society purporting to realize consensual purposes as if enacted by individuals and individuals alone.

Thus, even as the centrality of the economic sector within liberal society receded, the magical claim of markets—horizontal or vertical—to balance self-interest and collective priorities would maintain it as the paradigm for liberal institutional formation, the philosopher's stone reconciling freedom and systemic integration. The power of free market theory, however, must remain a paradoxical one. Despite the lingering conviction Americans have that they inhabit Locke's pre-transfer condition in a culture far more voluntarist than Locke's England, it is ironic that the celebrated "free economy" was built not on the success but on the failure of revolutionary liberal economic freedom. Liberalism could no more achieve "a free individual in a free economy" than it could institute the idyll anywhere else. The modern attempt at revision—"a market agent in an exchange society"— was abandoned at home by 1900, while the socialized version it now offers to the world is, though nowhere fully acknowledged, the achievement of a Protestant-liberal synthesis: "an organizational agent in an institutional economy."

13

John Dewey and the Modern Synthesis

In our age the fact of human association is more obtrusive and relatively more influential than in any previous epoch. . . . Men are more definitely and variously aware of each other than ever before. They are also more promiscuously perplexed by each other's presence.

    —Albion W. Small

The function of the church is to universalize itself, and thus pass out of existence. . . . [P]olitical, domestic and industrial institutions have become in fact an organized Kingdom of God on earth, making for the welfare of the individual *and* the unity of the whole.

    —John Dewey

American liberalism had come a long way from its revolutionary roots. By the last decades of the nineteenth century, it was necessary to acknowledge an ever-widening web of public, market, and community institutions with the coalescing of an urban organizational society. The liberal social sector had evolved during the century in two phases: first, through informally rigidifying norms and practices (the "social") arising in the period of decentralized communities; second, through the rise of an interconnected system of large-scale organizations complimenting and partially absorbing the "social" with more formally standardized behaviors and functions which would be called "society." As its primitive institutional sectors became increasingly interconnected, liberal society emerged as a single integrated order held together by cooperation and coordination. Within this vast array of associations, formal and informal, voluntary and unavoidable, an increasingly common ethos fostered by interconnection and interdependence was juxtaposed with ever more complex role differentiation and social stratification. Liberal authority, unprecedentedly constituted as the product of popular will, was effectively attaching to transcendent and worldly institutions.

Individuals were being integrated within this new order as active fulfillers of collective ends, and in principle, if much more slowly in fact, were offered the equivalent opportunity for a place within this order.

The achievement of "society" as an integrated sector represented the American culmination of agency liberalism as a fixed political cosmology of ordered conduct and motion, of prescribed means directed within a system of designated ends, initiating the triumphant phase of liberal civilization as a renaturalized reality in the twentieth century.[1] An increasing realism was leading liberal theory to settle for a conception of justice as institutions with some access to meritocratic opportunity, resorting to "bureaucratic . . . [ideas] peculiarly suited to the fluidity and impersonality of an urban-industrial world."[2] What was missing in this institutional vision was the original promise of American liberalism to be the "free society of free individuals." Confronted by a threat to the core national self-understanding, modern institutional liberalism faced its deepest challenge—whether its emerging operation could be reconciled under vastly altered historic circumstances to the revolutionary tradition of individual voluntarism. This conceptual integration was the achievement of John Dewey.

The Role of the Liberal Social Realm

Among the elements which would constitute the Newtonian-Hobbesian cosmology of liberal order, the social contributed the critical final element: reversal set the directional motion toward integration; liberal religion universalized the reversal motion and offered institutional membership and participation; the liberal economic realm effected universal participation and selectively provided a systemic place for the "worthy"; and the liberal social sector was the arena of inclusive ordering. The last remaining element of ordered motion was provided by a fixed trajectory within a directional system amounting to a stable orbit, or function, for each. Bringing "wider ethical interests" to bear "than economics provided," the social realm insisted on "a place in the social system" for "all its members."[3] This steady, predictable motion—which the economic sector, with its inducements to maximize velocity and its neglect of any impediments to movement, could not offer—was to be the specific ordered role or set of ongoing activities for each individual within the societal process.

Once so stabilized, this motion would appear as if a natural property indistinguishable from and originating within the moving bodies or participants.

Aligned with the channels of economic behavior already established and structured to stabilize individual motion, it seems to emerge from preinstitutional commitments without much necessity for intervention beyond hedges and political traffic controls to prevent deviations and collisions. Evolved liberal society thus comes understandably to seem alternatively everything (a cosmos of constructed motion) and nothing (merely natural motion of the units) depending on the perspective chosen, the two sides of its synthesis of voluntarism and cosmic order in the paradoxical universe of the "free agent." These contrary views of what Dorothy Ross calls the "new liberalism" of the organizational age are captured in critical social theory, on the one hand, with its claim that the social realm has appropriated all other sectors, including private and public space, through uniform social behavior and a structurally integrated society, and in positivist social science and rational choice theory, on the other hand, with the hypostatization of the individual will.[4]

From both perspectives, liberalism offers a vision of a humanly ordered world characterized by the withering away of fundamental conflicts of political power and ideology as universal agency is achieved through the processes of economic integration and social inclusion. The social realm achieved this culmination of liberal formation by constituting a framework that incorporated all other sector-specific priorities. As success within religious, economic, political, and informal civil institutions became increasingly identified with their transactional—social—currency and connected with the imperatives of maintaining one's relative place in the overall system, society emerged to provide the ultimate cohesion. It represented the final destination of the reversal, a secure place where one's autonomy could be subtly exchanged for an (unadmitted) agency, the chance to be a part, to be integrated. With the completion of the project of integrative motion, the self-authorizing core that challenges collective imperatives, repudiated at the moment of self-reversal, was finally sealed off by a systemically organized individualism. Effective inclusion would eliminate the need to locate an internal reading separate from one's social construction as agent with its external cues and road markers, its elision of inside and outside. In this way, the social served as a realm without any end other than to maintain and replicate its own patterns, and to stifle any fragmenting or countervailing tendencies to its ubiquitous and inclusive order.

Unlike nineteenth-century Europe, whose thinkers were drawn in a deeply stratified civilization to the consensual social realm, with its universal inclusion and stable practices as an antidote to (or refuge from) increasing modern contestations over caste and class prerogatives, in the United States the social realm represented the fulfillment of modernist developments. Rather than merely muting class and caste divisions through the leavening power of traditionally shared community structures, the social realm in American liberalism constituted, as Hume and Smith had foreseen, the inclusive institutional, normative, and behavioral consolidation of middle-class political and moral hegemony. That is, the project of universalizing character and then behavior drove liberalism when unencumbered by past divisions toward that sector which operates through consensus and informal conduct rather than conflict and formal mandates. Its very structural ambiguity, leaving it unclear whether individuals embrace or are fit into existing arrangements, whether they eschew fundamental institutional change or are not even conscious of its desirability, long rendered the social realm uncontroversial, enabling it to become the central institution of advanced liberal society. More recently, the recognition of this ambiguity has cast this sector at the center of the debate over the future of liberalism.

The Liberal Discovery of "Society"

The conception of a single American social reality arose after the Civil War among a few intellectuals and social reformers. This understanding initially stemmed less from perceptions of convergence among the vastly different subcultures and regions or emerging uniformity of values and behaviors than from the theoretical and political recognition that the Civil War, industrialization, and urbanization were producing a single interdependent society at a deeper functional level. This in turn led to two late-century movements concerned with the process of societal integration: reformers and social critics asserting the existence of a single moral collective with universal responsibility for its members; and social theorists tracing the emerging structure of a comprehensive societal system. The two groups, with overlapping membership, deviated similarly from traditional liberalism by acknowledging and explicitly validating the increasing power of inclusion, adaptation, and interdependence as an accurate reflection of postbellum realities.

The reformers surfaced first, emboldened by the new sense of collective responsibility arising from the Civil War and Reconstruction. Beyond earlier initiatives, the war highlighted the powerful role of "national authority" to address collectively major internal failings with "national purpose"[5] and to

act resolutely to solve them. Despite a "new enthusiasm," the problems precipitating the war had been only partly solved "by the overthrow of negro
slavery and the heresy of succession,"[6] while others were arising that "were
more numerous, novel, and difficult than any existing here" since the Revolution and founding.[7] Albion Small, a first-generation professor of sociology
at the University of Chicago, wrote:

> At the close of the war the intelligent people of the country were more so-
> phisticated than at its beginning. They realized in part that the country was
> not the primitive, simple affair which it had been when all its inhabitants
> were pioneers. They had been jostled a good deal in the fondest of Ameri-
> can illusions that a constitution and laws enacted in the pursuance thereof
> would automatically produce human welfare. They became acutely aware
> that life in the United States was not altogether a success. They perceived
> more or less distinctly that work was ahead to bring American conditions
> into tolerable likeness to American ideals.[8]

Calling on a public sense of a single society, not yet as a set of integrated
functions but as a growing web of communal obligations, a generation of
social reformers alongside Protestant social gospel activists addressing the
industrial crisis within the church and social economists seeking changes
within the productive and distributive mechanisms began to identify common problems. Founding the American Social Science Association (ASSA)
in 1865 and promoting "the revival" of "the theory and the practice or application of . . . *Social Science*" to advance such matters,[9] they hoped to
strengthen and expand this national will to address as a single community
the growing problems of industrial America.

The innovative aspect of this national association, which later gave rise to
the Progressive movement, nationwide legislative reform, and the American
professional social sciences, was the recognition of "Society" as the realm
which in its "comprehensiveness" with a distinct "constitution" and "welfare" had recast "man as a social being."[10] Earlier traditions of private and
group philanthropy and local forms of mutual aid were no longer viable,
given "the experience of our great cities," which required "a harmonious
system" of "public activity."[11] The ASSA from its inception through the end
of the century spurred the transition from values of idyllic antebellum individualism to the conception of an interdependent society: "combined into
great bodies," human "nature is very different in many respects from what it
is in individual men." The older vision of "liberty" which had "kept the

world in a blaze" was now "rather an ideal than a tangible good."[12] The earlier focus on "individual rights" represented a prior stage of society governed by the principle *"Every man for himself, and the Devil take the hindermost,"* which "for the word *'Devil'* substitute . . . want, misery, and privation."[13]

In a major address to the association in 1880, titled "Changes in American Society," Julia Ward Howe noted how the religious individualism and sectarian isolation of her youth had given way to "a sense of the dependence of human beings upon each other" and a necessity for a social "power corresponding to the needs involved in this interdependence."[14] The Reverend Samuel Dike in a sweeping 1881 paper identified the problematic legacy of "American *political* institutions": from a "nation . . . born in throes over the right of man as an individual" has come "a relative excess of individualism."[15] Combined with "the individualizing tendencies of modern law and modern economic forces," this reinforced "the destructive notion that the individual only is the true social unit," a "false notion of the structure of society" in which "civil life . . . easily becomes sheer individualism in conception, and its living intensely selfish and narrow."[16]

The transition, "guided as with Ariadne's clew, by that enticing word *social,*"[17] involved accepting "human society as a whole" which possessed a "good" of the "whole," a "composite unity" in which benefits to each "part" and to the "aggregate" were intertwined.[18] The collective was increasingly an "endless diversity" of "bonds," of "labor and capital . . . of law and justice, of administration and legislation, of public and private service, of crime and police, of health and disease, of poverty and charity," and so on.[19] Beginning in the 1880s, the growing environmental degradations and physical hazards no longer plausibly attributable to individuals, particularly in cities, were creating innocent victims with little choice over their situation—the young and old especially—as sacrifices to "a kind of biological furnace, which in the end consumes the lives supplied to it."[20]

This dawning understanding of a common enterprise suggested the need for common solutions. If some, more obvious, social conditions were the product of collective activity, was there not a deeper sense of continuing responsibility for the fate of all, particularly for the many burdens which large numbers of individuals neither created nor could overcome by themselves: long work hours, low wages, language and educational deprivation, disability, insanity, pauperism, machine politics, a lack of proper socialization, immigration inequities, exploitative female employment, lack of public services and amenities, health care neglect, and limited employment opportunities? If there was a collective process generating social dysfunction, it was clearly both possible and just to call on that collective as author to remedy its own failure: "One indispensable element of true civilizations is a common regard for the interests of every person composing the community." This sentiment, so distinct from that of the economic sector, involved "a deeper sympathy with human weakness" and "a nobler conception of human possibility."[21]

This movement foresaw a society not only of universal membership but of universal success as well, where social failure is actively prevented rather than taken as a personal judgment and "a larger number are enabled to compete successfully for the benefits of life."[22] The Reverend J. H. Jones declared in 1882 that "the primal law of all righteous society" is to create a "shape and structure" to "work out the welfare of all who compose it."[23] All who have been left out or forced out deserved to be brought in and helped to "a greater strength and efficiency" by policies of "improvement," designed to "educate, strengthen, and elevate." Benjamin Pierce, association president, proclaimed in 1880, "Let no man be wasted! is the rightful demand of society," the logical consequence of "universal suffrage."[24] Where problems occur on the community's watch, the shifting *burden* of responsibility now imposes a corresponding obligation.

The operational premises of this new realm of society were as yet unclear. For this group, liberal voluntarism remained a primary value, though as the actual availability of social options rather than an abstract independence, leading them to expand collective action to enhance opportunities for the less fortunate. At the same time, they wanted the "social" without the "socialist," a confusing "socialistic progress . . . toward greater liberty and more intimate social relations,"[25] cooperation without threatening the individual incentive to achieve: "If liberty is not afforded to all, rich and poor, high and low, to keep, and to use in whatever way they may see fit, that which they lawfully acquire . . . then the desire to acquire and accumulate property will be taken away."[26] Aspiring toward a synthesis of individual voluntarism and responsibility within liberal institutions that their own liberal heritage had not provided, they could only hope as practical thinkers that "the sociology of the future will devise" a "more equitable" model for integrating social and individual interests by shifting freedom from independence apart from institutions to opportunity *within* institutions.[27]

Their role was to elaborate the importance of opportunity. The equal chance for each and every citizen to fulfill one's capacity to seek collective ends was to be achieved not through market inequities but by altering the market's unacceptable results: "The first duty of a community like the American is not to feed the hungry and clothe the naked, but to prevent people from being hungry and naked." The responsibility of "the nation" was "to improve the opportunities of life" so that "free opportunities of self-development" for "mental and moral cultivation . . . be placed within reach of all,"[28] including recognition of "the aspirations and capacities of women."[29] The distinctions arising because individuals "are born with different natural capacities" and differential commitments to "industry and economy"[30] cannot be overcome by projects of social improvement. Yet everyone was entitled to a place in society, to be prepared for it and to be justly rewarded in it, even if the specific allocation must be earned. Civil service reform received enormous enthusiasm in the ASSA as a model for "free and open competition" within organizational systems. It suggested the means by which "the fittest" would have to be determined by a complex series of factors, including individuals' "comparative general intelligence," their "special knowledge of the particular . . . duties required," and their practical ability determined by an "actual trial in the performance of the duties."[31] In this way, the individual was to find an appropriate niche within ever "enlarged and more comprehensive . . . social organizations" while remaining "sovereign over himself."[32]

Liberal individualism was metamorphosing into meritocratic place. The optimal role for the state to universalize opportunity without determining outcomes was to prepare citizens for meritocratic competition and organizational roles. By emphasizing social justice, these reformers provided the moral basis for the transformation of liberalism into a doctrine of societal integration: the growing role of institutions in individuals' lives demanded universal inclusion as well as equitable principles of citizen preparation and resource distribution through collective responsibility and action. What they left for social theory to face was the conceptual justification of organizational society and its impact, with its hierarchies and unequal distribution of status and power, on early republican values. As Thomas Haskell has written, "The growing interdependence of nineteenth-century society not only supplied a uniformitarian social universe" but also replaced the conception of "human actors in the social universe" as "autonomous beings" with "individual behavior" as "largely a product of external circumstances."[33] The social science and social theory emerging from this shift would be forced to confront the seeming oxymoron of liberal interdependence.

Early Liberal Societal Theory and the Science
of Interdependence

The corresponding rise of a postbellum American social theory was driven by similar moral and conceptual goals: to grasp the underlying reality of a new systemic America and shape it by utilizing more just and universal principles. It sought to comprehend the emergence of a single community composed of equivalent individuals who pursued distinct functions within a highly differentiated system, and to explain its two sides of uni(formi)ty and differentiation, the complex harmony of modern industrial and organizational life, in a way consonant with core liberal values. Such liberal theories of society represented a major shift in American values. The other sectors, though forced to acknowledge the growing dominance of institutional reality, had continued to focus on sector-specific ends and their origin in individual will. Even the social realm as the sector of group norms was understood as informal and optional, while for the reformers society remained a moral construct. The transvaluation precipitated by societal theory was the recognition of not only fixed institutional processes but also fixed functional sectors themselves coordinated in a single collectivity, "society." Lester Ward called it "sociocracy," W. T. Harris *"the world of institutions,"* of "Man as distinguished from Nature."[34] The now "hopeless insufficiency of the isolated individual" meant the replacement of "wilfully compacting constituents" with an "organizational revolution" creating a nation featuring "organization and administration" in which few individuals might avoid "impotence and insignificance."[35]

Albion Small chronicled the emergence of "society" after the Civil War as "a child of its time" and "part of the orderly unfolding of native conditions" from "the primitive, simple affair" when "all its inhabitants were pioneers":

> *In our age the fact of human association is more obtrusive and relatively more influential than in any previous epoch. . . .* As industries become diversified, as division of labor becomes territorial and international . . . as occupations become more visibly affected by the actions of distant persons, as communication becomes accurate and rapid between groups of men industrially related though geographically separate, perception of dependence upon physical conditions ceases to be the dominant factor in human calculation. Perception of subjection to human devices or of advantage to be won by personal combination becomes decisive.[36]

Slowly waking up to this "complex web of man to man in modern society . . . of living and working together" that was growing around them, Americans were moving to reform its dysfunctions. Yet the deeper implications eluded them: other people were no longer avoidable *"meddlers one with another."* Suddenly "more definitely and variously aware of each other than ever before," people were still "promiscuously perplexed by each other's presence."[37]

Sociological theory emerged late in the century to provide and account for "an assurance of order in a natural universe" now composed of systems "suddenly removed from God."[38] All "orthodox moorings," including "historical, economic, political, philosophical, theological," were gone. Moreover, traditional efforts to isolate and explain human behavior within boundaries of discrete sectors, as "an affair of a single factor," no longer sufficed. The political-legal process and the economic system were merely aspects of complex and continuing collective relations, "in reality devices of groups of men who for generations and centuries have been dividing their time between struggling for economic gains at one moment and . . . legal adjustments at the next." Such "groups of men with economic interests and political interests were at the same time groups structuralized and motivated by topographical interests . . . and racial interests and creedal interests, and composite physical, intellectual, aesthetic, and moral interests of innumerable sorts." Referring to his own evangelical background, Small specified the limitations of earlier narrow and exclusivist explanatory frameworks.[39]

A "new attitude, a new procedure toward all problems of knowledge and conduct of human life" was needed, a "revolution" that would shift "the emphasis from the assumed individual agent to the *group* in which individuals are now seen as subordinate factors."[40] Henceforth it would be "elementary" that "human experience always and everywhere runs its course in and through groupings of persons." Inquiry must therefore focus on "recurrent group forms, group movements, group appraisals, and group controls," on the "forms, modes, methods, proportions, and intensities of these group processes."[41] The objective was a model, "a miniature, as we make reduced models of our physical world," of "the interaction of all Americans upon one another" suggested "in the term 'society.'"[42] The ultimate imperative of such knowledge was ethical—"adequate investigation and formulation of the conditions of human welfare" resulting in "credible programmes for the wholesale promotion of welfare."[43]

Developing the vision of an overarching societal network incorporating all sectors and promising not only membership and formal equivalence but also universal—though differential—place as suggested by the social reformers was the work of two broad groups: those proponents of the traditional European organicist model following Comte, Hegel, and the Germans; and those seeking to reconcile institutional society with liberal individualist values. The former included James O'Connell and Henry Hughes just before the war, George Frederick Holmes, William Strong, and W. T. Harris in the first postbellum generation, and influential figures such as G. H. Mead, C. H. Cooley, and L. L. Bernard in the later heyday of sociology. In the latter group of liberal sociologists were Robert Hamilton, R. J. Wright, and notably Lester Ward in the first postwar generation and Albion Small (for the most part) among the early-twentieth-century mainstream, with the great figure being John Dewey. Unlike the organicists, who posited society as the constitutive reality[44] leaving the individual as a mere part of "one living whole,"[45] liberal theorists would pursue a theoretical framework that sought despite its intrinsic tensions to reconcile institutional primacy with the cardinal principles of voluntarism and individualism.

For these latter theorists a satisfactory account of society was far more problematic. Not just freedom but the very *existence* of separate individuals was at stake. For liberalism, individuals were foundational to society in two ways—as the universal and equivalent constitutive elements of any larger system and as the ultimate beneficiaries of institutional processes. What it had never provided was a satisfactory model of societal institutions that were both functionally primary and yet circumscribed by an individualist constitution and telos. Early liberal theorists therefore "launched out on a quest of their own."[46] Driven by an urgency reflecting the perilous future of liberalism, Hamilton, Wright, and Ward among others asserted "the necessity of a total reorganization of thought . . . as radical and thorough" as the "new principles, new modes of thought" offered by Newton.[47] Such fierce originality led to extremes both imaginative and idiosyncratic.

They began by dismissing traditional liberalism as irrelevant to institutional society. Hamilton rejected the "error" of the "Political" and "Political-Economic" schools of thought for narrowly asserting the independence of their sectors. With institutions the "*outgrowths* of society," it is this larger "framework of man" that is "the primary object of consideration."[48] For Wright, the "overwhelming tendency to centralization . . . all over the civilized world" had replaced the earlier period of "uncivilized independence,"[49] creating for Ward the "great organizations in which we live" as

"the superstructure of our civilization" and the "distinguishing feature" between earlier and present times, "between man the low savage and man the
cultured, intellectual being." Individual activity was now to be understood
as "social functions" within "social structures" called *institutions,*" which
characterized "government" and "civilization," "every workshop, every factory, every hive of industry."[50] These "structures" are "not independent, but
are connected into one great system, which is society."[51]

A new comprehensive societal reality required an equally comprehensive
account using a new language, which they agreed was science. By seeking
"the laws and truths of Nature" which are "pervading the universe" in patterns "absolute and certain," it would "supersede" the superannuated ho-
lism of "theology."[52] The "great work" was to found "a science of Sociology
. . . a thorough Social Philosophy" which could "penetrate to CAUSES, to the
fundamental LAWS, which give rise to phenomena" and "DETERMINE THE SO-
CIAL CONDITION OF MANKIND."[53] Remarkably, the three theorists working independently arrived at similar, deeply suggestive though methodologically
problematic solutions which attempted to integrate Newtonian physics and
an optimistic variant of Darwinian-Spencerian evolution, each harnessed to
its author's quite distinctive reformist agenda. Rejecting organicism, these
theorists were attracted by the Newtonian conception of reality as collective
systems constituted and engaged in by the individual units which form the
sole tangible reality. By extension, society has "no corporate consciousness,"
operating through the ordered motion of "living units," each with "individual consciousness," to create "the SOCIAL COSMOS" through the "laws of social gravitation."[54]

Yet, as Ward understood most fully, Newtonian mechanics offered only a
partial solution because, as an essentially static model of systems composed
from individual parts, it failed to explain "social transformation" or the process of "change in social structure and human institutions."[55] Given the goal
of providing a scientific framework for progress and reform, the clearly applicable framework at the time for such systemic change was the "science of
dynamic biology."[56] Evolution provided these theorists with a language to
conceptualize systemic societal progress. The biological component, however, also posed problems, given its tendency "to subordinate the individual
to the society, nay, to *merge* the individual completely in the society."[57] The
answer, a conceptual synthesis, was evolutionary Newtonianism. Systemic
while preserving both the individual and the imperative of progress, this
synthesis by acknowledging purposive change further provided the basis for

a social theory of collective initiative directed by human intelligence. Yet the compilation of features produced unwieldy scientific hybrids. Evolutionary organic and static mechanical models were not reconcilable, nor were iron natural laws and ameliorative collective action. The theoretical imprecision of their models was in each case offset by an elaborated project to reinscribe individualism within a reshaped organizational liberalism. But the question remained whether freedom would survive the transformation.

The Theoretical Impasse: Freedom in an Organizational Age

These theorists hoped that liberal voluntarism could be preserved, both in their scientific theories and in the reconstructions of the liberal polity that flowed from them. Yet they were unpersuaded by their own claims of freedom. Institutional systems reconciled individuals with collective processes only by incorporating individual initiative within a tightly ordered world. In its quest for conceptual clarity, late-nineteenth-century social theory had unknowingly returned part of the way toward its origins: by means of ordered Newtonian motion to a Hobbesian systemic integration of the parts. Though Hobbes as an early modern regarded his constituent actors as free relative to traditional stasis, their conformable motion and directionality—however ontologically distinct—were less likely to be seen as voluntarist in a nation raised on proprietary individualism and Jeffersonian ideals.

The difficulty of preserving individualism in an industrial and urban age led some early sociological theorists to relinquish voluntarism as the core liberal value. Albion Small noted this great danger: "We have often erred on the side of magnifying 'society,' 'association,' 'activities,' and minimizing *socii*, people associating, people acting."[58] Systems of natural phenomena featuring individual motion could not be both voluntary and predictive, free and necessary, optional and ordered. Regularity, whether accounted for by the consistency of external forces or by internal adaptations of the operational units, presumed necessity, though science suggested a language more grounded and less controversial than religion. Hobbes's vision of ordered Newtonian motion, albeit with a progressive slant, was finally one of highly mobile parts carrying the burden of stability through their unquestioned engagement in the collectively authorized channels set forth.

With a better sense of the agency paradigm, it is possible to recognize the limits of the liberal search for scientific grounding. On the level of individuals, the Protestant commitment to an institutionally contained voluntarism had no equivalent in the scientific world of unmotivated particles. The basis of the freedom of the agent was a personal assumption by systemic units of their *duty* to act continuously and cooperatively in furtherance of collective ends, to undertake willingly conformable motion. On the systemic level, the conception of a universal process emerging in conjunction with individual activity which is itself dynamic, evolving, and purposive in an intelligent sense also had no scientific equivalent. Science was precisely the effort to divorce natural phenomena from the continued intervention of a guiding intelligence. But systemic change isolated from ulterior purpose could only with difficulty be framed as inherently progressive. The severe restraints imposed by the scientific paradigm on the purposive activity of both individuals *and* society, the two poles on whose integration agency civilization rested, undercut the American sense of common mission which sustained the willingness to be agents.

Liberalism needed voluntarism, for even as it generated expectations which threatened functional integration, so too it released a power and sense of purpose unavailable to organic societies to move individuals to undertake socially constructed roles and collective progress from their own internal assent. Ironically, the failure of the project of constituting a natural world whose parts were pre-instilled with systemic values sheds light on the source of its warrant, revealing an implicit turn not only toward Hobbes (and presumptively away from religion) but also in fact to Protestantism itself. For the Newtonian relinquishment of an active ordering intelligence had occurred only because this intelligence had already fully "bestowed" its dispensation in the form of "habits" of motion on its creation:

> Eighteenth-century social scientists propounded the laws of nature as "rules through which divine governance flowed," thus fusing the scientific view of law as observed regularities in nature with the older religious concept of natural law as the agency by which God governed the natural world. By the early and mid-nineteenth century, the divine presence was generally discounted, but the characteristics of divine law—its necessity, uniformity, and action as a governing agency—most often continued to adhere to the laws scientists discovered in nature.[59]

By reaching back not simply to a political Newtonianism but also to the broader legitimization of a cosmically evolving Newtonianism, these theorists in effect imported a veiled theological explanation for the progressive emergence and development of society.

This debt to "the metaphysicians and the theologians"[60] has not prevented modern theory from "a determination to develop natural knowledge on its own terms" in which "positivist science . . . set the terms of the agreement," framing "Social Science laws as human generalizations of historical and contemporaneous data."[61] Ever greater confidence about the "immanence" or indwelling of its basic theological conceptions produced an ever more antiseptic language: "This reification of scientific law . . . reflect[ed] both the need to rely on nature as divinity receded and a growing assurance in the scope and power of scientific investigation. . . . Once the chief dynamic factors had been specified, rooted in nature, and the trajectory of their action set, history developed by an *inner* logic along a precharted course."[62] The retreat from a discussion of ultimate ends and from conflict over societal means represented a successful "renaturing" and reshaping of citizens for this new interdependent world.[63] At the end of the century, the impetus to practical reform was producing the far-flung legislative initiatives of the Progressive movement, while the early theoretical work was giving rise to architectonic conceptions of the new industrial society in the works of George Herbert Mead, Charles Cooley, and Herbert Croly. The programmatic culmination in Theodore Roosevelt's "New Nationalism" demonstrated the extent to which a language of "public welfare" and "the general right of the community" had replaced the discourse of voluntarism, and accounts in part for the triumph of Woodrow Wilson's outdated but resonant "New Freedom."[64]

For the new generation of theorists, organizational society was an unavoidable but troubling reality. The cause of social justice and equal opportunity could never be achieved by breaking up the very organizations that defined modern society.[65] Croly called for an "acceptance by the state" of the reality of "corporate industrial organization" as the "only sound point of departure."[66] For Mead and Cooley, the conception of a "separate individual" was now merely "an abstraction," for "the individual is not separable from the human whole, but a living member of it."[67] An overarching "human community" composed of a "social matrix" of institutions had to replace the "old" view that "human societies have arisen out of individuals."[68] Freedom would in turn become a property that "exist[s] only in and through a social order" as the preparation and exercise of this "opportunity": "It is freedom to be disciplined in as rational a manner as you are fit for" in order to undertake "the free participation of the individual in the process."[69] In Croly's words, "The means . . . to reach a more desirable condition of individual independence" is "primarily and chiefly in a thoroughly zealous and competent performance of [one's] own particular job" in "the process of national fulfillment."[70]

These grand theoretical visions of interdependence and cohesion foreshadowed and gave direction to the later creation of a single society, still an abstraction or intimation when written. During the sixty years culminating after World War II, Americans came to terms with society as a wholistic entity with the awesome power to construct roles, define place, marginalize deviance, and incorporate selfhood. At the same time, partly out of the incommensurability of an integrated, inclusive society with revolutionary freedom, modern theorists largely accepted the sacrifice of individual freedom as the price for institutional maturation. The "free individual," the "free society," and the sense of national mission that produced them were all in jeopardy. The project of citizen and child formation also found itself at a loss to define the active agent for the modern liberal community. As these visions of regulatory and organizational liberalism gained influence, theories of radical structural change proliferated to compensate for the dramatic waning of the revolutionary vision.[71] At its very inception, then, American social theory was in danger of relinquishing the central discourse of voluntarism, reflecting the crisis for liberalism posed by the advent of organizational America.

The Architect of Liberal "Society"

In this crisis of coherence, the greatest since the Revolution and founding, liberalism would have to recover the second of its two great originating premises: not only that the ordering of the political universe was "scientific" but also that its Maker conceived it as a just order and effectively guaranteed the realization of that order through the "freedom" of its participants. The theorist who most fully identified the conceptual task and forged out of his Protestant and liberal background a voluntarist conception of organizational agency society was John Dewey. Dewey is understood to be America's great modern liberal philosopher. Neil Coughlan calls him "the philosopher par excellence of American liberalism."[72] Robert Westbrook regards him as "the most important philosopher in modern American history," who undertook "to revitalize and reconstruct the Anglo-American liberal tradition."[73] As "*the* philosopher of American liberalism in the first half of [the twentieth] century," he is placed by Alan Ryan in a "secular trinity" during "the high tide of American liberalism" along with the English philosophers Mill and Russell.[74]

With his deep roots in evangelical Protestantism, the liberal Dewey understood the complex synthesis that agency represented. Unmoved by the traditions of anti-institutional individualism, he believed agency to be the true shape of human nature and the foundational principle of social institutions. Unlike older forms of collectivism, agency society in his view shared with secular liberalism the centrality of voluntarism. The complex demands of agency could be realized only through self-willed and active engagement on the part of the subject. At the same time, since one could be strongly induced (if never forced) to be an agent, institutions had the responsibility to encourage individuals to enter willingly and fulfill their agency natures by internalizing and actively realizing common priorities.

While many shared with Dewey the creation of a modern institutional liberalism, his great genius was to forge a grand Protestant-liberal settlement by synthesizing liberal voluntarism and Protestant social integration within an inclusive vision incorporating all sectors of society and all of its members. Appropriating the language of "a free society of free individuals," Dewey saved and reinvigorated the liberal dream by recasting the discourse of secular modernity using the values of the Anglo-American past. Transforming freedom into the voluntary activity of individuals imbued with and fulfilling collective ends, modern liberalism became an inclusive and secularized version of the Protestant kingdom of self-willing agents, in substance "a liberal society of Protestant agents." Completed about 1895, this powerful settlement was presented as a vast new cosmic architecture, a self-moving order of interdependent individual constituents. Thus provided with an inevitability that at once reconciled the tensions of modern individualism and mitigated the fragility of Hobbes's "artifice," this political cosmology completed the liberal historical project: the "renaturalization" of agency civilization. This model, the center of Dewey's thinking over a long and productive career, would further orient progressive societal and pedagogical theory and practice for more than a half-century to come.

So revitalized and reconsecrated, liberalism would go on to unprecedented levels of institutional and theoretical cohesion. At the same time, Dewey's deft reframing of individuals as by nature agents and freedom as voluntarism within agency institutions should not blind us to the larger questions raised. This new cosmology, the product of centuries, was of course only one remarkably successful human ordering. An iron cage to some, to others the very air we breathe, it would in our time face the question whether modern organizational liberalism had produced a new liberal nature or simply a routinized and diminished individualism. Many have returned to Dewey to recover his agency settlement from the period of its optimistic ascendancy. Others would challenge the effort to turn any historic settlement into an accomplished fact and work to restore the dialectic of human possibility and worldly transformation.

In the dominant view, held by Dewey himself, he succeeded in producing a modernist liberalism in part because he gradually perceived the error of the strict and narrow religious beliefs of his upbringing and moved toward a broader view of American life. In so doing, he is assumed to exemplify the growing influence of liberal democracy during his lifetime and the triumph of secular liberal values over Protestant culture. Ryan cautiously claims that, as an adult, Dewey "slipped quietly out of orthodox Christianity into a secular faith in democracy." Though ready "to use the language of traditional Christianity . . . to communicate with" the "public," Dewey after his shift promoted "a view of the world that is commonly thought to be squarely at odds with religion," a "thoroughgoing naturalism . . . that subscribed to 'scientific politics.'"[75] For Westbrook, Dewey evolved into an apostle of democracy in part by replacing divine guidance with human empowerment: "As he chased the Absolute from his philosophy, he also stripped his social theory of all metaphysical and religious guarantees of progress toward his democratic ideal. . . . As long as mankind suffered from . . . impotency, it naturally shifted a burden of responsibility it could not carry over to the competent shoulders of the transcendent cause. Now, Dewey believed, man was able to carry this burden alone." In Coughlan's view, Dewey relinquished "what had passed for transcendent and supernatural" as he discovered it "to be a mystification of something finite and real." The resulting theory was a stronger and more probing "examination of human conduct and society."[76]

In Steven Rockefeller's 1991 book *John Dewey: Religious Faith and Democratic Humanism*, a deeper sense of Dewey's thought emerges which establishes his lifelong reliance on his early religious ideas. His major working concepts of the individual, society, history, and science as well as his pervasive and enduring effort at "unifying the ideal and the actual" were first formulated in the theological language of late-nineteenth-century liberal Protestantism, framed transitionally in a neo-Hegelian secular theology, and finally put into the language of sociological theory. In Rockefeller's view, Dewey believed that the "new humanism and ethical naturalism preserve the most important religious values in the Western tradition," and his "religious . . . ideals" and "values" continued to "pervade his entire philosophy of social reconstruction and individual liberation."[77] While Dewey certainly shifted from a Protestant formulation of his paradigm and agenda to a preeminently secular vision of liberal democracy, making his later writings more influential with those seeking the reconstruction of democracy, community, and individualism, Rockefeller is right that Dewey's liberal ideals never ventured far from their origins.

The persuasiveness of the Deweyan synthesis stemmed from his intuitive appreciation of the strengths and weaknesses of the two national discourses and his recognition that their power derived from their complementarity. Protestantism had transformed the individual into a willing and dynamic actor in the providential drama of the American mission, but its antidote for growing individualism and diversity was a restrictive and ritualized ecclesium that was counterproductively divisive in a voluntarist, heterogeneous society. Deeply committed to the national accession of an evolving millennial community, American Protestantism had been unwilling finally to put its mission in the hands of that community's citizens. Liberalism, by mobilizing citizens and expanding its membership over time, was in turn creating a society of unparalleled dynamism and allegiance. The Protestant sense of individual engagement almost eerily complemented the social dynamic of liberalism.

Dewey sensed this new unified civilization being created from the strands of nineteenth-century life and struggled to give its emerging aspirations a theoretical shape. Providing a virtually theological cast to the liberal processes of self-formation and institutional construction, he gave modern form to the traditions constituting the American experience. In a "liberalized" language, the nation was reconstituted as a just and inclusive society of agents and the American citizen as an active agent of the collective enterprise. Insisting that an evolved self and a realized society were achievable together, that the dynamism of each required and ensured the vitality of both, Dewey combined the uncommon power of both Anne Hutchinson and John Winthrop, Jefferson and Madison, Emerson and George Herbert Mead, as only Franklin, Whitman, and Lincoln had before. Mechanisms of order and authority inhered within the underlying structures of both self and society, permitting a full release of human energies. As a result, freedom and order would now grow from each other.

Rockefeller has directed our attention to Dewey's 1894 essay "Reconstruction" as the summation of a decade's work before he moved to the University of Chicago to focus on democracy, society, and education. I want to treat this essay as a culmination of Dewey's consuming project to that point in his life and a key moment in the history of American liberal culture. The essay boldly announced the realization of Protestant civilization in American life as "a cause already won": "The ideals with which Christianity started . . . must by this time have embodied themselves in the institutions and habits of practical life; they must have converted themselves into structure, into institutions, into a system of working means." Liberal society was now equated with "the Kingdom of God on earth," a continuation, expression, and fulfillment of American Protestantism. Dewey's embrace of liberalism must be understood in light of this sense of historic achievement; it was merely a new language applied to evolved Reformation forms of self and society. Moreover, with Protestant ends now embodied in the practices of liberal society, they were no longer accessible to human intervention. In his new political metaphysics, only the means remained for consideration: "The very success of the former ideal demands that we no longer go on striving for that ideal, but that we formulate a new principle of action."[78] His emerging philosophy of processual activity represented the very apotheosis of agency.

John Dewey was thus a Protestant and a liberal, the creator of a synthesis which was always the former and increasingly the latter. He was religiously guided in his construction of self and society while struggling to extend their applicability beyond the narrow frame of his early life to the national society being constituted. Dewey's shift in language is important not because of a transformed content but because it established the basis of a national settlement. In this light, I would suggest beyond Rockefeller that Dewey does more than merely restate his religious ideas in liberal rhetoric. With Continental organicism irrelevant and a socially embedded English liberalism inapplicable, American liberalism had no voluntarist institutional discourse. To provide these ideas with a secular frame was to *remake American liberalism as secular Protestantism*. The revolutionary-Lockean language of coercive institutions and the Hobbesian-Madisonian notion of forcible adaptation were dispensed with. In their place are the original formulations from which Anglo-American modernism began: agency individuals, engaged communities of spiritual equals, and a collective mission to realize common ideals. Reframed in the newer rhetoric of individual voluntarism, democratic community, and historical progress, American liberalism was able to complete the project of the English Reformation and Revolution while simultaneously preserving and adapting the revolutionary foundations of the American nation.

While emphasizing his religious preoccupations, therefore, we must be wary of treating Dewey, as Rockefeller suggests, as a lifelong religious seeker trying to heal the divisions between "the head and the heart, reason and faith, materialist and romanticist, naturalist and idealist, philosophy and theology, relativist and absolutist" by longing "to know for certain and realize in his own life experience the truth that reality is an organic unity."[79] This approach underestimates precisely the ways in which he was also very much a political philosopher. Having come to his own understanding relatively early, he functioned thereafter not as a quester for personal truth but as an architect of societal reality seeking to provide a common language for national consolidation. Given the scope and quantity of his early work, it is possible to trace the evolution of Dewey's thought to his 1894 resolution. Of primary concern is the nature of this bridge Dewey constructed linking the two cultures, and the precise ways in which the "free individual" had become the agent and the "free society" the liberal polity as the Protestant paradigm was reconfigured for liberal society.

Dewey's Religious Roots and His Yearning for Synthesis

Religion played a pervasive role in Dewey's early life. His mother, in his youth, had converted from liberal Congregationalism to evangelical Congregational pietism, and imbued her children with an overriding sense of religious vigilance, continually inquiring of them whether they were "right with Jesus."[80] From this upbringing Dewey gained a sense of the spiritual life as an active, strenuous, directed, and ambitious engagement with the direction of society. The expectation and responsibility of human agents was to engage in committed activity in the world—a stance which he maintained throughout his long life. The continual pressure to pursue scarcely attainable ideals, combined with the revivalist belief in sanctification for the persevering, left in Dewey a nearly unyielding but unavoidable quest for moral achievement. This spiritual tightrope was vividly conveyed in an 1884 talk: "Belief is not a privilege, but a duty—'whatsoever is not of faith is sin.' . . . We must seek in order to find, and we find that for which we seek. If the desire and will of man are for God, he will find God in all knowledge." If not, he continues, "he had been shut out from the start . . . his eyes will never see light," his knowledge "will never reach unto God."[81]

Another early shaping experience arose from Dewey's reaction to his mother's belief as a "confirmed 'partialist,'" in Westbrook's terms, that "only a select portion of humanity was destined for salvation." For her, the world was radically divided between the sacred and profane, believers' sect and secular society, inner spirit and quotidian passions, transcendent divinity and the unlit world. In personal matters, the demands of religious certitude required emotional self-denial fed by guilt, religious submission, and relentless self-criticism which Dewey called "an inward laceration."[82] He spoke critically in later life of traditional religion's "divisions by way of isolation of self from the world, of soul from body, of nature from God."[83] This lifelong need to lift the burdens of antebellum faith by reconciling divisions and announcing a common national faith encompassing self, society, and the world emerged from his early experience. In one of his earliest essays, "The New Psychology" (1884), Dewey stated his commitment to primordial interconnection which was to remain the center of his life's work. In the old psychology "schematism was supreme," premised on "self-subsistent individuals" whose "psychical life" was broken up into "atomic elements or independent powers." Understanding, however, lies not in discrete and unconnected apprehensions but in a unified psychological ground arising from "the mother soil of experience." Moreover "experience," suggesting subjective "realities" to some, is—and must be—by its nature *prior to all divisions*. "We know," he claims, that the subject's life "is bound up with the life of society, of the nation in the *ethos* and *nomos* . . . that he is closely connected with all the past by the lines of education, tradition, and heredity; we know that . . . life is a continuance, having no breaks . . . that our distinctions, however necessary, are unreal and largely arbitrary."[84]

This "new psychology" of wholistic experience in turn unifies both knowledge and the known reality of each system from self to universe. It reveals "mental life as an organic unitary process developing according to the laws of all life," and establishes "the organic relation of the individual to . . . organized social life" and to "other lives organized in society," all within a "teleological" process of life in which "immanent ideas or purposes are realizing themselves through the development of experience" on the "altar stairs which slope up to God."[85] Ideal purpose and real life for Dewey were from the outset inextricably linked in all dimensions. In a remarkable elaboration culminating in "Reconstruction," he asserted that endemic rents in the fabric of the individual, the society, and the world were no longer a falling away from transcendence desperately needing to be overcome but divisions already healed. It was as if the fear of being separated off in his own life coincided with his sense of a larger collective wish for inclusion to generate a vision of primal unity.

Dewey's capacity to move boldly beyond the divisions pervading the Protestantism of his youth and the antinomies of classic liberalism was a central element in his historic importance. The parallels between his search for national synthesis and emerging popular aspirations suggest an immense capacity to absorb the philosophical and cultural tendencies inchoate in the age. This defining moment witnessed the coalescence of a young and ambitious nation just unleashing its immense apparatus of industrial production and distribution. With its seeming power to surmount all worldly barriers, the energies of this dynamic and innovative society bred with a sense of millennial promise were pregnant with a conviction of transcendent achievement and realization of potential beyond anything previously imagined.

The sense of prophetic immanence in Dewey's work resonates with many voices of that period, including that of Henry James. A traditionalist who had fled his philistine homeland, James upon returning in 1904 to New York after twenty years away shed his customary reticence when faced with its immense potency. Suggesting Dreiser at his best, James experienced in this city of the future a "greatness" calling forth the "largest suggestion," a "ubiquitous American force, the most ubiquitous of all," making it a "gorgeous golden blur" difficult even for *him* to explain:

> The aspect the power wears . . . is indescribable; it is the power of the most extravagant of cities, rejoicing, as with the voice of the morning, in its might, its fortune, its unsurpassable conditions, and imparting to every object and element, to the motion and expression of every floating, hurrying panting thing . . . its sovereign sense of being "backed" and able to back. The universal *applied* passion struck me unprecedentedly . . . in the bigness and bravery and insolence, especially, of everything that rushed and shrieked.

The sense of coalescence was palpable: "This appearance of the bold lacing-together, across the waters, of the scattered members of the monstrous organism" as it "grows and grows" like "some unmannered large giant" created the sense of an "enormous system" held by "binding stitches" which "for ever fly further and faster and draw harder." The product was a colossus filling up the space "under the sky and over the sea."[86]

As Americans were rushing headlong to the urban centers of a newly forming common life, this nation was absorbing all other dreams as well as all who dreamed: "One was in the presence, as never before, of a realized ideal," a "society which had found . . . so exactly what it wanted." James experienced around him and even in his own diffident heart a "childlike rush to surrender to it and clutch" this "supremely gregarious" enterprise, opening its arms to all comers and "blissfully exempt from any principle or possibility of discord with itself." He concluded: "It was absolutely a fit to its conditions, those conditions which were both its heaven and its earth, and every part of the picture, every item of its immense sum, every wheel of the wondrous complexity, was on the best terms with all the rest."[87] The revival promise of merging heaven and earth had become a national faith reaching even sophisticated skeptics.

This wish for an inclusive national culture was reflected in the new intellectual currents which the younger Dewey absorbed and through which he gradually moved beyond the Protestantism and liberalism of his youth. His influential teachers in college and graduate school included several who reflected the growing liberal Christian shift from "the transcendent, inscrutable God of conservative Congregationalism" to "an immanent deity that worked its will through the laws of nature," bringing natural development into correspondence with transcendental progress in a single, unified moral reality.[88] In April 1884, while Dewey was a graduate student at Hopkins, Lester Ward, reflecting these currents, spoke to the Metaphysical Club of the inclusive organizational "society" grounded in "justice and right," evolving positive institutions through collective human intelligence: "Then, and only then, can man justly claim to have risen out of the animal and fully to have entered the human stage of development."[89] By that time, G. Stanley Hall, one of Dewey's important teachers at Hopkins, was already suggesting a new model of human development aiming at "unity with nature . . . the readjustment of instinct to conscience . . . restored harmony with self, reunion with God, newly awakened love for Jesus." The shaping of character was an ethical and spiritual enterprise enforcing a positive ethic of "moral freedom" designed to bring "inner unity to the mind, heart, and will" and integration into society. Hall was aware that "a decade ago" such education for "consensus" would have been impossible, given "the sects."[90] Now, however, the search for a spirit and language of reconciliation was everywhere in the air.

Dewey was determined to complete the healing work of revivalism by forging the terms of national reconciliation. Raised in a societally transformative religion which operated nevertheless to save the souls of the actors and beneficiaries one at a time, Dewey understood beyond the others of his age that an American synthesis had to provide the simultaneous realization of human individuality. His early writings indicate the presence of that individualism from the outset. The "new psychology" began from the perspective of individuals, not institutions, from "the living experience of the soul's development" which by individual commitment established bonds with others through an act of "the will." Yet the individual in this model must recognize its participation by "draw[ing] . . . mental and spiritual sustenance" through socialization and integration in the "organized social life into which he was born."[91] Collective inclusion thus presumed to drive late-century liberal individualism, though it could fail precisely because it was rooted in individual action and not ontologically guaranteed as in organicism: internally one could be "plunged into doubt and bitterness regarding the reality of all things . . . or . . . the very worth of life itself."[92] In collective life each "must perform his proper function or become a mental or moral wreck."[93] The individual wish for integration was so powerful within the culture that Dewey could increasingly assume it to be the incontrovertible basis of institutional formation. In true liberal fashion, then, personal engagement was the source and never merely a given effect of social organization.

Dewey's Early Agency Systems

Dewey's graduate experience was to suggest two ways out of the constricting Protestantism of his youth: the Hegelianism of his teacher G. S. Morris and the modernist experimental psychology of Hall, which would become, respectively, transitional and final frameworks for his larger system. Initially, though, Dewey retained the religious framework, expanding it in several early essays between 1884 and 1888 from sectarian to universal scope by boldly uniting "faith and reason," for there is "no reason which is not based on faith and no faith which is not rational in its origin and tendency."[94] In search of a comprehensive language, Dewey presented his writings as philosophy rather than theology, though the content is explicitly religious. The principles of systemic harmony operating universally in psychology, history, social life, and nature were consistent with a liberal Protestant framework and further assured by God: "All knowledge is one. It is all of God, the universe, say rather, of God; and if any set of facts are regarded as something in themselves, out of all relation to God and God's creatures, it is no knowledge. The whole world of nature and history . . . that science or philosophy is worthless" unless it is in "guiding relation with the living activity of man, and the end of all his striving—approach to God." Given his presumption that life demanded the realization of the ideal, and since the sole source of "knowledge" is the "will," knowledge by definition grasps the ideal one is proposing and committed to realizing: "We have separated [knowledge] from will. We have isolated truth from duty. We have forgotten that every fact demands something of us. . . . [K]nowledge does not become real knowledge until the commands which it lays upon the will have been executed."[95] To will what one is to know and then actualize is a "bootstrap" argument of immeasurable proportions, but once made, distinctions melt away.

Worldly systems are now identical with religious ideals. Because reality now *follows from and derives from* knowledge, the "Divine" and "Human," the "spiritual" and the "physical," are "one."[96] "Whatever banishes God from the heart of things . . . excludes the ideal, the ethical, from the life of man. . . . Can the ethical be regarded as one with the natural? . . . [G]ranted that this whole structure of the physical is only the garment with which the ethical has clothed itself, then we can see how . . . the garment shall finally manifest the living form within; but not otherwise." Because, he admits candidly, intrinsically "nature has no end, no aim, no purpose," and since without willing identity "the whole scheme empties itself of value," an "ideal end" must be posited "towards which man should direct his conduct."[97] "Ethics demands an ideal which says 'ought,' irrespective of the 'is.'" Transcendent human purpose—"an end which is *man's* end," which "he has himself the power of realizing"—must be merged with natural processes: "We must substitute a teleological theory of evolution for the mechanical: we must read physical causes in terms of rational purpose." The new result, "identical with the theological teachings of Christianity," is a "truly scientific ethics" of "the universe" as a "spiritual . . . reality" which is "tending towards a perfect unity in variety, a complete harmony."[98]

Society is also posited as a unitary reality based on the transcendent unity of purpose and existence: "The idea of democracy, the ideas of liberty, equality, and fraternity . . . represent a society in which the distinction between the spiritual and secular has ceased, and . . . as in the Christian theory of the Kingdom of God, the church and the state, the divine and the human organization of society are one." Inscribing an ideal individualism not of "isolated non-social atoms" but of "society in its unified and structural character" with "man" as "a social being," he says, "the fact" becomes that "democracy . . . not only does have, but must have, a common will."[99] Despite the organic language, however, this ethical collective, and indeed stable collectives generally, are by no means inevitable. Because for liberals "society exists for and by individuals," a "unity of purpose" cannot as in organicist theory be presumed as a "property procured from without. It must begin in the man himself" and arise out of "personal responsibility" and "individual initiation." Yet communities often emerge from principles that operate "to the detriment of the common good," amidst individuals uncaring of "connection or relation," who dwell in the "apparent selfishness, cruelty, and heedlessness" of "natural life."[100] Such lack of unity would drive the social universe "towards disintegration" into "infinitesimal fragments," into "anarchy" with "society dissolved, annihilated." Dewey responds by asserting "an ethical conception" of "the ideal . . . already at work in every personality" and "the unified spirit of the community" as the transcendent "ethical ideal of humanity." With democracy posited as the realized "ideal of all social organization" in which "individual and society" achieve a "thoroughly reciprocal" relation, "society" now possesses (by bootstrap) "a unified and articulate will."[101]

The same logic applies to internal individual unity. Regarding individualism as the triumph of the liberal tradition and ultimate goal of modern democratic society, the achievement of *"personality"* was "the first and final reality," "the one thing of permanent and abiding worth," "the supreme and only law, that every man is an absolute end in himself."[102] With God as the "perfect personality" and model for "the one perfect life," individuals by "striving" to "approach" God achieve inner *"harmony"* and "unity" as a capacity "indwell[ing] in every individual."[103] True knowledge becomes the power to "find God in all his knowledge" and shape "his will and desires toward God." This "infinite and universal possibility" is "everlastingly about us" and "under" personal "control" if one would "open" and "direct his eyes to the things of God."[104] Yet, as with Dewey's other ideal formulations of the "true," this ecstatic individuality does not correspond to actual emotional life, too often burdened with "a diseased soul . . . from drowsy torpor, from listless dreaming, from an empty and purposeless life." The "healthy psychological life," which is a sound "Christian life," must be attained by "the right conduct of the emotions": "It alone can call us out of the kingdom of drudgery and routine, and introduce us to the joy of the Kingdom of God."[105] Moreover, as such an individual has "concentrated" within himself the "intelligence and will" of the society, full self-expression becomes the simultaneous realization of the community's "ideal or spiritual life," its collective "spirit and will" *and* "the sovereignty of every elector" and "citizen."[106]

What is evident from Dewey's earliest system was not his pursuit of a philosophical exploration of modern life but his quest for a program for bringing the Kingdom of God into liberal society. Given his admission to being "one of those who believes that the real will never find an irremovable basis till it rests upon the ideal,"[107] the task was as Milton's to announce the Plan, to "justify the living ways of man to man,"[108] to shape the "real" by extrapolating from "fact" to overriding design. Yet because the admitted gaps between partial will and knowledge, partial knowledge and complete instantiation, could be overcome only by directed action, the realization of Dewey's kingdom depended on its human agents. Since reality derives from the will, whose commitment to transcendent ends is guaranteed by God, self-realization is recast as the determination to "awake and act," to realize not a narrow sectarian agenda but a world where no one is without a "share in society," where none are aliens in "their own commonwealth."[109] "Truth," no longer "confined to religious action," becomes "co-extensive with all action."[110]

With the "ideal" now "at work in every personality," each individual becomes a fully deputized institutional participant responsible for realizing collective reality on the basis of ethical norms: "Every man is a priest of God" who "embodies and realizes within himself the spirit and will of the whole organism." Dewey's formulation places total weight, in effect exclusive agency, on humans, with their agency accessibility to the divine project through rational comprehension and agency commitment to effective and directed action. By ensuring the optimal "stimuli and encouragements" of working together "in society" and initiative which "must begin in the man himself," God guarantees the liberal dream of a fully active and self-reliant role for both individuals and the community.[111]

Why should citizens confused about modernity and raised on voluntarist liberal values either feel confident about personal integration or pursue the path of institutional accommodation? Dewey reveals a revivalist ambiguity

between a promise, even a certainty of healing unities, and the need to continue working in a world that remains split. The sense of division still plagu-
ing his quest is thus a call, always, to greater action: for if "we find that for
which we seek," we "must seek in order to find."[112] Dewey is very much the
evangelist presenting "the fact of choice," for the "obligation to know God"
means that one must either "see the light" or remain "shut out."[113] This
choice involves severe moral consequences: "To fail to meet this obligation is
not to err intellectually, but to sin morally. Belief is not a privilege, but a
duty,—'what soever is not of faith is sin.'" Dewey adopted a similar lack of
compromise in his early political discourses: "The individual who acts in
conformity with [the law of society] is moral; the individual whose conduct [is not] . . . is immoral."[114] Recalling William Perkins, he urges, "We
must plant the seed and nourish it," and in time we "find this rude and
for the most part non-moral condition developing into higher and higher
moral states . . . but the flowering and fruitage of the moral germ." With
faith and patience, "the end" culminates in "a unity which binds together
every event, every existence. . . . [I]t is that which interprets, which gives
meaning to, which unifies all processes."[115]

As with the sectarian language of his youth, however, the broader language of liberal Protestant universality complicated and jeopardized
Dewey's inclusivist agenda. Overtly religious discourse was both too controversial among the religious community and aversive to the secular community. Dewey later articulated these precise concerns at the opening of his
Terry lectures at Yale: "Never before in history has mankind been so much of
two minds, so divided into two camps, as it is today." On the one side are
many who affirm "the necessity for a Supernatural Being and for an immor-
tality that is beyond the power of nature." They include "many Protestant
denominations" as well as believers of "the Greek and Roman Catholic
Church." On the other side are "those who think the advance of culture and
science has completely discredited the supernatural and with it all religions
that were allied with belief in it."[116] The religious formulations reflected
Dewey's continuing doubts that without supervening moral certitudes human agency could go awry. He could not yet dispense with transcendent
verities: neither with "society" as "a real whole," a "social organism" that
realizes "a common will," nor with citizens—otherwise at risk of being
"bare" and "abstract" "fragments"—as "member[s] of the organism" and
"the manifestation" of its "purpose."[117] Moreover, the language of liberal
voluntarism, though in evidence in more public presentations, was still too

easily associated with anti-institutional liberalism. His immersion in what he later called the "historical oddity" of Hegelianism[118] is indicative of the gap between the wish for national cohesion and the available discourses—prior to Dewey—of secular American liberalism.

Dewey's turn to Hegel during this period as the first of his secular reframings evinces his wish to relinquish the explicit religious discourse. For our purposes, the reasons for the shift are more important than tracing his efforts to rephrase his entire agenda in Hegelian metaphysics. Hegelianism propounded the Deweyan merger between the ideal and the real on all levels in philosophical terms. By turning the real into a systemic manifestation of spirit and making spirit the essential reality, the discourse framed the aspirations embodied within systemic goals as synonymous with the systemic process itself. The orderly and teleological progress toward comprehensive ideals, conceptually unavailable in the scientific paradigm of earlier theorists, is now presumed to accompany the operation of all processes. The immanentism of liberal Protestantism, which allows for a transcendental remnant in a deity not entirely embodied in the world, is replaced by a complete unification of world and spirit. Human accessibility is preserved through rationality because the movement is now intrinsically philosophical. The presence of transcendence fully in and of the world preserves and enhances human agency, for the elements of a system fully constitute it and embody its ends to realize its ideal nature.

Dewey's determination to make the human role—exclusive agency—the center led him to forge a Hegelian "liberalism" rooted not in the organic logic of the original but in the psychological realities of its constituents. In this revised Hegelianism, unity remains a property of the religious sphere, but now as the worldly product of the human "religious will": "It is religious will which performs the act of identification once for all. The will, as religious, declares that the perfect ideal will is the only reality . . . in the universe, and . . . in the individual life." The unity of reality is achieved by a movement of the individual will, its surrender in its religious mode in which it renounces its "own particular life as an unreality" and "declares that God, as the perfect Personality or Will, is the only Reality, and the Source of all activity." Through a *"faith"* which "transcends knowledge," the telos which is the "perfect personality—God" is found. Each individual then "merely appropriates the product of the wills of the community" and "reproduces social relations."[119]

The unavoidable if modified organicism of the Hegelian period reflected

Dewey's frustration over finding an acceptable liberal model of systemic integration. Given his pronounced doubt that an individualistic culture could embrace national institutions and purposes, he was driven to submerge individuality within a highly coercive and directive model. Personal reticence was admitted only as subjective resistance to the necessary movement of the whole. Even when subjects crave the realization of "the ideal" and wish "to obey," integration is not assured: "The impulses will not reach the end working blindly. They must be directed along certain channels by the intellect." Choice must produce a "*resolute* will" which "must persist in one choice to accomplish any thing." To be what one "should be" in "his own true being" one must inflexibly "fix the mind," be "tenacious," "evince" ever "more pertinacity or *perseverance*."[120] Freedom in turn depends entirely on the early provision of "channels" which have "habitually directed" the "imagination" to produce the "inhibition" of some "feeling" so that "the feelings which are not inhibited may be duly developed." Subjective life must become "subservient" to objective "intellect or will," producing "perfect prudential, practical self-control" toward a "comprehensive end which will lead" one to "inhibit all acts which are not in accordance with it, and to connect all successive acts so as to lead up to it." Character is perfect directionality, turning "its force in one direction," which further "does not recognize obstacles. [One's] eye is on the end, and upon that alone." One either moves as proposed, so that "choice is speedy" and movement becomes "more and more intuitive and spontaneous," or one is left behind in "weakness" and "instability," which represents a "lack of character."[121]

The Hegelian solution of predirected and largely determined unit action, for all its resonance to Protestant and Hobbesian individualism, was an unsatisfactory resolution to the liberal search for societal integration. The umbrella of Hegelian thinking guaranteed teleological unification in the language of secularized philosophy which imported hitherto unavailable possibilities to the discourse of American liberalism. But it was, as influential critics such as William James and G. S. Hall noted, a deductive system completely abstracted from experience and simply asserting Dewey's own priorities.[122] More damning to his goal of offering a vision of cohesion and solidarity in a discourse acceptable to and usable by American society was Dewey's inability to provide an adequate degree of either voluntarism or meaningful individualism. But Dewey did not yet trust that his own unitary realities, requiring both liberal verities and systemic structures, could be derived from experience.

The criticisms of Dewey's philosophical idealism provoked a major crisis in his thinking. In his decision to relinquish Hegelianism, he acknowledged that the "philosophy of a ready-made mind over against a physical world" and "manifested in social institutions" has "no empirical support" and has to be "dropped out." The period between 1888 and his early summa in the "Reconstruction" of 1894 involved his search for a convincing liberal frame for institutional context. His turn to "experience" and "the weight of actual material" represented this shift not toward pure induction, as he would have it, but toward the rhetoric of American liberalism for the expression of his synthetic vision.[123]

The Reframing of American Liberal Selfhood

The task of consolidating the reversal, of validating and shaping the irresistible movement of individuals toward systemic integration, represented a cultural transformation of American liberalism. As Dewey recognized, this involved its appropriation of nineteenth-century American Protestantism. Initiated by "the next religious prophet who will have a permanent and real influence on men's lives," the project involved "pointing out the religious meaning of democracy, the ultimate religious value to be found in the normal flow of life itself." Liberalism would in effect become secular Protestantism: "The function of the church is to universalize itself, and thus pass out of existence."[124] American individualism as self-direction together with negative freedom was redefined as an entirely new liberal doctrine of ethical selfhood leading to positive integration through "voluntary" participation in a free or "democratic" society. Democracy itself was in turn recast not as government by the decisions of all but as an encompassing society of active members who shared its ends and its operation by the principles of "inclusive meritocracy." The natural world was then shorn of its Darwinian associations and made part of human history as an internally purposive and evolving process.

As Dewey reframed the ground of systems in ordinary individual experience, he gradually relinquished his reliance on Hegel. "Moral theory," he claimed in his emerging ethical discourse, is merely "moral insight," or "the every-day workings of the same ordinary intelligence that measures drygoods, drives nails, sells wheat, and invents the telephone."[125] He was in full flight from disconnected generalities: "Metaphysics has had its day and if the truths which Hegel saw cannot be stated as direct, practical truths, they are not true."[126] In the beginning is not "the divine or transcendental" but only "a given act" of individuals: "Moral science is *not* a collection of abstract laws . . . it is only in the mind of the agent as an agent."[127] Dewey's turn to the "facts" represented his growing confidence that the harmonious functioning of all systems could be extrapolated from unit conduct, from the immanent principles of universal agency already inscribed in American experience.

Beginning with the individual, if the aim of ethics was no longer "to prescribe what men ought to do," that was because it was possible "to detect the element of obligation in conduct, to examine conduct to see what gives it its *worth*."[128] Personal conduct, in other words, remained as in the earlier iterations resolutely transcendental. Apart from "savages and babes" and "marginal" acts dismissed as "mere impulse," conduct is "executed insight," which means it is an "ideal act" which "realizes an idea, a conception."[129] Within the range of activity Dewey was willing to consider, subjects responsibly apply *"moral rules"* like the Golden Rule and "moral forces" such as "justice" and "love," making obligation a "kind of fact," one of "the actual forces of reality." Though he cautioned that this must be "taken at a certain angle and scope of working," it quickly becomes axiomatic: "The 'ought' always rises and falls back into the 'is,' and . . . is itself an 'is'—the 'is' of action." Relinquishing the "creaking, lumbering *Deus ex machina*" of Hegelianism, Dewey instead embedded the moral universe of ethical agency in human nature: "The law of gravitation indicates an order of physical fact in which matter behaves thus and so; the Golden Rule indicates an order of social fact, in which it is true that persons act thus and so, and not simply describable that they *should* act thus and so."[130]

The truth, no longer to be found in either theological or philosophical systems which abstract "in symbolic form" from the concrete "social relations of the community" and "mental attitude and habit of a people," was now experiential. Those ends ordained by "the very laws of God" were manifested as "the presence of God in the world," the "outworking of God in life" and in "the forces which unify society" for all to grasp. They were available to be apprehended in "consciousness" by each "individual" through "intelligence" acting *"in* men's thought and reason."[131] Individual conduct was in turn the teleological realization of these truths, the moral pursuit of an *"end"* which is "its real meaning." Responsibility was no longer extrinsic to the act but its very nature: "Consciousness of something to be done is the consciousness of duty. . . . Any being . . . whose conduct is the attempted realization of proposed ends—must conceive of these ends in terms of . . . obligation."[132] Subjects become by this reasoning "moral agents" engaging primarily in "conduct that really deserves the name of conduct," exceptions to which are "perverted" and "deflected." To "embody" the proper "end" is *"right,"* all else is "wrong." Such ethical embodiment is at the same time fully natural, for "man is so one with the truth" of the world "that it is not so much revealed *to* him as *in* him; he is its incarnation" by "appropriation of" and "identification with it."[133]

The self is now a natural—even preternatural—agent, as *agency and no more than agency is now possible.* Behaviorally, "man can[not] enact 'law' in the social sphere any more than in the so-called 'physical' sphere." Humans cannot create but only "discover" and "uncover" and "extend" the "truth" which is already operational.[134] Motivationally, agency becomes the only possible basis of human action. An ethics of mere hedonism or "just what the voluptuary does" fails because it legitimates the pursuit of untransformed ends, the "natural and brutal impulse being just that which insists upon itself irrespective of all other wants."[135] An impulse is valid only if one acts to "extend its range and to idealize it" by placing it into "connection with other impulses" to produce a "growing unity with the whole range of man's action" or "'spiritualizing' of the impulse" as the "active projection of character really and deeply" as a moral activity.[136] Organicist ethics, "conformity to abstract moral law," while rightly affirming the need to control desire in order to achieve principled action, also fails by demanding "obedience to law simply because it is law" without concern for the genuine satisfaction of the individual.[137]

The valid path "combines the one-sided truths of the other two," the satisfaction of the individual with communal norms through the *"satisfaction of desires according to law."* This synthesis fully preserves the claim of individualism, for "the moral end or the good is the realization by a person and as a person of individuality."[138] The individual triumphs, however, only by becoming that "character" or "self" which "includes and transforms all special desires," in order to make them "conformable" and "fitting-in" with the "whole man" and the "universal." Proceeding with "the inner disposition and inclination" of a "calling," one could achieve "the union of law and inclination in its pure form—love for the action in and of itself."[139] So infused with ethical certitudes, individualist warrants expanded, becoming rhetorically indistinguishable from or even a more extreme case of liberal self-referentiality. Referring in an 1893 essay to "self-realization" as *the* moral end," Dewey asserted "two necessary phases of the ethical ideal: that it cannot lie in subordination to any law outside itself; and that, starting with the self, the end is to be sought in the active, or volitional, rather than in the passive, or feeling, side." Yet, as always, "true" self-realization "require[s] that every act be an outlet of the whole self" through "complete functioning . . . in the highest and fullest activity possible at the time," which in action unites the actual "agent" and the "ideal self" into "the same self."[140]

Dewey before his 1894 vision of closure still acknowledged as a self-fulfilling prophecy the notion of an individual nature intrinsically attuned to universal principles of moral agency. Where "there is no organizing principle, no 'universal' on the basis of which various acts fall into a system or order," then "the moral life is left in a series of shreds and patches, where each act is torn off, as to its moral value, from every other" with "no centre, no movement." The loss of moral direction in the world "is almost sure to turn into a bitterness of feeling which leads" to a repudiation of this entire moral edifice and a "blind feeling that things should be overturned because they are not what they should be."[141] Presumably everyone potentially experiences being "double-minded," affected by "conflicting wills," for morality "always requires an effort." But one who hangs on to the lower self is a "bad man." The good person has "faith in the moral order" and the "constant willingness" to pursue "right action."[142] There is for each a "choice" as always—in revivalist terms a naked option of the will—pursuit of the "*ideal* or active good" or the refusal to recognize "the necessity of expansion and a wider environment."[143] Those unable to accept "this general idea of duty," namely "children" and "adults so far as their moral life is immature," will "need to have their moral judgments constantly reinforced" by "command" and "obedience," by being "continually required to perform such an act on the ground that it is *obligatory*." In this way, "the desires are socialized" to "reflect . . . the needs of the environment," resulting in "the unification of desire and duty." At this merger, "individuality" has achieved "realization" as the impulses "flow . . . in the channel of response to the demands of the moral environment."[144]

The presumption of a willing—if societally constructed—embrace of the ethical finally permitted Dewey to trust the personal spontaneity of the will. Once the Protestant dream of the agent's call to transcendent ends, this will henceforth constitutes the voluntarism that grounds Dewey's institutional liberalism. Humans now lack the power to formulate other than the inscribed collective and cosmological ends which are "continuously unfolding" as "the meaning of life." There at the same time must be sustained dedication to the demands of responsible voluntary activity: "So far as this occurs, the burden of the moral struggle is transformed into freedom of movement. There is no longer effort to bring the particular desire into conformity with a law, or a universal, outside of itself. The fitting-in of each desire . . . takes place without friction; as a natural re-adjustment. . . . The law is not an external ideal, but the principle of the movement."[145] With individual freedom—the "free individual"—as an attribute of all systemic conduct, one can be no other than both "agent" and "free," the "free agent" of mature liberal theory. Set within this circumscribed and directed universe, the individual out of its new "nature" or preformed character and from its own will necessarily produces the realized systems of the liberal world.

None of his skeptical colleagues could celebrate as Dewey could the advent of organizational society as a liberation, the "loosening of bonds, the wearing away of restrictions, the breaking down of barriers" through embracing the new role. By rising to become an agent of truth, as "the organ of the absolute Truth of the Universe," the individual "is free, free from negativity, free from sin, free positively, free to live his own life, free to express himself, free to play, without let or limitation upon the instrument given him." In this way, as "truth makes free," then "a life loyal to truth" will "bring freedom." The inevitable task for free agents is to bring truth and freedom into being everywhere: "The truth is not fully freed when it gets into some individuals' consciousness. . . . It is freed only when it moves in and through this favored individual to his fellows; when the truth which comes to consciousness in one, extends and distributes itself to all so that it becomes the Common-wealth, the Republic, the public affair." That "free society" which is the "cause worth battling for," a veritable "realization of the brotherhood of man," was in his liberal reframing to be called democracy.[146]

Liberal Democracy as a Collectivism

The second part of Dewey's project, to find a grounding for his conception of collective unity in experiential reality rather than in abstract collective will or being, was now possible. "Society," overarching institutions and processes, the nexus of "actual relations" and "actual demands" constantly operating on the individual,[147] could be acknowledged in its full scope within liberalism because with its foundation in free agents the very power and dynamism of society now arose from "man's own action, his own life movement" as an individual.[148] The web of society, "the mental attitude and habit of a people" that gives rise to "its ideas, its dogmas and mysteries," to "man's social organizations" and "social relationships," and even to religion itself, with "its source in the social and intellectual life of a community or race" as "an expression of the social relations of the community," is now a liberal web of individual origin.[149]

This new liberal network which Dewey called "democracy," the center of his social and political thought henceforth, involved a transformation of the concept virtually beyond recognition. In his hands it is neither the classical model of a direct share of political authority nor, as used in American idyllic liberalism, a form of government sufficiently weak and responsive to the popular will to protect its citizens from substantial intrusion. Merging the language of American individualism and self-governance with the institutional orientation previously associated only with Protestant assumptions of collectivism, it has become a wholistic community incorporating the many facets of individual life in its "community of ideas and interest through community of action . . . enacted in all departments of action." As "a spiritual fact," a "revelation" of "the incarnation of God in man," this "community of truth" in which "truth" is "brought down to life" forms "the ties which bind men together . . . the forces which unify society." With each individual a *"member"* with a "defined position in the whole," success at one's "social placing" and in one's "function" which "furthers the needs of society" entitles the "agent" to "merit" or "social desert." Each "doing his specific part" produces a higher "unity" of the community through "the co-operating activity of diverse individuals."[150]

This wholistic, inclusive, and incorporative society—"an objective ethical world realized in institutions"—would be "democratic" because it would embody the ethical priorities and productive results of all its members: "No argument is needed to show, theoretically, that any proposed moral criteria must, in order to be valid, harmonize the interests of different men, or to show, practically, that the whole tendency of the modern democratic and philanthropic movement has been to discover and realize a good in which men shall share on the basis of an equal principle."[151] A democratic "social system" was "a community of interests and ends" dedicated to forging a *"common good"* out of "the acts" and "the ends of the various agents who make up society." Because the democratic individual presumptively operates out of a sense of the common good, "realizing its spirit in himself," the collective becomes an expression of the "inner capacity" of each, a "living realization . . . in and through the will of the agent." Thus integration becomes a form of self-realization and self-constitution, a "*willing* the maintenance, and development of moral surroundings as *one's own ends*."[152]

By means of this logic of perfect integration, in which the individual "takes for his own end, ends already existing for the wills of others" and makes "*the environment*" of society "*a reality for oneself*," Dewey successfully provided for the institutional realm its essential identity as a "free society of free individuals": "It is absolutely required by the interests of a progressive society that it allow freedom to the individual to develop such functions as he finds in himself," the "fullest life possible" through "a complete and free development of capacities." Such freedom was available for all individuals who, as a "calling," pursued "the satisfaction of the entire moral order, the furthering of the community," not merely "the satisfaction of self." This individual citizen is the "AGENT WHO DULY SATISFIES THE COMMUNITY IN WHICH HE SHARES" and is able "BY THAT SAME CONDUCT" to "SATISF[Y] HIMSELF." Given the identity of individual freedom and "the realization of one's specific capacity" as "the realized activity, the full and unhindered performance of function," freedom could now be proclaimed as a very requirement of collective membership:

> Obligation and freedom . . . answer respectively to the two sides of function. On the one hand, the performing of a function realizes the social whole. Man is thus "bound" by the relations necessary to constitute this whole. He is subject to the conditions which existence and growth of the social unity impose. He is, in a word, under *obligation;* the performance of his function is duty owed to the community of which he is a member.
>
> But on the other hand, activity in the way of function realizes the individual; it is what makes him an individual, or distinct person. In the performance of his own function the agent satisfies his own interests and gains power. In it is found his *freedom.*
>
> Obligation thus corresponds to the *social* satisfaction, freedom to the *self*-satisfaction, involved in the exercise of function; and they can . . . [not] be separated. . . . One has to realize oneself as a member of a community. In this fact are found both freedom and duty.[153]

The perfect reciprocity Dewey posited between a realized agent and a realized ethical community produced an identity of individual and collective wills, and absent conceivable disparities between "moral self-satisfaction" and "social satisfaction," coercion was by definition impossible.

Doubts remained for Dewey that there was "no 'the Good,' but an aggregate of fragmentary ends" which are "irreducible to a common principle." The unacceptable result would be a "chasm in the self," "a feeble idealism" or "a pessimistic and fruitless discontent with things as they are—leading, in either case, to neglect of active and pressing duty." Dewey spun a Pascalian wager: "What is really good for men *must* turn out good for all, or else there is no good in the world at all." With "moral activity" now able to "feed itself into larger appetites and thus into larger life," democracy was to be regarded as a "progressive development" spreading as "truth . . . extends and distributes itself" throughout the community.[154] As "the outworking of God in life," the "incarnation of God in man" becoming "a living, present thing" through "the continuously unfolding, never ceasing discovery of the meaning of life," democratic society was by ever active and universally participating agents emerging as a collective process infused with flexibility, openness, and a spirit of self-determination.[155]

The American Instantiation: The Protestant Agent in Liberal Society

Given his continuing doubts, Dewey might have posited the "free society of free individuals" as an aspiration toward which individuals and communities must always strive. And there is a sense in his thought that no existing reality would ever entirely measure up. Yet one must face the sense of closure which propelled Dewey and American liberalism. With immanentism as the placement of divine responsibility fully within human grasp, any gap between present conditions and the coming Kingdom represented a harsh judgment on those offered God's generous grant of exclusive agency. American revivalism emboldened by the revolutionary legacy, unwilling to tolerate a separation from the ideal, had created an irresistible push for moral unification. If "democracy" is "the freeing of truth," and truth is "all that Christ called the Kingdom of God," then the Kingdom was at hand.[156] In his remarkable 1894 essay "Reconstruction," Dewey proclaimed the completion of the Protestant-liberal synthesis. The Protestant ideals of self and community which had long overflowed the boundaries of institutional religion were now fully realized as the essence of secular liberal society: "Any aim worth striving for is always at some definite period or other realized. . . . Unless the ideals with which Christianity started were immobile or inert, or unless they were so far away as to be out of relation to actual life, they must by this time have embodied themselves in the institutions and habits of practical life; they must have converted themselves into structure, into institutions, into a system of working means." With attainment "if not wholly" then "at least sufficiently realized," "that which is prophetic" has "fulfilled itself."[157]

Dewey announced the instantiation of the Christian ideal in the three areas for which he had pursued closure: the individual, society, and the historical-natural world. Modern American civilization had at the culmination of a long historical process finally realized and disseminated "one of the great thoughts of early Christianity . . . the value, the inalienable worth of the individual soul." The liberal individual now beyond doubt was the Protestant ethical self subject to higher direction and purpose, which being godly is incontrovertibly free: "The individual has now become to a considerable extent, in fact, what at the outset he was only in name; a being who is self-possessed, an end in himself, and whose life permits no law which does not spring out of its own basis and destiny."[158]

In the collective realm, liberal society has been actualizing the great Christian "Kingdom of God," the "common incarnate life, the purpose and interest animating all men and binding them into one harmonious whole of sympathy and action." That project has also "succeeded," with an inclusive, integrated, and just community becoming "a practical fact of life": "The means for lifting up the individual and binding men together in harmony are now found working in all forms of life . . . political, domestic and industrial institutions have become in fact an organized Kingdom of God on earth, making for the welfare of the individual *and* the unity of the whole." The individual and the collective now dwell within a final, harmonious, and nonconflictual integration. Finally, the increasing power of human understanding to grasp the immanent "revelation of absolute truth" has resulted in "open access to its inexhaustible stores." As a consequence, the secrets of the world have been revealed "living incarnate in the individual himself,"[159] and for a theorist such as Dewey the ultimate logic, direction, and strategies of the larger Plan to which human history assimilates itself can now be discerned. This progressive immanentism derived by spiritualizing the natural world allowed Dewey to transform science as well into a set of methods to study "the existing world of practice in all its concrete relationships" by tracking the emergence of "underlying unity."[160]

These great arenas are not fixed in the sense of being static: "Now, we see the universe as one all-comprehensive, interrelated scene of limited life and motion." They are dynamic processes, but processes in which are embedded already "the actual incarnation of truth in human experience," that is, "embodied" authoritative ideals to be acted upon with "the necessity for giving heed to it." The stated goal of the essay was to assist the institutional church and believers in reformulating the human project in light of the completion of this historico-cosmological mission: "This is a period of reconstruction. The very success of the former ideal demands that we no longer go on striving for that ideal, but that we form for ourselves a new principle of action."[161] Human activity was now to occur within—as framed by— a fully ethical individualism, moral community, and progressive universe. With this culmination Dewey rendered the ultimate Protestant-liberal synthesis, at once bringing liberalism back to its origins and forward into modern institutional society. With this mapping for America of the comprehensive vision of the agency civilization it had become, finally the great medieval achievement of an integrated cosmos, lost through more than three hundred years of civilizational crisis, had found its modernist equivalent.

For Dewey, the Jeffersonian promise of a "free society of free individuals" had, if in a most un-Jeffersonian way, been achieved. Where Protestantism and early liberalism had each failed at comprehensiveness, Dewey perceived underlying the dominant cultural tendency toward individual voluntarism within overarching institutional structures a framework for their merger. But the idyll had evolved far from its origins: the agent of transcendent responsibility has been incorporated within a heterogeneous, inclusive, and worldly society. The American promise, though the words remained the same, would henceforth connote "the Protestant agent in liberal society."

With this renaturalization of the liberal individual as Protestant agent and liberal society as the integrative community of agents, Dewey turned liberalism after 1894 toward a new historic task: the preparation of citizens for life within the new paradigm. He wrote presciently to his wife in 1894, "I sometimes think I will drop teaching philosophy directly, and teach it via pedagogy."[162] The maturation of agency institutions and model of character meant that the process of integration could itself be formalized. Social cohesion now could be advanced not through doctrine or institutional formation but by means of socialization. As he put it in an 1894 essay, "The Chaos in Moral Training," the task was instilling in the young the now clear principles and habits of agency, for the "formation" of "character" was more easily achieved in those not yet completely socialized. The child could be led to actively "reproduce" social priorities through the internalization of their mandates as the "desires" are "clothed upon" or shaped while they are "plastic to new wants and demands" so that the "identity of freedom and law" is achieved: "Everyone will admit without dispute that the question of the moral attitude and tendencies induced in youth by the motives for conduct habitually brought to bear is the ultimate question in all education whatever."[163] In his famous essay of 1897, "My Pedagogic Creed," Dewey elaborated the prophetic and nation-building role of education, concluding with the faith that "the teacher always is the prophet of the true God and the usherer in of the true kingdom of God."[164] With the theory incarnate, the future of liberalism was henceforth to be waged in the vineyards.

Dewey's achievement as the molder of a modern Protestant universalism was commensurate with the historical project that put human agency forward as a new human possibility and the foundation of an unprecedented societal reality. His vision of a progressively and transcendently realized liberal society invested early-twentieth-century liberalism with the powerful cultural legacy of Protestant millennialism. Giving voice to the dynamic of national coalescence, his words articulated the broader convictions and theoretical underpinnings for the spirit of the Progressive reform movement. As one Progressive wrote, "We were all Deweyites before we read Dewey."[165] Dewey, to be sure, was not alone. The springs of Progressivism in the "sensitive conscience" of "Protestant idealism," what Daniel Rodgers calls "socialized Protestantism," is well understood.[166] The logical outcome of their common origin in the revivalist vision of an integrated believers' community was the "moral" project of "the Great Community" of "shared ends."[167]

Underlying this project was the conviction of this "cooperative and just 'great community'" in America that all people including the most "ordinary" would act together as "agents of social reconstruction."[168] In furthering this vision through his incessant theoretical and popular writings, Dewey was the imposing figure. His work provided the certainty that this society of universal agency was fully compatible with and the fullest expression of liberal values of freedom, individualism, and democracy, and that they were surely on the ascendance even as organizational society was propounding institutional solutions for social justice, community, and moral virtue. He alone advanced this new liberalism on the pedagogical foundation of individual human development. And this faith spread through modernizing reformers seeking to reconcile the revolutionary dream with emerging institutional realities, from public intellectuals such as Herbert Croly and Walter Lippmann, to the legions of Progressive activists and Teddy Roosevelt and Woodrow Wilson, to the subsequent movements for inclusion in the twentieth century.

A major reason for the influence and resonance of Dewey's thought is his confidence that maximum self-realization and democratic governance were not merely compatible but complementary foundations of modern liberal society. His optimistic account derived from the Protestant understanding of exclusive human agency, in which God's world progresses through the work of individuals and they in turn act freely to fulfill God's vision for the nation and the world. The mutual fulfillment of individual and community with neither side constrained or diminished was the basis of Dewey's unyielding belief in the resolution of all antinomies: nationalism merged with a vibrant democracy; functional roles with effective public action; freedom and systemic conduct; progress as refinement of existing institutions; ethics with empirical observation; theology and social realism; scientific mastery and technocracy with participatory egalitarianism. In this model, power was somehow distributed among all the participants, who found their individually empowered, collectively authorized, and transcendentally motivated places in an active, unfolding harmony. Despite a theoretical imprecision nearly as vast as the system itself, Dewey's synthesis, unlike other theories of democracy, connected with a people constituting their nation jointly as never before in historical memory and was thus, despite apparent conceptual limitations, able to validate the great journey to this unprecedented collective.

As mature liberalism became convinced that integration within its structures fully vindicated the promise of American history, Dewey's influence was felt in the vast attention given in the first half of the twentieth century to socialization and education. Pressures for inclusion dominated this period as the excluded themselves demanded a greater role in the society, while the shaping of the young to this evolving liberal meritocracy became a national priority. The Progressive ethos achieved its greatest successes in the New Deal, which infused society with a new confidence that liberal values had survived the rise of organizational society. In his 1941 proclamation of the Four Freedoms, Franklin D. Roosevelt celebrated the modernist formulation of the American voluntarist idyll with a believing America, suggesting the reach of Dewey's transvaluation. As the universal right to agency moved to the center of social turmoil, a Protestantized liberalism was by World War II and the 1950s, beyond debate, the heir of the revolutionary faith.

Conclusion:
The Recovery of Agency

Pragmatism has come to be seen as an American alternative . . . [to]
theory . . . a search for method when the foundations have already
crumbled.

—Morris Dickstein

Every great civilization as a securely grounded moral order, so
Plato knew best, arises upon an inability to remember the forms of conviction not chosen and the privileging of those taken. As Locke grasped about
the process of individual development and John Dewey about the construction of democratic culture, the loss to memory of the reversal as the moment
of election into social role and popular institutions would be the liberal version of the Myth of Er. With the fading not only of the historical turn in early
America from nature to the collective, but even of its theoretical grounding
in a primordial and uninduced choice preserved fictionally in the rhetoric of
the social contract, liberalism insulated itself from the exercise of a no longer
recoverable self-authorization and thus from all the dangers (and hopes) of
"reconstruction." Absent a memory of founding, future possibilities as well
as past compromises would recede, leaving only the thickening web of the
liberal present. More recently, with the erosion of contemporary faith in the
liberal settlement, the effort to recover the liberal tradition as a source of inspiration has emerged from two aspirations: the first, to restore Dewey's
"common faith" in the American synthesis; the second, to regain access to
the original reversal as the moment of possibility that, once more, opens the
future.

Assessing the Deweyan Synthesis

Troubled by the unraveling of the Great Settlement principles, reformers of
a progressive bent now seek to revive its original spirit and rekindle the via-

537

bility of the synthesis. They turn in this effort to Dewey as a critical contemporary presence to revitalize their commitment to the American promise of a "liberalism that had to meet the demands of democracy."[1] From the secular pole, a neo-pragmatist return to the spirit of change, openness, democratic activism, and institutional flexibility is advocated against the weight of organizational rigidities.[2] Similarly from the religious pole, the settlement is revived to reinscribe Dewey's "good society" with its consensual "pursuit of the good in common" against the corrosive effects of modern individualism.[3] Those committed to completing the agency agenda in the face of a society rent with inequality and unequal opportunity, social marginalization and fragmentation, and an inadequate sense of social role and purpose might well appropriate his vision of a just meritocracy, an inclusive community without fear of sectarian divisions or self-authorizing individualism, and personal wholeness by actualizing with others our common ends.

To quibble with this apparently empowering faith in a time of doubt seems harsh and gratuitous. And yet, to represent Dewey's resolution as an emerging late- or postindustrial model of social organization would be to fail to understand its limits, perhaps to repeat its very errors with which we now contend. Dewey's work must be seen in historical context as a *summa theologica*—the great summation and culmination of the agency age. The secular return to "method" with "the loss of old certainties" after the "foundations have already crumbled" amidst the "exhaustion of the 'grand narrative'" in a "post-ideological" effort to skirt fundamental conflict seriously misreads the very power of postindustrial challenges to agency and their portent of fundamental debate.[4] The similarly conflict-aversive religious view neglects the implications of the spread of godly empowerment within a diverse community. The assumption that God's ends and overall plan would be known and read as a single Will resists the logic of agency. Political reconciliation hinges on the investment of one societal model with transcendental status, a troubling outcome in an increasingly global and multicultural setting.

Those seeking a discourse which advances the project of selfhood and democracy beyond the intrinsic limits of agency will find Dewey's work problematic. The central conundrum in interpreting Dewey and measuring his future viability is to ascertain the degree to which his fluidly described systems were open to collective as well as individual initiatives and reformulations. Do his continual references to the importance of new discoveries, new ideals, and new principles of action amount to a faith in continuing transformation? Or does the explicit dynamism of his processes simply reflect the ordered motion of that process orientation? Does his vision provide for the creative (and often destabilizing) tension, ferment, and conflict necessary for new openings, structures, and ends not yet evolved or even imagined to arise? Or merely the continuing application of available "means" of engagement and participation on behalf of ends already written into reality, the extension of existing channels to new challenges which change and chance will surely produce?

The thinker who emerged in the early 1890s undertook the bold shift from a religious to a liberal framework because he was convinced that the world, at least in its American variant, had come to immanently embody ultimate theological principles. The pervasive sense of philosophical closure lurking underneath his fluid images suggests a universe now operating according to its ultimate ends. In describing this "deep structure" of universal processes perfectly authorized and fulfilled by the units, and units with fully evolved places and functions in the whole, Dewey inscribed the agency cosmology as the final meaning of modernity. This completed vision of agents willing their own agency and their agency institutions forms a perfectly closed circle: the reopening of ends cannot even be formulated because reality itself proceeds by means of agency systems. Dewey, like Hobbes, realized that a permanent and stable attempt to create a dynamic nontraditional society of equally dynamic individuals required predictable motion, or at least stable channels for the motion provided by a common institutional authority. The cosmology avoids the determinism of Hobbes and later social theory by reflecting the cosmic intelligence and guarantees of individual voluntarism which Newton's God afforded Newton and the Protestant God provided liberalism.[5] Within this circle, ever greater "freedom" of the constituent parts and systemic fluidity can now be encouraged, for directed motion now reinforces and validates an operational agency universe. Through the popular recognition of ultimate principles, individuals would by the revivalist paradox willingly act together to realize the agency principles already inscribed in the world. Systems now deficient largely in their inclusivity and scope would mandate individuals to pursue inclusion, participation, a functional role, and above all harmony in this community of common ends, which is to say, maintaining and strengthening the processes.[6]

Reflective of his roots in the "radicalism" of the American project, Dewey equated movement and the lack of a traditional order with an openness that suggested common authorship by the members.[7] Yet processes because they involve universal motion are not necessarily open and self-governing.

To the contrary, without other substantial factors present, they represent precisely the genius of the liberal mechanism for reauthoring the polity. Dewey's liberalism, by mystifying the reality of authority through the language of collective involvement, merges with the radically modern Hobbesian-Newtonian conception of a *compliance fashioned as active adaptation*. But this is precisely the seduction of liberal "freedom" and authorship on which Hobbes presumed that participatory motion experienced as individual voluntarism would provide systemic validation. Moreover, individual voluntarism will not succeed more fully in being freedom simply by our *calling* it liberal rather than Protestant, nor in such fashion will political authority be more truly democratized nor community made more egalitarian. The limits, compromises, and adaptations as well as the possibilities of this shift from religious to secular terms are imposed by its structures of character formation and institutional authority, only minimally by the language in which they are framed.

The evidence for this view is that Dewey with increasing confidence treated process as an embodiment of fixed, authoritative values within which the component members, possessing "organs for the truth," utilize them to "get hold of . . . see and feel, the truth" and to move responsively rather than as originators. His unwillingness to open the processes to a consideration of first principles or the authority within them to reconstitution led him to consider individuals in largely adaptive terms. Thus, while "the self is not something fixed or rigid" but a "process" in which "progress is the ideal," a clear pattern of deference was emerging: "A cardinal virtue is not *a* virtue, but a spirit in which all acts are performed. It lies in the attitude which the agent takes toward the duty; his obedience to recognized forms, his readiness to respond to new duties, his enthusiasm in moving forward to new relations."[8] The expectation was an internalization of authoritative mandates, no longer as subservience to traditional rules, but as a way of ordering one's internal processes in correspondence with collective processes and parameters.

Dewey's embrace of the "apparent" dynamism of fixed or predictable motion was evident in his growing tolerance for repetitive behavior. He advised in "Reconstruction" that when "ideas finally become embodied in outward life," then purposes "become realized as habits."[9] He cautioned the reader elsewhere at this time "not . . . to deny that there is a mechanical side even to the moral life. A merchant, for example, may do the same thing over and over again, like going to his business every morning at the same hour. This is a moral act and yet it does not seem to lead to change in moral wants and surroundings."[10] Predictable conduct is now essential to selfhood. He wrote in 1894: "The agent is molded through education, unconscious and conscious, into certain habits of thinking and feeling as well as acting. His act, therefore, partakes of the aims and dispositions of his race and time. . . . Our acts are controlled by the demands made upon us . . . not simply the express requirements of other persons, but the customary expectations of the family, social circle, trade or profession." Individuals as social beings must learn to locate their acts in terms of predictable consequences, encouraged by "the rebuke or punishment for violating or coming short of social functioning." This "*power* of being influenced by the foreseen consequences" generates "a *habit*" of "substantial *responsibility*," producing a new nature, "an attainment, a conquest, not an original possession; it is a name for virtue or rightness of will."[11] An ethical education, instilling the "*typical features of every human interaction,*" that is, individual ethical duty and collective unity, will prepare the young for unconflicted assimilation within agency civilization. The result is a fixed system of "virtue" which is really "rational habit," patterns of predictive behavior in which "every habit is a dependent function of the whole organism . . . a member of a system of habits."[12]

Similarly, "democratic" society came to be increasingly a product of habit. Within a determinate process with fixed patterns ordering the activity of its parts, each member performed the function best suited to one's talents. Thus "progressive development" came to mean the steady realization of a "moral community" with an 'increase in number of those persons whose ideal is a 'common good.'"[13] This collective faith Dewey would increasingly call "culture," and the presence of a democratic culture became synonymous with "freedom" and "free political institutions." In effect, democracy existed if one—and one's fellow citizens—believed it did.[14]

As individualism beyond role and democratic initiative beyond process were replaced by "the freeing of impulse, of appetite, of desire, of power, by enabling them to flow in the channel of a unified and full end" as "the free service of the spirit,"[15] external pressure could be justified henceforth as Hobbes had imagined only in the "service" of this freedom. Given an essentialized self, the collective could legitimately force citizens to be free (as agents), or "free agents," as the fulfillment of their individual will. Adults must be expected and encouraged to express their "true" natures: "In other words, obligation or duty is simply the aspect which the good or moral end assumes, as the individual conceives of it. . . . It requires no further argument to show that obligation is at once self-imposed, and social in its content. It is self-imposed because it flows from the good, from the full idea of the activity of the individual's own will. It is no law imposed from without; but is his own law, the law of his own function, of his individuality."[16] Children similarly can be instructed and led by society's "constituting and teaching duties" to the realization of what one "must" want as the realization of his or her nature. The task of the educator is to inculcate the sense that the basis of such action is "free service," encouraging "the growth of feeling of duty" by activating the child's capacity to make "judgments" and to experience "the emotional accompaniment appropriate" to each act: "The community, in imposing its own needs and demands upon the individual, is simply arousing him to a knowledge of his relationships in life, to a knowledge of the moral environment in which he lives, and of the acts which he must perform if he is to realize his individuality." Those with "undeveloped" moral natures are to be otherwise motivated by "hope and fear" and the necessity of "pleasing others."[17] With freedom and coercion merging, images of a different order of possibility receded behind the veil of a completed self in a completed political cosmos.

Beyond the Veil of Lockean Forgetfulness

Dewey captured the American spirit in its formative age, the relentless building of a nation and its institutions which Tocqueville had witnessed, when individual enterprise seamlessly interwove with collective purpose, where individual will and collective destiny fed on and grew from each other. Individuality given the exigencies of carving out a land was agency, by its very nature implementation of community goals, as it was also participation in the work of framing and founding those goals. The irony is that Dewey wrote just as liberalism was hardening into a set of formalized institutions, functional roles, and ritualized behaviors. At the same time that Dewey was claiming to sustain liberalism on a course of continuing reinvention, Frederick Jackson Turner was suggesting that the American character was becoming static and rigid, losing its democratic openness and individual fluidity with the final settling of the society.

The neo-pragmatic revival, together with the contemporary "parties of liberty," by presuming the idyll as the foundation of national formation perpetuate the amnesia whose result is cultural and intellectual paralysis. Either the settlement has produced a Utopia Sustained of liberty regardless of constraints, or a Utopia Lost of false promises regarding freedom. That is, it is necessary either to accept society as constituted or to reverse modernity itself. It follows that either nothing *needs to be done* or nothing *can be done*. Lifting the veil of forgetfulness, even provisionally, from the disarming impact of Dewey's benign language would be to reopen the "iron logic of liberal election," to reconsider the benefits and sacrifices attending the agency structure of ends and means in our time. Through understanding its "gentler and subtler" processes of "control," it becomes possible to see "how" liberal "freedom is limited."[18] The comforting view of "conformism" as "the nemesis of American individualism" becomes less convincing as the specter of the organizationally shaped "social self" of contemporary liberalism is traced back to the Protestant saint situated within a morally directed and constraining community.[19] The pervading religious claim from the Puritans to Dewey to possess the "truth which shall make you free" meant that the truth could never be regarded as a restraint. Yet with ends so predetermined, the release of individualism from the responsibility and power regarding ends to focus on means has as an inevitable result the pervasive conformity and docility of American life.

Seemingly inexplicable for a project presumably rooted in liberty, the inevitable dependence of agents on a unitary author or plan and circumscribed means makes the underlying regularity of American life entirely comprehensible. With participation in the formulation of personal ends precluded, individuals were never to recover the power to reconsider their role as ethical agents or the kingdom of agency as defined, to act beyond the boundaries of the process. What could it mean to grow or develop further if one were already, as one should be, God's or society's agent except perhaps to expand one's repertoire or use of means *as an agent?* If the paths are made broad enough, as the universalist American faith meant them to be, one never gets to the edge or wishes to see beyond. Unable to be either more or less than an agent, one can only ask, "What kind?" and—absent any strategy of political reform—continue willing one's place in society. Given the liberal conflation of agency and liberty through an engagement in "voluntary" conformable conduct, Dewey's turn to socialization and to instrumental action stemmed not from a "faith" that "fell away" but from his belief that, where divinity and its ends are immanent, there remains only the active effort to improve and apply means.[20]

Regarding American society, focusing one's previously interdicted gaze on the primal construction of agency reveals similar illusions at the collective level. The notion that "the ethos of liberal democracy is equality" and that the decisive trend away even from equalized opportunity constitutes a failure of the settlement cannot be easily maintained.[21] Nor is it plausible, as James Morone suggests, that the "development of an administrative apparatus," the organizational society, as an inevitable consequence of popular "political mobilization" is the "unanticipated" product of the democratic "innocence of organizational dynamics," rendering the evident decline of citizen empowerment an avoidable tragedy of modern liberalism.[22] The enduring commitment of agency organizations to a stratified society of meritocratic differentiations of status and distribution follows from functional divergences in the talents, motivations, resources, and powers of individual agents. Similarly, the very project of agency inclusion within a single master authorizing system rendered institutional expansion and organizational hierarchies the necessary result. The emphasis within such a system on a secure place focuses personal incentives on maintaining one's role in and measuring rewards by the meritocracy. Similarly, the collective goal of over-arching regularity and stability explains trends toward defining "massive nonvoting, general lack of active political participation, and the apparent feebleness of public opinion" as "supports" of democracy.[23]

Moreover, populist rhetoric aside, agency principles by a truism of political architectonics lack the mechanism for altering themselves. Agency society never mandated making the rules, only an equal responsibility for acting on and in accordance with them. What might politics be in the Kingdom of God? Once the processes of this perfected system are set in their essentials, the actual areas of controversy contract, becoming a debate about means— "great freedom in details"—which leaves the consensually affirmed ends and structures untouched.[24] Dewey, it is suggested by some, was too much of a democrat to provide specifics. Yet it is more persuasive to note "his neglect of the politics necessary for the contemporary publics to solve their intellectual problem and to build a new state and his refusal to speculate on the forms this state might take."[25] Dewey rarely spoke of dissent for the "ordinary citizen" who "hardly does more than make his own the environment of ends and interests already sustained in the wills of others."[26] While every society, even the freest, requires a large degree of order and regularity, there is a common tendency of social systems toward containment of differences. Unless contrary options, including periodic and open consideration of collective values and goals and a personal power to dissent and resist conformity, are stressed and provided for, it is not unrealistic to think that these tendencies will prevail and that the theorist wants this to occur.[27] What

Dewey offered, thus, was not common authorship but the appearance of common authority veiling the reality of common agency. Borrowing freely from the language of democratic empowerment, he provided in the end that citizens were (at best) merely willing participants deferring to the structures (though not to their every decision) which defined their power as its adjunct: "Society is a society of individuals and the individual is always a social individual. He has no existence by himself. He lives in, for, and by society."[28]

Dewey's complex task was to sustain the sense of individual empowerment and vital contribution in a post-founding America, after the institutions were built and had developed agendas distinct from the wills and interests of their members. Dewey, like those he appeals to, wanted to believe that the transition from decentralized to organizational society, from the state of nature to social contract, could be held in a timeless equilibrium with open participation and systemic security equally available. But this is an ahistorical fantasy seeking to preserve the unintended benefits of America's early social conditions. His vision of a "free society of free individuals" being fulfilled in his time, though a noble one striking the deepest chords in the American liberal spirit, promoted a dangerously naive trust in existing arrangements. Given the realities of an American society ever less Deweyan, his faith in the growing power of participation, rejection of institutional critiques, denial of access to value formation beyond his just collective, and failure to protect citizens from institutional incursion verged on a blanket validation of liberal institutions and processes.[29]

Once religious authorization was elided into a societal validation, the religious vision of societal integration unavoidably became a transcendent defense of the collective. His call to recognize ultimate national values unfolding in a participatory process could easily be conflated with the prevalent if unrealistic public belief that the America arising as the first popular society embodied such an unquestioned consensus. To be sure, Dewey with his prophetic streak consistently urged liberalism toward a realization of an ideal self and society beyond its tendencies toward organizational hierarchies and pervasive compliance. Yet he never made his language of affirmation conditional on specific achievements. Given the fine line between validation of deep structures and legitimation of present institutions, Dewey left citizens fearing that broadly voluntarist liberal adaptation and systemic integration were to be the closest available approximations to genuine selfhood and democracy.

By proclaiming an ever-growing liberal democratic community and liberal free individuals along with an optimal if "implausible harmony both within the individual and among individuals" to "reconcile modern man to the modern world" and organizational society, Dewey made it nearly impossible to conjure other—perhaps more adaptively modern—alternatives.[30] The project of realizing genuine voluntarism, popular control, and societal equity in an increasingly organized collective thus remains to be addressed. Jefferson had seen the problem of closure—that institutions outlive their members, their agendas becoming less flexible, less responsive, forming in time a settled framework for new members. His wistful answer was periodic revolution. Hannah Arendt in our time recognized the same dilemma and called for a collectivity offering a permanent political space with only an intangible and hence provisional agenda. These twin efforts to destabilize political rigor mortis, one fantasy and one ritual, were attempts to provide a continual source of power for the citizenry who would otherwise come to feel dwarfed by institutions more permanent than themselves. Yet the result in the twentieth century, for all the vitality of American society, was a perception of constricting possibilities, of decreasing institutional options. This consolidation of organizational legitimacy culminated in Talcott Parsons's 1958 definition of "mental health" as the "capacity" to undertake "specific memberships in specific relational systems, *i.e.*, collectivities" and "to fulfill the expectations of such memberships."[31]

Though increasing the risk of deep political divisions from which Dewey retreated, recognizing the reach and limit of the present settlement would at the same time be a profound encouragement to both democratic and personal empowerment. Can the equilibrium between individual and collective intrinsic to a vital agency society be restored with institutions provisional enough to let each new generation redefine and reappropriate them? Or does the faith in a continuously reinventive liberalism like John Dewey's become inevitably operationalized through stable structures as in Mead or Cooley or Parsons? What if squaring the circle of "a free society of free individuals," providing cohesion on an unprecedentedly voluntarist foundation, requires that Americans speak of Jeffersonian principles while remaining firmly within Madisonian institutions, praising revolutionary self-authority while containing it tightly within the Protestant-liberal settlement?

The Future of Agency

The Protestant-liberal settlement became the center of the national consensus between 1895 and 1960 as the pursuit of integration within the nation of agents subsumed other voices in the celebrated "end of ideology." The unstated reversal with its submerged choices was noted by numerous cultural critics in the 1950s, but was left intact as the sustaining paradox of liberalism. Given its complex task of ordering individuals flattered with continual attributions of freedom, self-interest, and power, these saving confusions were thought to mute the structural tensions threatening the enterprise.[32] And yet, alternative traditions had, if quieted, never been silent. As American society had continued its unique trajectory in the "wilderness," Hobbes's automatic reversal into the social contract with alienability of authorship was weakened by the desocialized experience, mobile opportunities, and open setting of American society. His fictional memory of a collective primal election at the core of liberal legitimacy ironically stirred for this nation the reminder of real events and perhaps lost opportunities.

From the outset, American liberalism had offered an adult voluntarism only partly channeled, as the limited reach of early socialization and adult institutions opened an individualism deeper than that provided by the settlement. Moreover, even as the nation of agents was being initiated, Jefferson's suggestive vision of freedom began to haunt the American psychic landscape. Invoking these possibilities, three great waves of Emersonian self-authorization—each larger than the last—have flowed upon the land: in the Concord Renaissance, the pre–World War I "end of American innocence," and the 1960s. For if, it was reasoned, the dream of human freedom is not behind us, it lies before us yet, in institutions more open and lives more autonomous than anything we have yet dared to imagine. Thus, Emma Goldman wrote of women's achievement of inclusion in liberal society, "Now, woman is confronted with the necessity of emancipating herself from emancipation, if she really desires to be free."[33] For this tradition, the "truth" of given ends is not liberating but a constraint on the human power of self-formation and self-determination.

The latest challenge to the national consensus in the 1960s, the specter of the "end of the end of ideology," stemmed from the resurfacing on a broad scale of liberalism's repressed self-authorization. Its emergence at that time was largely the result of the unimaginable achievements of the agency world. The offer to Milton's Adam and Eve upon leaving the garden of servitude was of a vaster garden in the world. By applying their new powers faithfully, they would be able to create a garden of agency, an abundant paradise on earth now flowing from human self-reliance and initiative. And for all its limitations, America after World War II for many approached the fulfillment of this great promise. The very success of the narrative of human agency and its power to mobilize the creation of an earthly paradise opened in our time questions whether we had reached the "end of history" or of just one phase that might lead to new challenges and narratives.

The vacuity of our present political discourse derives from an unwillingness to confront this achievement and the challenges it presents. Questions once avoidable are no longer. Are there alternatives to social incorporation and adjustment, and if so, how are these to be exercised in our tightening corporate society? Does the garden of agency turn its inhabitants into abusers of abundance and their concerns to outlets in consumption, and are there other uses for this wealth? What if diversity, genuine community, self-actualization, and autonomy require our involvement in ends and structures as well as means? What if others emerge with different conceptions of the individual or the collective? What if we ourselves feel an urgent need to remake our community? What if we choose to dissent, or follow a path that few beside ourself see? How well equipped would the agent be to deal with these?

Some, including regenerated Protestants and uncompromising liberals, who trace the present predicament to flaws in the Grand Settlement itself, would undo it.[34] They would reopen the compact and return to their own distinct strand or tradition in order to restore core values. No settlement is forever. Yet a strong cultural and historical logic enabled a powerful modern synthesis linking complementary visions of the seen and the unseen worlds, of internal conviction and social practice, to evolve and prevail over its contributing strands. A return to the margins would not open greater opportunities now than in the nineteenth century, when neither Protestantism nor liberalism independently withstood the movement toward a national society. Their very own communities after all shaped the republic, their very own ideas infused it.

The view of the religious remnant that collective "ends" were diluted by liberalism ignores how Protestants invested agency with worldly power to realize God's will and proposed its immanentist realization in a national instantiation. Similarly, for liberals to insist on their commitment to unsullied "self-improvement and the opportunity to be self-made" in a society of "individual human rights" neglects their insistence on consensual conceptions of individualism, rights, and democracy.[35] Parading these anew to citizens already shaped to seek inclusion and integration simply masks the disingenuousness of efforts to revitalize the social contract. Claims of placing freedom or rights or rational choice in the hands of the many variants of the "free agent" from democratic citizen to market actor and entrepreneur under such circumstances do not magically dismantle the liberal collective. Rather such unsupported personal options become what they are systematically intended to be, mere "justiciable" types of "Interests," that is, powers of comparative acquisition within a settled system of ends.[36] A wide scope for preferences, compatible with reasonable bounds and fixed ends, is agency itself. Thus, proposals for a liberal-Protestant divorce, while always possible, are subject inevitably to the dreams which initially propelled the alliance and the logic of its settlement, as well as its provision for the children. One is never any longer the same.

Amidst resistance to confronting the settlement directly, increasing exposure of the origins of liberal adjustment and its dependence on agency character reversal opens new options. One result has been the fraying of the nearly seamless conflation of individual and collective interests into separate agendas. For insightful conservative defenders of institutional preeminence including Christopher Lasch, Richard Sennett, and Daniel Bell, a defense of agency society is now feasible which directly supports the systemic limitation on reformulating ends. Tracing these limits within historical liberalism, they insist on collective authority and internalized constraint utilizing the discourses of Freudian psychoanalysis and the Hobbesian variant of Protestant-liberalism. This has led to the recognition that economic constraint in adults and psychological reversal in the young, motivated by both fear and rewards, are indispensable to the liberal construction of character and to its containment of individualism within agency institutions. By accepting the agency foundation of modernity, they have been further able to promote its historic demand for a more just and meritocratic implementation of agency principles. The result has been a reinvigoration of agency discourse.

On the other side, the protean vision of individual authorization and democratic inventiveness with its challenge to settled institutions and values was destined to resurface. Theories of democracy, multiculturalism, and postindustrial cultural shifts, offering the opportunity to reconsider the agency paradigm, what it foreclosed and what now might be possible, continue the innovative spirit of the English Puritans. The Protestant-liberal synthesis is from this perspective neither refuge nor antagonist but forebear, the source out of which (in both senses) the contemporary world has grown. Facing what was excluded from this integrated universe of the mobilized Protestant community and Hobbes's cosmic political architecture encourages rethinking the viability of reversing from one's own path for a link to the collective by "authorizing and giving up" one's authority. If liberalism never involved autonomy or democracy as such, if the twentieth-century apotheosis of liberal society was the fulfillment and not the decline of liberalism, then what must be reevaluated is not the "free society" as such but the *liberal conception* of the "free society." In a world without a just or consensual collective author, where choice, dissent, and division exist, can we be merely agents in a Grand Community? Must we not in a fractured world be more than instruments, finding ways of balancing our agency with larger ends and institutions with personal values and in the final analysis responsibility for our own fate? As the later Lawrence Kohlberg realized and Dewey did not, the relation between the individual and society presents a value tension that cannot be resolved through a single unambiguous hierarchy of moral priorities. And, at the same time, even if individualism cannot be naively identified with societal cohesion, sustainable communities which nurture and confirm personal growth and meaningful self-direction in the world might still be promoted.

The agency paradigm, then, the deepest narrative of American nationhood attending to its modernist interweaving of individual and collective, searches for continued viability in the United States. The partial fracturing from systemic tensions of a synthesis both unprecedented and incomplete has produced the lurchings of late-twentieth-century American culture and the preeminent ideological divisions of our time. Perhaps the closing of the frontier, actual and psychic, justifies the claim of "the end of ideology" and "the end of history." Or perhaps the synthesis between ideal and real, of which agency was one stage on some greater journey, lies ahead to be newly imagined and pursued. Might not the quest for just democracy, genuine selfhood, and diversity within a cohesive community, while indebted to the immense developmental steps taken with creation of the agency world, be advanced through further reconstruction of the human setting? A "free individual in a free society" will not forever look like the Protestant agent in liberal society. Brilliant and long enduring though it was, it was only the first approximation.

NOTES

INDEX

NOTES

1. The American Narrative in Crisis

For the sake of clarity, a limited modernization of spelling and punctuation has been undertaken where necessary in quotations from older works.

1. Alexis de Tocqueville, *Democracy in America* (New York, 1954), 1:7.
2. Sydney E. Ahlstrom, "National Trauma and Changing Religious Values," *Daedalus* 107 *(A New America?)* (Winter 1978), 28, 20.
3. James Davison Hunter, *Culture Wars: The Struggle to Define America* (New York, 1991), 118.
4. Kevin Phillips, "Post-Conservative America," *New York Review of Books,* May 13, 1982, 31.
5. Todd Gitlin, *The Twilight of Common Dreams: Why America Is Wracked by Culture Wars* (New York, 1995), 3.
6. William J. Bennett, *The De-Valuing of America: The Fight for Our Culture and Our Children* (New York, 1992), 253, 35.
7. Robert Blauner, "Colonized and Immigrant Minorities," in *From Different Shores,* ed. Ronald Takaki (New York, 1994), 152. See also Eric Foner, ed., *The New American History* (Philadelphia, 1990).
8. Hayden White, *Metahistory: The Historical Imagination in Nineteenth-Century Europe* (Baltimore, 1973), 2.
9. Homi K. Bhabha, *The Location of Culture* (London, 1994), 37.
10. Eric Foner, "The Meaning of Freedom in the Age of Emancipation," *Journal of American History* 82 (September 1994), 460.
11. Ronald Takaki, *A Different Mirror: A History of Multicultural America* (Boston, 1993), 10.
12. Daniel T. Rodgers, "Republicanism: The Career of a Concept," *Journal of American History* 79 (June 1992), 37.
13. Louis Hartz, *The Liberal Tradition in America* (New York, 1955), 21, 39.
14. Ibid., 11, 58.
15. Ibid., 308.

16. Wesley Frank Craven, *The Legend of the Founding Fathers* (Ithaca, N.Y., 1965), 20, 25, 29.
17. Ibid., 203.
18. See ibid., 60–65, 134–136, 203–207.
19. Ibid., 203.
20. Louis Hartz, *The Founding of New Societies* (New York, 1964), 5, 6, 73.
21. Ibid., 81; see also Hartz, *Tradition*, 23, 40–41.
22. See, e.g., Daniel Bell, *The End of Ideology: On the Exhaustion of Political Ideas in the Fifties* (New York, 1962).
23. See Rodgers, "Republicanism," 33. I have used this article extensively in this discussion.
24. See Hannah Arendt, *On Revolution* (New York, 1965).
25. See Sheldon S. Wolin, *Politics and Vision: Continuity and Innovation in Western Political Thought* (Boston, 1960); Robert Bellah et al., *The Good Society* (New York, 1992); Michael J. Sandel, *Democracy's Discontent* (Cambridge, Mass., 1996).
26. Sandel, *Discontent*, 24.
27. Rodgers, "Republicanism," 38.
28. See John Patrick Diggins, *The Lost Soul of American Politics: Virtue, Self-Interest, and the Foundations of Liberalism* (New York, 1984); Foner, "Meaning of Freedom"; Isaac Kramnick, "Republican Revisionism Revisited," *American Historical Review* 87 (June 1982). See also Theda Skocpol, "The Legacies of New Deal Liberalism," in *Liberalism Reconsidered*, ed. Douglas MacLean and Claudia Mills (Totowa, N.J., 1983); Gordon S. Wood, *The Radicalism of the American Revolution* (New York, 1993).
29. Diggins, *Soul*, 5.
30. Joyce Appleby, Lynn Hunt, and Margaret Jacob, *Telling the Truth about History* (New York, 1994), 8, 156.
31. Eric Foner, *The Story of American Freedom* (New York, 1998), xiv, xviii.
32. Rodgers, "Republicanism," 34.
33. Gitlin, *Twilight*, 236.
34. David A. Hollinger, *Postethnic America* (New York, 1995), 125.
35. Gary B. Nash, "The Great Multicultural Debate," *Contention* (1992), 24.
36. Sheldon S. Wolin, *The Presence of the Past: Essays on the State and the Constitution* (Baltimore, 1989), 2.
37. Michael Lienesch, *New Order of the Ages: Time, the Constitution, and the Making of Modern Political Thought* (Princeton, 1988), 4.
38. See, e.g., Francis Fukuyama, *The End of History and the Last Man* (New York, 1992).
39. See Daniel Bell, ed., *The New American Right* (New York, 1955); Richard Hofstadter, *Anti-Intellectualism in American Life* (New York, 1963).
40. Daniel Lerner, *The Passing of Traditional Society: Modernizing the Middle East* (New York, 1958), 48.
41. David Riesman, *The Lonely Crowd: A Study of the Changing American Character* (New Haven, 1989), 251.

42. Alex Inkeles, "National Character and Modern Political Systems," in *Psychological Anthropology: Approaches to Culture and Personality,* ed. Francis Shu (Homewood, Ill., 1961), 196, 198.

43. See Erich Fromm, *Escape from Freedom* (New York, 1965); Riesman, *Crowd;* William H. Whyte, Jr., *The Organization Man* (Garden City, N.Y., 1957); Karen Horney, *The Neurotic Personality of Our Time* (New York, 1937).

44. See Herbert Marcuse, *Eros and Civilization: A Philosophical Inquiry into Freud* (Boston, 1966); N. O. Brown, *Life against Death: The Psychoanalytic Meaning of History* (New York, 1959); Theodore Roszak, *The Making of a Counter Culture* (Garden City, N.Y., 1969); Henry Malcolm, *Generation of Narcissus* (Boston, 1971); Kenneth Keniston, *Youth and Dissent* (New York, 1971).

45. See Christopher Lasch, *The Culture of Narcissism* (New York, 1978); Richard Sennett, *Authority* (New York, 1980); Philip Rieff, *The Triumph of the Therapeutic: Uses of Faith after Freud* (New York, 1966); Daniel Bell, *The Cultural Contradictions of Capitalism* (New York, 1976).

46. Seymour Martin Lipset, *The First New Nation: The United States in Historical and Comparative Perspective* (Garden City, N.Y., 1967), 156; see also David M. Potter, "The Quest for the National Character," in *History and American Society: Essays of David M. Potter,* ed. Don E. Fehrenbacher (New York, 1975).

47. See Clyde Kluckhohn, "Have There Been Discernible Shifts in American Values during the Past Generation?" in *The American Style: Essays in Value and Performance,* ed. Elting E. Morison (New York, 1958), 187.

48. Potter, "Quest for National Character," 243.

49. See, e.g., Riesman, *Crowd;* Robert Lane, "Political Character and Political Analysis," *Psychiatry* 16 (1953), 387–398.

50. See David Riesman, "Twenty Years After—A Second Preface," in *Crowd,* xiv; Christopher Lasch, *The True and Only Heaven: Progress and Its Critics* (New York, 1991); Sennett, *Authority.*

51. See, e.g., Sandel, *Democracy's Discontent;* Bellah et al., *The Good Society;* Jean Bethke Elshtain, *Democracy on Trial* (New York, 1995); Ronald Dworkin, "What Liberalism Isn't," *New York Review of Books,* January 20, 1983; Ronald Dworkin, "Why Liberals Should Believe in Equality," *New York Review of Books,* February 3, 1983.

52. Martin E. Marty, *The One and the Many: America's Struggle for the Common Good* (Cambridge, Mass., 1997), 145.

53. Foner, *American Freedom,* 435.

54. Nash, "Debate," 24, 25.

55. Takaki, *Mirror,* 6, 17.

56. Patricia Nelson Limerick, "Insiders and Outsiders: The Borders of the USA and the Limits of the ASA," Presidential Address to the American Studies Association, October 31, 1996, *American Quarterly* 49 (September 1997), 466.

57. Sacvan Bercovitch, *The American Jeremiad* (Madison, Wis., 1978), 11.

58. Wolin, *Presence,* 2.

59. Robert A. Nisbet, *Community and Power* (New York, 1962), 68.

60. John Higham, "The Future of American History," *Journal of American History* 81 (March 1994), 1298.

61. See, e.g., Jonathan Mahler, "Uprooting the Past: Israel's New Historians Take a Hard Look at Their Nation's Origins," *Lingua Franca* 7 (August 1997); François Furet, *Marx and the French Revolution* (Chicago, 1988); Enrique Krauze, "In Memory of Octavio Paz (1914–1998)," *New York Review of Books,* May 28, 1998, 25–26; André Liebich, *From the Other Shore: Russian Social Democracy after 1921* (Cambridge, Mass., 1998). For the American case, see David Brion Davis, *Revolutions: Reflections on American Equality and Foreign Liberations* (Cambridge, Mass., 1990).

62. Sandel, *Democracy's Discontent,* appeared in 1996.

63. Thomas L. Pangle, "The Retrieval of Civic Virtue: A Critical Appreciation of Sandel's *Democracy's Discontent,*" in *Debating Democracy's Discontent: Essays on American Politics, Law, and Public Philosophy,* ed. Anita L. Allen and Milton C. Regan, Jr. (Oxford, 1998); Will Kymlicka, "Liberal Egalitarianism and Civic Republicanism: Friends or Enemies?" ibid., 133; Ronald S. Beiner, "Introduction: The Quest for a Post-Liberal Public Philosophy," ibid., 4.

64. David M. Potter, *Freedom and Its Limitations in American Life* (Stanford, 1976), 48, 56, 41, 56, 46.

65. Daniel Walker Howe, *Making the American Self: Jonathan Edwards to Abraham Lincoln* (Cambridge, Mass., 1997), 10, 116; Daniel T. Rodgers, *Contested Truths: Keywords in American Politics since Independence* (New York, 1987), 216, 217.

66. Carl Becker, "Kansas," in *Everyman His Own Historian: Essays on History and Politics* (Chicago, 1966), 9.

67. Michael Zuckerman, *Almost Chosen People: Oblique Biographies in the American Grain* (Berkeley, 1993), 23.

68. James A. Morone, *The Democratic Wish: Popular Participation and the Limits of American Government* (New York, 1990), 13.

69. Adam B. Seligman, *Innerworldly Individualism: Charismatic Community and Its Institutionalization* (New Brunswick, N.J., 1994), 168.

70. Potter, *Freedom,* 51.

71. Foner, "Meaning," 435.

72. Gordon S. Wood, "Star-Spangled History," *New York Review of Books,* August 12, 1982, 4.

73. Geoff Eley and Ronald Grigor Suny, "Introduction: From the Moment of Social History to the Work of Cultural Representation," in *Becoming National,* ed. Geoff Eley and Ronald Grigor Suny (New York, 1966), 32.

74. Potter, *Freedom,* 11.

75. Higham, "Future," 1304.

76. Tocqueville, *Democracy,* 2:10, 336.

77. Ibid., 313, 335.

78. Ibid., 313, 277.

79. Ibid., 240.

80. Rodgers, *Truths,* 224, 223, 225.

81. Howe, *Self*, 116.
82. Charles Taylor, *Sources of the Self: The Making of the Modern Identity* (Cambridge, Mass., 1989), ix, 12, 33.
83. Ibid., 106, 39, 105.
84. Ibid., 306, 104.
85. Ibid., 104, 319.
86. Ibid., 315.
87. Howe, *Self*, 3.
88. Rodgers, *Truths*, 118.
89. Taylor, *Sources*, 319, 305.
90. Michael J. Lacey, "Introduction: The Academic Revolution and American Religious Thought," in *Religion and Twentieth-Century American Intellectual Life*, ed. Michael J. Lacey (Cambridge, 1991), 5.
91. See Taylor, *Sources*.
92. Cushing Strout, *The New Heavens and the New Earth: Political Religion in America* (New York, 1974), xi, 3, 11, 12.
93. Zuckerman, *People*, 23, 45.
94. Seligman, *Individualism*, viii, ix, 189.
95. Ibid., 217, 187, x.
96. Max Weber, *The Protestant Ethic and the Spirit of Capitalism* (New York, 1958), 160, 97, 98.
97. Ibid., 179, 160.
98. Michael Walzer, *The Revolution of the Saints: A Study in the Origin of Radical Politics* (New York, 1974), 3, 166, 30, 145.
99. Ibid., 7, 13, 198.
100. For an expression of this view, see Sandel, *Democracy's Discontent*, 4, and his citations in note 2.
101. Urian Oakes, *The Soveraign Efficacy of Divine Providence*, in *The American Puritans*, ed. Perry Miller (Garden City, N.Y., 1956), 193.
102. Samuel Willard, quoted in Perry Miller, *The New England Mind: The Seventeenth Century* (Boston, 1961), 375.
103. Samuel Johnson, quoted in Philip Greven, *The Protestant Temperament: Patterns of Child-Rearing, Religious Experience, and the Self in Early America* (New York, 1977), 239, 219, 221.
104. William Livingston, quoted ibid., 232, 218.
105. Charles Chauncy, quoted ibid., 219.
106. Alexander Garden, quoted ibid., 229.
107. John Perkins, *Theory of Agency, or, An Essay on the Nature, Source, and Extent of Moral Freedom* (Boston, 1771), 43, 39.
108. Daniel Shute, "An Election Sermon," in *American Political Writing during the Founding Era, 1760–1805*, ed. Charles S. Hyneman and Donald S. Lutz (Indianapolis, 1983), 1:111.
109. Levi Hart, "Liberty Described and Recommended: in a Sermon Preached to the Corporation of Freemen in Farmington," ibid., 308.

110. Timothy Dwight, quoted in Robert H. Abzug, *Cosmos Crumbling: American Reform and the Religious Imagination* (New York, 1994), 36.

111. See Samuel Rutherford, *Lex, Rex,* in *Puritanism and Liberty,* ed. A. S. P. Woodhouse (London, 1992), 201; "Two Letters from the Agents of the Five Regiments," ibid., 437.

112. Oakes, *Efficacy,* 194, 195.

113. See Perry Miller, *The New England Mind: From Colony to Province* (Boston, 1961), 57–67.

114. See Stephen Darwall, *The British Moralists and the Internal "Ought," 1640–1740* (Cambridge, 1995), 13–14.

115. See Harold Laski, *The Rise of European Liberalism* (London, 1962), 17–21, 30, 45–46; Kenneth R. Minogue, *The Liberal Mind* (New York, 1968), 25–26; Nathan O. Hatch, *The Sacred Cause of Liberty: Republican Thought and the Millennium in Revolutionary New England* (New Haven, 1977), 3–4; Edwin Scott Gaustad, *The Great Awakening in New England* (Chicago, 1957), 139–140.

116. See Douglas John Hall, *The Reality of the Gospel and the Unreality of the Churches* (Philadelphia, 1975); Stephen Holmes, *Passions and Constraints: On the Theory of Liberal Democracy* (Chicago, 1995).

117. Edward Everett, "Oration on the Peculiar Motives to Intellectual Exertion in America," in *The American Literary Revolution, 1783–1837,* ed. Robert E. Spiller (Garden City, N.Y., 1967), 288.

118. For a discussion of American exceptionalism in relation to the American religious tradition, see J. C. D. Clark, *The Language of Liberty, 1660–1832: Political Discourse and Social Dynamics in the Anglo-American World* (Cambridge, 1994), 13–14.

119. See the related perspective in Marty, *One and Many.*

2. The Early Puritan Insurgents and the Origins of Agency

1. See William Haller, *The Rise of Puritanism* (New York, 1957), 23–24.

2. This discussion is indebted to Haller, *Puritanism,* and to David Zaret, *The Heavenly Contract: Ideology and Organization in Pre-Revolutionary Puritanism* (Chicago, 1985). On the role of the laity, see also William Haller, *Liberty and Reformation in the Puritan Revolution* (New York, 1963).

3. See Haller, *Puritanism,* 174–175, 180, 375; J. Sears McGee, *The Godly Man in Stuart England* (New Haven, 1976), 254–255; Zaret, *Contract,* 14–15, 87, 116–121.

4. See Haller, *Puritanism,* 18–21; Zaret, *Contract,* 14–15, 24.

5. Peter Lake writes that the "pietistic, personal core had underlain the puritan impulse from the start," in *Moderate Puritans and the Elizabethan Church* (Cambridge, 1982), 284. See also John Spurr, *English Puritanism, 1603–1689* (New York, 1998), 3–6.

6. Haller, *Puritanism,* 172–173.

7. John Preston, *Life Eternal* (London, 1631), 166–167.

8. See Charles H. George and Katherine George, *The Protestant Mind of the English Reformation, 1570–1640* (Princeton, 1961), 3, 86–87; Lake, *Puritans,* 279–280.

9. See Walzer, *Revolution;* Haller, *Puritanism.*

10. Alexis de Tocqueville, *The Old Regime and the French Revolution,* trans. Stuart Gilbert (Garden City, N.Y., 1955), 204.

11. See Voltaire, *Philosophical Letters,* trans. Ernest Dilworth (Indianapolis, 1961), 26, 32, 39.

12. Tocqueville, *Old Regime,* 18, 19.

13. See Karl Marx, article from *Neue Rheinishe Zeitung,* December 15, 1848, reprinted in *The Revolutions of 1848,* ed. David Fernbach (New York, 1974), 192–193, and "Manifesto of the Communist Party," ibid., 98.

14. See Arendt, *Revolution.*

15. Wood, *Radicalism,* 6, 11, 7. To the English, Wood contrasts the Americans of the Revolution who "had become, almost overnight, the most liberal, the most democratic, the most commercially minded, and the most modern people in the world." Ibid., 6–7.

16. Christopher Hill, *The World Turned Upside Down* (New York, 1972), 14.

17. Christopher Hill, *Milton and the English Revolution* (New York, 1979), 459.

18. This approach, which emphasizes psychological shifts over shifts in economic thinking and other forms of institutional ideology, is of course traceable to the work of Max Weber, *Protestant Ethic.* See also Zaret, *Contract,* chap. 7.

19. See Peter Lake, *Anglicans and Puritans? Presbyterian and English Conformist Thought from Whitgift to Hooker* (London, 1988), 16–19; McGee, *Man,* 72, 270.

20. See Bernard Bailyn, *The Ideological Origins of the American Revolution* (Cambridge, Mass., 1967), 128–130.

21. See Haller, *Puritanism,* 173–175, 193; Haller, *Liberty,* 15, 78, 107, 153.

22. McGee, *Man,* 63, 60; Edward Hyde, "Contemplations and Reflections upon the Psalms of David," in *A Collection of Several Tracts of the Right Honourable Earl of Clarendon* (London, 1727), 411.

23. Janice Knight, *Orthodoxies in Massachusetts: Rereading American Puritanism* (Cambridge, Mass., 1994), 2, 4.

24. See Christopher Durston and Jacqueline Eales, "Introduction: The Puritan Ethos, 1560–1700," in *The Culture of English Puritanism, 1560–1700,* ed. Christopher Durston and Jacqueline Eales (New York, 1996), 9–10; Zaret, *Contract,* 128.

25. See M. M. Knappen, *Tudor Puritanism* (Chicago, 1970), 392; M. M. Knappen, introduction to *Two Elizabethan Puritan Diaries* (Chicago, 1933), 13; Zaret, *Contract,* 128, 153–154.

26. As Janice Knight suggests *(Orthodoxies),* doctrinal liberalization reflects the leadership vacuum demanding Puritan governance and containment of political disorder in New England and the Commonwealth.

27. See Durston and Eales, "Introduction," 12–13; John Spurr, "From Puritanism to Dissent, 1660–1700," in Durston and Eales, *Culture of English Puritanism.*

28. McGee suggests the existence of a single "English Protestant mind" during the period subject only to "differences in degrees of adherence to doctrines and in weight of emphasis upon doctrines." McGee, *Man*, 3–5.

29. An important characterological study of the Puritans, Michael Walzer's *Revolution of the Saints*, focusing on ideology, with character structure as its product, drastically separates Puritanism and liberalism. If character rather than ideas is foundational, different ideological formations represent stages in characterological development which produce shifting emphases.

30. *The Works of John Whitgift*, 3 vols. (Cambridge, 1851–1853), 3:420.

31. Ibid., 274–275.

32. William Laud, quoted in McGee, *Man*, 8.

33. Ibid., 144.

34. Ibid., 163.

35. William Chillingworth, *Works*, 3 vols. (New York, 1972), 3:31.

36. Jeremy Taylor, *The Whole Works*, 15 vols. (London, 1822), 6:cccxxii.

37. Clarendon, "Contemplations," 544.

38. Richard Hooker, *Of the Laws of Ecclesiastical Polity*, 2 vols. (London, 1907), 1:119.

39. Ibid., 137, 121.

40. Henry Hammond, *A Practical Catechism*, 14th ed. (London, 1700), 183.

41. Hooker, *Polity*, 2:16, 12.

42. Ibid., 16.

43. Ibid., 12, 36.

44. Ibid., 12.

45. Ibid., 1:124–125.

46. Stephen Gardiner, bishop of Winchester, *Contemptum humanae legis*, quoted in David Little, *Religion, Order, and Law: A Study in Pre-Revolutionary England* (New York, 1969), 132.

47. Hooker, *Polity*, 2:363, 362.

48. McGee, *Man*, 150. The foregoing discussion is indebted to McGee and Lake.

49. "The Diary of Richard Rogers," in Knappen, *Two Elizabethan Puritan Diaries*, 54.

50. Arthur Dent, *The Plain Man's Path-way to Heaven* (London, 1601), 57.

51. Rogers, "Diary," 55, 54, 53.

52. Ibid., 57, 53.

53. Ibid., 57, 54.

54. Richard Rogers, preface to *Seaven Treatises* (London, 1604).

55. Dent, *Path-way*, 23.

56. Stephen Egerton, "To the Christian Reader," in Rogers, *Treatises*.

57. Rogers, "Diary," 63, 64.

58. Dent, *Path-way*, 15, 9, 14, 7.

59. Richard Greenham, "Grave Counsels and Godly Observations," in *The Works of Richard Greenham*, 5th ed. (London, 1612), 12–13.

60. See, e.g., Dent, *Path-way*.

61. Rogers, "Diary," 65, 61.

62. Ibid., 61, 67, 55.

63. Ibid., 68, 70, 67, 58.

64. Ibid., 67, 61, 53.

65. Greenham, "Counsels," 13.

66. Dent, *Path-way,* 13.

67. Rogers, "Diary," 61, 53; Greenham, "Counsels," 13, 18.

68. Greenham, "Counsels," 5.

69. Dent, *Path-way,* 165, 174, 221, 194, 199.

70. Rogers, "Diary," 70.

71. Rogers, *Treatises,* 92–93.

72. Rogers, "Diary," 72.

73. Ibid., 53.

74. Rogers, preface to *Treatises.*

75. Dent, *Path-way,* 11, 8.

76. Rogers, *Treatises,* 157, 528, 165.

77. Dent, *Path-way,* 13, 160, 158.

78. Rogers, "Diary," 63.

79. Rogers, *Treatises,* 151.

80. Ibid., 169, 193.

81. Ibid., 199.

82. Ibid., 177.

83. Ibid., 154, 174, 180.

84. Ibid., 181, 155.

85. Ibid., 175.

86. Ibid., 153.

87. Ibid., 160, 248.

88. Ian Breward, introduction to *The Works of William Perkins* (Appleford, Berks., 1970), 25.

89. William Perkins, "How to Live, and at that Well," in *The Works of William Perkins* (London, 1603), 585.

90. William Perkins, "A Faithful and Plain Exposition upon Zephaniah 2.1–2," in *Works* (1970), 291–292.

91. William Perkins, "A Case of Conscience," in *Works* (1603), 517.

92. William Perkins, "A Discourse of Conscience," in *Works* (1603), 644.

93. Ibid., 659.

94. William Perkins, "The Whole Treatise of Cases of Conscience" (henceforth "Treatise"), in *William Perkins, 1558–1602: English Puritanist,* ed. Thomas F. Merrill (The Hague, 1966), 103.

95. Perkins, "Discourse," 539.

96. Perkins, "Treatise," 102; Perkins, "Discourse," 661.

97. Perkins, "Treatise," 94.

98. William Perkins, "A Treatise of Gods Free Grace and Mans Free Will," in *Works* (1603), 891.

99. Perkins, "Zephaniah," 294; William Perkins, "An Exposition of the Lord's Prayer," in *Works* (1603), 403. Perkins's embrace of the covenant and works

follows directly from the enlarged role of the human will. See Perkins, "Discourse," 121–127, 145–151; Perkins, "Case," 521.

100. Perkins, "Discourse," 92, 95; Perkins, "Zephaniah," 285.

101. William Perkins, "A Treatise Whether a Man be in the Estate of Damnation or in the Estate of Grace," in *Works* (1603), 438.

102. Perkins, quoted in Breward, introduction to *Works* (1970), 95.

103. Ibid.; William Perkins, "A Grain of Mustard Seed," ibid., 405.

104. Perkins, "Discourse," 661–662; Perkins, "Treatise," 104; Perkins, "Zephaniah," 288–289.

105. Perkins, "Zephaniah," 284.

106. William Perkins, "Two Treatises," in *Works* (1603), 543.

107. William Perkins, "A Treatise of the Vocations or Callings of Men," in *Works* (1970), 474, 473.

108. William Perkins, "An Instruction Touching Religious or Divine Worship," in *Works* (1970), 310, 311; Perkins, "Treatise Whether," 439.

109. Perkins, "Instruction," 315, 316; Perkins, "Treatise," 116–117.

110. Perkins, "Case," 106.

111. William Perkins, "To the Christian Reader," in *Works* (1603), unpaginated; Perkins, "Exposition," 408.

112. Perkins, "Treatise Whether," 465; Perkins, "Discourse," 112.

113. Perkins, "Treatise Whether," 436; William Perkins, "A Golden Chaine," in *Works* (1603), 91.

114. Perkins, "Treatise Whether," 440.

115. Perkins, "Treatise," 117; Perkins, "Chaine," 93; Perkins, "Treatise Whether," 432.

116. William Perkins, "Dialogue between Saved Sinner (Eusebius) and Questioner (Timotheus)," in *Works* (1603), 468.

117. Perkins, "Treatise Whether," 438.

118. Ibid., 432; Perkins, "Christian Reader," unpaginated.

119. Perkins, "Treatise," 91; Perkins, "Instruction," 312.

120. Perkins, "Gods Free Grace," 889.

121. Perkins, "Exposition," 422, 407; Perkins, "Treatise," 107, 110, 164; Perkins, "Treatise Whether," 440; Perkins, "Instruction," 313.

122. Perkins, "Case," 513.

123. Perkins, "Treatise Whether," 442.

124. Ibid.

125. Perkins, "Treatise," 113, 99.

126. Perkins, "Grain," 393; Perkins, "Treatise," 163.

127. Perkins, "Discourse," 92, 91; Perkins, "Chaine," 94.

128. Perkins, "Treatise Whether," 444, 441; Perkins, "Case," 513; Perkins, "Discourse," 646.

129. Perkins, "Dialogue," 461; Perkins, "Discourse," 645, 648.

130. Perkins, "Gods Free Grace," 892.

131. Ibid., 889, 891 (emphasis added).
132. Perkins, "Discourse," 666.
133. Perkins, "Grain," 384–385; Perkins, "Discourse," 634, 635.
134. Perkins, "Discourse," 635.
135. Ibid., 637; Perkins, "Instruction," 309.
136. Perkins, "Discourse," 633.
137. Perkins, "Grain," 410.
138. Perkins, "Discourse," 637, 632, 644.
139. See ibid., 644.
140. William Perkins, "A Dialogue of the State of a Christian Man Gathered Here and There Out of the Sweet and Savoury Writings of Master Tyndale and Master Bradford," in *Works* (1970), 382, 381.
141. Ibid., 381–382.
142. See ibid. 382–384.
143. Perkins, "Exposition," 406–407.
144. Perkins, "Zephaniah," 292–293.
145. Ibid., 293, 294, 296, 298.
146. Ibid., 292, 299; Perkins, "Two Treatises," 539.
147. Perkins, "Zephaniah," 295, 299, 301.
148. Perkins, "Case," 502.
149. Perkins, "Treatise Whether," 432, 441. A character in one of his dialogues reports, "I am certainly persuaded of the favor and mercy of God even to the salvation of my soul." The proof? "In my prayers I find great joy and comfort and exceeding favor of God. . . . Now from whence comes all this? From the devil? No. . . . [W]herefore these are the works of Gods spirit, and my conscience is thereby certified that God has given me the spirit of adoption, and . . . his favor and mercy . . . for ever." Perkins, "Dialogue between Saved Sinner," 459.
150. Perkins, "Discourse," 645, 655.
151. Perkins, "Grain," 391, 408.
152. Perkins, "Treatise," 115. The extensive list of these signs included specific keys associated with spiritual receptivity and humility, constancy of religious practice, moral rectitude, the desire to do God's work, conformity to his will, faith in God and personal sanctification, and the willingness to undertake "some lawful calling." Perkins, "Treatise Whether," 446. See also Perkins, "Grain," 405–410 (nineteen rules of behavior, seven rules of meditation).
153. Perkins, "Treatise Whether," 451.
154. Perkins, "Treatise," 149.
155. Ibid., 150, 151, 146.
156. Ibid., 151, 149, 121.
157. Perkins, "Case," 513, 517.
158. Perkins, "Treatise," 149.
159. One element conspicuously muted, suggesting an awareness of the fragility and vulnerability of the believer's journey, is the rhetoric of fear. Belying the

later image of the Puritan minister, it is primarily placed at the end of discourses in which Perkins's transformative process and the means for attaining it have been elaborated at length. See Perkins, "Dialogue between Saved Sinner"; Perkins, "Vocations," 476.

160. Perkins, "Dialogue between Saved Sinner," 469, 459, 460.
161. Perkins, "Treatise," 122.
162. Perkins, "Dialogue between Saved Sinner," 467, 465.
163. Perkins, "Discourse," 643–644; Perkins, "Instruction," 308, 346, 347; Perkins, "Case," 517.
164. Perkins, "Grain," 405; Perkins, "Vocations," 447.

3. The Protestant Revolutionaries and the Emerging Society of Agents

1. Richard Sibbes, "The Soul's Conflict with Itself," in *The Works of Richard Sibbes* (Edinburgh, 1862), 1:270, 261, 280–281.
2. John Preston, *Sermons Preached before his Majestie* (Cambridge, 1630), 87; John Preston, *The New Covenant*, 4th ed. (London, 1630), 182, 181, 166.
3. Robert Bolton, *Some General Directions for a Comfortable Walking with God*, 3d ed. (London, 1630), 28; Preston, *Covenant*, 11, 85.
4. Sibbes, "Conflict," 164, 214, 149, 162.
5. Ibid., 149, 142, 146.
6. Ibid., 174, 167, 212.
7. Ibid., 146; Preston, *Covenant*, 12.
8. Sibbes, "Conflict," 145, 144.
9. "The Life of Doctor Thomas Goodwin: Compos'd out of his own Papers and Memoirs," in *The Works of Thomas Goodwin*, vol. 5 (London, 1704), xiii.
10. Thomas Hooker, *The Soul's Preparation for Christ* (1640; reprint, Ames, Iowa, 1994), 128.
11. Sibbes, "Conflict," 161, 176, 220, 181; "Life of Goodwin," xiv; Richard Sibbes, *The Bruised Reed*, quoted in Haller, *Puritanism*, 160.
12. Hooker, *Preparation*, 159–160.
13. Preston, *Covenant*, 145.
14. "Life of Goodwin," xi.
15. Preston, *Covenant*, 333.
16. Sibbes, "Conflict," 159, 162.
17. Ibid., 150, 214.
18. Preston, *Covenant*, 2, 161, 226, 150, 273.
19. Ibid., 145, 192; Sibbes, "Conflict," 155, 216.
20. Preston, *Covenant*, 145.
21. "Life of Goodwin," xi; Sibbes, "Conflict," 149; Preston, *Covenant*, 108, 217.
22. Sibbes, "Conflict," 181; Preston, *Covenant*, 250.
23. Preston, *Covenant*, 222; "Life of Goodwin," xi.
24. John Cotton, *Gods Mercie Mixed with His Justice* (London, 1641), 42.
25. "Life of Goodwin," xi; Preston, *Covenant*, 118.

26. Preston, *Covenant,* 322.
27. Sibbes, "Conflict," 176, 162, 159; Preston, *Covenant,* 13.
28. Sibbes, "Conflict," 148, 159; "Life of Goodwin," xi.
29. Sibbes, "Conflict," 176, 204, 222; Cotton, *Mercie,* 65.
30. Hooker, *Preparation,* 128; Thomas Hooker, "The Carnal Hypocrit," in *Writings in England and Holland, 1626–1633* (Cambridge, Mass., 1975), 108.
31. Sibbes, "Conflict," 167; Cotton, *Mercie,* 64.
32. Preston, *Covenant,* 332, 124, 482; Preston, *Life Eternal,* pt. 2, 191.
33. Sibbes, "Conflict," 272, 262.
34. Ibid., 262, 161; Preston, *Covenant,* 235.
35. Sibbes, "Conflict," 247, 149, 159; Preston, *Covenant,* 116.
36. Sibbes, "Conflict," 149, 133.
37. Ibid., 161–162.
38. John Benbrigge, *Christ Above All Exalted* (London, 1645), 28–29.
39. Quoted in McGee, *Man,* 146.
40. Sibbes, "Conflict, 146; Preston, *Covenant,* 91, 92.
41. Cotton, *Mercie,* 118; Sibbes, "Conflict," 205.
42. Preston, *Covenant,* 186, 195.
43. Sibbes, "Conflict," 205.
44. Hooker, *Preparation,* 129; William Gouge, *The Saints Sacrifice* (London, 1632), 160.
45. Preston, *Sermons Preached,* 105; Sibbes, "Conflict," 205, 198, 209.
46. Preston, *Covenant,* 322, 511; Sibbes, "Conflict, 223–224, 281.
47. Sibbes, "Conflict, 242.
48. Preston, *Covenant,* 12; Gouge, *Saints,* 204; Sibbes, "Conflict," 281, 255.
49. Preston, *Covenant,* 462; Cotton, *Mercie,* 39.
50. Hooker, "Carnal Hypocrit," 94; Sibbes, "Conflict," 284; Preston, *Life Eternal,* 138.
51. Preston, *Covenant,* 259.
52. Ibid., 324; Sibbes, "Conflict," 162, 177; Hooker, *Preparation,* 128.
53. Sibbes speaks of "people . . . set at liberty from . . . bondage" who yet act with "child-like service," Gouge of "Saints" as "Gods servants." Sibbes, "Conflict," 258; Gouge, *Saints,* 214.
54. Sibbes, "Conflict," 153, 154, 161, 197.
55. Ibid., 153, 154.
56. Ibid., 210.
57. Hooker, *Preparation,* 128.
58. Preston, *Covenant,* 318–319, 320, 329.
59. Ibid., 395, 184, 182, 216, 183; Sibbes, "Conflict," 265.
60. Sibbes, "Conflict," 137, 165, 139, 177, 134.
61. Ibid., 149, 196. Others largely confirm "our own hearts" and otherwise likely set us back. Ibid., 196.
62. Sibbes, "Conflict," 155, 194, 147. See also Preston, *The Saints Daily Exercise* (London, 1629).

63. "Life of Goodwin," vii–viii.
64. Hooker, *Preparation*, 194–195.
65. Ibid., 100.
66. Sibbes, "Conflict," 289.
67. Preston, *Covenant*, 5, 61.
68. Sibbes, "Conflict," 203, 222.
69. "Life of Goodwin," xiii, xii.
70. Sibbes, "Conflict," 206.
71. Preston, *Covenant*, 49.
72. "Life of Goodwin," vi, x. This difference "made so strong an impression" that it convinced him regarding a preordained plan. Ibid., vi.
73. Sibbes, "Conflict," 138.
74. Preston, *Covenant*, 3.
75. Ibid., 12, 13.
76. Ibid., 316; Sibbes, "Conflict," 212.
77. Preston, *Covenant*, 316, 331.
78. Quoted in Zaret, *Contract*, 192, 160, 161.
79. Sibbes, "Conflict," 209; Thomas Hooker, "Faithful Covenanter," in *Writings*, 202.
80. See Gouge, *Saints*, 129.
81. Preston, *Life Eternal*, 150.
82. Gouge, *Saints*, 46, 13.
83. Sibbes, "Conflict," 159, 213, 161.
84. Hooker, *Preparation*, 12.
85. Ibid., 213, 168.
86. Gouge, *Saints*, 13.
87. Cotton, *Mercie*, 36.
88. Bolton, *Directions*, 317; Sibbes, "Conflict," 138, 226.
89. Hooker, *Preparation*, 191; Preston, *Covenant*, 12, 484.
90. Sibbes, "Conflict," 157–158, 143.
91. Preston, *Covenant*, 250; Sibbes, "Conflict," 231; Cotton, *Mercie*, 116.
92. See Sibbes, "Conflict," 138, 142, 279.
93. Ibid., 138, 252, 262; Preston, *Covenant*, 313; Cotton, *Mercie*, 36.
94. See Sibbes, "Conflict," 222.
95. Ibid., 221; Thomas Hooker, "The Church's Deliverance," in *Writings*, 67.
96. Cotton, *Mercie*, 29–30, 117–118.
97. Sibbes, "Conflict," 244, 249, 261, 276; Bolton, *Directions*, 1, 18; Thomas Hooker, "The Danger of Desertion," in *Writings*, 244.
98. Bolton, *Saints*, 1; Preston, *Life Eternal*, 195.
99. Sibbes, "Conflict," 270, 251. See also Hooker, "The Church's Deliverance," 86–88.
100. Cotton, *Mercie*, 122, 119–120.
101. Preston, *Covenant*, 603, 611–612.
102. Sibbes, "Conflict," 287, 168, 250.

103. Preston, *Covenant*, 607, 202, 191.

104. Sibbes, "Conflict," 156, 243.

105. Preston, *Covenant*, 202–203, 204; Sibbes, "Conflict," 243, 160.

106. "Life of Goodwin," xii; Sibbes, "Conflict," 144, 208.

107. Preston, *Covenant*, 126.

108. Ibid., 138–139; Sibbes, "Conflict," 243.

109. Preston, *Covenant*, 133.

110. Sibbes, "Conflict," 224, 141, 209; Preston, *Covenant*, 85.

111. Robert Bolton, "Epistle Dedicatory," in *Directions*.

112. Sibbes, "Conflict," 272, 211, 283, 149, 285.

113. Ibid., 280–281, 226.

114. Ibid., 159, 156.

115. Preston, *Covenant*, 601–602, 603, 605.

116. Ibid., 261, 178.

117. Sibbes, "Conflict," 260, 250, 265. Thus, many who disavowed separatism paradoxically left England to form a "national" church elsewhere. See Hooker, "Carnal Hypocrit," 110.

118. Haller, *Puritanism*, 174. Even Christopher Hill, an ardent champion, regards the extreme as a "lunatic fringe," if one with both method and madness. Hill, *World Turned*, 113.

119. Haller, *Puritanism*, 193.

120. Haller, *Liberty*, 108.

121. John Milton, "The Tenure of Kings and Magistrates," in *The Prose of John Milton* (Garden City, N.Y., 1967), 358.

122. Hanserd Knollys, "A Glimpse of Sion's Glory," in Woodhouse, *Puritanism and Liberty*, 233.

123. John Goodwin, "Right and Might Well Met," ibid., 213.

124. John Goodwin, *Christian Theology* (London, 1836), 115, 117; William Walwyn, "The Power of Love," in *Tracts on Liberty in the Puritan Revolution, 1638–1647*, ed. William Haller, 3 vols. (New York, 1933), 2:273.

125. Goodwin, *Theology*, 141, 235.

126. Walwyn, "Love," 296.

127. Goodwin, *Theology*, 263, 296, 265.

128. Ibid., 292, 267, 410, 412, 285.

129. Walwyn, "Love," 277, 290–295.

130. Goodwin, *Theology*, 205, 116; John Lilburne, "A Worke of the Beast," in Haller, *Tracts on Liberty*, 2:23.

131. Walwyn, "Love," 294–295; Goodwin, *Theology*, 263.

132. Thomas Collier, "A Discovery of the New Creation," in Woodhouse, *Puritanism and Liberty*, 391; Oliver Cromwell (Putney Debates), ibid., 16. All citations of Putney Debates are from this source.

133. Hill, *World Turned*, 67.

134. Ibid., 172, 254, 173.

135. Haller, *Liberty*, 298.

136. Henry Ireton (Putney Debates), 50; "A Declaration of the English Army Now in Scotland, 1st Aug. 1650," in Woodhouse, *Puritanism and Liberty*, 477, 478.

137. Robert Everard (Putney Debates), 42.

138. "Declaration of English Army," 475.

139. Collier, "Discovery," 395.

140. George Joyce (Whitehall Debates), in Woodhouse, *Puritanism and Liberty*, 176. All citations of Whitehall Debates are from this source.

141. Goodwin, *Theology*, 301, 291.

142. John Saltmarsh, "Smoke in the Temple," in Woodhouse, *Puritanism and Liberty*, 280, 281, 307, 300.

143. John Goodwin, "Independency God's Verity," ibid., 186; Collier, "Discovery," 394.

144. John Goodwin, "Right and Might Well Met," in Woodhouse, *Puritanism and Liberty*, 214–215.

145. [John Wildman], "A Call to all the Soldiers of the Army by the Free People of England," ibid., 440.

146. Goodwin, *Theology*, 259, 266, 306, 234, 307.

147. Ibid., 214, 291, 301.

148. Walwyn, "Love," 296; *The Ancient Bounds*, in Woodhouse, *Puritanism and Liberty*, 248; quoted in Woodhouse's introduction, ibid., 69.

149. Roger Williams, "The Bloody Tenet of Persecution," in Woodhouse, *Puritanism and Liberty*; 285; Milton, quoted in Haller, *Liberty*, 54.

150. William Goffe (Putney Debates), 20, 40; "Declaration of English Army," 475, 477; Collier, "Discovery," 390, 393, 394.

151. Saltmarsh, "Smoke," 184.

152. Walwyn, "Love," 282–283, 297.

153. William Ames, *Conscience with the Power and Cares Thereof* (Norwood, N.J., 1975), bk. 1, 55. See also William Bradshaw, "English Puritanisme," in *English Puritanism and Other Works* (Westmead, Hants., 1972), 3.

154. John Robinson, "A Justification of Separation," in *The Works of John Robinson* (Boston, 1851), 505, 473, 69.

155. Henry Robinson, "Liberty of Conscience," in Haller, *Tracts on Liberty*, 3:112, 115, 155–156.

156. Richard Overton, "The Araignement of Mr. Persecution," ibid., 3:224.

157. Williams, "Persecution," 266, 281–282, 247.

158. Goodwin, *Theology*, 215.

159. Quoted in Hill, *World Turned*, 166.

160. Goodwin, *Theology*, 116, 114, 186, 117.

161. Ibid., 406, 401, 396.

162. Quoted in Hill, *World Turned*, 137.

163. Goodwin, *Theology*, 197, 185. He later found predestination "ever . . . gravelish in my mouth, and corroding and fretting to my bowels." Quoted in Samuel Dunn, "The Life of John Goodwin," ibid., 22.

164. Ibid., 215, 411, 412, 197, 185, 424, 428, 425.

165. Milton, "Kings," 371; Milton, "Areopagitica," in *Prose of Milton,* 296.

166. Goodwin, *Theology,* 406, 424.

167. Goodwin, *Theology,* 372, 375, 216.

168. Hill, *World Turned,* 153.

169. Saltmarsh, "Smoke," 185.

170. Collier, "Discovery," 393.

171. Walwyn, "Love," 294, 282.

172. Ibid., 294, 289.

173. "Declaration of English Army," 476.

174. Haller, *Liberty,* 334.

175. Cromwell (Putney Debates), 9.

176. "Large Petition of the Levellers," in Haller, *Tracts on Liberty,* 3:399.

177. Ireton (Putney Debates), 26.

178. Goodwin, *Theology,* 200, 201, 203, 180.

179. Collier, "Discovery," 390, 391.

180. See Woodhouse, introduction to *Puritanism and Liberty,* 45, 65–66.

181. Ireton (Putney Debates), 151.

182. Goodwin, *Theology,* 234, 203; Walwyn, "Love," 288, 293.

183. Cromwell (Putney Debates), 16; Thomas Rainborough (Putney Debates), 61.

184. John Lilburne, "Englands Birth-right Justified," in Haller, *Tracts on Liberty,* 3:303, 295.

185. Collier, "Discovery," 395, 393.

186. Woodhouse, introduction to *Puritanism and Liberty,* 65.

187. Haller, *Puritanism,* 142, 141.

188. Milton, "Areopagitica," 329; John Milton, "Defensio Secunda," in Woodhouse, *Puritanism and Liberty,* 231.

189. Milton, "Areopagitica," 330–331.

190. Milton, "Kings," 347; John Milton, "Of Civil Power in Ecclesiastical Causes," in Woodhouse, *Puritanism and Liberty,* 226, 227, 228.

191. John Milton, "Pro Populo Anglicano Defensio," in Woodhouse, *Puritanism and Liberty,* 230.

192. Milton, "Kings," 347; Milton, "Power," 226, 228; Milton, "Defensio Secunda," 231.

193. Milton, "Defensio Secunda," 232; Milton, "Pro Populo," 229.

194. Milton, *Paradise Lost* (New York, 1985), 96, 103, 97.

195. Ibid., 307.

196. Ibid., 303.

197. See ibid., 293.

198. Ibid., 136, 115.

199. Ibid., 299, 293; cf. bks. 10, 12.

200. Martin Luther King, Jr., "Letter from Birmingham Jail," provides an interesting parallel.

201. Milton, *Paradise Lost,* 39, 131.

202. Ibid., 264, 307, 250, 251.

203. Ibid., 266.

204. "The Book of Q," in Burton Mack, *The Lost Gospel: The Book of Q and Christian Origins* (San Francisco, 1993), 96.

205. Milton, *Paradise Lost,* 306.

206. Ibid., 308.

207. John Goodwin, "Anti-Cavalierisme," in Haller, *Tracts on Liberty,* 2:222–223, 268–269, 263, 262.

208. Walwyn, "Love," 298.

209. Rainborough (Putney Debates), 13–14; Cromwell (Putney Debates), 15; "Declaration of English Army," 475.

210. Collier, "Discovery," 395.

211. Goodwin, *Treatise,* 327, 138.

212. Haller, *Puritanism,* 215.

213. Walwyn, "Love," 282.

214. Quoted in Hill, *World Turned,* 177.

215. Knollys, "Sion's Glory," 238; Saltmarsh, "Smoke," 180; Haller, *Puritanism,* 203.

216. Goodwin, *Theology,* 291, 293, 301–302.

217. Goodwin, "Anti-Cavalierisme," 231.

218. Cromwell (Putney Debates), 46, 49.

219. Ireton (Putney Debates), 21; Buff-Coat [Robert Everard] (Putney Debates), 36; Edward Sexby (Putney Debates), 69.

220. Rutherford, *Lex, Rex,* 212.

221. John Lilburne, "The Free-man's Freedom Vindicated," in Woodhouse, *Puritanism and Liberty,* 317. See Putney Debates, 53–56.

222. Lilburne, "Freedom Vindicated," 317; Rainborough (Putney Debates), 61.

223. Lilburne, "Freedom Vindicated," 317; Rainborough (Putney Debates), 56, 53. The question debated was the nature and extent of this equality, whether including political, economic, and legal rights, at the extreme demanding full political democracy and full distributional equity.

224. Saltmarsh, "Smoke," 185.

225. Goodwin, "Anti-Cavalierisme," 234, 221–222.

226. Captain Clarke (Whitehall Debates), 141; Captain Bishop (Putney Debates), 82.

227. Goodwin, "Anti-Cavalierisme," 256–257.

228. Putney Debates, 4, 24, 18, 12, 16, 23.

229. Ireton (Putney Debates), 29.

230. Putney Debates, 3, 89, 82, 121.

231. Everard (Putney Debates), 83.

232. See "Large Petition of the Levellers," in Woodhouse, *Puritanism and Liberty,* 318–319; Richard Overton, "An Appeal from the Commons to the Free People," ibid., 335–336.

233. John Wildman (Putney Debates), 24.

234. John Clarke (Putney Debates), 38; Cromwell (Putney Debates), 103, 105.

235. Goodwin, *Theology*, 259.
236. Hill, *World Turned*, 165; Thomas Hobbes, *Leviathan* (New York, 1962), 64.
237. William Dell, "The Way of True Peace and Unity," in Woodhouse, *Puritanism and Liberty*, 312.
238. Quoted in Woodhouse, introduction, ibid., 26.
239. Goffe (Putney Debates), 100–101; Cromwell (Putney Debates), 104.
240. Hobbes, *Leviathan*, 64.
241. Williams, "Persecution," 267.
242. Ibid., 269.
243. Rainborough (Putney Debates), 32.
244. Cromwell (Putney Debates), 37.
245. Joshua Sprigge (Whitehall Debates), 145.
246. Rainborough (Putney Debates), 33.
247. See Haller, *Tracts on Liberty*, 2:220, 224–225, 236–237, 257–258, 265; 3:377–378.
248. Wildman (Putney Debates), 122; Sprigge (Whitehall Debates), 136.
249. Thomas Goodwin and Phillip Nye, "To the Reader," in Thomas Hooker, *The Application of Redemption* (Cornhil, 1657), unpaginated.
250. Thomas Shepard, "A Wholesome Caveat for a Time of Liberty," in *The Works of Thomas Shepard* (Boston, 1967), 3:295.
251. Stephen Marshall, *The Right Understanding of the Times* (n.p., 1647), 36; see also Tom Webster, *Godly Clergy in Early Stuart England: The Caroline Puritan Movement, c. 1620–1643* (Cambridge, 1997).
252. Shepard, "Caveat," 295, 293.
253. Ibid., 336.
254. Williams, "Persecution," 267; John Goodwin, "Independency God's Verity," in Woodhouse, *Puritanism and Liberty*, 186; Williams, "Persecution," 267; *Ancient Bounds*, 259.
255. Milton's suggestive though utterly impractical response is the act setting events in motion—God's abdication to Jesus. God, traditionally distant leader of the obedient state, is replaced by a new style of leadership. Jesus, with "Armed Saints," was equipped for governing over a divided, individualistic world unleashed by modernity. He is a Son to deal with rebellious sons, an agent himself who understands agency, God with a human face. Milton, *Paradise Lost*, 139.
256. Cromwell (Putney Debates), 17, 8, 16.
257. *Ancient Bounds*, 25.
258. Putney Debates, 7—8.
259. Hill, *World Turned*, 292, 298.
260. Putney Debates, 20, 102, 127, 23
261. Ireton (Whitehall Debates), 131.
262. See Hill, *World Turned*, 299–300, 306–307.
263. Haller, *Liberty*, 154.

4. Thomas Hobbes and the Founding of the Liberal Politics of Agency

1. Laski, *Liberalism*, 11, 13; Diggins, *Lost Soul*, 31.
2. Laski, *Liberalism*, 14, 12, 79, 78.
3. See discussion in Chapter 1.
4. Hobbes, *Leviathan*, 506.
5. Ibid., 506, 157–158.
6. Ibid., 251, 158.
7. Thomas Hobbes, *Behemoth*, in *The English Works of Thomas Hobbes*, ed. Sir William Molesworth (London, 1840), 6:168, 257.
8. *Leviathan*, 99.
9. *Behemoth*, 196, 166.
10. Ibid., 167, 195; *Leviathan*, 249, 253.
11. *Behemoth*, 168–169.
12. Ibid., 169, 282.
13. *Leviathan*, 132, 31.
14. *Leviathan*, 80, 132; Thomas Hobbes, *De Cive*, in *Man and Citizen*, ed. Bernard Gert (Garden City, N.Y., 1972), 307. See also Don Herzog, *Happy Slaves: A Critique of Consent Theory* (Chicago, 1989), 79.
15. *Leviathan*, 131.
16. *De Cive*, 110n, 100.
17. *Leviathan*, 509.
18. Thomas Hobbes, *De Corpore*, in *The English Works of Thomas Hobbes*, ed. Sir William Molesworth (London, 1839), 1:ix.
19. *Leviathan*, 511.
20. Ibid., 511; *De Cive*, 90–91, 92, 98.
21. *De Cive*, 98, 92.
22. *Leviathan*, 511, 509, 248.
23. *Behemoth*, 166.
24. See Leo Strauss, *The Political Philosophy of Hobbes* (Chicago, 1963).
25. Thomas Hobbes, *Thucydides* (New Brunswick, N.J., 1975), 4.
26. Thomas Hobbes, "The Whole Art of Rhetoric," in *English Works*, 6:437, 429. See also Arlene W. Saxonhouse, "Hobbes and the Beginnings of Modern Political Thought," in Thomas Hobbes, *Three Discourses* (Chicago, 1995), 143–145.
27. "Rhetoric," 435–436.
28. *Leviathan*, 98.
29. *De Cive*, 225, 104, 234–235.
30. Ibid., 104, 234, 228, 113.
31. Ibid., 113, 225.
32. See, e.g., *Leviathan*, 143–146.
33. Ibid., 142, 140.
34. *De Cive*, 238–239, 103, 96.
35. Thomas Hobbes, *Elements of Law* (New York, 1969), xvii. Quentin Skinner dis-

cusses Hobbes's shift from science to rhetoric in *Leviathan* and his early attraction to rhetoric in *Reason and Rhetoric in the Philosophy of Hobbes* (Cambridge, 1996).

36. *De Cive*, 35.
37. *Elements of Law*, 17–18.
38. Bernard Gert, introduction to Hobbes, *Man and Citizen*, 3.
39. *De Cive*, 119, 113, 115.
40. See Skinner, *Reason*. For *Leviathan* as imaginative creation, see Herzog, *Slaves*, 99–101.
41. "Rhetoric," 423, 428, 473, 474.
42. *De Cive*, 310, 95, 97; cf. 224.
43. *Leviathan*, 90, 93, 51. "TRUE RELIGION" is given no content.
44. Ibid., 94, 261, 503, 61, 59.
45. *De Cive*, 112.
46. *Behemoth*, 220.
47. *De Cive*, 97, 93, 249, 96, 224, 245.
48. Ibid., 97, 93, 155, 175, 184, 276.
49. Ibid., 93, 184, 115, 175.
50. Ibid., 112.
51. Ibid., 117, 110n, 100.
52. Ibid., 184, 224, 89.
53. Ibid., 249, 246, 231, 174n, 150, 175.
54. Ibid., 384, 252, 332, 231.
55. *Leviathan*, 437, 101, 93.
56. "Rhetoric," 474.
57. The irrationality in Hobbes's theory is discussed in Stephen Holmes, *Passions and Constraint: On the Theory of Liberal Democracy* (Chicago, 1995).
58. *Leviathan*, 19, 236.
59. Ibid., 46, 248, 158, 45.
60. Thomas Hobbes, *Human Nature*, in *Body, Man, and Citizen* (New York, 1962), 215, 228.
61. Ibid., 188, 190, 183.
62. Ibid., 21, 20.
63. Ibid., 21, 22, 85. Blindness is often taken as the human condition. *Body, Man, and Citizen*, 53, 203; *De Cive*, 293.
64. *Leviathan*, 27, 24, 23, 25, 30, 31, 29.
65. Ibid., 101, 510, 20.
66. Ibid., 131.
67. Ibid., 103, 72, 80.
68. Ibid., 22.
69. Thomas Hobbes, "Of Liberty and Necessity," in *Body, Man, and Citizen*, 271; Thomas Hobbes, *De Corpore*, ibid., 117.
70. *De Corpore*, 121, 124; "Of Liberty," 272.
71. *Leviathan*, 23.

72. "Of Liberty," 273.
73. Ibid., 273, 259, 269, 261.
74. *Leviathan*, 160; "Of Liberty," 258.
75. *Leviathan*, 100; *De Cive*, 224.
76. *De Cive*, 98–99.
77. *De Corpore*, 72, 78, 74.
78. *De Corpore*, xiii.
79. *De Cive*, 92.
80. Ibid., 93, 250.
81. *Leviathan*, 129, 57, 42.
82. "Of Liberty," 248.
83. *Leviathan*, 45, 100, 64, 31.
84. Ibid., 45, 129.
85. *Elements*, 240, 237.
86. *Leviathan*, 19, 118.
87. *Elements*, 312.
88. *Leviathan*, 237.
89. Ibid., 57.
90. Ibid., 20, 62.
91. *De Cive*, 99.
92. *Leviathan*, 141, 22, 89.
93. Ibid., 87–88, 31.
94. Ibid., 274–275, 317.
95. Ibid., 239, 85–86, 64.
96. Ibid., 36–37.
97. Ibid., 56, 41, 62.
98. Ibid., 40.
99. Ibid., 48, 123.
100. Ibid., 55, 238–239.
101. Ibid., 99, 80, 63, 101.
102. Ibid., 98, 81.
103. Ibid., 120, 20, 101.
104. Ibid., 100–101. One week's newspaper references included Anthony Lake's characterization of his Senate confirmation hearings, a review of novels of urban violence, Mao's experiment with China, Thomas Friedman on the war in Albania.
105. See ibid., 102, 141.
106. Ibid., 104, 102.
107. Thomas Hobbes, *De Homine*, in Gert, *Man and Citizen*, 65.
108. *Leviathan*, 102, 120, 113.
109. Ibid., 159, 105.
110. One exception to the neglect of chap. 16 is Hanna Fenichel Pitkin, *The Concept of Representation* (Berkeley, 1967), chap. 2.
111. *Leviathan*, 125.

112. Ibid., 127, 105, 104.
113. Ibid., 127, 132.
114. Pitkin resolves the issue by suggesting that "somehow we have been tricked," that "something has gone wrong" and "representation" has "disappeared while our backs were turned," rather than asking the reasons for the trick, that is, for the liberal "inducement" to defer to one's created author. Pitkin, *Representation*, 34, 37.
115. *Leviathan*, 499, 213, 216.
116. *De Homine*, 76; *Leviathan*, 364.
117. *De Cive*, 149; *Leviathan*, 216.
118. See *Leviathan*, 164, 105.
119. Ibid., 132.
120. Ibid., 373.
121. Ibid., 491, 123, 364.
122. *De Cive*, 268.
123. See *Leviathan*, 117, 105.
124. Ibid., 131, 19. Herzog, neglecting psychological constructs, regards the sovereign as "a mirage." Herzog, *Slaves*, 100.
125. *Leviathan*, 132, 137, 239, 138.
126. Ibid., 139; cf. chap. 30.
127. See ibid., 220.
128. Ibid., 247, 136.
129. Ibid., 247. Hobbes's "wish" was that "supreme authority, would so temper themselves as to commit no wrong, but only minding their charges, contain themselves within the limits of the natural and divine laws." *De Cive*, 194n.
130. *Leviathan*, 159, 104, 120.
131. Ibid., 160; *De Cive*, 268.
132. *Leviathan*, 255–256.
133. *De Cive*, 260.
134. *Leviathan*, 160, 161.
135. *De Cive*, 169.
136. *Leviathan*, 255, 185. In *De Homine* and *De Cive*, Hobbes strenuously affirms new virtues of the market age, calling the "love of riches . . . greater than wisdom." *De Homine*, 49. "Work" is "good . . . truly a motive for life," while "idleness is torture. . . . There is nothing more afflicts the mind of man than *poverty*." *De Homine*, 51; *De Cive*, 251. In *Leviathan*, the escalating political crisis meant that individualism needed no encouragement. The emphasis was blockading all channels of public activity. The personal drive for "necessary things," to rather "naturally mind [one's] *own private*, than the *public* business," which directed citizens to "quietly enjoy that wealth which they have purchased by their own industry," had new usefulness. *De Cive*, 252, 232, 260.
137. See *Leviathan*, chaps. 26–28.
138. *De Cive*, 264.
139. *Leviathan*, 256, 253, 167.

140. Ibid., 248.
141. Ibid., 137, 247, 503, 253.
142. Ibid., 249, 251, 253, 503.
143. Ibid., 247.
144. Ibid., 250; see 155–156, 262.
145. See ibid., 140.
146. Ibid., 236.
147. Ibid., 124.
148. See ibid., 73.
149. Ibid., 237, 118–119, 115, 136.
150. *De Homine*, 55, 54, 64–65; *De Cive*, 265. The goal of "punishment" is a renewed commitment to orderly motion. *Leviathan*, 229.
151. *De Homine*, 65, 68, 70, 83, 76.
152. *Leviathan*, 123, 206.
153. *De Cive*, 258.
154. See Margaret C. Jacob, *The Newtonians and the English Revolution, 1689–1720* (Ithaca, N.Y., 1976).
155. Adam Smith, *Theory of Moral Sentiments* (Indianapolis, 1982), 85, 184, 212. Hobbes is summarily dispensed with for failing to grasp the internal "faculty . . . antecedent" to all coercion by "law or positive institution," that is, "reason," as the source of "virtue and vice." Ibid., 318, 319.
156. G. H. Mead, *Mind, Self, and Society* (Chicago, 1967), 277.
157. *Leviathan*, 160, 163, 215.
158. Ibid., 237.

5. John Locke and the Mythic Society of Free Agents

1. John Locke, *An Essay Concerning Human Understanding*, vol. 1 (New York, 1959), vol. 2 (London, 1964), 2:280, 296 (hereafter *Essay*).
2. John Locke, *On the Reasonableness of Christianity* (Chicago, 1965), 191; *Essay*, 1:29.
3. *Essay*, 1:25, 31–32, 30.
4. Ibid., 2:287; 1:31, 29.
5. Ibid., 1:29, 61, 125, 46.
6. Minogue, *Mind* 39, 25, 30.
7. Voltaire, *Philosophical Letters*, 54.
8. John Locke, *The Second Treatise of Government* (Indianapolis, 1952), 32, 31, 33; Laski, *Liberalism*, 78; *Essay*, 2:293, 295.
9. Peter Laslett, introduction to John Locke, *Two Treatises of Government* (New York, 1963), 95, 99.
10. *Essay*, 1:145.
11. Ibid., 1:29; 2:282. On the limited use of natural law, see ibid., 1:66–71; Laslett, introduction to *Two Treatises*, 93–95; Minogue, *Mind*, 39.
12. *Reasonableness*, 170–171.

13. *Essay,* 1:31; *Reasonableness,* 191.

14. *Essay,* 2:292.

15. *Reasonableness,* 9–10.

16. Wolin, *Politics,* 335–337.

17. John Locke, *Some Thoughts Concerning Education,* in *The Educational Writings of John Locke,* ed. James L. Axtell (Cambridge, 1968), 325, 114 (hereafter *Education*).

18. Laslett, introduction to *Two Treatises,* 105.

19. Letter to Mr. Thomas Man Randolph (May 30, 1790), in *The Life and Selected Writings of Thomas Jefferson,* ed. Adrienne Koch and William Peden (New York, 1944), 497.

20. Hartz, *Liberal,* 106.

21. *Second Treatise,* 4, 5–6.

22. Ibid., 44, 21, 20.

23. Ibid., 44.

24. Ibid., 17, 19, 18.

25. Ibid., 29, 28.

26. Ibid., 31, 27.

27. Ibid., 6, 7, 16.

28. Ibid., 32–33, 6, 20.

29. Ibid., 29, 31, 28.

30. See David Hume, *Political Essays* (Indianapolis, 1953).

31. *Second Treatise,* 6, 54, 50.

32. Ibid., 126, 139.

33. Ibid., 77, 76.

34. Ibid., 20, 71.

35. Ibid., 26, 17, 28.

36. Ibid., 25–26, 77, 73.

37. Ibid., 71.

38. *Education,* 112.

39. Ibid., 112, 197.

40. *Second Treatise,* 26, 27, 29.

41. See ibid., 68, 41.

42. Ibid., 65, 56, 71, 9, 72, 68. Locke's use of the narrative of origins to legitimate existing society would, though not generally recognized, influence his use in the American colonies to defend established local government, a role greater than the one typically accorded him as a defender of liberty.

43. Ibid., 21–22, 71, 68.

44. *Education,* 197; *Second Treatise,* 23.

45. *Second Treatise,* 10.

46. See ibid.

47. *Second Treatise,* 32.

48. *Essay,* 1:67–68.

49. Ibid., 1:70.

50. Ibid., 1:69; 2:247–248.
51. Ibid., 2:290; *Reasonableness*, 179, 193.
52. *Essay*, 2:290.
53. Ibid., 1:23, 43, 73n1, 125.
54. Ibid., 1:125, 86, 78.
55. Ibid., 1:71, 77.
56. Ibid., 1:45, 44, 31; 2:287.
57. Ibid., 2:291.
58. Ibid., 2:166.
59. Ibid., 2:291.
60. *Reasonableness*, 181, 184. While rejecting the doctrinal partiality and bias of each "peculiar sect or party" which sabotage consensual Christianity, he is adamant only that the triumph of Protestantism is part—and proof—of the narrative of the development of human agency. Locke provides a progressive Protestant account of the development in Judeo-Christianity from the religion based on the covenant or "law of works" to the "new covenant" based on "the law of faith." Ibid., 100, 10, 128. In Locke's model of religious evolution, individuals move from one "standing and fixed measure of life and death" to another, from one universal "moral" system with "weak and beggarly elements" to a moral system which is higher, "more full and strict." Ibid., 8, 13.
61. Ibid., 178.
62. Ibid., 186.
63. *Second Treatise*, 23.
64. See *Essay*, 1:487–535.
65. Ibid., 1:236; 2:167, 169, 168, 166. As if individuals were easily "to search and follow the clearer evidence and greater probability," Locke builds a pathway through the realms of confusion from the "clear and distinct perception" of "simple ideas," to "*clear* and *determinate*" ideas, to "compounded" ideas with "a *necessary* connexion and dependence one upon another." Ibid., 2:280; 1:145, 204, 237. The system, it turns out, depends not on universal mental operations but on "probability," or how "constant" and regular specific experiences are and the degree to which the same result is "attested by the concurrent report" of all "that mention it." Ibid., 2:250, 255. In other words, certainty arises largely from habit.
66. Ibid., 2:280, 289.
67. *Second Treatise*, 42, 53, 60–61, 64, 43. To defend the popular will in the Glorious Revolution, Locke must trace all authority to a consensual transfer of power, including a consensual justifiable initial transfer. This entails an original "golden age" when parental prerogative was judged by the offspring "fitter to be trusted" and "the ablest and most likely to rule well over them," before "monarchs" by "chance, contrivance, or occasions" gave in to "ambition and luxury" and "tyrannical domination." Ibid., 64, 59–60, 43, 61.
68. Ibid., 31–34.
69. Ibid., 67–68, 31.

70. Ibid., 38, 32, 36.
71. Ibid., 33, 32.
72. *Education*, 137–138, 114–115.
73. Ibid., 139, 214, 207.
74. Ibid., 146, 148, 150, 145.
75. Ibid., 138, 145, 147, 148, 139, 177.
76. Ibid., 148.
77. Ibid., 137, 138, 148, 207–208, 184.
78. Ibid., 140, 211, 144.
79. Ibid., 145, 178, 205, 146, 219.
80. Ibid., 182, 171, 164, 143, 145.
81. Ibid., 174.
82. Ibid., 151, 143, 208 (emphasis added).
83. Ibid., 173, 172, 174, 154, 179.
84. Ibid., 273–274, 275, 158, 309–310, 157, 163.
85. Ibid., 157–158, 168, 237, 314, 148, 288, 296.
86. Ibid., 162, 191, 253, 314, 153.
87. Ibid., 152–155.
88. Ibid., 198, 234, 235, 244, 192, 249, 247, 246, 241–242, 200–202, 232, 216, 174, 210, 238.
89. Ibid., 148, 246, 146, 160, 161.
90. Ibid., 194, 195, 146, 163, 321, 323, 197.
91. Ibid., 152.
92. Ibid., 143, 147, 184, 145, 205, 146.
93. Ibid., 211, 201, 173, 159, 145, 146, 157, 174, 191.
94. Ibid., 157, 180, 205.
95. Ibid., 246.

6. The Great Awakening and the Emergent Culture of Agency

1. Ralph Waldo Emerson, "Concord Hymn," in *Selected Prose and Poetry*, ed. Reginald L. Cook (New York, 1963), 427; Wood, *Radicalism*, 368, 336.
2. Thomas Paine, *Common Sense*, in *Selected Writings of Thomas Paine*, ed. Richard Emory Roberts (New York, 1945), 40, 30, 29. Paine called in *Common Sense* for "an open and determined DECLARATION FOR INDEPENDENCE." Ibid., 35.
3. Bernard Bailyn, *The Ideological Origins of the American Revolution* (Cambridge, Mass., 1967), 230.
4. Beard suggested this vision was "fulfilled in a surprising measure." Charles A. Beard and Mary Beard, *The Rise of American Civilization* (New York, 1927), 1:289.
5. John Higham, "America's Three Reconstructions," *New York Review of Books*, November 6, 1997, 56.
6. Stephen A. Marini, *Radical Sects of Revolutionary New England* (Cambridge,

Mass., 1982), 172; Charles L. Cohen, "The Post-Puritan Paradigm of Early American Religious History," *William and Mary Quarterly*, 3d ser., no. 54 (1997), 712; William McLoughlin, "The Role of Religion in the Revolution: Liberty of Conscience and Cultural Cohesion in the New Nation," in *Essays on the American Revolution*, ed. Stephen G. Kurtz and James H. Hutson (Chapel Hill, 1973), 198; Alan Heimert, *Religion and the American Mind: From the Great Awakening to the Revolution* (Cambridge, Mass., 1966), 14, 15.

7. See, e.g., Henry F. May, *The Enlightenment in America* (New York, 1976), xii–xiii; Gordon S. Wood, *The Creation of the American Republic, 1776–1787* (New York, 1969), 8, 17; McLoughlin, "Religion," 199, 202.

8. See Bailyn, *Origins*; Wood, *Radicalism*; Barry Shain, *The Myth of American Individualism: The Protestant Origins of American Political Thought* (Princeton, 1994), 195–196; Nathan Hatch, *The Sacred Cause of Liberty* (New Haven, 1977), 3, 58.

9. See citations in Timothy D. Hall, *Contested Boundaries: Itinerancy and the Reshaping of the Colonial American Religious World* (Durham, N.C., 1994), 145n 33.

10. Two recent summaries of the scholarship are Allen Guelzo, "God's Designs: The Literature of the Colonial Revivals of Religion, 1735–1760," in *New Directions in American Religious History*, ed. Harry S. Stout and D. G. Hart (Oxford, 1997); and Gordon S. Wood, "Religion and the American Revolution," ibid. The latter is in part an apologia for Wood's earlier neglect.

11. Wood, "Religion," 175.

12. Perry Miller, "From the Covenant to the Revival," in *The Shaping of American Religion*, vol. 1, *Religion in American Life*, ed. James W. Smith and A. Leland Jamison (Princeton, 1961), 343.

13. Clark, *Language*, 29 (emphasis added).

14. Ruth Bloch, "Religion, Literary Sentimentalism, and Popular Revolutionary Ideology," in *Religion in a Revolutionary Age*, ed. Ronald Hoffman and Peter J. Albert (Charlottesville, Va., 1994), 312.

15. Patricia U. Bonomi, *Under the Cope of Heaven: Religion, Society, and Politics in Colonial America* (New York, 1986), 6, 7. See also Roger Finke and Rodney Stark, *The Churching of America, 1776–1990: Winners and Losers in Our Religious Economy* (New Brunswick, N.J. 1992).

16. Wood, "Religion," 181.

17. Cohen, "Paradigm," 697, 699, 721, 722; Guelzo, "Designs," 148, 164.

18. Wood, "Religion," 198, 173.

19. Cohen, "Paradigm," 722.

20. Clark, *Language*, 13.

21. C. G. Goen, *Revivalism and Separatism in New England, 1740–1800* (Middletown, Conn., 1987), 200. See also Edwin Scott Gaustad, *The Great Awakening in New England* (Chicago, 1968).

22. See citations in Hall, *Boundaries*, 141n2.

23. May, *Enlightenment*, xii. The irony was that interpretations went in one direction, the populace of revolutionary America in another. Ibid., xvii–xviii.

24. See, e.g., Beard and Beard, *Rise*, 1:150; Hatch, *Cause*, 45–46. McLoughlin con-

cluded from his early efforts to study colonial dissenters "how neglected the Baptists (and other dissenters) have been despite all that has been written about early New England." William McLoughlin, *New England Dissent, 1630–1833* (Cambridge, Mass., 1971), 1:xvi.

25. Hatch, *Cause,* 3, 145n16.

26. Marini, *Sects,* 172. See Philip F. Gura, *A Glimpse of Sion's Glory: Puritan Radicalism in New England, 1620–1660* (Middletown, Conn., 1984), 327. On difficulties confronting a sectarian American history, see Martin E. Marty, *Righteous Empire: The Protestant Experience in America* (New York, 1970); Rhys Isaac, *The Transformation of Virginia, 1740–1790* (New York, 1982).

27. Butler's revisionist argument reflects this confusion. Jon Butler, "Enthusiasm Described and Descried: The Great Awakening as Interpretive Fiction," *Journal of American History* 69 (September 1982), 310–311.

28. Wood, "Religion," 198.

29. Hall, *Boundaries,* 138, 9, 2.

30. Isaac Backus, *A History of New England,* 2 vols. (Newton, Mass., 1871), 2:232.

31. Benjamin Franklin, *Poor Richard's Almanack* (Garden City, N.Y., n.d.), 4.

32. William Bradford, *Of Plymouth Plantation* (New York, 1981), 357, 356; John Winthrop, "A Modell of Christian Charity," in *Winthrop Papers,* 5 vols. (Boston, 1929–1947), 2:295.

33. Knight, *Orthodoxies,* 23, 4.

34. Bradford, *Plymouth,* 351.

35. Winthrop, "Modell," 283, 288; John Winthrop, "Little Speech on Liberty" (to the General Court), July 3, 1645, in *The History of New England from 1630 to 1649,* ed. James Savage, 2 vols. (Boston, 1853), 2:280–281.

36. Harry S. Stout, *The New England Soul: Preaching and Religious Culture in Colonial New England* (New York, 1986), 20, 22, 7.

37. See Michael Zuckerman, *Peaceable Kingdoms: New England Towns in the Eighteenth Century* (New York, 1970); Sacvan Bercovitch, *The Puritan Origins of the American Self* (New Haven, 1975); Timothy H. Breen and Stephen Foster, "The Puritans' Greatest Achievement: A Study of Social Cohesion in Seventeenth-Century Massachusetts," *Journal of American History* 60 (June 1975).

38. Knight, *Orthodoxies,* 14.

39. Thomas Shepard, *A Defence of the Answer made unto the Nine Questions or Positions Sent from New-England* (London, 1648), 4. See also David S. Lovejoy, *Religious Enthusiasm in the New World: Heresy to Revolution* (Cambridge, Mass., 1985), 63–64.

40. Increase Mather, *The Life and Death of that Reverend Man of God, Mr. Richard Mather* (Cambridge, Mass., 1670), 11; Cotton Mather, "A General Introduction," in Miller, *American Puritans,* 63.

41. *John Winthrop's Journal "History of New England," 1630–1649,* ed. James Kendall Hosmer (New York, 1908), 2:84.

42. Thomas Hooker, *The Application of Redemption: The Ninth and Tenth Books* (London, 1657), bk. 10, 53, 65, 455.

43. *The Diary of Michael Wigglesworth, 1653–1657,* ed. Edmund S. Morgan (New York, 1965), 47, 81, 13, 7.

44. Bradford, *Plymouth,* 55.

45. Hooker, *Application,* bk. 10, 63; Cotton Mather, *Magnalia Christi Americana,* in *Selections from Cotton Mather,* ed. Kenneth B. Murdock (New York, 1965), 12; Cotton Mather, *An Essay to Do Good* (Boston, 1845), 124.

46. Mather, *Magnalia,* 5; Edward Johnson, *Wonder-Working Providence of Sion's Savior in New England, 1628–1651* (New York, 1910), 25.

47. Johnson, *Providence,* 53; Shepard, *Defence,* 3; Bradford, *Plymouth,* 5, 6.

48. Donald Weber, *Rhetoric and History in Revolutionary New England* (New York, 1988), 16.

49. Philemon Robbins, "An Ordination Sermon," quoted ibid.; Thomas Shepard, "To the Reader," in Peter Bulkeley, *The Gospel-Covenant* (London, 1651), unpaginated (emphasis added).

50. Bradford, *Plymouth,* 34, 35, 37.

51. John Cotton, *An Exposition upon the Thirteenth Chapter of the Revelation* (London, 1655), 72; Thomas Hooker, "Hartford Election Sermon," in Miller, *American Puritans,* 89.

52. *Connecticut Records,* May 15, 1676, 2:281, quoted in James Axtell, *The School upon a Hill* (New York, 1974), 121; Bradford, *Plymouth,* 57.

53. Hooker, "Election Sermon," 89.

54. Winthrop, *Journal,* 2:83.

55. Stout, *Soul,* 24, 41.

56. Cotton, *Exposition,* 72; Stephen Buckingham, *Moses and Aaron,* quoted in Richard L. Bushman, *From Puritan to Yankee: Character and the Social Order in Connecticut, 1690–1765* (New York, 1967), 5.

57. Thomas Shepard, "1638 Election Sermon," quoted in Axtell, *School,* 142; *The New England Primer,* quoted ibid., 144.

58. Winthrop, "Little Speech," 280; John Woodward, quoted in Bushman, *Puritan,* 10, 12.

59. Stout, *Soul,* 26.

60. Winthrop, "Modell," 283; Johnson, *Providence,* quoted in Bercovitch, *Puritan Origins,* 126; Urian Oakes, *The Soveraign Efficacy of Divine Providence* (Boston, 1682), 6, 18.

61. Stout, *Soul,* 7.

62. Bulkeley, *Gospel-Covenant,* 15.

63. Stout, *Soul,* 54; Nathaniel Eells, quoted ibid., 162.

64. See "The Examination of Mrs. Anne Hutchinson at the Court at Newtown," in *The Antinomian Controversy, 1636–1638: A Documentary History,* ed. David D. Hall (Middletown, Conn., 1968), 311–348.

65. Johnson, *Providence,* 53; Shepard, *Defence,* 3; Winthrop, "Modell," 295.

66. James W. Jones, *The Shattered Synthesis: New England Puritanism before the Great Awakening* (New Haven, 1973), ix. See also Perry Miller, *The New England Mind: From Colony to Province* (Boston, 1961), 57–67.

67. See Patricia U. Bonomi, "Religious Dissent and the Case for American Exceptionalism," in Hoffman and Albert, *Religion in a Revolutionary Age*.

68. Bushman, *Puritan*, 143.

69. Winthrop, *Journal*, 2:228; Bradford, *Plymouth*, 133–134.

70. Bernard Bailyn, *Education in the Forming of American Society* (New York, 1960), 34, 25; Franklin, *Almanack*, 28.

71. Axtell, *School*, 287.

72. Bulkeley, *Gospel-Covenant*, 16.

73. Gura, *Glimpse*, 5. Ruth Bloch notes that these origins have not been well developed, in *Visionary Republic: Millennial Themes in American Thought, 1756–1800* (Cambridge, 1985), 3.

74. Gura, *Glimpse*, 4–5.

75. Cohen, "Paradigm," 710.

76. Johnson, *Providence*, quoted in Gura, *Glimpse*, 326.

77. See Thomas J. Curry, *The First Freedoms: Church and State in America to the Passage of the First Amendment* (New York, 1985).

78. Quoted in McLoughlin, *Dissent*, 70, 67.

79. Ibid., 100.

80. See Goen, *Revivalism*, 186–188; Gary Nash, *The Urban Crucible: Social Change, Political Consciousness, and the Origins of the American Revolution* (Cambridge, Mass., 1979).

81. Goen, *Revivalism*, 130; Ebenezer Frothingham, *The Articles of Faith and Practice* (Newport, 1750), 340.

82. McLoughlin, *Dissent*, 159; Marini, *Sects*, 19.

83. Petition to Massachusetts General Assembly, quoted in William McLoughlin, *Isaac Backus and the American Pietistic Tradition* (Boston, 1967), 56; Ebenezer Frothingham, *A Key to Unlock the Door* (n.p., 1767), 50.

84. Backus, *History*, 2:231–232.

85. Goen, *Revivalism*, 273 (referring to Backus).

86. McLoughlin, *Dissent*, 172.

87. See "The People Speak: Confessions of Lay Men and Women," in *God's Plot: Puritan Spirituality in Thomas Shepard's Cambridge*, ed. Michael McGiffert (Amherst, Mass, 1994), 165–166; Stout, *Soul*, 40–41.

88. "The Itinerarium of Dr. Alexander Hamilton," in *Colonial American Travel Narratives*, ed. Wendy Martin (New York, 1994), 183, 204, 201.

89. Jonathan Edwards, "Sinners in the Hands of an Angry God," in *The Works of President Edwards* (New York, 1842–1844), 4:317; Jonathan Edwards, "Narrative of Surprising Conversions," ibid., 3:236.

90. Jonathan Edwards, "Covenant with the People of Northampton, 1742," in *The Works of Jonathan Edwards*, 2 vols. (London, 1834), 1:cii; Edwards, "Sinners," 314; Jonathan Edwards, "The Distinguishing Marks of a Work of the Spirit," *Works* (1834), 1:549.

91. Jonathan Edwards, "A Dissertation on the Nature of True Virtue," in *The Works of Jonathan Edwards*, 2 vols. (London, 1845), 1:ciii.

92. See Guelzo, "Designs," 160; Stout, *Soul,* 189; Nathan O. Hatch and Harry S. Stout, introduction to *Jonathan Edwards and the American Experience,* ed. Nathan O. Hatch and Harry S. Stout (New York, 1988), 10.

93. See William Breitenbach, "Piety and Moralism: Edwards and the New Divinity," in Hatch and Stout, *Edwards,* 181–182; Catherine A. Brekus, *Strangers and Pilgrims: Female Preaching in America, 1740–1845* (Chapel Hill, 1998), 57–58; Gerald R. McDermott, *One Holy and Happy Society: The Public Theology of Jonathan Edwards* (University Park, Pa., 1992), 179.

94. See Bloch, *Republic,* 29–50; McDermott, *Society,* viii, 6, 77.

95. See Bloch, *Republic,* 18.

96. Mark A. Noll, "Jonathan Edwards and Nineteenth Century Theology," in Hatch and Stout, *Edwards,* 278; Donald Weber, "The Recovery of Jonathan Edwards," ibid., 62–65; Noll, "Edwards," 180–181.

97. Isaac Backus, *All True Ministers* (Boston, 1754), 18.

98. Daniel Wadsworth, *Diary of Rev. Daniel Wadsworth, 1737–47,* ed. George Leon Walker (Hartford, 1894), 7; Samuel Blair, *A Short and Faithful Narrative of the late Remarkable Revival of Religion* (Philadelphia, [1744]), 13, 8; "The Spiritual Travels of Nathan Cole," ed. Michael J. Crawford, *William and Mary Quarterly,* 3d ser., no. 33 (January 1976), 94; Blair, *Narrative,* 26, 8, 20.

99. Edwards, "Surprising Conversions," 235.

100. Michael J. Crawford, *Seasons of Grace: Colonial New England's Revival Tradition in Its British Context* (New York, 1991), 15.

101. See Frank Lambert, *Inventing the "Great Awakening"* (Princeton, 1999).

102. Hall, *Boundaries,* 69.

103. See Cedric B. Cowing, *The Saving Remnant: Religion and the Settling of New England* (Urbana, Ill., 1995); Harry S. Stout and Peter Onuf, "James Davenport and the Great Awakening in New London," *Journal of American History* 71 (December 1983).

104. Hermon Husband, "A New Government of Liberty," in "'A New Government of Liberty': Hermon Husband's Vision of Backcountry North Carolina, 1755," ed. A. Roger Ekirch, *William and Mary Quarterly,* 3d ser., no. 34 (October 1977), 644.

105. Finke and Stark, *Churching,* 58.

106. Elizabeth Ashbridge, "Some Account of the Fore Part of the Life of Elizabeth Ashbridge," in *Journeys in New Worlds: Early American Women's Narratives,* ed. William L. Andrews (Madison, Wis., 1990), 155; Isaac Backus, "A Discourse Showing the Nature and Necessity of an Internal Call to Preach the Everlasting Gospel," in *Isaac Backus on Church, State, and Calvinism: Pamphlets, 1754–1789,* ed. William G. McLoughlin (Cambridge, Mass., 1968), 106. Long memories made the "Reformation" "next to the Scripture History" in importance (Thomas Prince, quoted in Lambert, *"Great Awakening,"* 119), while the heroic "Oliver" (Cromwell, of course) was celebrated along with "our Forefathers, who left their Native Country." Alfred F. Young, "English Plebeian Culture and Eigh-

teenth-Century American Radicalism," in *The Origins of Anglo-American Radicalism*, ed. Margaret C. Jacob and James R. Jacob (Boston, 1984), 197; Solomon Paine, "A Short View of the Church of Christ," in *The Great Awakening*, ed. Alan Heimert and Perry Miller (Indianapolis, 1967), 418.

107. Isaiah Thomas, quoted in Lambert, *"Great Awakening,"* 119.

108. George Whitefield, quoted in Harry S. Stout, *The Divine Dramatist: George Whitefield and the Rise of Modern Evangelism* (Grand Rapids, Mich., 1991), 131; Samuel Finley, "Christ Triumphing, and Satan Raging," in Heimert and Miller, *Great Awakening*, 156–157; Stout, *Soul*, 194.

109. Backus, "Discourse," 114; Andrew Croswell, quoted in Leigh Eric Schmidt, "'A Second and Glorious Reformation': The New Light Extremism of Andrew Croswell," *William and Mary Quarterly*, 3d ser., no. 43 (April 1986), 223, 241, 233; Backus, "Discourse," 112.

110. Finley, "Christ," 157, 156; Backus, quoted in McLoughlin, introduction to *Backus on Church*, 37.

111. Hamilton, "Itinerarium," 298.

112. Paul Parke, quoted in Stout, *Soul*, 209; Edward Wigglesworth, *Some Distinguishing Characteristics of the Extraordinary and Ordinary Ministers of the Church of Christ* (Boston, 1754), 11, 14.

113. Charles Brockwell, letter of February 18, 1742, in W. S. Perry, *Historical Collections Relating to the American Colonial Church* (Hartford, Conn., 1873), 3:353.

114. Richard J. Hooker, *The Carolina Backcountry on the Eve of the Revolution: The Journal and Other Writings of Charles Woodmason, Anglican Itinerant* (Chapel Hill, 1953), 13.

115. Hall, *Boundaries*, 5; Benjamin Colman, quoted in Lambert, *"Great Awakening,"* 122; Finley, "Christ," 164.

116. Hermon Husband, "Remarks on Religion," in *Some Eighteenth Century Tracts Concerning North Carolina*, ed. William K. Boyd (Raleigh, N.C.,1927), 227, 229, 216; Backus, "Discourse," 73; Gaustad, *Awakening*, 113. See also Richard W. Pointer, *Protestant Pluralism and the New York Experience* (Bloomington, Ind., 1988), 50–51.

117. Cohen, "Paradigm," 709; Hall, *Boundaries*, 5, 110.

118. Jonathan Parsons, quoted in *The Christian History, Containing Accounts of the Revival and Propagation of Religion in Great Britain and America*, ed. Thomas Prince, Jr., 2 vols. (Boston, 1743–1745), 2:144; Joseph Fish, *The Church of Christ a Firm and Durable House* (New London, 1767), 119; Hamilton, "Itinerarium," 266, 265.

119. Goen, *Revivalism*, 35; McLoughlin, *Backus*, 11; Crawford, *Seasons*, 15.

120. Husband, "New Government," 645.

121. George Whitefield, *The Marraige of Cana*, in *Seventy-Five Sermons on Various Subjects*, 3 vols. (London, 1812), 2:101–102.

122. Stout, *Dramatist*, xx.

123. Philemon Robbins, quoted in Weber, *Rhetoric*, 29; Gilbert Tennent and Samuel Finley, both quoted in Bonomi, *Cope*, 158.

124. Frothingham, *Articles*, 181; McLoughlin, *Backus*, 174.

125. Solomon Williams, "The True State of the Question," in Heimert and Miller, *Great Awakening*, 439, 437; Backus, "Discourse," 73.

126. Whitefield, quoted in Hall, *Boundaries*, 79; Finley, "Christ," 173.

127. Ashbridge, "Account," 159, 160; Husband, "Remarks," 237.

128. Ashbridge, "Account," 253, 158; Husband, "Remarks," 223; "Nathan Cole," 96.

129. Husband, "Remarks," 238–239, 245, 233; Robbins, quoted in Weber, *Rhetoric*, 18; Isaac Backus, "A Short Description of the Difference between the Bond-woman and the Free," in McLoughlin, *Backus on Church*, 143; "Nathan Cole," 115, 113; Andrew Croswell, quoted in Schmidt, "Reformation," 418.

130. Isaac Backus, *A Fish Caught in His Own Net*, quoted in McLoughlin, *Dissent*, 337n7; Backus, quoted in McLoughlin, *Backus*, 31.

131. Isaac Backus, *A Fish Caught in His Own Net* (Boston, 1768), 113; Hall, *Boundaries*, 86; Gilbert Tennent, *The Danger of an Unconverted Ministry* (Boston, 1742), 2.

132. Ashbridge, "Account," 167, 166; Husband, "Remarks," 209.

133. John Graham, *Some Remarks* (Boston, 1733), 35.

134. Solomon Paine, "A Short View of the Church of Christ," in Heimert and Miller, *Great Awakening*, 421; Joseph Fish, *Christ Jesus the Physician and his Blood* (New London, 1760), 59.

135. Timothy Cutler, quoted in Gaustad, *Awakening*, 31–32; see also ibid., 113.

136. Thomas Paine, Jr., *The Christian History*, ed. Timothy Prince, Jr. (Boston, 1743–1745), 1:71; Hamilton, "Itinerarium," 286; George Whitefield, *Eighteen Sermons* (London, 1771), 22.

137. Marini, *Sects*, 12–13; McLaughlin, "Religion," 201–202.

138. Husband, "Remarks," 227; Lambert, "Great Awakening," 49; Frank Lambert, "Pedlar in Divinity": George Whitefield and the Transatlantic Revivals, 1737–1770 (Princeton, 1994), 21–22; Croswell, quoted in Schmidt, "Reformation," 230; see also Marilyn J. Westerkamp, *Triumph of the Laity: Scots-Irish Piety and the Great Awakening, 1625–1760* (New York, 1988), 209–212.

139. McLoughlin, introduction to *Backus on Church*, 55–56.

140. See Heimert, *Religion*, 39.

141. Husband, "Remarks," 246; McLaughlin, *Backus*, 227; Blair, *Narrative*, 8; Daniel Russell to Eleazar Wheelock, January 7, 1741, quoted in *Great Awakening*, ed. Richard L. Bushman (New York, 1970), 43.

142. Croswell, quoted in Schmidt, "Reformation," 234; Whitefield, *Journals*, 423; Mayhew, *Grace Defended*, 199; Blair, *Narrative*, 27.

143. Whitefield's Journals," 459; Blair, *Narrative*, 8.

144. "Nathan Cole," 97; Elisha Paine, in *A Letter from the Associated Ministers of the County of Windham* (Boston, 1745), 12; Frothingham, *Articles*, 177.

145. Quoted in Goen, *Revivalism*, 151.

146. Whitefield, "Letter," 296.

147. Ibid.; Whitefield, *Marriage*, 101.

148. Whitefield, *Marriage*, 99, 104, 101.

149. Blair, *Narrative*, 8; Whitefield, *Journals*, 459; Whitefield, *Marriage*, 99; "Nathan Cole," 94; Blair, *Narrative*, 26.

150. "Nathan Cole," 97.

151. The Reverend Caleb Hide, quoted in Goen, *Revivalism*, 152; Frothingham, *Articles*, 7; McLaughlin, *Backus*, 15.

152. McLoughlin, *Dissent*, 338; Frothingham, *Articles*, 354–355.

153. Frothingham, *Articles*, quoted in Goen, *Revivalism*, 153; Husband, "Remarks," 225.

154. Whitefield, *Marriage*, 100; Blair, *Narrative*, 15.

155. Frothingham, *Articles*, 424–425; Blair, *Narrative*, 20–21; Experience Mayhew, *Grace Defended* (Boston, 1744), 198.

156. Husband, "Remarks," 245.

157. Whitefield, "Letter," 296.

158. Whitefield, *Journals*, 471; Blair, *Narrative*, 16.

159. *An Invitation to the Reverend Mr. Whitefield, from the Eastern Consociation of the County of Fairfield* (Boston, 1745), quoted in Bushman, *Great Awakening*, 24 (emphasis added); Whitefield, "Letter," 296.

160. Whitefield, *Marriage*, 33.

161. Frothingham, *Articles*, 16.

162. Elisha Paine, in *A Letter from the Associated Members*, 11; Husband, "Remarks," 219; "Nathan Cole," 98, 108, 112.

163. Husband, "Remarks," 206; "Nathan Cole," 115; Croswell, quoted in Schmidt, "Reformation," 234.

164. Finley, "Christ," 173, 154; Andrew Croswell, "What is Christ to me, if he is not mine?" in Heimert and Miller, *Great Awakening*, 515; Croswell, quoted in Schmidt, "Reformation," 225.

165. Quoted in Goen, *Revivalism*, 94; Elisha Paine, in Ellen D. Larned, *History of Windham County, Connecticut* (Worcester, Mass., 1874), 2:40; "Nathan Cole," 97.

166. Mayhew, *Grace Defended*, 198; "Letter of Daniel Russell," in Bushman, *Great Awakening*, 43; cf. Frothingham, *Articles*, 107, 101, 425.

167. Whitefield, quoted in Lambert, *"Great Awakening,"* 22; "Nathan Cole," 113; Ashbridge, "Account," 158.

168. McLaughlin, *Backus*, 227–228.

169. Marini, *Sects*, 16; Husband, "Remarks," 214–215.

170. Whitefield, "The Holy Spirit Convincing the World of Sin," in *Memoirs of the Rev. George Whitefield*, ed. John Gillies (Middletown, Conn., 1829), 400–401.

171. "Nathan Cole," 94, 111; Husband, "Remarks," 215.

172. Mayhew, *Grace Defended*, 175; Joseph Fish, quoted in Goen, *Revivalism*, 177.

173. Cole, 107, 115; Backus, *Fish*, in McLaughlin, *Backus on Church*, 190, 191.

174. Backus, *Fish*, in McLaughlin, *Backus on Church*, 249; Frothingham, *Articles*, 7, 387.

175. Husband, "Remarks," 246; "Nathan Cole," 121; Croswell, quoted in Schmidt, "Reformation," 241.

176. Backus, "Short Description," 161; Frothingham, *Articles*, 462.

177. Solomon Paine, quoted in McLaughlin, *Backus*, 83; [Anonymous], "Letter," in

Isaac Backus, *A Letter to the Reverend Mr. Lord* (Providence, R.I., 1764), 55; *Records of the Preston Separate Church,* quoted in Goen, *Revivalism,* 233; Isaac Backus, *A Church History of New-England* (Philadelphia, 1839), 178.

178. Isaac Backus, *The Bond-Woman and the Free,* quoted in McLoughlin, *Backus,* 75; McLoughlin, *Dissent,* 1:574.

179. Jon Pahl, *Paradox Lost: Free Will and Political Liberty in American Culture, 1630–1760* (Baltimore, 1992), 132, 131, 130; Mayhew, *Grace Defended,* 175, 198.

180. "Nathan Cole," 110; Husband, "Remarks," 236; George Whitefield, *A Continuation of the Reverend Mr. Whitefield's Journal . . . the Seventh Journal* (London, 1744), 40.

181. Gilbert Tennent, "The Danger of an Unconverted Ministry," in Heimert and Miller, *Great Awakening,* 88; *Articles for the Church of Christ,* quoted in McLoughlin, *Backus,* 43.

182. Backus, "Discourse," 87, 89, 112; "Nathan Cole," 118, 117.

183. Isaac Backus, "An Appeal to the Public for Religious Liberty," in McLoughlin, *Backus on Church,* 309, 324.

184. Bushman, *Puritan to Yankee,* 187; McLoughlin, "Religion," 200.

185. "Nathan Cole," 118; Solomon Paine et al., "A Separate Petition," in Bushman, *Great Awakening,* 160; Backus, *Fish,* 82, 86.

186. Tennent, "Danger," 19, 21; Jared Ingersoll, "Historical Account of Some Affairs of the Church," quoted in Bushman, *Puritan,* 212; Philemon Robbins, *A Plain Narrative* (Boston, 1747), 40.

187. Isaac Backus, "Policy as Well as Honesty," in McLoughlin, *Backus on Church,* 377; Hannah Cory, quoted in Goen, *Revivalism,* 102.

188. Blair, *Narrative,* 26, 28.

189. Marini, *Sects,* 14; Rhys Isaac, "Evangelical Revolt: The Nature of the Baptists' Challenge to the Traditional Order in Virginia, 1765 to 1775," *William and Mary Quarterly,* 3d ser., no. 31 (1972), 354.

190. Frothingham, *Articles,* 459–460; Hall, *Boundaries,* 102; Mayhew, *Grace Defended,* 196, 136, 110.

191. Marini, *Sects,* 14.

192. Whitefield, *Journals,* 459; Frothingham, *Articles,* 343; "Two Separates in Prison," in Bushman, *Great Awakening,* 106; Lee, "Letter," 41.

193. Solomon Paine, *A Short View of the Difference between the Church of Christ* (Newport, 1752), 53.

194. See, e.g., Jack P. Greene, "Introduction: The Reappraisal of the American Revolution in Recent Historical Literature," in *The Reinterpretation of the American Revolution: 1763–1789* (New York, 1969).

195. Guelzo, "Design," 160; see also Mark A. Noll, "The American Revolution and Protestant Evangelism," *Journal of Interdisciplinary History* 23 (Winter 1993), 635.

196. Stout, *Dramatist,* 131; Tennent, "Danger," 95; "Nathan Cole," 120; Eldon Eisenach, "Cultural Politics and Political Thought: The American Revolution Remembered," *American Studies* 20 (1979), 78.

197. Hermon Husband, "Impartial Relation," in Boyd, *Tracts,* 258; Killingly Conven-

tion of Strict Congregational Churches, *An Historical Narrative, and Declaration* (Providence, R.I., 1781), 10; Paine, *Short View,* 52; Frothingham, *Articles,* 153.

198. Elisha Paine, in Backus, *Church History,* 175; Lee, "Letter," 41; Frothingham, *A Key,* 68.

199. Goen, *Revivalism,* 133, 129.

200. Solomon Paine, *A Short View* (Newport, 1752), 36; quoted in Nash, *Crucible,* 208.

201. Frothingham, *Articles,* 256–257, 351, 260.

202. The Society for the Progagation of the Gospel in Foreign Parts, in E. E. Beardsley, *The History of the Episcopal Church in Connecticut* (Boston, 1883), 133; Benjamin Throop, "1758 Election Sermon," quoted in Gaustad, *Awakening,* 126.

203. McLoughlin, "Religion," 200; Frothingham, *Articles,* 374–375; Tennent, "Danger," 93; Goen, *Revivalism,* 123.

204. William Shurtleff, "Letter to those who refuse to admit Whitefield," in Heimert and Miller, *Great Awakening,* 362; Gaustad, *Awakening,* 85.

205. *A Letter to the Clergy of the Colony of Connecticut* (New York, 1760), 5.

206. Quoted in McLoughlin, *Backus,* 52.

207. Backus, "Policy," 380.

208. Backus, "Truth is Great and Will Prevail," in McLoughlin, *Backus on Church,* 418; [Isaac Stiles], *The Declaration of the Association of the County of New-Haven in Connecticut* (Boston, 1745), 6.

209. Isaac Stiles, *A Prospect of the City of Jerusalem* (New London, 1742), 46.

210. "Testimony of the Church upon the Withdrawal of Sundry Baptist Brethren," quoted in Goen, *Revivalism,* 235.

211. Jonathan Edwards, "Humble Inquiry into the Rules of the Word of God," in *Works of President Edwards,* 1:86.

212. Solomon Williams, "The True State of the Question," in Heimert and Miller, *Great Awakening,* 439.

213. Joseph Bellamy, *True Religion Delineated* (Boston, 1853), 1:57. 337

214. Marini, *Sects,* 12; quoted in Weber, *Rhetoric,* 52.

215. Joseph Bellamy, *An Election Sermon (May 13, 1762),* in *The Works of Joseph Bellamy* (Boston, 1853), 1:586

216. Edwards, "Covenant," ciii.

217. Shain, *Myth,* 4, 125.

218. Ibid., 119.

219. Quoted in Backus, *Fish,* in McLoughlin, *Backus on Church,* 179; Croswell, quoted in Schmidt, "Reformation," 239.

220. Gaustad, *Awakening,* 126; McLoughlin, *Dissent,* 360, 338, 356.

221. Bushman, *Puritan,* 219–220.

222. Shain, *Myth,* 95.

223. Frothingham, *Articles,* 153.

224. Ezra Stiles, *A Discourse on the Christian Union* (Boston, 1760), 94; Elisha Williams, *The Essential Rights and Liberties of Protestants* (Boston, 1744), 8.

225. Noah Hobart, *Civil Government* (New London, 1751), 29.

226. Frothingham, *Articles*, 15.

227. Croswell, quoted in Schmidt, "Reformation," 237, 239; Backus, "Discourse," 89, 97.

228. Clark, *Language*, 44.

229. "Philanthropos," quoted in McLoughlin, *Backus*, 153.

230. Bushman, *Puritan*, 231.

231. McLoughlin, "Religion," 199; Isaac, "Evangelical Revolt," 363.

232. Harry S. Stout, "Religion, Communications, and the Ideological Origins of the American Revolution," *William and Mary Quarterly*, 3d ser., no. 34 (October 1977), 539.

233. McLoughlin, "Religion," 205.

234. Bloch, *Republic*, 15, 20; see McLoughlin, "Enthusiasm for Liberty," 67–68.

235. Whitefield, *Journals*, 475; Isaac Backus, "Articles for the Church of Christ," quoted in McLoughlin, *Backus*, 43.

236. Frothingham, *Articles*, 28–29.

237. Quoted in Bloch, *Republic*, 16.

238. Ibid., 18, 19.

239. John Adams, "Letter to Hezekiah Niles (1818)," in *The Works of John Adams*, ed. Charles Francis Adams, 10 vols. (Boston, 1856), 10:282.

7. The Revolutionary Triumph of Agency

1. Issac, *Transformation*, 5, 271, 137.

2. Wood writes: "To most of the Revolutionaries there was no sense of incompatibility in their blending of history, rationalism, and scripture." Wood, *Creation*, 8. See also Noll, "American Revolution," 615.

3. See Greene, "Introduction."

4. Clark, *Language*, 45.

5. See Heimert, *Religion*, 16–17.

6. See May, *Enlightenment*, 377n.

7. See T. H. Breen, *The Character of the Good Ruler: Puritan Political Ideas in New England, 1630–1730* (New York, 1970).

8. James Wilson, quoted in Wood, *Creation*, 11; Stamp Act Congress, quoted ibid.

9. J. H. Plumb, *The Growth of Political Stability in England, 1675–1725* (Baltimore, 1969), 187.

10. See John Trenchard and Thomas Gordon, *Cato's Letters*, in *The English Libertarian Heritage* (Indianapolis, 1965).

11. Darwall, *British Moralists*, 13.

12. Joseph Butler, *Five Sermons* (Indianapolis, 1983), 49, 54.

13. Daniel Defoe, *Robinson Crusoe* (New York, 1981), 59–60, 52, 55.

14. Ibid., 100, 115, 31, 86, 88.

15. See Daniel Defoe, *The Family Instructor*, 2 vols. (New York, 1973).

16. See Bloch, *Republic*.

17. Heimert, *Religion*, 17. See also May, *Enlightenment*, 93.

18. Jonathan Mayhew, *A Discourse Concerning Unlimited Submission and Non-Resis-*

tance to the Higher Powers (Boston, 1750), 21; Charles Chauncy, *Civil Magistrates must be just, ruling in the Fear of God* (London, 1747), 103.

19. John Wise, *A Vindication of the Government of New England Churches* (Boston, 1772), 30, 26, 27.

20. Ibid., 26, 24.

21. Ibid., 26, 30, 29, 24–25.

22. Ibid., 29.

23. Ibid., 31, 34, 35; John Wise, quoted in Breen, *Character,* 257.

24. Elisha Williams, *The essential Rights and Liberties of Protestants* (Boston, 1744), 5, 7.

25. Ibid., 43, 38, 42, 64.

26. Ibid., 4, 42.

27. See Chauncy, *Magistrates;* Mayhew, *Discourse.*

28. Chauncy, *Magistrates,* 24, 36; Mayhew, *Discourse,* 30, 29, 28, 25.

29. Jonathan Mayhew, quoted in Lawrence H. Leder, *Liberty and Authority: Early American Political Ideology, 1689–1763* (Chicago, 1968), 69.

30. Mayhew, *Discourse,* 37–38, 38n, 54.

31. Lemuel Briant, *The Absurdity* (Boston, 1749), 23.

32. Chauncy, *Magistrates,* 12.

33. Ibid., 47, 24, 25, 34, 42.

34. Ibid., 26, 35.

35. Ibid., 42.

36. Ibid., 66, 34.

37. Mayhew, *Discourse,* 55, 45.

38. Ibid., 25.

39. Ibid., 54–55.

40. Chauncy, *Magistrates,* 13; Jonathan Mayhew, *A Sermon Preached . . . May 29th, 1754* (Boston, 1754), 12.

41. Chauncy, *Magistrates,* 8; Mayhew, *Discourse,* 55.

42. Abraham Williams, "A Sermon Preach'd at Boston, before the Great and General Court or Assembly of the Province of the Massachusetts-Bay in New England, May 26, 1762," in *Puritan Political Ideas, 1588–1794,* ed. Edmund S. Morgan (Indianapolis, 1965), 341.

43. William Smith, "Sermon VIII," in *The Works of William Smith, D.D.* (Philadelphia, 1803), 2:168.

44. Mayhew, *Discourse,* 38n.

45. Jonathan Mayhew, *The Snare Broken,* in *The Patriot Preachers of the American Revolution,* ed. Frank Moore (New York, 1862), 26.

46. Jonathan Mayhew, *Seven Sermons* (Boston, 1749), 97; Ebenezer Gay, *Natural Religion as Distinguished from Revealed* (Boston, 1759), 10; William Hart, *A Discourse Concerning the Nature of Regeneration* (New London, 1742), 36.

47. Mayhew, quoted in Heimert, *Religion,* 47.

48. Briant, *The Absurdity,* 23.

49. Mayhew, *Submission,* 23, 30; John Tucker, *Magistrates Considered as Fellow-*

Workers (Boston, 1768), 23; Heimert, *Religion,* 279, quoting Mayhew, *Snare Broken,* 47; Jonathan Mayhew, *Christian Sobriety* (Boston, 1763), 25.

50. For the Puritan role in shaping elite political thought, see Mark A. Noll, *Christians in the American Revolution* (Washington, D.C., 1977), 150–151; Mark Valeri, *Law and Providence in Joseph Bellamy's New England: The Origins of the New Divinity in Revolutionary America* (New York, 1994); Mark Valeri, "The New Divinity and the American Revolution," *William and Mary Quarterly,* 3d ser., no. 46 (October 1989).

51. John Tucker, *A Sermon Preached at Cambridge* (Boston, 1754), 12; Mayhew, *Snare Broken,* 29, 11, 47; Charles Chauncy, *Good News,* quoted in John Wingate Thornton, *The Pulpit of the American Revolution* (Boston, 1860), 140.

52. Quoted in Leder, *Liberty,* 69.

53. Jonathan Mayhew, "Memorandum on 25 August 1765 Sermon," appended to Bernard Bailyn, "Religion and Revolution: Three Biographical Studies," in *Perspectives in American History* 4 (1970), 142.

54. [Henry Brooke?], *Liberty and Common-Sense to the People of Ireland, Greeting* (London, 1760), letter 2, 11.

55. William McClenachan, *The Christian Warrior* (Boston, 1745), 5.

56. Robert Smith, *A Wheel in the Middle of a Wheel* (Philadelphia, 1759), 40.

57. Joseph Sewall, *The Lamb Slain* (Boston, 1745), 34; Aaron Burr, *A Servant of God* (New York, 1763), 23; Samuel Finley, *The Curse of Meroz* (Philadelphia, 1757), 25.

58. Samuel Davies, "The Crisis: or, the Uncertain Doom of Kingdoms at Particular Times," in *Sermons on Important Subjects,* 4 vols. (London, 1815), 3:415.

59. Heimert, *Religion,* 327.

60. Hatch, *Cause,* 40, 17.

61. Samuel Davies, "The Mediatorial Kingdom and Glories of Jesus Christ," in *Political Sermons of the American Founding Era,* ed. Ellis Sandoz (Indianapolis, 1991), 183, 198, 190, 206, 205.

62. Samuel Dunbar, "The Presence of God with His People," in Sandoz, *Political Sermons,* 216, 213; cf. 220.

63. Williams, "Sermon," 343, 341.

64. Davies, "Kingdom," 194; Dunbar, "Presence," 225.

65. Williams, "Sermon," 336, 339, 343, 347, 349.

66. Ibid., 338, 336, 343, 341, 346.

67. Davies, "Kingdom," 194, 193, 203.

68. Dunbar, "Presence," 220, 214.

69. Williams, "Sermon," 346–348, 342.

70. James Cogswell, *God, or the Pious Soldier's Strength and Instructor* (Boston, 1757), 26; Hatch, *Cause,* 17.

71. Wood, *Radicalism,* 124.

72. Bloch, *Republic,* 55, 56.

73. James Otis, *The Rights of the British Colonies Asserted and Proved* (Boston, 1764), 9.

74. Ibid., 65, 15.

75. Ibid., 33, 37, 38, 41.
76. Ibid., 35; "The New York Petition to the House of Commons," in *Colonies to Nation, 1763–1789: A Documentary History of the American Revolution,* ed. Jack P. Greene (New York, 1967), 35.
77. "New York Petition," 34; Otis, *Rights,* 36–37.
78. "The Virginia Resolves," May 30, 1765, in *Journals of the House of Burgesses of Virginia, 1761–1765,* ed. John Pendleton Kennedy (Richmond, Va., 1905–1915), 360.
79. "New York Petition," 39.
80. John Dickinson, *Letters from a Farmer in Pennsylvania* (Philadelphia, 1774), letters 12, 4.
81. Ibid., letter 12.
82. John Adams, quoted in Greene, *Colonies to Nation,* 146; Charleston Sons of Liberty, *South Carolina Gazette,* April 19, 1770, ibid., 155; editorial comments, ibid., 147; Joseph Harrison to the Marquis of Rockingham, June 17, 1768, in "Joseph Harrison and the Liberty Incident," ibid., 136, 140.
83. "Remonstrance of the Back Country," ibid., 100, 102; "The Declaration of the Injured Frontier Inhabitants," in *The Minutes of the Provincial Council of Pennsylvania* (Philadelphia, 1762–1771), 9:145.
84. See Nash, *Crucible,* 343–344, 354–355.
85. Quoted ibid., 311; ibid., 342.
86. "The Diary of Josiah Quincy, Jr.," August 27, 1765, in *Proceedings of the Massachusetts Historical Society,* 1st ser., 4 (1858–1860), 51.
87. Quoted in Nash, *Crucible,* 352.
88. "The House of Representatives of Massachusetts to Speakers of Other Houses of Representatives," in *The Writings of Samuel Adams,* ed. Harry Alonzo Cushing, 4 vols. (New York, 1904–1908), 1:184–185.
89. See "The Preceptor," in Hyneman and Lutz, *American Political Writing,* 1:181–182.
90. Rusticus, "Liberty," in Greene, *Colonies to Nation,* 149. As Wood wrote, "They revolted not against the English constitution but on behalf of it." Wood, *Creation,* 10.
91. Rusticus, "Liberty," 148, 153.
92. Ibid.; "Brutus," letter to *Virginia Gazette,* June 1, 1769.
93. "The Tribune," in Hyneman and Lutz, *American Political Writing,* 1:92–94.
94. Ibid., 95.
95. "The Preceptor," 179.
96. Ibid., 180.
97. Chauncy, *Magistrates,* 50, 42; Daniel Shute, "An Election Sermon," in Hyneman and Lutz, *American Political Writing,* 1:125.
98. Shute, "Election Sermon," 113.
99. Chauncy, *Magistrates,* 63, 50, 42.
100. John Tucker, "An Election Sermon," in Hyneman and Lutz, *American Political Writing,* 1:171, 169.

101. Richard Bland, "An Inquiry into the Rights of the British Colonies," ibid., 1:73, 86; Silas Downer, "A Discourse at the Dedication of the Tree of Liberty," ibid., 101.

102. Bland, "Inquiry," 71, 73; [Silas Downer], "Son of Liberty," in Hyneman and Lutz, *American Political Writing*, 1:101.

103. Downer, "Son," 107.

104. See Nash, *Crucible*, 342–350; Heimert, *Religion*, 281.

105. Bushman, *Puritan*, 266; [Samuel Adams], "The Rights of the Colonists," in *Writings*, 363, 368, 360.

106. Continental Congress, "Appeal to the Inhabitants of Quebec," in Hyneman and Lutz, *American Political Writing*, 1:238.

107. James Wilson, "Considerations on the Nature and Extent of the Legislative Authority of the British Parliament," in *The Works of James Wilson*, ed. Robert Green McCloskey, 2 vols. (Cambridge, Mass., 1967), 2:734. Wilson and others argued that so long as Parliament "can persuade the people of England they are lightening their burdens thereby, they are under no motive of interest to abstain from loading" the colonies down with unbearable taxes and legislation "that all our landed property . . . revert to his majesty." Ebenezer Baldwin, "An Appendix Stating the heavy Grievances the Colonies labor under . . . ," in Greene, *Colonies to Nation*, 214

108. Greene, *Colonies to Nation*, 213.

109. Ibid., 217, 216.

110. "Exchange between Governor Thomas Hutchinson and the House of Representatives," in *Speeches of the Governors of Massachusetts from 1765 to 1775*, ed. Alden Bradford (Boston, 1818), 357–358; Thomas Jefferson, "A Summary View of the Rights of British America (1774)," in *The Life and Selected Writings of Thomas Jefferson*, ed. Adrienne Koch and William Peden (New York, 1944), 307.

111. Wood, *Radicalism*, 4.

112. Wilson, "Considerations," 741.

113. Jefferson, "Summary View," 300; cf. 307–308.

114. See Elisha Douglass, *Rebels and Democrats: The Struggle for Equal Political Rights and Majority Rule during the American Revolution* (Chicago, 1965), 12, 155, 253.

115. "Exchange," 363; Wilson, "Considerations," 741; Simeon Howard, "A Sermon Preached to the Ancient and Honorable Artillery Company in Boston," in Hyneman and Lutz, *American Political Writing*, 1:193, 195.

116. Massachusettensis [Daniel Leonard], "To All Nations of Men," in Hyneman and Lutz, *American Political Writing*, 1:212.

117. Jefferson, "Summary View," 311.

118. Howard, "Sermon," 197; Massachusettensis, "Nations," 216; Gad Hitchcock, "An Election Sermon," in Hyneman and Lutz, *American Political Writing*, 1:293.

119. Samuel Sherwood, "Scriptural Instructions to Civil Rulers," in Sandoz, *Political Sermons*, 386.

120. "Exchange," 357–358; Continental Congress, "Appeal," 235; Jefferson, "Summary View," 310.

121. Howard, "Sermon," 188; Massachusettensis, "Nations," 214–215; Continental Congress, "Appeal," 234.

122. Nathaniel Niles, "Two Discourses on Liberty," in Hyneman and Lutz, *American Political Writing*, 1:275; Hitchcock, "Election Sermon," 303; Levi Hart, "Liberty Described and Recommended in a Sermon Preached to the Corporation of Freemen in Farmington," in Hyneman and Lutz, *American Political Writing*, 1:312; Sherwood, "Instructions," 399.

123. Massachusettensis, "Nations," 215; Sherwood, "Instructions," 383, 395.

124. Douglass, *Rebels*, 7. See also Merrill Jensen, "Democracy and the American Revolution," in *Causes and Consequences of the American Revolution*, ed. Esmond Wright (Chicago, 1966), 272; David Freeman Hawke, *A Transaction of Free Men: The Birth and Course of the Declaration of Independence* (New York, 1989).

125. Hart, "Liberty," 308; Howard, "Sermon," 200; Hitchcock, "Election Sermon," 302, 301; Sherwood, "Instructions," 378.

126. Douglass, *Rebels*, 14, 149.

127. Niles, "Discourses," 269; Howard, "Sermon," 206, 207.

128. Douglass, *Rebels*, 160.

129. Carl L. Becker, *The History of Political Parties in the Province of New York, 1760–1776* (Madison, Wis., 1909), 31–32.

130. Ronald Hoffman, preface to *The Transforming Hand of Revolution: Reconsidering the American Revolution as a Social Movement*, ed. Ronald Hoffman and Peter J. Albert (Charlottesville, Va., 1995), viii. See also Joshua Miller, *The Rise and Fall of Democracy in Early America, 1630–1789* (University Park, Pa., 1991), 52–53.

131. McLoughlin, "Religion," 200, 202.

132. Clark, *Language*, 10.

133. Bonomi, *Cope*, 6–7.

134. Stephen Marini, "Religion, Politics, and Ratification," in Hoffman and Albert, *Religion*, 188, 217, 193.

135. Isaac, *Transformation*, 162, 291, 287.

136. Wood, *Revolution*, 87.

137. Curry, *Religion*, 177; Douglass, *Rebels*, 186.

138. Backus, "Appeal," 337; Isaac Backus, "Government and Liberty Described," in McLoughlin, *Backus on Church*, 353, 360.

139. Robert J. Taylor, *Western Massachusetts in the Revolution* (Providence, R.I., 1954), 33, 37.

140. Douglass, *Rebels*, 109; Bernard Mason, *The Road to Independence: The Revolutionary Movement in New York, 1773–1777* (Lexington, Ky., 1966), 174.

141. Isaac, *Transformation*, 173.

142. Backus, "Policy," 382; Isaac Backus, *A History of New England* (Newton, Mass., 1871), 2:vii.

143. *Pennsylvania Packet*, June 24, 1776.

144. Bonomi, *Cope*, 186.

145. Isaac, *Transformation*, 255, 279.

146. Stout, "Religion," 537.

147. Backus, "Appeal," 309.
148. Robert A. Ferguson, *The American Enlightenment, 1750–1820* (Cambridge, Mass., 1997), 60; Douglass, *Rebels,* 134, 213, 185.
149. Bloch, *Republic,* 114; Wood, *Revolution,* 87; quoted in Isaac, *Transformation,* 175.
150. Isaac, *Transformation,* 5.
151. Marc W. Kruman, *Between Authority and Liberty: State Constitution Making in Revolutionary America* (Chapel Hill, 1997), 45; see also Robert Allen Rutland, *The Birth of the Bill of Rights, 1776–1791* (New York, 1962), 88–89.
152. See Rutland, *Birth;* Marini, "Religion"; Curry, *Religion.*
153. Mecklenburg Instructions (1775), quoted in Douglass, *Rebels,* 127.
154. The Reverend Thomas Allen, quoted in J. E. A. Smith, *History of Pittsfield* (Boston, 1869), 343; Douglass, *Rebels,* 160, 176.
155. "Return of Northampton on the Franchise," quoted in Samuel Eliot Morison, "The Struggle over the Adoption of the Constitution of Massachusetts, 1780," in *Proceedings of the Massachusetts Historical Society* 50 (November 1916), 409; "Berkshire's Grievances (Statement of Berkshire County Representatives)," in Hyneman and Lutz, *American Political Writing,* 1:456–457.
156. Bonomi, *Cope,* 186, 161, 9, 168.
157. Marini, "Religion," 209, 215.
158. Miller, *Rise,* 55.
159. Isaac, *Transformation,* 164–165, 291.
160. "Pittsfield Petition Remonstrance and Address" to the General Court, December 26, 1775, in *The Popular Sources of Political Authority: Documents in the Massachusetts Constitution of 1780* (Cambridge, Mass., 1966), 63–64; Richard Honyman, quoted in Isaac, *Transformation,* 276.
161. Hoffman, preface to *Transforming,* x.
162. Pauline Maier, *American Scripture: Making the Declaration of Independence* (New York, 1997), 62, 69, 68.
163. Isaac, *Transformation,* 244.
164. Maier, *Scripture,* 68; Bonomi, *Cope,* 216.
165. Bonomi, *Cope,* 211; Maier, *Scripture,* 73.
166. Isaac, *Transformation,* 244, 253.
167. *Common Sense,* in *Selected Writings of Thomas Paine,* ed. Richard Emery Roberts (New York, 1945), 29, 40, 22.
168. Ibid., 19, 40, 10, 25.
169. Ibid., 26, 10, 12–13.
170. Ibid., 9, 10, 19, 26, 22.
171. Ibid., 30.
172. See May, *Enlightenment,* 163.
173. Paine, *Common Sense,* 29, 41.
174. John Hughes to Samuel and John Adams, quoted in Bernard Mason, *The Road to Independence* (Lexington, Ky., 1966), 113.
175. Jonathan Todd, *Civil Rulers and Ministers of God* (New London, 1749), 2; James

Lockwood, *The Worth and Excellence of Civil Freedom and Liberty* (New London, 1759), 16.

176. McLoughlin, *Dissent,* 1:555.

177. Isaac Backus to Baptist Churches (1773), quoted in McLoughlin, *Backus,* 121; Backus, quoted in Alvah Hovey, *A Memoir of the Life and Times of Isaac Backus* (Boston, 1859), 197.

178. Quoted in Douglass, *Rebels,* 82.

179. *The People the Best governors* (1776), in Frederick Chase, *History of Dartmouth College* (Cambridge, Mass., 1891), 654; "A.P.," quoted in Charles H. Lincoln, *The Revolutionary Movement in Pennsylvania* (Philadelphia, 1901), 93n.

180. Taylor, *Massachusetts,* 3.

181. Adams, *Works,* 2:507.

182. John Adams, quoted in Hawke, *Transaction,* 98, 108, 112.

183. James Allen, quoted in Douglass, *Rebels,* 254; Hughes to Samuel and John Adams, 112.

184. John Adams to John Sullivan, quoted in Richard B. Morris, "Class Struggle and the American Revolution," *William and Mary Quarterly,* 3d ser., no. 19 (1962), 7; see also Jensen, "Democracy," 271–272.

185. John Jay to Alexander McDougall, April 11, 1776, quoted in Mason, *Road,* 140; William Smith to Philip Schuyler, March 16, 1775, quoted ibid., 174; William Smith, memoirs, quoted ibid., 235n75.

186. Samuel Adams, quoted in Douglass, *Rebels,* 19; Jared Sparks, *The Life of Gouverneur Morris* (Boston, 1832), 1:25.

187. Samuel West, "Election Sermon," in Thornton, *Pulpit,* 267; James Otis, quoted in Richard B. Morris, "Class Struggle and the American Revolution," *William and Mary Quarterly,* 3d ser., no. 19 (1962), 6.

188. Landon Carter to George Washington, in John Hazelton, *The Declaration of Independence: Its History* (New York, 1906), 75–76; Maier, *Scripture,* 49. Maier has the same ambivalence; see 36, 49.

189. See Morris, "Struggle," 6, 27; Douglass, *Rebels,* 17, 118–119, 122, 246–248, 252–253.

190. V. P. Ashfield to Isaac Wilkins, November 4, 1775, quoted in Mason, *Road,* 112; Irving Mark, *Agrarian Conflicts in Colonial New York, 1711–1775* (New York, 1940), 151.

191. Backus, quoted in Douglass, *Rebels,* 571, 559; Jared Ingersoll, *Mr. Ingersoll's Letters Relating to the Stamp Act* (New Haven, 1766), 62.

192. Jacob Duché, "The American Vine," in Greene, *Colonies to Nation,* 264.

193. See Maier, *Scripture,* 48–49.

194. McLoughlin, "Religion," 205; William Henry Drayton, quoted in Maier, *Scripture,* 71.

195. "Proclamation of the General Court, January 23, 1776, in *The Popular Sources of Political Authority: Documents on the Massachusetts Constitution of 1780,* ed. Oscar Handlin and Mary Handlin (Cambridge, Mass., 1966), 63–64, 67.

196. See Heimert, *Religion,* 436–442.
197. Maier, *Scripture,* 87, xvii. She emphasizes unanimity even though the document was soon forgotten (xviii, 154, 160–161) and though it was necessary to mobilize the populace (59–73, 80).
198. Hawke, *Transaction,* 3, 173.
199. Maier, *Scripture,* 134.
200. Jensen, "Struggle," 272.
201. Thomas Jefferson, *Notes on the State of Virginia* (Chapel Hill, 1955), 158.
202. Some, like Patrick Henry, recognized this, declaring at the Continental Congress that as "government is dissolved," then "we are in a state of nature . . . government is at an end. All distinctions are thrown down. All America is thrown into one mass." Quoted in Clark, *Language,* 59.
203. Hawke speaks of Jefferson's "feat" as "an intriguing part of the Declaration's story," how it "passed the scrutiny of some fifty conservative gentlemen who had wanted old and tested ideas to justify their 'great revolution,' and . . . nothing more." Hawke, *Transaction,* 3, 203.
204. See Greene, *Colonies to Nation,* 212–213; Maier, *Scripture.*
205. Maier, *Scripture,* 141, 138.
206. John Adams, quoted ibid., 122.
207. See Douglass, *Rebels,* 252–253, 160.
208. Maier, *Scripture,* 131; Stout, "Religion," 534.
209. Jay Fliegelman, *Declaring Independence: Jefferson, Natural Language, and the Culture of Performance* (Stanford, 1993), 25.
210. Maier, *Scripture,* 131.
211. McLoughlin, *Dissent,* 1:516.
212. Clark, *Language,* 143; Jefferson, quoted in Maier, *Scripture,* 133.
213. See Maier, *Scripture,* 154–159.
214. Clark has written: "This retrospective homogenisation of the positions of colonial denominations acted to secularize the historical interpretation of the Revolution and to drain the role of the sects of its immense significance." Clark, *Language,* 390.
215. Backus, "Appeal to the Public," 339, 338; Ruth H. Bloch, "Religion," in Hoffman and Albert, *Religion,* 308–309, 328, 329, 330.
216. Noll, "American Revolution," 635.
217. Isaac, *Transformation,* 266–267.
218. Bonomi, "Religious Dissent," 31, 51.
219. Weber, *Rhetoric,* 133; see also Bloch, *Republic,* 87.
220. John F. Wilson, "Religion and Revolution in American History," *Journal of Interdisciplinary History* 23 (Winter 1993), 610–611; Bloch, "Religion," 630.
221. McLoughlin, "Enthusiasm for Liberty," 55.
222. McLoughlin, *Dissent,* 1:339; quoted in Bloch, *Republic,* 110.
223. McLoughlin, *Dissent,* 1:576.
224. John DeWitt, "Essay I," in *The Anti-Federalist Papers and the Constitutional Debate,* ed. Ralph Ketcham (New York, 1986), 191; speech by Patrick Henry, ibid., 200.

225. Wood, *Creation*, 120–121.

226. Abraham Keteltas, *God Arising and Pleading His People's Cause* (Newburyport, Mass., 1777), 20.

227. Hawke, *Transaction*, 189; Stout, "Religion," 539; Stout, *Soul*, 274.

228. Quoted in Wood, *Creation*, 55, 67.

229. Ibid., 54.

230. Quoted ibid., 67.

231. Quoted ibid., 102, 101, 117; cf. 12–24.

232. Ibid., 83.

233. Jensen, "Struggle," 280; McLoughlin, "Religion," 203; Stout, *Soul*, 312.

234. John M. Mecklin, *The Story of American Dissent* (New York, 1990), 297; see "Isaac Backus' Draft for a Bill of Rights for the Massachusetts Constitution, 1779," in McLoughlin, *Backus on Church*, 487–488.

235. William Manning, "The Key of Liberty," in *The Key of Liberty: The Life and Democratic Writings of William Manning, "A Laborer," 1747–1814*, ed. Michael Merrill and Sean Wilentz (Cambridge, Mass., 1993), 125, 130, 122.

236. Quoted in Douglass, *Rebels*, 179; "Philanthropos," *Independent Chronicle*, April 6, 1780.

237. Douglass, *Rebels*, 159, 161.

238. Hawke, *Transaction*, 187; Rutland, *Birth*, 75.

239. Taylor, *Massachusetts*, 73, 175; Bailyn, *Origins*, 230.

240. Hatch, *Cause*, 138.

241. Quoted in Wood, *Creation*, 369, 374, 368; John Quincy Adams, quoted in Robert A. East, *John Quincy Adams: The Critical Years, 1785–1794* (New York, 1962), 85.

242. Quoted in Wood, *Creation*, 397, 399, 403, 432.

243. Stout, *Soul*, 312; McLoughlin, "Religion," 207.

244. Douglass, *Rebels*, 133; Bonomi, *Cope*, 185–186.

245. Robert L. Ganyard, *The Emergence of North Carolina's Revolutionary State Government* (Raleigh, N.C., 1978), 85.

246. James Madison, quoted in Rutland, *Birth*, 206; Curry, *Religion*, 200.

247. Isaac, *Transformation*, 321.

248. Thomas Jefferson, "Inauguration Address," in Koch and Peden, *Jefferson*, 321, 324, 323.

249. Jack P. Greene, "Search for Identity: An Interpretation of the Meaning of Selected Patterns of Social Response in Eighteenth-Century America," *Journal of Social History* 3 (Spring 1970), 218–220.

250. Wood, *Radicalism*, 369, 368.

251. J. Hector St. John de Crèvecoeur, *Letters from an American Farmer* (New York, 1957), 36.

252. Ibid., 55–56, 57, 220, 40, 20, 36; cf. 52–53.

253. See Jay Fliegelman, *Prodigals and Pilgrims: The America Revolution against Patriarchal Authority, 1750–1800* (Cambridge, 1982), 67–83.

254. Shain, *Myth*, 289.

255. Thomas Jefferson, "A Declaration by the Representatives of the United States of America," in Koch and Peden, *Jefferson*, 22; John Jay, quoted in Hartz, *Tradition*, 51; Jefferson, "Inauguration Address," 323.

256. Tocqueville, *Democracy*, 1:7.

257. John Adams, quoted in Wood, *Creation*, 8.

258. Jon Elster, introduction to *Rational Choice*, ed. Jon Elster (New York, 1986), 27, 15.

259. For a modern understanding, see J. Donald Moon, *Constructing Community: Moral Pluralism and Tragic Conflict* (Princeton, 1993).

260. Wood, *Radicalism*, 359.

261. Ibid., 308, 296.

262. See Bailyn, *Origins*.

263. Wood, *Radicalism*, 169–170. See also, Harry S. Stout, "Rhetoric and Reality in the Early Republic: The Case of the Federalist Clergy," in *Religion and American Politics: From the Colonial Period to the 1980s*, ed. Mark A. Noll (New York, 1990).

264. Charles Nisbet, quoted in Wood, *Radicalism*, 305, 329.

265. Nathan B. Hatch, *The Democratization of American Christianity* (New Haven, 1989), 6, 23.

266. Paine, *Common Sense*, 41.

267. Washington Irving, "Rip Van Winkle," in *The Sketch Book of Geoffrey Crayon, GentN* (Philadephia, 1848), 52–56, 59.

268. George Wilson Pierson, *Tocqueville in America* (Garden City, N.Y., 1959), 49; Tocqueville, *Democracy*, 2:304, 240.

269. John Dickinson, quoted in Wood, *Creation*, 475.

270. James Madison, *Federalist* no. 10, in *The Federalist Papers* (New York, 1961).

271. This was his "great object"; ibid.

272. See Robert H. Wiebe, *The Opening of American Society* (New York, 1984).

273. John Adams, "Discourses on Davila," in *The Political Writings of John Adams*, ed. George A. Peek, Jr. (Indianapolis, 1954), 189, 194.

274. "Letters from the Federal Farmer," in Ketcham, *The Anti-Federalist Papers*, 260.

275. Hawke, *Transaction*, 174, 224.

276. Clark, *Language*, 279.

277. See Hatch, *Cause*, 16–22.

278. Wood, *Radicalism*, 336.

279. Richard Price, *Observations on the Importance of the American Revolution* (London, 1784), 1–2.

8. The Liberal Idyll amidst Republican Realities

1. Daniel Walker Howe, *Making the American Self: Jonathan Edwards to Abraham Lincoln* (Cambridge, Mass., 1997), 12.

2. Wood, *Radicalism*, 359.

3. Frederick Jackson Turner, "The Significance of the Frontier in American History," in *Frontier and Section: Selected Essays of Frederick Jackson Turner*, ed. Ray Al-

len Billington (Englewood Cliffs, N.J., 1961), 62, 61. See F. O. Matthiessen, *American Renaissance* (New York, 1968), 626–656.

4. Wood, *Radicalism*, 336, 333; Foner, *Story*, 57.

5. Robert H. Wiebe, *Self-Rule: A Cultural History of American Democracy* (Chicago, 1995), 39, 40.

6. Wood, *Radicalism*, 368.

7. Paine, *Common Sense*, 9, 25; Edward Everett, "Phi Beta Kappa Oration on 'The Peculiar Motives to Intellectual Exertion in America,'" in *American Literary Revolution*, 316.

8. Henry James, *Hawthorne* (New York, 1966), 47–48.

9. See R. W. B. Lewis, *The American Adam: Innocence, Tragedy, and Tradition in the Nineteenth Century* (Chicago, 1971), 13–14.

10. Manning, "Key," 139, 166, 142; Tocqueville, *Democracy*, 1:266, 277, 60.

11. Herman Melville, *Moby-Dick* (New York, 1981), 159.

12. Tocqueville, *Democracy*, 1:45.

13. Ibid., 1:49, 7; 2:240–241.

14. Pierson, *Tocqueville*, 86–87.

15. Jefferson, "Inauguration Address," 323.

16. Hugh Swinton Legaré, "The Idea of the Nation," in *Quest for America, 1810–1824*, ed. Charles L. Sanford (Garden City, N.Y., 1967), 7, 10, 20, 12.

17. See Abraham Lincoln, "Speech at Chicago, Illinois," in *Abraham Lincoln: Selected Speeches, Messages, and Letters*, ed. T. Harry Williams (New York, 1964), 89, 93.

18. Pierson, *Tocqueville*, 49, 78.

19. Everett, "Oration," 287.

20. Quoted in Lewis, *Adam*, 5.

21. Tocqueville, *Democracy*, 2:4, 3.

22. Ralph Waldo Emerson, "Experience," in *Essays* (New York, 1993), 87, 88, 91.

23. Ibid., 103; Ralph Waldo Emerson, "Self-Reliance," ibid., 22.

24. Benjamin Franklin, *The Autobiography*, in *The Autobiography and Other Writings* (New York, 1982), 75; Walt Whitman, "Song of Myself," in *Leaves of Grass, and Selected Prose* (New York, 1964), 23.

25. Herman Melville, *Redburn: His First Voyage* (Garden City, N.Y., 1957), 145, 150–151.

26. Wiebe, *Opening*, 293, 292.

27. George Sidney Camp, quoted in John William Ward, "Jacksonian Democratic Thought: 'A Natural Charter of Privilege,'" in *The Development of American Culture*, ed. Stanley Coben and Lorman Ratner (Englewood Cliffs, N.J., 1970), 57.

28. See, e.g., Glenn C. Altschuler and Stuart M. Blumin, "'Where Is the Real America?': Politics and Popular Consciousness in the Antebellum Era," *America Quarterly* 49 (June 1997).

29. Harry L. Watson, *Liberty and Power: The Politics of Jacksonian America* (New York, 1990), 252.

30. Merrill D. Peterson, *The Jeffersonian Image in the American Mind* (New York, 1962), 92; Wiebe, *Opening*, 353.

31. Andrew Jackson, "A Political Testament," in *Social Theories of Jacksonian Democracy: Representative Writings of the Period 1825–1850,* ed. Joseph L. Blau (Indianapolis, 1954), 17.

32. Charles Jared Ingersoll, "Inchiquin's Letters," in *The Rising Glory of America, 1760–1820,* ed. Gordon S. Wood (Boston, 1990), 384, 388.

33. Everett, "Oration," 291–292.

34. Charles Grandison Finney, *Lectures on Revivals of Religion* (Cambridge, Mass., 1960), 297.

35. Henry Ward Beecher, *Lectures to Young Men* (Philadelphia, 1896), 39.

36. Ibid., 40.

37. Ralph Waldo Emerson, "Politics," in *Selected Prose and Poetry,* ed. Reginald L. Cook (New York, 1963), 199.

38. William P. Sprague, *Letters to Young Men* (Albany, N.Y., 1847), 115–116.

39. William Leggett, "Democratic Editorials," in Blau, *Jacksonian Democracy,* 75.

40. Jackson, "Political Testament," 17, 8.

41. Leggett, "Editorials," 71; James Fenimore Cooper, *Home as Found* (New York, 1883), 274–275, 255.

42. Jefferson, "Inauguration Address," 324.

43. Camp, quoted in Ward, "Jacksonian Democratic Thought," 57; Jackson, quoted ibid., 49.

44. See Karl Polanyi, *The Great Transformation: The Political and Economic Origins of Our Time* (Boston, 1957), 225–226.

45. Crèvecoeur, *Letters,* 8, 40.

46. Leggett, "Editorials," 76–77.

47. Crèvecoeur, *Letters,* 36.

48. Michel Chevalier, *Society, Manners, and Politics in the United States* (Ithaca, N.Y., 1969), 336.

49. Ingersoll, "Inchiquin's Letters," 383–384.

50. See Peterson, *Image,* 91–92, 98.

51. Walt Whitman, "Democratic Vistas," in *Leaves,* 508n. See also Peterson, *Image,* 91–92, 98.

52. See Joseph Dorfman, *The Economic Mind in American Civilization, 1606–1865* (New York, 1953), 2:638, 641.

53. Paul Conkin, *Prophets of Prosperity: America's First Political Economists* (Bloomington, Ind., 1980), 3, 2, 82; Leummi Baldwin, *Thoughts on the Study of Political Economy, as Connected with the Population, Industry, and Paper Currency of the United States* (Cambridge, Mass., 1809), 2, 62.

54. Charles Stewart Daveis, "Popular Government," in Blau, *Jacksonian Democracy,* 42.

55. Baldwin, *Thoughts,* 66.

56. Ibid., 17.

57. Jefferson, *Virginia,* 164–165; see also Henry Nash Smith, *Virgin Land: The American West as Symbol and Myth* (New York, 1950), 144–145.

58. Smith, *Land,* 138.

59. See Conkin, *Prophets*, 173–188.

60. Ibid., 173. See also Peterson, *Image*, 209–210.

61. Erick Bollman, *Paragraphs on Banks* (Philadelphia, 1810), 9.

62. Thomas Jefferson, "Letter to John Jay," in Koch and Pederson, *Jefferson*, 377.

63. Pierson, *Tocqueville*, 86.

64. Editors of the *Democratic Review*, "An Introductory Statement of the Democratic Principle," in Blau, *Jacksonian Democracy*, 28.

65. Tocqueville, *Democracy*, 1:308.

66. Wood, *Radicalism*, 337.

67. Samuel Blodget, *Economica: A Statistical Manual for the United States of America* (Washington, D.C., 1806), 12, 20, 200.

68. Turner, "Significance," 61.

69. Cooper, *Home*, 190; Caroline Kirkland, *A New Home—Who'll Follow?* (New Haven, 1965), 53.

70. Alvin Johnson, *Pioneer's Progress* (Lincoln, Neb., 1960), 89.

71. Caroline Kirkland, *Western Clearings* (New York, 1845), 64.

72. Jeremy Belknap, *The Foresters: An American Tale* (Upper Saddle River, N.J., 1970), 16–17.

73. Crèvecoeur, *Letters*, 35–36.

74. Thomas Paine, "Rights of Man," in *Selected Writings*, 291, 295; Paine, *Common Sense*, 9.

75. Tocqueville, *Democracy*, 1:32, 14, 37; Pierson, *Tocqueville*, 78.

76. E. W. Howe, *The Story of a Country Town* (New York, 1964), 1.

77. Frederick Jackson Turner, "The Problem of the West," in Billington, *Frontier and Section*, 75, 69; Turner, "Significance," 57, 56.

78. Quoted in Polanyi, *Transformation*, 117.

79. The importance of this constructed logic for liberalism is discussed ibid., 114, 115. For Locke's recognition of this construction, see *Education*, 112–113, 238.

80. "David Ramsay on the Arts and Sciences in a New Republic," in *Theories of Education in Early America, 1655–1819*, ed. Wilson Smith (Indianapolis, 1973), 225, 228.

81. Joel Barlow, *The Columbiad*, in *The Connecticut Wits*, ed. Vernon Louis Parrington (New York, 1969), 321, 322; Ingersoll, "Inchiquin's Letters," 388.

82. Gilbert Vale, "Political Economy," in Blau, *Jacksonian Democracy*, 237.

83. Chevalier, *Society*, 335.

84. Tocqueville, *Democracy*, 2:161, 250.

85. Ibid., 39; Crèvecoeur, *Letters*, 65.

86. Tocqueville, *Democracy*, 2:43.

87. Crèvecoeur, *Letters*, 78.

88. Ibid., 57, 64, 56.

89. Chevalier, *Society*, 202, 201.

90. Pierson, *Tocqueville*, 75, 87.

91. Ingersoll, "Inchiquin's Letters," 388.

92. Frances Trollope, *Domestic Manners of the Americans* (New York, 1949), 405.

93. "Ramsay on Arts," 224.

94. Tocqueville, *Democracy,* 2:248.

95. Ibid., 1:259; Ingersoll, "Inchiquin's Letters," 388; Daveis, "Government," 48; George Bancroft, "The Office of the People," in Blau, *Jacksonian Democracy,* 267.

96. Pierson, *Tocqueville,* 86–87.

97. Tocqueville, *Democracy,* 2:240, 268, 258.

98. Ingersoll, "Inchiquin's Letters," 388.

99. Pierson, *Tocqueville,* 87; Tocqueville, *Democracy,* 2:138.

100. Tocqueville, *Democracy,* 2:240.

101. Trollope, *Manners,* 301; Chevalier, *Society,* 202, 262, 201.

102. Tocqueville, *Democracy,* 2:272.

103. Steven Watts, *The Republic Reborn: War and the Making of Liberal America, 1790–1820* (Baltimore, 1987), 14, 68.

104. Ibid., xviii, xxi.

105. Judicial regulation became the means for framing institutional formation as the incidental regulation of the actualization of participating individual wills. See Morton J. Horowitz, *The Transformation of American Law, 1780–1860* (Cambridge, Mass., 1977).

106. Francis Wayland, *The Elements of Moral Science* (Cambridge, Mass., 1963), 349.

107. See Kirkland, *Home,* 55.

108. Cooper, *Home,* 17, 186. See Karen Halttunen, *Confidence Men and Painted Women: A Study of Middle-Class Culture in America, 1830–1870* (New Haven, 1982).

109. Quoted in Wood, *Radicalism,* 328.

110. Chevalier, *Society,* 321.

111. Becker, "Kansas," 4, 9–10.

112. Cooper, *Home,* 187–191.

113. Kirkland, *Home,* 180.

114. Tocqueville, *Democracy,* 2:13.

115. Peterson, *Image,* 85.

116. Leggett, "Editorials," 82; Stephen Simpson, "Political Economy and the Workers," in Blau, *Jacksonian Democracy,* 144.

117. Leggett, "Editorials," 77; Simpson, "Economy," 148.

118. John W. Vethake, "The Doctrine of Anti-Monopoly," in Blau, *Jacksonian Democracy,* 211.

119. Leggett, "Editorials," 86, 76; Simpson, "Economy," 140.

120. Theophilus Fisk, "Capital against Labor," in Blau, *Jacksonian Democracy,* 199; Leggett, "Editorials," 87.

121. Leggett, "Editorials," 71, 67, 68.

122. See, e.g., Fisk, "Capital," 203.

123. Simpson, "Economy," 156.

124. Blau, introduction to *Jacksonian Democracy,* xxiii.

125. Simpson, "Economy," 155, 156.

126. Conkin, *Prophets,* xi.

127. Blau, introduction to *Jacksonian Democracy*, xxvi.

128. Henry Adams, *The Education of Henry Adams* (Boston, 1961), 381; Frank Norris, *The Octopus* (New York, 1958), 33.

129. Jack London, *The Iron Heel* (New York, 1971), 42, 40; Sherwood Anderson, *A Story Teller's Story: Memoirs of Youth and Middle Age* (New York, 1989), 220; Sherwood Anderson, *Poor White* (New York, 1966), 60.

130. James Fenimore Cooper, *The Pioneers* (New York, 1964), 93.

131. Kirkland, *Home*, 172; Sinclair Lewis, *Main Street* (New York, 1961), 76, 71.

132. Kirkland, *Home*, 179–180.

133. Kate Chopin, "The Point at Issue!" in *The Awakening and Selected Stories* (New York, 1976), 139.

134. Stephen Crane, "The Monster," in *Maggie and Other Stories* (New York, 1960), 95, 97.

135. Ibid., 98, 129.

136. Anderson, *Story*, 300, 301, 325.

137. Ibid., 187, 229, 196, 208, 190, 301.

138. Ibid., 300.

139. Lewis, *Main Street*, 432.

140. See Smith, *Land*, bk. 3.

141. Frederick Jackson Turner, "Contributions of the West to American Democracy," in Billington, *Frontier and Section*, 90; Smith, *Land*, 297.

142. Edward Atkinson, *The Margin of Profits* (New York, 1887), 18.

143. Herbert Croly, *The Promise of American Life* (New York, 1964), 50; see also Vernon L. Parrington, *Main Currents in American Thought, vol. 2, 1800–1860: The Romantic Revolution in America* (New York, 1954), 12–13, 464.

144. See Rodgers, *Contested Truths*.

9. From Liberation to Reversal

1. D. H. Lawrence, *Studies in Classic American Literature* (New York, 1961), 7, 3; Matthiessen, *Renaissance*, xv.

2. Of course, the space into which the republic spread was not empty either of people or of culture, and this willed ignorance had horrific consequences. See, e.g., Herman Melville, *The Confidence Man* (New York, 1990); Michael Paul Rogin, *Fathers and Children: Andrew Jackson and the Subjugation of the American Indian* (New York, 1975).

3. Robert H. Wiebe, *The Opening of American Society* (New York, 1984), xii, 251; John Higham, *From Boundlessness to Consolidation: The Transformation of American Culture, 1848–1860* (Ann Arbor, 1969), 13, 6, 14.

4. McLoughlin, "Religion," 208, 212; Robert A. Ferguson, "'We Hold These Truths': Strategies of Control in the Literature of the Founders," in *Reconstructing American Literary History*, ed. Sacvan Bercovitch (Cambridge, Mass., 1986), 4.

5. Everett, "Oration," 288, 286; Charles Jared Ingersoll, "A Discourse Concerning the Influence of America on the Mind," in Spiller, *American Literary Revolution*, 282, 283.

6. Melville, *Moby-Dick*, 13, 158, 105.

7. Pierson, *Tocqueville*, 49.

8. Higham, *Boundlessness*, 15.

9. Lewis, *Adam*, 115.

10. Smith, *Land*, 90, 91; Lewis, *Adam*, 5.

11. Leslie A. Fiedler, *Love and Death in the American Novel* (New York, 1966), 27, 24.

12. Lewis, *Adam*, 9; Smith, *Land*, 135; Fiedler, *Love*, 143.

13. Cathy N. Davidson, *Revolution and the Word: The Rise of the Novel in America* (New York, 1986), vii.

14. Jane Tompkins, *Sensational Designs: The Cultural Work of American Fiction, 1790–1860* (New York, 1985), xviii.

15. Annette Kolodny, *The Land before Her: Fantasy and Experience of the American Frontiers, 1630–1860* (Chapel Hill, 1984), xiii, 67.

16. See Edward Watts, *Writing and Postcolonialism in the Early Republic* (Charlottesville, Va., 1998).

17. Davidson, *Revolution*, 252.

18. Everett, "Oration," 286, 316, 314.

19. Toni Morrison, *Playing in the Dark: Whiteness and the Literary Imagination* (New York, 1993), 34–37.

20. Ibid., 36, 37. On the predominance of a violent and disordered world in this literature, see Shirley Samuels, *Romance of the Republic: Women, the Family, and Violence in the Literature of the Early American Nation* (New York, 1996); Richard Slotkin, *Regeneration through Violence: The Mythology of the American Frontier, 1600–1860* (New York, 1996).

21. William Hill Brown, *The Power of Sympathy* (New Haven, 1970), 36, 64, 67, 111, 112.

22. Hannah Foster, *The Coquette* (New Haven, 1970), 138, 133, 140.

23. Ibid., 153, 201, 150.

24. Charles Brockden Brown, *Arthur Mervyn* (New York, 1962), 326, 18, 8, 9.

25. Charles Brockden Brown, *Wieland, or, the Transformation* (New York, 1989), 28–30.

26. Cooper, *Prairie*, 383; James Fenimore Cooper, *The Pioneers* (New York, 1964), 434, 433, 436.

27. Kirkland, *Home*, 189, 211, 212, 203.

28. Robert Montgomery Bird, *Nick of the Woods* (New Haven, 1967), 344, 46.

29. Bayard Taylor, *Hannah Thurston: A Story of American Life* (Upper Saddle River, N.J., 1968), 385, 38, 40.

30. Nathaniel Hawthorne, *The Scarlet Letter* (New York, 1960), 106.

31. Edgar Allan Poe, *The Narrative of Arthur Gordon Pym* (New York, 1960), 5, 16.

32. Melville, *Redburn*, 3, 6, 12, 9.

33. Melville, *Moby-Dick*, 13, 16, 11.

34. Brown, *Power,* 110–112, 123.

35. Ibid., 62–63, 95, 121.

36. Foster, *Coquette,* 155, 143.

37. Ibid., 150, 177, 149.

38. Ibid., 223, 222, 242, 246, 251.

39. Royall Tyler, *The Algerine Captive* (New Haven, 1970), 43.

40. Ibid., 44.

41. Brown, *Mervyn,* 25, 135, 377, 317, 421, 48.

42. Charles Brockden Brown, *Edgar Huntly; or Memoirs of a Sleepwalker* (New Haven, 1973), 103, 130, 110.

43. Ibid., 218, 153, 182.

44. Ibid., 32, 33, 38.

45. Brown, *Wieland,* 21, 26, 18.

46. Ibid., 71, 73, 75.

47. George Leppard, *The Monks of Monk Hall* (New York, 1970), 370, 371.

48. Cooper, *Prairie,* 143, 14, 10, 13, 11, 27, 345, 382, 383.

49. Cooper, *Home,* 231, 230, 226.

50. Kirkland, *Home,* 210.

51. Bird, *Nick,* 95, 86. 343.

52. Hawthorne, *Letter,* 70.

53. Ibid., 317, 185, 178.

54. Ibid., 71, 227, 219.

55. Nathaniel Hawthorne, "Young Goodman Brown," in *The Birthmark and Other Stories* (New York, 1968), 13, 12.

56. Ibid., 21, 23, 28.

57. Poe, *Pym,* 23, 12, 94, 51, 120.

58. Melville, *Redburn,* 34, 163, 178.

59. Ibid., 62, 64, 178, 184.

60. Melville, *Moby-Dick,* 169, 160, 175, 171.

61. Ibid., 175 (emphasis added), 169, 16.

62. Brown, *Power,* 112, 111, 113.

63. Ibid., 96, 121, 67, 123.

64. Foster, *Coquette,* 153, 163.

65. Ibid., 259, 265.

66. Ibid., 178, 267, 263.

67. Ibid., 267, 240, 163, 164.

68. Tyler, *Algerine Captive,* 124, 224, 132 (emphasis added).

69. Ibid., 147, 151, 224.

70. Ibid., 200, 224.

71. Brown, *Edgar Huntly,* 153.

72. Brown, *Mervyn,* 11, 68.

73. Ibid., 65, 50, 326.

74. Ibid., 280, 80, 380, 281.

75. Kirkland, *Home,* 211.

76. Ibid., 229, 226, 180.

77. Bird, *Nick,* 61, 347.

78. Cooper, *Prairie,* 383; Cooper, *Pioneers,* 436.

79. Cooper, *Prairie,* 382, 362, 27.

80. Taylor, *Hannah Thurston,* 33, 458, 463.

81. Hawthorne, *Letter,* 316.

82. Poe, *Pym,* 169, 118n, 120, 119.

83. Melville, *Redburn,* 298, 299.

84. Melville, *Moby-Dick,* 160.

85. Brown, *Wieland,* 73, 11, 30.

86. Ibid., 30, 97, 87.

87. Ibid., 129, 130.

88. Ibid., 133, 196, 190, 276.

89. Melville, *Moby-Dick,* 161, 185, 157, 156.

90. Ibid., 157, 192, 16.

91. Ibid., 384–385; cf. 521.

92. The parallels between the fictional depiction of reversal and its presence in such important nonfiction works as *Walden* and *The Oregon Trail* suggest a pervasive cultural process. For a similar process evident in private journals during this period, see Roderick Nash, *Wilderness and the American Mind* (New Haven, 1973), 57–59. 65–66, 81.

93. Pierson, *Tocqueville,* 252; Tocqueville, *Democracy,* 1:198.

94. Pierson, *Tocqueville,* 106–107.

95. Tocqueville, 1:67, 76, 93.

96. Pierson, *Tocqueville,* 74.

97. Tocqueville, *Democracy,* 1:73, 67. Chevalier also notes the irony of an authority both invisible and ubiquitous. Chevalier, *Society,* 328.

98. Pierson, *Tocqueville,* 86, 105.

99. Tocqueville, *Democracy,* 1:7.

100. Pierson, *Tocqueville,* 363.

101. Tocqueville, *Democracy,* 1:334.

102. Pierson, *Tocqueville,* 87, 73.

103. Tocqueville, *Democracy,* 1:45.

104. Ibid.,1:251, 252, 46, 97, 60; 2:23, 135.

105. Ibid., 1:67, 73; 2:130, 137.

106. Ibid., 1:252, 251; 2:132, 131.

107. Ibid., 1:254, 255, 261, 260; cf. 1:252, 95–96, 98, 270–275; 2:3, 118, 127, 254–255.

108. Ibid., 1:265, 266, 180, 143, 195, 194.

109. Ibid., 1:275, 274.

110. Ibid., 1:260, 310, 308, 179.

111. Ibid., 2:109, 275, 308, 307, 312.

112. Ibid., 1:262; 2:149, 148, 104, 106.

113. Ibid., 2:274, 277, 239, 240, 336, 337, 307.

114. Ibid., 2:336.
115. Ibid., 2:9, 3, 4.
116. Ibid., 2:10, 11.
117. Ibid., 2:9, 10, 11, 311 (emphasis added).
118. Ibid., 2:10, 311, 101–102, 227.
119. Ibid., 2:100, 165, 12, 13, 265, 275, 267.
120. Ibid., 2:149, 337, 313, 336.
121. Ibid., 2:276, 277, 268, 271.

10. National Revival as the Crucible of Agency Character

1. Potter, *Freedom*, 40.
2. Tocqueville, *Democracy*, 2:144, 239; Finney, *Lectures*, 11, 10.
3. Henry George, quoted with approval in John Dewey, *Liberalism and Social Action* (New York, 1963), 68; ibid., 90.
4. Roger Friedland and Robert R. Alford, quoted in Harry S. Stout and D. Scott Cormode, "Institutions and the Story of American Religion: A Sketch of a Synthesis," in *Sacred Companies: Organizational Aspects of Religion and Religious Aspects of Organizations*, ed. N. J. Demerath III, Peter Dobkin Hall, Terry Schmitt, and Rhys H. Williams (New York, 1998), 70.
5. See Horowitz, *Transformation*.
6. Stout and Cormode, "Institutions," 73.
7. See T. J. Jackson Lears, *Fables of Abundance* (New York, 1994); Steward Ewen, *Captains of Consciousness: Advertising and the Social Roots of the Consumer Culture* (New York, 1977).
8. See Nathan O. Hatch, "The Democratization of Christianity and the Character of American Politics," in Noll, *Religion and American Politics*, 97, 96.
9. See Winthrop S. Hudson, "A Time of Religious Ferment," in *The Rise of Adventism*, ed. Edwin S. Gaustad (New York, 1974).
10. Perry Miller, *The Life of the Mind in America from the Revolution to the Civil War* (New York, 1965), 6, 7.
11. Max Weber, "The Protestant Sects and the Spirit of Capitalism," in *From Max Weber: Essays in Sociology*, ed. Hans H. Gerth and C. Wright Mills (New York, 1958), 302.
12. Jane Louise Mesick, *The English Traveller in America, 1785–1835* (New York, 1922), 246–248; Karl Theodor Griesinger, "A Historian's Forebodings," in *This Was America*, ed. Oscar Handlin (Cambridge, Mass., 1969), 260–261.
13. Philip Schaff, *America: A Sketch of the Political, Social, and Religious Character of the United States of North America*, quoted in Lipset, *New Nation*, 162; Max Berger, *The British Traveler in America* (New York, 1943), 134.
14. Robert Baird, *Religion in America* (New York, 1856), 366.
15. Ingersoll, "Inchiquin's Letters," 386.
16. Francis Grund, "Religion and Morality Preside over Their Councils," in *America*

in Perspective: The United States through Foreign Eyes, ed. Henry Steele Commager (New York, 1947), 92–93.

17. Moritz Busch, *Travels between the Hudson and the Mississippi, 1851–1852* (Lexington, Ky., 1971), 274, 275, 55.

18. Trollope, *Manners,* 107 and note; Ralph W. Emerson, *The Heart of Emerson's Journals,* ed. Bliss Perry (New York, 1958), 49.

19. Quoted in Miller, *Life,* 36.

20. Baird, *Religion,* 264, 367.

21. Charles Finney, *The Guilt of Sin* (Grand Rapids, Mich., 1965), 12–13.

22. Baird, *Religion,* 77.

23. Ibid., 79.

24. Ibid., 67.

25. Leggett, "Editorials," 79; editors of the *Democratic Review,* "Introductory Statement," 28.

26. See Baird, *Religion,* 400, 80.

27. Charles Finney, *True Submission* (Grand Rapids, Mich., 1967), 64, 52–54.

28. Philip Schaff, *America: A Sketch of the Political, Social, and Religious Character of the United States of North America* (New York, 1855), xviii, xvii, xviii; Harriet Martineau, *Society in America,* 3 vols. (London, 1837), 1:23.

29. Donald G. Mathews, "The Second Great Awakening as an Organizing Process, 1780–1830: An Hypothesis," *American Quarterly* 21 (Spring 1969), 27, 33, 32, 43, 29.

30. Randall A. Roth, *The Democratic Dilemma: Religion, Reform, and the Social Order in the Connecticut River Valley of Vermont, 1791–1850* (Cambridge, 1987), 81.

31. Daniel Walker Howe, "Protestantism, Voluntarism, and Personal Identity in Antebellum America," in Stout and Hart, *New Directions,* 209, 207, 226. See also Daniel Walker Howe, "The Evangelical Movement and Political Culture in the North during the Second Party System," *Journal of American History* 77 (March 1991).

32. George M. Thomas, *Revivalism and Cultural Change: Christianity, Nation Building, and the Market in the Nineteenth-Century United States* (Chicago, 1989), 78; Howe, "Movement," 1220.

33. Timothy L. Smith, *Revivalism and Social Reform: American Protestantism on the Eve of the Civil War* (New York, 1965), 153. See Finney, quoted in William G. McLoughlin, introduction to Finney, *Lectures,* xlv.

34. Miller, *Life,* 43.

35. See Baird, *Religion,* 534, 537; Richard Carwardine, "Unity, Pluralism, and the Spiritual Market-Place: Interdenominational Competition in the Early American Republic," in *Unity and Diversity in the Church,* ed. R. N. Swanson (Oxford, 1996).

36. See R. Laurence Moore, *Religious Outsiders and the Making of Americans* (New York, 1986); Sydney E. Ahlstrom, *A Religious History of the American People* (New Haven, 1972); Hatch, *Democratization.*

37. William G. McLoughlin, *Revivals, Awakenings, and Reform: An Essay on Religion*

and Social Change in America, 1607–1977 (Chicago, 1978), 22. McLoughlin employs Anthony Wallace's conception of "revitalization movements." Ibid., 10.

38. Ibid., 21.

39. Ahlstrom, *History,* 472; Whitney R. Cross, *The Burned-Over District: The Social and Intellectual History of Enthusiastic Religion in Western New York, 1800–1850* (New York, 1965), 257.

40. Finke and Stark, *Churching,* 54, 57.

41. See, e.g., Charles A. Johnson, *The Frontier Camp Meeting: Religion's Harvest Time* (Dallas, 1985); A. Gregory Schneider, *The Way of the Cross Leads Home: The Domestication of American Methodism* (Bloomington, Ind., 1993).

42. Richard Carwardine, "'Antinomians' *and* 'Arminians': Methodists and the Market Revolution," in *The Market Revolution in America: Social, Political, and Religious Expressions, 1800–1880,* ed. Melvyn Stokes and Stephen Conway (Charlottesville, Va. 1996), 290; Carwardine, "Unity," 308.

43. See Paul E. Johnson, *A Shopkeeper's Millennium: Society and Revivals in Rochester, New York, 1815–1837* (New York, 1978).

44. Miller, *Life,* 34.

45. Carwardine, "Unity," 330.

46. Curtis D. Johnson, *Redeeming America: Evangelicals and the Road to the Civil War* (Chicago, 1993), 57.

47. Richard McNemar, "The Kentucky Revival," in *Rising Glory,* ed. Gordon Wood (Boston, 1990), 82.

48. Ibid., 86–88.

49. Joseph Haroutunian, *Piety versus Moralism: The Passing of the New England Theology* (New York, 1932), xvii; McNemar, "Revival," 87–88.

50. Cross, *District,* 284.

51. Quoted in Carwardine, "Unity," 310.

52. T. Scott Miyakawa, *Protestants and Pioneers* (Chicago, 1964), 145.

53. Cross, *District,* 322, 318–319.

54. Finney, quoted in McLaughlin, *Revivals,* 130; Miyakawa, *Protestants,* 158, 157.

55. Paul E. Johnson and Sean Wilentz, *The Kingdom of Matthias: A Story of Sex and Salvation in the Nineteenth Century* (New York, 1994), 9. See also Michael Barkun, *Crucible of the Millennium: The Burned-Over District of New York in the 1840s* (Syracuse, 1986).

56. Cross, *District,* 257, 274.

57. John Leland, quoted in Goen, *Revivalism,* 289; Lorenzo Dow, quoted in Hatch, *Democratization,* 37.

58. Michael G. Kenny, *The Perfect Law of Liberty: Elias Smith and the Providential History of America* (Washington, D.C., 1994), 13–14.

59. C. C. Goss, *Statistical History of the First Century of American Methodism* (New York, 1866), 9, 171.

60. Roth, *Dilemma,* 144; John Barent Johnson, quoted in David G. Hackett, *The Rude Hand of Innovation: Religion and Social Order in Albany, New York, 1652–1836* (New York, 1991), 53, 54.

61. Terry D. Bilhartz, *Urban Religion and the Second Great Awakening: Church and Society in Early National Baltimore* (Rutherford, N.J., 1986), 116.

62. Jama Lazerow, *Religion and the Working Class in Antebellum America* (Washington, D.C., 1995), 151, 164, 180; Alexander Campbell, quoted in Nathan Hatch, "The Christian Movement and the Demand for a Theology of the People," *Journal of American History* 67 (December 1980), 558.

63. William Warren Sweet, *Religion in the Development of American Culture* (New York, 1952), 254; Cross, *District,* 137.

64. Captain Marryat, quoted in Martin Marty, *Righteous Empire: The Protestant Experience in America* (New York, 1970), 93.

65. Miller, *Life,* 34.

66. Howe, "Movement," 1221, 1236.

67. Goss, *History,* 147–148, 165, 173.

68. Finney, *Lectures on Revivals of Religion* (Albany, 1832), 9, 26, 16.

69. William Sprague, *Lectures,* 22, 3.

70. Baird, *Religion,* 428, 414, 404.

71. Ibid., 414.

72. McNemar, "Revival," 88.

73. Horace Bushnell, "Sermons on Living Subjects," in *Horace Bushnell Sermons,* ed. Conrad Cherry (New York, 1985), 28, 34; Finney, *Lectures,* 6, 9; Baird, *Religion,* 416, 420.

74. Charles Finney, *Sermons on Important Subjects* (New York, 1836), 80.

75. Sprague, *Lectures,* 3, 9–10.

76. Cross, *District,* 137; Finney, *Sermons,* 143.

77. Baird, *Religion,* 431. See also Orville Dewey, "Discourses on the Nature of Religion," in *Works,* 3 vols. (New York, 1848), 118–130; Horace Bushnell, *Christian Nurture* (New York, 1975).

78. Finney, *Sermons,* 187, 186.

79. Finney, *Lectures,* 11, 10.

80. Finney, *Lectures,* 272, 273, 269–270.

81. Goss, *History,* 163.

82. See Hatch, *Democratization,* 65.

83. McNemar, "Revival," 88.

84. Finney, *Submission,* 14, 11.

85. Finney, *Lectures,* 270.

86. Finney, *Sermons,* 3, 5–7.

87. Ibid., 5, 8–9, 36, 23; Finney, quoted in McLoughlin, *Revivals,* 125.

88. Reynolds, *Faith,* 27, 11.

89. "The Freedom of the Human Will," quoted in Hatch, *Democratization,* 231.

90. Peter Cartwright, *The Backwoods Preacher* (London, n.d.), 27, 10.

91. Smith, *Revivalism,* 88.

92. Timothy L. Smith, "Righteousness and Hope: Christian Holiness and the Millennial Vision in America, 1800–1900," *American Quarterly* 31 (Spring 1979), 31.

93. Smith, *Revivalism*, 91; *Methodist Quarterly Review*, quoted ibid., 92; Daniel Whedon, quoted ibid.

94. Cartwright, *Preacher*, 16.

95. Baird, *Religion*, 416.

96. Finney, *Sermons*, 207; Finney, *Lectures*, 173.

97. Baird, *Religion*, 415–416.

98. "Letters of Orceneth Fisher," in *Religion on the American Frontier, 1783–1840*, ed. William Warren Sweet (Chicago, 1946), 473; Cartwright, *Preacher*, 100.

99. "The Journal of Benjamin Lakin," in Sweet, *American Frontier*, 258.

100. "Letters of Orceneth Fisher," 473, 492.

101. Asa Mahan, *Spiritual Doctrine of Christian Perfection* (Boston, 1839), 164.

102. Finney, *Sermons*, 217; Finney, *Lectures*, 16.

103. Finney, *Lectures*, 10n2 (emphasis added).

104. Ibid., 409; Finney, *Sermons*, 20.

105. Finney, *Lectures*, 171, 172, 211.

106. Ibid., 171; Henry Ware, *The Formation of the Christian Character* (Boston, 1874), 24–26.

107. Baird, *Religion*, 420, 412.

108. Ware, *Formation*, 37–38.

109. Finney, *Lectures*, 336, 359.

110. Ibid., 334.

111. Ibid., 169, 170, 340.

112. Ibid., 358.

113. Finney, *Sermons*, 217; quoted in Baird, *Religion*, 413.

114. Finney, *Lectures*, 334, 423; Finney, *Sermons*, 180; Finney, quoted in Miller, *Life*, 33.

115. Finney, *Sermons*, 74, 132.

116. Baird, *Religion*, 406, 407; quoted ibid., 416.

117. Ibid., 412.

118. T. C. Upham, *Principles of the Interior or Hidden Life* (Boston, 1845), 387.

119. Finney, *Lectures*, 400; "Testimony of Rev. Titus," in *Pioneer Experiences, or, The Gift of Power Received by Faith*, ed. Phoebe Palmer (New York, 1984), 216.

120. Finney, *Sermons*, 144.

121. Ibid., 56, 220.

122. McNemar, "Revival," 88. See also "Testimony of B. F. Crary," in Palmer, *Pioneer Experiences*, 140; "Testimony of Titus," 216; "Testimony of Dr. A. Hill," ibid., 316.

123. Baird, *Religion*, 26; Finney, *Sermons*, 144.

124. "Testimony of Rev. W. H. Poole," in Palmer, *Pioneer Experiences*, 23.

125. Reynolds, *Faith*, 41.

126. Finney, *Lectures*, 372, 425.

127. "Testimony of Hill," in Palmer, *Pioneer Experiences*, 316; "Testimony of Rev. H. Neff," ibid., 340; Ware, *Formation*, 176.

128. William Boardman, *The Higher Christian Life* (New York, 1984), 282, 283.

129. Finney, *Lectures*, 358; Ware, *Formation*, 66.

130. Finney, *Sermons*, 54, 56.

131. Quoted in Hatch, *Democratization*, 172–173.

132. Bushnell, "Living Subjects," 166.

133. Finney, *Lectures*, 425, 388; Reynolds, *Faith*, 10.

134. Baird, *Religion*, 421, 420.

135. Bushnell, "Living Subjects," 166.

136. McNemar, "Revival," 82–84, 87.

137. Goss, *History*, 184–186.

138. Finney, *Submission*, 11.

139. Smith, *Revivalism*, 28.

140. Finney, quoted in McLoughlin, *Revivals*, 121; Finney, *Sermons*, 18, 8 (emphasis added).

141. Finney, *Sermons*, 17–18, 72, 31, 29.

142. Ware, *Formation*, 14; Mahan, *Doctrine*, 13, 10.

143. William Sprague, *Letters to Young Men* (Albany, N.Y., 1847), 37.

144. Bushnell, "Living Subjects," 31; Horace Bushnell, "Christ and His Salvation, in Sermons Variously Related Thereto," in *Sermons*, 157.

145. Horace Bushnell, "The Spirit in Man," in *Sermons*, 70–71.

146. Sprague, *Lectures*, 29, 268.

147. Ware, *Formation*, v, 2–4.

148. Finney, *Sermons*, 79, 77, 76.

149. Mahan, *Doctrine*, 80.

150. Cartwright, *Preacher*, 7, 8.

151. Bushnell, "Spirit," 70–71.

152. Boardman, *Life*, 215, 224.

153. Finney, *Sermons*, 55, 8, 21.

154. Ware, *Formation*, 442.

155. Smith, *Revivalism*, 92.

156. Finney, *Lectures*, 423, 403.

157. Bushnell, "Spirit," 57, 70.

158. Finney, *Lectures*, 386; Bushnell, "Spirit," 67.

159. Ware, *Formation*, 13; Boardman, *Life*, 288.

160. Finney, *Lectures*, 19.

161. Ibid., 377, 404.

162. Bushnell, "Spirit," 56, 92.

163. Finney, *Sermons*, 61; Goss, *History*, 182–183.

164. "Testimony of T. C. Upham," in Palmer, *Pioneer Experiences*, 98; Bushnell, "Living Subjects," 220, 226.

165. Finney, *Sermons*, 11, 57.

166. Ibid., 197.

167. Bushnell, "Spirit," 67.

168. Finney, *Lectures*, 38–39, 50–51, 377; Bushnell, *Sermons*, 70.

169. Ware, *Formation*, 41.

170. Finney, *Lectures,* 386, 404; Sprague, *Lectures,* 5.

171. Bushnell, "Spirit," 71.

172. Finney, *Lectures,* 388.

173. Ibid., 397.

174. Ibid., 397, 400.

175. Sprague, *Lectures,* 197.

176. Ware, *Formation,* 149, 154, 67–68; cf. 68–69, 81–83 (all second pagination).

177. Upham, *Principles,* 312, 318.

178. Bushnell, "Sermons for the New Life," in *Sermons,* 206.

179. Finney, *Lectures,* 175, 194.

180. Ibid., 397, 411.

181. Sprague, *Lectures,* 216.

182. Finney, *Lectures,* 399.

183. Sprague, *Lectures,* 196; Finney, *Lectures,* 398.

184. Ware, *Formation,* 170, 72 (second pagination).

185. Wayland, *Elements,* 85, 86.

186. Ware, *Formation,* 74–75.

187. Dewey, "Discourses," 119, 126, 128, 130, 141.

188. Finney, *Lectures,* 402; Sprague, *Lectures,* 191; Ware, *Formation,* 152, 150.

189. Finney, *Lectures,* 459, 413; Ware, *Formation,* 152.

190. See Finney, *Lectures,* 44–49; Ware, *Formation.*

191. Sprague, *Lectures,* 191, 203, 204.

192. Finney, *Lectures,* 403; Ware, *Formation,* 176.

193. Hackett, *Rude Hand,* 47; Roth, *Dilemma,* 158.

194. Thomas, *Revivalism,* 78; see also William R. Sutton, *Journeymen for Jesus: Evangelical Artisans Confront Capitalism in Jacksonian Baltimore* (University Park, Pa., 1998), 258.

195. Goss, *History,* 177; Mathews, "Awakening," 38.

196. Ellen Eslinger, *Citizens of Zion: The Social Origins of Camp Meeting Revivalism* (Knoxville, Tenn., 1999), 241.

197. Mathews, "Awakening," 35.

198. Baird, *Religion,* 80.

199. Paul K. Conkin, *Cane Ridge, America's Pentecost* (Madison, Wis., 1990), 87; Finke and Stark, *Churching,* 94.

200. Baird, *Religion,* 421; Trollope, *Manners,* 168, 79.

201. Finney, *Lectures,* 421.

202. Baird, *Religion,* 414–415, 417.

203. McNemar, "Revival," 83; Howe, *Story,* 28.

204. McNemar, "Revival," 85, 88–89.

205. Baird, *Religion,* 422–433.

206. Howe, *Story,* 28.

207. Finney, *Lectures,* 268 (emphasis added), 267, 18.

208. Goss, *History,* 179; Finney, *Lectures,* 16.

209. Cartwright, *Preacher,* 260.

210. Mathews, "Awakening," 43; Eslinger, *Citizens,* 239.

211. Finney, *Sermons,* 56.

212. Timothy L. Smith, "Social Reform: Some Reflections on Causation and Consequence," in Gaustad, *Rise,* 18.

213. Robert H. Abzug, *Cosmos Crumbling: American Reform and the Religious Imagination* (New York, 1994), 80.

214. Howe, "Movement," 1239.

215. See James H. Moorhead, "Social Reform and the Divided Conscience of Antebellum Protestantism," *Church History* 48 (1979), 427–428.

216. Ware, *Formation,* 15, 13, 3.

217. Phoebe Palmer, "Editor's Preface," in Palmer, *Pioneer Experiences,* vii.

218. Finney, *Lectures,* 418, 400–401.

219. Cartwright, *Preacher,* 258, 242; Goss, *History,* 180.

220. C. G. Finney, quoted in Moorhead, "Social Reform," 422.

221. Ibid., 424.

222. See McLoughlin, *Revivals,* 101–112.

223. Finney, *Lectures,* 306, 286, 308.

224. Ibid., 308. See also Cartwright, *Preacher,* 251, 252.

225. See Charles C. Cole, Jr., *The Social Ideas of the Northern Evangelicals* (New York, 1977).

226. Quoted in Smith, *Revivalism,* 175.

227. Quoted in Lois W. Banner, "Religious Benevolence as Social Control: A Critique of an Interpretation," *Journal of American History* 60 (1973), 34.

228. Quoted in Smith, *Revivalism,* 154.

229. See ibid., 179–181.

230. See Curtis Johnson, *Redeeming America: Evangelicals and the Road to Civil War* (Chicago, 1993).

231. Richard J. Carwardine, "Lincoln, Evangelical Religion, and American Political Culture in the Era of the Civil War," *Journal of the Abraham Lincoln Association* 18 (1997), 49, 50. See also Eric Foner, *Free Soil, Free Labor, Free Men: The Ideology of the Republican Party before the Civil War* (London, 1970); Daniel Walker Howe, *The Political Culture of the American Whigs* (Chicago, 1979).

232. Smith, *Revivalism,* 195; quoted ibid., 221.

233. Randall M. Miller, Harry S. Stout, and Charles Reagan Wilson, introduction to *Religion and the American Civil War,* ed. Randall M. Miller, Harry S. Stout, and Charles Reagan Wilson (New York, 1998), 16.

234. Abraham Lincoln, quoted in Allen C. Guelzo, "Abraham Lincoln and the Doctrine of Necessity," *Journal of the Abraham Lincoln Association* 18 (1997), 68–69. David Greenstone powerfully demonstrated in revising the Hartzian thesis how radical religious universalism was incorporated into Lincoln's transformative liberalism, though he did not distinguish the specific sectarian contribution, and was cut short from elaborating Lincoln's impact on subsequent institutional formation. J. David Greenstone, *The Lincoln Persuasion: Remaking American Liberalism* (Princeton, 1993).

235. Cole, *Ideas*, 219.

236. James H. Moorhead, *American Apocalypse: Yankee Protestants and the Civil War, 1860–1869* (New Haven, 1978), 22.

237. George M. Fredrickson, "The Coming of the Lord: The Northern Protestant Clergy and the Civil War Crisis," in Miller, Stout, and Wilson, *Religion and American Civil War*, 119–120.

11. From Sectarian Discord to Civil Religion

1. Bilhartz, *Religion*, 140.

2. Smith, *Revivalism*, 25.

3. Finney, *Lectures*, 423; Smith, *Revivalism*, 28.

4. Finney, *Sermons*, 38, 36, 33.

5. Sprague, *Lectures*, 204, 104.

6. Finney, *Sermons*, 16; Finney, *Lectures*, 397, 386.

7. Finney, *Lectures*, 419, 420, 402; Finney, *Sermons*, 16.

8. Sprague, *Lectures*, 104–105; Finney, *Lectures*, 420.

9. "The Journal of James Gilruth," in Sweet, *American Frontier*, 258.

10. Quoted in Smith, *Revivalism*, 115.

11. "The Journal of Benjamin Lakin," in Sweet, *American Frontier*, 258.

12. "The Edward Dromgoole Letters," ibid., 185; "Benjamin Lakin," 249.

13. Smith, *Revivalism*, 104.

14. Mahan, *Doctrine*, 30, 149.

15. Reverend Bishop Janes, introduction to Palmer, *Pioneer Experiences*.

16. "Testimony of Rev. R. W. Hawkins," ibid., 310–311; "Testimony of Rev. J. W. Horne," ibid., 204, 206.

17. Bushnell, "Spirit," 63, 69.

18. Ibid., 64.

19. Miller, *Life*, 33.

20. Finney, *Sermons*, 36 (second pagination); Finney, *Submission*, 87–88.

21. Upham, *Principles*, 187.

22. Bushnell, "Spirit," 66, 67.

23. Finney, *Lectures*, 306; Sprague, *Lectures*, 261, 278.

24. Mahan, *Doctrine*, 51; Bushnell, "Spirit," 70, 64.

25. Bushnell, *Christian Nurture*, 181, 180.

26. Quoted in McLoughlin, *Revivals*, 119.

27. Finney, *Lectures*, 11. See Sprague, *Lectures*, 236–237, 56, 225. Finney wrote in 1845: "I am inspired with the importance of keeping excitement down. . . . I have learned to . . . feel much more confidence in apparent conversions where there is greater calmness of mind." Quoted in McLoughlin, introduction to Finney, *Lectures*, 1.

28. Sprague, *Lectures*, 223, 224.

29. Johnson and Wilentz, *Kingdom*, 8.

30. Busch, *Travels*, 277.

31. Cross, *District*, 183–184.

32. Busch, *Travels*, 277–278, 56.

33. Sprague, *Lectures*, 226–228.

34. Finney, *Lectures*, 282.

35. Mahan, *Doctrine*, 175, 176; Upham, *Principles*, 266.

36. Quoted in Hatch, *Democratization*, 37, 43.

37. Quoted in Johnson and Wilentz, *Kingdom*, 6.

38. Hatch, *Democratization*, 77.

39. Schaff, *America*, xv; Busch, *Travels*, 275, 274.

40. Boardman, *Life*, 178, 174.

41. Hatch, *Democratization*, 65.

42. Cross, *District*, 185.

43. Quoted in Hatch, *Democratization*, 64.

44. Schaff, *America*, xii, xv, xiii, 12; Busch, *Travels*, 276, 57n, 277, 281.

45. Ingersoll, "Inchiquin's Letters," 388.

46. Hatch, *Democratization*, 206.

47. Roth, *Dilemma*, 223.

48. Quoted in Curtis D. Johnson, *Islands of Holiness: Rural Religion in Upstate New York, 1790–1860* (Ithaca, N.Y., 1989), 141.

49. Lazerow, *Religion*, 189.

50. Cross, *District*, 257.

51. "Benjamin Lakin," 228.

52. Bushnell, *Christian Nurture*, 109.

53. Dewey, "Discourses," 51.

54. Roth, *Dilemma*, 188.

55. Johnson, *Islands*, 149; Paul Conkin, *The Uneasy Center: Reformed Christianity in Antebellum America* (Chapel Hill, 1995), 87.

56. Carwardine, "'Antinomians' and 'Arminians,'" 301; Hatch, *Democratization*, 193.

57. Miyakawa, *Protestants*, 203.

58. Conkin, *Uneasy Center*, 87.

59. Hatch, *Democratization*, 202; Roth, *Dilemmas*, 225.

60. Finney, *Lectures*, 399, 414–415.

61. Mahan, *Doctrine*, 8; "Rev. W. H. Poole," 32.

62. [A Friend to Revivals}, "Historical Sketch of Revivals—No. IX," *New York Evangelist*, January 5, 1833, 1.

63. McLoughlin, *Revivalism*, 127.

64. Finney, *Lectures*, 395.

65. For a discussion of the turn to organizational religion in the all-important Methodists, see Schneider, *Way*, 204–208.

66. Finney, *Sermons*, 40 (second pagination).

67. Ibid., 93.

68. Finney, *Lectures*, 435, 444, 441.

69. Baird, *Religion*, 425.

70. Taylor, *John Godfrey's Fortunes,* 130, 125.

71. Cross, *District,* 254, 255.

72. Ibid., 274.

73. William Warren Sweet, *Religion in the Development of American Culture* (New York, 1952), 145.

74. Sprague, *Lectures,* 209.

75. Ibid., 207.

76. Finney, *Lectures,* 432, 454, 460.

77. Cartwright, *Preacher,* 242, 258.

78. Ibid., 113.

79. Ibid., 240.

80. Finney, *Sermons,* 241.

81. Ibid., 206; Finney, *Lectures,* 443, 454.

82. Finney, *Lectures,* 443, 444.

83. Finney, *Sermons,* 246.

84. Finney, *Lectures,* 435, 415, 418.

85. Cartwright, *Preacher,* 113.

86. Finney, *Sermons,* 247; Finney, *Lectures,* 149–150.

87. Finney, *Sermons,* 250.

88. Quoted in Lipset, *New Nation,* 189.

89. Finney, *Lectures,* 284.

90. Baird, *Religion,* 425.

91. Roth, *Dilemma,* 223.

92. Daniel Day Williams, *The Andover Liberals: A Study in American Theology* (New York, 1970), 120.

93. Miyakawa, *Protestants,* 203.

94. Busch, *Travels,* 280.

95. Schaff, *America,* xvii–xviii.

96. Cartwright, *Preacher,* 231.

97. Hatch, *Democratization,* 15, 68.

98. Bushnell, *Christian Nurture,* 149, 180, 181.

99. Baird, *Religion,* 435.

100. Quoted in Cross, *District,* 286.

101. Miller, *Life,* 74.

102. Paul Boyer, *Urban Masses and Moral Order in America, 1820–1920* (Cambridge, Mass., 1978), ix.

103. Smith, *Revivalism,* 148, 151, 149.

104. Boyer, *Masses,* 31; quoted ibid., 42.

105. Roth, *Dilemma,* 223–225.

106. Ibid., 225, 280.

107. Dewey, "Discourses," 122, 50, 52.

108. Quoted in Reynolds, *Faith,* 53–55, 55n.

109. Quoted ibid., 62.

110. Miller, *Life,* 94.

111. Johnson, *Islands*, 146; Roth, *Dilemma*.
112. See George M. Marsden, *Fundamentalism and American Culture: The Shaping of Twentieth-Century Evangelism, 1870–1925* (New York, 1982), 11–32.
113. See Sidney Fine, *Laissez Faire and the General-Welfare State: A Study of Conflict in American Thought, 1865–1901* (Ann Arbor, 1965), 167–197.
114. Abraham Lincoln, "Second Inaugural Address," in *Selected Speeches, Messages, and Letters*, ed. T. Harry Williams (New York, 1964), 283.
115. Arthur C. McGiffert, "The Historical Study of Christianity," in *American Protestant Thought: The Liberal Era*, ed. William R. Hutchison (New York, 1968), 75
116. Edward Beecher, "The Scriptural Philosophy of Congregationalism and of Councils," *Bibliotecha Sacra* 22 (April 1865), 287.
117. McGiffert, "Study," 73.
118. William Arthur, quoted in Smith, *Revivalism*, 154; Gilbert Haven, quoted ibid., 236, 235.
119. Ibid., 7.
120. William Arthur, quoted ibid., 154.
121. Henry May, *Protestant Churches and Industrial America* (New York, 1967), 42.
122. Jean B. Quandt, "Religious and Social Thought: The Secularization of Postmillennialism," *American Quarterly* 25 (1973), 396, 400, 399.
123. May, *Protestant*, 86.
124. George A. Coe, "Salvation by Education," in Hutchison, *Thought*, 121.
125. Ibid.
126. See William McLoughlin, *The Meaning of Henry Ward Beecher: An Essay on the Shifting Values of Mid-Victorian America, 1840–1870* (New York, 1970), chap. 5.
127. Barbara Cross, *Horace Bushnell: Minister to a Changing America* (Chicago, 1958), 45.
128. McLoughlin, *Beecher*, 101; Henry Ward Beecher, quoted ibid., 116.
129. Cartwright, *Preacher*, 260.
130. Quoted in Marty, *Empire*, 109, 108
131. Dewey, "Discourses," 150–151.
132. Miyakawa, *Protestants*, 83, 140.
133. Dewey, "Discourses," 191, 310, 154, 161, 162, 167.
134. Ibid., 193, 220–221.
135. Ibid., 12, 190, 207, 208.
136. Quoted in Fine, *Laissez Faire*, 124.
137. See Baird, *Religion*, 235–260, 297–306, 662–665.
138. Quoted in John Cawelti, *Apostles of the Self-Made Man: Changing Concepts of Success in America* (Chicago, 1965), 186.
139. Quoted ibid., 179.
140. Quoted in Robert T. Handy, *A Christian America: Protestant Hopes and Historical Realities* (New York, 1974), 97–98.
141. Quoted ibid., 102.
142. Fine, *Laissez Faire*, 117, 118.

143. Quoted in May, *Churches*, 53.

144. Dewey, "Discourses," 212, 215, 210.

145. Baird, *Religion*, 386.

146. Bushnell, "Spirit," 69, 67, 187.

147. Richard Rabinowitz, *The Spiritual Self in Everyday Life: The Transformation of Religious Experience in Nineteenth-Century New England* (Boston, 1989), 231.

148. Roth, *Dilemma*, 288, 289, 300.

149. Cross, *District*, 356.

150. Hatch, *Democratization*, 189.

151. William M. Evarts, "Oration," in *Popular Culture and Industrialism, 1865–1890*, ed. Henry Nash Smith (Garden City, N.Y., 1967), 5, 13.

152. Ibid., 12–13, 18; Handy, *America*, 113; Marty, *Empire*, 154; Franklin Hamlin Littell, *From State Church to Pluralism: A Protestant Interpretation of Religion in American History* (Chicago, 1962), 97.

12. The Protestant Agent in Liberal Economics

1. Ingersoll, "Inchiquin's Letters," 383; Arthur Lathan Perry, *Principles of Political Economy* (New York, 1891), 18.

2. Ralph Waldo Emerson, "Self-Reliance," in *Essays*, 37; Henry David Thoreau, *Walden* (New York, 1980), 8, 9.

3. John R. Commons, *Social Reform and the Church* (New York, 1894), 72.

4. Judy Hilkey, *Character Is Capital: Success Manuals and Manhood in Gilded Age America* (Chapel Hill, 1997), 167, 170. See also Richard Bushman, *The Refinement of America: Persons, Houses, Cities* (New York, 1993).

5. Tocqueville, *Democracy*, 2:144, 145.

6. William Mathews, *Getting On in the World: or, Hints on Success in Life* (Chicago, 1879), 70.

7. Orison Swett Marden, *Pushing to the Front or, Success under Difficulties* (New York, 1894), 301.

8. Daniel T. Rodgers, *The Work Ethic in Industrial America, 1850–1920* (Chicago, 1979), xiii, 241.

9. See, e.g., Van Wyck Brooks, "America's Coming of Age," in *Essays on America* (New York, 1970); Stuart Chase, *The Economy of Abundance* (New York, 1934).

10. T. E. C. Leslie, "Political Economy in the United States," *Fortnightly Review*, October 1, 1880, 488.

11. See Hilkey, *Character*.

12. Ibid., 133.

13. Robert H. Wiebe, *The Search for Order, 1877–1920* (New York, 1967), 135, 134.

14. Henry Steele Commager, *The American Mind: An Interpretation of American Thought and Character since the 1880s* (New Haven, 1971), 201; James T. Kloppenberg, *Uncertain Victory: Social Democracy and Progressivism in European and American Thought, 1870–1950* (New York, 1986), 173.

15. Fine, *Laissez Faire*, 79.

16. Ibid., 58.

17. Simon Newcomb, *Principles of Political Economy* (New York, 1886), 7.

18. W. D. Wilson, *First Principles of Political Economy with Reference to Statesmanship and the Progress of Civilization* (Philadelphia, 1882), 107; Richard T. Ely, *An Introduction to Political Economy* (New York, 1889), 19–20.

19. Arthur Lathan Perry, *Elements of Political Economy* (New York, 1866), 25.

20. Francis Bowen, *American Political Economy* (New York, 1877), 76, 15, 78; Ely, *Introduction*, 29.

21. Edward Atkinson, *The Margin of Profits* (New York, 1887), 21.

22. Newcomb, *Principles*, 7.

23. Bowen, *Economy*, 25; Atkinson, *Margin*, 48; Simon Newcomb, *A Plain Man's Talk on the Labor Question* (New York, 1886), 13.

24. Perry, *Elements*, 142.

25. Amasa Walker, *The Science of Wealth: A Manual of Political Economy* (Philadelphia, 1872), 36.

26. Newcomb, *Principles* 7; Perry, *Elements*, 27–28.

27. Edward Atkinson, *The Industrial Progress of the Nation: Consumption Limited, Production Unlimited* (New York, 1889), 25.

28. Wilson, *Principles*, 183; Perry, *Elements*, 75.

29. Newcomb, *Principles*, 142, 36.

30. Walker, *Science*, 23; Perry, *Elements*, 57.

31. Perry, *Elements*, 33–35, 31.

32. John Stuart Mill, quoted in Bowen, *Economy*, 11.

33. Perry, *Elements*, 31.

34. Walker, *Science*, 23.

35. Bowen, *Economy*, 27.

36. Ely, *Introduction*, 26.

37. Perry, *Elements*, 50–51; Bowen, *Economy*, 27.

38. Ely, *Introduction*, 14; Walker, *Science*, 35; Bowen, *Economy*, 14; Perry, *Elements*, 75.

39. Bowen, *Economy*, 22.

40. Newcomb, *Principles*, 5.

41. Hobbes, *Leviathan*, 131; Newcomb, *Principles*, 8; Ely, *Introduction*, 44.

42. Perry, *Elements*, 77.

43. Newcomb, *Principles*, 5, 8; Newcomb, *Talk*, 17.

44. Bowen, *Economy*, 18, 17.

45. Wilson, *Principles*, 22, 21; Newcomb, *Principles*, 9.

46. Walker, *Science*, 19; Bowen, *Economy*, 2; Wilson, *Principles*, 25.

47. Atkinson, *Industrial Progress*, 387.

48. Walker, *Science*, 23, 36.

49. Newcomb, *Principles*, 10; Walker, *Science*, 19; Newcomb, *Principles*, 7.

50. Wilson, *Principles*, 55; Bowen, *Economy*, 15.

51. Newcomb, *Principles*, 11.

52. Perry, *Elements*, 77.

53. Ibid., 6.

54. Atkinson, *Industrial Progress*, 377; Walker, *Science*, 81. See Albert O. Hirschman, *The Passions and the Interests* (Princeton, 1977).

55. Bowen, *Economy*, 3–4, 26; Wilson, *Principles*, 5–7, 55.

56. Bowen, *Economy*, 59.

57. Newcomb, *Principles*, 536; Bowen, *Economy*, 58–59; Wilson, *Principles*, 109, 106.

58. Freedley noted in 1853 "the number of books on the principles of money-making" as "few—none to serve as models." Edwin T. Freedley, *A Practical Treatise on Business* (Philadelphia, 1853), 6.

59. Ibid., 47.

60. William Wirt, quoted ibid., 56.

61. Freeman Hunt, *Worth and Wealth: A Collection of Maxims, Morals, and Miscellanies for Merchants and Men of Business* (New York, 1856), vii, 120, 297, 493–494, 462, 185.

62. Marden, *Pushing*, 107. As worry grew about increased social divisions, the idea shifted to "all can make it." See Atkinson, *Industrial Progress*.

63. Russell Conwell, *Acres of Diamonds* (New York, 1978), 20; Wilbur F. Crafts, *Successful Men of To-Day and What They Say of Success* (New York, 1883), 31, 28.

64. Mathew, *Getting*, 125–126.

65. Orison Swett Marden, *The Progressive Business Man* (New York, 1913), 153.

66. Freedley, *Treatise*, 242.

67. Bowen, *Economy*, 18.

68. Anderson, *Story*, 219.

69. Mathews, *Getting*, 126; Ely, *Introduction*, 83.

70. Conwell, *Acres*, 10; Marden, *Progressive*, 153.

71. Bowen, *Economy*, 17

72. Newcomb, *Principles*, 13, 446, 142; Bowen, *Economy*, 17, 18.

73. Walker, *Science*, 17, 79, 19, 36.

74. Ely, *Introduction*, 74; Perry, *Elements*, 28, 27, 81.

75. Atkinson, *Industrial Progress*, 388, 5, 387.

76. Ibid., 11.

77. Newcomb, *Principles*, 11; Walker, *Science*, 18–19.

78. Bowen, *Economy*, 2; Walker, *Science*, 19; Wilson, *Principles*, 23.

79. Perry, *Elements*, 1.

80. Hunt, *Worth*, 121. This was an early "scientization" of the claim that "in our country every man is a trader." Ibid., 55; see also Freedley, *Treatise*, 96.

81. Bowen, *Economy*, 3.

82. Perry, *Elements*, 77.

83. Walker, *Science*, 449.

84. Bowen, *Economy*, 26.

85. Perry, *Elements*, 24.

86. Bowen, *Economy*, 14, 15; Hunt, *Worth*, 54, 57; Newcomb, *Principles*, 6; Perry, *Principles*, 18.

87. Bowen, *Economy*, 14; Hunt, *Worth*, viii, 115; Walker, *Science*, 448.

88. Marden, *Progressive*, 5; Bowen, *Economy*, 18.

89. Perry, *Elements*, 23–24; Bowen, *Economy*, 27.

90. Newcomb, *Principles*, 12.

91. Wilson, *Principles*, 56.

92. Walker, *Science*, 449, 395, 396; Bowen, *Economy*, 27, 41; Newcomb, *Principles*, 535

93. Walker, *Science*, 340; Newcomb, *Principles*, 530.

94. Newcomb, *Principles*, 444; Bowen, *Economy*, 22.

95. William Graham Sumner, "The Forgotten Man," in *Social Darwinism: Selected Essays of William Graham Sumner* (Englewood Cliffs, N.J., 1963), 122.

96. See Fine, *Laissez Faire*, 177–195.

97. Newcomb, *Principles*, 7 (called, respectively, "savage" and "civilized").

98. Fine, *Laissez Faire*, 52. I have utilized this work throughout this section.

99. Leslie, "Economy," 496, 497.

100. Walker, *Science*, 449, 19; Newcomb, *Principles*, 1.

101. Bowen, *Economy*, 18, 15; Perry, *Elements*, 1.

102. Perry, *Elements*, 26, 27; Atkinson, *Industrial Progress*, 387; Wilson, *Principles*, 351.

103. Perry, *Elements*, 89, 76, 25, 27, 28.

104. Ibid., 27.

105. Atkinson, *Industrial Progress*, 388; Walker, *Science*, 17; Newcomb, *Principles*, 446, 443; Perry, *Elements*, 28; Wilson, *Principles*, 348, 344.

106. Bowen, *Economy*, 17, 27; Atkinson, *Margins*, 17, 50; Newcomb, *Principles*, 447; Wilson, *Principles*, 340; Perry, *Elements*, 80–81, 77.

107. Bowen, *Economy*, 17, 27; Atkinson, *Margins*, 17, 50; Newcomb, *Principles*, 447; Wilson, *Principles*, 340; Perry, *Elements*, 80–81, 77.

108. Bowen, *Economy*, 110; Walker, *Science*, 445.

109. Walker, *Science*, 448; Perry, *Elements*, 1.

110. Bowen, *Economy*, 15.

111. Newcomb, *Talk*, 187; Walker, *Science*, 448; Bowen, *Economy*, 15.

112. Bowen, *Economy*, 105, 107, 108; Newcomb, *Principles*, 5.

113. Wilson, *Principles*, 349; Bowen, *Economy*, 107, 18.

114. Walker, *Science*, 449; Atkinson, *Industrial Progress*, 2.

115. Walker *Science*, 449; Bowen, *Economy*, 18.

116. Walker, *Science*, 20; Bowen, *Economy*, 18; Newcomb, *Principles*, 13.

117. Bowen, *Economy*, 19

118. Wilson, *Principles*, 29, 347–349.

119. Perry, *Principles*, 45, 3, 31, 2, 42, 76, 78–79.

120. See Jean B. Quandt, "Religion and Thought," *American Quarterly* 25 (1973), 398–401; Dorothy Ross, *The Origins of American Social Science* (Cambridge, 1991); Mary O. Furner, *Advocacy and Objectivity: A Crisis in the Professionalization of American Social Science, 1865–1905* (Lexington, Ky., 1975).

121. Realizing they were fighting a cultural war, the prewar economists parried: Why should business pursuits be stigmatized as low? they asked, referring to "a distinguished divine, who makes $3500 per annum out of his religious sentiments." Freedley, *Treatise*, 23–25.

122. Marden, *Progressive*, 3.

123. Marden, *Pushing*, 25; Atkinson, *Industrial Progress*, 378, 379, 386; Mathews, *Getting*, 58, 349.

124. Reverend F. E. Clark, *Danger Signals: The Enemies of Youth, from the Business Man's Standpoint* (Boston, 1883), 10–12.

125. Crafts, *Men*, 98, 105, 100, 106.

126. Ibid., 77, 81.

127. Conwell, *Acres*, 10.

128. Bruce Barton, *The Man Nobody Knows* (New York, 1925), preface.

129. Marden, *Progressive*, 8, 1.

130. Atkinson, *Industrial Progress*, 2, 379, 14; Mathews, *Getting*, 350; Marden, *Pushing*, 109.

131. Newcomb, *Talk*, 121.

132. Freedley, *Treatise*, 27.

133. Hilkey, *Character*, 4, 126–141, 169.

134. Conwell, *Acres*, 22, 20, 23.

135. Wilson, *Principles*, 84.

136. Newcomb, *Principles*, 449; Wilson, *Principles*, 28.

137. Crafts, *Men*, 80; Marden, *Pushing*, 25.

138. Quandt, "Thought," 400.

139. Marden, *Progressive*, 147.

140. Cawelti, *Apostles*, 168; see also Irvin Wyllie, *The Self-Made Man in America* (New York, 1966), chap. 7.

141. Marden, *Progressive*, 16.

142. John R. Commons, "Progressive Individualism," *American Magazine of Civics* 1 (June 1895), 565–567.

143. Atkinson, *Margin*, 48, 50.

144. See Edward Bellamy, *Looking Backward* (New York, 1960); Simon Patten, *The New Basis of Civilization* (Cambridge, Mass., 1968), 186; Kenneth M. Roemer, *The Obsolete Necessity: America in Utopian Writings, 1888–1900* (Kent, Ohio, 1976). Ironically, the laissez-faire theorists themselves first proclaimed the age of abundance from an ever-expanding market system. Wilson, *Principles*, 105.

145. James Livingston, *Pragmatism and the Political Economy of Cultural Revolution, 1850–1940* (Chapel Hill, 1994), 66–67.

146. Beyond Fine, see John Rutherford Everett, *Religion in Economics: A Study of John Bates Clark, Richard T. Ely, Simon Patten* (Morningside Heights, N.Y., 1946); Bradley W. Bateman and Ethan B. Kapstein, "Retrospectives: Between God and the Market: The Religious Roots of the American Economic Association," *Journal of Economic Perspectives* 13 (Fall 1999); Bradley W. Bateman, "Clearing the Ground: The Demise of the Social Gospel Movement and the Rise of Neoclassicism in American Economics," in *From Interwar Pluralism to Postwar Neoclassicism*, ed. Mary S. Morgan and Malcolm Rutherford (Durham, N.C., 1998); R. A. Gonce, "The Social Gospel, Ely, and Common's Initial Stage of Thought," *Journal of Economic Issues* 30 (September 1996).

147. Ely, *Introduction*, 14.

148. Quoted in Fine, *Laissez Faire*, 173.

149. Richard Ely, *The Social Law of Service* (New York, 1896), 21, 139.

150. Richard Ely, "Ethics and Economics," in *Social Aspects of Christianity, and Other Essays* (New York, 1889), 131.

151. Ely, *Law*, 20; Richard Ely, *The Labor Movement in America* (New York, 1886), 312.

152. Ely, *Introduction*, 318.

153. E. Benjamin Andrews, "Individualism as a Sociological Principle," *Yale Review* 2 (1894), 16.

154. Ely, *Introduction*, 71–72.

155. Quoted in Fine, *Laissez Faire*, 210. See also Lester Ward, "Dynamic Sociology," in *Lester Ward and the Welfare State*, ed. Henry Steele Commager (Indianapolis, 1967), 48–50.

156. For the legal transformation to a "corporate" society, see William J. Novak, *The People's Welfare: Law and Regulation in Nineteenth-Century America* (Chapel Hill, 1996); Morton J. Horowitz, *The Transformation of American Law, 1870–1960: The Crisis of Legal Orthodoxy* (New York, 1992).

157. Commons, "Progressive Individualism," 571.

158. Andrews, "Individualism," 23.

159. Ward, "Dynamic Sociology," 53.

160. Lester Ward, "Applied Sociology," in *Ward*, 346–347.

161. Ward, "Dynamic Sociology," 53.

162. Ely, *Introduction*, 13; Ward, "Applied Sociology," 367.

13. John Dewey and the Modern Synthesis

1. See Michael Walzer, "The Idea of Civil Society: A Path to Social Reconstruction," in *Community Works: The Revival of Civil Society in America*, ed. E. J. Dionne (Washington, D.C., 1998).

2. Wiebe, *Opening*, 145. See also Robert B. Westbrook, *John Dewey and American Democracy* (Ithaca, N.Y., 1991), 537–552.

3. Ross, *Origins*, 222, 241; Albion Small, quoted in ibid., 126.

4. Ross, *Origins*, 91.

5. F. S. Sanborn, "The Work of Social Science, Past and Present," *Journal of Social Science* 8 (May 1876), 23 (henceforth *JSS*).

6. F. S. Sanborn, "History of the American Social Science Association in a Letter to Its Present Secretary, I. F. Russell, New York," *JSS* 46 (December 1909), 3.

7. Ibid.

8. Albion W. Small, "Fifty Years of Sociology in the United States," *American Journal of Sociology* 21 (May 1916), 784–785.

9. Sanborn, "History," 2–3.

10. "Introductory Note," *JSS* 1 (June 1869), 1, 2, 4.

11. F. S. Sanborn, "The Supervision of Public Charities," *JSS* 1 (June 1869), 72.

12. E. L. Godkin, "Legislation and Social Science," *JSS* 3 (1871), 123, 115.
13. David A. Wells, "Influence of the Production and Distribution of Wealth on So-
    cial Development," *JSS* 8 (May 1876), 5.
14. Julia Ward Howe, "Changes in American Society," *JSS* 13 (March 1881), 176.
    Whereas once "religious people were supposed to live out of the world," the
    new model was to "have saints *in* the world." Ibid., 176 (emphasis added).
15. Reverend Samuel W. Dike, "The Effect of Lax Divorce Legislation upon the
    Stability of American Institutions," *JSS* 14 (November 1881), 152, 162, 160,
    159.
16. Ibid., 160, 159.
17. F. S. Sanborn, "Papers of the Social Economy Department: Address of the
    Chairman," *JSS* 22 (June 1887), 98.
18. F. S. Sanborn, "Society and Socialism," *JSS* 33 (November 1895), 24.
19. Benjamin Pierce, "The National Importance of Social Science in the United
    States," *JSS* 12 (December 1880), xiv.
20. Henry Ling Taylor, M.D., "American Childhood from a Medical Standpoint,"
    JSS 30 (October 1892), 44.
21. Lucy Larcom, "American Factory Life—Past, Present, and Future," *JSS* 16 (De-
    cember 1882), 145; Sanborn, "Past and Present," 39.
22. Henry Dwight Chapin, M.D., "The Struggle for Subsistence: How Can It Be
    Most Efficiently Aided?" *JSS* 25 (December 1888), 93.
23. Reverend J. H. Jones, "Ten Hours," *JSS* 16 (December 1882), 150.
24. Chapin, "Struggle," 95; Pierce, "National Importance," xvii.
25. Sanborn, "Society and Socialism," 25.
26. Wells, "Influence," 13.
27. Chapin, "Struggle," 95.
28. Pierce, "National Importance," xviii; Larcom, "Factory Life," 146, 145.
29. Sanborn, "The Work of Social Science in the United States," 43.
30. Wells, "Production and Distribution," 16, 22.
31. George William Curtin, "Civil-Service Reform," *JSS* 14 (November 1881), 49.
32. Lorin Blodget, "Waste of Existing Social Systems," *JSS* 4 (1871), 18; Wells,
    "Influence," 22.
33. Thomas L. Haskell, *The Emergence of Professional Social Science: The American Social
    Science Association and the Nineteenth-Century Crisis of Authority* (Urbana, Ill.,
    1977), 43.
34. W. T. Harris, "The Study of Method in Social Science," *JSS* 10 [labeled 9] (De-
    cember 1879), 28.
35. R. Jackson Wilson, *In Quest of Community: Social Philosophy in the United States,
    1860–1920* (New York, 1968), 30, 174, 173.
36. Small, "Fifty Years," 725; Albion W. Small, "The Era of Sociology," *American
    Journal of Sociology* 1 (July 1895), 1.
37. Graham Taylor, quoted in Small, "Era," 4; ibid., 2.
38. Ross, *Origins*, 93.

39. Small, "Fifty Years," 753, 844.

40. Albion W. Small, *Origins of Sociology* (Chicago, 1924), 326; Small, "Fifty Years," 723.

41. Small, *Origins,* 334.

42. Small, "Fifty Years," 753, 725, 843.

43. Small, "Era," 7.

44. See L. L. Bernard and Jessie Bernard, *Origins of American Sociology: The Social Science Movement in the United States* (New York, 1943).

45. George Frederick Holmes, *A Science of Society* (Charlottesville, Va., 1884), 10.

46. Small, "Fifty Years," 753. For the roots of the social reformism of early American sociology in Protestantism, see Arthur J. Vidich and Stanford M. Lyman, *American Sociology: Worldly Rejections of Religion and Their Directions* (New Haven, 1985).

47. Robert S. Hamilton [Leland A. Webster, pseud.], *Present Status of the Philosophy of Society: A Treatise Designed to Show the Insufficiency of Existing Systems of Thought, and the Tendencies toward a Larger System* (New York, 1866), 93.

48. Ibid., 46, 171, 86.

49. R. J. Wright, *Principia of Political Science: Upon a Reverent, Moral, Liberal, and Progressive Foundation* (Philadelphia, 1876), 22, 127.

50. Lester A. Ward, "Organization," *Glimpses of the Cosmos* 1 (1913), 167; Lester A. Ward, "Static and Dynamic Sociology," *Glimpses of the Cosmos* 5 (1917), 185.

51. Lester A. Ward, "The Establishment of Sociology," *Glimpses of the Cosmos* 6 (1918), 263.

52. Lester A. Ward, "The Situation," *Glimpses of the Cosmos* 1 (1913), 44; "Editorial: The Present Age," ibid., 48; "What Has Been Gained? No. 2," ibid., 78; "Science vs. Theology," ibid., 53; "The Rising School," ibid., 112.

53. Hamilton, *Philosophy,* 314–315.

54. Ibid., 264, viii.

55. Lester A. Ward, "The Establishment of Sociology," 264.

56. Lester A. Ward, "The Gospel of Action," in Commager, *Lester Ward,* 273.

57. Hamilton, *Philosophy,* 236.

58. Small, "Fifty Years," 849.

59. Ross, *Origins,* 16–17.

60. Bernard and Bernard, *Origins,* 309.

61. Ross, *Origins,* 57; Bernard and Bernard, *Origins,* 713.

62. Ross, *Origins,* 17, 18 (emphasis added).

63. See Raymond Seidelman, *Disenchanted Realists: Political Science and the American Crisis, 1884–1984* (Albany, N.Y., 1985).

64. President Theodore Roosevelt, quoted in Charles Forcey, *The Crossroads of Liberalism: Croly, Weyl, Lippmann, and the Progressive Era, 1900–1925* (London, 1967), 133, 134.

65. See ibid., 145.

66. Herbert Croly, *The Promise of American Life* (New York, 1964), 369.

67. Charles Horton Cooley, *Human Nature and the Social Order* (New York, 1964), 35. Cooley continues, "Long solitude as in the case of sheepherders on the Western plain . . . often produces imbecility."

68. G. H. Mead, *Mind, Self, and Society* (Chicago, 1967), 233.

69. Cooley, *Human Nature*, 431, 425–427.

70. Croly, *Promise*, 428.

71. See Roemer, *Necessity*.

72. Neil Coughlan, *Young John Dewey: An Essay in American Intellectual History* (Chicago, 1975), 86.

73. Westbrook, *Dewey*, ix, 430.

74. Alan Ryan, *John Dewey and the High Tide of American Liberalism* (New York, 1995), 11, 36.

75. Ibid., 19, 20.

76. Westbrook, *Dewey*, 79, 80; Coughlan, *Young Dewey*, 9, 85.

77. Steven C. Rockefeller, *John Dewey: Religious Faith and Democratic Humanism* (New York, 1991), 2, 217, 18.

78. John Dewey, "Reconstruction," in *John Dewey: The Early Works, 1882–1898*, 5 vols. (Carbondale, Ill., 1967–1972), 4:98, 105, 97.

79. Rockefeller, *Dewey*, 22, 74.

80. See Westbrook, *Dewey*, 3.

81. John Dewey, "The Obligation to Knowledge of God," in *Early Works*, 1:61–63.

82. Westbrook, *Dewey*, 3; John Dewey, quoted ibid., 3.

83. Quoted in Coughlan, *Young Dewey*, 6.

84. John Dewey, "The New Psychology," in *Early Works*, 1:48, 60, 49.

85. Ibid., 56, 60.

86. Henry James, *The American Scene* (Bloomington, Ind., 1968), 72–75, 106, 102.

87. Ibid., 104.

88. Westbrook, *Dewey*, 24.

89. Lester Ward, "Mind as a Social Factor," *Glimpses of the Cosmos* 3 (1913), 372, 371, 379.

90. G. Stanley Hall, "The Moral and Religious Training of Children," *JSS* 15 (February 1882), 57, 60–62.

91. Dewey, "New Psychology," 59, 60, 56.

92. Quoted in Rockefeller, *Dewey*, 51.

93. Dewey, "New Psychology," 56.

94. Ibid., 60.

95. Dewey, "Obligation," 61.

96. John Dewey, "Ethics and Physical Science," in *Early Works*, 1:205, 209.

97. Ibid., 209, 212–213, 218.

98. Ibid., 218, 225, 209, 226.

99. John Dewey, "The Ethics of Democracy," in *Early Works*, 1:248–249, 232.

100. Ibid., 236, 243, 240, 242; John Dewey, "Psychology in High-Schools from the Standpoint of the College," in *Early Works*, 1:83.

101. Dewey, "High-Schools," 232, 231; Dewey, "Ethics of Democracy," 243, 248, 237, 239.
102. Dewey, "Ethics of Democracy," 244, 245.
103. John Dewey, "The Place of Religious Emotion," in *Early Works*, 1:92, 91; Dewey "Obligation," 62; John Dewey, "Psychology," in *Early Works*, 2:361; Dewey, "Ethics of Democracy," 244.
104. Dewey, "Obligation," 62, 63; Dewey, "Ethics of Democracy," 246.
105. Dewey, "Religious Emotion," 90.
106. Dewey, "Ethics of Democracy," 235–237.
107. James Russell Lowell, quoted ibid., 249.
108. John Dewey, "Ethics and Physical Science," in *Early Works*, 1:226.
109. Dewey, "Ethics of Democracy," 237. Accorded "that place" for which "he is best fitted," the individual will be enabled to exercise "the function proper to that place." Economically, unity will produce "a community of good (though not necessarily of goods)," "a democracy of wealth" achieved not through distributional equality but by distributional equity. This community will allow the individual "completest development," a "chance which is truly infinite, the chance to become a person." Dewey, "Religious Emotion," 243, 247, 246.
110. Dewey, "Religious Emotion," 90.
111. Dewey, "Ethics of Democracy," 243, 237, 236, 244.
112. Dewey, "Obligation," 62.
113. Dewey, "Physical Science," 210; Dewey, "Obligation," 61, 63.
114. Dewey, "Obligation," 61; Dewey, "Physical Science," 211.
115. Dewey, "Religious Emotion," 91; Dewey, "Physical Science," 217, 223.
116. John Dewey, *A Common Faith* (New Haven, 1962), 1.
117. Dewey, "Ethics of Democracy," 232–235.
118. Ryan, *Dewey*, 64.
119. Dewey, "Psychology," 360, 361, 331.
120. Ibid., 316, 347, 317, 339, 338.
121. Ibid., 336, 340, 341, 338, 353–355.
122. See Westbrook, *Dewey*, 27–30; Coughlan, *Young Dewey*, 57–58.
123. Quoted in Ryan, *Dewey*, 78, 81.
124. John Dewey, "The Relation of Philosophy to Theology: Appendix to *The Study of Ethics: A Syllabus*," in *Early Works*, 4:367.
125. John Dewey, "Moral Theory and Practice," in *Early Works*, 3:94–95.
126. Quoted in Westbrook, *Dewey*, 61.
127. Dewey, "Moral Theory," 95, 99. He continued: "There is no more halo about the insight that determines what I should do in this catastrophe of life when the foundations are unheaving and my bent for eternity lies waiting to be fixed, than in that which determines whether commercial conditions favor heavy or light purchases." To "bow" in front of "intelligence" or "baptize moral intelligence" is now mere "sentimentalism." Ibid., 95.
128. John Dewey, "Outlines of a Critical Theory of Ethics," in *Early Years*, 3:241.
129. Dewey, "Moral Theory," 96, 99, 95.

130. Ibid., 100, 105, 108, 106 (emphasis added).

131. John Dewey, "Christianity and Democracy," in *Early Works*, 4:3, 9, 7.

132. Dewey, "Outlines," 241; Dewey, "Moral Theory," 108, 109.

133. Dewey, "Outlines," 242–243; Dewey, "Christianity and Democracy," 5.

134. Dewey, "Christianity and Democracy," 8.

135. Dewey, "Outlines," 256.

136. Ibid., 255, 256, 259. The pursuit of pleasure without "a tribunal of judgment" and a "standard of measurement" is "suicidal" because it "is to deprive life of all unity, all system . . . all standard." Ibid., 273.

137. Ibid., 249, 259, 300.

138. Ibid., 249, 300, 301.

139. Ibid., 301, 304, 364.

140. John Dewey, "Self-Realization as a Moral Ideal," in *Early Works*, 4:42 (emphasis added), 50, 51, 53.

141. Dewey, "Outlines," 263, 377; Dewey, "Moral Theory," 107. This allows the "character" to be left to suffer "disorganization" and "disintegration," to "relapse, to slip down into" a "low, degraded, sensual self" with "no desire high, none low." Dewey, "Outlines," 377–378.

142. Dewey, "Outlines," 380, 372, 373.

143. Ibid., 374, 375.

144. Ibid., 387, 388.

145. Dewey, "Christianity and Democracy," 4; Dewey, "Outlines," 387.

146. Dewey, "Christianity and Democracy," 5, 7–10.

147. Dewey, "Moral Theory," 107.

148. Dewey, "Christianity and Democracy," 7.

149. Ibid., 3, 7.

150. Ibid., 9, 8; Dewey, "Outlines," 239, 380, 326.

151. Dewey, "Outlines," 239, 273.

152. Ibid., 261, 282, 314, 313.

153. Ibid., 313, 318, 321–323, 383, 327.

154. Ibid., 315, 321, 320, 370; Dewey, "Christianity and Democracy," 8–9.

155. Dewey, "Christianity and Democracy," 9, 4.

156. Ibid., 8, 9.

157. Dewey, "Reconstruction," 97, 98.

158. Ibid., 98, 99.

159. Ibid., 100, 101 (emphasis added).

160. Dewey, "Moral Theory," 99; John Dewey, "Renan's Loss of Faith in Science," in *Early Works*, 4:12.

161. Dewey, "Moral Theory," 103, 97.

162. Quoted in Westbrook, *Dewey*, 95.

163. Quoted ibid., 104, 101; Dewey, "Outlines," 386; John Dewey, "The Chaos in Moral Training," in *Early Works*, 4:113.

164. John Dewey, "My Pedagogic Creed," in *Early Works*, 5:15.

165. Quoted in Forcey, *Crossroads*, 21.

166. Clyde Griffen, "The Progressive Ethos," in Coben and Ratner, *Development*, 123; Daniel Rodgers, "In Search of Progressivism," *Reviews in American History* 10 (1982), 126.

167. Jean B. Quandt, *From the Small Town to the Great Community: The Social Thought of Progressive Intellectuals* (New Brunswick, N.J., 1970), 24; see also Eldon J. Eisenach, *The Lost Promise of Progressivism* (Lawrence, Kans., 1994); Andrew Feffer, *The Chicago Pragmatists and American Progressivism* (Ithaca, N.Y., 1993); Louise L. Stevenson, *Scholarly Means to Evangelical Ends: The New Haven Scholars and the Transformation of Higher Learning in America, 1830–1890* (Baltimore, 1986).

168. Feffer, *Pragmatists*, 252.

Conclusion

1. Westbrook, *Dewey*, xvi.

2. See David A. Hollinger, "The Problem of Pragmatism in American History," *Journal of American History* (1980); James Campbell, *The Community Reconstructs: The Meaning of Pragmatic Social Thought* (Urbana, Ill., 1992); Sandra B. Rosenthal, Carl R. Hausman, and Douglas R. Anderson, eds., *Classic American Pragmatism: Its Contemporary Vitality* (Urbana, Ill., 1999); Morris Dickstein, ed., *The Revival of Pragmatism: New Essays on Social Thought, Law, and Culture* (Durham, N.C., 1998); Westbrook, *Dewey*, 537–552.

3. Robert Bellah et al., *The Good Society* (New York, 1992), 9.

4. Morris Dickstein, "Introduction: Pragmatism Then and Now," in Dickstein, *Revival*, 16, 11, 17.

5. See Leila Zenderland, *Measuring Minds: Henry Herbert Goddard and the Origins of American Intelligence Testing* (New York, 1998).

6. See Westbrook, *Dewey*, 42–44.

7. See John Dewey, *The Public and Its Problems* (Denver, 1954), 147, 184.

8. Dewey, "Outlines," 343, 387, 384.

9. Dewey, "Reconstruction," 97.

10. Dewey, "Outlines," 370.

11. John Dewey, "The Study of Ethics: A Syllabus," in *Early Works*, 4:229, 343, 344.

12. John Dewey, "Teaching Ethics in the High School," ibid., 58; Dewey, "Study of Ethics," 356, 348.

13. Dewey, "Outlines," 370, 371.

14. John Dewey, *Freedom and Culture* (New York, 1939), 6, 13; see also Edward A. Purcell, *The Crisis of Democratic Theory: Scientific Naturalism and the Problem of Value* (Lexington, Ky., 1973).

15. Dewey, "Outlines," 337.

16. Dewey, "Christianity and Democracy," 336.

17. Dewey, "Outlines," 362, 367, 363, 339.

18. Potter, *Freedom*, 56, 61.

19. Robert N. Bellah et al., *Habits of the Heart: Individualism and Commitment in American Life* (Berkeley, 1985), 162.
20. Ryan, *Dewey*, 37.
21. Philip Green, *The Pursuit of Inequality* (New York, 1981), 2.
22. Morone, *Wish*, 9, 335.
23. Purcell, *Crisis*, 216.
24. Dewey, "Teaching Ethics," 58.
25. Westbrook, *Dewey*, 316.
26. Dewey, "Outlines," 314. Even G. H. Mead, from whom Dewey gained his concept of the social nature of the self, understood better the importance of artists and other "individuals . . . divergent from the point of view" of "the prejudices of the community" as forces which may "enlarge the environment." Mead, *Mind*, 217. See also Ryan, *Dewey*, 123.
27. See J. S. Mill, *On Liberty* (Indianapolis, 1956).
28. Dewey, "Ethical Principles Underlying Education," in *Early Works*, 5:55.
29. See Westbrook, *Dewey*, 363–364.
30. Ryan, *Dewey*, 85, 34.
31. Talcott Parsons, "Definitions of Health and Illness in the Light of American Values and Social Structure," in *Social Structure and Personality* (New York, 1970), 258.
32. For a recent version of the argument, see James T. Kloppenberg, *The Virtues of Liberalism* (New York, 1998), 7–8, 19–20.
33. Emma Goldman, "The Tragedy of Woman's Emancipation," in *Red Emma Speaks: Selected Writings and Speeches by Emma Goldman*, ed. Alix Kates Shulman (New York, 1972), 135.
34. On the liberal presumption of detachment from religion, see Ronald Dworkin, *Taking Rights Seriously* (Cambridge, Mass., 1977); John Rawls, *A Theory of Justice* (Cambridge, Mass., 1971); George Kateb, *Individualism and Democratic Culture* (Ithaca, N.Y., 1992). On the religious retreat from liberal society, see Douglass John Hall, *The Reality of the Gospel and the Unreality of the Churches* (Philadelphia, 1975); Stanley Hauerwas, *Against the Nations: War and Survival in a Liberal Society* (Minneapolis, 1985); Michael Budde, *The Two Churches: Catholicism and Capitalism in the World System* (Durham, N.C., 1992).
35. Howe, *Self*, 268; Dworkin, *Rights*, vii.
36. Rodgers, *Truths*, 220, 222.

INDEX

Abzug, Robert H., 419

Acres of Diamonds (Conwell), 486

Adam, 44, 56, 95–96, 98–102, 547

Adams, Henry, 293, 326

Adams, John: on change in religious sentiments before Revolution, 183, 231–232; on continuation of existing social relationships, 258; on cultivating sensations of freedom, 251; on Declaration of Independence, 274; on independence, 256; on participation in government, 257; on the popular revolution, 269; on populism sweeping away elites, 293; sharpening rhetorical divisions, 255; on willing obedience, 280

Adams, Sam, 252, 258, 269, 271

Adult baptism, 218, 226

Agency: American Revolution as revolution for, 31, 234–237; American Revolution as triumph of, 233–296; in Anglo-American Protestant discourse, 24–25; ascendancy in America, 181–296; becoming worldly, 449–454; common author in world of, 142–145; creation of a civilization of, 367–535; culture of voluntarist agency emerging, 219–222; as developmental process, 95–98; Dewey's early agency systems, 517–524; dictionary definition of, 23; and dynamic of reversal, 25–26; early Puritan insurgents and origins of, 39–68; English transformation to, 26–27; as existing only in reference to authority, 23; First Great Awakening and emergent culture of, 183–232; as foundation of Locke's politics, 30, 157–159; freedom as precondition of exercise of, 94–95; freedom as voluntarism within agency institutions for Dewey, 509–510; full bond of, 86–90; future of, 546–550; as hidden premise of Declaration of Independence, 275–278; Hobbes and founding of liberal politics of, 111–152; Hobbes's *Leviathan* as narrative of, 126–128; Hobbes's reconciliation with, 116–118; humans as God's agents, 24–25; liberal idyll amidst republican realities, 299–331; liberty of empowered agents, 90–95; Locke and mythic society of free agents, 152–180; making a nation of agents, 387–390; Milton's agency cosmology, 97–102; national revival as crucible of, 369–423; in Perkins's theology, 61–63; political crisis of, 106–109; politicization of Protestant, 102–106; Protestant agent in liberal economics, 459–492; Protestant agent in liberal society, 531–535; Protestant-liberal synthesis in transformation to, 20, 27–29; Protestant revolutionaries and emerging society of agents, 69–110; public instruction for securing, 145–150; recovering, 20–25, 537–550; and Reformation shift in conception of human nature, 22–23; in reform of market